John Willis

Screen World

2000

Volume 51

Associate Editor
BARRY MONUSH

APPLAUSE
NEW YORK • LONDON

LIBRARY OF CONGRESS CARD NO. 50-3023
ISBN: 1-55783-430-X (CLOTH)
ISBN: 1-55783-431-8 (PAPER)

Mary Poppins

The Americanization of Emily

The Sound of Music

Torn Curtain

Thoroughly Modern Millie

Star!

Darling Lili

The Tamarind Seed

10

To
JULIE ANDREWS

who has lit up the screen with her special blend of warmth, magic, charm and grace, proving to be not only one of the great musical performers of our time, but an outstanding dramatic and comedic actress.

FILMS: *Mary Poppins* (1964; Academy Award for Best Actress), *The Americanization of Emily* (1964), *The Sound of Music* (1965; Academy Award nomination), *Hawaii* (1966), *Torn Curtain* (1966), *Thoroughly Modern Millie* (1967), *Star!* (1968), *Darling Lili* (1970), *The Tamarind Seed* (1974), *10* (1979), *Little Miss Marker* (1980), *S.O.B.* (1981), *Victor/Victoria* (1982; Academy Award nomination), *The Man Who Loved Women* (1983), *That's Life* (1986), *Duet for One* (1986), *A Fine Romance* (1992), *Relative Values* (2000)

Little Miss Marker

Victor/Victoria

Duet for One

Kevin Spacey, Annette Bening in *American Beauty*
Academy Award Winner for Best Picture of 1999
©DreamWorks

CONTENTS

EDITOR: JOHN WILLIS

ASSOCIATE EDITOR: BARRY MONUSH

Staff: Marco Starr Boyajian, William Camp, Jim Hollifield, II,

Tom Lynch, John Sala

Acknowledgements: Tom Amorosi, Anthology Film Archives, Ed Arentz, Artistic License, Benjamin Barrett, Castle Hill, Castle Rock Entertainment, John Cicero, City Cinemas, Cline & White, Joanne Coloma, Richard D'Attile, Samantha Dean, DreamWorks, Brian Durnin, The Film Forum, First Look, First Run Features, Fox Searchlight, Adrian Goycoolea, Gramercy Pictures, Kino International, Legacy Releasing, Leisure Time Features, LIVE Entertainment, Mike Maggiore, Shona McCarthy, Robert Milite, Jr., Miramax Films, New Line Cinema/Fine Line Features, New Yorker Films, October Films, Paramount Pictures, Phaedra Cinema, PolyGram, 7th Art Releasing, Sony Pictures Entertainment, Sheldon Stone, Strand Releasing, Paul Sugarman, Twentieth Century Fox, Universal Pictures, Richard Valley, Walt Disney Pictures, Robert Ward, Glenn Young, Zeitgeist Films.

1. Julia Roberts

2. Tom Hanks

3. Adam Sandler

4. Bruce Willis

5. Mike Myers

6. Tom Cruise

7. Will Smith

8. Mel Gibson

9. Meg Ryan

10. Sandra Bullock

TOP BOX OFFICE STARS OF 1999

6

1999 RELEASES

January 1 Through December 31, 1999

VARSITY BLUES

(PARAMOUNT) Producer, Tova Laiter, Mike Tollin, Brian Robbins; Executive Producers, David Gale, Van Toffler; Director, Brian Robbins; Screenplay, W. Peter Iliff; Photography, Charles Cohen; Designer, Jaymes Hinkle; Editor, Ned Bastille; Costumes, Wendy Chuck; Co-Producers, Herbert W. Gains, Ruben Hostka; Music, Mark Isham; Casting, Bob Krakower, Sarah Halley Finn; a Marquee Tollin/Robbins production in association with Tova Laiter Productions; Presented in association with MTV Films; Dolby; Deluxe color; Rated R; 104 minutes; Release date: January 15, 1999

James Van Der Beek, Jon Voight, Ron Lester

CAST

Jonathan "Mox" Moxon	James Van Der Beek
Coach Bud Kilmer	Jon Voight
Lance Harbor	Paul Walker
Billy Bob	Ron Lester
Tweeter	Scott Caan
Joe Harbor	Richard Lineback
Collette Harbor	Tiffany C. Love
Julie Harbor	Amy Smar
Wendell	Eliel Swinton
Sam Moxon	Thomas F. Duffy
Mo Moxon	Jill Parker Jones
Kyle Moxon	Joe Pichler
Chet McNurty	Mark Walters
Sheriff Bigelow	Brady Coleman
Murray	James Harrell
Darcy	Ali Larter
Miss Davis	Tonie Perensky
Tommy Harbor	Jesse Plemons
Cashier	Sam Pleasant
Coach Bates	Tim Crowley

and Joe Stevens, Don Cass (Young Deputies), James Michael O'Brien (Brett), Robert Ellis (Referee), Robert S. Lott (Middle Aged Fan), Barry Switzer (Bronco Coach), Mona Lee (Old Miss Logan), Kevin Reid (Wilkes), Eric Jungmann (Elliot), Laura Olson, Ryan Allen (Teen Babes), Bristi Havins (Cute Naked Girl), John Hyrns (Bald Guy), Rome Azzaro (Young Father), Marco Perella (Dr. Benton), Doyle Carter (Doctor/Field), Tony Frank (Clerk), Sue Rock (Minnie), Olin Buchanan (Reporter), David Williams (Coyote Player), John Gatins (Smiling Man)

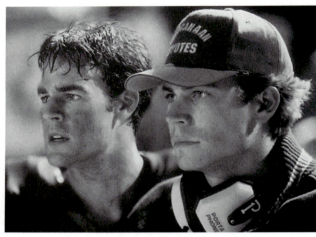

James Van Der Beek, Paul Walker

17-year-old Mox is promoted to first-string quarterback of his high school football team despite his disapproval of the coach's relentless drive to win and his small Texas town's blind emphasis on the importance of the sport.

Amy Smart, James Van Der Beek, Ali Larter

(clockwise from bottom center) James Van Der Beek, Amy Smart, Eliel Swinton, Paul Walker, Ali Larter, Ron Lester, Scott Caan

Val Kilmer, Mira Sorvino, Steven Weber

AT FIRST SIGHT

Val Kilmer, Mira Sorvino

(**MGM**) Producers, Irwin Winkler, Rob Cowan; Director, Irwin Winkler; Screenplay, Steve Levitt; Based on the story *To See and Not See* by Oliver Sacks, M.D.; Photography, John Seale; Designer, Jane Musky; Editor, Julie Monroe; Costumes, John Dunn; Line Producer, Roger Paradiso; Music, Mark Isham; Song: *Love Is Where You Are* by Mark Isham (music), Alan & Marilyn Bergman (lyrics)/performed by Diana Krall; Casting, Billy Hopkins, Suzanne Smith, Kerry Barden; Dolby; Deluxe color; Rated PG-13; 128 minutes; Release date: January 15, 1999

CAST

Virgil Adamson	Val Kilmer
Amy Benic	Mira Sorvino
Jennie Adamson	Kelly McGillis
Duncan Allanbrook	Steven Weber
Dr. Charles Aaron	Bruce Davison
Phil Webster	Nathan Lane
Virgil's Father	Ken Howard
Betsy Ernst	Laura Kirk
Nancy Bender	Margo Winkler
Singer	Diana Krall
Ethan	Brett Robbins
Jack Falk	Willie Carpenter
Health Instructor	Charles Winkler
Caroline	Drena De Niro
Susan	Kelly Chapman Meyer
Dr. Goldman	Jack Dodick
Christie Evans	Nina Griscom
Homeless Man	Mortimer B. Zuckerman
Marshall	Gene Kirkwood

Kelly McGillis, Val Kilmer

and Richard Euell (Carl Kipling), Carl Matusovich (Tommy), John W. Guidera (Virgil's Co-Worker), Jack Cooper (Overweight Man), Jennifer Wachtell (Eva), Marty Davey (School Mother), Ben Wolfe (Bass Player), Casey W. Harris (Casey), Ricky Trammell (Loft D.J.), J.P. Patterson (Waiter), Bonnie Deutsch (Worker), Sheryl Allington Carter, Oliver Saks, Angela Wang, Claude Ravier (Reporters)

Amy Benic meets and falls in love with a blind man, Virgil Adamson, whom she encourages to agree to a surgical procedure that will restore his sight.

© Metro-Goldwyn-Mayer Pictures Inc.

Nathan Lane, Val Kilmer

Annette Bening

Aidan Quinn, Stephen Rea

Robert Downey, Jr.

IN DREAMS

(**DREAMWORKS**) Producer, Stephen Woolley; Director, Neil Jordan; Screenplay, Bruce Robinson, Neil Jordan; Based upon the novel *Doll's Eyes* by Bari Wood; Co-Producer, Redmond Morris; Photography, Darius Khondji; Designer, Nigel Phelps; Editor, Tony Lawson; Costumes, Jeffrey Kurland; Music, Elliot Goldenthal; Special Effects Supervisor, Yves De Bono; Underater Photography, Peter Romano; Casting, Janet Hirshenson, Jane Jenkins; a Stephen Woolley production; Dolby; Panavision; Technicolor; Rated R; 99 minutes; Release date: January 15, 1999

CAST

Claire Cooper ....Annette Bening
Vivian Thompson ....Robert Downey, Jr.
Dr. Silverman ....Stephen Rea
Paul Cooper ....Aidan Quinn
Detective Jack Kay ....Paul Guilfoyle
Dr. Stevens ....Dennis Boutsikaris
Rebecca Cooper ....Katie Sagona
Ruby ....Krystal Benn
Mary ....Prudence Wright
HolmesEthel...Pamela Payton-Wright
Nurse Floyd...Margo Martindale
Snow White..Kathleen Langlois
Hunter ....Jennifer Berry
Prince ....Amelia Claire Novotny
Wicked Stepmother...Kristin Sroka
Man at School Play ....Robert Walsh
Woman at School Play...Denise Cormier
Policeman ....John Fiore
Paramedic ....Ken Cheeseman
Vivian Thompson (as boy) ....Devon Cole Borisoff
Nurse Rosco ....Lonnie Farmer
and June Lewin (Kindly Nurse), Dorothy Dwyer (Foster Mother), Geoff Wigdor (Vivian Thompson—as teenager), Wally Dunn (Walter), Eric Roemele (Security Man—1970s), Dossy Peabody (Vivian's Mother), John Michael Vaughn (Helicopter Pilot), Brian Goodman (Policeman in Squad Car), Michael Cavanaugh (Voice of Judge), Pete ("Dobie"), Emma J. Brown, Jennifer Dragon, Samantha Kelly, Jennifer Caine Natenshon, Bethany M. Paquin, Erica Sullivan (Dwarves)

Claire Cooper begins having bizarre visions of a missing girl and an underwater town, disturbing images that seem to connect her to a serial killer on the loose.

© DreamWorks LLC

Annette Bening, Robert Downey, Jr.

SHE'S ALL THAT

(**MIRAMAX**) Producers, Peter Abrams, Robert L. Levy, Richard N. Gladstein; Executive Producers, Bob Weinstein, Harvey Weinstein; Director, Robert Iscove; Screenplay, R. Lee Fleming, Jr.; Co-Executive Producers, Jeremy Kramer, Jill Sobel Messick; Co-Producers, Jennifer Gibgot, Richard Hull; Photography, Francis Kenny; Designer, Charles Breen; Editor, Casey O. Rohrs; Costumes, Denise Wingate; Music, Stewart Copeland; Music Supervisor, Amanda Scheer-Demme; Line Producer, Louise Rosner; a Tapestry Films/Film Colony production; Dolby; Technicolor; Rated PG-13; 95 minutes; Release date: January 29, 1999

Rachael Leigh Cook, Freddie Prinze, Jr.

CAST

Zack Siler	Freddie Prinze, Jr.
Laney Boggs	Rachael Leigh Cook
Brock Hudson	Matthew Lillard
Dean Sampson	Paul Walker
Taylor Vaughan	Jodi Lyn O'Keefe
Wayne Boggs	Kevin Pollak
Mackenzie Siler	Anna Paquin
Simon Boggs	Kieran Culkin
Jesse Jackson	Elden Henson
Campus D.J.	Usher Raymond
Alex	Kimberly "Lil' Kim" Jones
Katie	Gabrielle Union
Preston Harrison	Dulé Hill
Chandler	Tamara Mello
Misty	Clea DuVall
Harlan Siler	Tim Matheson
Ms. Rousseau	Debbi Morgan
Mitch	Alexis Arquette

Dave Buzzotta (Jeffrey Munge Rylander), Chris Owen (Derek Funkhouser Rutley), Charlie Dell (Elderly Man), Michael Milhoan (Principal Stickley), Carlos Jacott (Prom Photographer), Ashlee Levitch (Melissa), Vanessa Lee Chester (Girl #2), Patricia Charbonneau (Lois Siler), Katherine Towne (Savannah), Wendy Fowler (Harmony), Flex Alexander (Kadeem), Bob Baglia (Beatnik), Debbie Lee Carrington (Felicity), Clay Rivers (Gustave), Sara Rivas (Vampire Girl), Amon Bourne, Takbir Bashir, Anthony "Click" Rivera (Rappers), Jarrett Lennon (Naylon), Milo Ventimigilia (Soccer Player), Kenté Scott (Sophomore Boy), Kim Cotton, T.J. Espinoza, Brian Friedman, Tony Fugate, Caroline Girvin, Alicia Gilley, Scott Hislop, Jennifer Keyes, Richard Kim, Stephanie Landwehr, Dani Lee, Joe Loera, Mayah McCoy, Yesha Orange, Robert Schultz, Josh Seffinger, Sarah Smith, Christopher Smith, Bree Turner, Christine Vincent, Jerry "Flo" Randolph (Dancers), Sarah Michelle Gellar (Girl in Cafeteria)

Kieran Culkin, Kevin Pollak

Devestated that his girlfriend has dumped him, popular high school teen Zack Siler, now dateless for the prom, takes a wager that he can turn the shy, unpopular Laney into the prom queen.

© Miramax Films

Paul Walker, Dulé Hill, Freddie Prinze, Jr.

Jodi Lyn O'Keefe, Freddie Prinze, Jr.

Wendell Pierce, Marianne Jean-Baptiste

THE 24 HOUR WOMAN

Rosie Perez

(**ARTISAN**) Producers, Richard Guay, Larry Meistrich, Peter Newman; Executive Producers, Steve Carlis, Donald C. Carter, Daniel J. Victor; Director, Nancy Savoca; Screenplay, Nancy Savoca, Richard Guay; Photography, Teresa Medina; Co-Producer, Rosie Perez; Designer, Bob Shaw; Editor, Camilla Toniolo; Music, "Little" Louie Vega, Kenny "Dope" Gonzalez; Line Producer, Diana Schmidt; Casting, Sheila Jaffe, Georgianne Walken; a Shooting Gallery presentation of a Redeemable Features/Exile Films production in association with Dirt Road Productions; Dolby; Color; Rated R; 95 minutes; Release date: January 29, 1999

CAST

Grace Santos	Rosie Perez
Madeline Labelle	Marianne Jean-Baptiste
Joan Marshall	Patti LuPone
Margo Lynn	Karen Duffy
Eddie Diaz	Diego Serrano
Roy Labelle	Wendell Pierce
Dr. Suzanne Pincus	Melissa Leo
Brenda	Aida Turturro
Linda	Rosana DeSoto
Patty	Alicia Rene Washington
Crystal	Reno
Young Woman	Bianca Bakija
Nurse	Elizabeth Bracco
Deanne	Samantha Buck
Phil	Dale Carman
Security Guard	Nicky Cappodanno
Cook	Olga Divina
Suzanne Pincus' Publicist	Michael Cumpsty
Lori	Drena De Niro

Diego Serrano

and Brandi & Jade DiCesare, Daniel Hernandez, Madison Valdes (Lily—newborn), Wally Dunn (Ray), Daryl Edwards (Dr. Walker), Carla Gallo (Pantyhose Victim), Richard Guay (Jim—New Director), Cari Gorostiza (Abuela), Jayne Haynes (Dr. Huffington), Beth Littleford (Lynn Shapiro), Marianne Leone, Alan Pottinger (Cable Executives), Angie Martinez (Herself), Marcus Matthews (Derek Labelle), Ivan J. Moffitt (Leon), Jay Potter (John Garson), Sandra Prosper (Press Agent), Angie Utt, Sixto Ramos (Audience Members), Blake Ramsey (Carvel Clerk), Steven Randazzo (Security Guard—CBS), Jose Ramon Rosario (Candy Store Manager), Jordana & Olivia Rosenzweig (Lily—age 1), Carl Savoca (Police Officer), Kristin Sentman (Cheryl), Jerry Springer (Himself), Corey Twitty (TJ Labelle), Kianna Underwood (Taneesha Labelle), Rick Washburn (Police Officer—CBS), J.D. Williams (Toy Store Clerk)

When television producer Grace Santos reveals her pregnancy on the air of her local New York morning show, her ratings-hungry executive producer decides to cash in on the event by focusing the program on the baby's upcoming delivery.

©TSG Pictures

Alicia Rene Washington, Patti LuPone, Aida Turturro

PAYBACK

(**PARAMOUNT**) Producer, Bruce Davey; Executive Producer, Stephen McEveety; Director, Brian Helgeland; Screenplay, Brian Helgeland, Terry Hayes; Based on the novel *The Hunter* by Richard Stark; Photography, Ericson Core; Designer, Richard Hoover; Editor, Kevin Stitt; Costumes, Ha Nguyen; Music, Chris Boardman; Casting, Marion Dougherty; an Icon production; Dolby; Super 35 Widescreen; Deluxe color; Rated R; 102 minutes; Release date: February 5, 1999

CAST

Porter	Mel Gibson
Val Resnick	Gregg Henry
Rosie	Maria Bello
Stegman	David Paymer
Detective Hicks	Bill Duke
Lynn	Deborah Kara Unger
Phil	John Glover
Carter	William Devane
Pearl	Lucy Alexis Liu
Detective Leary	Jack Conley
Bronson	Kris Kristofferson
Fairfax	James Coburn
Johnny's Friends	Nathan Effron, Mark Alfa
Radioman	Kwame Amoaku
Michael the Bartender	Justin Ashforth
Fairfax Bodyguards	Len Bajenski, Michael Skewes
Counter Girl	Kate Buddeke
Bronson's Heavies	Price Carson, Art Cohan
Chow Thug's	Michael Ingram, Roddy Chiong
Whipping Boy	Andrew Cooper
Tailor	James Deuter
Fatboy	Doc Duhame
Doctor	David Dunard

and Tom Equin, Daniel Patrick Sullivan (Razor Cleans), Brian Heinberg (Bartender #2), Alex Henteloff (Varrick's Manager), Jeff Imada (Chow's Bodyguard), Robert Kim (Chow's Courier), Robert Kurcz (Oakwood Arms Manager), Turk Muller (Black Suit), Chet Nichols, Alex Skuby (Oakwood Arms Toughs), George O'Mara (Driver), Yasen Peyankov (Panhandler), Ed Pfeifer (Ed Johnson), Katrina Phillips (Teller), Freddy Rodriguez (Punk Messenger), Trevor St. John (Johnny), Lee Stepp (Bar Patron), Tedd Taskey (Waiter), Manu Tupou (Pawnbroker), Marc Vann (Gray)

Porter, left for dead by his cohort after commiting a heist, survives and becomes singularly determined to get his share of the money, no matter who stands in his way. Earlier film version was Point Blank (MGM, 1967) starring Lee Marvin.

© Icon Distribution, Inc.

Mel Gibson, Gregg Henry

Mel Gibson, David Paymer

Mel Gibson, Gregg Henry, Lucy Alexis Liu

Maria Bello, Mel Gibson

BLAST FROM THE PAST

(**NEW LINE CINEMA**) Producers, Renny Harlin, Hugh Wilson; Executive Producers, Amanda Stern, Sunil Perkash, Claire Rudnick Polstein; Director, Hugh Wilson; Screenplay, Bill Kelly, Hugh Wilson; Story, Bill Kelly; Co-Producer, Mary Kane; Photography, Jose Luis Alcaine; Designer, Robert Ziembicki; Editor, Don Brochu; Costumes, Mark Bridges; Music, Steve Dorff; Casting, Denise Chamian; a Midnight Sun Pictures production; Dolby; Super 35 Widescreen; Deluxe color; Rated PG-13; 111 minutes; Release date: February 12, 1999

Alicia Silverstone, Brendan Fraser

CAST

Adam Webber	Brendan Fraser
Eve Rostokov	Alicia Silverstone
Calvin Webber	Christopher Walken
Helen Webber	Sissy Spacek
Troy	Dave Foley
Soda Jerk	Joey Slotnick
Mom	Dale Raoul
Adam age 3 1/2	Hayden Tank
Adam age 11	Douglas Smith
Adam age 8	Ryan Sparks
Jerry	Don Yesso
Young Psycho	Scott Thomson
Navy Pilot	Ted Kairys
Dave	Rex Linn
Betty	Cynthia Mace
Bob	Harry S. Murphy
Ruth	Wendel Meldurm
Guest	Richard Gilbert Hill
Harold	Steve Bean

and Ann Ryerson (Woman Guest #1), Donovan Scott (Ron), Hugh Wilson (Levy), John Roselius (Atkinson), Bill Gratton (Boss), Bill Duffy, Bill Stevenson (Workmen), J. Bruce Eckert (Realtor), Karen Geraghty, Christopher Holloway (Buyers), Harrison Young (Bum), Jazzmun (Streetwalker), Hannah Kozak (Drunken Hag), Dori Mizrahi (Pakistani), Fred Pierce, Hubert Hodgin (Bystanders), Annie O'Donnell (Woman), Caroline Wilson (Child), Julie Zelman (Mother), Monty Ash (Old Jewish Man), Sheila Shaw (Bakery Clerk), Michael Hagiwara (Japanese Produce Clerk), Todd Susman (Butcher), Rosalee Mayeux (Hotel Registration Clerk), Danny Zorn (Bellboy), Rod Britt (Hotel Desk Clerk), Robb Skyler (Marine Manager), Nathan Fillion (Cliff), Todd Robert Anderson (Jason), Michael Gallagher (Jonathan), Carmen Moré (Sophie), Deborah Kellner (Miss Sweet), Mary Ann Hermanson (Heather), Jenifer Lewis (Dr. Aron), Jonathan Stockwell Baker (Broker), Brian Blondell (Mr. Brown), Sonya Eddy (Postal Worker), Mary Portser (Woman Guest #2), Gary Cruz (Low Rider), Robert Sacchi (Bogart DJ)

Dave Foley

Sissy Spacek

Adam Webber, born and raised in an underground fallout shelter, is sent out into modern day Los Angeles at the age of 35 where his innocence charms the jaded Eve Rostokov.

© New Line Productions, Inc.

Ryan Sparks, Sissy Spacek, Christopher Walken

Christopher Walken

MY FAVORITE MARTIAN

(**WALT DISNEY PICTURES**) Producers, Robert Shapiro, Jerry Leider, Mark Toberoff; Executive Producer, Barry Bernardi; Director, Donald Petrie; Screenplay, Sherri Stoner, Deanna Oliver; Based on the television series created by John L. Greene and produced by Jack Chertok; Photography, Thomas Ackerman; Designer, Sandy Veneziano; Editor, Malcolm Campbell; Co-Producer, Daryl Kass; Visual Effects Supervisors, Phil Tippett, John T. Van Vliet; Animatronic Martian Effects Designers and Creators, Alec Gillis, Tom Woodruff Jr.; Costumes, Hope Hanafin; Music, John Debney; Casting, Janet Hirshenson, Jane Jenkins; a Jerry Leider/Robert Shapiro production; Dolby; Technicolor; Rated PG; 93 minutes; Release date: February 12, 1999

Daryl Hannah, Jeff Daniels

CAST

Uncle Martin	Christopher Lloyd
Tim O'Hara	Jeff Daniels
Brace Channing	Elizabeth Hurley
Lizzie	Daryl Hannah
Coleye	Wallace Shawn
Mrs. Brown	Christine Ebersole
Mr. Channing	Michael Lerner
Armitan	Ray Walston
Voice of Zoot	Wayne Knight
Felix	Shelley Malil
Billy	Jeremy Hotz
Lenny	T.K. Carter

and Dawn Maxey (Salesgirl), Steven Anthony Lawrence (Nurplex Kid), Michael Chieffo (Earl Metz), Troy Evans (Captain Dalton), Arthur Senzy (Cmdr. Murdoch), Charles Chun (Radar Controller), Michael Dempsey (Van Gundy), David St. James (Prescott), Dee Anne Helsel (Dressing Room Woman), Joe Garrett (Hardware Store Employee), Lorin McRaley (Cool Dude), Ken Thorley (KTSC Floor Manager), Tom Hallick (Howard Greenly), Barry Pearl (News Director), Buck Kartalian (Muscle Man), Steve Bond (The SETI Group Driver), Sylvester "Bear" Terkay (Huge Guard), Michael Bailey Smith (Big Guard), Jean-Luc Martin (Guard at Gate), Christian Keiber (Guard at Clearing), Richard Kleber (Mr. Butz), Debra Christofferson (Mrs. Butz), Howard H. Ross (Newspaper Man), Allan Kolman, Robert Rigamonti, Pamela Gordon, Beau Billingslea, Michael Adler (Scientists), Frank Cavestani (Tanning Contest Emcee)

Television reporter Tim O'Hara stumbles upon a Martian and intends to expose the alien to the media until the spaceman convinces Tim to help him repair his ship and return to Mars. Based on the television series that ran on CBS from 1963 to 1966 and starred Ray Walston and Bill Bixby. Walston makes an appearance in this film.

Christopher Lloyd

Julia Sweeney

GOD SAID, "HA!"

(**MIRAMAX**) Producer, Rana Joy Glickman; Executive Producer, Quentin Tarantino; Director/Screenplay, Julia Sweeney; Based on her stage play; Co-Producer, Greg Kachel; Line Producer, Dawn Todd; Associate Producer, Mark Friedman; Designer, Gail Bennett; Music, Anthony Marinelli; Photography, John Hora; Editor, Fabienne Rawley; a presentation of Oh Brother Productions; Dolby; FotoKem color; Rated PG-13; 83 minutes; Release date: February 12, 1999.

A one-woman performance piece by Julia Sweeney relating how her life unraveled after her brother became sick and moved in with her, prompting her parents to move in as well.

Kevin Costner, Robin Wright Penn

MESSAGE IN A BOTTLE

(**WARNER BROS.**) Producers, Denise Di Novi, Jim Wilson, Kevin Costner; Director, Luis Mandoki; Screenplay, Gerald DiPego; Based on the novel by Nicholas Sparks; Photography, Caleb Deschanel; Designer, Jeffrey Beecroft; Music, Gabriel Yared; Editor, Steven Weisberg; Costumes, Bernie Pollack; Casting, Amanda Mackey Johnson, Cathy Sandrich; Presented in association with Bel-Air Entertainment; a Tig Production in association with Di Novi Pictures; Dolby; Panavision; Technicolor; Rated PG-13; 132 minutes; Release date: February 12, 1999

CAST

Garret Blake	Kevin Costner
Theresa Osborne	Robin Wright Penn
Dodge Blake	Paul Newman
Johnny Land	John Savage
Lina	Illeana Douglas
Charlie	Robbie Coltrane
Jason	Jesse James
Marta Land	Bethel Leslie
Hank Land	Tom Aldredge
Alva	Viveka Davis
Andy	Raphael Sbarge
Chet	Richard Hamilton
Helen at the B&B	Rosemary Murphy
David	Steven Eckholdt
Catherine	Susan Brightbill
Annie	Patricia Belcher
Man on Dock	Steve Mellor
Man on Sinking Boat	Lance Gilbert
Woman on Sinking Boat	Jennifer Lamb
Girl on Sinking Boat	Hayden Panettiere
Pete the Cop	Walt MacPherson

and Justin DiPego (Typewriter Repairman), Meagan Riley-Grant (Mary), Karen Fowler (Mother in Car), Caleb Deschanel (Man at the B&B), Mauricio Ochmann (Mail Boy), Anthony Genovese (Photographer), Elizabeth Guindi (Christine), Donald Watson, Clapham Murray (Diner Patrons), Gregg Trzaskowski, Robert E. Tarlow (Johnny Friends), Philip Traynor (Boy in Car), Daniel V. Trefts (Policeman on Boat), Christina Bergstrom, Norman Fessler (Officer Workers)

Theresa Osborne discovers a love letter inside a bottle on the beach and tracks down the sender, a reclusive sailboat builder who is still trying to cope with the loss of his wife.

© Warner Bros.

Kevin Costner, Paul Newman

Robin Wright Penn, Kevin Costner

Kevin Costner, Paul Newman

Chris Cooper, Jake Gyllenhaal

Jake Gyllenhaal, Laura Dern

Chad Lindberg, William Lee Scott, Jake Gyllenhaal, Chris Owen

William Lee Scott, Jake Gyllenhaal, Chris Owen, Chad Lindberg

© Universal Studios

OCTOBER SKY

(**UNIVERSAL**) Producers, Charles Gordon, Larry Franco; Executive Producers, Marc Sternberg, Peter Cramer; Director, Joe Johnston; Screenplay, Lewis Colick; Based on the book *Rocket Boy*s by Homer H. Hickam, Jr.; Photography, Fred Murphy; Designer, Barry Robison; Editor, Robert Dalva; Music, Mark Isham; Costumes, Betsy Cox; Casting, Nancy Foy; a Charles Gordon production; Dolby; Panavision; Deluxe color; Rated PG; 108 minutes; Release date: February 19, 1999

CAST

Homer Hickam ....Jake Gyllenhaal
John Hickam ....Chris Cooper
Miss Riley ....Laura Dern
Quentin ....Chris Owen
Roy Lee ....William Lee Scott
O'Dell..Chad Lindberg
Elsie Hickam ....Natalie Canerday
Jim Hickam ....Scott Miles
Leon Bolden...Randy Stripling
Principal Turner...Chris Ellis
Ike Bykovsky...Elya Baskin
Dorothy Platt ....Courtney Fendley
Jake Mosby...David Dwyer
Mr. Dantzler..Terry Loughlin
Valentine Carmina..Kaili Hollister
Coach Gainer...David Copeland
Jensen ....Don Henderson Baker
Lenny...Tom Kagy
and Donald Thorne (Trooper One), Justin Whitsett (Kid), Larry Rue, Neva Howell, Terry Nienhuis (Neighbors), Brady Coleman (Anderson), Rick Forrester (Roper), Terrence Gibney (Basil Thorpe), Doug Swander (Corvette Guy), Keeli Hale Kimbro (Corvette Girl), Mark Jeffrey Miller (Vernon), Blaque Fowler (Reverend), Don Tilley (Rescue Worker), Rockford Davis (Chemistry Teacher), John Bennes (Doctor), Jonathan Fawbush (Barney), Larry Black (Fred Smith), Frank Schuler (Moonshiner), Tommy Smetzler (Man at Mine), Charles Lawlor, Tom Turbiville (Miners), Ida Ginn (Quentin's Mom), Richard Lumpkin (Judge at Welch), Mark Whitman Johnson, Don Taylor (Union Officials), Don G. Campbell (Mr. Morris), Elizabeth Byler (Ivy League Girl), Bradford Ryan Lund (Ivy League Boy), Frank Hoyt Taylor (Judge at Indy), Dvid Hager (Head Judge), Ray Elder (Tom Webster), Andy Stahl (Jack Palmer), Joey DiGaetano (Wernher Von Braun), Thomas Taylor (Miner in Elevator), David Ducey (Man in Crowd), Jenny Patterson (Nurse), O. Winston Link (Locomotive Engineer)

Inspired by the 1957 flight of the Soviet satellite Sputnik, young Homer Hickam sets his sights on a future in the space program rather than become the coal miner his father expects him to be.

Gary Cole, Ron Livingston

Ajay Naidu, David Herman

© Twentieth Century Fox

Jennifer Aniston, Ron Livingston

Ron Livingston, David Herman, Ajay Naidu

OFFICE SPACE

(**20TH CENTURY FOX**) Producers, Michael Rotenberg, Daniel Rappaport; Executive Producer, Guy Riedel; Director/Screenplay, Mike Judge; Based upon his "Milton" animated shorts; Photography, Tim Suhrstedt; Designer, Edward McAvoy; Editor, David Rennie; Costumes, Melinda Eshelman; Music, John Frizzell; Casting, Nancy Klopper; Dolby; Deluxe color; Rated R; 89 minutes; Release date: February 19, 1999

CAST

Peter Gibbons ....Ron Livingston
Joanna ....Jennifer Aniston
Michael Bolton ....David Herman
Samir ....Ajay Naidu
Lawrence...Diedrich Bader
Milton..Stephen Root
Bill Lumbergh...Gary Cole
Tom Smykowski...Richard Riehle
Anne ....Alexandra Wentworth
Dom Portwood...Joe Bays
Bob Slydell ....John C. McGinley
Bob Porter...Paul Willson
and Kinna McInroe (Nina), Todd Duffey (Chotchkie's Waiter), Greg Pitts (Drew), Micheal McShane (Dr. Swanson), Linda Wakeman (Laura Smykowski), Jennifer Jane Emerson (Temp), Josh Bond (Initech Security Guard), Kyle Scott Jackson (Rob Newhouse), Orlando Jones (Steve), Barbara George-Reiss (Lumbergh's Secretary), Tom Schuster (Construction Foreman), Ruperto Reyes, Jr. (Mexican Waiter), Jackie Belvin, Gabriel Folse (Swanson's Patients), Jesse De Luna (Cop at Fire), William King (Chotchkie's Manager), Justin Possenti (Spectator), Jack Betts (Judge)

Hoping to get himself fired, computer programmer Peter Gibbons begins showing up at work on his own designated hours only to find himself getting a promotion.

8MM

(COLUMBIA) Producers, Gavin Polone, Judy Hofflund, Joel Schumacher; Executive Producer, Joseph M. Caracciolo; Director, Joel Schumacher; Screenplay, Andrew Kevin Walker; Photography, Robert Elswit; Designer, Gary Wissner; Editor, Mark Stevens; Music, Mychael Danna; Co-Producer, Jeff Levine; Costumes, Mona May; Casting, Mali Finn; a Hofflund/Polone production; Dolby; Super 35 Widescreen; Technicolor; Rated R; 123 minutes; Release date: February 26, 1999

Nicolas Cage, Chris Bauer, Peter Stormare

CAST

Tom Welles ....Nicolas Cage
Max California...Joaquin Phoenix
Eddie Poole ....James Gandolfini
Dino Velvet...Peter Stormare
Longdale ....Anthony Heald
Machine...Chris Bauer
Amy Welles ....Catherine Keener
Mrs. Christian...Myra Carter
Mrs. Mathews ....Amy Morton
Mary Anne Mathews ....Jenny Powell
Senator ....Anne Gee Byrd
Butler...Jack Betts
Archive Director...Luis Oropeza
Neighbor ....Rachel Singer
Mr. Anderson...Don Creech
Warren Anderson ....Norman Reedus
Nuns ....Fran Bennett, Wilma Bonet
Manny ....Luis Saguar
and Walter K. Jordan, Norm Compton, Brian Keith Russell (Thugs), John Robb (Porn Dealer), Devan Brown (Flea Market Woman), Doris Brent (Machine's Mother), Robert Amico (Casting Director), Kiva Dawson, Eva Minemar, Rachel Dara Wolfe (Girls in Hall), Suzy Nakamura (Computer Wizard), Torsten Voges (Stick), Tahitia Dean (Hollywood Prostitute), Terri Larid (Dino's Redhead), Vernon Guichard (Porn Guy), Emily Patrick (Porn Girl), Nancy Lynn Vaughn (Porno Make-up Artist), Lisa Vanasco (Topless Ticket Taker), Bridgett Vera (Ticket Taker), Jennifer Harris, Burton Richards, Jovanna Vitiello (Strip Club Dancers), David U. Hodges (Surveillance Man), William Lawrence Mack (Bouncer), Lorena Martinez (Prostitute), Connie Mercurio (Nurse), William Buck (Mr. Christian), Kerry Corcoran (Cheating Son-in-Law), Mario Ernesto Sanchez (Taxi Driver), Claudia Aros (Miami Girlfriend)

Nicolas Cage

Hired by the widow of a millionaire to determine whether the "snuff film" found in her late husband's vault is authentic, surveillance specialist Tom Welles finds himself being drawn deeper into the dangerous world of underground pornographic filmmaking.

Nicolas Cage, Joaquin Phoenix

James Gandolfini

JUST THE TICKET

(**UNITED ARTISTS**) Producers, Gary Lucchesi, Andy Garcia; Executive Producers, Andie MacDowell, Yoram Pelman; Director/Screenplay, Richard Wenk; Photography, Ellen Kuras; Designer, Franckie Diago; Costumes, Susan Lyall; Editor, Christopher Cibelli; Music, Rick Marotta; Co-Producer, John H. Starke; Casting, Amanda Mackey Johnson, Cathy Sandrich; a CineSon production; Dolby; Deluxe color; Rated R; 115 minutes; Release date: February 26, 1999

CAST

Gary Starke	Andy Garcia
Linda Paliski	Andie MacDowell
Benny Moran	Richard Bradford
Mrs. Paliski	Elizabeth Ashley
Zeus	Fred Asparagus
Casino	André Blake
San Diego Vinnie	Patrick Breen
Gerrard (Culinary Director)	Ronald Guttman
Realtor	Donna Hanover
Cyclops	Laura Harris
Ray Charles	Bill Irwin
Alex	Chris Lemmon
Barry the Book	Ron Leibman
Harry the Head	Louis Mustillo
Rhonda	Paunita Nichols
Tony	Don Novello
Arty	Abe Vigoda
Mrs. Haywood	Irene Worth
Himself	Joe Frazier

and Sullivan Cooke ("Blinker"), Alice Drummond (Lady with Cash), Anita Elliott (Refund Lady at the Met), Michael Willis (TV Customer), Jack Cafferty (Newscaster), Molly Wenk (Catholic Schoolgirl Fanny), Daniella Garcia-Lorido (Catholic Schoolgirl Lucy), Michael P. Moran (Fat Max), Helen Carey (Food Critic), Bobo Lewis (Mrs. Dolmatch), Brian Schwary (College Kid in Jail), Davenia McFadden (Social Security Checker), Lenny Venito (Stanley), Richard Wenk ("Good Call Johnny" D.J.), George Palermo (Undercover Cop), Anthony DeSando (Kenny Paliski), Robert Castle (Uncle Donald), Sully Boyar (Uncle Tony), Luis Aponte (Maury—Funeral Director), Joe Drago (Father V. Crespo), Alfredo Alvarez Calderon (Yankee Stadium Security Chief), Gene Greytak (The Pope), Joanna P. Adler (Vickie), John Tormey (Taxi Cab Driver), Michael Higgins (Confessional Priest), Austin Lyall Sansone (Baby in Womb)

Gary Starke, a street smart ticket scalper, figures he can win back his fed-up girlfriend Linda if he can make a killing on one last score, setting his sights on the Pope's Easter Mass at Yankee Stadium.

© MGM Distribution Co.

Andie MacDowell, Andy Garcia

Martha Plimpton, Brian McCardie, Catherine Kellner

Paul Rudd, Janeane Garofalo

200 CIGARETTES

(**PARAMOUNT**) Producers, Betsy Beers, David Gale, Van Toffler; Executive Producers, Tom Rosenberg, Mike Newell, Alan Greenspan, Ted Tannebaum, Sigurjon Sighvatsson; Director, Risa Bramon Garcia; Screenplay, Shana Larsen; Photography, Frank Prinzi; Editor, Lisa Zeno Churgin; Designer, Ina Mayhew; Costumes, Susan Lyall; Music, Bob and Mark Mothersbaugh; Music Supervisor, Randall Poster; Co-Producers, Cecilia Kate Roque, Andrew Lamal, Steven L. Bernstein; Casting, Deborah Aquila, Sarah Halley Finn; a Lakeshore Entertainment presentation in association with MTV Films and Dogstar Films; Dolby; Deluxe color; Rated R; 101 minutes; Release date: February 26, 1999

CAST

Bartender	Ben Affleck
Tom	Casey Affleck
Disco Cabbie	Dave Chappelle
Dave	Guillermo Diaz
Caitlyn	Angela Featherstone
Ellie	Janeane Garofalo
Stephie	Gaby Hoffman
Cindy	Kate Hudson

and Courtney Love (Lucy), Jay Mohr (Jack), Martha Plimpton (Monica), Christina Ricci (Val), Paul Rudd (Kevin) Jennifer Albano (Cheryl), Jenny Blong (Cheryl's Friend), Morgan Brown (French Rocker), Caleb Carr (Cynical Bar Patron), Elvis Costello (Himself), Patrick Frederic (Tiki Sobbing Man), David Johansen (Tiki Bartender), Catherine Kellner (Hillary), Kiran Merchant (Restaurant Owner), Brian McCardie (Eric), James Murphy (Drag Queen), Nicole Parker (Bridget), Patricia Wible (Ace Bar Patron)

A comedy following various young couples and friends whose lives ultimately intersect in an East Village loft on New Year's Eve, 1981.

© Paramount Pictures/Lakeshore Pictures

THE OTHER SISTER

(TOUCHSTONE) Producers, Mario Iscovich, Alexandra Rose; Executive Producer, David Hoberman; Director, Garry Marshall; Screenplay, Garry Marshall, Bob Brunner; Story, Alexandra Rose, Blair Richwood, Garry Marshall, Bob Brunner; Co-Producer, Ellen H. Schwartz; Photography, Dante Spinotti; Designer, Stephen J. Lineweaver; Editor, Bruce Green; Music, Rachel Portman; Costumes, Gary Jones; Casting, Gretchen Rennell Court; a Mandeville Films production; Dolby; Super 35 Widescreen; Technicolor; Rated PG-13; 129 minutes; Release date: February 26, 1999

Giovanni Ribisi, Juliette Lewis

CAST

Carla Tate	Juliette Lewis
Elizabeth Tate	Diane Keaton
Radley Tate	Tom Skerritt
Danny McMahon	Giovanni Ribisi
Caroline Tate	Poppy Montgomery
Heather Tate	Sarah Paulson

and Linda Thorson (Drew), Joe Flanigan (Jeff), Juliet Mills (Winnie), Tracy Reiner (Michelle), Hope Alexander-Willis (Marge), Harvey Miller (Dr. Johnson), Hector Elizondo (Ernie), The Tech School: Almayvonne (Rachel), Marvin Braverman (Uncle Sam Teacher), Laura D'Arista (Statue of Liberty Teacher), Linda Hawkins (Student Marilyn), James Emery (Computer Teacher), Steve Lipinsky (Tough Guy Phil), Giuseppe Andrews (Tough Guy Trevor), Jake Wall (School Registration Man), Zaid Faird (Tech Principal), Debra Wiseman (Tech School Student Alice), Sunny Hawks (Broken Toe Student); The Weddings: Dennis Creaghan (Caroline's Minister), Jim Meskimen (Carla's Minister), Julie Paris (Wedding Coordinator), Pierson Blaetz (Assistant Coordinator Mark), Steve Restivo (Bakery Boss Vitello), Shannon Wilcox (Danny's Mom Ruthie), Phil Redrow (Ruthie's Boyfriend Tex), Adrienne Smith (Bridesmaid Ginger), Gretchen Bingham, Mariah Dobson (Bridesmaids), Tom Hines (Best Man), Gregg Goulet (Cousin Teddy), David Sterns, Benjamin Linder, Ryan Hart (Ushers), Connie Engel (Cousin Anne), Barbara Marshall (Guest Cynthia), Frank Campenella (Guest William), Norma Jean Jahn (Guest Grace); The Country Club: Allan Kent (Country Club Bartender), Joe Ross (Maitre'D), Catherine McGoohan, Julia Hunter (Country Club Ladies), Stephanie Kissner (Country Club Member Stephanie), Joy Rosenthal (Country Club Member Joy); The Other Players: Patrick Richwood (Real Estate Agent), Jeanette Lee (Pool Player—Black Widow), Cassie Rowell (Truck Girl Jenny), Anthony Russell (Train Passenger), Bob Brunner (Train Conductor), Richard Stahl (Train Ticket Seller), Steven Daniel (Band Master), Gerald Miller III (Drum Major), Bud Markowitz (Roselake Juggler), Jodi Johnson (Roselake School Teacher), Shiri Appleby (Free Sample Girl), Steve Moloney, David Ketchum (College Maintenance Men), Monette Magrath (Store Clerk), Jason Cottle (Dog Trainer), Jenna Byrne, Ali Gage (Stewardesses), Robert Malina (Bus Driver), Bill Ferrell (Bus Station Bartender), Charles Guardino (Limo Driver), Kendra Krull (Young Carla), Brooke Garrett (Young Caroline), Brighton McCloskey (Young Heather), Jennifer Leigh Warren (Dr. Johnson's Secretary), Colin MacDonald (Mean Young Boy), Dina Merrill

Possessive mother Elizabeth Tate fears the worst when her 24-year-old mentally challenged daughter Carla falls in love with Danny, an equally challenged young man.

© Touchstone Pictures

Sarah Paulson, Poppy Montgomery, Juliette Lewis

Tom Skerritt, Diane Keaton, Juliette Lewis

Hector Elizondo, Giovanni Ribisi

Robert De Niro, Billy Crystal, Lisa Kudrow

Robert De Niro, Billy Crystal

ANALYZE THIS

(**WARNER BROS**.) Producers, Paula Weinstein, Jane Rosenthal; Executive Producers, Billy Crystal, Chris Brigham, Bruce Berman; Director, Harold Ramis; Screenplay, Peter Tolan, Harold Ramis, Kenneth Lonergan; Story, Kenneth Lonergan, Peter Tolan; Photography, Stuart Dryburgh; Designer, Wynn Thomas; Editor, Christopher Tellefsen; Co-Producer, Len Amato; Music, Howard Shore; Associate Producer, Suzanne Herrington; Costumes, Aude Bronson-Howard; Casting, Ellen Chenoweth, Laura Rosenthal; Presented in association with Village Roadshow Pictures and NPV Entertainment; a Baltimore/Spring Creek Pictures/Face/Tribeca production; Dolby; Technicolor; Rated R; 103 minutes; Release date: March 5, 1999

CAST

Paul Vitti	Robert De Niro
Dr. Ben Sobel	Billy Crystal
Laura MacNamara	Lisa Kudrow
Primo Sindone	Chazz Palminteri
Jelly	Joe Viterelli
'50s Gangster	Kresimir Novakovic
Young Vitti	Bart Tangredi
Young Manetta	Michael Straka
Manetta	Joe Rigano
Jimmy	Richard Castellano
Caroline	Molly Shannon
Nicky Shivers	Max Casella
Tuna	Frank Pietrangolare
Michael Sobel	Kyle Sabihy
Isaac Sobel	Bill Macy
Dorothy Sobel	Rebecca Schull
Salvatore Masiello	Pat Cooper
Carlo Mangano	Leo Rossi
Dr. Shulman	Aasif Mandvi
Carl	Neil Pepe
Moony	Tony Darrow
Producer	R.M. Haley
Soundman	Ian Marioles
Sheila	Donnamarie Recco
Tino	Vince Cecere
FBI Agent Steadman	Jimmie Ray Weeks
FBI Agent Ricci	Robert Cea
FBI Agent Provano	William Hill
Scott MacNamara	Ira Wheeler
Belinda MacNamara	Luce Ennis

and Elizabeth Bracco (Marie Vitti), Gina Gallagher (Theresa Vitti), Francesca Mari (Anna Vitti), Vincent Vella, Jr. (Anthony Vitti), Mickey Bruno (Miami Soldier), Dave Corey (Miami Hall Guard), Fred Workman (Justice of the Peace), Daniel W. Barringer, John J. Polce (Dream Sequence Gunmen), Drew Eliot (Priest), Grace DeSena (Tommy Angels' Widow), "New York Joe" Catalfumo (Exuberant Mourner), Michael Guarino, Jr. (Stevie Beef), Michael Harkins, Paula Raflo, Ondine Harris, Matthew Vega (Paretti's Family), Clem Caserta (Handsome Jack), Tony Ray Rossi (Potatoes), Judith Kahan (Elaine Felton), Ted Neustadt (Rabbi), Pasquale Cajano (Joe Baldassare), Gene Ruffini (Frank Zello), Alfred Sauchelli, Jr. (Mo-Mo), Tony DiBenedetto (Johnny "Bigs"), Frank Aquilino (Eddie "Cokes"), Tony Bennett (Himself)

Robert De Niro, Billy Crystal

About to become the head of a powerful crime family, Paul Vitti has sudden self-doubts, causing him to seek help from psychiatrist Ben Sobol, who is horrified at the thought of serving as personal analyst to a mobster.

Robert De Niro, Billy Crystal

CRUEL INTENTIONS

(**COLUMBIA**) Producer, Neal H. Moritz; Executive Producer, Michael Fottrell; Director/Screenplay, Roger Kumble; Suggested by the novel *Les Liaisons Dangereuses* by Choderlos De Laclos; Photography, Theo Van de Sande; Designer, Jon Gary Steele; Editor, Jeff Freeman; Music, Edward Shearmur; Costumes, Denise Wingate; Co-Executive Producers, William Tyrer, Bruce Mellon, Chris J. Ball; Co-Producer, Heather Zeegen; Casting, Mary Vernieu, Anne McCarthy; a Neal H. Moritz production, presented in association with Original Film and Newmarket Capital Group; Dolby; Deluxe color; Rated R; 95 minutes; Release date: March 5, 1999

CAST

Kathryn Merteuil	Sarah Michelle Gellar
Sebastian Valmont	Ryan Phillippe
Annette Hargrove	Reese Witherspoon
Cecile Caldwell	Selma Blair
Helen Rosemond	Louise Fletcher
Blaine Tuttle	Joshua Jackson
Greg McConnell	Eric Mabius
Ronald Clifford	Sean Patrick Thomas
Dr. Greenbaum	Swoosie Kurtz
Bunny Caldwell	Christine Baranski
Nurse	Alaina Reed Hall
Mrs. Michalak	Deborah Offner
Marci Greenbaum	Tara Reid
Mrs. Sugarman	Herta Ware
Mai-Lee	Hiep Thi Le
Court Reynolds	Charlie O'Connell
Meter Maid	Fred Norris
Clorissa	Ginger Williams
Headmaster Hargrove	Drew Snyder

Womanizing teen Sebastian Valmont makes a wager with his manipulative stepsister Kathryn that he can seduce the virginal Annette Hargrove Previous film versions of Les Liaision Dangereuses were released in the U.S. in 1960 (starring Gerard Philipe and Jeanne Moreau), 1988 (Dangerous Liaisions, with John Malkovich and Glenn Close), and 1989 (Valmont, with Colin Firth and Annette Bening).

Ryan Phillippe, Reese Witherspoon, Sarah Michelle Gellar, Selma Blair

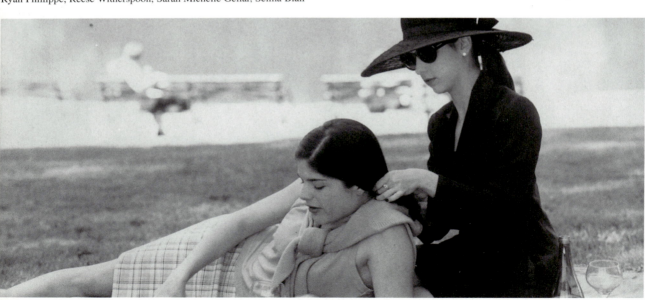

Selma Blair, Sarah Michelle Gellar

Sarah Michelle Gellar, Ryan Phillippe

Ryan Phillippe, Swoosie Kurtz

Sean Patrick Thomas, Selma Blair

Selma Blair, Christine Baranski

Joshua Jackson, Ryan Phillippe

Cory Buck, Michelle Pfeiffer

Jonathan Jackson, Michelle Pfeiffer

Treat Williams, Michelle Pfeiffer

Ryan Merriman, Michelle Pfeiffer

THE DEEP END OF THE OCEAN

(**COLUMBIA**) Producers, Kate Guinzberg, Steve Nicolaides; Executive Producer, Frank Capra III; Director, Ulu Grosbard; Screenplay, Stephen Schiff; Based on the book by Jacquelyn Mitchard; Photography, Stephen Goldblatt; Designer, Dan Davis; Editor, John Bloom; Costumes, Susie DeSanto; Music, Elmer Bernstein; Casting, Lora Kennedy; a Mandalay Entertainment presentation of a Via Rosa production; Dolby; Technicolor; Rated PG-13; 108 minutes; Release date: March 12, 1999

CAST

Beth Cappadora ....Michelle Pfeiffer
Pat Cappadora...Treat Williams
Detective Candy Bliss..Whoopi Goldberg
Vincent Cappadora (age 16)...........................Jonathan Jackson
Vincent Cappadora (age 7) ....Cory Buck
Sam (Ben) ....Ryan Merriman
Kerry Cappadora (age 9) ....Alexa Vega
Jimmy Daugherty...Michael McGrady
Ellen ....Brenda Strong
Ben Cappadora..Michael McElroy
Angelo ....Tony Musante
Rosie ....Rose Gregorio
George Karras...John Kapelos
Laurie ....Lucinda Jenney
Bastokovich...John Roselius
Theresa ....K.K. Dodds
Schaffer ....Joey Simmrin
Martha ....Holly Towne
Cecil Lockhart...Maryanne Summers
Cheerleaders ....Susie Spear, Lisa Maris
Hotel Manager...Daniel Hagen
Cop ....McNally Sagal
Joey...Robert Cicchini
and Frank Marocco (Bandleader), Aison McMillian (Desk Clerk), Stephanie Feury (Waitress), Wayne Duvall (McGuire), Father Gerald McSorley (Father Cleary), Mickey Swenson (Cop Tommy/Cop #1), Todd Jeffries (Cop Ricky), Steve Ireland, Scott William McKinlay, Wylie Small, Ana Gabriel, Nancy Sullivan, Timothy Davis-Reed, Robert Clotworthy (Reporters), Ken Magee (Cop #2), Van Epperson (Guard), Jennifer Reznikoff (Waitress), Ron Von Gober (Police Officer), Steve Blalock, Mike Watson (ND Cops), Jim James, Emidio Antonio, Patricia M. Leahy (Zoo Employees), Pete Sutton (Community Center Volunteer)

Beth Cappadora's family is devestated when their younger son Ben disappears while they are attending Beth's high school reunion, a situation that plunges her into despair for the next nine years until a small boy appears in their neighborhood who might possibly be her missing child.

© Mandalay Entertainment

Michelle Pfeiffer, Whoopi Goldberg, Cory Buck

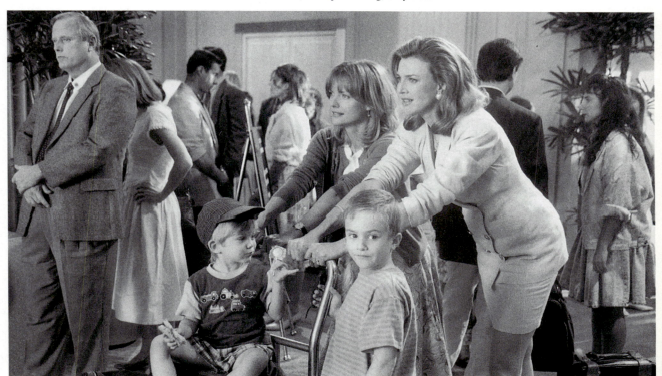

Cory Buck, Michelle Pfeiffer, Michael McElroy, Brenda Strong

THE CORRUPTOR

(**NEW LINE CINEMA**) Producers, Dan Halsted; Executive Producers, Oliver Stone, Terence Chang, Bill Carraro, Jay Stern; Director, James Foley; Screenplay, Robert Pucci; Photography, Juan Ruiz-Anchia; Designer, David Brisbin; Editor, Howard E. Smith; Costumes, Doug Hall; Music, Carter Burwell; Co-Executive Producers, Jonathan Krauss, Brian Witten; Casting, Mary Vernieu, Anne McCarthy; an Illusion Entertainment Group production; Dolby; Panavision; Deluxe color; Rated R; 110 minutes; Release date: March 12, 1999

Mark Wahlberg, Chow Yun-Fat

CAST

Nick Chen	Chow Yun-Fat
Danny Wallace	Mark Wahlberg
Henry Lee	Ric Young
Schabacker	Paul Ben-Victor
Jack	Jon Kit Lee
Willy Ung	Andrew Pang
Louise Deng	Elizabeth Lindsey
Sean Wallace	Brian Cox
Bobby Vu	Byron Mann
Benny Wong	Kim Chan
Vince Kirkpatrick	Bill MacDonald
Amy San	Susie Trinh
Black Eyes	Ho Chow
Tai	Olivia Yap
Kim	Lynda Chiu
May	Marie Matiko
Phan Ho	Pak-Kong Ho
Lackey	Tim Progosh
Captain Stan Klein	Beau Starr
Guard One	LeRoy Allen
Lawyer	Simon B. Cotter
Large Agent	Frank Pellegrino
U.S. Attorney Margaret Wheeler	Tovah Feldshuh
Sumo Guard	Tig Fong

and Chuck Scarborough (Himself), Karen Huie (Woman in Brothel), Mike Jung (Doctor), Howard Hoover (Smaller Agent), Lucille Soong (Elderly Immigrant), Mark Williams (Co. Captain), Alice Poon (Masseuse), Jason Ting (Young Boy), Arthur Lo (Man on Street), Alice Lee Chun (Frightened Woman)

Chow Yun-Fat

Because of a turf war between the Triads and the Fukienese Dragons in New York's Chinatown, the NYPD assigns young cop Danny Wallace to the Asian Gang Unit where he discovers that his partner, Nick Chen, has risen up the ranks with help from the Triads.

© New Line Cinema Inc.

Mark Wahlberg

Chow Yun-Fat, Mark Wahlberg

Ben Affleck, Sandra Bullock

FORCES OF NATURE

Ben Affleck, Sandra Bullock

(**DREAMWORKS**) Producers, Susan Arnold, Donna Arkoff Roth, Ian Bryce; Director, Bronwen Hughes; Screenplay, Marc Lawrence; Photography, Elliot Davis; Designer, Lester Cohen; Editor, Craig Wood; Costumes, Donna Zakowska; Music, John Powell; Casting, Junie Lowry Johnson; a Roth/Arnold production; Dolby; Panavision; Technicolor; Rated PG-13; 104 minutes; Release date: March 19, 1999

CAST

Sarah	Sandra Bullock
Ben	Ben Affleck
Bridget	Maura Tierney
Alan	Steve Zahn
Viriginia	Blythe Danner
Hadley	Ronny Cox
Richard	Michael Fairman
Barbara	Janet Carroll
Joe	Richard Schiff
Steve	David Strickland
Debbie	Meredith Scott Lynn
Max	George D. Wallace
Jack	Steve Hytner
Carl	John Doe
Vic	Jack Kehler
Emma	Anne Haney
Ned	Bert Remsen
Beth	Julie Ivey
Sandy	Maia Lien
Dr. Keller	Taylor Gilbert
Bus Driver	Francisco De Ramirez
Florence	Pat Crawford Brown
Murray	Bill Erwin
Herman	William Marquez

and Carter Reedy, Rafiki Smith, Franklin H.D. Ecker (Groomsmen), Antone Calandra, Tommy Chappelle, James Chirbas, Bill Coates, Vivian Edwards-Ashford, Damon Frost, Jean Gates, Joan Glover, Winnie Hammer, Bob King, Leon Lamar, Judith Maltenfort, Eddie Miller, Mali Miller, Danny Nelson, Joanne Pankow, Ginnie Randall, Beverly Shelton, George Stoba, Jacki Wilson (Sunseekers), Michael Cudlitz (Bartender), Athena Bitzis (Juanita the Bull Tamer), Libby Whittemore (Car Rental Agent), Dan Albright (Officer McDonnell), Marshall Rosenbloom (Ticket Vendor), Mike Pniewski (Conductor), Wes Kennemore (Thief), Brandon McLaughlin (Delivery Man), Marc McPherson (Hotel Manager), Justin Michael Benassi (Sarah's Son), Shelly DeSai (Cabbie), Cordell Nichols (Child on Train), Dan Biggers (Justice of the Peace), Lester Cohen (Port Authority Spokesman), Natalie Hendrix (Airport Reporter), Scott Pierce (News Anchor), Shannon Welles (Lady in Wheelchair)

Meredith Scott Lynn, Steve Zahn

Ben, a young man traveling from New York to Savannah for a marriage about which he is uncertain, encounters Sarah, an eccentric woman with whom he shares an eventful road trip after a mishap on the airport runway.

Maura Tierney, Blythe Danner, David Strickland, Ronny Cox

Robert Carlyle, Guy Pearce

Jeremy Davies, Robert Carlyle

Robert Carlyle

Jeffrey Jones

RAVENOUS

(**20TH CENTURY FOX**) Producers, Adam Fields, David Heyman; Executive Producer, Tim Van Rellim; Director, Antonia Bird; Screenplay, Ted Griffin; Photography, Anthony B. Richmond; Designer, Bryce Perrin; Editor, Neil Farrell; Music, Michael Nyman, Damon Albarn; Costumes, Sheena Napier; a Fox 2000 Pictures presentation of an Adam Fields/Heyday Films production; Dolby; Super 35 Widescreen; Deluxe color; Rated R; 98 minutes; Release date: March 19, 1999

CAST

Captain John Boyd	Guy Pearce
Colqhoun/Ives	Robert Carlyle
Toffler	Jeremy Davies
Hart	Jeffrey Jones
General Slauson	John Spencer
Knox	Stephen Spinella
Reich	Neal McDonough
Cleaves	David Arquette
Martha	Sheila Tousey
Lindus	Bill Brochtrup
George	Joseph Running Fox

and Fernando Becerril, Gabriel Berthier, Pedro Altamirano (Mexican Commanders), Joseph Boyle (U.S. Blond Soldier), Damian Delgado, Fernando Manzano (Mexican Sentries), Alfredo Escobar, Gerardo Martinez (Soldiers), David Heyman (James), Tim Van Rellim (Mr. MacCready), Miezl Sungu (Jones), Abel Woolrich (Borracho)

In a desolate outpost in the Sierra Nevadas in 1847, a man on the verge of death arrives with tales of how his party of settlers resorted to cannibalism to survive.

David Arquette, Joseph Running Fox

TRUE CRIME

(**WARNER BROS.**) Producers, Clint Eastwood, Richard D. Zanuck, Lili Fini Zanuck; Director, Clint Eastwood; Screenplay, Larry Gross, Paul Brickman, Stephen Schiff; Based upon the novel by Andrew Klavan; Photography, Jack N. Green; Executive Producer, Tom Rooker; Designer, Henry Bumstead; Editor, Joel Cox; Music, Lennie Niehaus; Casting, Phyllis Huffman; a Zanuck Company/Malpaso production; Dolby; Technicolor; Rated R; 127 minutes; Release date: March 19, 1999

Clint Eastwood, Sydney Poitier

CAST

Steve Everett	Clint Eastwood
Frank Beechum	Isaiah Washington
Bob Findley	Denis Leary
Bonnie Beechum	Lisa Gay Hamilton
Alan Mann	James Woods
Luther Plunkitt	Bernard Hill
Barbara Everett	Diane Venora
Reverend Shillerman	Michael McKean
Dale Porterhouse	Michael Jeter
Michelle Ziegler	Mary McCormack
Mrs. Russel	Hattie Winston

and Penny Bae Bridges (Gail Beechum), Francesca Fisher-Eastwood (Kate Everett), John Finn (Reedy), Laila Robins (Patricia Findley), Sydney Poitier (Jane March), Erik King (Pussy Man), Graham Beckel (Arnold McCardle), Frances Fisher (Cecilia Nussbaum), Marissa Ribisi (Amy Wilson), Christine Ebersole (Bridget Rossiter), Anthony Zerbe (Henry Lowenstein), Nancy Giles (Leesha Mitchell), Tom McGowan (Tom Donaldson), William Windom (Neil the Bartender), Don West (Dr. Roger Waters), Lucy Alexis Liu (Toy Store Girl), Dina Eastwood (Wilma Francis), Leslie Griffith, Dennis Richmond (TV Anchors), Frank Somerville (Afternoon News Anchor), Dan Green (Field Producer), Nicolas Bearde (Reuben Skycock), Frances Lee McCain (Mrs. Lowenstein), Rev. Cecil Williams (Reverend Williams), Casey Lee (Warren Russel), Jack Kehler (Mr. Ziegler), Colman Domingo (Wally Cartwright), Linda Hoy (Counter Woman), Danny Kovacs (Atkins), Kelvin Han Yee (Zachary Platt), Kathryn Howell (Nurse), Beulah Stanley (Guard), George Maguire (Fredrick Robertson), Bill Wattenburg (Radio Announcer), Cathy Fithian (Nancy Larson), Roland Abasolo (Guard—First Night), Michael Halton (Guard—Execution Day), Jade Marx-Berti (Waitress), Velicia Marie Davis (Purse Whacker), John B. Scott (Col. Drummond), Edward Silva (Col. Hernandez), Jordan Sax (Col. Badger), Rob Reece (Executioner), Walter Brown (Beechum Family Member)

Investigative reporter Steve Everett is assigned to conduct a final inter-view with a condemned San Quentin inmate, whom he begins to suspect might actually be innocent.

© Warner Bros.

Clint Eastwood, Frances Fisher

Isaiah Washington

THE KING AND I

(**WARNER BROS**.) Producers, James G. Robinson, Arthur Rankin, Peter Bakalian; Executive Producer, Robert Mandell; Director, Richard Rich; Screenplay, Peter Bakalian, Jacqueline Feather, David Seidler; Additional Dialogue, Brian Nissen; Conceived and Adapted for Animation by Arthur Rankin; Adapted from the musical by Richard Rodgers (music) and Oscar Hammerstein II (lyrics); Co-Producers, Terry L. Noss, Thomas J. Tobin; Supervising Editor, James D. Koford; Character Design, Bronwen Barry; Supervising Animators, Patrick Gleeson, Colm Duggan; Casting, Geoffrey Johnson, Vincent Liff; a James G. Robinson presentation of a Morgan Creek production in association with Rankin/Bass Productions and Nest Entertainment; Dolby; Color; Rated G; 87 minutes; Release date: March 19, 1999

Anna Leonowens, The King of Siam

VOICE CAST

Anna Leonowens	Miranda Richardson
Anna (singing voice)	Christiane Noll
The King of Siam	Martin Vidnovic
The Kralahome	Ian Richardson
Master Little	Darrell Hammond
Prince Chululongkorn	Allen D. Hong
Prince (singing voice)	David Burnham
Tuptim	Armi Arabe
Tuptim (singing voice)	Tracy Venner Warren
Louis Leonowens	Adam Wylie
Sir Edward Ramsay	Sean Smith
First Wife	J.A. Fuji
Captain Orton	Ken Baker

and Ed Trotta (Sir Edward's Captain), Anthony Mozdy (Burmese Emissary), Alexandra Lai (Princess Ying), Katherine Lai (Princess Naomi), Mark Hunt (Steward), B.K. Tochi (Soldier)

British schoolteacher Anna Leonowens arrives in mid-19th Century Siam to serve as teacher to the many children of the stubborn but charismatic king. Other versions of the story: Anna and the King of Siam (20th Century Fox, 1946) with Irene Dunne and Rex Harrison; The King and I (20th Century Fox, 1956) with Deborah Kerr and Yul Brynner; and Anna and the King (20th Century Fox, 1999) with Jodie Foster and Chow Yun-Fat.

Tuptim, Prince Chululongkorn, Louis Leonowens
© Morgan Creek Productions, Inc.

DOUG'S 1ST MOVIE

(**WALT DISNEY PICTURES**) Producers, Jim Jinkins, David Campbell, Melanie Grisanti, Jack Spillum; Director, Maurice Joyce; Creator, Jim Jinkins; Screenplay, Ken Scarborough; Editors, Alysha Nadine Cohen, Christopher K. Gee; Music, Mark Watters; Associate Producer, Bruce Knapp; Design Supervisors, Freya Tanz, Pete List, Eugene Salandra; Design Coordinator, Marcus Pauls; Animation Production, Plus One Animation Inc.; a Jumbo Pictures production; Dolby; Technicolor; Rated G; 77 minutes; Release date: March 26, 1999

VOICE CAST

Doug Funnie/Lincoln	Thomas McHugh
Skeeter/Mr. Dink/Porkchop/Ned	Fred Newman
Roger Klotz/Boomer/Larry/Mr. Chiminy	Chris Phillips
Patti Mayonnaise	Constance Shulman
Herman Melville	Frank Welker
Mr. Funnie/Mr. Bluff/Willie/Chalky/Bluff Agent #1	Doug Preis
Guy Graham	Guy Hadley
Beebe Bluff/Elmo	Alice Playten
Al & Moo Sleech/RoboCrusher	Eddie Korbich

and David O'Brien (Stentorian —Quailman— Announcer), Doris Belack (Mayor Tippi Dink), Becca Lish (Judy Funnie/ Mrs. Funnie/Connie), Greg Lee (Principal White), Bob Bottone (Bluff Assistant), Bruce Bayley Johnson (Mr. Swirley), Fran Brill (Mrs. Perigrew), Melissa Greenspan (Briar Langolier)

12-year-old Doug faces a dual dilemma: trying to save an endangered "mythical" monster from Lucky Duck Lake, and working up the nerve to take Patti Mayonnaise to the school dance. Based on the "Doug" series that premiered on Nickelodeon in 1991 and transferred to ABC in 1996.

Doug Funnie, Skeeter
© Jumbo Pictures, Inc.

EDTV

(**UNIVERSAL**) Producers, Brian Grazer, Ron Howard; Executive Producers, Todd Hallowell, Michel Roy, Richard Sadler; Director, Ron Howard; Screenplay, Lowell Ganz, Babaloo Mandel; Based on the motion picture *Louis XIX: Roi Des Ondes*, written by Emile Gaudreault & Sylvie Bouchard, directed by Michel Poulette; Photography, John Schwartzman; Designer, Michael Corenblith; Editors, Mike Hill, Dan Hanley; Music, Randy Edelman; Associate Producers, Aldric La'Auli Porter, Louisa Velis; Costumes, Rita Ryack; Casting, Jane Jenkins, Janet Hirshenson; an Imagine Entertainment presentation of a Brian Grazer production; Dolby; Deluxe color; Rated PG-13; 122 minutes; Release date: March 26, 1999

Matthew McConaughey, Woody Harrelson

CAST

Ed Pekurny	Matthew McConaughey
Shari	Jenna Elfman
Ray	Woody Harrelson
Jeanette	Sally Kirkland
Al	Martin Landau
Cynthia	Ellen DeGeneres
Whitaker	Rob Reiner
Hank	Dennis Hopper
Jill	Elizabeth Hurley
John	Adam Goldberg
Ken, The Director	Clint Howard
Marcia	Viveka Davis

and Geoffrey Blake (Keith), Gail Boggs (Wife), Jenna Byrne (Felicia), Merrin Dungey (Ms. Seaver), Ian Gomez (McIlvaine), Gavin Grazer (Cliff), Chris Hogan (Paul), Arianna Huffington (Panel Member), Larry Jenkins (Husband), Wendle Josepher (Rita), Scott LaRose (Desipio), John Livingston (Terry), Mitzi McCall (Fig Lady), Jim Meskimen (Dr. Geller), Don Most (Benson), Rick Overton (Barry), James Ritz (Tad), RuPaul, Jay Leno (Themselves), Rusty Schwimmer (Alice), Steven Shenbaum (Jack), Gedde Watanabe (Greg), Steve Kehela, Googy Gress (Reporters), Jo McGinley (Tracy), John Pirruccello (Kevin), Charles Berg, Anthony Jensen (Party Goers), Joe Bellan (Lou), Brian Michael Erlich, Marcus J. Oliver (Video Store Clerks), Sam Rubin (Entertainment Reporter), Mark Thompson (Anchor), Barry Wiggins (Sports Anchor), Michael Parsons (Kid), Zidu Chen (Dental Patient), Eric Shinn (Camera Truck Tech Driver), Robert Pastoriza (Carlos), Jeffrey Schecter (Utility—1st Team), Michael Esposito (Camera Operator—1st Team), Connie Campbell-Gott, Louie Mejia (Camera Operators—2nd Team), Crystall Carmen (Utility—2nd Team), Matt Morrissey (Director—2nd Team), Marilyn Pittman (Woman in Window), Sommer Saqr, Jennifer Elise Cox, Alexandra Holden (College Girls), Mark Wheeler (Bartender), Kathleen Marshall (Hygienist), Harry Shearer (Moderator), Michael Moore, Merrill Markoe, George Plimpton (Panel Members), Geoff Bolt (Drunk Guy), Azalea Stanley, Ezra Stanley (Teenagers), Anna Karin (Snapple Girl), Todd Hallowell (Interviewer), Cyndi Pass (Cassie), Jen Moe, Velina Brown (Girls), Rod Tate (Moe), Todd Krainin (Younger Man), Zeidy Martinez, Azura Skye, Daisy Clarke (Interview Teenagers), Lombardo Boyar, Rainbow Borden, David Quane (New York Guys), Christian Kane (P.A.), Gina Hecht, Cheryl Howard, Louisa Marie (Party Girls), Mike Grief (Repairman), Jason Kim, King Alexander, Dublin James, T.J. Tyne (Frat Guys), Laurel Moglen (Underwear Woman), Wade J. Robson, Sy Hearn, Nathan Paul (Teenage Boys), Bill Maher (Host), Anita Morales (Nurse), Lowell Ganz (Lawyer), Bob Sarlatte (Motorcycle Cop), Ashley Clarke (Girl), William M. Connor (Toilet Man), Roberta Callahan (Cat Advocate), William Bagnell (Presidential Aide), Julie Rose Stevens, Brigitte Jacoby-Baker (Ken Groupies), Joe Mazza (Vet), Mel Berger (Confused Man), Diane Amos (Autograph Mom), James Brooks (Delivery Man), Luke Esterkyn (Band Member), Mark Marking, Tom Turpel (Ed's Fans), Sun St. Pierre (Well-Wisher), Roger L. Jackson (Mama's Boy), Julie Donatt (Reporter), Thomas Barg (Boom Box Boy), Glenn E. Schuldt (Paramedic), Curtis Davis (Whoop Boy), William Dance (Beauty Salon Owner), Sonia Bhalla (Ticket Taker), Todd P. McCormick (P.I. Guest), Jordan Harrleson (Audition Guy), Tony Harras, Vince Lozano, Rolando Molina (Warehouse Workers), Alberto Vazquez (Grave Digger), Lydee Walsh (College Girl), Veronica Moody (College Dorm Girl)

Matthew McConaughey, Elizabeth Hurley

An affable, aimless video store clerk agrees to be the star of a round-the-clock television show that captures every mundane moment of his everyday life, a decision he eventually regrets.

© Universal Studios

Jenna Elfman, Matthew McConaughey

Viggo Mortensen, Diane Lane

Diane Lane, Anna Paquin

A WALK ON THE MOON

(**MIRAMAX**) Producers, Dustin Hoffman, Tony Goldwyn, Jay Cohen, Neil Koenigsberg, Lee Gottsegen, Murray Schisgal; Executive Producers, Graham Burke, Greg Coote, Josette Perotta; Director, Tony Goldwyn; Screenplay, Pamela Gray; Photography, Anthony Richmond; Editor, Dana Congdon; Music, Mason Daring; Music Supervisor, Stephan R. Goldman; Designer, Dan Leigh; Costumes, Jess Goldstein; Casting, Billy Hopkins, Suzanne Smith, Kerry Barden, Ann Goulder; a Punch Production in association with Village Roadshow Pictures—Groucho Film Partnership; Dolby; Technicolor; Rated R; 107 minutes; Release date: March 26, 1999

CAST

Pearl Kantrowitz	Diane Lane
Walker Jerome	Viggo Mortensen
Marty Kantrowitz	Liev Schreiber
Alison Kantrowitz	Anna Paquin
Lilian Kantrowitz (Bubbie)	Tovah Feldshuh
Daniel Kantrowitz	Bobby Boriello
Neil Leiberman	Stewart Bick
Herb Fogler	Jess Platt
Mrs. Dymbort	Mahee Paiment
Rhoda Leiberman	Star Jasper
Eleanor Gelfand	Ellen David
Norma Fogler	Lisa Bronwyn Moore
Selma Levitsky	Vicky Barkoff
Wendy Green	Tamar Kozlov
Myra Naidell	Lisa Jakub
Ross Epstein	Joseph Perrino
Carl Applebaum	Jesse Lavendel
Jeffrey Fogler	James Liboiron
Sheldon Dymbort	Howard Rosenstein
Comedian	Mal Z. Lawrence
Sid Shapiro	Joel Miller
Customers	Bill Brownstein, Sam Gesser
Voice of Camp Social Director	Julie Kavner

In the summer of 1969, restless housewife Pearl Kantrowitz travels to the Catskills with her children and meets hippie Walker Jerome with whom she begins an affair.

© Miramax Films

Diane Lane, Liev Schreiber

Viggo Mortensen, Diane Lane

THE MATRIX

(**WARNER BROS.**) Producer, Joel Silver; Executive Producers, Barrie Osborne, Andrew Mason, Andy Wachowski, Larry Wachowski, Erwin Stoff, Bruce Berman; Co-Producer, Dan Cracchiolo; Directors/Screenplay, Andy Wachowski, Larry Wachowski; Photography, Bill Pope; Designer, Owen Paterson; Editor, Zach Staenberg; Music, Don Davis; Costumes, Kym Barrett; Visual Effects Supervisor, John Gaeta; Conceptual Designer, Geofrey Darrow; Kung Fu Choreographer, Yuen Wo Ping; Makeup Special Effects, Bob McCarron; Stunts, Glenn Boswell; Casting, Mali Finn, Shauna Wolifson; a Village Roadshow Pictures-Groucho Film Partnership of a Silver Pictures production; Dolby; Panavision; Technicolor; Rated R; 136 minutes; Release date: March 31, 1999

CAST

Neo	Keanu Reeves
Morpheus	Laurence Fishburne
Trinity	Carrie-Anne Moss
Agent Smith	Hugo Weaving
Oracle	Gloria Foster
Cypher	Joe Pantoliano
Tank	Marcus Chong
Apoc	Julian Arahanga
Mouse	Matt Doran
Switch	Belinda McClory
Dozer	Anthony Ray Parker

Paul Goddard (Agent Brown), Robert Taylor (Agent Jones), David Aston (Rhinehart), Marc Gray (Choi), Ada Nicodemou (Dujour), Deni Gordon (Priestess), Rowan Witt (Spoon Boy), Elenor Witt, Tamara Brown, Janaya Pender, Adryn White, Natalie Tjen (Potentials), Bill Young (Lieutenant), David O'Connor (FedEx Man), Jeremy Ball (Businessman), Fiona Johnson (Woman in Red), Harry Lawrence (Old Man), Steve Dodd (Blind Man), Luke Quinton (Security Guard), Lawrence Woodward (Guard), Michael Butcher (Cop Who Captures Neo), Bernie Ledger (Big Cop), Robert Simper, Chris Scott (Cops), Nigel Harbach (Parking Cop)

The mysterious Trinity leads Neo into an alternate underworld where he hopes to find the secret of the Matrix, a power he believes is controlling his life.

1999 Academy Award-winner for Best Visual Effects, Editing, Sound, and Sound Effects Editing.

© Warner Bros./Village Roadshow Films

Keanu Reeves, Carrie-Anne Moss

Keanu Reeves, Hugo Weaving

Heath Ledger, Julia Stiles

Joseph Gordon-Levitt, David Krumholtz

10 THINGS I HATE ABOUT YOU

(**TOUCHSTONE**) Producer, Andrew Lazar; Executive Producers, Jeffrey Chernov, Seth Jaret; Director, Gil Junger; Screenplay, Karen McCullah Lutz, Kirsten Smith; Photography, Mark Irwin; Designer, Carol Winstead Wood; Editor, O. Nicholas Brown; Co-Producer, Jody Hedien; Associate Producer, Greg Silverman; Costumes, Kimberly A. Tillman; Music, Richard Gibbs; Casting, Marcia Ross, Donna Morong, Gail Goldberg; a Mad Chance/Jaret Entertainment production; Dolby; Technicolor; Rated PG-13; 97 minutes; Release date: March 31, 1999

CAST

Joseph Gordon-Levitt, Larisa Oleynik

Patrick Verona	Heath Ledger
Katarina Stratford	Julia Stiles
Cameron James	Joseph Gordon-Levitt
Bianca Stratford	Larisa Oleynik
Michael Eckman	David Krumholtz
Joey Donner	Andrew Keegan
Mandella	Susan May Pratt
Chastity	Gabrielle Union
Walter Stratford	Larry Miller
Mr. Morgan	Daryl "Chill" Mitchell
Ms. Perky	Allison Janney
Mr. Chapin	David Leisure
Scurvy	Greg Jackson
Bogey Lowenstein	Kyle Cease
Derek	Terence Heuston
Trevor	Cameron Fraser
Audio Visual Guy	Eric Reidman
Beautiful Jock	Quinn Maixner
Coffee Kids	Demegio Kimbrough, Todd Butler
Cohort	Dennis Mosley
Coffee Girl	Bianca Kajlich

Nick Vukelic (Drugged Out Loser), Benjamin Laurance (Wimpy Loser), Aidan Kennedy (Laughing Loser), Jelani Quinn (Crying Loser), Jesse Dyer (Screaming Loser), Aaron Therol (Detention Student), Carlos Lacamara (Bartender), Heather Taylor (Drunken Girl), Joshua Thorpe (Jock), J.R. Johnson (MBA Guy at Party), Wendy Gottlieb (Heather), Brian Hood (Clem), Travis Miller (Cowboy), Ari Karczag (Kissing Guy), Laura Kenny (Judith), Alice Evans (Perky Girl), Jesper Inglis (Buckaroo Bartender), Nick Brown (Biker), Monique Powell, Brian Mashburn (Save Ferris Singers), Kay Hanley, Michael Eisenstein (Letter to Cleo Singers)

When Bianca Stratford is told that she cannot date until her ill-tempered older sister Kat does, her boyfriend bribes Patrick Verona to woo and win over Kat.

Heath Ledger, Andrew Keegan

THE OUT-OF-TOWNERS

Steve Martin, Goldie Hawn, Oliver Hudson

(**PARAMOUNT**) Producers, Robert Evans, Teri Schwartz, Robert Cort, David Madden; Executive Producers, Christine Forsyth-Peters, Philip E. Thomas; Director, Sam Weisman; Screenplay, Marc Lawrence; Based upon the screenplay by Neil Simon; Photography, John Bailey; Designer, Ken Adam; Editor, Kent Beyda; Costumes, Ann Roth; Co-Producer, Andrew La Marca; Music, Marc Shaiman; Casting, Ilene Starger; a Robert Evans production in association with Cherry Alley productions and the Cort/Madden Company; Dolby; Color; Rated PG-13; 92 minutes; Release date: April 2, 1999

CAST

Henry Clark	Steve Martin
Nancy Clark	Goldie Hawn
Mr. Mersault	John Cleese
Greg	Mark McKinney
Alan Clark	Oliver Hudson
Stewardess	Valerie Perri
Passengers	Steve Mittleman, Randall Arney
Airline Representative	Carlease Burke
Lost Baggage Clerk	William Duell
Boston Cab Driver	J.P. Bumstead
Sweeper Woman	Peggy Mannix
Woman in Bathroom	Anne Haney
Janitor on Train	Charlie Dell
Rental Car Clerk	Jordan Baker
Andrew Lloyd Webber	Tom Riis Farrell
Michelle	Dani Klein
Desk Clerks	Daniel T. Parker, Karen Elizabeth White
Shoplifters	Alyson Palmer, Elizabeth Ziff
Korean Grocer	Diane Cheng
Paranoid Man	Christopher Durang
Paranoid Woman	Mo Gaffney
Dominatrix	Mary Testa
Supermodel	Monica Birt
Deli Guy	John Elsen
Well Dressed Woman	Babo Harrison
Dr. Faber	Josh Mostel
Edward	Gregory Jbara
Edward's Friend	Amy Ziff
Sheena	Cynthia Nixon
Sexaholic	French Napier
Mr. Wellstone	Joseph Maher
Mrs. Wellstone	Constance McCashin
Greg's Friend	Steve Bean

James Arone (Room Service Waiter), Philip Earl Johnson (Hotel Security Man), Ernie Sabella (Getaway Driver), Jack Willis (Robber), John Pizzarelli (Band Leader), Mayor Rudolph Giuliani (Mayor), Scotty Bloch (Florence Needleman), Chris McKinney, Joe Grifasi (Arresting Cops), Jerome Preston Bates, Jacinto Taras Riddick (Prisoners), Jack McGee (Sergeant Jordan), L.B. Fisher (Howard the Bellman), Janna Lapidus (Central Park Woman), T. Scott Cunningham (Paul), Mandy Sigfried (Receptionist), Jenn Thompson (Lisa Tobin), John Gould Rubin (Bill), Christopher Duva (Barry the Bellman), Arthur French (Cab Driver), Jessica Cauffiel (Susan Clark).

Steve Martin, Goldie Hawn

Midwestern couple Henry and Nancy Clark journey to New York so that Henry might interview for a job only to find themselves facing every problem and set-back possible during a 24-hour period. Remake of the 1970 Paramount film that starred Jack Lemmon and Sandy Dennis.

© Paramount Pictures

John Cleese, Steve Martin, Goldie Hawn

COOKIE'S FORTUNE

(**OCTOBER**) Producers, Robert Altman, Etchie Stroh; Co-Producers, David Levy, James McLindon; Executive Producer, Willi Baer; Director, Robert Altman; Screenplay, Anne Rapp; Photography, Toyomichi Kurita; Editor, Abraham Lim; Designer, Stephen Altman; Costumes, Dona Granata; Music, David A. Stewart; Casting, Pam Dixon Mickelson; a Sandcastle 5 and Elysian Dreams production; Dolby; CFI Color; Rated PG-13; 118 minutes; Release date: April 2, 1999

CAST

Camille Dixon	Glenn Close
Cora Duvall	Julianne Moore
Emma Duvall	Liv Tyler
Jason Brown	Chris O'Donnell
Willis Richland	Charles S. Dutton
Jewel Mae "Cookie" Orcutt	Patricia Neal
Lester Boyle	Ned Beatty
Otis Tucker	Courtney B. Vance
Jack Palmer	Donald Moffat
Manny Hood	Lyle Lovett
Billy Cox	Danny Darst
Eddie "The Expert" Pitts	Matt Malloy
Patrick Freeman	Randle Mell
Wanda Carter	Niecy Mash
Theo Johnson	Rufus Thomas
Josie Martin	Ruby Wilson
Ronnie Freeman	Preston Strobel

and Ann Whitfield (Mrs. Henderson/Herodias), Hank Worsham (Tigellinus), Kenny Pillow, Derek Guyer (Soldiers), Emily Sindelar (Marlene), Heath Lail (Prop Boy), Shari Schneider (Mrs. Tippett), John Sullivan (Mr. Tippett), Red West (Mr. Henderson), Ferguson Reid, Chris Coulson (Deputies), Cheryl Cole (Picnic Lady), Fred Sanders (Guitarist), Jimmy Ellis (Drummer), Solomon McDaniel (Keyboardist), Terris Tate (Bass Guitarist)

When Camille finds her estranged aunt Cookie dead, she plots to make the suicide look like murder, a move that winds up implicating Cookie's loyal handyman Willis in the crime.

©October Films

Charles S. Dutton, Liv Tyler

Patricia Neal

Glenn Close

Chris O'Donnell, Liv Tyler

GO

(**COLUMBIA**) Producers, Paul Rosenberg, Mickey Liddell, Matt Freeman; Director/Photography, Doug Liman; Screenplay, John August; Designer, Tom Wilkins; Editor, Stephen Mirrione; Music, BT; Music Supervisor, Julianne Kelley; Costumes, Genevieve Tyrrell; Casting, Joseph Middleton; a Banner Entertainment production in association with Saratoga Entertainment; Dolby; Super 35 Widescreen; Deluxe color; Rated R; 100 minutes; Release date: April 9, 1999

Sarah Polley, Scott Wolf, Jay Mohr, Katie Holmes

CAST

Claire Montgomery	Katie Holmes
Ronna Martin	Sarah Polley
Stringy Haired Woman	Suzanne Krull
Simon Baines	Desmond Askew
Mannie	Nathan Bexton
Switterman	Robert Peters
Adam	Scott Wolf
Zack	Jay Mohr
Todd Gaines	Timothy Olyphant
Ballerina Girl	Jodi Bianca Wise
Burke	William Fichtner
Dancing Register Woman	Rita Bland
Track Suit Guy	Tony Denman
Raver Dude	Scott Hass
Anorexic Girl	Natasha Melnick
Skate Punk Guy	Manu Intiraymi
Spider Marine	Josh Paddock
Marcus	Taye Diggs
Tiny	Breckin Meyer
Singh	James Duval
Boy	Courtland Mead
Becky	Katharine Towne
Rebecca	Marisa Morell

Ken Kupstis (Sports Car Man), Nikki Fritz (Noelle), Tane McClure (Holly), Jimmy Shubert (Victor Jr.), J.E. Freeman (Victor Sr.), Jay Paulson (Loop), Jane Krakowski (Irene), Melissa McCarthy (Sandra), Shann Beeman (Jimmy), Willie Amakye (Waiter), Princess Leah Lucky Buttons (Alley Cat)

Sarah Polley

During a 24-hour period, three diverse groups—supermarket checkout clerks Ronna and Claire; Las Vegas partiers Simon and Marcus; and tv soap actors Adam and Zack—all find themselves somehow involved in events surrounding a botched drug deal.

© Columbia Pictures Industries Inc.

Nathan Bexton, Katie Holmes

Taye Diggs, Desmond Askew

NEVER BEEN KISSED

(20TH CENTURY FOX) Producers, Sandy Isaac, Nancy Juvonen; Executive Producer, Drew Barrymore; Director, Raja Gosnell; Screenplay, Abby Kohn, Marc Silverstein; Photography, Alex Nepomniaschy; Designer, Steven Jordan; Editors, Debra Chiate, Marcelo Sansevieri; Co-Producer, Jeffrey Downer; Music, David Newman; Costumes, Mona May; Casting, Justine Baddeley, Kim Davis; a Fox 2000 Pictures presentation of a Flower Films/Bushwood Pictures production; Dolby; Super 35 Widescreen; Deluxe color; Rated PG-13; 107 minutes; Release date: April 9, 1999

CAST

Josie Geller	Drew Barrymore
Rob Geller	David Arquette
Sam Coulson	Michael Vartan

Sun-Times:

Anita	Molly Shannon
Gus	John C. Reilly
Rigfort	Garry Marshall
Merkin	Sean Whalen

Cress Williams (George), Octavia L. Spencer (Cynthia), Sarah DeVincentis (Rhoda), Allen Covert (Roger in Op/Ed), Rock Reiser (Dutton), David Doty (Hairplug Bruns), Derrick Morgan (Armcast Henson), Kathleen Marshall (Sun-Times Worker), Jenny Bicks (Miss Haskell)

South Glen South:

Aldys	Leelee Sobieski
Guy Perkins	Jeremy Jordan
Kirsten	Jessica Alba
Kristin	Marley Shelton
Gibby	Jordan Ladd

Katie Lansdale (Tracy), Branden Williams (Tommy), James Edward Franco (Jason), Gregory Sporleder (Coach Romano), Martha Hackett (Mrs. Knox), Jennifer Parsons (P.E. Teacher), Andrew Wilson (School Guard), Giuseppe Andrews (Denominator), Alex Solowitz (Brett), Niesha Trout (Sera), Chad Christian Haywood (Matz), Cory Hardrict (Packer), Chad Todhunter, Daniel Louis Rivas (Stoners), Mark Edwards (School Guard #2);

and Denny Kirkwood (Billy Prince), Marissa Jaret Winokur (Sheila), Carmen Llywellyn (Rob's Girlfriend), Sara Downing (Billy's Prom Date), Mike G. Moyer (Monty Malik), Steven Wilde (Bouncer), Maya McLaughlin (Lara), David Douglas (Rasta), Russell Bobbitt (Carny), Tara Skye (Tyke), Mark Allen (D.J.), Conor O'Neil (Gibby's Prom Date), Joe Ochman, Don Snell (Prom Judges), Jason Weissbrod (Big Bad Wolf), Tinsley Grimes (Little Red Riding Hood), Joshua Fitzgerald (Tarzan), Amanda Wilmshurst (Fruit Headdress Woman); Ozomatli: Band Members: Willy Abers, Ullses Bella, Jose Espinoza, Lucas MacFadden, William Marruto, Raul Pacheco, Justin Porie, Asdru Sierra, Charles Stewart, Jiro Yamaguchi.

For her first job as a reporter, Josie Geller is assigned to go undercover and pose as a high school student, a task that has her dreading reliving her life as an unpopular teenager.

© Twentieth Century Fox

Drew Barrymore, Leelee Sobieski

Michael Vartan

John C. Reilly, Molly Shannon

Drew Barrymore, David Arquette

LIFE

Martin Lawrence, Bernie Mac

(UNIVERSAL) Producers, Brian Grazer, Eddie Murphy; Executive Producers, Karen Kehela, James D. Brubaker; Director, Ted Demme; Screenplay, Robert Ramsey, Matthew Stone; Photography, Geoffrey Simpson; Designer, Dan Bishop; Editor, Jeffrey Wolf; Special Make-Up and Effects, Rick Baker; Music, Wyclef Jean; Music Supervisor, Amanda Scheer-Demme; Costumes, Lucy Corrigan; Casting, Margery Simkin; an Imagine Entertainment presentation of a Brian Grazer production; Dolby; Deluxe color; Rated R; 108 minutes; Release date: April 16, 1999

CAST

Rayford Gibson ....Eddie Murphy
Claude Banks ....Martin Lawrence
Willie Long ....Obba Babatundé
Sgt. Dillard ....Nick Cassavetes
Cookie ....Anthony Anderson
Pokerface ....Barry Shabaka Henley
Hoppin' Bob ....Brent Jennings
Jangle Leg ....Bernie Mac
Biscuit ....Miguel A. Nuñez, Jr.
Goldmouth ....Michael "Bear" Taliferro
Radio..Guy Torry
Can't Get Right ....Bokeem Woodbine
Dexter Wilkins ....Ned Beatty
Sylvia...Lisa Nicole Carson
Superintendent Abernathy ....O'Neal Compton
Stan Blocker ....Noah Emmerich
Spanky..Rick James
Winston Hancock ....Clarence Williams III
Jake ....Heavy D
Leon ....Bonz Malone
Young Sheriff Pike ....Ned Vaughn
Older Sheriff Pike ....R. Lee Ermey
Daisy ....Sanaa Lathan
Young Mae Rose ....Allyson Call
Older Mae Rose ....Poppy Montgomery
Judge ....James D. Brubaker
Slim ....Walter Jordan
Billy's Mama ....Brooks Almy
Billy ....Hal Havins
Nurse Doherty ....Hildy Brooks
Isaac ....Kenn Whitaker
Bathroom Attendant..Ernie Banks
Doctor...David Alexander
Blind Reverend Clay ....Johnny Brown
Mrs. Clay ....Armelia McQueen
Juke Bartender ....Nate Evans
Deputy at Mansion ....Todd Everett
Man with Lantern ....Don Harvey
Juke Joint Waitress..............................Venus De Milo Thomas
and Zaid Farid, Keith Burke (Shady Cardplayers), Haskell Vaughn Anderson III (Junkie), Steven Barr, Pete Zahradnick (Firemen), Kenneth White (Deputy), Leonard O. Turner (Superintendent Burke), Garcelle Beauvais (Yvette), Augie Blunt (Man in Prison), Keith Burke, Quantae Love, Sean Lampkin (Trustees at Line), James Emory, Jr. (Goldmouth's Son), Bill Gratton (Fire Inspector), Reamy Hall (Mrs. Dillard), Corrie Harris, Ayanna Maharry (Sylvia's Girls), George Hartmann (Prison Guard), Zack Helvey (Captain Tom Burnette), Kimble Jemison, Jordan Mahome (Gang Bangers), William Taylor, Jay Arlen Jones (Bagmen), Oscar Jordan (Juke Joint Guitarist), Jordan Lund (Funeral Chaplain), Bridget Morrow (Cocktail Waitress), Ronald Lee Moss (Bouncer), Betty Murphy (Mrs. Abernathy), Walter Powell, Jr. (Waiter), Chris Prevost (Pilot), Joseph Rappa (Disgruntled Fan), Dawn Robinson (Club Crooner), Leon Sanders (Barkeep)

Martin Lawrence, Eddie Murphy

Ray Gibson, a small-time hustler, and Claude Banks, a bank teller with a gambling debt, team up to do a bootlegging job and wind up falsely accused of murder, leading to their being sentenced to life imprisonment. This film received an Oscar nomination for makeup.

© Universal Studios

Eddie Murphy, Michael "Bear" Taliferro

GOODBYE LOVER

(**WARNER BROS.**) Producers, Alexandra Milchan, Patrick McDarrah, Joel Roodman, Chris Daniel; Executive Producers, Arnon Milchan, Michael G. Nathanson; Director, Roland Joffé; Screenplay, Ron Peer, Joel Cohen, Alec Sokolow; Story, Ron Peer; Photography, Dante Spinotti; Designer, Stewart Starkin; Editor, William Steinkamp; Line Producer, Gerald T. Olson; Music, John Ottman; Associate Producer, Van Spurgeon; Costumes, Theodora Van Runkle; Casting, Shari Rhodes, Joseph Middleton; a Regency Enterprises presentation of an Arnon Milchan/Gotham Entertainment Group/Lightmotive production; Dolby; Super 35 Widescreen; Technicolor; Rated R; 102 minutes; Release date: April 16, 1999

CAST

Sandra Dunmore	Patricia Arquette
Jake Dunmore	Dermot Mulroney
Peggy Blane	Mary-Louise Parker
Rita Pompano	Ellen DeGeneres
Rollins	Ray McKinnon
Detective Crowley	Alex Rocco
Ben Dunmore	Don Johnson
Reverend Finlayson	Andre Gregory
Bradley	John Neville
Evelyn	Jo Nell Kennedy

and Akane Nelson (Receptionist), Kevin Cooney (Company Man #1), Will Foster Stewartv (Dennis), Nina Siemaszko (Newscaster), David Brisbin (Mr. Brodsky), Lisa Eichhorn (Mrs. Brodsky), George Furth (Mr. Merritt), Barry Newman (Senator Lassetter), Michael Krawic (Medical Examiner), Max Perlich (Will), Quincy Samuel Smith (Larry), Andi Chapman (Cop), John Prosky (Forensic Cop), Richard T. Jones (Detective One), Michael P. Byrne (Detective Two), Michael William James (Detective Three), Frances Bay (Old Woman), Pavel Cerny (Cabbie), Ernie Lively (Sheriff), Danny Goldring (Forensic Officer), Rob LaBelle (Minister), Leslie Jordan (Homer), Lou Myers (Police Captain), Doug Spinuzza (Gang-Banger), Lee Weaver (Old Codger), Newell Alexander (Minister), Molly Hager, Erin Keim (Young Girls), Gerald T. Olson (Politician), Kenny Moskow (Commerical Guy), Bruce Rogers (Choir Conductor), Mary Lippman (Joan), Ken Lam (Coroner's Assistant), Darrick Lam, Marcus M. Shirey (Police Officers), Charles Gladney (Cop at College), Lisa Cohen (Battered Woman), Chic Daniel (Detective Daniel), Jay B. Yarnel (Detective Yarnell), Mike Singer, Gary Sear (Company Men), Angela Blattenberger, Bianca Davis, Demi Dustman, Jenna Escoto, Courtney Hansen, Candace Kovacic, Juliana Kubicki, Brittany Mahurin, Kellie Roberson, Julie Shapiro, Ashley Thornton, Natalie Thornton (Girls Chorus)

Ben Dunmore, who is carrying on with both his brother's wife and his brother's secretary, takes a fall from his high rise apartment leading Detective Rita Pompano to suspect foul play.

Dermot Mulroney, Patricia Arquette

SLC PUNK

(**SONY PICTURES CLASSICS**) Producers, Sam Maydew, Peter Ward, James Merendino; Executive Producers, Michael Peyser, Andrea Kreuzhage, Jan De Bont; Director/Screenplay, James Merendino; Photography, Greg Littlewood; Designer, Charlotte Malmlöf; Editor, Esther P. Russell; Costumes, Fiora; Casting, Risa Bramon Garcia, Randi Hiller; a Beyond Films presentation of a Blue Tulip production; Dolby; Panavision; Color; Rated R; 98 minutes; Release date: April 23, 1999

CAST

Stevo	Matthew Lillard
Bob	Michael Goorjian
Trish	Annabeth Gish
Sandy	Jennifer Lien
Father	Christopher McDonald
Sean	Devon Sawa
Mike	Jason Segel
Brandy	Summer Phoenix
John "The Mod"	James Duval
Mark	Til Schweiger
Eddie	Adam Pascal
Jennifer	Chiara Barzini
Chris	Kevin Breznahan
Jamie	Christina Karras
Jones	Ross Peacock
Young Stevo	Christopher Ogden
Young Bob	Francis Capra

and McNally Sagel (Mom), Scott Brady (Bouncer), Vaughn McBride (Liquor Store Man), Janice Knickrehm (Liquor Store Woman), Marcia Dangerfield (Liquor Store Lady), Tom Jacobson (Liquor Store Fellow), Stephanie Shumway (Jules), Eric Robertson (Doctor), Micaela Nelligan (Nurse), Mary Bishop (Sean's Mother), Dominic Gortat (Poser), Elizabeth Westwood (Hot Babe), Glade Quinn, Brad Jersey (Cowboys), Don Walsh (Bob's Dad), Adam Lawson (Russ), Brandon Klock (Tom), Kassandra Metos (Little Girl), Brad Slocum (Teller), Joyce Cohen (Clothing Store Woman), Tracey Pfau (Fast Food Clerk), The 8 Bucks Experiment: Dan Epstein, Evan O'Meara, Paige O'Meara, Preston O'Meara (Extreme Corporal Punishment)

Following high school graduation, Salt Lake City teen Stevo is faced with the decision of going to Harvard Law School or staying true to his devotion to the punk scene.

© Sony Pictures Entertainment Inc.

Michael Goorjian, Annabeth Gish

PUSHING TIN

(20TH CENTURY FOX) Producer, Art Linson; Executive Producers, Alan Greenspan, Michael Flynn; Director, Mike Newell; Screenplay, Glen Charles, Les Charles; Based upon the article "Something's Got to Give" by Darcy Frey; Photography, Gale Tattersall; Designer, Bruno Rubeo; Editor, Jon Gregory; Costumes, Marie-Sylvie Deveau; Music, Anne Dudley; a Fox 2000 Pictures and Regency Enterprises presentation of an Art Linson production; Dolby; Super 35 Widescreen; Deluxe color; Rated R; 124 minutes; Release date: April 23, 1999

Cate Blanchett, Billy Bob Thornton, Angelina Jolie, John Cusack

CAST

Nick Falzone	John Cusack
Russell Bell	Billy Bob Thornton
Connie Falzone	Cate Blanchett
Mary Bell	Angelina Jolie
Barry Plotkin	Jake Weber
Ed Clabes	Kurt Fuller
Tina Leary	Vicki Lewis
Ron Hewitt	Matt Ross
Leo Morton	Jerry Grayson
Pat Feeney	Michael Willis
Paul	Philip Akin
Pete	Mike O'Malley
Tom	Neil Crone
Ken	Matt Gordon
Mark	Joe Pingue
New Controller	Shaun Majumder
Veteran Controller	Dwight McFee
Bob	Rob Smith
Tanya Hewitt	Catherine Lloyd Burns
Julie Clabes	Star Jasper
Crystal Plotkin	Molly Price

and Sarah Knowlton (Beverly), Kiersten Warren (Karen), Andrew Dan (Diner Cook), Tennyson Loeh (Diner Waitress), Michael Hyatt (Trudy), Jillian Cameron (Falzone Girl), Michael Cameron (Falzone Boy), Carolyn Scott (Mrs. Connor), Cody Jones (Timmy), Jimmy Ruderman (Scared Student), Paul Brogren (Supermarket Clerk), Gene DiNovi (Enzo Sorrento), Emile Belcourt (Tenor), Robyn Stevan (Sara), Amanda Delaney (Bodybuilder), Ferne Downey (Sorrento Customer), Joe Matheson (Announcer), Gina Clayton (Dynajet Flight Attendant), Matthew Bennett (Dynajet Steward), Jim Millington (Dynajet Captain), Ramona Milano (TV Reporter), Ray Paisley (K-9 Cop), Rita Tuckett (Lady Sparta), Bob Bidaman (Near Miss Pilot), Dick Callahan (TRACON Guard), Brian King (Honeymoon Man), Julia Paton (Honeymoon Woman), Jenny Parsons (Flight Attendant), John Lefebvre (Pilot), John Robinson (Co-Pilot), Todd Faithful (Tina's Boyfriend), Richard Bauer, Jim Codrington, William Colgate, Craig Eldridge, Peter Graham, Peter James Howarth, Ray Kahnert, Robert B. Kennedy, Shawn Lawrence, Markus Parilo, Martin Roach, Jonathan Whittaker (Pilot Voices)

Billy Bob Thornton, Angelina Jolie

Reigning air traffic controller Nick Falzone finds his status challenged when unorthodox Russell Bell arrives to fill a new position on the TRA-CON staff, prompting a rivalry between the two men.

© Twentieth Century Fox/Monarchy Enterprises/Regency Entertainment

Cate Blanchett, John Cusack

Kurt Fuller, Jake Weber, Matt Ross, Vicki Lewis

Matthew Broderick, Reese Witherspoon

Jessica Campbell, Frankie Ingrassia

Matthew Broderick

Chris Klein

Matthew Broderick, Molly Hagan

ELECTION

(**PARAMOUNT**) Producers, Albert Berger, Ron Yerxa, David Gale, Keith Samples; Executive Producer, Van Toffler; Director, Alexander Payne; Screenplay, Alexander Payne, Jim Taylor; Based on the novel by Tom Perrotta; Co-Producers, Jacobus Rose, Jim Burke; Photography, James Glennon; Designer, Jane Ann Stewart; Editor Kevin Tent; Costumes, Wendy Chuck; Music, Rolfe Kent; Music Supervisor, Dondi Bastone; Casting, Lisa Beach; an MTV Films production in association with Bona Fide productions; Dolby; Panavision; CFI color; Rated R; 103 minutes; Release date: April 23, 1999

Reese Witherspoon

CAST

Jim McAllister	Matthew Broderick
Tracy Flick	Reese Witherspoon
Paul Metzler	Chris Klein
Tammy Metzler	Jessica Campbell
Dave Novotny	Mark Harelik
Diane McAllister	Molly Hagan
Linda Novotny	Delaney Driscoll
Tracy's Mother	Colleen Camp
Lisa Flanagan	Frankie Ingrassia
Principal Walt Hendricks	Phil Reeves
Custodian	Loren Nelson
Girl in Crisis	Emily Martin
Classroom Students	Jonathan Marion, Amy Falcone
"Eat Me" Boy	Matt Justesen
Eat Me" Boy's Buddy	Nick Kenny
Adult Video Actors	Brian Tobin, Christa Young
Tracy's Friend Eric	David Wenzel
Jerry Slavin	Joel Parks
Vice-Principal Ron Bell	Matt Malloy
Chemistry Teacher	Larry Kaiser
Dick Metzler	Holmes Osborne
Jo Metzler	Jeanine Jackson
Carver Office Lady	Marilyn Tipp
Faculty Ballot-Giver	Jeannie Brayman
Larry Fouch	Nick D'Agosto
Motel Clerk	James Devney
Spanish Teacher	L. Carmen Novoa
Kids in the Hall	Jason Paige, Matt Golden, Heather Koenig
Jillian	Jillian Crane

High school teacher Jim McAllister, determined to see ambitious Tracy Flick challenged in her campaign to win the student election, encourages affable jock Paul Metzler to run against her. This film received an Oscar nomination for screenplay adaptation.

© Paramount Pictures

Matthew Broderick

Delaney Driscoll, Molly Hagan

Nguyen Ngoc Hiep, Don Duong

Nguyen Huu Duoc

Zoë Bui

Harvey Keitel

THREE SEASONS

(**OCTOBER**) Producers, Jason Kliot, Joana Vicente, Tony Bui; Executive Producer, Harvey Keitel; Director/Screenplay, Tony Bui; Story, Tony Bui, Timothy Linh Bui; Co-Executive Producer, Charles Rosen; Co-Producer, Timothy Linh Bui; Photography, Lisa Rinzler; Editor, Keith Reamer; Designer, Wing Lee; Line Producer, Trish Hofmann; Music, Richard Horowitz; Costumes, Ghia Ci Fam; Casting, Quan Lelan; an Open City Films production in association with The Goatsingers; Dolby; Color; Not rated; 113 minutes; Release date: April 30, 1999

CAST

Hai	Don Duong
Kien An	Nguyen Ngoc Hiep
Teacher Dao	Tran Manh Cuong
James Hager	Harvey Keitel
Lan	Zoë Bui
Woody	Nguyen Huu Duoc
Truck Driver	Minh Ngoc
Huy	Hoang Phat Trieu
Singing Lotus Woman	Diem Kieu
Giang	Kieu Hanh
Binh	Le Hong Son
Don	Nguyen Ba Quang
Ngon	Tran Huu Su
Minh	Luong Duc Hung

and Hoang Trieu, Tran Long (Men Who Chase Lan), Bui Tuong Trac (Man Who Buys Lotus Flowers), Huynh Kim Hong (Woman on the Balcony), Michael Salamon (Man Who Steals Case), Nguyen Van Son (Shoeshine Boy), A Lu, Hong Phu Quang (Street Guardians), Tran Quang Hieu ("Fagan"), Duong Tan Dung (Cyclo Race Promoter), Ho Van Hoang (Khoi), Thach Thi Kim Trang (Little Girl), Ho Kieng (Restaurant Owner), Ngo Quang Hai (Man in Taxi), Hong Khac Dao (Parlor Manager), Oliver Thai (Parlor Friend), Othello Khanh (Phuong's Drunk Boyfriend), Lola Guimond (Phuong—Amerasian Daughter), Nguyen Thanh Son (Cyclo Race Official), Nguyen Thi Ngoc (Teacher Dao's Servant), Nguyen Thi Lien (Grandmother)

Four strangers in Saigon find themselves struggling to make their way in the New Vietnam as their paths slowly begin to merge.

© October Films

Jeremy Northam, Rebecca Pidgeon

THE WINSLOW BOY

(**SONY PICTURES CLASSICS**) Producer, Sarah Green; Director/Screenplay, David Mamet; Based on the play by Terence Rattigan; Photography, Benoit Delhomme; Designer, Gemma Jackson; Editor, Barbara Tulliver; Music, Alaric Jans; Costumes, Consolata Boyle; Casting, Ros and John Hubbard; Dolby; Color; Rated G; 104 minutes; Release date: April 30, 1999

CAST

Arthur Winslow ....Nigel Hawthorne
Sir Robert Morton ....Jeremy Northam
Catherine Winslow ....Rebecca Pidgeon
Grace Winslow ....Gemma Jones
Ronnie Winslow ....Guy Edwards
Dickie Winslow..Matthew Pidgeon
Desmond Curry..Colin Stinton
John Watherstone..Aden Gillett
Violet..Sarah Flind
First Lord of the Admiralty..Neil North
Miss Barne ....Sara Stewart
Fred, a Photographer..Perry Fenwick
Mr. Michaels..Alan Polanski
Commons Reporter..Duncan Gould
Colleague ....Jim Dunk
Local Reporter ....Ian Soundy
Suffragette ....Eve Bland
MP..Chris Porter

When young Ronnie Winslow is expelled from school after being accused of stealing a postal order, his father hires leading defense lawyer Sir Robert Morton to clear the boy's name. Previous 1948 film version starred Robert Donat, Margaret Leighton, and Cedric Hardwicke and was released in the U.S. in 1950 by Eagle Lion Films. Neil North, who played Ronnie in that version, appears here as the First Lord of the Admiralty.

© Sony Pictures Entertainment Inc.

Nigel Hawthorne, Guy Edwards

Rebecca Pidgeon, Nigel Hawthorne, Colin Stinton

Gemma Jones, Rebecca Pidgeon, Nigel Hawthorne

ENTRAPMENT

(**20TH CENTURY FOX**) Producers, Sean Connery, Michael Hertzberg, Rhonda Tollefson; Executive Producers, Iain Smith, Ron Bass, Arnon Milchan; Director, Jon Amiel; Screenplay, Ron Bass, William Broyles; Story, Ron Bass, Michael Hertzberg; Photography, Phil Meheux; Designer, Norman Garwood; Editor, Terry Rawlings; Music, Christopher Young; Costumes, Penny Rose; Stunts, Vic Armstrong, Jim Dowdall; Casting, Michelle Guish, Donna Isaacson; a Regency Enterprises presentation of a Fountainbridge Films and a Michael Hertzberg production; Dolby; Panavision; Deluxe color; Rated PG-13; 112 minutes; Release date: April 30, 1999

CAST

Robert "Mac" MacDougal...Sean Connery
Virginia "Gin" Baker...Catherine Zeta-Jones
Thibadeaux ....Ving Rhames
Cruz..Will Patton
Conrad Greene ....Maury Chaykin
Haas ....Kevin McNally
Quinn ....Terry O'Neill
Security Chief ....Madhav Sharma
Chief of Police ....David Yip
Millennium Man ....Tim Potter
Waverly Technician ....Eric Meyers
Cruz's Man ....Aaron Swartz
Computer Technician ....William Marsh
Banker ....Tony Xu
Director ....Rolf Saxon
Operator ....Tom Clarke-Hill
Technician...David Howard
Doctor ....Stuart Ong
Security Guards ....Ravin Ganatra, Rhydian Jai-Persad, Hari Dhillon

Gin Baker, an insurance investigator sent to trap master art thief Mac MacDougal, forms an alliance with him instead as they scheme to pull off a daring multi-billion dollar heist on the eve of the millennium.

© Twentieth Century Fox Film Corp.

Sean Connery, Catherine Zeta-Jones

Catherine Zeta-Jones

Sean Connery, Catherine Zeta-Jones

Sean Connery, Ving Rhames

Arnold Vosloo

Brendan Fraser, Rachel Weisz, John Hannah

The Mummy, Rachel Weisz, Brendan Fraser

THE MUMMY

(**UNIVERSAL**) Producers, James Jacks, Sean Daniel; Director/Screenplay, Stephen Sommers; Screen Story, Stephen Sommers, Lloyd Fonvielle, Kevin Jarre; Photography, Adrian Biddle; Designer, Allan Cameron; Editor, Bob Ducsay; Executive Producer, Kevin Jarre, Co-Producer, Patricia Carr; Special Visual Effects, Industrial Light & Magic; Special Effects Supervisor, Chris Corbould; Live Action Creature Effects Supervisor, Nick Dudman; Associate Producer, Megan Moran; Stunts, Simon Crane; an Alphaville production; Dolby; Panavision; Deluxe color; Rated PG-13; 124 minutes; Release date: May 7, 1999

CAST

Rick O'Connell	Brendan Fraser
Evelyn	Rachel Weisz
Jonathan	John Hannah
Beni	Kevin J. O'Connor
Imhotep	Arnold Vosloo
Egyptologist	Jonathan Hyde
Ardeth Bay	Oded Fehr
Warden	Omid Djalili
Curator	Erick Avari
Pharaoh Seti	Aharon Ipale
Anck Su Namun	Patricia Velasquez
Hook	Carl Chase
Henderson	Stephen Dunham
Daniels	Corey Johnson
Burns	Tuc Watkins
Winston Havelock	Bernard Fox
Hangman	Mohammed Afifi
Camel Trader	Abderrahim El Aadili

An Egyptologist and her brother enlist adventurer Rick O'Connell to help them find the ruins of Hamunaptra where the 3,000 year-old remains of the cursed Imhotep lie waiting to be unleashed into the modern world. Previous film versions were released by Universal in 1932 (starring Boris Karloff) and Hammer Films in 1959 (starring Christopher Lee). This film received an Oscar nomination for sound.

© Universal Studios

Brendan Fraser, Rachel Weisz

Chris Stafford, Anderson Gabrych

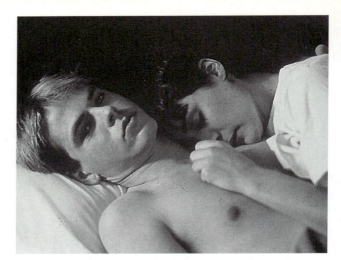

Chris Stafford, Tina Holmes

Chris Stafford, Anderson Gabrych

Chris Stafford, Lea DeLaria

EDGE OF SEVENTEEN

(**STRAND**) Producers, David Moreton, Todd Stephens; Director, David Moreton; Screenplay, Todd Stephens; Co-Producer, Michael Wolfson; Associate Producer, Karen Jaroneski; Photography, Gina Degirolamo; Designer, Ivor Stillen; Editor, Tal Ben-David; Music, Tom Bailey; Line Producer, Craig Shepherd; Costumes, Ane Crabtree; Casting, Tim Kaltenecker, Richard Whobrey; a Blue Steak Films & Luna Pictures presentation; Color; Not rated; 100 minutes; Release date: May 14, 1999

CAST

Eric Hunter	Chris Stafford
Maggie	Tina Holmes
Rod	Andersen Gabrych
Mom	Stephanie McVay
Angie	Lea DeLaria
Dad	John Eby
Andy	Antonio Carriero
Steve	Jason Sheingross
Gregg	Tony Maietta
Jonathan	Jeff Fryer
Chuckie	Kevin J. Kelley
Foodtown	Mark Gates
Ruby Rogers	Stevie Reese Desmond
Frieda	Barbie Marie
Irate Customer	Craig Shepherd
Security Guard	Doug Millon
Ed	Clay Van Sickle
Scott	Jason Griffiths

and Jimmy Mack (Bartender), Justin Leach (Tall Blond Guy), Jeff Abramson (Dan McAllister), Don Mitri (Teacher), Mike Roth (Wrestling Jock), Adam Penton (Joe Plonsky, Jr.), Tal Ben-David (Waitress), Dina Anderson, Karen Brooks, Shannon Constantine (Bitchy Girls), Edd Martin (Drag Queen), Gregg Long (Mr. Johnson), Ryan Florio (Randy), Twiggy (Marlene Dicktrick), Dominic Carrion (Miss Anita Mann), Jesse Adams (Drag Atrocity), Joshua Elrod (Rod's Roommate), Khalid Abdelrasoul, Sally Law, Jarred J. Nichols, Mark Jay Warschak (Grubbers), Diva (Herself)

During the summer of 1984, teenager Eric Hunter has his first sexual experience with another guy, leading him to explore an alternate lifestyle and come to terms with his homosexuality.

© Strand Releasing

WILLIAM SHAKESPEARE'S A MIDSUMMER NIGHT'S DREAM

(FOX SEARCHLIGHT) Producers, Leslie Urdang, Michael Hoffman; Executive Producer, Arnon Milchan; Director/Screenplay, Michael Hoffman; Based on the play by William Shakespeare; Photography, Oliver Stapleton; Designer, Luciana Arrighi; Co-Producer, Ann Wingate; Music, Simon Boswell; Costumes, Gabriella Pescucci; Associate Producer, Nigel Goldsack; Editor, Garth Craven; Casting, Lora Kennedy; a Regency Enterprises presentation; Dolby; PLC Widescreen; Deluxe color; Rated PG-13; 116 minutes; Release date: May 14, 1999

CAST

Nick Bottom	Kevin Kline
Titania	Michelle Pfeiffer
Oberon	Rupert Everett
Puck	Stanley Tucci
Helena	Calista Flockhart
Hermia	Anna Friel
Demetrius	Christian Bale
Lysander	Dominic West
Theseus	David Strathairn
Hippolyta	Sophie Marceau
Peter Quince	Roger Rees
Robin Starveling	Max Wright
Snug	Gregory Jbara
Tom Snout	Bill Irwin
Francis Flute	Sam Rockwell
Egeus	Bernard Hill
Philostrate	John Sessions

and Deirdre A. Harrison (Hard-eyed Fairy), Heather Elizabeth Parisi (Bottom's Wife), Annalisa Cordone (Cobweb), Paola Pessot (Mustardseed), Solena Nocentini (Moth), Flaminia Fegarotti (Peaseblossom), Valerio Isidori (Master Antonio), Daniele Finizio, Damiano Salvatori (Dangerous Boys), Chomoke Bhuiyan (Changeling Boy)

A pair of mismatched lovers and a troupe of would-be actors converge in the woods outside of Athens where a playful gathering of enchanted spirits works mischief and magic. Previous film versions include the 1935 Warners Bros. release with James Cagney, Mickey Rooney, Dick Powell, and Olivia de Havilland.

© Twentieth Century Fox/Monarchy Enterprises/Regency Entertainment

Stanley Tucci, Rupert Everett

Michelle Pfeiffer

Kevin Kline, Michelle Pfeiffer

Calista Flockhart, Christian Bale

Natalie Portman

Ray Park

STAR WARS EPISODE 1: THE PHANTOM MENACE

(20TH CENTURY FOX) Producer, Rick McCallum; Executive Producer/Director/Screenplay, George Lucas; Photography, David Tattersall; Designer, Gavin Bocquet; Costumes, Trisha Biggar; Editor, Paul Martin Smith; Music, John Williams; Special Visual Effects & Animation, Industrial Light & Magic; Creature Effects, Nick Dudman; Visual Effects Supervisors, Dennis Muren, Scott Squires, John Knoll; Stunts/Swordmaster, Nick Gillard; Casting, Robin Gurland; a Lucasfilm production; Dolby; Panavision; Deluxe color; Rated PG; 133 minutes; Release date: May 19, 1999

CAST

Qui-Gon Jinn ....Liam Neeson
Obi-Wan Kenobi...Ewan McGregor
Queen Amidala ....Natalie Portman
Anakin Skywalker ....Jake Lloyd
Senator Palpatine/Darth Sidious....................Ian McDiarmid
Shmi Skywalker ....Pernilla August
Jar Jar Binks/Senator (voice) ....Ahmed Best
Yoda...Frank Oz
Mace Windu ....Samuel L. Jackson
Darth Maul ....Ray Park
Captain Panaka ....Hugh Quarshie
Ric Olie ....Ralph Brown
C-3PO ....Anthony Daniels
Sio Bibble ....Oliver Ford Davies
Chancellor Finis Valorum.....................................Terence Stamp
R2-D2 ....Kenny Baker
Wald/Grimy Man/Weazel ....Warwick Davis
Boss Nass ....Brian Blessed
Nute Gunray/Ki-Adi-Mundi/Lott Dodd ....Silas Carsons
Kitster ....Dhruv Chanchani
Jira ....Margaret Towner
Seek ....Oliver Walpole
Rabé ....Karol Cristina daSilva
Rune Haako/Mas Amedda/Oppo Rancisis/
Horox Ryyder/Orn Free Taa/
Graxol Kelvyyn/Trade Federation Delegate ....Jerome Blake
Captain Tarpals...Steven Speirs
Bravos ....Benedict Taylor, Clarence Smith, Celia Imrie
Fode Annodue ....Greg Proops
Beed Annodue...Scott Capurro
Eirtaé...Friday "Liz" Wilson
Saesee Tiin ....Khan Bonfils
Even Piell ....Michaela Cottrell
Aks Moe ....Mark Coulier
TC-14 ....John Fensom
Watto...Andrew Secombe
Sebulba (voice)..Lewis Macleod
Plo Koon/Daultay Dofine ....Alan Ruscoe
Senate Guard ....Dominic West
Yané..Candice Orwell
Saché ....Sofia Coppola
Sabé ....Kiera Knighley
Radian VII Captain...Bronagh Gallagher
and Jenna Green (Amee), Megan Udall (Melee), Hassani Shapi (Eeth Koth), Gin Clarke (Adi Gallia), Michelle Taylor (Yarael Poof), Dipika O'Neill Joti (Depa Billaba), Phil Eason (Yaddle), Lindsay Duncan (TC-14—voice), Peter Serafinowicz (Darth Maul—voice), James Taylor (Rune Haako—voice), Toby Longworth (Lott Dodd—voice), Robert Sundback (R-23—voice), Chris Sanders (Daultay Dofine—voice), Marc Silk (Aks Moe—voice), Tyger (Tey How—voice)

Jedi knights Quin-Gon Jinn and Obi-Wan Kenobi arrive on the planet Naboo to aide Queen Amidala whose planet the Trade Federation plans to invade in order to extend its dominance over the galaxy. Prequel to the 20th Century Fox films Star War (1977), The Empire Strikes Back (1980), and Return of the Jedi (1983), all of which also featured Anthony Daniels and Kenny Baker. This became the highest grossing movie released in 1999. This film received Oscar nominations for visual effects, sound, and sound effects editing.

Jake Lloyd, Pernilla August

Liam Neeson, R2-D2, Jake Lloyd, Ewan McGregor

Yoda, Samuel L. Jackson

Liam Neeson, Jake Lloyd, Watto

Droids

Natalie Portman, Jar Jar Binks

THE LOVE LETTER

(**DREAMWORKS**) Producers, Sarah Pillsbury, Midge Sanford, Kate Capshaw; Executive Producers, Beau Flynn, Stefan Simchowitz; Director, Peter Ho-Sun Chan; Screenplay, Maria Maggenti; Based on the novel by Cathleen Schine; Photography, Tami Reiker; Designer, Andrew Jackness; Editor, Jacqueline Cambas; Costumes, Tracy Tynan; Music, Luis Bacalov; Co-Producer/Production Manager, Karen Koch; Casting, Mali Finn; a Sanford/Pillsbury production; Dolby; Technicolor; Rated PG-13; 88 minutes; Release date: May 21, 1999

Julianne Nicholson, Tom Everett Scott

CAST

Helen MacFarquhar	Kate Capshaw
Lillian	Blythe Danner
Janet	Ellen DeGeneres
Miss Scattergoods	Geraldine McEwan
Jennifer	Julianne Nicholson
Johnny	Tom Everett Scott
George Mathias	Tom Selleck
Eleanor	Gloria Stuart
Officer Dan	Bill Buell
Postal Clerk	Alice Drummond
Ray	Erick Jensen
Selma	Margaret Ann Brady
Kelly	Jessica Capshaw
Post Office Customer	Walter Covell
Bookstore Customer	Patrick Donnelly
Garbage Men	Lucas Hall, Christian Harmony, Christopher Nee
Vivian	Marilyn Rockafellow
Emily	Breanne Smith
Girl with Sparkler	Sasha Spielberg

In the quiet New England town of Loblolly by the Sea, an unsigned love letter is found leading some of the town's principals to wonder if they were the intended recipient.

© DreamWorks LLC

Blythe Danner

Gloria Stuart

Kate Capshaw, Ellen DeGeneres, Tom Selleck

George Dzundza, Cuba Gooding, Jr.

INSTINCT

(**TOUCHSTONE**) Producers, Michael Taylor, Barbara Boyle; Executive Producers, Wolfgang Petersen, Gail Katz; Director, Jon Turteltaub; Screen Story and Screenplay, Gerald DiPego; Suggested by the novel *Ishmael* by Daniel Quinn; Photography, Philippe Rousselot; Designer, Garreth Stover; Editor, Richard Francis-Bruce; Co-Producers, Richard Lerner, Brian Doubleday, Christina Steinberg; Special Character Effects, Stan Winston; Music, Danny Elfman; Costumes, Jill Ohanneson; Primate Choreographer, Peter Elliott; Casting, Renee Rousselot; a Spyglass Entertainment presentation of a Barbara Boyle and Michael Taylor production; Dolby; Panavision; Technicolor; Rated R; 123 minutes; Release date: June 4, 1999

Anthony Hopkins, Cuba Gooding, Jr.

CAST

Ethan Powell..Anthony Hopkins
Theo Caulder...Cuba Gooding, Jr.
Ben Hillard..Donald Sutherland
Lyn Powell...Maura Tierney
Dr. John Murray..George Dzundza
Guard Dacks..John Ashton
Warden Keefer...John Aylward
Pete..Thomas Q. Morris
Nicko...Doug Spinuzza
Bluto...Paul Bates
Guard Alan..Rex Linn
Guard Anderson..Rod McLachlan
Guards ....Kurt Smildsin, Jim Coleman
Annie...Tracey Ellis
Lester Rodman...Kim Ingram
Tom Hanley...Paul Collins
Foley..Marc Macaulay
Boaz..Jim Grimshaw
Federal Marshal...Gary Bristow
and Rus Blackwell, Bruce Borgan (Government Aides), Louanne Stephens (Marjorie Powell), Ajie Kirkland (Captain Kagona), Chike Kani Omo (David), Christopher John Harris (William), Ivonne Coll (Dr. Marquez), Pat McNamara (Dr. Josephson), Vivienne Sendaydiego (Catherine), Roger Floyd (Gilbert), Dave Deever (Man in Car), Tim Goodwin (Helmet Man), Alex City, Jimmy Dipisa, Manwell Hendrix, Kevin McNally, Kevin Moore, Joe Tacke, Bertram Wallace (Prisoners), John Travis (Bartender Mike), David Anthony, John Munro Cameron, Jay Caputo, Garon Michael, Misty Rosas, David St. Pierre, Verne Troyer (Gorilla Performers)

Psychiatrist Theo Caulder attempts to find out how primatologist Ethan Powell has ended up in prison, accused of the murder of two park rangers while living among the mountain gorillas of Rwanda.

Donald Sutherland, Cuba Gooding, Jr.

Maura Tierney, Cuba Gooding, Jr.

Mary Elizabeth Mastrantonio, David Strathairn

LIMBO

(**SCREEN GEMS**) Producer, Maggie Renzi; Director/Screenplay/Editor, John Sayles; Photography, Haskell Wexler; Designer, Gemma Jackson; Music, Mason Daring; Costumes, Shay Cunliffe; Casting, Lizzie Martinez; a Green/Renzi production; Distributed through Sony Pictures Releasing; Dolby; CFI color; Rated R; 126 minutes; Release date: June 4, 1999

CAST

Donna De Angelo	Mary Elizabeth Mastrantonio
Joe Gastineau	David Strathairn
Noelle De Angelo	Vanessa Martinez
Smilin' Jack	Kris Kristofferson
Bobby Gastineau	Casey Siemaszko
Frankie	Kathryn Grody
Lou	Rita Taggart
Harmon King	Leo Burmester
Albright	Michael Laskin
Ricky	Herminio Ramos
Audrey	Dawn McInturff
Baines	Tom Biss
Randy Mason	Jimmy MacDonell
Stacy	Märit Carlson-Van Dort
Corky	Monica Brandner
Denise	Maria Gladziszewski
X-Man	Dan Rinner
Vic	Stephen James Lang
Cruise Director	Ron Clarke
Loan Officer	Charlotte Carroll
Teacher	Joaqlin Estus
Bad Guys	Andy Spear, Dave Hunsaker

In a small Alaskan fishing village on the brink of possible redevelopment, nightclub singer Donna De Angelo takes up with a world-wearied fisherman-turned-handyman, Joe Gastineau.

© Screen Gems

Mary Elizabeth Mastrantonio, David Strathairn, Vanessa Martinez

Mary Elizabeth Mastrantonio, Vanessa Martinez, David Strathairn

DESERT BLUE

(**SAMUEL GOLWYN CO.**) Producers, Andrea Sperling, Nadia Leonelli, Michael Burns; Executive Producers, Leanna Creel, Marc Butan, Kip Hagopian; Director/Screenplay, Morgan J. Freeman; Co-Producers, Gill Holland, A. Carter Pottash; Photography, Enrique Chediak; Designer, David Doernberg; Editor, Sabine Hoffman; Music, Vytas Nagisetty; Costumes, Trish Summerville; Casting, Susan Shopmaker; an Ignite Entertainment production; Dolby; Panavision; Color; Rated R; 90 minutes; Release date: June 4, 1999

CAST

Blue	Brendan Sexton III
Skye	Kate Hudson
Lance	John Heard
Ely	Christina Ricci
Pete	Casey Affleck
Sandy	Sara Gilbert
Cale	Ethan Suplee
Billy	Peter Sarsgaard
Deputy Keeler	Lee Holmes
Sheriff Jackson	Daniel Von Bargen
Agent Summers	Aunjanue Ellis
Dr. Gordon	René Rivera
Haley	Isidra Vega
Caroline	Lucinda Jenney
Agent Bellows	Michael Ironside
Insurance Agent	Jerry Agee
Truck Driver	Richmond Arquette
Agent Red	Nate Moore
Agent Green	Ntare Mwine
KBLU Radio DJ Voices	Fred Schneider
Mickey Moonday	Liev Schreiber
Telly Clems	MacDaddy Beefcake

Restless teenager Blue and his friends find themselves stuck in their dead-end California town when a truck spills a mysterious and possibly dangerous chemical, resulting in a quarantine.

©Samuel Goldwyn Films

Christina Ricci, Casey Affleck

Brendan Sexton III

RETURN WITH HONOR

(**OCEAN RELEASING**) Producers/Directors, Freida Lee Mock, Terry Sanders; Screenplay, Freida Lee Mock, Terry Sanders, Christine Z. Wiser; Photography, Eddie Marritz, Terry Sanders; Editor, Greg Byers; Music, Charles Bernstein; Co-Producer, Christine Wiser; a Tom Hanks presentation of a Sanders & Mock/American Film Foundation production; a Playtone presentation; Dolby; Color; Not rated; 102 minutes; Release date: June 11, 1999. Documentary looks back on several American pilots who were shot down over North Vietnam and spent several years as POWs.

WITH

Lt. jg. Everett "Ev" Alvarez, USN; Lt. Cmdr. Bob Shumaker, USN; Cmdr. Jeremiah "Jerry" Denton, USN; Cmdr. James "Jim" Stockdale, USN; Lt.. Col. Robinson "Robbie" Risner, USAF; Lt. Cmdr. John McCain, USN; Capt. Douglas "Pete" Peterson, USAF; Maj. Fred Cherry, USAF; Capt. George McKnight, USAF; Maj. Sam Johnson, USAF; Lt. Paul Galanti, USN; Lt. Ron Bliss, USAF; Lt. Tom McNish, USAF; Lt. Cmdr. Richard Stratton, USN; Seaman Douglas Hegdahl, USN; Col. Tom Madison, USAF; Lt. Ed Mechenbier, USAF; Lt. Kevin McManus, USAF; Lt. John "Mike" McGrath, USN; Maj. George "Bud" Day, USAF; Sybil Stockdale, Henry Etta Madison, Alice Stratton, Phyllis Galanti, Marlene McGrath, Lorraine Shumaker.

© AFF

Lt. Mike McGrath

Mike Myers, Heather Graham

Verne J. Troyer, Mike Myers

Seth Green

Kristen Johnston, Mike Myers

Heather Graham

Robert Wagner

AUSTIN POWERS:
THE SPY WHO SHAGGED ME

(**NEW LINE CINEMA**) Producers, John Lyons, Mike Myers, Suzanne Todd, Jennifer Todd, Demi Moore, Eric McLeod; Executive Producers, Erwin Stoff, Michael De Luca, Donna Langley; Director, Jay Roach; Screenplay, Mike Myers, Michael McCullers; Based on characters created by Mike Myers; Photography, Ueli Steiger; Designer, Rusty Smith; Editors, Jon Poll, Debra Neil-Fisher; Costumes, Deena Appel; Music, George S. Clinton; Music Supervisor, John Houlihan; Associate Producer, Emma Chasin; Casting, Juel Bestrop, Jeanne McCarthy; an Eric's Boy, Moving Pictures and Team Todd production; Dolby; Super 35 Widescreen; Deluxe color; Rated PG-13; 95 minutes; Release date: June 11, 1999

CAST

Austin Powers/Dr. Evil/Fat Bastard	Mike Myers
Felicity Shagwell	Heather Graham
Basil Exposition	Michael York
Number Two	Robert Wagner
Young Number Two	Rob Lowe
Scott Evil	Seth Green
Frau Farbissina	Mindy Sterling
Mini-Me	Verne J. Troyer
Vanessa	Elizabeth Hurley
Robin Swallows	Gia Carides
Themselves	Burt Bacharach, Elvis Costello, Woody Harrelson, Willie Nelson, Rebecca Romijn Stamos, Jerry Springer
Mustafa	Will Ferrell
Ivana Humpalot	Kristen Johnston
General Hawk	Charles Napier
The President	Tim Robbins
Mission Commander	Fred Willard
British Colonel	Oliver Muirhead
Chinese Teacher	George Kee Cheung
Chinese Student	Jeffrey Meng
Klansman	Muse Watson
Klansman's Son (Bobby)	Scott Cooper
Man (Pecker)	Douglas Fisher
Norad Colonel	Kevin Cooney
Radar Operator Peters	Clint Howard
Pilot	Brian Hooks
Co-Pilot	David Koechner
Guitarist with Willie Nelson	Frank Clem
Sargeant	Herb Mitchell
Umpire	Steve Eastin
Woman (Pecker)	Jane Carr
Assassin	Kevin Durand
Chick #1 at Party	Melissa Justin
Captain of the Guard	Nicholas Walker
Guard at Jail Cell	Steve Hibbert
Private Army Soldier	Eric Winzenried

and Tim Bagley (Friendly Dad), Colton James (Friendly Son), Mike Hagerty (Peanut Vendor), Jack Kehler (Circus Barker) Kirk Ward (Soldier), Jeff Garlin (Cyclops) David Coy, David Crigger, Tom Ehlen, Dennis Wilson (Carnaby Street Band), Rachel Wilson (Fan), Jennifer Coolidge (Woman at Football Game), John Mahon (NATO Colonel), Michael McDonald (NATO Soldier), Jeanette Miller (Teacher), Mary Jo Smith (Unibrau), Carrie Ann Inaba, Jennifer Hamilton, Ayesha Orange, Natalie Willes (Felicity's Dancers), John Corella, Alison Faulk, Michelle Elkin, Shealan Spencer, Tovaris Wilson (Party Dancers), Bree Turner, Marisa Gilliam, Mark Meismer, Sal Vassallo, Jason Yribar (Dancers), Chekesha Van Putten, Tara Mouri, Gigi Yazicioglu (Go-Go Dancers), Sarah Smith, Faune A. Chambers, Gabriel Paige (Scene Break Dancers), Jim Boensch (Queen's Guard), Ron Ulstad (Chief of Staff), Tim Watters (Bill Clinton Look-Alike), Todd M. Schultz, Steve Wilkos (Jerry Springer's Bodyguards)

Swinging secret agent Austin Powers must travel back to 1969 after the nefarious Dr. Evil steals Powers' mojo as part of his plan to destroy the world. Sequel to the 1997 New Line Cinema release Austin Powers: International Man of Mystery, which also featured Mike Myers, Robert Wagner, Michael York, Seth Green, Mindy Sterling, Will Ferrell, Clint Howard, and Burt Bacharach. Charles Napier returns in a different role. This film received an Oscar nomination for makeup.

Mindy Sterling, Mike Myers

Rob Lowe

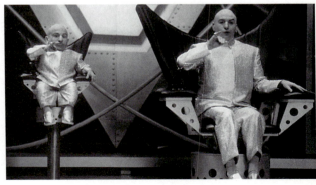

Verne J. Troyer, Mike Myers

Jane

Tantor, Terk

Jane, Professor Porter, Clayton

Kala

TARZAN

(WALT DISNEY PICTURES) Producer, Bonnie Arnold; Directors, Kevin Lima, Chris Buck; Screenplay, Tab Murphy, Bob Tzudiker, Noni White; Based on the story *Tarzan of the Apes* by Edgar Rice Burroughs; Songs, Phil Collins; Music Score, Mark Mancina; Associate Producer, Christopher Chase; Art Director, Daniel St. Pierre; Editor, Gregory Perler; Artistic Supervisors: Associate Art Director, Dan Cooper; Story, Brian Pimental; Layout, Jean Christophe Poulain; Backgrounds, Doug Ball; Clean-Up, Marshall Lee Toomey; Visual Effects, Peter De Mund Computer Graphics, Eric Daniels; Production Manager, Jean Luc Florinda; Executive Music Producer, Chris Montan; Artistic Coordinator, Fraser MacLean; Distributed by Buena Vista Pictures; Dolby; Technicolor; Rated G; 88 minutes; Release date: June 16, 1999

VOICE CAST

Clayton ....Brian Blessed
Kala ....Glenn Close
Jane Porter ....Minnie Driver
Tarzan ....Tony Goldwyn
Professor Porter ....Nigel Hawthorne
Kerchak ....Lance Henriksen
Tantor ....Wayne Knight
Young Tarzan ....Alex D. Linz
Terk ....Rosie O'Donnell
and Beth Anderson, Jack Angel, Joseph Ashton, Robert Bergen, Billy Warren Bodine, Hillary Brooks, Roger Bumpass, Lily Collins, Kat Cressida, Jim Cummings, Aria Curzon, Jennifer Darling, Taylor Dempsey, Debi Derryberry, Patti Deutsch, Paul Eiding, Blake Ewing, Francesca Falcone, Michael Geiger, Scott Gershin, Sam Gifaldi, Amy Gleason, Jackie Gonneau, Debbie Hall, Jonnie Hall, Sandie Hall, Tina Halvorson, Linda Harmon, Karen Harper, Micah Hauptman, Jennifer L. Hughes, Grady Hutt, Luana Jackman, Adam Karpel, Theo Lebow, Brandon Lucas, Ricky Lucchese, James Lively, Sherry Lynn, Melissa Mackay, Danny Mann, Ilana Marks, Jason Marsden, Mickie T. McGowan, Donna Medine, Nils Montan, Bobbi Page, Brandon Pollard, Phil Proctor, Scott Record, Michael Reagan, Ian Redford, Jessica Rotter, Chris Sanders, Stephanie Sawyer, Laurie Schillinger, Brianne Siddall, Frank Simms, Susan Stevens Logan, Shane Sweet, Tiffany Takara, Dominic Thiroux, Jamie Torcellini, Eric Von Detten, Joe Whyte, Danielle Wiener (Additional Voices)

A baby, left alone in the jungle after his parents are killed, is raised by apes to be one of their own. Previous versions of Tarzan of the Apes include those in 1918 (Elmo Lincoln), 1932 (Tarzan the Ape Man, MGM; Johnny Weissmuller); 1959 (Tarzan the Ape Man, MGM; Denny Miller); and 1984 (Greystoke: The Legend of Tarzan, Lord of the Apes, WB; Christopher Lambert).

1999 Academy Award winner for Best Original Song ("You'll Be in My Heart").

©Burroughs and Disney

Jane, Tarzan

Tarzan, Professor Porter

Tarzan

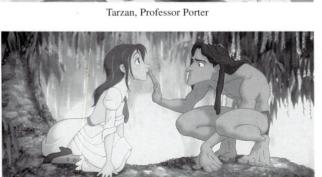

Jane, Tarzan

Terk

John Travolta, Madeleine Stowe, Timothy Hutton

THE GENERAL'S DAUGHTER

John Travolta, James Woods

(**PARAMOUNT**) Producer, Mace Neufeld; Executive Producer, Jonathan D. Krane; Director, Simon West; Screenplay, Christopher Bertolini, William Goldman; Based on the novel by Nelson DeMille; Photography, Peter Menzies, Jr.; Editor, Glen Scantlebury; Designer, Dennis Washington; Costumes, Erica Edell Phillips; Co-Producer, Stratton Leopold; Associate Producer, Lis Kern; Music, Carter Burwell; Casting, Mindy Marin; a Mace Neufeld and Robert Rehme production, a Jonathan D. Krane production; Dolby; Panavision; Deluxe color; Rated R; 116 minutes; Release date: June 18, 1999

CAST

Paul Brenner ....John Travolta
Sarah Sunhill ....Madeleine Stowe
General Joe Campbell ....James Cromwell
Colonel William Kent ....Timothy Hutton
Captain Elisabeth Campbell ....Leslie Stefanson
Chief Yardley ....Daniel von Bargen
Colonel George Fowler ....Clarence Williams III
Colonel Robert Moore ....James Woods
Belling ....Peter Weireter
Elkins ....Mark Boone Junior
Colonel Donald Slesinger ....John Beasley
Captain Elby..Boyd Kestner
Captain Bransford ....Brad Beyer
Captain Goodson ....John Benjamin Hickey
Cal Seiver..Rick Dial
PFC Robbins ....Ariyan Johnson
General Sonnenberg ....John Frankenheimer
CNN Anchor ....Katrina vanden Heuvel
Deputy Yardley..Chris Snyder

Steve Danton, Rich Jackson (Bomb Van Soldiers), Joshua Stafford, Darius Montgomery (Soldiers Who Find Elisabeth), Mark Ivie (Fencing Loser), Michael Terry Swiney (Lockup Sergeant), Lisa A. Tripp (Work Detail Leader), Tait Ruppert (Young Tech), Scott Rosenberg, Jared Chandler, James Paul Morse, Paul Ware (MP Guards), James O. Evans, Chris Grayson, Sy Leopold, Fred Tate (Sex Video Officers), Steve Goyen (Honor Guard Commander), Pablo Espinosa (Color Guard Commander), Levin Handy, Jr., Jason M. Luevano (Airborne Soldiers), Gustavo A. Perdomo (Drill Team NCO), Rodney Mitchell, Ryan D. Kirkland (Ranger Instructors), Michael Gerald Jones, Jr. (Soldier in Locker Room), Matt Anderson (Firing Party Commander), Cooper Huckabee (Colonel Weems), Cliff Fleming, Chris Saunders, Bruce Benson, Rick Shuster, Corey Fleming (Pilots)

John Travolta, Leslie Stefanson

Criminal Investigator Paul Brenner, assigned to solve the brutal rape and murder of Captain Elisabeth Campbell, uncovers a military scandal of epic size.

© Paramount Pictures

Clarence Williams III, John Travolta, Timothy Hutton

Rob Schneider, Cole/Dylan Sprouse, Adam Sandler

Leslie Mann, Jon Stewart

Joey Lauren Adams, Adam Sandler

Peter Dante, Allen Covert

BIG DADDY

(**COLUMBIA**) Producers, Sid Ganis, Jack Giarraputo; Executive Producers, Adam Sandler, Robert Simonds, Joseph M. Caracciolo; Director, Dennis Dugan; Screenplay, Steve Franks, Tim Herlihy, Adam Sandler; Story, Steve Franks; Photography, Theo Van de Sande; Designer, Perry Andelin Blake; Editor, Jeff Gourson; Music, Teddy Castellucci; Costumes, Ellen Lutter; Co-Producer, Alex Siskin; Casting, Roger Mussenden; an Out of the Blue Entertainment/Jack Giarraputo production; Dolby; Technicolor; Rated PG-13; 95 minutes; Release date: June 25, 1999

CAST

Sonny Koufax...Adam Sandler
Layla..Joey Lauren Adams
Kevin Gerrity...Jon Stewart
Julian..Cole Sprouse, Dylan Sprouse
Mr. Brooks ....Josh Mostel
Corinne..Leslie Mann
Phil...Allen Covert
Delivery Guy ....Rob Schneider
Vanessa...Kristy Swanson
Mr. Koufax..Joseph Bologna
Tommy...Peter Dante
Mike...Jonathan Loughran
Homeless Guy ....Steve Buscemi
Singing Kangaroo..Tim Herlihy
Old Man ....Edmund Lyndeck
Restaurant Owner..Larkin Malloy
Employee ....Samantha Brown
Customer ....Neal Huff
Sid...Geoffrey Horn
NYU Student ....Greg Haberny
Waitress ....Jacqueline Titone
Elderly Driver ....George Hall
and Peggy Shay (Lady at Tollbooth), Alfonso Ramirez (George),.Salvatore Cavaliere (Angry Motorist), Kelly Dugan (Kelly), Jared Sandler (Jared), Jillian Sandler (Jillian), Helen Lloyd Breed (Ms. Foote), Chloé Hult (Schoolteacher), Carmen DeLavallade (Judge), Steve Brill (Castelluci), Glen Trotiner (Bailiff) Jorge Buccio (Himself), Cat Jagar (Receptionist), Deborah S. Craig (Paralegal), Nicholas Taylor (Older Kid), Cole Hawkins (Cole), Gabriel Jacobs (Jeff), Michael Arcate (Broken Arm Kid), Gaetano Lisi (Hot Dog Vendor), Michael Giarraputo (Hoboken Motorist), Steven Glenn (Guy at Party), Dennis Dugan (Halloween Dad)

32-year-old Sonny Koufax, who has spent most of his adult life avoiding responsibilities, makes a misguided attempt to impress his girlfriend by adopting a five-year-old boy.

© Columbia Pictures Industries, Inc.

WILD WILD WEST

(**WARNER BROS.**) Producers, Jon Peters, Barry Sonnenfeld; Executive Producers, Bill Todman, Jr., Joel Simon, Kim LeMasters, Tracy Glaser, Barry Josephson; Director, Barry Sonnenfeld; Screenplay, S.S. Wilson, Brent Maddock, Jeffrey Price, Peter S. Seaman; Story, Jim Thomas, John Thomas; Photography, Michael Ballhaus; Designer, Bo Welch; Editor, Jim Miller; Co-Producer, Graham Place; Music, Elmer Bernstein; Song: *Wild Wild West* by Stevie Wonder, Will Smith and Mohanndas DeWese/performed by Will Smith; Costumes, Deborah L. Scott; Special Visual Effects, Industrial Light & Magic; Visual Effects Supervisor, Eric Brevig; Casting, David Rubin, Ronna Kress; a Peters Entertainment/Sonnenfeld-Josephson production, in association with Todman, Simon, LeMasters productions; Dolby; Technicolor; Rated PG-13; 107 minutes; Release date: June 30, 1999

Will Smith, Salma Hayek

CAST

James West	Will Smith
Artemus Gordon/President Grant	Kevin Kline
Dr. Arliss Loveless	Kenneth Branagh
Rita Escobar	Salma Hayek
Coleman	M. Emmet Walsh
General McGrath	Ted Levine
Amazonia	Frederique van der Wal
Munitia	Musetta Vander
Miss Lippenreider	Sofia Eng
Miss East	Bai Ling
Girl in Water Tower	Garcelle Beauvais
Big Reb	Mike McGaughy
Other Reb	Jerry Wills
Hudson	Rodney A. Grant
Eye-Crossed Reb	Buck Taylor
Mr. Pinkerton	E.J. Callahan
Dora Lookalike	Debra Christofferson

James Lashly, Dean Rader-Duval (Rebs), Christian Aubert (French Dignitary), Orestes Matacena (Spanish Dignitary), Ian Abercrombie (British Dignitary), Ismael "East" Carlo (Mexican Dignitary), Bob Rumnock (Whitehouse Aide), Carlos "Gary" Cervantes (Rita's Husband), Jerry Potter (George Washington), Mik Scriba (Guard), Michael Sims (Morton)

Government agents James West and Artemus Gordon team to stop diabolical madman Dr. Arliss Loveless from assassinating President Grant with the aide of his deadly mechanical invention, the Tarantula. Based on the television series that ran on CBS from 1965 to 1969, and starred Robert Conrad and Ross Martin.

© Warner Bros.

Kenneth Branagh

Kevin Kline, Will Smith

Salma Hayek, Kevin Kline

SOUTH PARK: BIGGER, LONGER & UNCUT

(PARAMOUNT/WARNER BROS.) Producers, Trey Parker, Matt Stone; Executive Producers, Scott Rudin, Adam Schroeder; Director, Trey Parker; Screenplay, Trey Parker, Matt Stone, Pam Brady; Co-Producers, Anne Garefino, Deborah Liebling; Music/Lyrics, Trey Parker; Music Score/Additional Music & Lyrics, Marc Shaiman; Director of Animation, Eric Stough; a Scott Rudin and Trey Parker/Matt Stone production; Presented in association with Comedy Central; Dolby; Color; Rated R; 81 minutes; Release date: June 30, 1999

Cartman, Kyle, Stan, Kenny

VOICE CAST

Stan Marsh/Eric Cartman/Mr. Garrison/
Mr. Hat/Officer Barbrady ....Trey Parker
Kyle Broflovski/Kenny McCormick/Pip/Jesus/Jimbo ....Matt Stone
Mrs. Cartman/Sheila Broflovski/Sharon Manson/
Wendy Testaburger/Principal Victoria ....Mary Kay Bergman
Chef ....Issac Hayes
Ike ....Jesse Howell, Anthony Cross-Thomas, Francesca Clifford
Bebe ....Jennifer Howell
Dr. Gouache ....George Clooney
Conan O'Brien ....Brent Spiner
Dr. Vosknocker ....Eric Idle
Brooke Shields ....Minnie Driver
The Baldwin Brothers...Dave Foley
and Bruce Howell (Man in Theatre), Deb Adair (Woman in Theatre), Saddam Hussein (Himself), Nick Rhodes (Canadian Fighter Pilot), Toddy E. Walters (Winona Ryder), Stewart Copeland, Stanley G. Sawicki (American Soldiers), Mike Judge (Kenny's Goodbye)

When three children are corrupted by the R-rated movie they sneaked in to see, their parents' anger leads to censorship which, in turns, leads to war with Canada. Based on the Comedy Central series South Park which debuted in 1997. This film received an Oscar nomination for original song ("Blame Canada").

© Paramount Pictures/Viacom International Inc.

Ike, Kyle, Cartman

BROKEN VESSELS

(UNAPIX/ZEITGEIST) Producers, Roxana Zal, Scott Ziehl; Director, Scott Ziehl; Screenplay, David Baer, John McMahon, Scott Ziehl; Co-Producers, David Baer, Robyn Knoll, Todd Field; Associate Producers, Vidette Schine, John Sjogren; Photography, Antonio Calvache; Editors, David Moritz, Chris Figler; Designer, Rodrigo Castillo; Costumes, Roseanne Fiedler; Casting, Robyn Knoll; a Ziehl and Zal presentation; Dolby; Deluxe color; Not rated; 90 minutes; Release date: July 2, 1999

CAST

Jimmy...Todd Field
Tom...Jason London
Elizabeth ....Roxana Zal
Susy..Susan Traylor
Mr. Chen..James Hong
Gramps..Patrick Cranshaw
Brent David Fraser (Jed), Stephanie Feury (Jill), Dave Nelson (Rick), William Smith (Bo), Charley Spradling London (Ginger), Ashley Rhey (Karen), Rodrigo Castillo (Oscar), David Baer (Bob), Al Isreal (Detective McMahon), Bobby Harwell (Detective Baer), Shashawnee Hall (Crazy Sword Man/Ricky), Rose Marie (Mr. Chen's Secretary), Rose Powell (Earl's Wife), Rita Solomon (Waitress), Herman Solomon (Gambler), Robert Kropt (Earl), Justin Herwick (Mike), Gerald Lee (Lance), Vidette Schine (Lawyer), John McMahon (Scotty), Ron Jeremy, Marcia Gray (Porn Stars), Christopher Gallivan, Jenny White Buffalo Clay (Ravers), Solo Scott, Ron Lunceford, Craig Alsop, Lisa Warsniak, Joey Gold (Crackhouse), Dolores Anderson (Mother of Crazy Man), Lisa Davis (Hooker), Eugene Pagano, Alfred Pagano (Bartenders), Kevin O'Connell (Fire Captain), Barbara Volz, Joseph Ortiz (Firefighters), Kevin Brown (Drug Dealer), George Gunderson (Chester)

Naive Tom becomes a paramedic sidekick to L.A. ambulance driver Jimmy who drags the young man into a world of corruption and drugs.

Jason London, Todd Field

John Leguizamo, Mira Sorvino, Arthur Nascarella

Adrien Brody, John Leguizamo

SUMMER OF SAM

(TOUCHSTONE) Producers, Jon Kilik, Spike Lee; Executive Producers, Michael Imperioli, Jeri Carroll-Colicchio; Director, Spike Lee; Screenplay, Victor Colicchio, Michael Imperioli, Spike Lee; Photography, Ellen Kuras; Designer, Therese DePrez; Editor, Barry Alexander Brown; Music, Terence Blanchard; Music Supervisor, Alex Steyermark; Costumes, Ruth E. Carter; Casting, Aisha Coley; a 40 Acres and a Mule Filmworks production of a Spike Lee Joint; Dolby; Technicolor; Rated R; 142 minutes; Release date: July 2, 1999

CAST

Vinny	John Leguizamo
Ritchie	Adrien Brody
Dionna	Mira Sorvino
Ruby	Jennifer Esposito
Joey T	Michael Rispoli
Woodstock	Saverio Guerra
Bobby Del Fiore	Brian Tarantina
Anthony	Al Palagonia
Brian	Ken Garito
Gloria	Bebe Neuwirth
Helen	Patti LuPone
Eddie	Mike Starr
Detective Lou Petrocelli	Anthony LaPaglia
Detective Curt Atwater	Roger Guenveur Smith
Luigi	Ben Gazarra
Tony Olives	Joe Lisi
Crony	James Reno
Mario	Arthur Nascarella
Simon	John Savage
Himself	Jimmy Breslin
Son of Sam	Michael Badalucco
John Jeffries	Spike Lee

and Lucia Grillo (Chiara), Nelson Vasquez (Officer Cruz), Darielle Gilad (Debbie Cadabra), Michael Harper (Raygun), Jessica Galbreath (Fire), Evan Cohen (Bite), George Tabb (Spider), Michael Imperioli (Midnight), Victor Colicchio (Chickie), Peter Maloney (Detective Timothy Dowd), Christopher Wynkoop (Sam Carr), John Turturro (Voice of Harvey the Black Dog), Ernie Anastos, Jim Jensen (Anchormen), Melba Tolliver (Anchorwoman), Phil Rizuto (Yankee Broadcaster), Reggie Jackson (Himself), Danielle Burgio, Lisa France (Girls in Parked Car), Peter Epstein (Chuckie), Jill Stokesberry (Rose), Joseph Lyle Taylor (Ron), Kim Director (Dee), Bill Raymond (Father Cadilli), Mildrid Clinton, Emelise Aleandri (Italian Women at Murder Site), Michael Sorvino, Phil Campanella (Bowlers at Diner), William H. Burns, Ernest Mingione (Officers), Frank Fortunato (Doorman), Dan Zappin, Murielle Cohen, Christina Kolbe (Simon's Friends), Charlotte Colavin (Neighbor), Clayton Barber (Punk), Joie Lee, Rome Neal, Mark Breland, Susan Batson (Bed Stuy Interviews), Evander Holyfield (Man in Riot), Toneda Laiwan (Dot, Atwater's Girlfriend), Janet Paparazzo, Jodi Michelle Pynn (Young Women Shot by Son of Sam), Jennifer S. Badger (Woman Victim), Jeff DeRocker (Man in Car), Nick Oddo (Husband), Damian Achilles (Wounded Man), Joanne Lamstein (Woman in Car), Gabriel Barre (Johnny Nasso), Tara McNamee (Victim), John Michael Brown, Damian Branica, Lorne Behrman, Curtis Gove, James Baggs (L.E.S. Stitches Band), Rozie Bacchi (Brian's Girlfriend), Grace Desena (Joe T's Girlfriend), Zoe Bournelis (Anthony's Girlfriend), Ashleigh Closs (Princess), Frank Cadillac (Patty a.k.a. Man with Weird Eyes), Daniel J. Courtenay (Guitar Store Owner), Michael Prozzo (Rocco), Kathryn Hudd (Rocco's Girlfriend), Antonio Torres (Man Pulled from Car), Pamela Wehner (Lady at Block Party), Dionna Colicchio, Victoria Galasso, Danielle Tutelian (Girls at Block Party), Mario Macaluso (Italian Chef), Andrew Lasky (Officer Cruz Partner), Richard Paul (Detective with Decoy Dummy), Ray Carlson (Crime Scene Cop), Alexander J. Vega (Bouncer), Steven Croft (Limo Driver), Mary Jo Todaro, Jacqueline Margolis (Ladies in Window), Iris Alten (Lady in Car Window), Valerie Mazzonelli (Lady with Dog), Hal Sherman (Arresting Detective), Nicholas Brown (Young Detective Petrocelli), Christopher Gaspari (Pizzeria Owner)

The inhabitants of a closeknit Italian American community in the Bronx experience personal tensions and traumas during the sweltering summer of 1977 when a deranged killer calling himself Son of Sam was murdering young women.

© Touchstone Pictures

Jennifer Esposito, Adrien Brody

Adrien Brody, Jennifer Esposito, John Leguizamo, Mira Sorvino

Jennifer Esposito, Adrien Brody

John Leguizamo, Mira Sorvino

Bebe Neuwirth, John Leguizamo

Saverio Guerra, Brian Tarantina, John Leguizamo,
Ken Garito, Michael Rispoli

Jason Biggs, Shannon Elizabeth, Chris Klein, Thomas Ian Nicholas

Natasha Lyonne, Tara Reid

Seann W. Scott, Eden Riegel

Jason Biggs, Alyson Hannigan

Jason Biggs

AMERICAN PIE

(**UNIVERSAL**) Producers, Warren Zide, Craig Perry, Chris Moore, Chris Weitz; Director, Paul Weitz; Screenplay, Adam Herz; Photography, Richard Crudo; Designer, Paul Peters; Editor, Priscilla Nedd-Friendly; Co-Producers, Louis G. Friedman, Chris Bender; Music, David Lawrence; Music Supervisor, Gary Jones; Casting, Joseph Middleton; a Zide/Perry production; Dolby; Deluxe color; Rated R; 95 minutes; Release date: July 9, 1999

Molly Cheek, Eugene Levy, Jason Biggs

CAST

Jim	Jason Biggs
Stifler's Mom	Jennifer Coolidge
Nadia	Shannon Elizabeth
Michelle	Alyson Hannigan
Oz	Chris Klein
English Teacher	Clyde Kusatsu
Jim's Dad	Eugene Levy
Jessica	Natasha Lyonne
Kevin	Thomas Ian Nicholas
Sherman	Chris Owen
Coach Marshall	Lawrence Pressman
Vicky	Tara Reid
Stifler	Seann W. Scott
Heather	Mena Suvari
Finch	Eddie Kaye Thomas
Jim's Mom	Molly Cheek
Band Member	Christina Milian
Party Guy	Woody Schultz
Drinking Buddy	Casey Erklin
Party Girl	Annika Hays
Sophomore Chick	Eden Riegel
"MILF" Guys	Justin Isfeld, John Cho
Central Girl	Alexandra Adi
Vocal Jazz Girls	Veronica Lauren, Monica McSwain
Vocal Jazz Group	Fletcher Sheridan, Robyn Roth, Jamar Cargo
Vocal Jazz Teacher	Akuyoe Graham
Enthralled Girl	Katie Lansdale
Sushi Customer	Jay Rossi
Vicky's Mom	Linda Gehringer
Vicky's Dad	Ashton Dane
Random Cute Girl	Sahsa Barrese
Albert	Eric Lively
Stifler's Younger Brother	Eli Marienthal
Computer Nerd	Travis Cody Aimer
Garage Band	Mark Hoppus, Thomas M. Delonge, Scott Raynor
Guy with Monkey	Danny Spink
Enthusiastic Guy	James Debello
Computer Girls	Amber Phillips, Clementine Ford
Girl Holding Out	Hilary Salvatore
Bathroom Girls	Jasmine Stocken, Jillian Bach
Prom Band Singer	David Kuhn
Lacrosse Referees	Dan Coronel, Pete Pallad, J.D. Doyle, Lito Coronel

Four high school friends make a pact to lose their virginity on prom night.

© Universal Studies

(clockwise from center) Jason Biggs, Natasha Lyonne, Alyson Hannigan, Eddie Kaye Thomas, Chris Klein, Seann W. Scott, Mena Suvari, Thomas Ian Nicholas, Tara Reid

Eddie Kaye Thomas, Jennifer Coolidge

ARLINGTON ROAD

(**SCREEN GEMS**) Producers, Peter Samuelson, Tom Gorai, Marc Samuelson; Executive Producers, Tom Rosenberg, Sigurjon Sighvatsson, Ted Tannebaum; Director, Mark Pellington; Screenplay, Ehren Kruger; Co-Executive Producers, Judd Malkin, Ed Ross; Photography, Bobby Bukowski; Editor, Therese DePrez; Editor, Conrad Buff; Costumes, Jennifer Barrett-Pellington; Music, Angelo Badalamenti, Tomandandy; Co-Producers, Jean Higgins, Richard S. Wright; Casting, Ellen Chenoweth; a Gorai/Samuelson production, presented in association with Lakeshore Entertainment; Distributed by Sony Pictures releasing; Dolby; Panavision; Deluxe color; Rated R; 119 minutes; Release date: July 9, 1999

Jeff Bridges

CAST

Michael Faraday ....Jeff Bridges
Oliver Lang ....Tim Robbins
Cheryl Lang ....Joan Cusack
Brooke Wolfe ....Hope Davis
FBI Agent Whit Carver ....Robert Gossett
Brady Lang ....Mason Gamble
Grant Faraday ....Spencer Treat Clark
Dr. Archer Scobee ....Stanley Anderson
Nurse ....Vivianne Vives
Orderly ....Lee Stringer
Troopmaster ....Darryl Cox
Delivery Man ....Loyd Catlett
Phone Technician ....Sid Hillman
Hannah Lang ....Auden Thornton
Daphne Lang ....Mary Ashleigh Green
Ponytail Girl..Jennie Tooley
Student Kemp ....Grant Garrison
Student O'Neill ....Naya Castinado
Leah Faraday...Laura Poe
Chris Dahlberg (Buckley, FBI), Gabriel Folse (Merks, FBI), Hunter Burkes (Hutch Parsons), Diane Peterson (Ma Parsons), Josh Ridgway (18-Year-Old Parsons), Hans Stroble (16-Year-Old Parsons), Michelle Du Bois (Parsons Girl), Steve Ottesen, Harris Mackenzie (TV Reporters), John Hussey (Accident Detective), Charles Sanders, Todd Terry (Camp Officials), Gina Santori (Party Girl/Student), Denver Williams, Willie Dirden (FBI Guards), Paul Pender, Charlie Webb (FBI Van Agents), Billy D. Washington (FBI Agent), Cindy Hom, Dave Allen Clark (TV Reporters), Ken Manelis (Reporter Charles Bell), Deborah Swanson (Bomb Site Reporter), Homer Jon Young (Student)

College professor Michael Faraday begins to suspect that his new next door neighbors might be involved in terrorist activities.

© Screen Gems

Hope Davis, Jeff Bridges

Tim Robbins, Joan Cusack

Jeff Bridges, Tim Robbins

Heather Donahue

Joshua Leonard

Michael Williams

Heather Donahue

THE BLAIR WITCH PROJECT

(**ARTISAN ENTERTAINMENT**) Producers, Gregg Hale, Robin Cowie; Directors/Screenplay/Editors, Daniel Myrick, Eduardo Sanchez; Executive Producers, Bob Eick, Kevin J. Foxe; Co-Producer, Michael Monello; Photography, Neal Fredericks; Music, Antonio Cora; Deisgner, Ben Rock; a Haxan Films production; Dolby; Color; Rated R; 75 minutes; Release date: July 14, 1999

CAST

Heather ....Heather Donahue
Mike ....Michael Williams
Josh..Joshua Leonard
Interviews....................................Bob Griffith, Jim King, Sandra Sanchez,
Ed Swanson, Patricia Decou

A mock-documentary account of what happened to three student filmmak-ers who disappeared while trying to make a film about the legendary Blair Witch.

Joshua Leonard, Michael Williams

Jeffrey Tambor, Gonzo

Josh Charles, Miss Piggy

MUPPETS FROM SPACE

(COLUMBIA) Producers, Brian Henson, Martin G. Baker; Executive Producers, Kristine Belson, Stephanie Allain; Director, Tim Hill; Screenplay, Jerry Juhl, Joseph Mazzarino, Ken Kaufman; Photography, Alan Caso; Designer, Stephen Marsh; Editors, Michael A. Stevenson, Richard Pearson; Producer of Visual Effects, Thomas G. Smith; Co-Producers, Timothy M. Bourne, Alex Rockwell; Music, Jamshied Sharifi; Casting, Michael Fenton, Allison Cowitt; a Jim Henson Pictures presentation; Dolby; Deluxe color; Rated G; 82 minutes; Release date: July 14, 1999

CAST

Gonzo/Bunsen Honeydew/Waldorf/The Birdman ....Dave Goelz
Kermit the Frog/Rizzo the Rat/Beaker/Cosmic Fish #1 .....Steve Whitmire
Pepe the Prawn/Bobo as Rentro/Bubba the Rat/Johnny Fiama/
Cosmic Fish #2...Bill Barretta
Robin/Statler/Ubergonzo...Jerry Nelson
Dr. Phil Van Neuter/Sal Minella ....Brian Henson
Clifford ....Kevin Clash
Miss Piggy/Fozzie Bear/Animal/Sam Eagl...................Franz Oz
K. Edgar Singer ....Jeffrey Tambor
Noah...F. Murray Abraham
TV Producer ....Rob Schneider
Agent Barker..Josh Charles
Gate Guard ....Ray Liotta
Dr. Tucker..David Arquette
Shelley Snipes..Andie MacDowell
Armed Guard...Kathy Griffin
General Luft ....Pat Hingle
Man in Black ....Hollywood Hogan
and Veronica Alicino (TV Stage Manager), David Lenthall (Mikey the Cameraman), Richard Fullerton, Mark Joy (Gate Guards), Carl Espy (TV Associate Producer), Deron Barnett (Child), Christina Mullins (Little Girl), Elaine Nalee (Mashed Potato Lady), Joshua Jackson, Katie Holmes (Beach Kids)

Gonzo, on a quest to find his real family, comes to the conclusion that his relatives are actually aliens from a distant planet.

© Jim Henson Pictures Inc.

Kermit, Ray Liotta, Pepe the Prawn, Miss Piggy

Bobo the Bear, Hollywood Hogan

LAKE PLACID

(20TH CENTURY FOX) Producers, David E. Kelley, Michael Pressman; Executive Producer, Peter Bogart; Director, Steve Miner; Screenplay David E. Kelley; Photography, Daryn Okada; Designer, John Willett; Editors, Marshall Harvey, Paul Hirsch; Music, John Ottman; Creature Effects, Stan Winston Studio; Costumes, Jori Woodman; Casting, Lisa Beach; a Fox 2000 Pictures presentation from Phoenix Pictures of a Rocking Chair production; Dolby; Panavision; Color; Rated R; 82 minutes; Release date: July 16, 1999

CAST

Jack Wells	Bill Pullman
Kelly Scott	Bridget Fonda
Hector Cyr	Oliver Platt
Sheriff Hank Keough	Brendan Gleeson
Mrs. Delores Bickerman	Betty White
Walt Lawson	David Lewis
Stephen Daniels	Tim Dixon
Janine	Natassia Malthe
Myra Okubo	Mariska Hargitay
Deputy Sharon Gare	Meredith Salenger
Deputy Burke	Jed Rees
Deputy Stevens	Richard Leacock
Officer Coulson	Jake T. Roberts
Paramedic	Warren Takeuchi
State Trooper	Ty Olsson
Kevin	Adam Arkin
Airplane Pilot	Steve Miner

Paleontologist Kelly Scott arrives in a small town in northern Maine to find out what sort of creature dwelling in the lake has been attacking the locals.

© Twentieth Century Fox

Richard T. Jones, Taye Diggs, Omar Epps

Bridget Fonda, Bill Pullman

THE WOOD

(PARAMOUNT) Producers, Albert Berger, Ron Yerxa, David Gale; Executive Producer, Van Toffler; Director/Screenplay, Rick Famuyiwa; Story, Rick Famuyiwa, Todd Boyd; Photography, Steven Bernstein; Designers, Roger Fortune, Maxine Shepard; Co-Producer, Douglas Curtis; Editor, John Carter; Costumes, Darryle Johnson; Music Supervisor, Pilar McCurry; Casting, Mali Finn, Emily Schweber; an MTV Films production in association with Bona Fide productions; Dolby; Color; Rated R; 106 minutes; Release date: July 16, 1999

CAST

Roland	Taye Diggs
Mike Fleming	Omar Epps
Slim	Richard T. Jones
Young Mike	Sean Nelson
Young Slim	Duane Finley
Young Roland	Trent Cameron
Young Alicia	Malinda Williams
Stacey	De'Aundre Bonds
Alicia	Sanaa Lathan
The Bride	Lisaraye
Tanya	Tamala Jones

and Elayn Taylor (Roland's Mother), Patricia Belcher (Mrs. Hughes), Cynthia Martells (Mike's Mother), Wyking Jones (Cashier in Nelson's), Jascha Washington (Mike's Brother), Aiysha Sinclair (Tracey), Melvin Lyons (Gang Member), Samuel Hiona (Cashier in Nelson's 1986), Antwon Tanner (Boo), John Wesley, Oscar Dillon (Police Officers), Tia Gainer (Girl at Dance), Howard Thompson (DJ at Dance), Douglas Shamburger (DJ on Radio), Brandi Wilson, Christina Milian (Girls at Dance), Dawnn Lewis (Woman in Cleaners), Crystal Grant (Girl with Slim), La'Myia Good (Monica), Alecia Smith (Girl with Roland), Kongit Farrell (Girl with Slim), Stacey Arnell (Woman with Stacey), Telma Hopkins (Slim's Mother), Basil Wallace (Lisa's Father), Todd Boyd (Reverend Parker)

While Slim has second thoughts about his upcoming wedding, he and his best friends, Mike and Roland, look back on their youth and the growth of their friendship.

© Paramount Pictures

73

Tom Cruise, Nicole Kidman

Todd Field

Nicole Kidman

Sydney Pollack

Tom Cruise

EYES WIDE SHUT

(**WARNER BROS.**) Producer/Director, Stanley Kubrick; Screenplay, Stanley Kubrick, Frederic Raphael; Inspired by the novel *Traumnovelle* by Arthur Schnitzler; Executive Producer, Jan Harlan; Co-Producer, Brian W. Cook; Photography, Larry Smith; Designers, Les Tomkins, Roy Walker; Editor, Nigel Galt; Music, Jocelyn Pook; Costumes, Marit Allen; Casting, Denise Chamian, Leon Vitali; Dolby; Deluxe color; Rated R; 158 minutes; Release date: July 16, 1999

Tom Cruise

CAST

Dr. William Harford	Tom Cruise
Alice Harford	Nicole Kidman
Victor Ziegler	Sydney Pollack
Marion	Marie Richardson
Carl	Thomas Gibson
Milich's Daughter	Leelee Sobieski
Nick Nightingale	Todd Field
Milich	Rade Sherbedgia
Sandor Szavost	Sky Dumont
Desk Clerk	Alan Cumming
Helena Harford	Madison Eginton
Roz	Jackie Sawiris
Illona	Leslie Lowe
Bandleader	Peter Benson
Ziegler's Secretary	Michael Doven
Gayle	Louise Taylor
Nuala	Stewart Thorndike
Harris	Randall Paul
Mandy	Julienne Davis
Lisa	Lisa Leone
Lou Nathanson	Kevin Connealy
Rosa	Mariana Hewett
Rowdy College Kids	Dan Rollman, Gavin Perry, Chris Pare, Adam Lias, Christian Clarke, Kyle Whitcombe
Naval Officer	Gary Goba
Domino	Vinessa Shaw
Maitre D'—Cafe Sonata	Florian Windorfer
Japanese Men	Togo Igawa, Eiji Kusuhara
Cab Driver	Sam Douglas
Gateman #1	Angus MacInnes
Mysterious Woman	Abigail Good
Tall Butler	Brian W. Cook
Red Cloak	Leon Vitali
Waitress at Gillespie's	Carmela Marner
Sally	Fay Masterson
Stalker	Phil Davies
Girl a Sharky's	Cindy Dolenc
Hospital Receptionist	Clark Hayes
Morgue Orderly	Treva Etienne

and Colin Angus, Karla Ashley, Kathryn Charman, James DeMaria, Anthony DeSergio, Janie Dickens, Laura Fallace, Vanessa Fenton, Georgina Finch, Peter Godwin, Abigail Good, Joanna Heath, Lee Henshaw, Ateeka Poole, Adam Pudney, Sharon Quinn, Ben De Sausmarcz, Emma Lou Sharratt, Paul Spelling, Matthew Thompson, Dan Travers, Russell Trigg, Kate Whalin (Masked Party Principals)

Tom Cruise, Nicole Kidman

Following his wife's confession of her desires for a stranger she glimpsed fleetingly, Dr. William Harford finds himself on a nocturnal trip through New York during which he has several disturbing neo-sexual encounters.

© Warner Bros.

Sydney Pollack, Tom Cruise

Catherine Zeta-Jones, Owen Wilson, Lili Taylor, Liam Neeson

Lili Taylor, Liam Neeson

Lili Taylor

THE HAUNTING

(**DREAMWORKS**) Producers, Susan Arnold, Donna Arkoff Roth, Colin Wilson; Executive Producer/Director, Jan De Bont; Screenplay, David Self; Based upon the novel *The Haunting of Hill House* by Shirley Jackson; Photography, Karl Walter Lindenlaub; Designer, Eugenio Zanetti; Editor, Michael Kahn; Music, Jerry Goldsmith; Visual Effects Supervisors, Phil Tippett, Craig Hayes; Costumes, Ellen Mirojnick; Casting, Randi Hiller; a Roth/Arnold production; Dolby; Panavision; Technicolor; Rated PG-13; 114 minutes; Release date: July 23, 1999

CAST

Dr. David Marrow	Liam Neeson
Theo	Catherine Zeta-Jones
Luke Sanderson	Owen Wilson
Nell	Lili Taylor
Mr. Dudley	Bruce Dern
Mrs. Dudley	Marian Seldes
Mary Lambetta	Alix Koromzay
Todd Hackett	Todd Field
Jane	Virginia Madsen
Dr. Malcolm Keogh	Michael Cavanaugh
Lou	Tom Irwin
Hugh Crain	Charles Gunning
Ritchie	Saul Priever
Large Man	M.C. Gainey
Carolyn Crain	Hadley Eure
Rene Crain	Kadina Halliday

and Alessandra Benjamin, Karen Gregan, Brandon Jarrett, Mary McNeal, William Minkin (Psych Patients)

Dr. David Marrow, determined to delve into the tragic history of Hill House, brings three subjects to the mansion where they experience terrifying visitations from past spirits. Earlier film version was released in 1963 by MGM and starred Julie Harris, Claire Bloom, Richard Johnson, and Russ Tamblyn.

© DreamWorks LLC

TRICK

(**FINE LINE FEATURES**) Producers, Eric d'Arbeloff, Jim Fall, Ross Katz; Executive Producers, Anthony Bregman, Mary Jane Skalski; Co-Executive Producer, Mark Beigelman; Director, Jim Fall; Screenplay, Jason Schafer; Co-Producer, Robert Hawk; Photography, Terry Stacey; Editor, Brian A. Kates; Music, David Friedman; Music Supervisor, Tracy McKnight; Song: *Enter You* by Jason Schafer/performed by Tori Spelling, Christian Campbell; Designer, Jody Asnes; Costumes, Mary Gasser; Casting, Susan Shopmaker; a Roadside Attractions/Good Machine production; Dolby; DuArt color; Rated R; 89 minutes; Release date: July 23, 1999

John Paul Pitoc, Christian Campbell

CAST

Gabriel	Christian Campbell
Mark Miranda	John Paul Pitoc
Katherine Lambert	Tori Spelling
Perry	Steve Hayes
Rich	Brad Beyer
Judy	Lorri Bagley
Perry's Ex	Kevin Chamberlin
Miss Coco Peru	Clinton Leupp
Genevieve	Lacey Kohl
Business Woman	Abbey Hope
Yolanda	Becky Caldwell
Ridiculous Writer	Kate Flannery
Dude	Will Keenan
Ex Go-Go Boy	Joey Dedio
Scary Man	Ricky Ritzel
Woman on the Subway	Lissette Gutierrez
Stoop Cruiser	Kevin Andrew
Lester Sinclair	Bobby Peaco

and Eric Bernat (Funky Stage Manager), Missi Pyle (Actress with Flowers), Debbie Troché (Actress with Videotape), Michelle Brilliant (Little Dyke), Nat DeWolfe (Gay Reveler), Scottie Epstein (Muscley Chest Guy), Jamie Gustis (Dino), Helen Hanft (Greasy Spoon Waitress)

A shy Manhattan songwriter hooks up with a hunky go-go dancer only to spend the entire evening trying to find a place to have sex.

© Fine Line Features

John Paul Pitoc, Christian Campbell, Tori Spelling

Christian Campbell, John Paul Pitoc

Christian Campbell, John Paul Pitoc

INSPECTOR GADGET

Matthew Broderick

(**WALT DISNEY PICTURES**) Producers, Jordan Kerner, Roger Birnbaum, Andy Heyward; Executive Producers, Jon Avnet, Barry Bernardi, Ralph Winter, Aaron Meyerson, Jonathan Glickman; Director, David Kellogg; Screenplay, Kerry Ehrin, Zak Penn; Story, Dana Olsen, Kerry Ehrin; Based on characters created by Andy Heyward, Jean Chalopin, Bruno Bianchi; Photography, Adam Greenberg; Designers, Michael White, Leslie Dilley; Costumes, Mary Vogt; Editors, Thom Noble, Alan Cody; Special Animatronic Effects, Stan Winston Studio; Visual Effects, Dream Quest Images; Visual Effects Supervisor, Richard Hoover; Co-Producers, Lou Arkoff, Jean Chalopin; Music, John Debney; Music Supervisor, Peter Afterman; Casting, Amanda Mackey Johnson, Cathy Sandrich; an Avnet Kerner/Roger Birnbaum/DIC production, presented in association with Caravan Pictures; Dolby; Technicolor; Rated PG; 77 minutes; Release date: July 23, 1999

CAST

Inspector Gadget (John Brown)/RoboGadget...............Matthew Broderick
Sanford Scolex (Claw)..Rupert Everett
Dr. Brenda Bradford ....Joely Fisher
Penny...Michelle Trachtenberg
Kramer..Andy Dick
Mayor Wilson...Cheri Oteri
Sikes ....Michael G. Hagerty
Chief Quimby ....Dabney Coleman
Gadgetmobile Voice ....D.L. Hughley
Artemus Bradford..Rene Auberjonois
Thelma..Frances Bay
Bus Driver..Cliff Emmich
Boy on Bike...Brian Tibbetts
Robotic Foot Dancer ....W. Bob Gaynor
Docto ....Richard Penn
Mayor's Assistant ....J.P. Manoux
Officer McMurphy ....Sam Brown
Officer Johnson ....Brad Blaisdell
Young Girls ....Jennifer Ingersoll, Haley Harper, Vichany
        Sam, Ivory Dilley, Brielle Blount, Hailey Peitzman
Hospital Secretary ....Sonya Eddy
Nurses in Hallway..............................Katsy Chappell, Kathleen M. Darcy
Guru...Brian George
Businessman...Alexander Witt
and E.J. Callahan (Hot Dog Vendor), Chad Parker (Assistant Car Thief), Frank Masi (Photographer), Mary Chris Wall (News Anchor), Linda Cevallos, Lora-Lyn Peterson (Showgirls), Amy Derrick (Zoftig Woman), William Smith (Little Man), Jim Thiel, Jeff Thiel (Bartenders), David Page, Jacob Avnet, Dorothy David, Huch Hackstedt (Party Guests), Matthew Murray (Autograph Kid), Mark Leahy (Father of Kid), Rick LaFond (News Reporter), Tadao Tomomatsu (Japanese Tourist), Adrienne Wehr (Waitress on Bridge), Richard Rauh (Man with Toupee), Will Blount, Josh Kuhn, Kylle Ross Collingsworth, Jesse Yoshimura, Michael Fossatt (RoboBrenda Aerobics Group), Don Adams (Voice of Brain); The Minion Recovery Group: Richard Kiel (Jaws), Mr. T, Aaron Meyerson (Themselves), Richard Lee-Sung (Odd Job), Robert N. Bell (Tattoo), Hank Barrera (Tonto), Keith Morrison (Igor), Bob Bell (Peter Lorre), John Kim (Number One Son), Jesse Yoshimura (Kato)

After an accident has destroyed most of his working parts, a security guard is reconstructed as Inspector Gadget, a robotic crime fighter whose first duty is to stop the crazed Claw from destroying the world. Based on the animated television series that originally ran in syndication from 1983 to 1985, then was re-run by both Nickelodeon cable (1987-92) and CBS (1991-92).

© Disney Enterprises, Inc.

Rupert Everett, Matthew Broderick, Joely Fisher

Michael G. Hagerty, Michelle Trachtenberg, Dabney Coleman

Saffron Burrows

Saffron Burrows, LL Cool J, Thomas Jane

Michael Rapaport, Samuel L. Jackson, Saffron Burrows

DEEP BLUE SEA

(**WARNER BROS.**) Producers, Akiva Goldsman, Tony Ludwig, Alan Riche; Executive Producers, Duncan Henderson, Bruce Berman; Director, Renny Harlin; Screenplay, Duncan Kennedy, Donna Powers, Wayne Powers; Photography, Stephen Windon; Designer, William Sandell; Editors, Frank J. Urioste, Derek G. Brechin, Dallas S. Puett; Co-Producer, Rebecca Spikings; Music, Trevor Rabin; Costumes, Mark Bridges; Visual Effects Supervisor, Jeffrey A. Okun; Shark Action Supervisor, Walt Conti; Special Effects Supervisor, John Richardson; Stunts, R.A. Rondell; Underwater Photography, Pete Romano; Special Visual Effects & Animation, Cinesite, Industrial Light & Magic; Presented in asssociation with Village Roadshow Pictures, Groucho III Film Partnership of an Alan Riche, Tony Ludwig/Akiva Goldsman production; Dolby; Super 35 Widescreen; Technicolor; Rated R; 105 minutes; Release date: July 28, 1999

CAST

Carter Blake ....Thomas Jane
Dr. Susan McAlester...Saffron Burrows
Russell Franklin ....Samuel L. Jackson
Janice Higgins...Jacqueline McKenzie
Tom Scoggins ....Michael RapaportJim
Whitlock...Stellan Skarsgård
Preacher..LL Cool J
Brenda Kerns..Aida Turturro
Boat Captain..Cristos
and Daniel Rey (Helicopter Pilot), Valente Rodriguez (Helicopter Co-Pilot), Brent Roam (Helicopter Winch Operator), Eyal Podell, Dan Thiel (Boys), Erinn Bartlett, Sabrina Geerinckx (Girls), Tajsha Thomas (Friend of Janice), Mary Kay Bergman (Voice of Parrot), Frank Welker (Parrot Noises), Ronny Cox (Executive), Renny Harlin (Worker), Sarah Kelly (Shark Victim)

At a floating scientific laboratory, Dr. Susan McAlester's attempts to find a cure for Alzheimer's disease by altering the DNA of mako sharks, causes unexpected havoc as the creatures become predatory monsters.

© Warner Bros./Village Roadshow

Thomas Jane

Michele Hicks, Mark Polish, Michael Polish

Patric Bauchau, Michele Hicks

Michele Hicks

Mark Polish, Michael Polish

TWIN FALLS IDAHO

(**SONY PICTURES CLASSICS**) Producers, Marshall Persinger, Rena Ronson, Steven J. Wolfe; Executive Producer, Joyce Schweickert; Director, Michael Polish; Screenplay, Mark Polish, Michael Polish; Photography, M. David Mullen; Co-Producer, Paul Torok; Editor, Leo Trombetta; Designer, Warren Alan Young; Music, Stuart Matthewman; Costumes, Bic Owen; a Seattle Pacific Investments and the Fresh Produce Company in association with Steven J. Wolfe and Sneak Preview Entertainment presentation; Dolby; Color; Rated R; 110 minutes; Release date: July 30, 1999

CAST

Blake Falls	Mark Polish
Francis Falls	Michael Polish
Penny	Michele Hicks
Francine	Lesley Ann Warren
Miles	Patrick Bauchau
Jay	Jon Gries
Jesus	Garrett Morris
Surgeon	William Katt
Sissy	Teresa Hill
D'Walt	Robert Beecher
Waitress	Jill Andre
Tre	Ant
Flamboyant at Party	Holly Woodlawn
Miss America	Sasha Alexander
Guadelupe	Socorro Mora
Nurse	Mary-Pat Green
June	Patty Maloney

An unorthodox woman finds herself being drawn to Blake Falls who is co-joined with his identical twin brother Francis.

© Sony Pictures Entertainment, Inc.

RUNAWAY BRIDE

(**PARAMOUNT/TOUCHSTONE**) Producers, Ted Field, Tom Rosenberg, Scott Kroopf, Robert Cort; Executive Producers, Ted Tannebaum, David Madden, Gary Lucchesi; Director, Garry Marshall; Screenplay, Josann McGibbon, Sara Parriott; Photography, Stuart Dryburgh; Designer, Mark Friedberg; Editor, Bruce Green; Costumes, Albert Wolsky; Music, James Newton Howard; Co-Producers, Ellen H. Schwartz, Mario Iscovich, Karen Stirgwolt, Richard Wright; Casting, Gretchen Rennell Court; an Interscope Communications production in association with Lakeshore Entertainment; Dolby; Super 35 Widescreen; Technicolor; Rated PG; 116 minutes; Release date: July 30, 1999

Julia Roberts, Richard Gere

CAST

Maggie Carpenter..Julia Roberts
Ike Graham ....Richard Gere
Peggy Flemming ....Joan Cusack
Fisher..Hector Elizondo
Ellie ....Rita Wilson
Walter ....Paul Dooley
Coach Bob ....Christopher Meloni
Priest Brian...Donal Logue
George Bug Guy..Reg Rogers
Dead Head Gill..Yul Vasquez
Mrs. Pressman ....Jane Morris
and Lisa Roberts Gillan (Elaine from Manhattan), Kathleen Marshall (Cousin Cindy), Jean Schertler (Grandma), Tom Hines (Cory Flemming), Tom Mason (Final Wedding Pastor),Garrett Wright (Student Dennis), New York: Sela Ward (Pretty Bar Woman), Marvin Braverman (T-Shirt Vendor), Yvonne Pollack (T-Shirt Lady), Joy Rosenthal (Limo Woman), John Goldman (Construction Man), Sandra Taylor (Model Shelby), Thong Nguyen (Fashion Shoot Photographer), Karen Stirgwolt (Office Worker Francis); Hale Townspeople: Lee McKenna (Mrs. Whittenmeyer), Patrick Richwood (TV Host), Marty Nadler (Traveling Salesman), Allan Kent (Mr. Trout), Kevin Murray (Pete), James Richardson (Mr. Paxton), Duncna Lam (Dragged Little Boy), Julie Paris, Dina Napoli, Jacqui Allen, Jack Hoffman, Cheryl Frazel, Tiffany Paulsen (Reporters), Gregg Goulet (Church Organist), Shannon Wilcox (Luau Lady), Diana Kent (Hula Girl), Diane Frazen (Wedding Guest Diane), Karla Pattur (Church Teacher Karla), Linda Larkin (Gill's Girlfriend), William Todd Crosby, Robert Lee Jones, Joseph William Andrews, Eugene Walker Jackson Jr. (Barbershop Quartet), Garry Marshall (Ballplayer)

Rita Wilson, Richard Gere

Maggie Carpenter's habit of panicking at the last minute and leaving her grooms at the altar brings the attention of the media, including cynical reporter Ike Graham, who arrives in Maggie's small town to see if she will bolt from her latest planned nuptials.

© Paramount Pictures/Touchstone Pictures

Richard Gere, Hector Elizondo

Julia Roberts, Joan Cusack

DICK

(**COLUMBIA**) Producer, Gale Anne Hurd; Executive Producer, David Coatsworth; Director, Andrew Fleming; Screenplay, Andrew Fleming, Sheryl Longin; Photography, Alexander Gruszynski; Designer, Barbara Dunphy; Editor, Mia Goldman; Music, John Debney; Music Supervisor, Ralph Sall; Costumes, Deborah Everton; Casting, Pam Dixon Mickelson; a Phoenix Pictures presentation of a Pacific Western production; Dolby; Technicolor; Rated PG-13; 95 minutes; Release date: August 4, 1999

Michelle Williams, Kirsten Dunst

CAST

Betsy Jobs	Kirsten Dunst
Arlene Lorenzo	Michelle Williams
Dick Nixon	Dan Hedaya
Bob Woodward	Will Ferrell
Carl Bernstein	Bruce McCulloch
Helen Lorenzo	Teri Garr
Bob Haldeman	Dave Foley
John Dean	Jim Breuer
Rose Mary Woods	Ana Gasteyer
G. Gordon Liddy	Harry Shearer
Henry Kissinger	Saul Rubinek
Larry Jobs	Devon Gummersall
Roderick	Ted McGinley
Chip	Ryan Reynolds
Ben Bradlee	G.D. Spradlin
Kay Lawson	Shannon Lawson
Frank Jobs	Karl Pruner
Mrs. Spinnler	Brenda Devine
G-Men	Jonathan Ranells, Paulino Nunes
Burglars	Michael Dyson, Jerry Schaefer
Fat Freddy	Jack Mosshammer
The Interviewer	French Stewart

and Karen Waddell (White House Secretary), Richard Fitzpatrick (John Erlichman), Cole Barrington (Student #1), Scott Wickware (White House Guard), Mark Lutz (Hunky Secret Service Man), Kedar Brown (Mr. Samovar), Paul Wildbaum (Shredder Man), Kerry Dorey (Payola Man), Len Doncheff (Leonid Brezhnev), Igor Portnoi (Russian Translator), Jennifer Wigmore (Washington Post Receptionist), Jane Moffat (Kissing Secretary), Rob Nickerson, Bernard Browne (Police Officers), Rummy Bishop (Newsstand Guy), Deborah Grover (Pat Nixon), Stephen Robert (FBI Agent), Michael Kramer (TV News Reporter), Mike Anscombe (TV News Anchor), Brunswick (Checkers the Dog)

Dan Hedaya, Dave Foley

A pair of well-meaning but none-too-bright teenage girls become dog walkers for President Nixon and find themselves inadvertently blowing the lid off the Watergate scandal.

Bruce McCulloch, Will Ferrell

Michelle Williams, Kirsten Dunst

Hogarth Hughes, The Iron Giant

THE IRON GIANT

(WARNER BROS.) Producers, Allison Abbate, Des McAnuff; Executive Producer, Pete Townshend; Director/Screen Story, Brad Bird; Screenplay, Tim McCanlies; Based on the book *The Iron Man* by Ted Hughes; Music, Michael Kamen; Associate Producer, John Walker; Editor, Darren T. Holmes; Designer, Mark Whiting; Art Director, Alan Bodner; Head of Animation, Tony Fucile; Artistic Coordinator, Scott F. Johnston; Dolby; Celco-Widescreen; Technicolor; Rated PG; 86 minutes; Release date: August 4, 1999

Annie Hughes, Hogarth Hughes, Dean McCoppin

VOICE CAST

Annie Hughes ....Jennifer Aniston
Dean McCoppin...Harry Connick, Jr.
The Iron Giant...Vin Diesel
Foreman Marv Loach/Floyd Turbeaux ....James Gammon
Mrs. Tensedge ....Cloris Leachman
Kent Mansley ....Christopher McDonald
General Rogard..John Mahoney
Hogarth Hughes ....Eli Marienthal
Earl Stutz..M. Emmet Walsh

In 1957, in the town of Rockport, Maine, nine-year-old Hogarth Hughes stumbles upon a gigantic iron man who has come from a distant world.

© Warner Bros.

The Iron Giant, Hogarth Hughes

THE SIXTH SENSE

(**HOLLYWOOD PICTURES**) Producers, Frank Marshall, Kathleen Kennedy, Barry Mendel; Executive Producer, Sam Mercer; Director/Screenplay, M. Night Shyamalan; Photography, Tak Fujimoto; Designer, Larry Fulton; Editor, Andrew Mondshein; Music, James Newton Howard; Costumes, Joanna Johnston; Casting, Avy Kaufman; a Spyglass Entertainment presentation of a Kennedy/Marshall/Barry Mendel production; Dolby; Technicolor; Rated PG-13; 107 minutes; Release date: August 6, 1999

CAST

Malcolm Crowe..Bruce Willis
Cole Sear...Haley Joel Osment
Lynn Sear...Toni Collette
Anna Crowe ....Olivia Williams
Tommy Tammisimo ....Trevor Morgan
Vincent Gray ....Donnie Wahlberg
Darren ....Peter Tambakis
Bobby ....Jeffrey Zubernis
Stanley Cunningham ....Bruce Norris
Sean ....Glenn Fitzgerald
Mr. Collins ....Greg Wood
Kyra Collins..Mischa Barton
Mrs. Collins ....Angelica Torn
Bridesmaid..Lisa Summerour
Young Man Buying Ring ....Firdous Bamji
Young Woman Buying Ring ....Samia Shoaib
Darren's Mom...Hayden Saunier
Kitchen Woman ....Janis Dardaris
Kyra's Sister ....Samantha Fitzpatrick
Society Ladies.......................................Holly Rudkin, Kate Kearney-Patch
Woman at Accident ....Marilyn Shanok
Dr. Hill...M. Night Shyamalan
and Neill Hartley, Sarah Ripard, Heidi Fischer, Kadee Strickland, Michael J. Lyons (Visitors), Wes Heywood (Commerical Narrator), Nico Woulard (Hanged Child), Carol Nielson (Hanged Female), Keith Woulard (Hanged Male), Jodi Dawson (Burnt Teacher), Tony Donnelly (Gunshot Boy), Ronnie Lea (Secretary), Carlos X. López (Spanish Ghost on Tape), Gino Inverso (Young Vincent), Ellen Sheppard (Mrs. Sloan), Tom McLaughlin (Anna's Father), Candy Aston Dennis (Anna's Mother), Patrick F. McDade (Shaken Driver), Jose L. Rodriguez (Husband)

Child psychologist Malcolm Crowe tries to help 8-year-old Cole Sear who is regularly visited by ghosts. This film received Oscar nominations for picture, director, supporting actor (Haley Joel Osment), supporting actress (Toni Collette), original screenplay, and editing.

Haley Joel Osment, Bruce Willis

Haley Joel Osment

Bruce Willis

Bruce Willis, Haley Joel Osment

Haley Joel Osment

Bruce Willis, Olivia Williams

Toni Collette, Haley Joel Osment

Haley Joel Osment, Toni Collette

Aleksa Palladino, Adrian Grenier

Adrian Grenier

THE ADVENTURES OF SEBASTIAN COLE

(**PARAMOUNT CLASSICS**) Producers, Jasmine Kosovic, Karen Barber; Director/Screenplay, Tod Williams; Photography, John Foster; Editor, Affonso Gonçalves; Costumes, Eric Daman; Music, Elizabeth Swados; Casting, Ann Goulder; a Culpan production; Color; Rated R; 104 minutes; Release date: August 6, 1999

CAST

Sebastian Cole	Adrian Grenier
Hank/Henrietta Cole	Clark Gregg
Mary	Aleksa Palladino
Joan Cole	Margaret Colin
Hartley	John Shea
Jessica	Marni Lustig
Grandmother	Joan Copeland
Grandfather	Tom Lacy
Troy	Gabriel Macht
Wayne	Russel Harper
Jimmy	Greg Haberny
Principal	Peter McRobbie
Susan	Merritt Wever
Chinatown	Rory Cochrane
Juvie Bob	Levon Helm
Fiona	Famke Janssen

and Marisol Padilla Sanchez (Woman in Desert), Graeme Malcolm (John), Dan Tedlie (Hall Monitor), Miguel Nájera (Man in Desert), Joe Lisi (Concrete Guy)

Sebastian Cole's troubled life as a high school underachiever is further complicated when his step-father announces his plans to become a woman.

Clark Gregg

Greg Haberny, Russel Harper, Adrian Grenier

MYSTERY MEN

(**UNIVERSAL**) Producers, Lawrence Gordon, Mike Richardson, Lloyd Levin; Executive Producer, Robert Engelman; Director, Kinka Usher; Screenplay, Neil Cuthbert; Based on the Dark Horse Comic Book Series Created by Bob Burden; Photography, Stephen H. Burum; Designer, Kirk M. Petruccelli; Editor, Conrad Buff; Co-Producer, Steven Gilder; Costumes, Marilyn Vance; Music, Stephen Warbeck; Music Supervisor, Karyn Rachtman; Visual Effects Supervisor, Lori J. Nelson; Casting, Mindy Marin; Stunts, Mickey Gilbert; a Lawrence Gordon presentation of a Golar/Lloyd Levin/Dark Horse production; Dolby; Deluxe color; Rated PG-13; 120 minutes; Release date: August 6, 1999

William H. Macy, Ben Stiller, Hank Azaria

CAST

The Blue Raja	Hank Azaria
The Bowler	Janeane Garofalo
The Shoveler	William H. Macy
Invisible Boy	Kel Mitchell
The Spleen	Paul Reubens
The Furious	Ben Stiller
The Sphinx	Wes Studi
Captain Amazing/Lance	Greg Kinnear
Tony P	Eddie Izzard
Tony C	Prakazrel Michel
Dr. Annabel Leek	Lena Olin
Casanova Frankenstein	Geoffrey Rush
Ted	Ernie Lee Banks
Banyon	Gerry Becker
Funk	Ned Bellamy
Butch	Corbin Bleu
Roland	Philip Bolden
Thugs	Jake Cross
Monica	Claire Forlani

and Ricky Jay (Vic Weems), Louise Lasser (Violet), Emmy Laybourne, Chris Mugglebee (Reporters), Jenifer Lewis (Lucille), Mason Lucero (Young Kid), Monet Mazur (Becky Beaner), Joel McCrary (Funk), Olivia Lauren Todd (Tracy), Frederick Usher (Thug), Kinka Usher (Moe), Gayle Vance (Sally), Tom Waits (Dr. Heller), Adrian Armas, Gichi Gamba, Thomas Lake, Robert Musselman, Solo Scott, Erik Michael Tristan (Disco Boys), James Duke (Big Tobacco), Andreea Radutoiu, Ungela Brockman, Kimberly James, Angelica Bridges (Furriers), Michael Bay, Riki Rachtman, Noah Blake (Frat Boys), Robert Barnett aka T-Mo, Willie Knighton Jr. aka Khujo, Thomas Burton aka Cee-Lo, Cameron Gipp aka Gipp (Rappers), Michael Chieffo, Gil Christner, Carl Strano (Suits), John Brantley Cole, Robert Chow, Steven Jang, Sung Kang (Susies), Jody Watley, Shane Johnson, Sunny Gorg, Jennifer Lee Keyes, Sasha Bray, Marie Matiko (Disco Girls), Artie Lange (Big Red), Margaret Wheeler (Old Lady), Bill Beck, Robert Lieb (Old Men), Sarah Kane, Florence Stone Fevergeon (Old Party Goers), Ed Denette (Old Veteran), Kiyoko Yamaguchi, Kiko Kiko, Nori T. Gehr (Back-Up Singer)s, Mark Mothersbaugh (Band Leader), Nancye Ferguson (Singer), Katie Adams, Shirley Bowden, Lu Gay, Helen Etting, Crystal Gaer White, Valerie Gitter, Mae Greenstein, C. Elane Innes, Irene Kamsler, Miriam R. Lawless, Teresa MacLean, Joanne McDermott (Dancers), Stacey Travis, Joann Richter (Powerwomen), Larkin Campbell (Supervacman), Oliver Clark (Reverse Psychologist), Jack Plotnick (Mr. Pups), Dane Cook (Waffler), Robert Musselman (Ballerinaman), Vince Melocchi (Mailman), Doug Jones (Pencilhead), Vincent Bowman (Son of Pencilhead), Vylette Fagerholm (Little Miss Vengeance), Dana Gould (Squeegeeman), Branden Williams (Maintainer), Aaron Priest (The Artiste), Robert B. Martin, Jr. (Big Billy Hill Billy), Gabrielle Conferti (PMS Avenger), Jeff Z. Danziger (Radio Man), Wilbert Sampson, Kenneth W. Watts (Pigs), Elliot Durant III (Martial Artist), Anthony Sebastian Marinelli (Gorilla), Drinda E. Shaneyfelt (Evil Devil Woman), Felix Castro (Globalman), Michael Craig (Gardener), Ronald Lasky (Bullfighter), David Still (Stilt Man), Jonathan Khan (Fisherman), Jerry Farmer (Thirstyman)

Greg Kinnear

When Champion City's resident superhero, Captain Amazing, is captured by his nemesis Casanova Frankenstein, a rag-tag group of pseudo-super-heros with questionable skills and powers join forces to fight the villain and save the day.

Paul Reubens, Tom Waits, Janeane Garofalo

Pierce Brosnan, Rene Russo

Denis Leary

Rene Russo, Pierce Brosnan

Pierce Brosnan, Rene Russo

Faye Dunaway

THE THOMAS CROWN AFFAIR

(**MGM**) Producers, Pierce Brosnan, Beau St. Clair; Executive Producer, Michael Tadross; Director, John McTiernan; Screenplay, Leslie Dixon, Kurt Wimmer; Story, Alan R. Trustman; Co-Producer, Roger Paradiso; Photography, Tom Priestley; Designer, Bruno Rubeo; Editor, John Wright; Costumes, Kate Harrington; Visual Effects, John Sullivan; Music, Bill Conti; Casting, Pat McCorkle; an Irish DreamTime production; Dolby; Panavision; Deluxe color; Rated R; 111 minutes; Release date: August 6, 1999

Pierce Brosnan

CAST

Thomas Crown	Pierce Brosnan
Catherine Banning	Rene Russo
Michael McCann	Denis Leary
Andrew Wallace	Ben Gazzara
Paretti	Frankie Faison
John Reynolds	Fritz Weaver
Golchan	Charles Keating
Knutzhorn	Mark Margolis
Psychiatrist	Faye Dunaway
Proctor McKinley	Michael Lombard
Proctors	Bill Ambrozy, Michael S. Bahr, Robert Novak, Joe Lamb
Paul Cheng	James Saito
Anna Knutzhorn	Esther Cañadas
Crown's Driver	Mischa Hausserman
Petru	Daniel Oreskes
Dimetri	Dominic Chianese, Jr.
Janos	Ritchie Coster
Iggy	Gregg Bello

and John P. McCann (Senior Detective), Gino Lucci (Freight Truck Driver), George Christy (Senior Museum Guard), Mike Danner (Forklift Operator), James J. Archer (J.J. the Security Guard), John Elsen (New York City Cop), Robert Spillane (Crown Security Guard), Daniel Jamal Gibson (Sam), Cynthia Darlow (Crown's Secretary), Sherry Koftan, Jane DeNoble, Gene Bozzi, Ryan Hecht, Paul Simon (Crown Employees), Tom Tammi (Businessman), Mark Zeisler, Mark Zimmerman (Bulldogs), Dan Southern, James Yaegashi (Crown Executives), Ira Wheeler (Old Man)

Rene Russo

Investigator Catherine Banning becomes determined to prove that self-made Manhattan billionaire Thomas Crown is behind the theft of a priceless painting. Remake of the 1968 United Artists release that starred Steve McQueen and Faye Dunaway. Dunaway also appears in this film. The Oscar-winning song from the original film, The Windmills of Your Mind, is also heard here.

Pierce Brosnan

Pierce Brosnan, Esther Cañadas, Rene Russo

ILLUMINATA

(**ARTISAN**) Producers, John Penotti, John Turturro; Executive Producers, Giovanni Di Clemente, Ellen Little, Robert Little; Director, John Turturro; Screenplay, Brandon Cole, John Turturro; Based on the play by Brandon Cole; Photography, Harris Savides; Line Producer, Carol Cuddy; Editor, Michael Berenbaum; Music, William Bolcom, Arnold Black; Designer, Robin Standefer; Costumes, Donna Zakowska; Casting, Todd Thaler; an Overseas Filmgroup presentation in association with CDI Compagnia Distribuzione Internationale JVC, Sogepaq of a Greenstreet Films production; Dolby; Technicolor; Rated R; 111 minutes; Release date: August 6, 1999

CAST

Rachel	Katharine Borowitz
Astergourd	Beverly D'Angelo
Old Flavio	Ben Gazzara
Pallenchio	Donal McCann
Celimene	Susan Sarandon
Dominique	Rufus Sewell
Tuccio	John Turturro
Bevalaqua	Christopher Walken
Beppo	Leo Bassi
Simone	Georgina Cates
Marco	Bill Irwin
Piero	Matthew Sussman
Orlandini	David Thornton
Marta	Aida Turturro
Pitou	Henri Behar
Passerby	Maurizio Benazzo
Boys	Amedeo Turturro, Fernando Bolles, Chris Papadopoulos
Duke	Jeff Braun
Journalist	David Cale
Scruffy Man	Kenny Cranna
Jailor	George DiCenzo

Timothy Doyle (Aristocrat #1), Alexander Goodwin (Crying Boy), Amo Gulinello (Pupo), Joe Paparone (Grand Inquisitor), William Preston (Old Toothless Man), Mary Lou Rosato (Duchessa), Suzanne Shepherd (Marco's Mother), Rocco Sisto (Prince), Richard Spore (Stagehand), June Stein (Angry Woman), Henry Stram (Captain), Kohl Sudduth, Arjun Bhasin, (Concubines),

In turn of the century New York, anxious playwright Tuccio hopes to have his new, unfinished work premiered by his repertory company.

© Artisan Entertainment Inc.

John Turturro, Susan Sarandon

Christopher Walken

Donal McCann, Beverly D'Angelo

Katherine Borowitz, John Turturro

Kate Beckinsale, Claire Danes

Lou Diamond Phillips. Bill Pullman

Kate Beckinsale, Claire Danes

BROKEDOWN PALACE

(20TH CENTURY FOX) Producer, Adam Fields; Executive Producer, A. Kitman Ho; Director, Jonathan Kaplan; Screenplay, David Arata; Story, Adam Fields, David Arata; Photography, Newton Thomas Sigel; Designer, James Newport; Editor, Curtiss Clayton; Costumes, April Ferry; Music, David Newman; Casting, Julie Selzer; a Fox 2000 Pictures presentation of an Adam Fields production; Dolby; Super 35 Widescreen; Deluxe color; Rated PG-13; 100 minutes; Release date: August 13, 1999

CAST

Alice Marano...Claire Danes
Darlene Davis...Kate Beckinsale
Hank Greene ....Bill Pullman
Yon Greene...Jacqueline Kim
Roy Knox..Lou Diamond Phillips
Nick Parks...Daniel Lapaine
Doug Davis ....Tom Amandes
Beth Ann Gardener ....Aimee Graham
Bill Marano ....John Doe
Chief Detective Jagkrit ....Kay Tong Lim
Guard Velie ....Beulah Quo
Emissary to Crown ....Henry O
Jamaican Prisoner ....Bahni Turpin
English Prisoner...Amanda De Cadenet

and Indhira Charoenpura (Prisoner Shub), Lilia Cuntapay (Old Prisoner), Somsuda Chotikasupa (Glasses Guard), Maya Elise Goodwin (Mary), Chad Todhunter (Ferg), Lori Lethin (Lori Davis), Hayley Palmer (Heidi Davis), Rhency Padilla (Pool Boy), Victor Neri (Bellhop), Ermie M. Concepcion (Paku), Nopachai Israngkur Na Ayudhya, Ayutthaya A. Payakkapong (Cabbies), Kawee Sirikhanaerut (Shouting Soldier), Sahajak Boonthanakit (Sgt. Choy), Mario Valentino Victa (Lt. Tung), Joonee Gamboa (Attorney Montree), Phikun M. Sabino (Guard Sorhirun), Toun Tolentino (Old Dorm Guard), Tawewan Promgontha (Young Dorm Guard), Sawan Edo (Guard Sawalee), Sudarat L. Gaoat (Guard Mangman), Tawatchai Teeranusoon, M. Tom Visvachat (Thai Judges), Tony Carney (Doug's Translator), Pichada De Jesus (Darlene's Translator), Sutagorn Jaiman (Prosecutor), Pathompong Supalert (Defense Attorney), Achavasak Phitak (Officer Deesom), Songkran Somboon (Officer Changjarung), Harry E. Northup (Leon Smith), Johnny Ray McGhee (DEA Agent), Phanom Promguntha (Customs Supervisor), Jake De Asis (Royal Thai Guard), Olympio D. Franco (Sick Prisoner), Ronnie Lazaro (Security), Parinya Pattamadilok (Shop Owner), Yuthana Kaewdaeng (Thai Vendor)

Two vacationing teenage girls are arrested when heroin is found in their luggage, an act that finds them imprisoned in Thailand where there is little hope of release.

© Twentieth Century Fox

Claire Danes, Kate Beckinsale, Daniel Lapaine

BOWFINGER

(**UNIVERSAL**) Producer, Brian Grazer; Executive Producers, Karen Kehela, Bernie Williams; Director, Frank Oz; Screenplay, Steve Martin; Photography, Ueli Steiger; Designer, Jackson DeGovia; Editor, Richard Pearson; Costumes, Joseph G. Aulisi; Music, David Newman; Music Supervisor, Pilar McCurry; Casting, Margery Simkin; an Imagine Entertainment presentation of a Brian Grazer production; Dolby; Deluxe color; Rated PG-13; 96 minutes; Release date: August 13, 1999

CAST

Bobby Bowfinger	Steve Martin
Kit Ramsey/Jiff Ramsey	Eddie Murphy
Daisy	Heather Graham
Carol	Christine Baranski
Dave	Jamie Kennedy
Kit's Agent	Barry Newman
Afrim	Adam Alexi-Malle
Slater	Kohl Sudduth
Terry Stricter	Terence Stamp
Jerry Renfro	Robert Downey, Jr.
Sanchez	Alejandro Patino
Martinez	Alfred De Contreras
Hector	Ramiro Fabian
Luis	Johnny Sanchez
Freddy	Claude Brooks
LA Cop	Kevin Scannell
MindHead Executive	John Prosky
Camera Security Guard	Michael Dempsey
Federal Express Man	Walter Powell
Actor at Audition	Phill Lewis

and Marisol Nichols (Young Actress at Audition), Nathan Anderson (Clothing Sales Clerk), Brogan Roche (Renfro's Executive), John Cho (Nightclub Cleaner), Lloyd Berman (Camera Store Clerk), Zaid Farid (Kit's Limo Driver), Aaron Brumfield, Kevin Grevioux (Kit's Bodyguards), Kimble Jemison (Kit's Assistant), Alex Craig Mann (Studio Executive), Laura Grady (E Channel Interviewer), Reamy Hall (Farrah), Michelle Boehle, Kimberly Baum, Megan Denton, Janet Jaeger, Hope Wood, Addie Yungmee, Andrea Toste (Laker Girls), Mindy (Betsy, Bowfinger's Dog)

In a last desperate bid to make it in Hollywood, third-rate filmmaker Bobby Bowfinger decides to shoot a script starring action star Kit Ramsey without Ramsey even knowing he is being filmed.

© Universal Studios

Eddie Murphy, Steve Martin

Jamie Kennedy

Adam Alexi-Malle

Christine Baranski

Terence Stamp

Heather Graham

Jeanne Tripplehorn, Hugh Grant

James Caan, Hugh Grant

MICKEY BLUE EYES

(**WARNER BROS.**) Producers, Elizabeth Hurley, Charles Mulvehill; Director, Kelly Makin; Screenplay, Adam Scheinman, Robert Kuhn; Photography, Donald E. Thorin; Editor, David Freeman; Music, Basil Poledouris; Designer, Gregory Keen; Costumes, Ellen Mirojnick; Casting, Laura Rosenthal; a Castle Rock Entertainment presentation of a Simian Films production; Dolby; Technicolor; Rated PG-13; 103 minutes; Release date: August 20, 1999

CAST

Michael Felgate	Hugh Grant
Frank Vitale	James Caan
Gina Vitale	Jeanne Tripplehorn
Vito Graziosi	Burt Young
Philip Cromwell	James Fox
Vinnie	Joe Viterelli
Agent Connell	Gerry Becker
Carol	Maddie Corman
Angelo	Tony Darrow
Ritchie Vitale	Paul Lazar
Al	Vincent Pastore
Sante	Frank Pellegrino
Agent Lewis	Scott Thompson
Johnny Graziosi	John Ventimiglia
Helen	Margaret Devine
Mrs. Horton	Beatrice Winde
Gene Morganson	Mark Margolis
Emily Basset	Helen Lloyd Breed
Luigi	Carmine Parisi
Caroline Cromwell	Sybil Lines

and Alexis Brentani, Rose Caiola, Felicia Scarangelo (Bridesmaids), Joseph R. Gannascoli (Gina's Doorman), Rocco Musacchia (Carmine), John DiBenedetto (Harold Green), Bruno Gioiello (Technician), Rich Topol (FBI Chief—Truck), Frank Senger (Delivery Driver), Lori Tan Chinn (Chinese Waitress), Marsha Dietlein (Customer), Steve Mellor (FBI—Chef Leader), John DiResta (Traffic Cop), Ephraim Benton (Student), Ed Wheeler (Reporter), Aida Turturro (Waitress), Tony Sirico (First Risolli Man), Lorri Bagley (Antoinette), Brian Davies (Priest), Melissa Marsala (Carla), Joe Rigano (Mr. Risoli), Michael Kennealy (Jeffrey), Leonardo Sessa, Andy Redmond (FBI Chefs), Chris McGinn, David McConeghey (Tourists), Stephen Dym (Cromwell Employee), Shelagh Ratner, Tori King (Art Patrons), Sara Colton, Kevin Kean Murphy (Auction Bidders)

Hugh Grant, Jeanne Tripplehorn

A Manhattan art dealer proposes to his girlfriend, only to find out that her father is a Mafia chieftan.

James Caan, Burt Young

IN TOO DEEP

Omar Epps, LL Cool J, Veronica Webb

Pam Grier

Stanley Tucci, Omar Epps

(**DIMENSION**) Producers, Paul Aaron, Michael Henry Brown; Executive Producers, Bob Weinstein, Harvey Weinstein, Jeremy Kramer, Amy Slotnick, Don Carmody; Director, Michael Rymer; Screenplay, Michael Henry Brown, Paul Aaron; Photography, Ellery Ryan; Designer, Dan Leigh; Editor, Dany Cooper; Music, Christopher Young; Music Supervisor, Frank Fitzpatrick; Costumes, Shawn Barton; Casting, Aisha Coley; a Suntaur Entertainment Company production; Distributed by Miramax Films; Dolby; Super 35 Widescreen; Color; Rated R; 104 minutes; Release date: August 25, 1999

CAST

Det. Jeff Cole (J. Reid)	Omar Epps
Dwayne Gittens "God"	LL Cool J
Myra	Nia Long
Preston	Stanley Tucci
Breezy T	Hill Harper
Det. Angela Wilson	Pam Grier
Pam	Veronica Webb
Ray-Ray	Lloyd Adams
Minister	Philip Akin
Esperanza Batista	Anna Alvim
G.G.	Karina Arroyave
Officers	Richard Blackburn, Howard Hoover
Wesley	Richard Brooks
Dr. Bratton	Ron Canada
O'Hanlon	Kevin Chapman
Mrs. Batista	Ivonne Coll
Lookout	Chris Collins
Batista Cops	Shane Daly, Brian Furlong
Mrs. Coy	Brenda Thomas Denmark
Miguel Batista	Guillermo Diaz
Melvin	Jermaine Dupri
Denise	Aujanue Ellis
Grandmother	Dolores Etienne
Ozzie	Sticky Fingaz
Mrs. Connelly	Wendji Fulford
Frisco	Gano Grills
Mrs. Johnson	Jackie Hargrave
Murphy	Don Harvey
Professor	Edward Heeley
Connelly (4 years)	Tatum Hunter
Doreen	Camille James
Connelly (2 years)	Claire Johnson
Latique	Hassan Iniko Johnson
Rick Scott	David Patrick Kelly
Felipe Batista	Robert Lasardo
Marcus (8 years)	Dustin Leonard
Marcus (3 years)	Jordan Leonard
Cadet	Latoya Lesmond
Lisa	Yvette Martin
Martha	Michi Mi
Loretta	Mya
Red-Haired Cadet	Toby Proctor
Dancer	Alex Restrepo
Romeo Concepcion	Victor Rivers
Che	Shyheim
2nd Cop	Stephen Graham Simpson
K. Dee	David Spates
Angie	Lenore Thomas
Ramon	Angel Torres
Judge	Katherine Trowell
Gashman	Avery Kidd Waddell
Pam	Veronica Webb
Daniel Connelly	Jake Weber

Detective Jeffrey Cole goes undercover to trap a dangerous crimelord who calls himself "God" only to find that his infiltration might threaten the operation altogether.

© Dimension Films

THE SOURCE

(WINSTAR) Producer/Director/Screenplay/Editor, Chuck Workman; Executive Producer, Hiro Yamagata; Photography, Tom Hurwitz, Don Lenzer, Jose Luis Mignone, Nancy Schreiber, Andrew Dintenfass; Music, Various Artists; Color; Not rated; 88 minutes; Release date: August 25, 1999. Documentary on the Beats and the Beat Generation.

Dramatized Performance Sequences: Johnny Depp, Dennis Hopper, John Turturro

Documentary Sequences Interviews: Allen Ginsberg, William S. Burroughs, Timothy Leary, Lawrence Ferlinghetti, Michael McClure, Ken Kesey, Gregory Corso, Ed Sanders, Amiri Baraka, Tom Hayden, Gary Snyder, Robert Creeley, Phillip Glass, David Amram; Archival Material and Interviews: Jack Kerouac, Jerry Garcia, Bob Dylan, Shirley Clarke, Diane di Prima, Robert Motherwell, Norman Mailer, Terry Southern, Neal Cassady.

Jack Kerouac, Allen Ginsberg, William S. Burroughs

Brendan Fraser, Sarah Jessica Parker

Alfred Molina

DUDLEY DO-RIGHT

(UNIVERSAL) Producers, John Davis, Joseph M. Singer, J. Todd Harris; Director/Screenplay/Executive Producer, Hugh Wilson; Based on characters developed by Jay Ward; Photography, Donald E. Thorin; Designer, Bob Ziembicki; Editor, Don Brochu; Co-Producer, Mary Kane; Costumes, Lisa Jensen; Associate Producer, Kathy Zimmer; Music, Steve Dorff; Dudley Do-Right Theme, Fred Steiner; Casting, Denise Chamian; a Davis Entertainment/Joseph Singer Entertainment/Todd Harris production; Dolby; Super 35 Widescreen; Deluxe color; Rated PG; 79 minutes; Release date: August 27, 1999

CAST

Dudley Do-Right ....Brendan Fraser
Nell Fenwick ....Sarah Jessica Parker
Snidley Whiplash ....Alfred Molina
The Prospector...Eric Idle
Inspector Fenwick ....Robert Prosky
The Chief..Alex Rocco
The Voice of the Announcer...Corey Burton
Howard ....Jack Kehler
and Louis Mustillo (Standing Room Only), Don Yesso (Kenneth), Jed Rees (Lavar), Brant Von Hoffmann (Barry), P. Adrien Dorval, Mark Acheson (Locals), Richard Side (Barber), L. Harvey Gold (Baker), Susan Astley (Baker's Wife), Douglas Newell (Bank President), Haig Sutherland (Teller), Jake T. Roberts, Scott Nicholson (Mounties), Kevin Griffin-Park (Bartender), Michael McCarty (Local Banker), Nicole Robert (Mother), Rondel Reynoldson, Rick Poltaruk, Kevin Blatch (Townspeople), Regis Philbin (Regis), Kathie Lee Gifford (Kathie Lee), Ernie Grunwald, Jennifer Clement (Customs Officers), Brian Arnold (Anchor), Joanna Piros (Fernandez), Paul Barsanti (Caitlin), Forbes Angus (Leader), Eddie Moore (Lefty), Eric Breker (Husband), Jennifer Rockett (Wife), Robert C. Saunders (Another Guy), C. Ernst Harth (Shane), Betty Linde (Secretary), Gerard Plunkett (Spinworthy), Greg Rogers, Bob Dawson (FBI Types), William Samples, Nick Misura, Alex Diakun (Gentlemen), Michael Suchanek (Ten Year Old Boy), Brent Butt (A Bad Guy in Back), John Destrey (Another Bad Guy), David Fredericks (Yet Another Bad Guy), William MacDonald (In the Back), Robin Mossley (In the Way Back), Oscar Goncalves (Indian), Emmanuelle Vaugier (Indian Maiden), Jessica Schreier (Mrs. Darling), Kevin Mundy (Jim Darling), Justen Harcourt (Chad Darling), Nathan Bennett, Isis Johnson (Mother's Kids), Daniel Bacon, Jayme Knox (Miners), Art Irizawa (Asian Golfer)

Bumbling Mountie Dudley Do-Right tries to prevent his arch enemy Snidley Whiplash from taking over Semi-Happy Valley. Based on the animated shorts that ran on The Bullwinkle Show and later as their own ABC series, The Dudley Do-Right Show (1969-70).

Antonio Banderas

Antonio Banderas, Omar Sharif

THE 13TH WARRIOR

(**TOUCHSTONE**) formerly *Eaters of the Dead*; Producers, John McTiernan, Michael Crichton, Ned Dowd; Executive Producers, Andrew G. Vajna, Ethan Dubrow; Director, John McTiernan; Screenplay, William Wisher, Warren Lewis; Based on the novel *Eaters of the Dead* by Michael Crichton; Co-Producer, Lou Arkoff; Photography, Peter Menzies, Jr.; Designer, Wolf Kroeger; Editor, John Wright; Visual Effects Supervisor, John Sullivan; Costumes, Kate Harrington; Music, Jerry Goldsmith; Casting, Pat McCorkle; a Crichton/McTiernan production; Distributed by Buena Vista Pictures; Dolby; Panavision; Technicolor; Rated R; 103 minutes; Release date: August 27, 1999

CAST

Ahmed Ibn Fahdlan	Antonio Banderas
Queen Weilew	Diane Venora
Herger the Joyous	Dennis Storhoi
Buliwyf	Vladimir Kulich
Melchisidek	Omar Sharif
Wigliff, King Hrothgar's Son	Anders T. Andersen
Skeld the Superstitious	Richard Bremmer
Weath the Musician	Tony Curran
Rethel the Archer	Mischa Hausserman
Roneth the Horseman	Neil Maffin
Halga the Wise	Asbjørn Riis
Helfdane the Large	Clive Russell
Edgtho the Silent	Daniel Southern
Haltaf the Boy	Oliver Sveinall
King Hrothgar	Sven Wollter

and Albie Woodington (Hyglak the Quarrelsome), John DeSantis (Ragnar the Dour), Eric Avari (Caravan Leader), Maria Bonnevie (Olga), Richard Ooms (One-Eyed Old Man), (Screaming Boy), Dylan Gray Woodley, Bjorn Ove Pedersen (Wulfgar, the Boy-Messenger), Scott Elam (Herald), Ghoncheh Tazmini (Shaharazhad, Arabian Beauty), Joe Bulatti (Shaharazhad's Husband), Mina Erian Mina (The Caliph), Mona Storhoi (Sacrificial Woman), Turid Balke (Oracle, Old Woman), Suzanne Bertish (Hulda), Susan Willis (Wendol Mother), Yolande Bavan (Wendol Mother Companion), Claire Lapinski (Freyda), Tarik Batal (Arab Page), Brett Reyez (Caravan Lieutenant), Akesh Gill, Natalia Mohammed MacLeod, Kaaren De Zilva, Layla Alizada (Serving Girls), Sven-Ole Thorsen (Would Be King), Alaina Lander (Sleeping Girl), Jeremy Van Der Driesen, Al Hachlaf (Arab Generals), Brian Jensen, Michael Brynjolfson, Alex Zahara, Mark Acheson, John Bear Curtis, Andrew A. Kavadas (Norsemen), Gunnar Skjavestad (Norseman on Ship), Malcolm Jolly (Wulfgar Retainer), Owen Walstrom (Wendol Guard)

Ibn Fahdlan, banished from his homeland, joins a band of Norse warriors who are battling against a deadly and mysterious band of creatures who are destroying everything in their path.

© Touchstone Pictures

Vladimir Kulich, Dennis Storhoi

Maria Bonnevie, Antonio Banderas

Jeff Bridges, Albert Brooks

Sharon Stone, Albert Brooks

Andie MacDowell, Albert Brooks

Sharon Stone

THE MUSE

(**USA FILMS**) Producer, Herb Nanas; Director, Albert Brooks; Screenplay, Albert Brooks, Monica Johnson; Executive Producer, Barry Berg; Photography, Thomas Ackerman; Music, Elton John; Designer, Dina Lipton; Costumes, Betsy Cox; Editor, Peter Teschner; Casting, Victoria Burrows; an October Films presentation; Dolby; Deluxe color; Rated PG-13; 97 minutes; Release date: August 27, 1999

CAST

Steven Phillips ....Albert Brooks
Sarah ....Sharon Stone
Laura Phillips...Andie MacDowell
Jack Warrick...Jeff Bridges
Josh Martin ....Mark Feuerstein
Stan Spielberg ....Steven Wright
Hal ....Bradley Whitford
European Man ....Mario Opinato
Dr. Jacobson...Dakin Matthews
Nurse Rennert ....Concetta Tomei
Themselves ....Cybill Shepherd, Lorenzo Lamas, Jennifer Tilly,
Rob Reiner, Wolfgang Puck,
James Cameron, Martin Scorsese
Julie Phillips ....Monica Mikala
Mary Phillips ....Jamie Alexis
Jennifer ....Marnie Shelton
Anne ....Catherine MacNeal
Universal Studio Guard ....Skip O'Brien
and Aude Charles, Ange Billman, Gannon Daniels (Spielberg Secretaries), Jennie Ventriss (Older Secretary), Bobby Ender (Boy at Sarah's House), Stacy Travis (Phyllis), Michele Crosby Jones (Tiffany Saleswoman), Paul C. Jensen (Four Seasons Porter), Steve Valentine (Four Seasons Assistant Manager), Greg Grunberg (Four Seasnos Hotel Security), Alexandra Kaplan (Rob Reiner's Daughter), Steven Anthony Lawrence (Rob Reiner's Son), Jill Tobin (Attendant), Mario Opinato (European), Walter Williamson (Bruno), A.J. Orta (Boy in Cookie Store)

Experiencing writers' block and told by executives that he has lost his edge, Hollywood screenwriter Steven Phillips seeks the help of a mysterious woman named Sarah, who claims to be an actual Greek muse.

© October Films

OUTSIDE PROVIDENCE

(**MIRAMAX**) Producers, Michael Corrente, Peter Farrelly, Bobby Farrelly, Randy Finch; Director, Michael Corrente; Screenplay, Peter Farrelly, Michael Corrente, Bobby Farrelly; Based upon the novel by Peter Farrelly; Executive Producers, Bob Weinstein, Harvey Weinstein; Co-Producer, Marisa Polvino; Associate Producer, Libby Langdon; Photography, Richard Crudo; Editor, Kate Sanford; Designer, Chad Detwille; Costumes, Annie Dunn; Music, Sheldon Mirowitz; Music Supervisor, Peter Afterman; Casting, Sheila Jaffe, Georgianne Walken; an Eagle Beach production; Dolby; Color; Rated R; 103 minutes; Release date: September 1, 1999

Alec Baldwin, George Wendt

CAST

Timothy Dunphy	Shawn Hatosy
Old Man Dunphy	Alec Baldwin
Jane Weston	Amy Smart
Joey	George Wendt
Mousy	Jonathan Brandis
Jack Wheeler	Gabriel Mann
Drugs Delaney	Jon Abrahams
Irving Waltham	Jack Ferver
Billy Fu	Alex Toma
Mr. Funderberk	Timothy Crowe
Jackie Dunphy	Tommy Bone
Barney	Richard Jenkins
Caveech	Mike Cerrone
Fran	Robert Turano
Tommy the Wire	Adam Lavorgna
Decenz	Jesse Leach
"Clops"	Samantha Levigne
Bunny Cote	Kristen Shorten
Dean Mort	George Martin
Brackett	Chris Jewett

and Sean Gildea (Math Teacher), Bernie Sheredy (History Teacher), Jimmy Landi (Ticket Taker), Amy Van Nostrand (Mrs. Weston), Mark O'Connell, Seth Meier (Jizz Flashback Older Boys), Nicholas Cardi, Vincent Mesolella, Joshua Moore, Scott Rabideau, David Vaillancourt (Cornwall Students), Libby Langdon (Mrs. Dunphy), Johnny O'Hern (Young Tim Dunphy), Kyle Pepi, Ryan Pepi (Young Jackie Dunphy), Gus Albero (Stoner), T.J. Paolino (Maggie), Eric Brown (English Teacher), Robert W. Jordan (Shorty), Harry Cooper, Steve Cerrone (Men at Bar), Johnny Cicco (Jensen), Kevin Gilmore (Kelleher), Max Ricci (Student in Dining Hall), Kate Lohman (Secretary), Nigel Gore (Dean John S. Rogers, Jr.)

Shawn Hatosy

Fed up with Timothy's constant drug use and worthless lifestyle, his blue collar dad packs him off to a prep school where the boy feels seriously out of place.

© Miramax Films

Amy Smart, Shawn Hatosy

Shawn Hatosy, Jack Ferver, Chris Jewett

THE MINUS MAN

(**ARTISAN**) Producers, David Bushell, Fida Attieh; Director/Screenplay, Hampton Fancher; Based upon the novel by Lew McCreary; Executive Producers, Larry Meistrich, Steve Carlis, Joseph J. DiMartino, Keith Abell; Associate Producer, Mary Vernieu; Photography, Bobby Bukowski; Editor, Todd Ramsay; Designer, Andrew Laws; Costumes, Kimberly Adams-Galligan; Music, Marco Beltrami; Casting, Mary Vernieu, Anne McCarthy; The Shooting Gallery and Fida Attieh Productions presentation in association with Donald C. Carter; Dolby; Color; Rated R; 112 minutes; Release date: September 10, 1999

CAST

Vann Siegert	Owen Wilson
Ferrin	Janeane Garofalo
Doug	Brian Cox
Jane	Mercedes Ruehl
BlaiR	Dwight Yoakam
Graves	Dennis Haysbert
Casper	Sheryl Crow
State Trooper	Alex Warren
Karen (age 18)	Chloe Black
Gene	Eric Mabius
Paul	Larry Miller
Lois	Lois Gerace
Coach	Erik Holland
Arthur	Daniel "Big Black" Rey
Joe La Moine	Axel Overgaard
Chief of Police	Brent Briscoe
Priest	John Vargas
Man in Diner	Lew McCreary
Wendy	Shannon Kies
Karen (age 5)	Madeleine Ignon
Irene	Meg Foster
Anchorwoman	Maria Diaz
Pate	David Warshofsky
Creech	Mark Derwin
Arresting Officer	Matt Gerald

Vann Siegert, a mysterious drifter of vague personality, settles down in a small coastal town, after which several of the locals beginning disappearing.

© TSG

Janeane Garofalo, Owen Wilson

Gabriel Byrne, Patricia Arquette

STIGMATA

(**MGM**) Producer, Frank Mancuso, Jr.; Director, Rupert Wainwright; Screenplay, Tom Lazarus, Rick Ramage; Story, Tom Lazarus; Photography, Jeffrey L. Kimball; Designer, Waldemar Kalinowski; Line Producer, Vikki Williams; Editors, Michael R. Miller, Michael J. Duthie; Costumes, Louise Frogley; Makeup Effects Supervisor, Ve Neill; Music, Billy Corgan, Elia Cmiral; Casting, Wendy Kurtzman; an FGM Entertainment production; Dolby; Super 35 Widescreen; Deluxe color; Rated R; 103 minutes; Release date: September 10, 1999

CAST

Frankie Paige	Patricia Arquette
Father Andrew Kiernan	Gabriel Byrne
Cardinal Daniel Houseman	Jonathan Pryce
Donna Chadway	Nia Long
Father Durning	Thomas Kopache
Marion Petrocelli	Rade Sherbedgia
Father Dario	Enrico Colantoni
Father Gianni Delmonico	Dick Latessa
Jennifer Kelliho	Portia de Rossi
Steven	Patrick Muldoon
Dr. Reston	Ann Cusack
Doctor	Shaun Toub
Nurse	Tom Hodges
Attending Nurse	Lydia Hazan
Dr. Eckworth	Duke Moosekian
Woman with a Baby	Valarie Trapp
Cheryl	Kessia Kordelle
Donna's Customer	Frankie Thorn
Sister Angela	Mariah Nunn
MTA Man	Tom Fahn
Homeless Woman	Marilyn Pitzer
Father Paulo Alameida	Jack Donner

and Richard Conti (Valet Priest), Mary Linda Phillips (Sister Agnes), Liz Cruz, Faith Christopher (Waitresses), Joe Ruffo, Federico Scutti (Guards), William Howell, Kristopher Davis (Aerialists), Devin Unruh (Flower Boy), Vera Yell (Jennifer's Costumer), Mary Marshall (Nun), Daniel Escalzo, Michael P. Dearth (Italian Businessmen), Mark Adair Rios (Deacon)

After receiving a rosary from Brazil, Frankie Paige, a Pittsburgh hairdresser, begins experiencing bizarre and unexplainable seizures, prompting the Vatican to investigate the matter.

© Metro-Goldwyn-Mayer Pictures, Inc.

Kevin Bacon

Kevin Bacon

Illeana Douglas

Kathryn Erbe, Kevin Bacon

STIR OF ECHOES

(**ARTISAN ENTERTAINMENT**) Producers, Gavin Polone, Judy Hofflund; Executive Producer, Michele Weisler; Director/Screenplay, David Koepp; Based on the novel *A Stir of Echoes* by Richard Matheson; Photography, Fred Murphy; Designer, Nelson Coates; Editor, Jill Savitt; Costumes, Leesa Evans; Music, James Newton Howard; Casting, Mary Colquhoun; a Hofflund/Polone production; Dolby; Color; Rated R; 110 minutes; Release date: September 10, 1999

CAST

Tom Witzky ....Kevin Bacon
Maggie Witzky ....Kathryn Erbe
Lisa..Illeana Douglas
Debbie Kozac..Liza Weil
Frank McCarthy..Kevin Dunn
Harry Damon..Conor O'Farrell
Samantha..Jennifer Morrison
Jake Witzky..Zachary David Cope
Sheila..Lusia Strus
Bobby..Stephen Eugene Walker
Vanessa..Mary Kay Cook
Lenny..Larry Neumann, Jr.
Neighborhood Man..Richard Cotovsky
Kurt..Steve Rifkin
Adam..Chalon Williams
Security Guard..George Ivey
Debbie's Mother..Lisa Lewis
and Mike Bacarella, Christian Stolte (Train Station Cops), Eddie Bo Smith, Jr. (Neil the Cop), Hyowon K. Yoo (Korean Woman), Jim Andelin (Elderly Man), Karen Vaccaro (Upset Woman), Antonio Polk (Homey), Rosario Varela (Latin Woman), Duane Sharp (Polish Priest)

After Tom Witzky is hypnotized, he begins behaving irrationally due to the weird visions he keeps experiencing which seem to be sending him a message.

©Artisan Entertainment Inc.

BLUE STREAK

(**COLUMBIA**) Producers, Neal H. Moritz, Toby Jaffe; Executive Producers, Daniel Melnick, Allen Shapiro; Director, Les Mayfield; Screenplay, Michael Berry, John Blumenthal, Steve Carpenter; Photography, David Eggby; Designer, Bill Brzeski; Editor, Michael Tronick; Co-Producers, Michael Fottrell, Peaches Davis; Music, Edward Shearmur; Costumes, Denise Wingate; Casting, Lynn Kressel; an IndieProd/Neal H. Moritz/Jaffe production; Dolby; Deluxe color; Rated PG-13; 95 minutes; Release date: September 17, 1999

Martin Lawrence, Luke Wilson

CAST

Miles Logan	Martin Lawrence
Det. Carlson	Luke Wilson
Deacon	Peter Greene
Tulley	Dave Chappelle
Melissa Green	Nicole Ari Parker
Rizzo	Graham Beckel
Glenfiddish	Robert Miranda
LaFleur	Olek Krupa
Benny	Saverio Guerra
Uncle Lou	Richard C. Sarafian
Janiece	Tamala Jones
Agent Gray	Steve Rankin
Captain Penelli	Carmen Argenziano
Eddie	John Hawkes
Frank	Frank Medrano
Hardcastle	William Forsythe
Shawna	Octavania L. Spencer
Cop in Alley	Timothy Dale Agee

and Bayani Ison (Uniform Outside Station), Scott Sowers (Prison Guard #37), Christopher J. Stapleton (K-9 Cop), Eddy Donno (Guard One), Troy Gilbert (Guard Two), Kenny Endoso (Clerk), Googy Gress (Desk Sergeant), Robert Lasardo (Twitchy Suspect), Bill Ferrell (Cop in Elevator), Billy Williams (Cop in Gem Store Elevator), Greg Montgomery (Cop in Precinct), Jason Kravits (Customs Guy), Henry Hayashi (FBI Tech), James Gavin (Helicopter Pilot), Anne Marie Howard (Officer), Jane Carr (Museum Official), Brandon Michael DePaul (Little Friend), Amy Oberer (Terrified Woman), Ash Winfield (Briefing Room Detective), Erik Rondell (Francois), J. Kenneth Campbell (Peterson), Joel Hurt Jones (Tipsy Cop), Darryl Brunson (Office Porter), Shawn Elaine Brown Chiquette (Friendly Officer), Christian J. Christiensen, Michael A. Grasso, John McCarthy (Swat Team), Jeff Xander, Damian Foster (Thugs), Yetta Ginsburg (Repelled Passer-By), Daniel Rogerson (Chinese Delivery Man)

Dave Chappelle

Jewel thief Miles Logan returns from prison with the intention of recovering the $20 million diamond he had hidden in a construction site, only to discover that the finished building is a police precinct.

William Forsythe, Martin Lawrence

Martin Lawrence

BREAKFAST OF CHAMPIONS

(HOLLYWOOD PICTURES) Producers, David Blocker, David Willis; Director/Screenplay, Alan Rudolph; Based on the novel by Kurt Vonnegut, Jr.; Photography, Elliot Davis; Designer, Nina Ruscio; Costumes, Rudy Dillon; Editor, Suzy Elmiger; Music, Mark Isham; Songs Performed by Martin Denny; Additional Songs Performed by Lukas Haas; Casting, Pam Dixon Mickelson; a Flying Heart Films presentation; Dolby; CFI color; Rated R; 110 minutes; Release date: September 17, 1999

CAST

Dwayne Hoover	Bruce Willis
Kilgore Trout	Albert Finney
Harry Le Sabre	Nick Nolte
Celia Hoover	Barbara Hershey
Francine Pefko	Glenne Headly
Bunny Hoover	Lukas Haas
Wayne Hoobler	Omar Epps
Fred T. Barry	Buck Henry
Grace Le Sabre	Vicki Lewis
Eliot Rosewater	Ken Campbell
Bill Bailey	Jake Johannsen
Moe	Will Patton
Andy Wojeckowzski	Chip Zien
Gilbert	Ken Campbell
Monte Rapid	Owen Wilson
Maria Maritmo	Alison Eastwood
Bonnie MacMahon	Shawnee Smith
Howell	Michael Jai White
Vernon Garr	Keith Joe Dick
Rosemary Garr	Diane Dick

and Michael Duncan (Eli), Lahmard Tate (Elmore), Kurt Vonnegut, Jr. (Commerical Director), Dawn Didawick (Lottie), Bill Nagel (EPA Lawyer), Karl Wiedergott (Homer), Patti Allison (Blossom), Alexa Robbins (Art Hostess "Kaye"), Debra Dusay (Art Hostess "Faye"), Tom Robbins (Pesky Webber), Raymond O'Connor (Rabo Karebekian), Tisha Sterling (Beatrice Keedsler), Matt Callahan (Zeke the Gas Station Attendant), Tracey Lee Mapstone (Mailwoman), Mary Kennedy (Waitress), Greg Walker (Highway Patrolman), David Blampied (Prison Guard), Greg Moore (Porn Store Patron), Doug Hamblin (Mugger), Patrice Thomas (NY Policewoman), Nancy Volle (Marlo), Danielle Kennedy (Motel Clerk), Scout Willis (Young Girl), Nicolas Small (Young Boy); On Camera Commericals: Denise Simone ("Blue Monday" Housewife), Russell Wilson ("Blue Monday" Doctor), Scott Beauchemin ("Trypepton" Husband), Kassandra Kay ("Trypepton" Wife), Ken Odom ("Prodigal Life" Husband), Erica Evans ("Prodigal Life" Wife), David Kyle ("Prodigal Life" Child), Richard Sheehan (Voice-Over)

Improverished science fiction author Kilgore Trout journeys to the town of Midland City where successful car salesman Dwayne Hoover is teetering on the edge of a nervous breakdown.

© Sugar Creek Productions, Inc.

Bruce Willis, Nick Nolte

Lukas Haas

Albert Finney

TAXMAN

(PHAEDRA CINEMA) Producers, Avi Nesher, Kathy Jordan; Executive Producers, Pascal Borno; Director, Avi Nesher; Screenplay, Avi Nesher, Roger Berger; Photography, Jim Denault; Designer, Michael Krantz; Editor, Alexander Hall; Music, Roger Neill; Co-Producers, Joana Vicente, Jason Kliot; a Counterclock Pictures production in association with Open City Film; Dolby; Color; Rated R; 101 minutes; Release date: September 17, 1999

CAST

Al Benjamin	Joe Pantoliano
Joseph Romero	Wade Dominguez
Nadia Rubakov	Elizabeth Berkley
Andre Rubakov	Michael Chiklis
Peyton Cody	Robert Townsend
Abrasha Topolev	Casey Siemaszko
Mike Neals	Mike Starr
Kenneth Green	Fisher Stevens

and Michael Raynor (Mason Buckley), Jack Shearer (Captain Nunzio), Rick Washburn (Sergei Utisov), Glenn Palmer-Smith (Joe Lutz), David Deblinger (John Kravitz), Mark Giordano (Agent Johanson), Ian O'Donnell (Misha Baruchin), Jeffrey Ross (Tax Collector), Elizabeth Rouse (Taxpayer), Mick O'Rourke (Scarface), Vicor Tatarkin (Glasses), Ralph Cefarello (Detective Phil), Izrail Katsyv (Grisha Gold), Irina Zaagornova (Mrs. Rubakov), Molly Shulman (Natalia), Ernest Barseqov (Sasha), Buzz Roddy, Jack McLaughlin, Raymond Cassar (Policemen), Tony Ray Rossi (Truck Driver), David Stepanovskiy (Rabbi), Lia Chang (Receptionist), William Severs (Judge), Tom Myler (Court Clerk), Bunny Levine (Jury Foreman), Bernie Friedman (Old Man), Izia Sklar (Laundromat Owner), Igor Zinoviev (Andre's Bodyguard), Daniel M. Wong (Karaoke Singer), Alexei Cheburin, Polina Griffith (Russian Wedding Singers), Michael "Moe" Bernstein (Utisov's Driver), Phil Salvatore (Deck Hand), Jerry Jordan (Pool Security Guard)

In the Russian immigrant community in Brighton Beach, Brooklyn, a tax investigator and a NYPD patrolman team to track down a mysterious con man operating a multi-million dollar tax fraud.

© Phaedra Cinema

Joe Pantoliano, Elizabeth Berkley

FOR LOVE OF THE GAME

(**UNIVERSAL**) Producers, Armyan Bernstein, Amy Robinson; Executive Producers, Ron Bozman, Marc Abraham; Director, Sam Raimi; Screenplay, Dana Stevens; Based on the novel by Michael Shaara; Photography, John Bailey; Designer, Neil Spisak; Editors, Eric L. Beason, Arthur Coburn; Costumes, Judianna Makovsky; Music, Basil Poledouris; Casting, Lynn Kressel; a Beacon Pictures/Tig Productions/Mirage Enterprises production; Dolby; Panavision; Deluxe color; Rated PG-13; 137 minutes; Release date: September 17, 1999

Kevin Costner, Kelly Preston

CAST

Billy Chapel	Kevin Costner
Jane Aubrey	Kelly Preston
Gus Sinski	John C. Reilly
Heather	Jena Malone
Gary Wheeler	Brian Cox
Frank Perry	J.K. Simmons
Themselves	Vin Scully, Steve Lyons
Kent Strout	Carmine D. Giovinazzo
Davis Birch	Bill Rogers
Mike Udall	Hugh Ross
Tow Truck Driver	Domenick Lombardozzi
Airport Bartender	Arnetia Walker
Yankee Fan in Bar	Larry Joshua

and Detroit Tigers: Greer Barnes (Mickey Hart), Scott Bream (Brian Whitt), Jose Mota (Jose Garcia), Earl Johnson (Marcus Ransom), Chris Lemonis (Lee Giordano), Jesse Ibarra (Dennis Skinner), Pedro Swann (Juan Vasquez), Michael Rivera (Jimmy Pena), David Eiland (Relief Pitcher), Joe Lisi (Pete), Jim Colborn (3rd Base Coach), Paul Bradshaw (Tiger Pitching Coach), Gene Kirley (Tiger Bench Coach), Chris Fischer, Jonathan Marc McDonnell, Barry Bradford, Kevin Craig West, Wes Said Drake, Luis Moro (Tiger Bench); New York Yankees: Michael Papajohn (Sam Tuttle), John Darjean, Jr. (Jonathan Warble), Donzell McDonald (Lenny Howell), Scott Pose (Matt Crane), Vick Brown (Jesus Cabrillo), Chris Ashby (Nardini), Bill Masse (Mike Robinson), Mike Buddie (Jack Spellman), Eric Knowles (Ted Franklin), Ricky Ledee (Ruiz), Juan Nieves (Francisco Delgado), Augie Garrido (Yankee Manager), Rick Reed (Home Plate Umpire), Rich Garcia (1st Base Umpire), Jerry Crawford (2nd Base Umpire), Robert Leo Shepard (Yankee Stadium Announcer), Eddie Layton (Yankee Stadium Organist), Robinson Frank Adu (Locker Room Attendant); T. Sean Ferguson, Victor Colicchio, David Mucci (Hecklers), Jacob Reynolds (Wheeler's Nephew), Maurice Shrog (Yankee Stadium Usher), Karen Williams (Kisha Birch), Tracy Middendorf (Blond Player's Wife), William Newman (Fitch), P.J. Barry (Waldorf Doorman), Frank Girardeau (Waldorf Bellhop), Caterina Zapponi (Waldorf Singer), Monty Alexander (Waldorf Pianist), Daniel Dae Kim (ER Doctor), Judith Drake (ER Nurse), Bill Vincent (X-Ray Technician), Billy V. Costner (Billy's Father), Sharon Rae Costner (Billy's Mother), Mark Thomason (Billy's Father—Early Years), Laura Cayouette (Masseuse), Christopher Cousins (Ian), Ted Raimi, Michael Emerson (Gallery Doormen), Shelly Desai (Taxi Driver), Lucinda Faraldo (Airline Ticket Agent), Ed Morgan (Man at Cafe), Brian Donald Hickey, Tracy Perry (Autograph Seekers)

While pitching his final game as a player for the Detroit Tigers, Billy Chapel looks back on how his relationship with Jane Aubrey began, and what led her to walk out on him.

©Universal Studios

John C. Reilly, Kevin Costner

Kevin Costner

103

SUGAR TOWN

(OCTOBER) Producer, Daniel Hassid; Directors/Screenplay, Allison Anders, Kurt Voss; Co-Producers, Nancy Griffin, Nanda Rao; Photography, Kristian Bernier; Designer, Alyssa Coppelman; Editor, Chris Figler; Costumes, Anita Cabada; Music, Larry Klein; a Film Four presentation of a Jack n' Zack production; Dolby; Fotokem color; Rated R; 92 minutes; Release date: September 17, 1999

CAST

Rick	Richmond Arquette
Eva	Rosanna Arquette
Nerve	Vincent Berry
Rocio	Lumi Cavazos
Jane	Beverly D'Angelo
Nick	Michael Des Barres
Carl	John Doe
Gwen	Jade Gordon
Kate	Lucinda Jenney
Jonesy	Martin Kemp
Burt	Larry Klein
Liz	Ally Sheedy
Clive	John Taylor
In Utero Baby	Marion Moseley
Viole	Veronica Nommenson
Rose	Elena Nommenson
Daisy	Amelia Nommenson
Masseuse	Nicholas Walker
Kevin	Jeff McDonald
Groupies	Catherine Munro, Kristina Hayes, Alyse Pozzo
Journalist	Michael Rodgers
Nerve's Mom	Paige Dylan
Maggie	Polly Platt
Aaron	Chris Mulkey
Band Members	Simon Bonney, Kelly Jones
Maya	Antonia Bogdanovich
Alex	Kia Lennox
Monte	Kadu Lennox
Autograph Girl	Bijou Phillips
Tracy	Ursula Brooks
Groupie #4	Lacey Rodine
Karate Instructor	Phillip Tan

A look at the lives of some show business professionals whose heyday has passed them by, specifically the members of a once-hot rock band who are trying desperately to find a backer for their new recording.

© October Films

Ally Sheedy, Rosanna Arquette

Rosanna Arquette, John Taylor

Beverly D'Angelo, Michael Des Barres

Michael Des Barres, John Taylor, Larry Klein, Martin Kemp

Bob Balaban, Armin Mueller-Stahl, Robin Williams

Robin Williams, Hannah Taylor Gordon

JAKOB THE LIAR

(**COLUMBIA**) Producers, Marsha Garces Williams, Steven Haft; Executive Producer, Robin Williams; Director, Peter Kassovitz; Screenplay, Peter Kassovitz, Didier Decoin; Based on the book by Jurek Becker; Photography, Elemér Ragályi; Designer, Luciana Arrighi; Editor, Claire Simpson; Costumes, Wieslawa Starska; Co-Producer, Nick Gillott; Music, Edward Shearmur; Casting, Billy Hopkins, Suzanne Smith, Kerry Barden; a Blue Wolf productions with Kasso Inc. presentation; Dolby; Deluxe color; Rated PG-13;   114 minutes; Release date: September 24, 1999

CAST

Jakob	Robin Williams
Lina	Hannah Taylor Gordon
Lina's Mother	Eva Igo
Lina's Father	Istvan Balint
Preuss	Justus von Dohnanyi
Hooker	Kathleen Gati
Kowalsky	Bob Balaban
Frankfurter	Alan Arkin
Avron	Michael Jeter
Fajngold	Mark Margolis
Samuel	Janos Gosztonyi
Mischa	Liev Schreiber
Kirschbaum	Armin Mueller-Stahl
The Whistler	Adam Rajhona
Peg-Leg	Antal Leisen
Herschel	Mathieu Kassovitz
Roman	Peter Rudolf
Young German	Jan Becker
Nathan	Zanos Kulka
Blumenthal	Gregg Bello
Rosa	Nina Siemaszko

and Grazyna Barszczewska (Mrs. Frankfurter), Judit Sagi (Mrs. Avron), Ilona Psota (Grandmother), Agi Margitai (Miss Esther), and Ivan Darvas (Hardtloff), Laszlo Borbely (Doctor), Zolí Anders (Meyer), Miroslaw Zbrojewicz, György Szkladányi (SS Oficers), Jozef Mika (Soldier), Zofia Saretok (Neighbor), Michael Mehlmann (Escaping Man), Mirtill Micheller, Orsolya Pflum, Beatrix Bisztricsan (3 Lady Singers)

To help build morale in a Nazi-occupied Jewish ghetto in Poland, Jakob pretends he has access to a radio and begins making up fictious news about the Allies' victorious advances against the Nazis. Remake of the 1974 German film Jacob the Liar, which was released in the U.S. in 1977 by Macmillan Films, and also featured Armin Mueller-Stahl.

© Columbia Pictures Industries Inc.

Robin Williams

Michael Jeter (back to camera), Armin Mueller-Stahl, Alan Arkin

Ashley Judd, Tommy Lee Jones

Tommy Lee Jones

Bruce Greenwood, Ashley Judd

Benjamin Weir, Annabeth Gish, Ashley Judd

DOUBLE JEOPARDY

(**PARAMOUNT**) Producer, Leonard Goldberg; Director, Bruce Beresford; Screenplay, David Weisberg, Douglas S. Cook; Co-Producer, Richard Luke Rothschild; Photography, Peter James; Editor, Mark Warner; Designer, Howard Cummings; Music, Normand Corbeil; Costumes, Rudy Dillon, Linda Bass; Casting, Deborah Aquila, Sarah Halley Finn; a Leonard Goldberg production; Dolby; Panavision; Deluxe color; Rated R; 105 minutes; Release date: September 24, 1999

CAST

Travis Lehman	Tommy Lee Jones
Libby Parsons	Ashley Judd
Nick Parsons	Bruce Greenwood
Angie	Annabeth Gish
Margaret Skolowski	Roma Maffia
Evelyn Lake	Davenia McFadden
Matty, Age 4	Benjamin Weir
Bobby	Jay Brazeau
Rudy	John MacLaren
Warren	Edward Evanko

and Bruce Campbell (Bartender at Party), Brennan Elliott (Yuppie Man), Angela Schneider (Yuppie Girl), Michael Gaston (Cutter), Gillian Barber (Rebecca Tingely), Tom McBeath (Coast Guard Officer), David Jacox (Deputy Ben), Betsy Brantley (Prosecutor), Woody Jeffreys (Watch Stander), French Tickner (Judge), Maria Bitamba (Prisoner at Phone), Ben Bodé (Karl Carruthers), Robin J. Kelley (Parole Board Member), Dana Owen Still (Drug Counselor), Gabrielle Rose (Georgia), Daniel LaPaine (Handsome Internet Expert), Maria R. Herrera (Libby's Roommate), Babz Chula (Ruby), Enuka Okuma (Parolee), Captain Peter Kimmerly (Ferry Captain), George Gordon (Emergency Room Doctor), David Fredericks (Trucker), Anna Hagan (Libby's Mother), Fulvio Cecere (BMW Salesman), Tracy Vilar (Orbe), Addison Ridge (Boy at Door), Crystal Verge (Housewife), Joy Coghill (Neighbor in Garden), Bernard Cuffling (Gallery Owner), Barth C. Phillips, Reginald Ringo, Jerome Alexander, George Hunter (Singers in Jackson Square), Barth C. Phillips, Reginald Ringo, Jerome Alexander, George Hunter (Singers in Jackson Square), Roger R. Cross (Hotel Manager), Pamela Perry (Mrs. Kritch), Tim McDermott (Bell Hop), Keegan Tracy (Boutique Saleswoman), Dave Hager (Mangold), Jason Douglas (Detective), Jeannie Grelier Church (Scarf Woman), Austin B. Church (Scarf Woman's Husband), Michael Shannon Jenkins (Doorman), Joe Simon (Singer at Auction), Charlie Detraz (Auctioneer), Susan LeCourt-Barbe, Ramona Tyler, C. Barrett Downing (Bidders), Michelle Stafford (Suzanne Monroe), Greg Di Leo, Lance Spellerberg (Bachelors at Auction), George Touliatos (New Orleans Bartender), Deryl Hayes (New Orleans Cop), Brent Woolsey (Mounted Cop), Eliza Murbach (Co-ed with Umbrella), Roland "Bob" Harris (Preacher), George Montgomery II (Matty Pretender), Lossen Chambers (Lucy), Harold Evans (New Orleans Cabbie), Thomas M. Mathews, Gordon Starling, Jr. (Coaches), Spencer Treat Clark (Matty, Age 11)

Libby Parsons, unjustly sent to prison for the murder of her husband, finds out that not only is her spouse still alive but had set her up to take the fall for the crime, prompting Libby to seek revenge once she is released.

© Paramount Pictures

MUMFORD

(TOUCHSTONE) Producers, Charles Okun, Lawrence Kasdan; Director/Screenplay, Lawrence Kasdan; Co-Producers, Steve Dunn, Linda Goldstein Knowlton, Jon Hutman; Photography, Ericson Core; Designer, Jon Hutman; Editors, Carol Littleton, William Steinkamp; Costumes, Colleen Atwood; Music, James Newton Howard; Casting, Jennifer Shull; a Kasdan Pictures production; Distributed by Buena Vista Pictures; Dolby; Super 35 Widescreen; Deluxe color; Rated R; 112 minutes; Release date: September 24, 1999

Loren Dean, Jason Lee

CAST

Dr. Mumford	Loren Dean
Sofie Crisp	Hope Davis
Skip Skipperton	Jason Lee
Lily	Alfre Woodard
Althea Brockett	Mary McDonnell
Henry Follett	Pruitt Taylor Vince
Nessa Watkins	Zooey Deschanel
Lionel Dillard	Martin Short
Dr. Ernest Delbanco	David Paymer
Dr. Phyllis Sheeler	Jane Adams
Mrs. Crisp	Dana Ivey
Mr. Crisp	Kevin Tighe
Jeremy Brockett	Ted Danson
Martin Brockett	Jason Ritter
Katie Brockett	Elisabeth Moss
Gregory	Kirk Fox
Ben Crisp	Scott N. Stevens
Himself	Robert Stack

and Eddie Allen (Gilroy), Rick Dial (Correctional Officer), Joy Carlin (Judge Otto), Helene Cardona (Candy), Priscilla Barnes (Landlady), Kelly Monaco (Landlady's Daughter), Steven Sennett (Young Pharmacist), Amanda Carlin(Mumford's Sister), Randall King (Revenue Officer McLure), Arell Blanton (Brother Timothy), Eddie McClintock (Unsolved Mumford), Molly Schaffer (Attractive Date), Simon Helberg (College Roommate), Lucie Laurier (Pretty Coed), Sam Sako (Edmond Warris), Penny Safranek (Mrs. Warris), David Doty (Samuel Gorbeck), Pamela Paulshock (Sutter's Young Wife), Kathryn Howell (Co-Worker, IRS), Sulo Williams (Gas Station Co-Worker), Simone Kerrick (Lionel's Teacher), Barbara E. Tuss (Elizabeth), Ronald B. Morefield (Factory Co-Worker), Dick Mallon (Dino), Gea Carr (Jennifer), Chase Allen, Bryan Close, Jim Hiser (Toughs), Tim Hayes (Prosecutor), Roger Oyama (Revenue Officer), Naomi Sample (Janitor), Joe Peer (Garbage Co-Worker), Ron Kaell (Pest Control Co-Worker), T.J. Blair (Irate Taxpayer), Holt McCallany (Newcomer), Charles Okun (Charlie)

Hope Davis, Loren Dean

Dr. Mumford proves to be a most helpful therapist for the troubled citizens of the small town of Mumford, despite the fact that secretly he is not even licensed to do the job.

© Touchstone Pictures

Alfre Woodard, Loren Dean

Martin Short, Loren Dean

Sarah Polley, Stephen Rea

GUINEVERE

(**MIRAMAX**) Producers, Jonathan King, Brad Weston; Executive Producers, Avi Lerner, Danny Dimbort, Trevor Short, Bob Weinstein, Harvey Weinstein, Beau Flynn, Stefan Simchowitz, John Thompson, Boaz Davidson; Director/Screenplay, Audrey Wells; Line Producer, Tani Cohen; Photography, Charles Minsky; Editor, Dody Dorn; Costumes, Genevieve Tyrrell; Music, Christophe Beck; Casting, Linda Lowy; a Jonathan King and Bandeira Entertainment production, presented in association with Millennium Films; Dolby; CFI color; Rated R; 104 minutes; Release date: September 24, 1999

CAST

Harper Sloane	Sarah Polley
Cornelius "Connie" Fitzpatrick	Stephen Rea
Patty	Carrie Preston
Zack	Tracy Letts
Billie	Gina Gershon
Deborah Sloane	Jean Smart
Susan	Emily Procter
Leslie	Sharon McNight
Ed	Gedde Watanabe
Jay	Carlton Wilborn
Cindy	Sandra Oh
Alan Sloane	Francis Guinan
Gary	Oded Gross
April	Grace Una
Linda	Jasmine Guy
Denise (Jazz Singer)	Michelle Aurthor
French Diva	Dorit Sauer
Toilet Paper Woman	Rose Mallett
Pretty Woman	Kim Flowers
Transsexual	Scott Kaske
Walter	Paul Dooley
Jeremy	Trevor Edmond
Cop	Danny Kovaks

and Brian Frank, Debra Engle (Wedding Guests), Kevin Breif (Dentist), Martin Yu (Modern Boyfriend), Paulina Sahagan (Mexican Seamstress), Kai Ephron (Positano's Regular), Alexandra Hilden (Angelic Girl)

On the brink of attending Harvard Law School, young Harper Sloane finds her life plans disrupted when she unexpectedly falls in love with photographer Cornelius Fitzpatrick, who is thirty years her senior.

© Miramax Films

Jean Smart

Stephen Rea, Sarah Polley

Sarah Polley, Gina Gershon

HAPPY, TEXAS

(**MIRAMAX**) Producers, Mark Illsley, Rick Montgomery, Ed Stone; Executive Producer, Jason Clark; Director, Mark Illsley; Screenplay, Ed Stone, Mark Illsley, Phil Reeves; Co-Producer, Glenn S. Gainor; Photography, Bruce Douglas Johnson; Designer, Maurin Scarlata; Editor, Norman Buckley; Music, Peter Harris; Music Supervisors, Emily Kaye, Alex Patsavas; Costumes, Julia Schklair; Choreographer, Kelly Devine; Casting, Joe Garcia; an Illsley/Stone Production, presented in association with Marked Entertainment; Dolby; Fotokem color; Rated PG-13; 99 minutes; Release date: October 1, 1999

CAST

Harry Sawyer	Jeremy Northam
Wayne Wayne Wayne Jr.	Steve Zahn
Sheriff Chappy Dent	William H. Macy
Joe McClintock	Ally Walker
Ms. Schaefer	Illeana Douglas
Bob Maslow	M.C. Gainey
Nalhober	Ron Perlman
Mrs. Bromley	Mo Gaffney
The Judge	Paul Dooley
Madison	Jillian Berard
Jency	Scarlett Pomers
Other Happy Girls	Melissa Arnold, Cassie Silva, Tiffany Takara
David	Tim Bagley
Steven	Michael Hitchcock
Alton	Ed Stone
Ely	Rance Howard
Bully Boy	Derek Montgomery
Pageant Judge	Kiva Lawrence
"Little Light Girl"	Carly Fink
Varnel	David Shackelford
Guard	Kim Story

A pair of escaped cons find themselves in the sleepy town of Happy, Texas, where they are forced to pose as a pair of gay pageant coordinators for a group of little girls.

© Miramax Films

Illeana Douglas, Steve Zahn

William H. Macy

Ally Walker, Jeremy Northam

Steve Zahn

THREE KINGS

(**WARNER BROS.**) Producers, Charles Roven, Paul Junger Witt, Edward L. McDonnell; Executive Producers, Gregory Goodman, Kelley Smith-Wait, Bruce Berman; Director/Screenplay, David O. Russell; Story, John Ridley; Co-Producers, Douglas Segal, Kim Roth; Photography, Newton Thomas Sigel; Editor, Robert K. Lambert; Music, Carter Burwell; Designer, Catherine Hardwicke; Costumes, Kym Barrett; 2nd Unit/Stunts, Dan Bradley; Casting, Mary Vernieu, Anne McCarthy; Presented in association with Village Roadshow Pictures/Village-A.M. Film Partnership of a Coast Ridge Films/Atlas Entertainment production; Dolby; Super 35 Widescreen; Technicolor; Rated R; 115 minutes; Release date: October 1, 1999

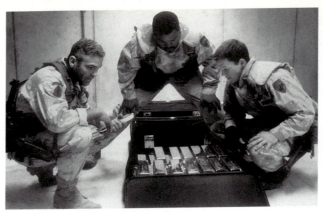

George Clooney, Ice Cube, Mark Wahlberg

CAST

Archie Gates	George Clooney
Troy Barlow	Mark Wahlberg
Chief Elgin	Ice Cube
Conrad Vig	Spike Jonze
Adriana Cruz	Nora Dunn
Walter Wogaman	Jamie Kennedy
Col. Horn	Mykelti Williamson
Amir Abdullah	Cliff Curtis
Capt. Sa'id	Said Taghmaoui
Cathy Daitch	Judy Greer
Debbie Barlow	Liz Stauber
Capt. Van Meter	Holt McCallany
Teebaux	Christopher Lohr
Paco	Jon Sklaroff
Amir's Wife	Marsha Horan
Amir's Daughter	Alia Shawkat
Hairdressing Twins	Jabir Algarawi, Ghanem Algarawi
Western Dressed Village Woman	Bonnie Afsary
Traditional Village Woman	Jacqueline Abi-Ad
Deserter Leader	Fadil Al-Badri
Kaied	Al No-Omani
Iraqi Tank Major	Sayed Badreya
Iraqi Trooper Carrier Major	Magdi Rashwan
Iraqi First Kill Soldier	Alex Dodd
Berm. Soldier/Truck Driver	Larry "Tank" Jones
Berm. Soldiers	Patrick O'Neal Jones, Shawn Pilot, Bret Bassett
Soldier	Jim Gaffigan
Camp Soldiers/Truck Drivers	Al Whiting, Brian Patterson
Camp Soldiers	Scott Dillon, Kwesi Okai Hazel, Mark Rhodes, Randy W. McCoy, Joseph Richard Romanov, Scott Pearce
Civil Affairs Company Clerk	Gary Parker
Saudi Translator	Haidar Alatowa
Iraqi Soldier with Map	Salah Salea
Dead Iraqi Soldier	Doug Jones
Iraqi Civilian Mother with Baby	Farinaz Farrokh
Bunker 1—Friendly Iraqis	Omar "Freefly" Alhegelan, Hassan Allawati
Pleading Civilian Woman	Sara Aziz
Iraqi Civilian Man	A. Halim Mostafa
Bunker 2 Store Room Captain	Al Mustafa
Iraqi Interrogation Sergeant	Anthony Batarse
Bunker 2 Iraqi Rifle Loader	Mohamad Al-Jalahma
Iraqi Soldier	Mohammed Sharafi
Bunker 2 Store Room Guard	Hillel Michael Shamam
Iraqi Radio Operator	Joey Naber
Black Robe Leader	Basim Ridha

Mark Wahlberg, George Clooney

and Peter Macdissi, Tony Shawkat, Joseph Abi-Ad (Oasis Bunker Iraqi Republican Guards), Fahd Al-Ujaimy, Derick Qaqish (Oasis Bunker—Troy's Interrogation Guards), Hassan Bach-Agha Fadi Sitto (Oasis Bunker—Troy's Republican), Ali Alkind, Abdullah Al-Dawalem, Rick Mendoza (Deserters), Jassim Al-Khazraji (Oasis Bunker—Republican Roof Guard), Haider Alkindi, Kalid Mustrafa, Ghazwyn Ramiawi, Raad Thomasian, Wessam Saleh (Oasis Bunker—Fleeing Republican Guards), Jay Giannone (Oasis Bunker Republican), Sam Hassan (Oasis Bunker Republican Guard/Sniper), Brian Bosworth (Action Star), Donte Delila, Dylan Brown (Iraqi Children)

At the close of the Persian Gulf war, a group of American soldiers venture into Iraqi territory to locate a stash of Kuwaiti gold bullion stolen by the Iraqi army, and find themselves facing the dangerous political situation at hand.

George Clooney, Spike Jonze, Mark Wahlberg

George Clooney, Mark Wahlberg, Ice Cube, Spike Jonze

Fadil Al-Badri, Ice Cube, George Clooney, Cliff Curtis

THE ADVENTURES OF ELMO IN GROUCHLAND

(COLUMBIA) Producers, Alex Rockwell, Marjorie Kalins; Executive Producers, Brian Henson, Stephanie Allain, Martin G. Baker; Director, Gary Halvorson; Screenplay, Mitchell Kriegman, Joseph Mazzarino; Story, Mitchell Kriegman; Photography, Alan Caso; Designer, Alan Cassie; Music, John Debney; Editor, Alan Baumgarten; Co-Producers, Kevin Clash, Timothy M. Bourne; Costumes, Polly Smith; Puppeteer Captain, Kevin Clash; a Children's Television Workshop production; Dolby; Deluxe color; Rated G; 77 minutes; Release date: October 1, 1999

Elmo, Zoe

CAST

Elmo/Pestie/Grouch Jailer/Grouch Cab Driver	Kevin Clash
Huxley	Mandy Patinkin
Queen of Trash	Vanessa Williams
Maria	Sonia Manzano
Gordon	Roscoe Orman
Zoe/Pestie/Prairie Dawn	Fran Brill
Grizzy/Pestie	Stephanie D'Abruzzo
Humongous Chicken	Dave Goelz
Bug	Joseph Mazzarino
Count/Pestie/Grouch Mayor/Grouch Cop	Jerry Nelson
Rosita	Carmen Osbahr
Telly/Pestie	Martin P. Robinson
Baby Bear/Caterpillar/Pestie/ Collander Stenchman/Ice Cream Customer	David Rudman
Big Bird/Oscar	Caroll Spinney
Ernie/Stuckweed/Football Stenchman/ Ice Cream Vendor/Parrot	Steve Whitmire
Bert/Grover/Cookie Monster	Franz Oz
Gina	Alison Bartlett-O'Reilly
Ruthie	Ruth Buzzi
Luis	Emilio Delgado
Susan	Loretta Long
Bob	Bob McGrath

and Drew Allison, Bill Barretta, John Boone, R. Lee Bryan, Leslie Carrera, Lisa Consolo, Jodi Eichelberger, Rowell Gormon, Mary Harrison, Rob Killen, Bruce Lanoil, Bob Lynch, Ed May, Tim Parati, Annie Peterle, Andy Stone, Lisa Sturz, Kirk Thatcher, Matt Vogel, Matt Yates (Additional Muppet Performers)

While trying to retrieve his beloved blanket from a trash can, Elmo finds himself sucked into Grouchland, the most disgusting place on earth.

© Jim Henson Pictures, Inc.

Adrian Grenier, Melissa Joan Hart

Bug, Mandy Patinkin

DRIVE ME CRAZY

(20TH CENTURY FOX) formerly *Next to You*; Producer, Amy Robinson; Director, John Schultz; Screenplay, Rob Thomas; Based on the novel *How I Created My Perfect Prom Date* by Todd Strasser; Photography, Kees van Oostrum; Designer, Aaron Osborne; Editor, John Pace; Costumes, Genevieve Tyrrell; Music, Greg Kendall; Music Supervisors, Tom Wolfe, Manish Raval; Casting, Sheila Jaffe, Georgianne Walken; an Amy Robinson production; Dolby; Deluxe color; Rated PG-13; 91 minutes; Release date: October 1, 1999

CAST

Nicole Maris	Melissa Joan Hart
Chase Hammond	Adrian Grenier
Mr. Maris	Stephen Collins
Mr. Rope	Mark Metcalf
Mr. Hammond	William Converse-Roberts
Mrs. Maris	Faye Grant
Alicia	Susan May Pratt
Ray Neeley	Kris Park

and Ali Larter (Dulcie), Mark Webber (Dave), Gabriel Carpenter (Brad), Lourdes Benedicto (Chloe Frost), Keri Lynn Pratt (Dee Vine), Natasha Pearce (Sue), Derrick Shore (Tom), Jordan Bridges (Eddie Lampell), Keram Malicki-Sanchez (Rupert), Andrew Roach (Big Fred), Joey Lopez (Student TV Director), Jessica Frandsen (Drena), Kristy Wu (Liz), Lee Holmes (Joshua), Jacque Gray (Kathy), Ivey Lloyd (Pretty Girl), Terry Cain (Diner Waitress), Lauren Renei Boyer, Elizabeth Hart (Vixens), Doug McMillan (Mr. Webb), Mary A. Daniel (Faculty Sponsor), Holly Swain (Nordic Blonde), Maya Ford, Torrance Castellano, Allsion Robertson, Brett Anderson (Electrocutes), Marc Valasquez, Brendon Te, Tone Te, Darby Bailey (Pit Band)

Nicole and Chase, neighbors who are worlds apart in the high school social scheme, plan to attend a school dance together with the purpose of reuniting Chase with his old girlfriend.

© Twentieth Century Fox

MYSTERY, ALASKA

(HOLLYWOOD) Producers, David E. Kelley, Howard Baldwin; Executive Producer, Dan Kolsrud; Director, Jay Roach; Screenplay, David E. Kelley, Sean O'Byrne; Photography, Peter Deming; Editor, Jon Poll; Costumes, Deena Appel; Music, Carter Burwell; Co-Producers, Karen Baldwin, Richard Cohen, Jack L. Gilardi, Jr.; Designer, Rusty Smith; Casting, Linda Lowy; a Baldwin/Cohen-Rocking Chair production; Dolby; Panavision; Technicolor; Rated R; 118 minutes; Release date: October 1, 1999

CAST

John Biebe	Russell Crowe
Charles Danner	Hank Azaria
Donna Biebe	Mary McCormack
Judge Walter Burns	Burt Reynolds
Mayor Scott Pitcher	Colm Meaney
Mary Jane Pitcher	Lolita Davidovich
Bailey Pruitt	Maury Chaykin
"Skank" Marden	Ron Eldard
Stevie Weeks	Ryan Northcott
Connor Banks	Michael Buie
"Tree" Lane	Kevin Durand
"Birdie" Burns	Scott Grimes
Bobby Michan	Jason Gray-Stanford
Kevin Holt	Brent Strait
Ben Winetka	Leroy Peltier
Galin Winetka	Adam Beach
"Tinker" Connolly	Cameron Bancroft

and Michael McKean (Mr. Walsh), Rachel Wilson (Marla Burns), Beth Littleford (Janice Pettiboe), Megyn Price (Sarah Heinz), Judith Ivey (Joanne Burns), Stephen Hair (Jack Danby), Joshua Silberg (Michael Biebe), Regan Sean O'Byrne MacElwain (Joey Biebe), Terry David Mulligan (Dr. Henry Savage), Rod Jarvis (Referee), Lindsay Jarvis (Linesman), Mike Myers (Donnie Shulzhoffer), Jim Fox, Doug McLeod, Phil Esposito, Little Richard, Steve Levy, Barry Melrose (Themselves), Betty Linde (Mirabelle Houle), Randall Arney (TV Director), Gary Murdoch (Bodyguard), Genevieve Fraser (Student Charlotte), Taylor Smith (Student Tommy), Matt Clarke (Joe), Scott Olynek (Bob), Zane Snow (Jeff), Joe Turvey (Walt), Brenda Shuttleworth (Deputy Betty Fisher), Michael Auger (Gordon Herrod), Shaun Johnston (D.A. Dollof), Karen Gartner (Jury Foreman), Bruce Nozick (NHL Lawyer), Gerry Becker (Players' Union Lawyer), L. Scott Caldwell (Judge McGibbons), Warren Beckett, Mike Church, Beau Evans, Ryan Haggins, Fred Hettle, Travis Hulse, Todd Karman, Dale Kushner, Marty Lacroix, Dave Lovsin, George Maniotakis, Darren Morrison, Dean Payne, Jason Peipmann, Justin Sather, Jason Smith, Travis Stephenson, Brad Turner, Grant Van Laar, Jim Wheatcroft, Cory Wills, Jason Wist (Hockey Players)

The tiny, snowbound town of Mystery, Alaska, suddenly finds itself in the public eye when the citizens accept the challenge to play their non-professional team of hockey players against the New York Rangers.

© Hollywood Picture Company

Michael Buie, Ryan Northcott, Russell Crowe, Kevin Durand

Russell Crowe, Burt Reynolds

Ron Eldard, Russell Crowe, Michael Buie

Lolita Davidovich, Colm Meaney, Russell Crowe, Mary McCormack

Chloë Sevigny, Hilary Swank

Peter Sarsgaard, Hilary Swank, Brendan Sexton III

BOYS DON'T CRY

(**FOX SEARCHLIGHT**) Producers, Jeffrey Sharp, John Hart, Eva Kolodner, Christine Vachon; Executive Producers, Pamela Koffler, Jonathan Sehring, Caroline Kaplan, John Sloss; Director, Kimberly Peirce; Screenplay, Kimberly Peirce, Andy Bienen; Photography, Jim Denault; Designer, Michael Shaw; Costumes, Victoria Farrell; Editors, Lee Percy, Tracy Granger; Music, Nathan Larsen; Co-Producer, Morton Swinsky; Casting, Billy Hopkins, Suzanne Smith, Kerry Barden, Jennifer McNamara; a Killer Films/Hart-Sharp production; Presented in association with the Independent Film Channel; Dolby; Deluxe color; Rated R; 116 minutes; Release date: October 8, 1999

CAST

Brandon Teena (Teena Brandon)	Hilary Swank
Lana Tisdal	Chloë Sevigny
John Lotter	Peter Sarsgaard
Tom Nissen	Brendan Sexton III
Candace	Alicia Goranson
Kate	Alison Folland
Lana's Mom	Jeannetta Arnette
Brian	Rob Campbell
Lonny	Matt McGrath
Nicole	Cheyenne Rushing
Trucker	Robert Prentiss
Kwik Stop Cashier	Josh Ridgway
Trucker at Kwik Stop	Craig Erickson
April	Stephanie Sechrist
Judge	Jerry Haynes
Sheriff	Lou Perryman
Pam	Lisa Wilson
Sam Phillips	Jackson Kane
Tom	Joseph Gibson
Nerdy Teen	Michael Tripp
Girl in Car	Shana McClendon
Nurse	Libby Villari
Dave (Deputy)	Paige Carl Griggs
Clerk	Gail Cronauer

The true story of how Teena Brandon passed herself off as a young man, Brandon Teena, in a small Nebraska town, a deception that eventually led to tragedy.

1999 Academy Award-winner for Best Actress (Hilary Swank). This film received an additional Oscar nomination for supporting actress (Chloë Sevigny).

© Fox Searchlight Pictures

Hilary Swank

Chloë Sevigny

Peter Sarsgaard, Alison Folland, Brendan Sexton III, Hilary Swank, Alicia Goranson, Chloë Sevigny

Harrison Ford, Kristin Scott Thomas

Harrison Ford, Kristin Scott Thomas

RANDOM HEARTS

(**COLUMBIA**) Producers, Sydney Pollack, Marykay Powell; Executive Producers, Ronald L. Schwary, Warren Adler; Director, Sydney Pollack; Screenplay, Kurt Luedtke; Adapted by Darryl Ponicsan from the novel by Warren Adler; Photography, Philippe Rousselot; Designer, Barbara Ling; Editor, William Steinkamp; Music, Dave Grusin; Costumes, Bernie Pollack; Ms. Thomas' Clothing Designer, Ann Roth; Casting, David Rubin; a Rastar/Mirage Enterprises production; Dolby; Deluxe color; Rated R; 131 minutes; Release date: October 8, 1999

CAST

Dutch Van Den Broeck	Harrison Ford
Kay Chandler	Kristin Scott Thomas
Alcee	Charles S. Dutton
Wendy Judd	Bonnie Hunt
Detective George Beaufort	Dennis Haysbert
Carl Broman	Sydney Pollack
Truman Trainor	Richard Jenkins
Dick Montoya	Paul Guilfoyle
Peyton Van Den Broeck	Susanna Thompson
Cullen Chandler	Peter Coyote
Richard Judd	Dylan Baker
Phyllis Bonaparte	Lynne Thigpen
Molly Roll	Susan Floyd
Marvin	Bill Cobbs
Jessica Chandler	Kate Mara
Shyla Mumford	Ariana Thomas
Silvio Coya	Nelson Landrieu
Sarah	Brooke Smith
Laurie	Christina Chang
Susan	Michelle Hurd
Mary Claire Clark	Reiko Aylesworth
Officer Clayton Williams	Ray Anthony Thomas
Janice	Edie Falco
Nea	S. Epatha Merkerson
David Dotson	Jack Gilpin
Steven Driker	Mark Zeisler
Peyton's Father	John Carter
Cassie	Davenia McFadden
Maureen	Barbara Gulan
Alice Beaufort	Molly Price
Tad Baker	Brian Schwary
Susan's Customer	Priscilla Shanks
Nurse Nancy	Lynette Du Pre
Peter Suchet	Ken Kay
Claire Suchet	Susan Hatfield
Sally Gabriel	Jenna Stern
Dick Shulte	Tom McCarthy
Joe Parella	Jan Austell

and Aasif Mandvi (Electronics Store Salesman), Todd Malta (Supermarket Stockboy), Jordan Lage (Assistant Prosecutor), Judith Knight Young (Clara), Fenton Lawless (Officer Lawrence), Deirdre Lovejoy (Officer Isabel), Terry Serpico (Evidence Technician), Liam Craig (Waiter at DC Restaurant), C.S. Lee (Luncheonette Counterman), Ellen Foley (Young Woman at Fundraiser), Judy Jamison, Steven Mark Friedman, Becky Veduccio (TV Reporters at Hospital), Susan Allenback (Airline Spokesperson), Don Scott, Dina Napoli, Tracey Neale (News Anchors), Will Thomas (Field Reporter), Andy Fowle (Orderly), Robert Zajonc (Helicopter Pilot—Camera), Alan Purwin (Helicopter Pilot—TV News), Roy R. Taylor, Jr. (Helicopter Pilot—WJZ Pilot)

After their respective spouses are killed in an airline crash, internal affairs investigator Dutch Van Den Broeck and congresswoman Kay Chandler discover that their marital partners had been having an affair, a revelation that bonds the two survivors.

©Columbia Pictures Industries, Inc.

Charles S. Dutton, Harrison Ford

Terence Stamp

Peter Fonda

THE LIMEY

(**ARTISAN ENTERTAINMENT**) Producers, Scott Kramer, John Hardy; Director, Steven Soderbergh; Screenplay, Lem Dobbs; Photography, Ed Lachman; Editor, Sarah Flack; Designer, Gary Frutkoff; Music, Cliff Martinez; Costumes, Louise Frogley; Casting, Debra Zane; Dolby; CFI Color; Rated R; 89 minutes; Release date: October 8, 1999

CAST

Wilson	Terence Stamp
Valentine	Peter Fonda
Elaine	Lesley Ann Warren
Ed	Luis Guzman
Adhara	Amelia Heinle
Avery	Barry Newman
Stacy	Nicky Katt
Uncle John	Joe Dallesandro
Jennifer	Melissa George
Warehouse Foreman	William Lucking
Tom	Matthew Kimbrough
Rick	John Robotham
Larry	Steve Heinze
Lady on Plane	Nancy Lenehan
Pool Hall Creep	Wayne Pe're'
DEA Guys	John Cothran, Jr., Ousan Elam, Dwayne McGee, Brian Bennet
Gordon	Allan Graf
Warehouse Thugs	Carl Ciarflio, George Ruge, Lincoln Simonds
Warehouse Sweeper	Rainbow Borden
Young Jennifer	Michaela Gallo
Teen Gun Dealers	Jose Perez, Alex Perez
Excited Guy	Brandon Keener
Party Guys	Jim Jenkins, Mark Gerschwin
Valet	Johnny Sanchez
Child Actress	Brook Marie Bridges

Wilson, a British ex-con, arrives in Los Angeles to take revenge on those responsible for the death of his daughter. Terence Stamp plays the same character he did in director Ken Loach's 1967 film Poor Cow (released in the U.S. in 1968 by National General Pictures). Scenes from that film are used here.

Terence Stamp, Luis Guzman

Terence Stamp, Peter Fonda

SUPERSTAR

(**PARAMOUNT**) Producer, Lorne Michaels; Executive Producers, Robert K. Weiss, Susan Cavan; Director, Bruce McCulloch; Screenplay, Steven Wayne Koren; Based on a character created by Molly Shannon; Photography, Walt Lloyd; Designer, Gregory Keen; Editor, Malcolm Campbell; Co-Producers, Erin Fraser, Steven Wayne Koren; Costumes, Eydi Caines-Floyd; Music, Michael Gore; Music Supervisors, Elliot Lurie; Casting, Phyllis Huffman; a Lorne Michaels production; Presented in association with SNL Studios; Dolby; Panavision; Deluxe color; Rated PG-13; 82 minutes; Release date: October 8, 1999

Molly Shannon

CAST

Mary Katherine Gallagher	Molly Shannon
Sky Corrigan/Jesus	Will Ferrell
Evian	Elaine Hendrix
Slater	Harland Williams
Father Ritley	Mark McKinney
Grandma	Glynis Johns
Howard	Jason Blicker
Father John	Gerry Bamman
Helen	Emmy Laybourne
Maria	Jennifer Irwin
Thomas	Rob Stefaniuk
Autum	Natalie Radford
Summer	Karyn Dwyer
Dylan	Tom Green
Owen	Chuck Campbell
Mr. Feinstein	Jack Newman
Mrs. Corrigan	Donna Hanover
Freaky Freddy	Dan Redican
Crucifix Nun	Joan Massiah
Moira	Jean Howell
George	Frank Scott
Little Mary	Mallory Margel

and Deirdre McCloskey (Rosemary Gallagher), David Warrack (Father David), Aiden Kelly (Thornton Gallagher), Jane Moffat (Sister Eileen), Tracy Wright (Sister Ann), Robert Clarke (Little Boy Slater), Rick Campanelli, Ariel Manson-Wagner (Reporters), Boyd Banks (Weatherman), Sal Scozzari, Christina Gordon, Susie Dias, David Meinke (Special Ed Kids), Tina Campbell, Christine Nowland, Carol Mackereth (Cheerleaders), Michael McCloskey (Shamus O'Shea), Siobhan Donaghy (Una O'Shea), Blake Brooker (Man with Cake)

Hopelessly clumsy and insecure catholic school girl Mary Katherine Gallagher sets her mind on receiving her first kiss from popular Sky Corrigan, a goal she hopes to achieve by becoming a superstar.

Harland Williams

Will Ferrell

Bruce Willis, Michelle Pfeiffer

Michelle Pfeiffer, Rita Wilson

Red Buttons, Betty White, Bruce Willis, Michelle Pfeiffer,
Jayne Meadows, Tom Poston

Bruce Willis, Rob Reiner

THE STORY OF US

(**UNIVERSAL**) Producers, Rob Reiner, Jessie Nelson, Alan Zweibel; Executive Producers, Jeffrey Stott, Frank Capra III; Director, Rob Reiner; Screenplay, Alan Zweibel, Jessie Nelson; Photography, Michael Chapman; Designer, Lilly Kilvert; Editors, Robert Leighton, Alan Edward Bell; Costumes, Shay Cunliffe; Music, Eric Clapton, Marc Shaiman; Song: (I) Get Lost written and performed by Eric Clapton; a Castle Rock Entertainment presentation; Dolby; Panavision; Deluxe color; Rated R; 94 minutes; Release date: October 15, 1999

CAST

Katie Jordan	Michelle Pfeiffer
Ben Jordan	Bruce Willis
Rachel	Rita Wilson
Liza	Julie Hagerty
Dave	Paul Reiser
Marty	Tim Matheson
Stan	Rob Reiner
Erin Jordan	Colleen Rennison
Josh Jordan	Jake Sandvig
Arnie	Red Buttons
Dot	Jayne Meadows
Harry	Tom Poston
Lillian	Betty White
Dr. Rifkin	Ken Lerner
Dr. Hopkins	Victor Raider-Wexler
Dr. Siegler	Albert Hague
Josh at Two and a Half	Casey Boersma
Josh at Three	Dylan Boersma
Josh at Seven	Daniel Henson
Erin at Five	Tara Blanchard
Camper	Adam Zweibel
Uncle Shelly	Alan Zweibel
Andy Kirby	Bill Kirchenbauer
Joanie Kirby	Lucy Webb
Realtor	Jessie Nelson
Cooking Teacher	Tommy Tang

and Yaping (Stove Clerk), James J. Ritz (Maitre d'), Ryan Townsend, Michael Chapman (Waiters), Jordan Lund (Clergyman), Robert Alan Beuth (Obstetrician), Marci Rosenberg (Sonia), Art Evans (George), Renée Ridgeley (Sara), Matthew Moreno (Taxi Driver)

Facing a break-up, Katie and Ben Jordan look back on their fifteen-year marriage to examine the good and bad in their relationship and find out what went wrong.

© CR FIlms, LLC

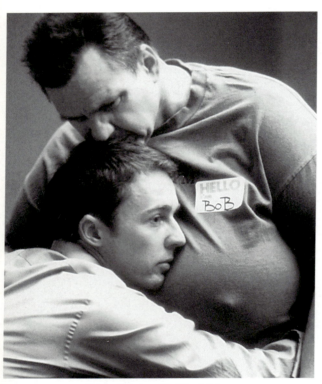

Edward Norton

Edward Norton, Meat Loaf Aday

FIGHT CLUB

(20TH CENTURY FOX) Producers, Art Linson, Cean Chaffin, Ross Grayson Bell; Executive Producer, Arnon Milchan; Director, David Fincher; Screenplay, Jim Uhls; Based on the novel by Chuck Palahniuk; Photography, Jeff Cronenweth; Designer, Alex McDowell; Editor, James Haygood; Music, The Dust Brothers (Michael Simpson, John King); Costumes, Michael Kaplan; Special Make-up Effects Supervisor, Rob Bottin; Casting, Laray Mayfield; a Fox 2000 Pictures and Regency Enterprises presentation of a Linson Films production; Dolby; Super 35 Widescreen; Technicolor; Rated R; 138 minutes; Release date: October 15, 1999

CAST

Tyler Durden	Brad Pitt
Narrator	Edward Norton
Marla Singer	Helena Bonham Carter
Robert Paulsen	Meat Loaf Aday
Angel Face	Jared Leto
Richard Chesler (Regional Manager)	Zach Grenier
Intern at Hospital	Richmond Arquette
Thomas at Remaining Men Together	David Andrews
Group Leader—Remaining Men Together	George Maguire
Weeping Woman—Onward and Upward	Eugenie Bondurant
Leader—Partners in Positivity	Christina Cabot
Speaker—Free and Clear	Sydney "Big Dawg" Colston
Chloe	Rachel Singer
Airline Check-In Attendant	Christie Cronenweth
Federated Motor Co. Inspector Bird	Tim deZarn
Federated Motor Co. Inspector Dent	Ezra Buzzington
Business Woman on Plane	Dierdre Downing-Jackson
Airport Security Officer	Robert J. Stephenson
Doorman at Pearson Towers	Charlie Dell
Man in Suit	Rob Lanza
Walter	David Lee Smith
The Mechanic	Holt McCallany
Food Court Maitre d'	Joel Bissonnette
Ricky	Eion Bailey
"Steph"	Evan Mirand
Next Month's Opponent	Robby Robinson
Cop at Marla's Building	Lou Beatty, Jr.
Detective Stern	Thom Gossom, Jr.
Cosmetics Buyer	Valerie Bickford
Lou	Peter Iacangelo
Lou's Body Guard	Carl N. Ciarfalio
Car Salesman	Stuart Blumberg
Men at Auto Shop	Todd Peirce, Mark Fite
Seminary Student	Matt Winston
Raymond K. Hessel	Joon B. Kim
Bus Driver with Broken Nose	Bennie E. Moore, Jr.
Channel 4 Reporter	W. Lauren Sanchez
Commissioner Jacobs	Pat McNamara
Banquet Speaker	Tyrone R. Livingston
Airport Valet	Owen Masterson
Policeman	David Jean-Thomas
Salvator—Winking Bartender	Paul Carafotes
Proprietor of Dry Cleaners	Christopher John Fields
Bruised Bar Patrons	Anderson Bourell, Scotch Ellis Loring
Bartender in Halo	Michael Shamus Wiles
Hotel Desk Clerk	Andi Carnick
Waiter at Clifton's	Edward Kowalczyk
Desk Sergeant	Leonard Termo
Detective Andrew	Van Quattro
Detective Kevin	Markus Redmond
Detective Walker	Michael Girardin

A man, deeply disillusioned with his routine life, meets soap manufacturer Tyler Durden who convinces him to help start a secret fight club where they and other men can release their pent-up hostility. This film received an Oscar nomination for sound effects editing.

Edward Norton, Brad Pitt

Brad Pitt

Edward Norton, Brad Pitt

Helena Bonham Carter

Helena Bonham Carter, Edward Norton

Brad Pitt, Edward Norton

THE STRAIGHT STORY

(**WALT DISNEY PICTURES**) Producers, Mary Sweeney, Neal Edelstein; Executive Producers, Pierre Edelman, Michael Polaire; Director, David Lynch; Screenplay, John Roach, Mary Sweeney; Photography, Freddie Francis; Designer, Jack Fisk; Editor, Mary Sweeney; Costumes, Patricia Norris; Music, Angelo Badalamenti; Casting, Jane Alderman, Lynn Blumenthal; Presented in association with Alain Sarde, a Picture Factory Production in association with Le Studio Canal+ and Film Four; U.S.-French; Dolby; Panavision; Fotokem color; Rated G; 111 minutes; Release date: October 15, 1999

CAST

Alvin Straight	Richard Farnsworth
Rose Straight	Sissy Spacek
Lyle Straight	Harry Dean Stanton
Tom, the John Deere Dealer	Everett McGill
Thorvald	John Farley
Harald	Kevin Farley
Dorothy	Jane Galloway Heitz
Bud	Joseph A. Carpenter
Sig	Donald Wiegert
Nurse	Tracey Maloney
Doctor Gibbons	Dan Flannery
Brenda	Jennifer Edwards-Hughes
Pete	Ed Grennan
Apple	Jack Walsh
Farm Dog	Max the Wonder Dog
Bus Driver	Gil Pearson
Woman on Bus	Barbara June Patterson
Crystal	Anastasia Webb
Steve	Max Guidry
Rat	Bill McCallum

and Barbara Robertson (Deer Woman), James Cada (Danny Riordon), Sally Wingert (Darla Riordon), Barbara Kingsley (Janet Johnson), Jim Haun (Johnny Johnson), Wiley Harker (Verlyn Heller), Randy Wiedenhoff, Jerry E. Anderson (Firemen), John Lordan (Priest), Garrett Sweeney, Peter Sweeney, Tommy Fahey, Matt Fahey, Dan Fahey (Boys in Truck), Russ Reed (Mt. Zion Bartender), Ralph Feldhacker (Farmer on Tractor)

Finding out that his estranged brother has suffered a stroke, 73-year-old Alvin Straight, whose failing eyesight will not allow him to drive a car, hops on a John Deere lawnmower and rides from Laurens, Iowa to Mt. Zion, Wisconsin to visit his ailing sibling. This film recieved an Oscar nomination for actor (Richard Farnsworth).

© The Straight Story, Inc.

Richard Farnsworth, Sissy Spacek

James Cada, Richard Farnsworth

Richard Farnsworth

John Leguizamo, Noah Fleiss

Noah Fleiss, Val Kilmer

Ethan Hawke

JOE THE KING

(**TRIMARK**) Producers, Robin O'Hara, Scott Macaulay, Jennifer Dewis, Lindsay Marx; Executive Producers, Janet Grillo, John Leguizamo; Director/Screenplay, Frank Whaley; Photography, Michael Mayers; Designer, Dan Ouellette; Editors, Melody London, Miran Miosic; Music, Robert Whaley, Anthony Grimaldi; Costumes, Richard Owings; Co-Producer, Kathy De Marco; Casting, Billy Hopkins, Suzanne Smith, Kerry Barden; a 49th Parallel Productions/Forensic-391 Films/Lower East Side Films production; Dolby; Color; Rated R; 101 minutes; Release date: October 15, 1999

CAST

Joe Henry .... Noah Fleiss
Theresa Henry .... Karen Young
Mrs. Basil .... Camryn Manheim
Winston .... Austin Pendleton
Jorge .... John Leguizamo
Len Coles .... Ethan Hawke
Bob Henry .... Val Kilmer
Mike Henry .... Max Ligosh
Ray .... James Costa
Little Joe .... Peter Tambakis
Dawn .... Harlee Ott
Rory .... Travis Feretic
Little Ray .... Benjamin Stix
Alice .... Alice Blythe
Mrs. Williams .... Linda Key
Little Mike .... Rob Bergenstock
Roy .... Richard Bright
Mary .... Amy Wright
and Michael Taylor (Man in Jerry's Apartment), Lori Eastside (Woman in Jerry's Apartment), Robert Whaley (Jerry), Craig Levine (Dave), Kate Mara (Allyson), Rachel Miner (Patty), Lyn Nagel (Jenny), Sarah Vitale (Brandy), Laura Ligosh (Fooseball Girl), Raymond De Fellita (Mr. Brazer), Jack McNamara (Mr. Dawson), Christopher Wynkoop (Mr. Margolis), Reggie Montgomery (Andy), Anthony Todisco (Kenny Orzo), Caitlin Clarke (Pat), Raynor Scheine (Doctor), Mitchell Fleiss (Cop #1), Louis Zorich (Judge), Danny Wiseman (Ticket Taker), Guy Griffis (Old Man), Jenny Robertson (Waitress), PJ Pesce (Detention Security)

The hostile environment of his homelife, caused by his frustrated mother and violent father, leads teenager Joe Henry into a life of rebellion and petty crime.

© Trimark Pictures

Max Ligosh, Noah Fleiss, Karen Young

CRAZY IN ALABAMA

(**COLUMBIA**) Producers, Meir Teper, Linda Goldstein Knowlton, Diane Sillan Isaacs, Debra Hill; Executive Producer, James R. Dyer; Director, Antonio Banderas; Screenplay, Mark Childress, based on his novel; Photography, Julio Macat; Designer, Cecilia Montiel; Editors, Maysie Hoy, Robert C. Jones; Music, Mark Snow; Costumes, Graciela Mazon; Casting, Mindy Marin; a Green Moon production in association with a Meir Teper production; Dolby; Super 35 Widescreen; Deluxe color; Rated PG-13; 104 minutes; Release date: October 22, 1999

Lucas Black, Louis Miller

CAST

Lucille	Melanie Griffith
Dove Bullis	David Morse
Peejoe	Lucas Black
Earlene Bullis	Cathy Moriarty
Sheriff John Doggett	Meat Loaf Aday
Judge Mead	Rod Steiger
Norman	Richard Schiff
Nehemiah Jackson	John Beasley
Harry Hall	Robert Wagner
Sheriff Raymond	Noah Emmerich
Meemaw	Sandra Seacat
Mackie	Paul Ben-Victor
Jack	Brad Beyer
Sally	Fannie Flagg
Joan Blake	Elizabeth Perkins
Madelyn	Linda Hart
Walter Schwegmann	Paul Mazursky

and Holmes Osborne (Larry Russell), William Converse Roberts (Murphy), David Speck (Wiley), Philip Carter (Deputy Tyrone), Carl Le Blanc, III (David Jackson), Louis Miller (Taylor Jackson), Marion Zinser (Saleswoman), John Fleck (Jake), Jack Stephens (Conventioneer), Mark Whitman Johnson (Pool Manager), Tom McCleister (Croupier), J.R. Dyer (Gambling Man), Tony Amendola (Casino Boss), Milly Ericson (Cashier), Jim Antonio (Dr. Ward), Thurn Hoffman (Bellhop Ted), Michael Arata (Photographer), Lance Spellerberg (Interviewer), Madison Mason (Alexander Powell), Amanda Aday (Assistant at Bewitched), Randal Kleiser (Bob), Charlie Dell (Darrin's Stand-In), Oliver Clark (Endora's Stand-In), Tracy Griffith (Samantha's Stand-In), Dudley F. Craig II (Reverend), Barbara Tasker (Organizer), Brent Briscoe (Jury Foreman/Chester's Voice), Sidney J. Lodrigue, Urisino Frank Lourino (Hecklers on Balcony), Kirk Fox (Patrolman), Wayne Ferrara, Jerry Lee Leighton, Don Thomas (Reporters), Marva Wright (Singer at Pool), Dane Le Blanc (Marlon), Dexter Le Blanc (Farley), Emily Guidry (Judy), Jess Bryan (Cary), Dakota Jackson (Sondra), Stella Banderas (Marilyn), Jackson Isaacs (Rock), Lia Chapman (Woman on Phone)

Rod Steiger, Lucas Black

After killing her hateful husband, Lucille takes off for Hollywood hoping for career in movies, leaving behind her small Alabama town where racial tensions are mounting after a bigoted sheriff has caused the death of a black boy. This marked the feature directorial debut of actor Antonio Banderas.

© Columbia Pictures Industries, Inc.

Lucas Black, David Morse

Lucas Black, Melanie Griffith

BATS

(DESTINATION) Producers, Brad Jenkel, Louise Rosner; Executive Producers, Steve Stabler, Brent Baum, John Logan, Dale Pollack; Director, Louis Morneau; Screenplay, John Logan; Photography, George Mooradian; Designer, Philip L.C. Duffin; Editor, Glenn Garland; Music, Graeme Revell; Special Effects Coordinator, Eric Allard; Special Make-up and Animatronic Effects, K.N.B. EFX Group Inc.; Visual Effects Designer, Netter Digital Entertainment, Inc.; Casting, Laura Schiff; Dolby; Clairmont-Scope; Technicolor; Rated PG-13; 91 minutes; Release date: October 22, 1999

CAST

Sheriff Emmett Kimsey .... Lou Diamond Phillips
Dr. Sheila Casper .... Dina Meyer
Jimmy Sands .... Leon
Dr. Alexander McCabe .... Bob Gunton
Dr. Tobe Hodge .... Carlos Jacott
Deputy Munn .... David Shawn McConnell
Mayor Branson .... Marcia Dangerfield
Dr. Swanbeck .... Oscar Rowland
Quint .... Tim Whitaker
Emma .... Juliana Johnson
Sergeant James .... James Sie
Major Reid .... Ned Bellamy
Private Cheswick .... George Gerdes
Bartender .... Joel Farar

A pair of zoologists try to stop a swarm of genetically altered bats from terrorizing a small Texas town.

© Destination Film Distribution

Dina Meyer, Lou Diamond Phillips

Leon

Matthew Perry, Neve Campbell. Dylan McDermott

THREE TO TANGO

(WARNER BROS.) Producers, Bobby Newmyer, Jeffrey Silver, Bettina Sofia Viviano; Executive Producers, Lawrence B. Abramson, Bruce Berman; Director, Damon Santostefano; Screenplay, Rodney Vaccaro, Aline Brosh McKenna; Story, Rodney Vaccaro; Co-Producers, John M. Eckert, Keri Selig; Photography, Walt Lloyd; Designer, David Nichols; Editor, Stephen Semel; Music, Graeme Revell; Costumes, Vicki Graef; Casting, Marion Dougherty; Presented in association with Village Roadshow Pictures and Village—Hoyts Film Partnership; an Outlaw production; Dolby; Technicolor; Rated PG-13; 98 minutes; Release date: October 22, 1999

CAST

Oscar Novak .... Matthew Perry
Amy Post .... Neve Campbell
Charles Newman .... Dylan McDermott
Peter Steinberg .... Oliver Platt
Kevin Cartwright .... Cylk Cozart
Strauss .... John C. McGinley
Decker .... Bob Balaban
Lenore .... Deborah Rush
Olivia Newman .... Kelly Rowan
Rick .... Rick Gomez
Zack .... Patrick van Horn
Bill .... David Ramsey
and Kent Staines (Gallery Owner), Ho Chow (Cabbie), Michael Proudfoot, Diner Waiter), Shaun Smyth, Robin Brûlé, Brett Heard (Interns), Les Porter, Andrew Dolha, Ned Vukovic (Peter's Friends), Keith Kemps, Lowell Conrad (Dinner Guests), Rumina Abadjieva (Reception Guest), Lindsey Connell (Newspaper Reporter), Katherine Steen (Beautiful Girl), Steve Richard (Weight Lifter), Stephanie Belding (Joanne), Ray Kahnert (Jonas), Sven van de Ven (Meeting Leader), Glen Peloso (Business Man), Barbara Gordon (Jenny Novak), Roger Dunn (Edward Novak), Meredith McGeachie (Megan), Marni Thompson, Deborah Pollitt, Anais Granofsky (Amy's Girlfriends), Ed Sahely (George), Lindsay Leese (Sandy), Tom Forrest (Kissed Guy), Barbara Radecki (TV Reporter), Shemekia Copeland (Blues Singer)

Eager to impress Chicago tycoon Charles Newman, with whom he has landed a architectural contract, Oscar Novak agrees to spy on Newman's mistress Amy. Oscar falls in love with Amy only to find out that both Newman and Amy feel comfortable with him being around because they believe he is gay.

© Warner Bros./Village Roadshow

THE BEST MAN

(**UNIVERSAL**) Producers, Spike Lee, Sam Kitt, Bill Carraro; Director/Screenplay, Malcolm D. Lee; Photography, Frank Prinzi; Designer, Kalina Ivanov; Editor, Cara Silverman; Music, Stanley Clarke; Music Supervisors, Bonnie Greenberg, Lisa Brown; Casting, Robi Reed-Humes; a 40 Acres and a Mule Filmworks production; Dolby; Deluxe Color; Rated R; 120 minutes; Release date: October 22, 1999

CAST

Harper Stewart	Taye Diggs
Jordan Armstrong	Nia Long
Lance	Morris Chestnut
Murch	Harold Perrineau
Quentin	Terrence Howard
Robin	Sanaa Lathan
Mia	Monica Calhoun
Shelby	Melissa De Sousa
Anita	Victoria Dillard
Cand	Regina Hall
Uncle Skeeter	Jim Moody
Wayne	Jarrod Bunch
Fandango	Stu "Large" Riley
Strippers	Liris Crosse, Lady Madonna
Wedding Coordinator	Linda Powell
Pastor	Willie Carpenter
Emcee	Malcolm D. Lee
Themselves	Doug Banks, DeDe McGuire
Groomsmen	Renton Kirk, Patrick Malcolm
Bridesmaids	Nikki Tillman, Lena Moore, Rebecca Brody, Gena Lue Sang
Lance's Parents	Linda Murrell, Willie Gaskins
Mia's Parents	Emilie Gaskins, Don Clark Williams
Flower Girls	Charltina "Chasha" Banks, Aleisha Allen
Broom Bearer	Vance Allen

Writer Harper Stewart arrives at a wedding to serve as best man, not realizing that one of the bridesmaids has gotten an advance copy of Harper's new book, which contains characters who bear uncomfortable resemblances to his real life friends.

Taye Diggs, Nia Long

Morris Chestnut, Taye Diggs

Monica Calhoun, Nia Long, Sanaa Lathan

Taye Diggs, Nia Long

BRINGING OUT THE DEAD

(PARAMOUNT/TOUCHSTONE) Producers, Scott Rudin, Barbara De Fina; Executive Producers, Adam Schroeder, Bruce S. Pustin; Director, Martin Scorsese; Screenplay, Paul Schrader; Based upon the novel by Joe Connelly; Photography, Robert Richardson; Designer, Dante Ferretti; Editor, Thelma Schoonmaker; Costumes, Rita Ryack; Music, Elmer Bernstein; Co-Producers, Joseph Reidy, Eric Steel; Casting, Ellen Lewis; a Scott Rudin—Cappa/De Fina production; Dolby; Panavision; Deluxe color; Rated R; 120 minutes; Release date: October 22, 1999

Patricia Arquette, Nicolas Cage, Marc Anthony

CAST

Frank Pierce	Nicolas Cage
Mary Burke	Patricia Arquette
Larry	John Goodman
Marcus	Ving Rhames
Tom Wolls	Tom Sizemore
Noel	Marc Anthony
Nurse Constance	Mary Beth Hurt
Cy Coates	Cliff Curtis
Dr. Hazmat	Nestor Serrano
Nurse Crupp	Aida Turturro
Kanita	Sonja Sohn
Rose	Cynthia Roman
Griss	Afemo Omilami
Mr. Burke	Cullen Oliver Johnson
Captain Barney	Arthur Nascarella
Dispatcher (Voice)	Martin Scorsese
Sister Fetus	Julyana Soelistyo
Neighbor Women	Graciela Lecube, Marylouise Burke
Mrs. Burke	Phyllis Somerville
Neighbor Woman	Mary Diveny
John Burke	Tom Riis Farrell
Arguing Russians	Aleks Shaklin, Leonid Citer
Man with Bloody Foot	Jesus A. Del Rosario, Jr.
Cokehead	Larry Fessenden
Big Feet	Bernie Friedman
Prostitutes	Theo Kogan, Fuschia Walker
Mr. Oh	John Heffernan
Mr. Oh's Friends	Matthew Maher, Bronson Dudley, Marilyn McDonald
Homeless Men in Waiting Room	Ed Jupp, Jr., J. Stanford Hoffman
Concerned Hispanic Aunt	Rita Norona Schrager
Naked Man	Don Berry
Street Punk	Mtume Gant
Grunt	Michael A. Noto
Bystander	Omar Sharif Scroggins
Voice in Crowd	muMs
Drug Dealer	Michael Kenneth Williams
Stanley	Andrew Davoli
Miss Williams	Charlene Hunter
Club Doorman	Jesse Malin
I.B. Bangin'	Harper Simon
Drummer	Joseph Monroe Webb
Club Bystander	Jon Abrahams
I.B.'s Girlfriend	Charis Michelson

and Lia Yang (Dr. Milagros), Antone Pagán (Arrested Man), Melissa Marsala (Bridge & Tunnel Girl), Betty Miller (Weeping Woman), Rosemary Gomez (Pregnant Maria), Luis Rodriguez (Carlos), Sylva Kelegian (Crackhead), Frank Ciornei (Dr. Mishra), Catrina Ganey (Nurse Odette), Jennifer Lane Newman (Nurse Advisor), John Bal, Raymond Cassar (Police in Hospital), Tom Cappadona, Jack O'Connell, Randy Foster (Drunks), Richard Spore (Homeless Suicidal), James Hanlon, Chris Edwards (Firemen), Mark Giordano (Police Sergeant), Michael Mulheren, David Zayas (Cops in Elevator), Terry Serpico, Brian Smyj, Floyd Resnick (Cops), Megan Leigh (Surgeon), David Vasquez (Screaming Man), Judy Reyes (ICU Nurse), Joseph Reidy (ICU Doctor), Queen Latifah (Voice of Dispatcher Love)

Nicolas Cage (back to camera), Ving Rhames

A look at the nightmarish existence of New York City paramedic Frank Pierce during a fifty-six hour period as he attempts to hold onto his sanity while trying to save lives in an urban jungle on the graveyard shift.

John Goodman, Nicolas Cage

BODY SHOTS

(NEW LINE CINEMA) Producers, Harry Colomby, Jennifer Keohane; Executive Producers, Michael Keaton, Guy Riedel, Michael De Luca, Lynn Harris; Director, Michael Cristofer; Screenplay, David McKenna; Photography, Rodrigo Garcia; Designer, David J. Bomba; Editor, Eric Sears; Music, Mark Isham; Costumes, Carolyn Leigh Greco; Casting, Junie Lowry Johnson, Libby Goldstein; a Colomby/Keaton production; Dolby; Panavision; Deluxe color; Rated R; 102 minutes; Release date: October 22, 1999

CAST

Rick Hamilton	Sean Patrick Flanery
Michael Penorisi	Jerry O'Connell
Jane Bannister	Amanda Peet
Sara Olswang	Tara Reid
Trent	Ron Livingston
Whitney Bryant	Emily Procter
Shawn Denigan	Brad Rowe
Emma Cooper	Sybil Temchen

and Joe Basile (Bartender), Scott Burkholder (Man in Bar), Liz Coke, Allison Dunbar (Girls), Edmond Genest (Sara's Dad), Adam Gordon (Burger Joint Cop), Mark Hicks (Bodyguard), Larry Joshua (Detective Richards), Elizabeth Liebel (Mrs. Drofsky), Marc Lynn (Disco Bartender), Lou Paget (Oral Sex Instructor), Adina Porter (Detective Thompson), Benny Quan (Burger Joint Manager), Wendy Schenker (Doctor), Nick Spano (Jeff the Doorman)

Eight twenty-somethings spend a night of club hopping through Los Angeles' nightlife, an evening that ends in one of the women accusing one of the men of rape.

© New Line Cinema Inc.

Sybil Temchen, Amanda Peet, Tara Reid, Emily Procter

Brad Rowe, Sean Patrick Flanery, Jerry O'Connell

Cipriano Garcia, Leticia Herrera

THE CITY (LA CIUDAD)

(ZEITGEIST) Producers, David Riker, Paul S. Mezey; Executive Producers, Andrew Hurwitz, Doug Mankoff, Robin Alper; Director/Screenplay/Editor, David Riker; Photography, Harlan Bosmajian; Designers, Ariane Burgess, Roshelle Berliner; Music, Tony Adzinikolov; a North Star Films production; Ultra-Stereo; Black and white; Not rated; 88 minutes; Release date: October 22, 1999

CAST

Bricks: Moises Garcia (Abel), Marcos Martinez Garcia (Armando), Fernando Reyes (Jose), Ricardo Cuevas, Mateo Gomez, Cesar Monzon, Harsh Nayyar, Victor Sierra, Carlos Torrentes (The Men), Anthony Rivera (The Boy), Joe Rigano (The Contractor), Miguel Maldonado (The Organizer), Maite Bonilla (Voiceover)
Home: Cipriano Garcia (Francisco), Leticia Herrera (Maria)
The Puppeteer: Jose Rabelo (Luis), Stephanie Viruet (Dulce), Gene Ruffini (The City Worker), Eileen Vega (The Health Worker), Denia Brache (The Friend), Marta De La Cruz (The School Registrar)
Seamstress: Silvia Goiz (The Seamstress), Rosa Caguana, Guillermina De Jesus, Betty Mendoza, Angeles Rubio, Teresa Venque, Valentina Zea (Her Friends), Hyoung Taek Limb, Jawon Kim (The Sweatshop Managers), Maria Galante (The Designer), Monica Cano, Ernesto Lopez (Workers in Hallway), Galo Rodin Schneider (The Cousin), Jaime Sanchez (The Dress Store Manager)
The Photo Studio: Antonio Peralta (The Photographer)

A look at the struggles of various Latin American immigrants living in New York.

© Zeitgeist Films

HOUSE ON HAUNTED HILL

(**WARNER BROS.**) Producers, Robert Zemekis, Joel Silver, Gilbert Adler; Executive Producers, Dan Cracchiolo, Steve Richards; Director, William Malone; Screenplay, Dick Beebe; Story, Robb White; Photography, Rick Bota; Designer, David F. Klassen; Editor, Anthony Adler; Co-Producer, Terry Castle; Costumes, Ha Nguyen; Music, Don Davis; Special Make-up Effects, Robert Kurtzman, Gregory Nicotero, Howard Berger; Special Effects, Bellissimo/Belardinelli Effects Inc.; Casting, Lora Kennedy; a Dark Castle Entertainment; Dolby; Panavision; Technicolor; Rated R; 96 minutes; Release date: October 29, 1999

CAST

Stephen Price	Geoffrey Rush
Evelyn Price	Famke Janssen
Eddie	Taye Diggs
Dr. Blackburn	Peter Gallagher
Watson Pritchett	Chris Kattan
Sara Wolfe	Ali Larter
Melissa Marr	Bridgette Wilson
Schecter	Max Perlich
Dr. Vannacutt	Jeffrey Combs
Male Nurse	Dick Beebe
Twisted Nurse	Slavitza Jovan
Channel 3 Reporter	Lisa Loeb
Channel 3 Cameraman	James Marsters
Price's Secretary	Jeannette Lewis
Girl on Wires	Janet Tracy Keijser
Himself	Peter Graves

Decades after the Vannacutt Institute for the Criminally Insane was shuttered for the unethical treatment of its inmates, Stephen Price invites five strangers to spend a night there, promising them a million dollar reward if they survive. Remake of the 1958 Allied Artists release that starred Vincent Price.

© Warner Bros.

Geoffrey Rush, Famke Janssen, Ali Larter, Taye Diggs, Peter Gallagher

MAN OF THE CENTURY

(**FINE LINE FEATURES**) Producers, Gibson Frazier, Adam Abraham; Director, Adam Abraham; Screenplay, Adam Abraham, Gibson Frazier; Photography, Matthew Jensen; Designer, Zeljka Pavlinovic; Costumes, Claudia Hill; Editor, Frank Reynolds; Music, Michael Weiner; Dolby; Black and white; Rated R; 80 minutes; Release date: October 29, 1999

CAST

Johnny Twennies	Gibson Frazier
Samantha Winter	Susan Egan
Timothy Burns	Anthony Rapp
Virginia Clemens	Cara Buono
Victor Young	Brian Davies
Richard Lancaster	Dwight Ewell
Roman Navarro	Frank Gorshin
Mr. Meyerscholtz	David Margulies
Chester	Bobby Short
Gertrude	Marisa Ryan
Hastings	Michael Allinson
Jeffrey Pitzer	Gary Beach
Dottie Lausenger	Nicole Brier
Tyrus	Alan Davidson
Lester	Lester Lanin
Reporter	Sean Patrick Reilly

and Michael Squicciarini (Maurice), Donald Symington (Rev. Sheehan), Michael Weiner (Milo), Kevin Weisman (Squibb), Ian Edwards (Clarence), Yul Vazquez (Brooding Artist), Brian Kite (Messenger), Alfred Hyslop (Public Official), David Anzuelo (Degenerate), Francis Dumaurier (Maitre D'), Cornelius Patrick Byrne (Coachman), William Meisle (Bartlett), Ken Leung (Mike Ramsey), Liza Politi (Denis Bradden), Alan Zachary (Pianist), Diana Georger (Shopper), Douglas Huch (Taxi Driver), Francis Cruz, Ron Domingo, Michael Minn, Wayland Quintero, Perry Yung (Chinese Boys), Robert Lin (Chinese Mob Boss), Ron Garcia (Obnoxious Guy), Anne Jackson (Johnny's Mother)

Johnny Twennies, a columnist for the New York Sun-Telegram who lives in the mind-set of the 1920s, is told he must find a hot story in order to hold on to his job and winds up tangling with the mob.

© Fine Line Features

Susan Egan, Gibson Frazier

Meryl Streep

Aidan Quinn, Meryl Streep

MUSIC OF THE HEART

(**MIRAMAX**) formerly *Fifty Violins*; Producers, Walter Scheuer, Allan Miller, Susan Kaplan, Marianne Maddalena; Executive Producers, Bob Weinstein, Harvey Weinstein, Amy Slotnick; Director, Wes Craven; Screenplay, Pamela Gray; Inspired by the documentary *Small Wonders*; Co-Producer, Stuart M. Besser; Photography, Peter Deming; Designer, Bruce Alan Miller; Editors, Patrick Lussier, Gregg Featherman; Music, Mason Daring; Music Supervisor, Sharon Boyle; Song: Music of the Heart by Diane Warren/performed by Gloria Estefan and N'Sync; Costumes, Susan Lyall; Casting, Avy Kafuman; a Craven/Maddalena Films production; Dolby; Deluxe color; Rated PG; 124 minutes; Release date: October 29, 1999

CAST

Roberta Guaspari	Meryl Streep
Janet Williams	Angela Bassett
Brian Sinclair	Aidan Quinn
Assunta Guaspari	Cloris Leachman
Dorothea von Haeften	Jane Leeves
Nick (young)	Michael Angarano
Nick (teen)	Charlie Hofheimer
Lexi (young)	Henry Dinhoffer
Lexi (teen)	Kieran Culkin
Dan Paxton	Jay O. Sanders
Lawrence	Cole Hawkins
Isabel Vasquez	Gloria Estefan
Naeem Adisa (young)	Justin Spaulding,
DeSean (young)	Jade Yorker
Guadalupe (young)	Zoe Sternbach-Taubman
Rachel	Melay Araya
Lucy (young)	Victoria Gomez
Ramon Olivas	Jean Luke Figueroa
Becky Lamb	Lucy Nonas-Barnes
Lucy's Mother	Socorro Santiago
Supervisor	Robert Ari
Taxi Driver	Teddy Coluca
Bongo Kid	Justin Pierre Edmund
Dennis Rausch	Josh Pais
Manuelo Olivas	Mateo Gomez

and Gideon Jacobs (Headlock Boy), French Napier (Painter #1), Dominic Walters (Justin Brady), Eva Loomis (Vanessa Klein), Asease Korankyi (Shandra Wilson), Asha Sapp (Tanisha), Olga Merediz (Concepcion), Ian Quinlan (Carlos), Leilani Irvin (Myesha), Sam Fox Royston (Leonard Hood), Betsy Aidem (Mrs. Lamb), Scott Cumberbatch (Lawrence), Willie Stiggers (Henry), Rosalyn Coleman (Mrs. Adisa), Sarallen (Old Woman in Tenement Bldg.), Myra Lucretia Taylor (Beverly Wilson), Hazel J. Medina (Alice Crowley), Christopher Lopez (Adam), Jraida Polanco (Landlady), Arthur French (Ernie the Electrician), Naeem Jones (Toussaint), Christian Berreondo (Pedro), Adam Lefevre (Mr. Klein), Arnold Steinhardt, Karen Briggs, Itzhak Perlman, Isaac Stern, Mark O'Connor, Diane Monroe, Michael Tree, Joshua Bell, Charles Veal Jr., Jonathan Feldman (Themselves), Kirby Mitchell (New York Times Reporter), Leon Addison Brown (Mr. Adams), Majid R. Khaliq (Naeem Adisa—teen), Omari Toomer (DeSean—teen), Molly Gia Foresta (Guadalupe—teen), Cristina Gomez (Lucy—teen), Isabel Segovia (Guadalupe's Grandmother), Isaiah Sheffer (Carnegie Hall Staff Person), John McGinty (Naval Officer), Edmund Wilkinson (Man #1 with Sheetrock), Tarik Lowe, Justin Daly (Teammates), Kevin Miller (Hall Boy), Julie Janney (Flight Attendant), Barbara Gonzalez (Janet's Secretary), Anibal Crooklyn Cuevas (Frog Hair Boy), Rosalyn Benniman (Woman at Opus Meeting), Sam Deutch, Ruben Jared Seraballs, Lucy Little, Andrew Mayer, Chantilly Mariani, Rafael John Alan Hines, Amanda Muchnick, Jordan Ware, Sophia Guaspari, Rebecca Dinhoffer, Jose Miguel Rojas, Thomas Martin, Christopher Katrandjian, Ama Korankyi (Violin Students)

Determined to move on with her life after her husband walks out on her, Roberta Guaspari accepts a job in an East Harlem school where she teaches violin to a number of young children over the course of ten years, until the school board cancels her funding. This film received Oscar nominations for actress (Meryl Streep) and original song ("Music of My Heart").

© Miramax Films

Gloria Estefan, Meryl Streep, Angela Bassett

Gloria Estefan, Meryl Streep, Angela Bassett

Meryl Streep

Catherine Keener, John Cusack

John Malkovich

John Cusack, Catherine Keener, Cameron Diaz

John Cusack

Orson Bean

BEING JOHN MALKOVICH

(**USA FILMS**) Producers, Michael Stipe, Sandy Stern, Steve Golin, Vincent Landay; Executive Producers, Charlie Kaufman, Michael Kuhn; Director, Spike Jonze; Screenplay, Charlie Kaufman; Photography, Lance Acord; Designer, K.K. Barrett; Editor, Eric Zumbrunnen; Costumes, Casey Storm; Music, Carter Burwell; Puppeteer, Phillip Huber; Casting, Kim Davis-Wagner, Justine Baddeley; a Gramercy Pictures presentation of a Propaganda Films/Single Cell Pictures production; Dolby; Color; Rated R; 112 minutes; Release date: October 29, 1999

CAST

Craig Schwartz	John Cusack
Lottie Schwartz	Cameron Diaz
Maxine	Catherine Keener
Dr. Lester	Orson Bean
Floris	Mary Kay Place
John Horatio Malkovich	John Malkovich
Derek Mantini	Ned Bellamy
Father at Puppet Show	Eric Weinstein
Daughter at Puppet Show	Madison Lanc
Woman in Elevator	Octavia L. Spencer
Wendy	K.K. Dodds
Don	Reggie Hayes
Captain Mertin	Byrne Piven
Tiny Woman	Judith Wetzell
Cab Driver	Kevin Carroll
Guy in Restaurant	Willie Garson
First J.M. Inc. Customer	W. Earl Brown
Charlie	Charlie Sheen
Sad Man in Line	Gerald Emerick
Mr. Hiroshi	Bill M. Ryusaki
Larry the Agent	Carlos Jacott
Student Puppeteer	James Murray
Johnson Heyward	Richard Fancy
Malkovich's Mother	Patti Tippo
Boy Malkovich	Daniel Hansen
Girl Creeped Out by Malkovich	Mariah O'Brien
Drunk at Bar	Gregory Sporleder
Emily	Kelly Teacher

and Jacqueline Benoit, William N. Buck, Christine D. Coleman, Jeanne Diehl, Audrey Gelfand, Yetta Ginsburg, Sylvester Jenkins, Roy C. Johnson, Eddie J. Low, Ralph W. Spaulding, David Wyler, Flori Wyler (Lester's Friends), Sean Penn, Andy Dick, Isaac Hanson, Winona Ryder, Brad Pitt (Themselves)

A struggling puppeteer takes a job at a weird office building where he discovers a hidden portal that grants temporary access into the head of actor John Malkovich. This film received Oscar nominations for supporting actress (Catherine Keener), director, and original screenplay.

© Universal Studios, Inc.

Catherine Keener, John Cusack

Catherine Keener, John Cusack

Orson Bean, Cameron Diaz

THE BACHELOR

(**NEW LINE CINEMA**) Producers, Lloyd Segan, Bing Howenstein; Executive Producers, Michael De Luca, Chris O'Donnell, Donna Langley; Director, Gary Sinyor; Screenplay, Steve Cohen; Based on the play *Seven Chances* by Roi Cooper Megrue and the screenplay by Clyde Bruckman, Jean Havez, and Joseph Mitchell; Co-Producers, Leon Dudevoir, Stephen Hollocker; Line Producer, Gene Levy; Photography, Simon Archer; Designer, Craig Stearns; Editor, Robert Reitano; Costumes, Terry Dresbach; Music, David A. Hughes, John Murphy; Casting, Valerie McCaffrey; a Lloyd Segan Company production in association with George Street Pictures; Dolby; Deluxe color; Rated PG-13; 101 minutes; Release date: November 5, 1999

CAST

Jimmie Shannon ....Chris O'Donnell
Anne ....Renée Zellweger
Marco ....Artie Lange
Gluckman ....Edward Asner
O'Dell ....Hal Holbrook
Priest ....James Cromwell
Natalie ....Marley Shelton
Grandad ....Peter Ustinov
Monique ....Katharine Towne
Stacey..Rebecca Cross
Zoe...Stacy Edwards
Ilana..Mariah Carey
Carolyn ....Sarah Silverman
Daphne ....Jennifer Esposito
Buckley ....Brooke Shields

Lydell M. Cheshier (Sanzel), Robert Kotecki (Hodgman), Pat Finn (Bolt), Timothy Paul Perez (Stone), Romy Rosemont (Rita), Kelly Jean Peters (Waitress), Jane L. Powell (Starlight Room Singer), Jim Jackman (Nervous Guy), Christopher Carroll (Maitre d'), Kevin Jones (Florist), Michael Deeg, Erik Kever Ryle, Brian Leonard (Customers), Mary J. White (Florist Assistant), Edith Fields (Edith), Joe Meek, Michael Lee Merrins (Traders), Lisa Nalen ("Anne" on the Street), Brantley Bush (Stagehand), Nicholas Pryor (Dale), Maree Cheatham (Mona), Mark Norby (Suspect), Ken Baldwin, Gustavo Vargas (Salsa Dancers), Natalie Bartlett (O'Dell's Daughter), Cheri Rae Russell (Biker Bride), Jodi Taylor (Older Bride), Jenni Pulos (Big Hair Bride), Rebecca Gray, Kiva Dawson (Punk Brides), Anastasia Horne (Preppy Bride), Niecy Nash (African-American Bride), T.L. Brooke (Big Bride), Marnie Alexenberg (Brunette Bride), Lea Moon Llovio (Latina Bride), Robin Lyon, Elizabeth Guber, Nancy O'Dell (Questioning Brides), Marnie Schneider (Muslim Bride), Louis Ganapoler (Baker)

After his girlfriend Anne rejects his marriage proposal as insincere, perennial bachelor Jimmie Shannon suddenly realizes he must come up with a bride in 24-hours in order to inherit the $100 million promised by his grandfather. Remake of the 1925 MGM film Seven Chances that starred and was directed by Buster Keaton.

© New Line Cinema Inc.

Renée Zellweger, Chris O'Donnell

Chris O'Donnell

Peter Ustinov, Chris O'Donnell

Edward Asner, Hal Holbrook, Chris O'Donnell

Miriam Frost, Mark Borchardt, Robert Jorge, Sherri Beaupre, Tom Schimmels

Mike Schank, Mark Borchardt

Uncle Bill Borchardt, Mark Borchardt

AMERICAN MOVIE

(**SONY PICTURES CLASSICS**) Producers, Sarah Price, Chris Smith; Director/Photography, Chris Smith; Co-Producers, Jim McKay, Michael Stipe; Music, Mike Schank; Editors, Barry Poltermann, Jun Diaz, Chris Smith; a C-Hundred Film Corp and Civilian Pictures presentation of a Bluemark Production; Dolby; Color; Rated R; 104 minutes; Release date: November 5, 1999

SUBJECTS OF THE FILM

Filmmaker..Mark Borchardt
Friend/Musician ....Mike Schank
Mark's Uncle/Executive Producer.............................Uncle Bill Borchardt
Mark's Mom ....Monica Borchardt
Mark's Dad ....Cliff Borchardt
Mark's Brother..Chris Borchardt
Mark's Brother ....Alex Borchardt
Friend/Associate Producer ....Ken Keen
Mark's Girlfriend/Associate Producer.......................................Joan Petrie

Filmmaker Mark Borchardt chronicles his efforts to get his first movie made, with his family and various citizens of the town of Menomonee Falls, Wisconsin, lending a hand.

© Sony Pictures Entertainment, Inc.

THE INSIDER

(**TOUCHSTONE**) Producers, Michael Mann, Pieter Jan Brugge; Director, Michael Mann; Screenplay, Eric Roth, Michael Mann; Based on the *Vanity Fair* article "The Man Who Knew Too Much" by Marie Brenner; Photography, Dante Spinotti; Designer, Brian Morris; Costumes, Anna Sheppard; Editors, William Goldenberg, Paul Rubell, David Rosenbloom; Music, Lisa Gerrard, Pieter Bourke; Co-Producer, Michael Waxman; Casting, Bonnie Timmerman; Distributed by Buena Vista Pictures; a Mann/Roth production of a Forward Pass Picture; Dolby; Panavision; Technicolor; Rated R; 157 minutes; Release date: November 5, 1999

CAST

Lowell Bergman	Al Pacino
Jeffrey Wigand	Russell Crowe
Mike Wallace	Christopher Plummer
Liane Wigand	Diane Venora
Don Hewitt	Philip Baker Hall
Sharon Tiller	Lindsay Crouse
Debbie De Luca	Debi Mazar
Eric Kluster	Stephen Tobolowsky
Richard Scruggs	Colm Feore
Ron Motley	Bruce McGill
Helen Caperelli	Gina Gershon
Thomas Sandefur	Michael Gambon
John Scanlon	Rip Torn
Mrs. Williams	Lynne Thigpen
Barbara Wigand	Hallie Kate Eisenberg
Norman the Cameraman	Michael Paul Chan
Mrs. Wigand	Linda Hart
Mark Stern	Robert Harper
FBI Agent Robertson	Nestor Serrano
NY Times Reporter	Pete Hamill
Tobacco Lawyer	Wings Hauser
Sheikh Fadlallah	Clifford Curtis
Deborah Wigand	Renee Olstead
Themselves	Michael Moore, Jack Palladino
Sandefur's Lawyer	Gary Sandy
John Harris	Willie C. Carpenter
Charlie Phillips	Paul Butler
Sandra Sutherland	Megan Odabash
Seelbach Hotel Manager	Roger Bart
Hezbollah Interpreter	Alan DeSatti
Hezbollah Head Gunman	Sayed Badreya
Doug Oliver (FDA)	Chris Ufland
Private Investigator	Doug McGrath
Intense Young Intern	Bill Sage
Baldo the Editor	Joseph Hindy
FBI Agents	Dennis Garber, Tim Grimm
Geologist/FBI Man	Paul Perri
Geologist/FBI Woman	Wanda De Jesus
Policeman	Robert Brink
Bill Felling	V.J. Foster
FBI Agent #3	James Harper

and Eyal Podell (Lowell's Son), Breckin Meyer (Sharon's Son), David Roberson (John Telafarro), Gregg E. Muravchick (Private Security Guard), William P. Bradford II (Subpoena Man), David Carr (Local Newscaster), Ann Reskin (Seelbach Hotel Desk Clerk), Claire Slemmer (Edie Magnus), Steve Salge (Dan Rather), Derrick Jones (Mississippi Reporter), Donald F. Burbrink II (B&W Male Security Officer), Vyto Ruginis (Junior Lawyer), George R. Parsons (B&W Uniformed Security Officer), Isodine Loury (Mississippi Court Stenographer), Charlene Bosarge (Mr. Scruggs' Assistant), Saemi Nakamura (Japanese Waitress), Ronal G. Yokley (Police Detective), Bob Lazarus (Stage Manager), Robert Ragno, Jr. (Photographer—New Media), Alvin L. Welch (Judge), Nathan Lewis Hill (Production Assistant), Paula Bisbikos (Mike Wallace's Assistant), Christ Evans (CBS News Producer), Knox Grantham White (Soundman), Amy L. Caudill (A Student)

Former Brown & Williamson employee Jeffrey Wigand agrees to disclose important inside information about the tobacco industry to 60 Minutes only to discover that his interview has triggered a controversy within the executive offices of CBS. This film received Oscar nominations for picture, director, actor (Russell Crowe), screenplay adaptation, cinematography, editing, and sound.

© Touchstone Pictures

Al Pacino

Russell Crowe

Philip Baker Hall, Al Pacino, Christopher Plummer

Russell Crowe, Al Pacino

Debi Mazar, Al Pacino, Philip Baker Hall, Christopher Plummer

Christopher Plummer

Debi Mazar

Diane Venora

Michael Moore

Russell Crowe, Diane Venora

Denzel Washington, Angelina Jolie

Mike McGlone, Ed O'Neill, Angelina Jolie

THE BONE COLLECTOR

(**UNIVERSAL/COLUMBIA**) Producers, Martin Bregman, Louis A. Stroller, Michael Bregman; Executive Producers, Michael Klawitter, Dan Jinks; Director, Phillip Noyce; Screenplay, Jeremy Iacone; Based on the novel by Jeffery Deaver; Photography, Dean Semler; Designer, Nigel Phelps; Associate Producer, Bo Dietl; Costumes, Odette Gadoury; Music, Craig Armstrong; Casting, Bernard Telsey, William Cantler, David Vaccari; a Bregman production; Dolby; Panavision; Deluxe color; Rated R; 118 minutes; Release date: November 5, 1999

CAST

Lincoln Rhyme	Denzel Washington
Amelia Donaghy	Angelina Jolie
Thelma	Queen Latifah
Captain Howard Cheney	Michael Rooker
Detective Kenny Solomon	Mike McGlone
Eddie Ortiz	Luis Guzman
Richard Thompson	Leland Orser
Dr. Barry Lehman	John Benjamin Hickey
Steve	Bobby Cannavale
Detective Paulie Sellitto	Ed O'Neill
Lt. Carl Hanson	Richard Zeman
Lindsay Rubin	Olivia Birkelund
Alan Rubin	Gary Swanson
Train Engineer	Jim Bulleit
Grandfather	Frank Fontaine
Granddaughter	Zena Grey
NYU Student	Daniel C. Brochu
Taxi Inspector	Desmond Campbell
Young Boy	Christian Veliz
Ortiz's Mother	Mercedes Gomez
Girlfriend in Nightclub	Mary Hammett
Girl in Nightclub	Amanda Gay
Gas Workers	Steve Adams, Larry Day
Police Instructor	Burke Lawrence

and Terry Simpson, Eric Davis (Cops in Apartment), Arthur Holden (Bookstore Clerk), Yashmin Daviault (Rhyme's Sister), Keenan MacWilliam (Rhyme's Niece), David Warshofsky (Amelia's Partner), Mateo Gomez (Hot Dog Vendor), Ted Whittall (Ortiz's Assistant), Peter Michael Dillon (Homicide Detective), Jonathan Stark (Detective), Fulvio Cecere (Forensics Expert), Hal Sherman (Fingerprint Cop), Russell Yuen (Forensics Worker), Andy Bradshaw (Uniform Cop), Jean Marc Bisson, Christopher Bregman (Rescue Workers), Sonya Biddle (Nurse)

A leading criminologist, paralyzed in a freak accident, helps a police-woman track down a brutal serial killer.

© Universal Studios

Angelina Jolie

Queen Latifah, Angelina Jolie

DOGMA

(**LIONS GATE**) Producer, Scott Mosier; Director/Screenplay, Kevin Smith; Co-Producer, Laura Greenlee; Photography, Robert Yeoman; Designer, Robert "Ratface" Holtzman; Costumes, Abigail Murray; Editors, Kevin Smith, Scott Mosier; Music, Howard Shore; Special Visual Effects, Station X Studios; Visual Effects Supervisor, Richard "Dickie" Payne; a View Askew production; Dolby; Super 35 Widescreen; Deluxe color; Rated R; 129 minutes; Release date: November 12, 1999

Matt Damon, Ben Affleck

CAST

Bartleby	Ben Affleck
Cardinal Glick	George Carlin
Loki	Matt Damon
Bethany	Linda Fiorentino
Serendipity	Salma Hayek
Azrael	Jason Lee
Jay	Jason Mewes
Metatron	Alan Rickman
Rufus	Chris Rock
Silent Bob	Kevin Smith
John Doe Jersey	Bud Cort
Stygian Triplets	Barrett Hackney, Jared Pfennigwerth, Kitao Sakurai
Reporter	Brian Christopher O'Halloran
Nun	Betty Aberlin
Priest at St. Stephens	Dan Etheridge
Clinic Girl	Janeane Garofalo
Protestors	Bryan Johnson, Walter Flanagan
Mrs. Reynolds	Nancy Bach
Waiter	Armando Rodriguez
Married Man	Scott Mosier
Kane	Dwight Ewell
God	Alanis Morisette

and Benjamin Cain, Richard Baderinwa, Javon Johnson, Derrick Sanders (Gangsters), Mark Joy (Whitland), Ethan Suplee (Voice of Norman), Guinevere Turner (Bus Station Attendant), Jon Gordon (Blanket Boy on Train), Matthew Maher (Bartender), Robert "Ratface" Holtzman (Officer McGee)

Chris Rock, Jason Mewes, Salma Hayek

A heavenly messenger enlists an abortion clinic worker to stop two fallen angels from re-entering Heaven, an act that will obliterate all human existence.

© Lions Gate Films

Chris Rock, Kevin Smith, Jason Mewes, Linda Fiorentino

Linda Fiorentino

LIBERTY HEIGHTS

Ben Foster, Adrien Brody

Rebekah Johnson, Ben Foster

(**WARNER BROS.**) Producers, Barry Levinson, Paula Weinstein; Executive Producer, Patrick McCormick; Director/Screenplay, Barry Levinson; Photography, Chris Doyle; Designer, Vincent Peranio; Editor, Stu Linder; Music, Andrea Morricone; Music Supervisors, Joel Sill, Allan Mason; Casting, Ellen Chenoweth; a Baltimore/Spring Creek Pictures production; Dolby; Technicolor; Rated R; 127 minutes; Release date: November 17, 1999

CAST

Van Kurtzman	Adrien Brody
Ben Kurtzman	Ben Foster
Little Melvin	Orlando Jones
Ada Kurtzman	Bebe Neuwirth
Nate Kurtzman	Joe Mantegna
Sylvia	Rebekah Johnson
Yussel	David Krumholtz
Charlie	Richard Kline
Pete	Vincent Guastaferro
Trey	Justin Chambers
Dubbie	Carolyn Murphy
Sylvia's Father	James Pickens, Jr.
Rose	Frania Rubinek
Scribbles	Anthony Anderson
Annie	Kiersten Warren
Sheldon	Evan Neuman
Alan	Kevin Sussman
Murray	Gerry Rosenthal
Louie	Charley Scalies
Ted	Shane West
Gail	Cloie Wyatt Taylor
Teacher #2	Susan Duvall
James Brown	Carlton Smith
Mary	Elizabeth Ann Bennett
Anne Whittier	Ellyn O'Connell
Assistant D.A.	Doug Roberts
Bailiff	Al Brown
Burlesque Comic	Kenny Raskin
Butler	Peter Wilkes
Buxom Nurse	Kimberlee Suerth
Women in Court	Mary Lynn Ray, Patsy Grady Abrams
Defense Attorney	Marty Lodge
Ben—8 Years Old	Gideon Jacobs
Judge	Jan Austell
Nick	Timothy J. Scanlin, Jr.
Phil	Ralph Tabakin
Box Office Attendant	Shelley Stokes
Matt	Jay Hillmer
Morris	Stan Brandorff
Mrs. Johnson	Katie Finneran
Nurse	Kate Kiley
Turk	Jake Hoffman
Lenny	Joseph Patrick Abel
Halloween Stripper	Sekiya Billman
Singer	Brenda Russell
Cantor	Barry Black

and Rabbi Dennis N. Math (Rabbi), Judith Knight Young (Teacher #1—1944), Stephen Williams (Wilbert Mosley), Ty Robbins (Sylvia's Mother), Emily Chamberlain (Ben's Teacher), Christian T. Dockins, Kenny Pitt, Zahmu Sankofa (The Three Flames)

In 1954 Baltimore, Nate and Ada Kurtzman and their sons Van and Ben confront issues of race, class and religious distinction.

© Warner Bros.

Adrien Brody, Carolyn Murphy

Ben Foster, Bebe Neuwirth, Frania Rubinek

Ben Foster, Bebe Neuwirth, Joe Mantegna, Adrien Brody

Johnny Depp, Christina Ricci, Marc Pickering

Johnny Depp, Casper Van Dien, Christina Ricci

Johnny Depp, Christina Ricci, Marc Pickering

Miranda Richardson

Michael Gambon, Johnny Depp, Richard Griffiths, Ian McDiarmid

SLEEPY HOLLOW

(PARAMOUNT) Producers, Scott Rudin, Adam Schroeder; Executive Producers, Francis Ford Coppola, Larry Franco; Director, Tim Burton; Screenplay, Andrew Kevin Walker; Screen Story, Kevin Yagher, Andrew Kevin Walker; Based upon the story *The Legend of Sleepy Hollow* by Washington Irving; Photography, Emmanuel Lubezki; Designer, Rick Heinrichs; Editor, Chris Lebenzon; Costumes, Colleen Atwood; Music, Danny Elfman; Visual Effects Supervisor, Jim Mitchell; Special Visual Effects, Industrial Light & Magic; Co-Producer/Human and Creature Special Effects Creator, Kevin Yagher; Casting, Ilene Starger, Susie Figgis; Stunts, Nick Gillard; a Mandalay presentation of a Scott Rudin/American Zoetrope production; Dolby; Deluxe color; Rated R; 105 minutes; Release date: November 19, 1999

Johnny Depp

CAST

Ichabod Crane	Johnny Depp
Katrina Van Tassel	Christina Ricci
Lady Van Tassel/Crone	Miranda Richardson
Baltus Van Tassel	Michael Gambon
Brom Van Brunt	Casper Van Dien
Reverend Steenwyck	Jeffrey Jones
Magistrate Philipse	Richard Griffiths
Doctor Lancaster	Ian McDiarmid
Notary Hardenbrook	Michael Gough
Hessian Horseman	Christopher Walken
Young Masbath	Marc Pickering
Lady Crane	Lisa Marie
Killian	Steven Waddington
Beth Killian	Claire Skinner
Burgomaster	Christopher Lee
High Constable	Alun Armstrong
Jonathan Masbath	Mark Spalding
Sarah	Jessica Oyelowo
Van Ripper	Tony Maudsley
Lord Crane	Peter Guinness
Glenn	Nicholas Hewetson
Theodore	Orlando Seale
Thomas Killian	Sean Stephens
Doctor Lancaster's Wife	Gabrielle Lloyd
Dirk Van Garrett	Robert Sella
Peter Van Garrett	Martin Landau
Spotty Man	Michael Feast
Thuggish Constable	Jamie Foreman
Constable One	Philip Martin Brown
Young Ichabod	Sam Fior
Young Lady Van Tasse	ITessa Allen-Ridge
Young Crone	Cassandra Farndale
Girl 2	Lily Phillips
Little Girl	Bianca Nicholas
Rifleman	Paul Brightwell

Johnny Depp

New York City constable Ichabod Crane arrives in Sleepy Hollow to investigate the mysterious beheadings of several of the town's citizens, ghastly crimes that are attributed to the legendary Headless Horseman. Previous film adaptations of Irving's story include the 1949 Walt Disney-RKO release The Adventures of Ichabod and Mr. Toad.

1999 Academy Award-winner for Best Art Direction. This film received additional nominations for cinematography and costume design.

Christopher Walken

ANYWHERE BUT HERE

(20TH CENTURY FOX) Producer, Laurence Mark; Executive Producer, Ginny Nugent; Director, Wayne Wang; Screenplay, Alvin Sargent; Based on the novel by Mona Simpson; Photography, Roger Deakins; Designer, Donald Graham Burt; Editor, Nicholas C. Smith; Costumes, Betsy Heimann; Music, Danny Elfman; Casting, Victoria Thomas; a Fox 2000 Pictures presentation of a Laurence Mark production; Dolby; Super 35 Widescreen; Deluxe color; Rated PG-13; 114 minutes; Release date: November 12, 1999

CAST

Adele August	Susan Sarandon
Ann August	Natalie Portman
Carol	Bonnie Bedelia
Benny	Shawn Hatosy
Josh Spritzer	Hart Bochner
Janice	Heather McComb
Peter	Corbin Allred
Gail Letterfine	Caroline Aaron
Lillian	Eileen Ryan
Ted	Ray Baker
Jimmy	John Diehl
Hisham	Faran Tahir
Voice of Hisham	Shishir Kurup
4 Year Old Ann	Samantha Goldstein
Man with Mercedes	Scott Burkholder
Assistant Hotel Manager	Yvonna Kopacz
Girls on TV	Eva Amurri, Kieren Van Den Blink, Jennifer Castle
Mrs. Rush	Bebe Drake
George Franklin	Paul Guilfoyle
Teacher	Allison Sie
Real Estate Agent	Sharona Alperin
Homeowner	Mary Elen Trainor

and Elisabeth Moss (Rachel), Ashley Johnson (Sarah), Heather DeLoach (Ellen), Stephanie Niznik (Waitress), Lindley Harrison (Janice's Mother), Michael Milhoan (Cop), Bob Sattler (Bernie), Nina Leichtling (Josh's Wife), Jay Harrington (Waiter), Andrew Bowles (Mourner), Rick Hurst (Reverend), Rachel Wilson (Sylvia), Stephen Berra (Hal), Nina Barry (Casting Assistant), Cricky Long (Casting Executive), Lillian Adams (Jack's Mother), John Carroll Lynch (Jack Irwin), Megan Mullally (Woman Buying Car), George Peck (Man with Luggage)

Adele August uproots herself and her reluctant, 14-year-old daughter Ann and moves to Beverly Hills, hoping to make her dreams of a better life come true.

© Twentieth Century Fox

Susan Sarandon, Natalie Portman

Natalie Portman, Susan Sarandon

Hart Bochner, Susan Sarandon, Natalie Portman

Natalie Portman, Susan Sarandon

Robin Tunney, Arnold Schwarzenegger

END OF DAYS

(**UNIVERSAL**) Producers, Armyan Bernstein, Bill Borden; Executive Producers, Marc Abraham, Thomas A. Bliss; Director/Photography, Peter Hyams; Screenplay, Andrew W. Marlowe; Designer, Richard Holland; Editor, Steven Kemper; Music, John Debney; Music Supervisor, G. Marq Roswell; Costumes, Bobbie Mannix; Creature Effects Supervisor, Stan Winston; Co-Producers, Paul Deason, Andrew W. Marlowe; Special Makeup Effects, Kurtzman, Nicotero & Berger EFX Group; Viusal Effects Supervisor, John "D.J." Desjardin; Stunts, Steve M. Davison; a Beacon Pictures presentation; Dolby; Panavision; Deluxe color; Rated R; 120 minutes; Release date: November 24, 1999

Arnold Schwarzenegger, Gabriel Byrne

CAST

Jericho Cane	Arnold Schwarzenegger
The Man	Gabriel Byrne
Chicago	Kevin Pollak
Christine York	Robin Tunney
Det. Margie Francis	CCH Pounder
Father Kovak	Rod Steiger
Thomas Aquinas	Derrick O'Connor
Mabel	Miriam Margolyes
Head Priest	Udo Kier
Albino	Victor Varnado
Cardinal	Michael O'Hagan
Pope	Mark Margolis
OB/GYN	David Weisenberg
Christine's Mother	Rainer Judd
Pope's Advisor	Luciano Miele
Kellogg	Jack Shearer
Old Woman	Eve Sigall
Carson	Robert Lesser
ConEd Worker #1	Lloyd Garroway
Utility Worker	Gary Anthony Williams
Hospital Cop	John C. Nielsen
Skateboarder	Yannis Bogris
Thomas' Doctor	Elliot Goldwag
Anchor	Elaine Corral Kendall
Emily	Denice D. Lewis

and Rebecca Renee Olstead (Amy), Matt Gallini (Monk), Marc Lawrence (Old Man), Van Quattro (Satan Priest), Charles A. Tamburro (Helicopter Pilot), Lynn Marie Sager (Head Priest's Wife), Linda Pine (Evie Abel), David Franco (Assistant Priest), Steve Kramer (Businessman), Melissa Mascara (Businessman's Wife), John Timothy Botka (Cop at Thomas'), Walter von Huene (Motorman), Father Michael Rocha (Father Mike), Kassandra Kay (Nun), Frankie Ray (Squatter)

Arnold Schwarzenegger, Kevin Pollak

Satan shows up in Manhattan on the eve of the millennium to mate with Christine York, an act that will bring about the destruction of mankind unless ex-cop Jericho Cane can stop him.

Robin Tunney, Victor Varnado

Woody, Buzz Lightyear

TOY STORY 2

(**WALT DISNEY PICTURES**) Producers, Helene Plotkin, Karen Robert Jackson; Executive Producer, Sarah McArthur; Director, John Lasseter; Co-Directors, Lee Unkrich, Ash Brannon; Screenplay, Andrew Stanton, Rita Hsiao, Doug Chamberlin, Chris Webb; Story, John Lasseter, Pete Docter, Ash Brannon, Andrew Stanton; Photography, Sharon Calahan; Designer, William Cone, Jim Pearson; Music, Randy Newman; Editors, Edie Bleiman, David Ian Salter, Lee Unkrich; Supervising Technical Director, Galyn Susman; Story Supervisors, Dan Jeup, Joe Ranft; Supervising Animator, Glenn McQueen; Layout Supervisors, Rikki Cleland-Hura, Ewan Johnson; Casting, Ruth Lambert; a Pixar Animation Studios Film; Dolby; Technicolor; Rated G; 92 minutes; Release date: November 19, 1999

VOICE CAST

Woody	Tom Hanks
Buzz Lightyear	Tim Allen
Jessie	Joan Cusack
Prospector	Kelsey Grammer
Mr. Potato Head	Don Rickles
Slinky Dog	Jim Varney
Rex	Wallace Shawn
Hamm	John Ratzenberger
Bo Peep	Annie Potts
Al McWhiggin	Wayne Knight
Andy	John Morris
Andy's Mom	Laurie Metcalf
Mrs. Potato Head	Estelle Harris
Sarge	R. Lee Ermey
Barbie	Jodi Benson
The Cleaner	Jonathan Harris
Wheezy	Joe Ranft
Emperor Zurg	Andrew Stanton
Aliens	Jeff Pidgeon

Realizing that Woody is a valuable collectable from the 1950s, toy collector Al McWhiggin kidnaps him, an action that prompts Buzz Lightyear and the other toys from Andy's room to attempt a daring rescue. Sequel to the 1995 Disney release Toy Story, with most of the cast repeating their vocals. This film received an Oscar nomination for original song ("When She Loved Me").

Woody, Jessie

Mr. Potato Head, Hamm, Rex, Buzz Lightyear, Slinky Dog

Woody, Wheezy

Kimberly J. Brown, Janet McTeer

Gavin O'Connor, Janet McTeer

Kimberly J. Brown, Janet McTeer

Kimberly J. Brown, Janet McTeer, Gavin O'Connor

TUMBLEWEEDS

(**FINE LINE FEATURES**) Producer, Gregory O'Connor; Executive Producers, Ted Demme, Joel Stillerman, Gavin O'Connor, Thomas J. Mangan IV; Director, Gavin O'Connor; Screenplay, Gavin O'Connor, Angela Shelton; Story, Angela Shelton; Photography, Dan Stoloff; Editor, John Gilroy; Music, David Mansfield; Designer, Bryce Elric Holtshousen; Costumes, Mimi Maxmen; Casting, Todd Thaler; a Solaris production in association with River One Films, presented in association with Spanky Pictures; Dolby; Color; Rated PG-13; 104 minutes; Release date: November 24, 1999

CAST

Mary Jo Walker	Janet McTeer
Ava Walker	Kimberly J. Brown
Dan Miller	Jay O. Sanders
Jack Ranson	Gavin O'Connor
Laurie Pendleton	Laurel Holloman
Ginger	Lois Smith
Mr. Cummings	Michael J. Pollard
Zoe Broussard	Ashley Buccille
Adam Riley	Cody McMains
Mrs. Boman	Linda Porter
Winston Jackson	Brian Tahash
Billy Jo	Josh Carmichael
Check-out Clerk	Dennis Ford
Rachel Riley	Sara Downing
Vice Principal	Joel Polis
Rachel's Boyfriend	Christian Payne
Gas Attendant	Harry Gradzhyan
Captain Nemo's Waitress	Renelouise Smith
Zoe's Mom at Cast Party	Kelly Rodgers
Lady Capulet	Stephanie Zajac
Nurse	Jennifer Paige
Diner Waitress	Lisa Persky

Running from her latest failed relationship, irresponsible Mary Jo Walker and her 12 year old daughter wind up in Southern California where they hope to start anew, until Mary Jo's new lover, Jack, threatens to tear apart the bond between mother and daughter. This film received an Oscar nomination for actress (Janet McTeer).

© Fine Line Features

Jeffrey Wright, Tobey Maguire, Jewel

Jewel, Skeet Ulrich

Jonathan Rhys Meyers, Jim Caviezel

RIDE WITH THE DEVIL

(USA FILMS) Producers, Ted Hope, Robert F. Colesberry, James Schamus; Director, Ang Lee; Screenplay, James Schamus; Based on the novel *Woe to Live On* by Daniel Woodrell; Executive Producer, David Linde; Photography, Frederick Elmes; Designer, Mark Friedberg; Editor, Tim Squyres; Music, Mychael Danna; Costumes, Marit Allen; Associate Producer, Anne Carey; Casting, Avy Kafuman; a Universal Pictures presentation of a Good Machine production; Dolby; Panavision; Deluxe color; Rated R; 138 minutes; Release date: November 24, 1999

CAST

Jake Roedel	Tobey Maguire
Jack Bull Chiles	Skeet Ulrich
Sue Lee Shelley	Jewel
Daniel Holt	Jeffrey Wright
George Clyde	Simon Baker
Pitt Mackeson	Jonathan Rhys Meyers
Black John	James Caviezel
Riley Crawford	Thomas Guiry
Cave Wyatt	Jonathan Brandis
Orton Brown	Tom Wilkinson
Minister	Glenn Q. Pierce
Mrs. Chiles	Kathleen Warfel
Asa Chiles	David Darlow
Horton Lee, Sr.	Michael Nash
Otto Roedel	John Judd
George	Don Shanks
Ted	Jay Thorson
Turner Rawls	Matthew Faber
Mrs. Clark	Celia Weston
Alf Bowden	Mark Ruffalo
Babe Hudspeth	Stephen Mailer
Mr. Evans	Zack Grenier
Mrs. Evans	Donna Thomason
Mary Evans	Cassie Mae Sears
Wilma Brown	Margo Martindale
Quantrill	John Ales
Guards	Jeremy W. Auman, Scott C. Sener
Wedding Musicians:	Zan McLeod (Guitar), John Whelan (Accordian), Roger Landes (Mandolin), Jeffrey Dover, Tyler Johnson (Drummers), Kelly Werts (Fiddle)
Storekeeper	Dean Vivian
Storekeeper's Wife	Cheryl Weaver
Clark Girl	Amber Griffith
Federals at Farm	Ric Averill, Buck Baker
Encampment Singer	Martin E. Liebschner, Jr

and Marvin Frank Schroeder, Steven Price, David L. Asher (Encampment Musicians), James Urbaniak, David Rees Snell (Poker Players), Dave Wilson (Quantrill's Lieutenant), Larry Greer (Federal Captain), Kevin Fewell (Federal Lieutenant), John Durbin (Skaggs), Michael Owen (Federal Recruits Captain), Jim Shelby, Addison Myers (Southern Gentlemen), Michael Linsley Rapport (Drunk Raider), Joseph Moynihan (Mr. Riggs), Jennie Nauman (Mrs. Riggs), Christine Brandt (Pleading Woman), Bill Grivna (Dulinski), Nora Denney (Elderly Woman), Harry Gibbs (Old Man), Clayton Vest (Young Boy), Roger Denesha, Jacob Kozlowski, David Lee Burnos, Jr. (Lawrence Raiders), Jennifer Ackland (Grace Shelley Chiles), T. Max Graham (Reverend Wright)

On the Kansas/Missouri border at the start of the Civil War, longtime friends Jake Roedel and Jack Bull Chiles join the conflict as Bushwhackers, engaging in guerilla warfare and executing daring raids on Northern soldiers and sympathizers.

© Universal Studios, Inc.

FLAWLESS

(**MGM**) Producers, Joel Schumacher, Jane Rosenthal; Executive Producer, Neil Machlis; Director/Screenplay, Joel Schumacher; Photography, Declan Quinn; Designer, Jan Roelfs; Editor, Mark Stevens; Costumes, Daniel Orlandi; Music, Bruce Roberts; Co-Producers, Caroline Baron, Amy Sayres; Casting, Mali Finn; a Tribeca production; Dolby; Panavision; Deluxe color; Rated R; 111 minutes; Release date: November 24, 1999

CAST

Walt Koontz	Robert De Niro
Rusty	Philip Seymour Hoffman
Leonard Wilcox	Barry Miller
Jacko	Chris Bauer
Tommy	Skipp Sudduth
Cha-Cha	Wilson Jermaine Heredia
Amazing Grace	Nashom Benjamin
Ivana	Scott Allen Cooper
Pogo	Rory Cochrane
Tia	Daphne Rubin-Vega
Raymond Camacho	Vincent Laresca
Amber	Karina Arroyave
Sonny	John Enos
Detective Noonan	Jude Ciccolella
Mrs. Spivak	Mina Bern
Karen	Wanda De Jesus

Madhur Jaffrey (Dr. Nirmala), Mark Margolis (Vinnie), Shiek Mahmud-Bey (Vance), Luis Saguar (Mr. Z), Kyle Rivers (LeShaun), Sammy Rhee (Mr. Pim), Hyunsoo Lee (Mrs. Pim), Richie LaMontagne (Carmine), Penny Balfour (Cristal), Winter B. Uhlarik (Tasha), Raven O (Notorious F.A.G.), Joey Arias (Stormy), Jackie Beat (Gypsy), Blake Willett, Ingrid Rivera (Cops), Craig Braun (Paulie), John Doumanian (Mr. Terzola), Melissa Osborn (Tourist), John Contratti (Customer), Stacy Highsmith (Denise), Rod Rodriguez, Alice Williams (Lesbians), Antonette Schwartzberg (Mrs. Terzola), Hamilton De Oliveira (Hotel Janitor), Logan McCall, John E. Mack (EMS Technicians), John R. Corcoran (Physical Therapist), Matt Merchant (Man in Crowd), Kevin Aviance, Coco LaChine, Jose Angel Garcia, Bruce Roberts (Singers), Al Marz (Cristal's Boyfriend), Michelle Robinson, Nina Sonja Peterson (Dancers), Larry Marx (Bar Patron), Mitchell Lichtenstein (Gay Republican Spokesperson), John Fink (Gay Republican Lawyer), Bret Kropp (Drag Queen), Cooley (Cop), Constance Boardman (Reporter), Lucy Cerezo-Scully, Al Thompson (Paramedics)

After suffering a stroke, homophobic ex-security guard Walt Koontz reluctantly turns to his drag queen neighbor Rusty to give him singing lessons to help him restore his speech.

© Metro-Goldwyn-Mayer Pictures Inc.

Philip Seymour Hoffman, Robert De Niro

Anjelica Huston, Marion O'Dwyer

AGNES BROWNE

(**USA FILMS**) Producers, Jim Sheridan, Arthur Lappin, Anjelica Huston, Greg Smith; Executive Producers, Morgan O'Sullivan, Tom Palmieri, Laurie Mansfield, Gerry Browne; Director, Anjelica Huston; Screenplay, John Goldsmith, Brendan O'Carroll; Based on the novel *The Mammy* by Brendan O'Carroll; Line Producer, Paul Myler; Photography, Anthony B. Richmond; Designer, David Brockhurst; Editor, Eva Gardos; Costumes, Joan Bergin; Music, Paddy Moloney; Casting, Maureen Hughes; an October Films presentation of a Hell's Kitchen production; Dolby; Color; Rated R; 91 minutes; Release date: December 3, 1999

CAST

Agnes Browne	Anjelica Huston
Marion Monks	Marion O'Dwyer
Mark Browne	Niall O'Shea
Frankie Browne	Ciaran Owens
Cathy Browne	Roxanna Williams
Simon Browne	Carl Power
Dermot Browne	Mark Power
Rory Browne	Gareth O'Connor
Trevor Browne	James Lappin
Mr. Billy	Ray Winstone
Pierre	Arno Chevrier
Mr. Aherne	Gerard McSorley
Himself	Tom Jones

June Rodgers (Fat Annie), Jennifer Gibney (Winnie the Mackerel), Gavin Kelty (Micko), Richie Walker (Jacko the Box), Sean Fox (Liam the Sweeper), Paul McCreery, Chrissie McCreery (Women in Market), Virginia Cole (Woman with Jumpers), Buster (Sparticus the Dog), Steve Blount (Tommo Monks), Noirin Ni Riain (Church Soprano), Arthur Lappin (Priest), Paddy McCarney (Hearse Driver), Terry Byrne (Carmichael), Joe Hanley (Rooney), Joanne Sloane (The Widow Clarke), Cristen Kauffman (Woman Buying Fish), Joe Gallagher (Post Office Clerk), Frank Melia (Shopkeeper), Keith Murtagh (Market Spiv), Clodagh Long (Mary Dowdall), Aedin Moloney (Shop Assistant), Eamonn Hunt (Mr. Foley), Jim Smith (Butcher), Olivia Tracey (Posh Customer with Dog), Tara Van Zyl (Shop Assistant), Tallis Music Services (Band on Seaside Pavilion), Peter Dix (Man in Pub), Anna Megan (Woman in Pub), Anne Bushnell (Singer in Restaurant), Pat Fitzpatrick, Patrick Collins, Michael Flynn (Restaurant Band), Frank McCusker (Tom O'Toole), Doreen Keogh (Nun in Mortuary), Sandra Corbally (Nurse in Mortuary), Joe Pigott (Wally the Ticket Tout), Maria Hayden (Receptionist at the Shelbourne Hotel), Cecil Bell (Mr. O'Dwyer), Don Archell (Tom Jones' Minder), Peter Adaus, Ian Thompson, Keith Airey, Steve Pearce (The Tom Jones Band)

Following the unexpected death of her husband, Agnes Browne becomes determined to make ends meet for herself and her seven children in their Dublin neighborhood. This was the first theatrical film directed by actress Anjelica Huston.

© October Films

SWEET AND LOWDOWN

Sean Penn

Sean Penn, Samantha Morton

(**SONY PICTURES CLASSICS**) Producer, Jean Doumanian; Executive Producer, J.E. Beaucaire; Co-Executive Producers, Jack Rollins, Charles H. Joffe, Letty Aronson; Director/Screenplay, Woody Allen; Co-Producer, Richard Brick; Photography, Zhao Fei; Designer, Santo Loquasto; Editor, Alisa Lepselter; Costumes, Laura Cunningham Bauer; Music Arranger/Conductor, Dick Hyman; Casting, Juliet Taylor, Laura Rosenthal; a Sweetland Films presentation of a Jean Doumanian production; Dolby; DuArt color; Rated PG-13; 95 minutes; Release date: December 3, 1999

CAST

Al Torrio	Anthony LaPaglia
Bill Shields	Brian Markinson
Ellie	Gretchen Mol
Hattie	Samantha Morton
Emmet Ray	Sean Penn
Blanche	Uma Thurman
Harry	James Urbaniak
Mr. Haynes	John Waters
Sid Bishop	Vincent Guastaferro
Hazel (Hooker #1)	Constance Schulman
Iris (Hooker #2)	Kellie Overbey
Omer	Mark Damon Johnson
Don	Darryl Alan Reed
Chester Weems	Dick Monday
Themselves	Woody Allen, Ben Duncan, Nat Hentoff, Douglas McGrath
Movie Director	Josh Mowery
William Weston	Fred Goehner
Django Reinhardt	Michael Sprague
Joe Bedloe	Brad Garrett
A.J. Pickman	Daniel Okrent
Boss	Dan Moran
Ben	Tony Darrow
Ace-PoolPlayer	Chris Bauer
Alvin	Ron Cephas Jones
Musician Friends	Steve Bargonetti, Benjamin Franklin Brown
Bass Player #1	Vince Giordano

and Emme Kemp, Clark Gayton, Macus McLaurin (Jam Session Musicians), Carolyn Saxon (Phyllis), Drummond Erskine, Joe Ambrose (Hobos), Molly Price (Ann), Joe Rigano (Stagehand), Denis O'Hare (Jake), Dennis Stein (Dick Ruth—Club Owner), Katie Hamill (Mary), Kaili Vernoff (Gracie), Carole Bayeux (Rita—Opium Party Hostess), Paula Parrish, Cory Solar, Lexi Egz, Yvette Mercedes, Peter Leung (Party Guests), William Addy (Master of Ceremonies), Mary Stout (Felicity Thomson—Amateur Singer), Dick Mingalone (Birdman), Mr. Spoons (Spoon Player), Carol Woods (Helen Minton), Eddy Davis (Bass Player #2), Ralph Pope (Panhandler), Jerome Richardson, Earl P. McIntyre, James Williams, Frank Wellington Wess, Al Bryant (Club Musicians), Ray Garvey (Club Manager), Sally Placksin (Sally Jillian), Lola Pashalinski (Blanche's Friend), Simon Wettenhall, Orange Kellin, Brooks Giles III (Jam Session Musicians), Alfred Sauchelli, Jr. (Ned—Pool Player), Michael Bolus (Lynch—Bar Room Friend), Mick O'Rourke, John P. McLaughlin (Holdup Men), Chuck Lewkowicz (Police Officer), Rick Mowat (Flat Tire Man), Ted Wilkins (Gas Station Proprietor)

Some jazz enthusiasts relate the story of brilliant-but-forgotten guitarist Emmet Ray and his thoughtless treatment of those closest to him. This film received Oscar nominations for actor (Sean Penn) and supporting actress (Samantha Morton).

© Sony Pictures Entertainment

Sean Penn, James Urbaniak

Marc Donato, Chloë Sevigny

Sigourney Weaver, David Strathairn

A MAP OF THE WORLD

(**FIRST LOOK PICTURES**) Producers, Kathleen Kennedy, Frank Marshall; Executive Producer, Willi Bär; Co-Producer, Lisa Niedenthal; Director, Scott Elliott; Screenplay, Peter Hedges, Polly Platt; Based on the novel by Jane Hamilton; Photography, Seamus McGarvey; Editors, Craig McKay, Naomi Geraghty; Designer, Richard Toyon; Music, Pat Metheny; Costumes, Suzette Daigle; Casting, Avy Kaufman; a Kennedy/Marshall production, presented in association with Cinerenta Filmproduktion; Dolby; Color; Rated R; Dolby; Deluxe color; Rated R; 125 minutes; Release date: December 3, 1999

Sigourney Weaver

CAST

Alice Goodwin	Sigourney Weaver
Theresa Collins	Julianne Moore
Howard Goodwin	David Strathairn
Paul Reverdy	Arliss Howard
Carole Mackessy	Chloë Sevigny
Nellie	Louise Fletcher
Debbie	Sara Rue
Dyshett	Aunjanue Ellis
Sherry	Nicole Ari Parker
Lynelle	Bruklin Harris
Dan Collins	Ron Lea
Emma	Dara Perlmutter
Claire	Kayla Perlmutter
Robbie Mackessy	Marc Donato
Susan Durkin	Lisa Emery
Audrey	Hayley Lochner
Lizzie	Victoria Rudiak
Judge Patterson	John Bourgeois
Detective Grogan	Nancy Mcalear

Alice Goodwin, a farmer and part-time school nurse, faces a double crises when her neighbor's child drowns under Alice's care, and a boy at school accuses her of sexual abuse.

David Strathairn, Julianne Moore

CRADLE WILL ROCK

Philip Baker Hall, Susan Sarandon, John Cusack

Cary Elwes, Adele Robbins, Hank Azaria, Angus Macfadyen

Joan Cusack, Bill Murray

(**TOUCHSTONE**) Producers, Jon Kilik, Lydia Dean Pilcher, Tim Robbins; Executive Producers, Louise Krakower, Frank Beacham, Allan Nicholls; Director/Screenplay, Tim Robbins; Photography, Jean Yves Escoffier; Designer, Richard Hoover; Editor, Geraldine Peroni; Costumes, Ruth Meyers; Music, David Robbins; Songs from *The Cradle Will Rock* by Marc Blitzstein; Casting, Douglas Aibel; a Havoc production; Distributed by Buena Vista Pictures; Dolby; Panavision; Technicolor; Rated R; 134 minutes; Release date: December 8, 1999

CAST

Marc Blitzstein	Hank Azaria
Diego Rivera	Ruben Blades
Hazel Huffman	Joan Cusack
Nelson Rockefeller	John Cusack
John Houseman	Cary Elwes
Gray Mathers	Philip Baker Hall
Hallie Flanagan	Cherry Jones
Orson Welles	Angus Macfadyen
Tommy Crickshaw	Bill Murray
Countess La Grange	Vanessa Redgrave
Margherita Sarfatti	Susan Sarandon
John Adair	Jamey Sheridan
Aldo Silvano	John Turturro
Olive Stanton	Emily Watson
Harry Hopkins	Bob Balaban
Sid	Jack Black
Larry	Kyle Gass
Carlo	Paul Giamatti
Frank Marvel	Barnard Hughes
Sophie Silvano	Barbara Sukowa

and Maxine Elliot's: Victoria Clark (Dulce Fox), Erin Hill (Sandra Mescal), Daniel Jenkins (Will Geer), Timothy Jerome (Bert Weston), Chris McKinney (Canada Lee), Henry Stram (Hiram Sherman), Adele Robbins (Augusta Weissberger), Lee Arenberg (Abe Feder), Allan Nicholls (George Zorn), Rob Carlson (National Guardsman), Alison Tatlock (Reporter), Dina Platias (Lucille Schly), Pamela D. Henry (Alma Dixon), Emma Smith Stevens (Stagehand), Steven Tyler (Lehman Engel), Charles Giordano (Accordion), Jeffrey Kievit (Trumpet), Kenneth Finn (Trombone), Kenneth Hitchcock (Clarinet), David D'Angelo (Alto Saxaphone), David Ratajczak (Percussion); Federal Theatre: Stephen Spinella (Donald O'Hara), Brenda Pressley (Rose), Brian Brophy (Pierre De Rohan), David Costabile (Beaver Man), Marla Schaffel (Beaver Woman), Dominic Cortese (Beaver Accordion Accompanist); Power: John Carpenter (William Randolph Hearst), Gretchen Mol (Marion Davies), Gil Robbins (Congressman Starnes), Harris Yulin (Chairman Martin Dies), Ned Bellamy (Paul Edwards), V.J. Foster (James), William Duell (Butler), Albert Macklin (Tailor), Scott Sowers, Bobby Amore (Reporters); Silvano: Lynn Cohen (Mama), Dominic Chianese (Papa), Peter Jacobson (Uncle), Evan Katz (Joey), Alysia Zucker (Chance), Sarah Hyland (Giovanna), Stephanie Roth (Marta); Vaudeville: Spanky McHugh (Melvin), Todd Stockman (Puppeteer), Patrick Husted (Vaudeville Theatre Manager), Jay Green (Plate Twirler), Carolyn West (Assistant Plate Twirler); Blitzstein: Steven Skybell (Bertolt Brecht), Susan Heimbinder (Eva Blitzstein), Audra McDonald ("Joe Worker" Singer), Robert Ari, Michele Pawk (Liberty Committee), Gregg Edelman (Dream Larry Foreman), Matthew Bennett (Dream Cop), Carolyn West (Dream Larry Foreman), Matthew Bennett (Dream Cop); Rockefeller Center: Brian Powell (Aide), Jack Willis (Lawyer), Gilbert Cruz (Mendez), Robert Hirschfeld (Sol), P.J. Brown (Guard), Michael Rivkin, Keira Naughton (Protesters), Taylor Stanley (Claire), Tommy Allen (Pete); Diego: Corina Katt (Frida Kahlo), Josie Whittlesey, Sandra Lindquist, Tamika Lamison (Models); Opening: Edward James Hyland (Worker in Theatre), Boris McGiver (Man on Street); WPA: Chris Bauer (Carpenter), Leonardo Cimino (Man in Line), Patti Tippo (Clerk), Carrie Preston (Administrator), Mary Robbins, Chris Talbott, Susan Bruce, Ian Bagg (Disgruntled Workers); Riot: Tony Amendola (Carl Jaspar), Charles Page (Guard), Jennifer Lamb, Derrick Simmons, Lisa Cain, Keith Siglinger, Brian Smyj, Mike Russo (Cops)

While the government tries to stop funding for the WPA's Federal Theatre project, the company members attempt to put on a production of the pro-labor musical The Cradle Will Rock.

Cary Elwes, Adele Robbins, Angus Macfadyen, Cherry Jones, John Turturro

Emily Watson, John Turturro

Ruben Blades

Vanessa Redgrave

Hank Azaria, Cary Elwes

Tom Hanks, David Morse

Doug Hutchison, David Morse, Tom Hanks

Sam Rockwell

Mr. Jingles. Michael Jeter

Tom Hanks, Michael Clarke Duncan

Bonnie Hunt, Tom Hanks

THE GREEN MILE

(**WARNER BROS.**) Producers, David Valdes, Frank Darabont; Director/Screenplay, Frank Darabont; Based on the novel by Stephen King; Photography, David Tattersall; Designer, Terence Marsh; Editor, Richard Francis-Bruce; Costumes, Karyn Wagner; Music, Thomas Newman; Visual Effects, Industrial Light & Magic; Casting, Mali Finn; a Castle Rock Entertainment presentation of a Darkwoods production; Dolby; Technicolor; Rated R; 187 minutes; Release date: December 10, 1999

Tom Hanks, Barry Pepper, David Morse

CAST

Paul Edgecomb ....Tom Hanks
Brutus "Brutal" Howell...David Morse
Jan Edgecomb..Bonnie Hunt
John Coffey...Michael Clarke Duncan
Warden Hal Moores..James Cromwell
Eduard Delacroix ....Michael Jeter
Arlen Bitterbuck ....Graham Greene
Percy Wetmore ....Doug Hutchison
"Wild Bill" Wharton ....Sam Rockwell
Dean Stanton...Barry Pepper
Harry Terwilliger...Jeffrey DeMunn
Melinda Moores..Patricia Clarkson
Toot-Toot..Harry Dean Stanton
Old Paul Edgecomb ....Dabbs Greer
Elaine Connelly..Eve Brent
Klaus Detterick ....William Sadler
Orderly Hector ....Mack C. Miles
Man in Nursing Home ....Rai Tasco
Lady in Nursing Home ....Edrie Warner
Marjorie Detterick ....Paula Malcomson
Howie Detterick..Christopher Ives
Kathe Detterick ....Evanne Drucker
Cora Detterick..Bailey Drucker
Sheriff McGee...Brian Libby
Bill Dodg...Brent Briscoe
Jack Van Hay..Bill McKinney
Burt Hammersmith ....Gary Sinise
Cynthia Hammersmith..Rachel Singer
Hammersmith's Son...Scotty Leavenworth
Hammersmith's Daughter..........................Katelyn Leavenworth
Earl the Plumber ....Bill Gratton
Woman at Del's Execution ....Dee Croxton
Wife at Del's Execution ....Rebecca Klingler
Husband at Del's Execution...Gary Imhoff
Police Officer ....Van Epperson
Reverend at Funeral.....................................Reverend David E. Browning

Tom Hanks

In a Southern prison in 1935, guard Paul Edgecomb develops a relationship with John Coffey, a massive, gentle and naive man convicted of brutally murdering two young girls. This film received Oscar nominations for picture, supporting actor (Michael Clarke Duncan), screenplay adaptation, and sound.

©CR Films, LLC

Jeffrey DeMunn, Tom Hanks, Michael Clarke Duncan

Rob Schneider, William Forsythe

Arija Bareikis, Rob Schneider

Gabrielle Tuite, Oded Fehr

Eddie Griffin, Rob Schneider

DEUCE BIGALOW:
MALE GIGOLO

(**TOUCHSTONE**) Producers, Sid Ganis, Barry Bernardi; Executive Producers, Adam Sandler, Jack Giarraputo; Director, Mike Mitchell; Screenplay, Harris Goldberg, Rob Schneider; Photography, Peter Lyons Collister; Designer, Alan Au; Editors, George Bowers, Lawrence Jordan; Costumes, Molly Maginnis; Co-Producers, Alex Siskin, Harris Goldberg; Music, Teddy Castellucci; Casting, Marcia Ross, Donna Morong, Gail Goldberg; Distributed by Buena Vista Pictures; a Happy Madison production in association with Out of the Blue...Entertainment; Dolby; Panavision; Technicolor; Rated R; 88 minutes; Release date: December 10, 1999

CAST

Deuce Bigalow	Rob Schneider
Detective Chuck Fowler	Wiliam Forsythe
T.J. Hicks	Eddie Griffin
Kate	Arija Bareikis
Antoine Laconte	Oded Fehr
Claire	Gail O'Grady
Bob Bigalow	Richard Riehle
Elaine Fowler	Jacqueline Obradors
Jabba Lady	Big Boy
Ruth	Amy Poehler
Bergita	Dina Platias
Tina	Torsten Voges
Carol	Deborah Lemen
Allison	Bree Turner
Neil	Andrew Shaifer

and Allen Covert (Restaurant Manager), Elle Tanner Schneider (Girl of America), Barry Cutler (Dr. Rosenblatt), Jacqueline Titone (Sally), Karlee Holden (Megan), Chloé Hult (Amber), Natalie Garner (Natalie), Robb Skyler (District Attorney), Jason Wall (Bailiff), John Harrington Bland (Patient), Caroline Ambrose (Mother), Louise Rapport (Old Woman in Line), Pilar Schneider (Old Lady at Restaurant), Shain Holden (Waiter at Pool), Gabrielle Tuite (Beautiful Porsche Woman), Charlie Curtis (Half Dressed Girl), Thomas Bellin (Elderly Man in Car), Flora Burke (Elderly Woman in Car)

In order to pay for an expensive aquarium he's destroyed while housesitting, hapless fish-tank cleaner Deuce Bigalow launches a new career as a gigolo.

©Touchstone Pictures

DIAMONDS

(**MIRAMAX**) Producer, Patricia T. Green; Executive Producer, Gerald Green; Co-Executive Producers, Rainer Bienger (Cinerenta), Andrew Somper; Director, John Asher; Screenplay, Allan Aaron Katz; Line Producer, Hannah Hempstead; Photography, Paul Elliott; Designer, Vance Lorenzini; Editor, C. Timothy O'Meara; Music, Joel Goldsmith; Costumes, Vicki Sanchez; Casting, Dan Parada; a Total Film Group/Cinerenta presentation; U.S.-German; Dolby; Color; Rated PG-13; 91 minutes; Release date: December 10, 1999

Lauren Bacall, Kirk Douglas

CAST

Harry Agensky	Kirk Douglas
Lance Agensky	Dan Aykroyd
Michael Agensky	Corbin Allred
Sin-Dee	Lauren Bacall
Moses	Kurt Fuller
Sugar	Jenny McCarthy
Tiffany	Mariah O'Brien
Roseanne	June Chadwick
Border Guard	Lee Tergesen
Tarzan	Val Bisiglio
Mugger	Allan Aaron Katz
Pit Boss	Roy Conrad
Gambler	John Landis
June (Waitress)	Joyce Bulifant
Roxanne	Liz Gandara
Glory	Rebecca Thorpe
Penelope	Pamela Coleman
Kim	Kamla Greer
Ellie	Jacqueline Collen
Bev	Karen Mal
Damon	James Russo

A one-time welterweight champion, recovering from a stroke, travels with his estranged son and grandson to Las Vegas to uncover a valuable stash of diamonds.

©Miramax Films

Jenny McCarthy

Kirk Douglas, Corbin Allred, Dan Aykroyd

Tobey Maguire

Tobey Maguire, Charlize Theron

THE CIDER HOUSE RULES

(**MIRAMAX**) Producer, Richard N. Gladstein; Executive Producers, Bob Weinstein, Harvey Weinstein, Bobby Cohen, Meryl Poster; Director, Lasse Hallström; Screenplay, John Irving, based upon his novel; Co-Producers, Alan C. Blomquist, Leslie Holleran; Photography, Oliver Stapleton; Designer, David Gropman; Editor, Lisa Zeno Churgin; Costumes, Renée Ehrlich Kalfus; Music, Rachel Portman; Casting, Hopkins, Smith & Barden; a Filmcolony production; Dolby; Super 35 Widescreen; Deluxe color; Rated PG-13; 125 minutes; Release date: December 10, 1999.

CAST

Homer Wells	Tobey Maguire
Candy Kendall	Charlize Theron
Mr. Rose	Delroy Lindo
Wally Worthington	Paul Rudd
Dr. Wilbur Larch	Michael Caine
Nurse Edna	Jane Alexander
Nurse Angela	Kathy Baker
Rose Rose	Erykah Badu
Buster	Kieran Culkin
Olive Worthington	Kate Nelligan
Peaches	Heavy D
Muddy	K. Todd Freeman
Mary Agnes	Paz De La Huerta
Ray Kendall	J.K. Simmons
Jack	Evan Dexter Parke
Vernon	Jimmy Flynn
Hero	Lonnie R. Farmer
Fuzzy	Erik Per Sullivan
Curly	Spencer Diamond
Copperfield	Sean Andrew
Steerforth	John Albano
Hazel	Sky McCole-Bartusiak
Clara	Clare Daly
Major Winslow	Colin Irving
Carla	Annie Corley
Adopting Father	Patrick Donnelly
Adopting Mother	Edie Schechter
12 Year Old Girl	Kasey Berry
Big Dot	Mary Bogue
Debra	Victoria Stankiewcz
Florence	Christine Stevens
Dr. Holtz	Earle C. Batchelder
Mrs. Goodhall	Norma Fine
Adopted Child	Daniel Walsh
Little Girl	Kathleen E. Broadhurst
Station Master	John Irving

Homer Wells, raised in an orphanage where he was taught the ways of life by doctor and illegal abortionist Wilbur Larch, leaves behind the only life he has known to find his place in the world.

1999 Academy Award-winner for Best Supporting Actor (Michael Caine) and Screenplay Adaptation. This film received additional Oscar nominations for picture, director, editing, original score, and art direction.

©Miramax Films

Delroy Lindo, Tobey Maguire

Michael Caine, Tobey Maguire

Tobey Maguire

Erykah Badu, Charlize Theron

Charlize Theron, Tobey Maguire

Michael Caine

SIMPATICO

(FINE LINE FEATURES) Producers, Dan Lupovitz, Timm Oberwelland, Jean-Francois Fonlupt; Executive Producers, Greg Shapiro, Joel Lubin, Sue Baden-Powell; Director, Matthew Warchus; Screenplay, Matthew Warchus, David Nicholls; Based on the play by Sam Shepard; Associate Producer, Leon Melas; Photography, John Toll; Designer, Amy B. Ancona; Costumes, Karen Patch; Editor, Pasquale Buba; Music, Stewart Copeland; Casting, Daniel Swee, Karen Meisels; an Axiom Entertainment, Emotion Pictures, Kingsgate Films production; Dolby; Color; Rated R; 106 minutes; Release date: December 15, 1999

Catherine Keener, Albert Finney

CAST

Vinnie Webb	Nick Nolte
Lyle Carter	Jeff Bridges
Rosie	Sharon Stone
Cecilia	Catherine Keener
Simms	Albert Finney
Young Vinnie	Shawn Hatosy
Young Rosie	Kimberly Williams
Young Carter	Liam Waite
Jess	Whit Crawford
Louis	Bob Harter
5 Year Old Kid	Angus T. Jones
Charlie	Ken Strunk
Kelly	Ashley Gutherie
Airport Attendant	Maria Carretero
Flight Attendant	Nicole Forester
Bartender	Joseph Hindy
Passenger (Pete)	Loyd Catlett

and Brigitta Simone (First Class Flight Attendant), Christina Cabot (Waitress), Mack Dryden (Rosie's Father), Kristen Knickerbocker (Becky), Barb Rossmeisl (Woman #1), Roxana Brusso (Checkout Girl), Jeannine Corbo (Ostario Attendant), Malina Moye (Receptionist), Dan Willoughby (Official), Kaizaad Kptwal, Ayman Elsebaet, Adham Sager, Randy Cohlmia (Arab Businessmen), Trevor Denman, Allan Bochdahl (Race Callers)

Nick Nolte

Lyle Carter, a billionaire who has built his fortune on breeding and training thoroughbreds, is contacted by a past friend, Vinnie, who wants desperately to make ammends for a scam he and Carter pulled on race commissioner Simms some twenty years earlier.

© Fine Line Features

Jeff Bridges

Shawn Hatosy, Kimberly Williams, Liam Waite

Robin Williams, Oliver Platt, Kiersten Connelly

BICENTENNIAL MAN

Embeth Davidtz, Robin Williams, Embeth Davidtz

(**TOUCHSTONE/COLUMBIA**) Producers, Wolfgang Petersen, Gail Katz, Laurence Mark, Neal Miller, Chris Columbus, Mark Radcliffe, Michael Barnathan; Director, Chris Columbus; Screenplay, Nicholas Kazan; Based upon the short story by Isaac Asimov, and the novel *The Positronic Man* by Isaac Asimov and Robert Silverberg; Executive Producer, Dan Kolsrud; Photography, Phil Meheux; Designer, Norman Reynolds; Editor, Neil Travis; Costumes, Joseph G. Aulisi; Music, James Horner; Song: Then You Look at Me by James Horner (music), Will Jennings (lyrics)/performed by Celine Dion; Visual Effects, Dream Quest Images; Robotic Effects, Steve Johnson's XFX Inc.; Old Age Make-up Effects Designer, Greg Cannom; Visual Effects Supervisor, James E. Price; Casting, Janet Hirshenson, Jane Jenkins; a 1492 Production in association with Laurence Mark Productions and Radiant Productions; Dolby; Technicolor; Rated PG; 131 minutes; Release date: December 17, 1999

CAST

Andrew Martin	Robin Williams
Sir (Richard Martin)	Sam Neill
Adult Little Miss/Portia	Embeth Davidtz
Rupert Burns	Oliver Platt
Ma'am	Wendy Crewson
Little Miss, 7 Yrs. Old (Amanda)	Hallie Kate Eisenberg
Dennis Mansky	Stephen Root
Female President	Lynne Thigpen
Lloyd	Bradley Whitford
Galatea Robotic/Human	Kiersten Warren
Bill Feingold	John Michael Higgins
Male President	George D. Wallace
Miss, 9 Yrs. Old	Lindze Letherman
Miss (Grace)	Angela Landis
Lloyd, 10 Yrs. Old	Igor Hiller

and Joe Bellan, Brett Wagner (Robot Delivery Men), Scott Waugh (Motorcycle Punk), Quinn Smith (Frank), Kristy Connelly (Monica), Jay Johnston (Charles), Ples Griffin (Zimbabwe Representative), Marcia Pizzo (Lloyd's Wife), Paula Dupré Pesmen (Feingold's Assistant), Clarke Devereux (Priest), Bruce Kenneth Wagner (Engagement Party Guest), Paula West (Singer), Kevin "Tiny" Ancell, Richard Cross (Restoration Worker), Adam Bryant (Humanoid Head)

Robin Williams

Andrew, a robot purchased by the Martin family to be their servant, begins showing increasingly human characteristics, prompting him on a 200 year journey to discover the intricacies of humanity, life and love. This film received an Oscar nomination for makeup.

Robin Williams, Sam Neill

Stuart Little, Hugh Laurie, Jonathan Lipnicki, Geena Davis

Stuart Little

Monty

Camille Stout, Reginald Stout

Stuart Little

STUART LITTLE

(**COLUMBIA**) Producer, Douglas Wick; Executive Producers, Jeff Franklin, Steve Waterman, Jason Clark; Director, Rob Minkoff; Screenplay, M. Night Shyamalan, Greg Brooker; Based on the book by E.B. White; Photography, Guillermo Navarro; Designer, Bill Brzeski; Editor, Tom Finan; Music, Alan Silvestri; Song: Walking Tall by Burt Bacharach, Tim Rice/performed by Lyle Lovett; Costumes, Joseph Porro; Senior Visual Effects Supervisor, John Dykstra; Special Visual Effects, Sony Pictures Imageworks; Cat Visual Effects, Rhythm & Hues, Inc.; Casting, Debra Zane; a Douglas Wick and Franklin/Waterman production; Dolby; Deluxe color; Rated PG; 85 minutes; Release date: December 17, 1999

Geena Davis, Snowbell, Jonathan Lipnicki, Stuart Little, Hugh Laurie

CAST

Voice of Stuart Little	Michael J. Fox
Mrs. Little	Geena Davis
Mr. Little	Hugh Laurie
George Little	Jonathan Lipnicki
Voice of Snowbell	Nathan Lane
Voice of Smokey	Chazz Palminteri
Voice of Monty	Steve Zahn
Voice of Lucky	Jim Doughan
Voice of Red	David Alan Grier
Voice of Mr. Stout	Bruno Kirby
Voice of Mrs. Stout	Jennifer Tilly
Voice of Race Announcer	Stan Freberg
Uncle Crenshaw	Jeffrey Jones
Aunt Tina	Connie Ray
Aunt Beatrice	Allyce Beasley
Cousin Edgar	Brian Doyle-Murray
Grandma Estelle	Estelle Getty
Grandpa Spencer	Harold Gould
Uncle Stretch	Patrick O'Brien
Mrs. Keeper	Julia Sweeney
Dr. Beechwood	Dabney Coleman

and Miles Marsico (Anton), Jon Polito (Officer Sherman), Jim Doughan (Officer Allen), Joe Bays (Race Starter), Taylor Negron (Salesman), Kimmy Robertson (Race Spectator), Tannis Benedict (Hot Dog Vendor), Chuck Blechen, Westleigh Michael Styer (Skippers), Larry Goodhue (Boat Registrar)

Stuart Little

The Little family sets out to adopt a brother for their son George, and returns from the orphanage with a talking mouse named Stuart. This film received an Oscar nomination for visual effects.

© Columbia Pictures Industries

Geena Davis, Stuart Little

Stuart Little, Snowbell

ANNA AND THE KING

Jodie Foster, Chow Yun-Fat

(20TH CENTURY FOX) Producers, Lawrence Bender, Ed Elbert; Executive Producer, Terence Chang; Director, Andy Tennant; Screenplay, Steve Meerson, Peter Krikes; Based upon the diaries of Anna Leonowens; Photography, Caleb Deschanel; Designer, Luciana Arrighi; Editor, Roger Bondelli; Costumes, Jenny Beavan; Co-Producers, Jon Jashni, G. Mac Brown; Music, George Fenton; Casting, Priscilla John; a Fox 2000 Pictures presentation of a Lawrence Bender production; Dolby; Panavision; Deluxe color; Rated PG-13; 147 minutes; Release date: December 17, 1999

CAST

Anna Leonowens ....Jodie Foster
King Mongkut...Chow Yun-Fat
Tuptim ....Bai Ling
Louis ....Tom Felton
The Kralahome ....Syed Alwi
General Alak ....Randall Duk Kim
Princess Chowfa ....Lim Kay Siu
Princess Fa-Ying ....Melissa Campbell
Prince Chulalongkorn ....Keith Chin
Moonshee..Mano Maniam
Beebe..Shanthini Venugopal
Lady Thiang...Deanna Yusoff
Lord John Bradley ....Geoffrey Palmer
Lady Bradley..Ann Firbank
Mycroft Kincaid...Bill Stewart
Khun Phra Balat..Sean Ghazi
and K.K. Moggie (Phim), Dharma Harun Al-Rashid (Noi), Harith Iskander (Nikorn), Yusof B. Mohd Kassim(Pitak), Afdlin Shauki (Interpreter), Swee-Lin (Lady Jao Jom Manda Ung), Ramli Hassan (King Chulalongkorn), Robert Hands (Captain Blake), Lim Yu-Beng (Scarfaced Leader), Kenneth Tsang (Justice Phya Phrom), Kee Thuan Chye (Second Judge), Patrick Teoh (Third Judge), Aimi Aziz, Ellie Suriaty Omar, Tina Lee Siew Ting, Wong Chui Ling, Zaridah Abdul Malik (Ladies of Court), Fariza Azlina (La-Ore), Ahmad Mazlan, Mohd Razib Saliman (Scouts), Zaibo (Siamese Trader), Pak Ling (Shipping Dock Woman), Mahmud Ali Basah (Mercenary), Zulhaila Siregar (Distraught Villager).

English schoolteacher Anna Leonowens arrives in Siam to instruct the fifty-eight children of King Mongkut and finds herself at first clashing then forming a special bond with the charismatic ruler. Previous film versions of this story were Anna and the King of Siam (20th Century-Fox, 1946, with Irene Dunne and Rex Harrison), The King and I (20th Century-Fox, 1956, with Deborah Kerr and Yul Brynner), and the animated film The King and I (WB, 1999). This film received Oscar nominations for art direction and costume design.

© Twentieth Century Fox

Chow Yun-Fat, Melissa Campbell

Chow Yun-Fat, Jodie Foster

Jodie Foster

Bai Ling

Tom Cruise, Jason Robards

John C. Reilly, Melora Walters

MAGNOLIA

(**NEW LINE CINEMA**) Producer, Joanne Sellar; Executive Producers, Michael De Luca, Lynn Harris; Co-Producer, Daniel Lupi; Director/Screenplay, Paul Thomas Anderson; Photography, Robert Elswit; Designers, William Arnold, Mark Bridges; Editor, Dylan Tichenor; Costumes, Mark Bridges; Songs, Aimee Mann; Song: *Wise Up* by Aimee Mann/performed by the cast principals; Music, Jon Brion; Visual Effects Supervisor, Joe Letteri; Special Visual Effects/Animation, Industrial Light & Magic; Casting, Cassandra Kulukundis; a Joanne Sellar/Ghoulardi Film Company production; Dolby; Panavision; Deluxe color; Rated R; 188 minutes; Release date: December 17, 1999

CAST

Stanley Spector	Jeremy Blackman
Frank T.J. Mackey	Tom Cruise
Rose Gator	Melinda Dillon
Gwenovier	April Grace
Luis	Luis Guzman
Jimmy Gator	Philip Baker Hall
Phil Parma	Philip Seymour Hoffman
Burt Ramsey	Ricky Jay
Worm	Orlando Jones
Quiz Kid Donnie Smith	William H. Macy
Solmon Solomon	Alfred Molina
Linda Partridge	Julianne Moore
Alan Kligman, Esq.	Michael Murphy
Officer Jim Kurring	John C. Reilly
Earl Partridge	Jason Robards
Claudia Wilson Gator	Melora Walters
Rick Spector	Michael Bowen
Thurston Howell	Henry Gibson
Cynthia	Felicity Huffman
Dixon	Emmanuel I. Johnson
Dr. Landon	Don McManus
Mary	Eileen Ryan
Dick Jennings	Danny Wells
Sir Edmund William Godfrey/Young Pharmacist	Pat Healy
Mrs. Godfrey	Genevieve Zweig
Joseph Green	Mark Flannagan
Stanley Berry	Neil Flynn
Daniel Hill	Rod McLachlan
Firefighter	Allan Graf
Delmer Darion	Patton Oswalt

and Raymond "Big Guy" Gonzales (Reno Security Guard), Brad Hunt (Craig Hansen), Jim Meskimen (Forensic Scientist), Chris O'Hara (Sydney Barringer), Clement Blake (Arthur Barringer), Miriam Margolyes (Fay Barringer), Frank Elmore (1958 Detective), John Kraftz Seitz (1958 Policeman), Cory Buck (Young Boy), Tim "Stuffy" Sorenen (Infomercial Guy), Jim Ortlieb (Middle Aged Guy), Thomas Jane (Young Jimmy Gator), Holly Houston (Jimmy's Showgirl), Benjamin Niedens (Little Donnie Smith), Veronica Hart, Melissa Spell (Dentist Nurses), James Kiriyama-Lem (Dr. Lee), Jake Cross, Charlie Scott (Pedestrians), Juan Medrano (Nurse Juan), John Pritchett (Police Captain), Cleo King (Marcie), Michael Shamus Wiles (Captain Muffy), Jason Andrews (Doc), John S. Davies (Cameraman), Kevin Breznahan (Geoff, Seminar Guy), Miguel Perez (Avi Solomon), David Masuda (Coroner Man), Neil Pepe (Officer #1), Lionel Mark Smith (Detective), Annette Helde (Coroner Woman), Lynne Lerner (Librarian), Scott Burkett, Amy Brown (WDKK Pages), Bob Brewer (Richard's Dad), Julie Brewer (Richard's Mom), Nancy Marston (Julia's Mom), Maurey Marston (Julia's Dad), Jamala Gaither, Meagan Fay (Dr. Diane), Patricia Forte (Mim), Patrick Warren (Todd Geronimo), Virginia Pereira (Pink Dot Girl), Craig Kvinsland (Brad the Bartender), Patricia Scanlon (Cocktail Waitress), Natalie Marston (Julia), Bobby Brewer (Richard), Clark Gregg (WDKK Floor Director), Art Frankel (Old Pharmacist), Matt Gerald (Officer #2), Guillermo Melgarejo (Pink Dot Guy), Paul F. Tompkins (Chad—Seduce & Destroy), Mary Lynn Rajskub (Janet—Frank's Assistant), Jim Beaver, Ezra Buzzington, Denise Woolfork (Smiling Peanut Patrons), New World Harmonica Trio (Harmonica Players), Bob Downey, Sr. (WDKK Show Director), William Mapother (WDKK Director's Assistant), Larry Ballard (WDKK Medic), Brett Higgins, Brian Higgins (Mackey Disciple Twins), Michael "Jocco" Phillips (Mackey Disciple in Middle), Lillian Adams (Donnie's Old Neighbor), Steven Bush, Mike Massa, Dale Gibson (Paramedics), Scott Alan Smith (ER Doctor)

A series of seemingly unrelated stories come together on one random day in the San Fernando Valley. This film received Oscar nominations for supporting actor (Tom Cruise), original screenplay, and original song ("Save Me").

© New Line Cinema Inc.

Jeremy Blackman, Michael Bowen, Felicity Huffman

Philip Baker Hall, Eileen Ryan

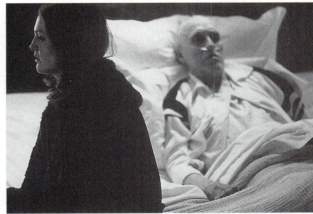

Julianne Moore, Jason Robards

Melinda Dillon

Philip Seymour Hoffman

Craig Kvinsland, William H. Macy, Henry Gibson

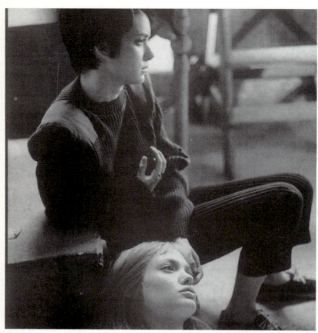

Winona Ryder, Angelina Jolie

Brittany Murphy

Angela Bettis

Vanessa Redgrave

Clea Duvall

Whoopi Goldberg

GIRL, INTERRUPTED

(**COLUMBIA**) Producers, Douglas Wick, Cathy Konrad; Executive Producers, Carol Bodie, Winona Ryder; Director, James Mangold; Screenplay, James Mangold, Lisa Loomer, Anna Hamilton Phelan; Based on the book by Susanna Kaysen; Photography, Jack Green; Designer, Richard Hoover; Editor, Kevin Tent; Costumes, Arianne Phillips; Music, Mychael Danna; Co-Producer, Georgia Kacandes; Casting, Lisa Beach; a Douglas Wick production; Dolby; Deluxe color; Rated R; 127 minutes; Release date: December 21, 1999

Winona Ryder, Angelina Jolie

CAST

Susanna Kaysen	Winona Ryder
Lisa	Angelina Jolie
Georgina	Clea Duvall
Daisy	Brittany Murphy
Polly	Elisabeth Moss
Tobias Jacobs	Jared Leto
Dr. Potts	Jeffrey Tambor
Dr. Wick	Vanessa Redgrave
Valerie	Whoopi Goldberg
Janet	Angela Bettis
Cynthia	Jillian Armenante
M-G	Drucie McDaniel
Gretta	Alison Claire
Margie	Christina Myers
Annette	Joanna Kerns
John	Travis Fine
Older Catatonic	Gloria Barnhart
Mrs. McWilley	Josie Gammell
Prof. Gilcrest	Bruce Altman
Mrs. Gilcrest	Mary Kay Place
Mr. Kaysen	Ray Baker
Bonnie Gilcrest	KaDee Strickland
Ronny	Christian Monroe
Dr. Crumble	Kurtwood Smith
Cabby—Monty Hoover	David Scott Taylor
ER Nurse	Janet Pryce
ER Resident	C. Scott Grimaldi
Arleen	Ginny Graham
Art Teacher	Richard Domeier
Jack	John Kirkman
Maureen	Sally Bowman
Tony	Misha Collins
Van Driver	John Lumia
Italian Shop Keeper	Marilyn Brett
Josh	Alex Rubin
Miss Plimack	Marilyn Spanier
Miss Paisley	Linda Gilvear
Principal	Allen Strange
British Teacher	Spencer Gates
Lillian	Rebecca Derrick
Nurse	Anne Connors
Medic	Steve Altes
Cop	Joe Gerrety
Dance Therapist	Anne Lewis
Naked Man	Donny Martino, Jr.
ER Doctor	John Levin
Connie	Irene Longshore
Tiffany	Katie Rimmer
Tough Guy	Jonathan Martin Spirk

Winona Ryder

A confused seventeen-year-old girl is diagnosed with Borderline Personality Disorder and sent to Claymore Hospital where she must help herself come to terms with her problems.

1999 Academy Award-winner for Best Supporting Actress (Angelina Jolie).

©Columbia Pictures Industries, Inc.

Elisabeth Moss, Winona Ryder

Al Pacino, Cameron Diaz

Jamie Foxx

ANY GIVEN SUNDAY

(**WARNER BROS.**) Producers, Lauren Shuler Donner, Clayton Townsend, Dan Halsted; Executive Producers, Richard Donner, Oliver Stone; Director, Oliver Stone; Screenplay, John Logan, Oliver Stone; Screen Story, Daniel Pyne, John Logan; Co-Producers, Eric Hamburg, Jonathan Krauss, Richard Rutowski; Photography, Salvatore Totino; Editors, Tom Nordberg, Keith Salmon, Stuart Waks, Stuart Levy; Music, Robbie Robertson, Paul Kelly, Richard Horowitz; Music Supervisor, Budd Carr; Designer, Victor Kempster; Costumes, Mary Zophres; Second Unit/Stunts/Football Coordinator, Allan Graf; Casting, Billy Hopkins, Mary Vernieu; an Ixtlan/The Donners' Company production; Dolby; Panavision; Technicolor; Rated R; 162 minutes; Release date: December 22, 1999

CAST

Tony D'Amato	Al Pacino
Christina Pagniacci	Cameron Diaz
Jack "Cap" Rooney	Dennis Quaid
Dr. Harvey Mandrake	James Woods
Willie Beamen	Jamie Foxx
Julian Washington	L L Cool J
Dr. Ollie Powers	Matthew Modine
Montezuma Monroe	Jim Brown
AFFA Football Commissioner	Charlton Heston
Margaret Pagniacci	Ann-Margret
Nick Crozier	Aaron Eckhart
Jack Rose	John C. McGinley
Luther "Shark" Lavay	Lawrence Taylor
Jimmy Sanderson	Bill Bellamy
Patrick "Madman" Kelly	Andrew Bryniarski
Cindy Rooney	Lauren Holly
Vanessa Struthers	Lela Rochon
Mandy Murphy	Elizabeth Berkley

and James Karen, Gianni Russo (Christina's Advisers), Duane Martin (Willie's Agent), Clifton Davis (Mayor Tyrone Smalls), John Daniel (Suitor in Christina's Box), Patrick O'Hara (Tyler Cherubini), Jerry A. Sharp (McKenna), Marty Wright ("Beastman"), Mazio Royster, Todd Smith (Wide Receivers), Jamie Williams, Craig Thompson, Greg Orvis (Tight Ends), Rick Johnson (Dallas Quarterback), Bjorn Nittmo (Kicker), Matt Martinez (Shark Fullback), Pete Ohnegian (Shark Center), John Clark, Brian O'Neal (Shark Linebackers), Robert L. Goff, Joseph Unitas, J.V. Goodman, Skip McClendon, Derrick Lassic, Fred Lester, Eric Miller, Todd Eric Yeaman, C. Ashley Shearman, Connell Spain Jr., Otis Mounds, Matt Storm, Michael Osuna, Connell Maynor, Marty Hochertz, Robert Gordon, Barry Wagner, Richard McKenzie, Sean Hamlet, Robert Grogan, Nyle Wiren, Michael Groh III, Len Johnson, Basil Proctor, Matthew Keneley, Kevin Reid (Additional Players), Tony Egués, Marc Claus, Michelle A. Porachan, Tyler Cravens, James A. Bachand, Jason Rubenstein (Shark Trainers), Art Young, William Hanlon, Allan Graf, Joseph W. Underwood, Timothy F. Crowley (Referees), Steve Raulerson (Shark Chaplain), Oliver Stone (Tug Kowalski, TV Announcer #1), Phl Latzman (Kevin Branson, TV Announcer #2), Barry Switzer (Dallas Announcer), Mark Ellis (Quarterback Coach), Anthony L. Tanzi, Joseph A. Wilson (Shark Coaches), Margaret Betts (Mayor's Aide), Antares Davis (Mayor's PR Woman), Liz Petterson (Society Lady at Mayor's Party), Lester "The Mighty Rasta" Speight (Shark's Security Guard), Daniel Marino, Alexandra L. Hellman, Hunter White (Cap Rooney's Children), Kirsten Kreuger, Tonya Oliver, Mary Fanaro, Kathy Davis Alzado, Nikki Novak, Lisa Ann Phillips, Joanna Theobalds, Amy Dorris, Sarah Penman, Sacha Voski, Michelle Bernard, Cat Akselrad, Carin Abnathy (Players' Wives/Girlfriends), Micah West ("Madman's" Wife), Christy Trummond (Dr. Mandrake's Girlfriend), Eva Tamargo, Debbie Howard, Tucker Brown (Tunnel Reporters, Game 3), Bob St. Clair (Opposing Coach, Game 1), Y.A. Tittle, Pat Toomay (Opposing Coaches, Game 2), Dick Butkus (Opposing Coach, Game 3), Warren Moon (Opposing Coach, Game 4), Johnny Unitas (Opposing Coach, Game 5), Bruce C. Hardy (Dallas Knights Chaplain), Terrell Owens, Irving Fryar, Joe Schmidt, Ricky Watters (Special Appearances), Meira Moet, Rhonda Adams, Glynnis Lawson, Jessie Aleander, Melissa Jayne, Sarah Bredell, Michelle Beisner, Cleo Bayla, Luna Abdi Mohamed, Olivia Fullerton, Bibi Mbayi, Jaime Bergman, Dawn Crawford, Gwendolyn Osborne, Celia Evans, Nichole Robinson, "Jaman" Janet Manns, Andrea Horka, Hermine Kraljevic, Mercy Lopez, Maria E. Heredia, Jeannie Mustelier, Delia Sheppard, Donna Preudhomme (Party Girls), Jack Spirtos, Mauricio De La Vega, Sean C. Stone, Michael Stone, Tara Stone, Frank J. Adler, Doug Cowden, Antoni Cornacchione (Fans), Drew Rosenhaus (TV Announcer, Willie's Apartment), Hunter Reno (Reporter at Mayor's Party), Dorothy J. Morrison (Willie's Mom), Vincent DiFatta, Jim Gasser, Allen Reidel ("Fan" Businessmen at Mayor's Party), Luciano Armellino (Tony's Bartender), Myriam Davoisne-Bruni, Rosa Iveth Cortez, Melinda Renna, Doris Cóndom (Friends, Owner's Box)

Following a losing streak, Sharks president and co-owner Christina Pagniacci announces that star player Jack Rooney is to be replaced by up-and-coming reserve quarterback Willie Beamen, a decision that challenges the team's long-time coach Tony D'Amato.

© Warner Bros.

Dennis Quaid, James Woods

Jamie Foxx, Al Pacino, L L Cool J

Dennis Quaid, Jamie Foxx, Al Pacino

Cameron Diaz, Ann-Margret

Lauren Holly, Dennis Quaid

Dennis Quaid, Jim Brown, Al Pacino

Al Pacino

Jim Carrey

Paul Giamatti, Jim Carrey

Jim Carrey, Howdy Doody

Jim Carrey

Jim Carrey

MAN ON THE MOON

(UNIVERSAL) Producers, Danny DeVito, Michael Shamberg, Stacey Sher; Executive Producers, George Shapiro, Howard West, Michael Hausman; Director, Milos Forman; Screenplay, Scott Alexander, Larry Karaszewski; Photography, Anastas Michos; Designer, Patrizia von Brandenstein; Editors, Christopher Tellefsen, Lynzee Klingman; Co-Executive Producer, Bob Zmuda; Costumes, Jeffrey Kurland; Music, R.E.M.; Title song by Bill Berry, Peter Buck, Mike Mills, Michael Stipe/performed by R.E.M.; Music Supervisor, Anita Camarata; Casting, Francine Maisler; a Mutual Film Company presentation of a Jersey Films/Cinehaus production in association with Shapiro/West Productions; Dolby; Panavision; Deluxe color; Rated R; 118 minutes; Release date: December 22, 1999

Danny DeVito, Jim Carrey

CAST

Andy Kaufman/Tony Clifton......................................Jim Carrey
George Shapiro ....Danny DeVito
Lynne Margulies..Courtney Love
Bob Zmuda...Paul Giamatti
Stanley Kaufman ....Gerry Becker
Janice Kaufman ....Leslie Lyles
Maynard Smith ....Vincent Schiavelli
Ed Weinberger...Peter Bonerz
Himself...Jerry Lawler

Greyson Pendry (Little Michael Kaufman), Brittany Colonna (Baby Carol Kaufman), Bobby Boriello (Little Andy Kaufman), George Shapiro (Mr. Besserman), Bud Friedman (Himself), Tom Dreesen (Wiseass Comic), Thomas Armbruster (Improv Piano Player), Pamela Abdy (Diane Barnet), Wendy Polland (Little Wendy), Cash Oshman (Yogi), Melanie Vesey (Carol Kaufman), Michael Kelly (Michael Kaufman), Richard Belzer, Lorne Michaels, Randall Carver, Howdy Doody, David Letterman, Paul Shaffer, J. Alan Thomas (Themselves), Marilu Henner, Jeff Conaway, Christopher Lloyd, Judd Hirsch, Carol Kane (Taxi Cast Members), Norm MacDonald (Michael Richards), Matt Price, Christina Cabot (Meditation Students), Miles Chapin (SNL Assistant), Dr. Isadore Rosenfeld (ABC Executive), Molly Schaffer (Maynard Smith's Assistant), Howard West, Greg Travis, Maureen Mueller (ABC Executives), Phil Perlman (Mama Rivoli's Angry Guy), Jessica Devlin (Mama Rivoli's Diner), Jeff Thomas (Andy Stand-In), Howard Keystone (Taxi Marching Man), Brent Briscoe (Heavyset Technician), Ray Bokhour, Patton Oswalt (Blue Collar Guys), Caroline Gibson (Sorority Girl), Conrad Roberts (College Promoter), Jeff Zabel (College Student), Marilyn Sokol (Madame), Angela Jones, Krystina Carson (Hookers), Gerry Robert Byrne (Taxi AD/Stage Manager), Mark Davenport (LA Times Reporter), Bert F. Balsam, Lonnie Hamilton, Ron Sanchez, Billy Lucas (Taxi Security Guards), Patricia Scanlon (Ed Weinberger's Secretary), Max Alexander (Harrah's Booker), Ed Mitchell (Harrah's Conductor), Reiko Aylesworth (Mimi), Michael Villani (Merv Griffin), Maria Maglaris (Irate Merv Spectator), Heath Hyche (Merv's Guest Coordinator), Robert Holeman (Boxing Trainer), James Ross (Wrestling Commentator), Tamara Bossett (Foxy Jackson), Gene Lebell (Foxy Jackson Referee), Bob Zmuda (Jack Burns), Brian Peck (Fridays Announcer), Caroline Rhea (Fridays' Melanie), Mary Lynn Rajskub (Fridays' Mary), Phil Lenkowsky (Fridays Tech Director), Rob Steiner (Fridays Control Booth Tech), Claudia Jaffee (Fridays Floor Director), Mando Guerrero (Jerry Lawler Referee), Lance Russell (Ring Announcer), Ladi Von Jansky (Stadium Photographer), K.P. Palmer, Mark Majetti, Deana Ann Aburto (Memphis Paramedics), Mews Small, David Elliott (TM Administrators), Fredd Wayne (Bland Doctor), Tracey Walter (National Enquirer Editor), David Koechner, Jeanine Jackson (National Enquirer Reporters), Johnny Legend (Wild-Haired Guru), Doris Eaton Travis (Eleanor Gould), Greg Sutton (Carnegie Hall Conductor), Sydney Lassick (Crystal Healer), Yoshi Jenkins (Jun Roxas), Lance Alarcon (Comedy Store Patron), D.J. Johnson (Comedy Store Waiter), Melissa Carrey (Comedy Store Waitress), Michiko Nishiwaki (Karate Fighter), Stacey Carter (Lawyer's Girlfriend), Nicholas Wilde (Waiter), Danielle Burgio, Karen Martin, Linda Cevallos, Tabatha Mays, Betsy Chang, Katie Miller, Jennifer Chavarria, Jessica Moore, Shirry Dolgin, Tara Nicole, Lisa Eaton, Mia Pitts, Melanie Gage, Kelly Sheerin, Catherine Hader, Alison Simpson, Betsy Harris, Melinda Songér, Kelly Jones, Michon Suyama, Tricia Lilly, Michelle Swanson, Natalie Webb (New York City Rockettes), Jacqueline Case, Natalie Mills, Karen Blake Challman, April Nixon, Teresa Chapman, Tiffany Olson, Kelly Cooper, Kathryn Rossberg, Penny Fisher, Karissa Seaman, Eva Jenickova, Lea Sullivan, Lindsay Lopez, Amy Tinkham, Kristin K. Willits (Tony Clifton Dancers)

Jim Carrey

The true story of performer Andy Kaufman, whose unpredictable behavior and often maddening routines and stunts made him a controversial figure in show business during his very short career.

Courtney Love, Jim Carrey

Youki Kudoh, Ethan Hawke

Youki Kudoh, Ethan Hawke

SNOW FALLING ON CEDARS

(**UNIVERSAL**) Producers, Harry J. Ufland, Ron Bass, Kathleen Kennedy, Frank Marshall; Executive Producers, Carol Baum, Lloyd A. Silverman; Director, Scott Hicks; Screenplay, Ron Bass, Scott Hicks; Based on the novel by David Guterson; Photography, Robert Richardson; Designer, Jeannine Oppewall; Editor, Hank Corwin; Music, James Newton Howard; Co-Producers, Richard Vane, David Guterson; Costumes, Renee Erlich Kalfus; Casting, David Rubin; a Harry J. Ufland/Ron Bass-Kennedy/Marshall production; Dolby; Panavision; Alpha Cine Lab Color; Rated PG-13; 126 minutes; Release date: December 22, 1999

CAST

Ishmael Chambers	Ethan Hawke
Hatsue Miyamoto	Youki Kudoh
Young Ishmael Chambers	Reeve Carney
Young Hatsue Imada	Anne Suzuki
Kazuo Miyamoto	Rick Yune
Nels Gudmundsson	Max von Sydow
Alvin Hooks	James Rebhorn
Judge Fielding	James Cromwell
Sheriff Art Moran	Richard Jenkins
Susan Marie Heine	Arija Bareikis
Carl Heine, Jr.	Eric Thal
Etta Heine	Celia Weston
Carl Heine, Sr.	Daniel von Bargen
Hisao Imada	Akira Takayama
Fujiko Imada	Ako
Zenhichi Miyamoto	Cary-Hiroyuki Tagawa

and Zak Orth Deputy (Abel Martinson), Max Wright (Horace Whaley), Sam Shepard (Arthur Chambers), Caroline Kava (Helen Chambers), Jan Rubes (Ole Jurgensen), Sheila Moore (Liesel Jurgensen), Zeljko Ivanek (Dr. Whitman), Seiji Inouye (Young Kazuo Miyamoto), Saemi Nakamura (Sumiko Imada), Mika Fujii (Yukiko Imada), Dwight McFee (Bus Driver), Bill Harper (Levant), Xi Reng Jiang "Henry O." (Nagaishi), Myles Ferguson (German Soldier), Noah Heney (Ship's Doctor), John Destrey (Bailiff), A. Arthur Takemoto (Buddhist Priest), Ken Takemoto (Monk), Larry Musser (Gas Station Attendant), Jamie Kang (Singing Girl), Lili Marshall (Strawberry Girl), Lisa Mena (Strawberry Woman), Jethro Heysen-Hicks (Parade Boy with Stick), Tom Heaton, Frank C. Turner, Marilyn Norry (Jurors), Peter Crook, Ron Snyder, Mark Ainsworth Farrell (Fishermen), Jay Brazeau, Tom Scholte, Tim Burd (Reporters), Gareth Williams, Anthony Harrison (FBI Agents), Adam Pospisil, Johnny Brynelsen (Heine Children)

In a small fishing village on San Piedro Island, Ishmael Chambers is assigned to cover the murder trial of Kazuo Miyamoto whose wife Hatsue had once been Ishamel's lover. This film received an Oscar nomination for cinematography.

Youki Kudoh

Max von Sydow, Rick Yune

PLAY IT TO THE BONE

Antonio Banderas, Woody Harrelson, Lolita Davidovich

(**TOUCHSTONE**) Producer, Stephen Chin; Executive Producer, David Lester; Director/Screenplay, Ron Shelton; Photography, Mark Vargo; Designer, Claire Jenora Bowin; Editor, Paul Seydor; Associate Producer, Kellie Davis; Music, Alex Wurman; Music Supervisors, Dawn Soler, Sterling Meredith; Costumes, Kathryn Morrison; Presented in association with Shanghai'd Films; Dolby; Panavision; Technicolor; Rated R; 124 minutes; Release date: December 25, 1999

CAST

Cesar Dominguez	Antonio Banderas
Vince Boudreau	Woody Harrelson
Grace Pasic	Lolita Davidovich
Joe Domino	Tom Sizemore
Lia	Lucy Liu
Hank Goody	Robert Wagner
Artie	Richard Masur
Cappie Caplan	Willie Garson
Rudy	Cylk Cozart
Dante Solomon	Jack Carter
Mad Greek Waitress	Aida Turturro

and Louie Leonardo (Freddy Green), Slade Barnett (Vegas Cop), Cameron Milzer (Vegas Paramedic), Julio Garcia (Chiquito Rosario), Johnny Ortiz (Gym Owner), Jordy Oakland (Julie), Will Utay (Sal), Joseph Arsenault (Bobby), Fred Lewis, Maurice Singer (Vegas Lawyers), Robert Sale (Robert Velario), Joe Cortez (Garden Referee), Bruce Buffer (Garden Ring Announcer), Teddy Atlas (Cesar's Garden Trainer), Dana Lee (Man with Ferrari), Rob Ingersoll (Jesus), Robby Robinson (Skeeter Lewis), Mitch Halpern (Vince's Big Fight Referee), Chuck Hull (Vince's Big Fight Ring Announcer), Jim Lampley (HBO Commentator), Al Bernstein, Reynaldo Rey (Sportwriters), Eloy Casados (Vince's Trainer), Henry G. Sanders (Cesar's Trainer), Vasil Chuck Bodak (Cesar's Cutman), Jacob "Stitch" Duran (Vince's Cutman), Al Benner (Cesar's Cornerman), Pat Barry (Vince's Cornerman), Steve Lawrence, Mike Tyson, Rod Stewart, George Foreman, Larry Merchant (HBO Commentators), Darrell Foster (Referee), Michael Buffer (Ring Announcer), Bill Caplan (Dr. Velvil Ginsberg), Marc Ratner (Boxing Commissioner), Jane Broadfoot, Carlos Padilla (Timekeepers), Debbie Caplan, Elizabeth Caplan (Press Assistants), Denise Pernula, Veronica Becerra (Ring Card Girls), Tamara Gibler, Fulvia Sanchez, Faye Mangabang (Fantasy Girls), Alison Walsh (Bartender), Ana Divac (Grace's Party Friend), Tom Todoroff (Croupier), Kevin Costner, Wesley Snipes, James Woods, Natasha Gregson Wagner, Drew Carey, Jennifer Tilly, Tony Curtis, Bob and Lovey Arum, Angel and Yvette Manfredy (Ringside Fans), Buddy Greco, Lezlie Anders, Dick Williams, Patricia Ford, Gennifer Flowers, Steve Schirripa, Tony Tucker, Bo Bolinski, Joey Maxim, John Momot (Party Guests), Bill Dwyre, Steve Springer, Bruce Trampler, Rick Reilly, Bert Sugar, Jason Levin, Royce Feour, Ron Borges, Michael Katz, Doug Kirkorian, Randy Harvey, Tim Smith, Michael Rosenthal, George Kimball, Bernard Fernandez, Timothy Dahlberg, Tim Graeham, Joe Hawk, Chris Thorne (Ringside Sportswriters)

Vince Boudreau and Cesar Dominguez, a pair of down-in-their luck boxers, head for a bout in Las Vegas with girlfriend Grace Pasic and a sultry hitchhiker, Lia, in tow.

Woody Harrelson, Antonio Banderas

Tom Sizemore, Robert Wagner

Woody Harrelson, Lucy Liu, Antonio Banderas

Gwyneth Paltrow, Jude Law, Matt Damon

Philip Seymour Hoffman

Rosario Fiorello, Matt Damon, Jude Law

Jack Davenport, Gwyneth Paltrow, Matt Damon

Cate Blanchett

THE TALENTED MR. RIPLEY

(PARAMOUNT/MIRAMAX) Producers, William Horberg, Tom Sternberg; Executive Producer, Sydney Pollack; Director/Screenplay, Anthony Minghella; Based on the novel by Patricia Highsmith; Photography, John Seale; Designer, Roy Walker; Editor, Walter Murch; Costumes, Ann Roth; Music, Gabriel Yared; Co-Producer, Alessandro von Normann, Paul Zaentz; Associate Producer, Steve Andrews, Casting, David Rubin; a Mirage Enterprises/Timnick Films productions; Dolby; Deluxe color; Rated R; 139 minutes; Release date: December 25, 1999

Matt Damon

CAST

Tom Ripley...Matt Damon
Marge Sherwood ....Gwyneth Paltrow
Dickie Greenleaf..Jude Law
Meredith Logue ....Cate Blanchett
Freddie Miles ....Philip Seymour Hoffman
Peter Smith-Kingsley ....Jack Davenport
Herbert Greenleaf ....James Rebhorn
Inspector Roverini...Sergio Rubini
Alvin MacCarron ....Philip Baker Hall
Aunt Joan ....Celia Weston
Fausto ....Rosario Fiorello
Silvana...Stefania Rocca
Colonnello Verrecchia..................................Ivano Marescotti
Signora Buffi..Anna Longhi
Sergeant Baggio...Alessandro Fabrizi
Emily Greenleaf...Lisa Eichhorn
Fran ....Gretchen Egolf
Greenleaf Chauffeur ....Jack Willis
Fran's Boyfriend ....Frederick Alexander Bosche
Police Officer ....Dario Bergesio
Uncle Ted...Larry Kaplan
Gucci Assistant ....Claire Hardwick
American Express Clerk ....Nino Prester
Bus Driver ....Lorenzo Mancuso
Priest ....Onofrio Mancuso
Immigration Officer..Massimo Reale
American Express Clerk....................Emanuele Carucci Viterbi
Dahlia...Caterina De Regibus
Ermenlinda..Silvana Bosi
Desk Manager Aldo.......................................Gianfranco Barra
Tailor ....Renato Scarpa
Fighting Neighbors ....Deirdre Lovejoy, Brian Tarantina
Silvana's Fiance..Beppe Fiorello
Silvana's Brother..Marco Quaglia
Silvana's Mother....................................Alessandra Vanzi
Photographer ....Marco Rossi

and Napoli Jazz Septet: Guy Barker (trumpet), Bernardo Sassetti (piano), Perico Sambeat (alto sax), Gene Calderazzo (drums), Joseph Lepore (double bass), Rosario Giuliuni (tenor sax), Eddy Palermo (electric guitar); San Remo Jazz Sextet: Byron Wallen (cornet), Pete King (alto sax), Clark Tracey (drums), Jean Toussaint (tenor sax), Geoff Gascogne (bass), Carlo Negroni (piano); Eugene Onegin Players: Roberto Valentini (Onegin), Francesco Bovino (Lensky), Stefano Canettieri (Zaretsky); Marco Foti (Guillot), Ludovica Tinghi (Fausto's Fiancée), Nicola Pannelli (Dinelli's Cafe Waiter), Pietro Ragusa (Record Store Owner), Simone Empler (Boy Singer), Gianluca Secci, Manuel Ruffini, Pierpaolo Lovino (Policemen), Roberto Di Palma (San Remo Hotel Desk Clerk)

Cate Blanchett, Matt Damon

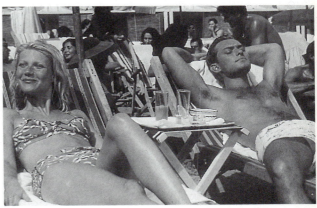

Gwyneth Paltrow, Jude Law

Sent to Italy by Dickie Greeneleaf's father in hopes of coaxing the young man out of his idle lifestyle, Tom Ripley finds himself drawn to this life of leisure and wealth, grabbing the opportunity to take over Dickie's identity. Previous film version of the Highsmith novel was the French Plein Soleil, starring Alain Delon as Ripley, which was released in the United States as Purple Noon in 1960. This film received Oscar nominations for supporting actor (Jude Law), screenplay adaptation, original score, costume design, and art direction.

TITUS

Anthony Hopkins

Alan Cumming

(**FOX SEARCHLIGHT**) Producers, Jody Patton, Conchita Airoldi, Julie Taymor; Executive Producer, Paul G. Allen; Co-Executive Producers, Ellen Little, Robert Little, Stephen K. Bannon; Director/ Screenplay, Julie Taymor; Based on the play *Titus Andronicus* by William Shakespeare; Co-Producers, Adam Leipzig, Michiyo Yoshizaki; Associate Producer, Karen L. Thorson; Photography, Luciano Tovoli; Designer, Dante Ferretti; Costumes, Milena Canonero; Music, Elliot Goldenthal; Editor, Françoise Bonnot; Visual Effects Supervisor, Kent Houston; Casting, Irene Lamb, Ellen Lewis; a Clear Blue Sky presentation, in association with Overseas Filmgroup, of a Urania Pictures and NDF Intl. production; Dolby; Super 35 Widescreen; Deluxe color; Rated R; 162 minutes; Release date: December 25, 1999

CAST

Titus Andronicus	Anthony Hopkins
Tamora	Jessica Lange
Saturninus	Alan Cumming
Aaron	Harry Lennix
Marcus	Colm Feore
Lucius	Angus Macfadyen
Chiron	Jonathan Rhys Meyers
Demetrius	Matthew Rhys
Lavinia	Laura Fraser
Bassianus	James Frain
Young Lucius	Osheen Jones
Quintus	Kenny Doughty
Mutius	Blake Ritson
Aemilius	Constantine Gregory
Martius	Colin Wells
Nurse	Geraldine McEwan

Dario D'Ambrosi (Clown), Raz Degan (Alarbus), Ettore Geri (Priest), Tresy Taddei (Little Girl), Bah Souleymane (Infant),Antonio Manzini (Publius), Leonardo Treviglio (Caius), Giacomo Gonnella (Sempronius), Carlo Medici (Valentin), Emanuele Vezzoli (Goth Leader), Herman Weiskopf, Cristopher Ahrens (Goth Soldiers), Vito Fasano (Goth General), Maurizio Rapotec (Goth Lieutenant), Bruno Bilotta (Roman Captain)

After Roman general Titus Andronicus executes one of her sons, Goth Queen Tamora swears vengeance upon him, resulting in a bloodbath between these two enemies and their families. This film received an Oscar nomination for costume design.

© Fox Searchlight Pictures

Harry Lennix, Angus Macfadyen

Alan Cumming, Anthony Hopkins

Harry Lennix

Matthew Rhys, Jonathan Rhys Meyers

Jessica Lange

Jessica Lange, Alan Cumming

Shane Murray Corcoran, Joe Breen, Emily Watson,
Robert Carlyle, Ben O'Gorman

Ciaran Owens (c)

ANGELA'S ASHES

(**PARAMOUNT/UNIVERSAL**) Producers, Scott Rudin, David Brown, Alan Parker; Executive Producers, Adam Schroeder, Eric Steel; Director, Alan Parker; Screenplay, Laura Jones, Alan Parker; Based upon the book by Frank McCourt; Line Producer, David Wimbury; Photography, Michael Seresin; Designer, Geoffrey Kirkland; Editor, Gerry Hambling; Costumes, Consolata Boyle; Music, John Williams; Casting, John and Ros Hubbard, Juliet Taylor; a David Brown/Scott Rudin/Dirty Hands production; Dolby; Technicolor; Rated R; 145 minutes; Release date: December 25, 1999

CAST

Angela McCourt	Emily Watson
Malachy McCourt	Robert Carlyle
Young Frank McCourt	Joe Breen
Middle Frank McCourt	Ciaran Owens
Older Frank McCourt	Michael Legge
Grandma Sheehan	Ronnie Masterson
Aunt Aggie	Pauline McLynn
Uncle Pa Keating	Liam Carney
Uncle Pat	Eanna MacLiam
Narrator	Andrew Bennett
Young Malachy	Shane Murray Corcoran
Middle Malachy	Devon Murray
Older Malachy	Peter Halpin
New Born Michael	Aaron Geraghty
Baby Michael	Sean Carney Daly, Oisin Carney Daly
Middle Michael	Shane Smith
Older Michael	Tim O'Brien
Newborn Alphie	Blaithnaid Howe
Baby Alphie	Kiara O'Leary, Caroline O'Sullivan
Older Alphie	Ryan Fielding
Margaret Mary	Daire Lynam
Eugene	Ben O'Gorman
Oliver	Sam O'Gorman
Young Paddy Clohessy	Frank Lavery
Middle Paddy Clohessy	James Mahon
Older Paddy Clohessy	Laurence Kinlan
Willie Harold	Lucas Neville
Fintan Slattery	Walter Mansfield
Mr. Benson	Des McAleer
Dotty O'Neill	Sean Kearns
Mr. O'Dea	Les Doherty
Mr. O'Halloran	Brendan Cauldwell
Mr. Hannon	Shay Gorman
Seamus	Johnny Murphy
Lavatory Man	Jon Kenny
Sister Rita	Susan Fitzgerald
Toby Mackey	Brendan McNamara
Bridey Hannon	Maria McDermottroe

and Olivier Maguire (Confession Priest), Daithi O'Suilleabhain (Young Priest), Eileen Pollock (Mrs. Finucane), Alvaro Lucchesi (Laman Griffin), Mark O'Regan (Dr. Troy), Moira Deady (Mrs. Purcell), Kerry Condon (Theresa), Gerard McSorley (Father Gregory), Garrett Keogh (Mr. Hegarty), Eamonn Owens (Quasimodo), John Anthony Murphy (Redemptionist Priest), Phelim Drew (Rent Man), Brendan O'Carroll (Funeral Carriage Driver), Maggie McCarthy (Miss Barry), Bairbre Ni Chaoimh (Mrs. O'Connell), Nuala Kelly (Dance Teacher), Brian Clifford (Telegram Boy), Edward Murphy (Young Mikey Molloy), Kieran Maher (Older Mikey Molloy), James McClatchie (Bishop), Patrick Bracken (Younger Question Quigley), Terry O'Donovan (Older Question Quigley), Danny O'Carroll (Clarke), David Ahern (Cyril Benson), Marcia DeBonis (Mrs. Leibowitz), Helen Norton (Delia), Eileen Colgan (Philomena), Alan Parker (Dr. Campbell), Stephen Marcus (English Agent), Pauline Shanahan (Eye Nurse), Gerry Walsh (Farmer), Brendan Morrissey (Brother Murray), Darragh Neill (Heffernan), Sarah Pilkington (Minnie MacAdorey), Donncha Crowley (Sacristan), Veronica O'Reilly (Mrs. Carmody), Ann O'Neill (Mrs. Dooley), Phil Kelly (Father Gory), Jaz Pollock (Roden Lane Neighbour), Paddy Scully, J.J. Murphy, Frankie McCafferty, Jack Lynch (St. Vincent Men), Patrick David Nolan (Travel Agent), Gerard Lee (Carmody Priest), Martin Benson (Christian Brother), Birdy Sweeney (Old Priest), Owen O'Gorman (Sleeping Sailor), Pat McGrath (Butcher), Ray McBride (Mill Foreman), John Sheedy (Coal Yard Foreman), Sam Ryan, Donnacha Gleeson (Shaved Head Boys), Jim McIntyre, Richard Walker (Gravediggers), Mary Ann Spencer, Kathleen Lambe, Jer O'Leary (Parents)

Frank McCourt recounts his growing up in poverty in Limerick, Ireland. This film received an Oscar nomination for original score.

© Paramount Pictures/Polygram Holding, Inc.

Michael Legge

Emily Watson, Shane Murray Corcoran

Michael Legge

Joe Breen

Emily Watson, Robert Carlyle

Joe Breen, Robert Carlyle

Michael Legge

181

Sigourney Weaver, Alan Rickman, Tim Allen, Tony Shalhoub

Tim Allen, Pig Lizard

GALAXY QUEST

Sigourney Weaver

(**DREAMWORKS**) Producers, Mark Johnson, Charles Newirth; Director, Dean Parisot; Screenplay, David Howard, Robert Gordon; Story, David Howard; Executive Producer, Elizabeth Cantillon; Photography, Jerzy Zielinski; Designer, Linda DeScenna; Editor, Don Zimmerman; Costumes, Albert Wolsky; Alien Make-Up and Creature Effects, Stan Winston; Visual Effects Supervisor, Bill George; Special Visual Effects and Animation, Industrial Light & Magic; Music, David Newman; Co-Producers, Suzann Ellis, Sona Gourgouris; Casting, Debra Zane; a Mark Johnson production; Dolby; Panavision; Technicolor; Rated PG; 104 minutes; Release date: December 25, 1999

CAST

James Nesmith ("Commander Peter Quincy Taggart")...............Tim Allen
Gwen DeMarco ("Lt. Tawny Madison").......................Sigourney Weaver
Alexander Dane ("Dr. Lazarus") ....Alan Rickman
Fred Kwan ("Tech Sergeant Chen").................................Tony Shalhoub
Guy Fleegman ("Crewman #6")...Sam Rockwell
Tommy Webber ("Laredo")...Daryl Mitchell
Mathesar..Enrico Colantoni
Sarris...Robin Sachs
Quellek ....Patrick Breen
Laliari ....Missi Pyle
Teb..Jed Rees
Brandon ....Justin Long
Kyle...Jeremy Howard
Katelyn...Kaitlin Cullum
Hollister..Jonathan Feyer
Tommy (age 9) ....Corbin Bleu
Lathe ....Wayne Péré
Neru ....Samuel Lloyd
Shy Girl ....Jennifer Manley
and Bill Chott, Morgan Rusler, Gregg Binkley, Brandon Michael DePaul, Paul G. Kubiak, Greg Colbrook (Fans), John Patrick White, Todd Giebenhain (Teens in the Bathroom), J.P. Manoux (Excited Alien), Dan Gunther (Navigator), Matt Winston, Brandon Keener (Technicians); Dian Bachar (Nervous Tech), Rainn Wilson (Lahnk), Susan Egan (Teek), Heidi Swedberg (Brandon's Mom), Isaac C. Singleton, Jr. (Sarris' Guard), Jerry Penacoli (Reporter), Joel McKinnon Miller (Warrior Alien), Kevin Hamilton McDonald (Announcer), Daniel T. Parker (Alien Fan), Dawn Hutchins (Inventory Clerk), Joe Frank (Voice of the Computer), Lawrence Richards, Mic Tomasi (Thermian Greeters)

Space aliens arrive on Earth requesting help from the cast of the long-cancelled sci-fi television series Galaxy Quest, whom they have mistaken for real-life galaxy heroes.

©DreamWorks LLC

Enrico Colantoni, Tim Allen

Alan Rickman

Sigourney Weaver

Tim Allen

Robin Sachs, Tim Allen

Tony Shalhoub

Daryl Mitchell

Sam Rockwell

Vicellous Reon Shannon, Denzel Washington

Denzel Washington

THE HURRICANE

(**UNIVERSAL**) Producers, Armyan Bernstein, John Ketcham, Norman Jewison; Executive Producers, Irving Azoff, Tom Rosenberg, Rudy Langlais, Thomas A. Bliss, Marc Abraham, William Teitler; Director, Norman Jewison; Screenplay, Armyan Bernstein, Dan Gordon; Based upon the books *The 16th Round* by Rubin "Hurricane" Carter and *Lazarus and the Hurricane* by Sam Chaiton and Terry Swinton; Photography, Roger Deakins; Designer, Philip Rosenberg; Editor, Stephen Rivkin; Costumes, Aggie Guerard Rodgers; Music, Christopher Young; Music Supervisor, G. Marq Roswell; Casting, Avy Kaufman; a Beacon Pictures presentation of an Azoff Films/Rudy Langlais production; Dolby; Deluxe color; Rated R; 149 minutes; Release date: December 29, 1999

CAST

Rubin "Hurricane" Carter	Denzel Washington
Lesra Martin	Vicellous Reon Shannon
Lisa Peters	Deborah Kara Unger
Sam Chaiton	Liev Schreiber
Terry Swinton	John Hannah
Detective Vincent Della Pesca	Dan Hedaya
Mae Thelma	Debbi Morgan
Lt. Jimmy Williams	Clancy Brown
Myron Beldock	David Paymer
Leon Friedman	Harris Yulin
Judge Sarokin	Rod Steiger
Mobutu	Badja Djola
Alfred Bello	Vincent Pastore
Warden	Al Waxman
U.S. Court Prosecutor	David Lansbury
John Artis	Garland Whitt
Earl Martin	Chuck Cooper
Alma Martin	Brenda Thomas
DenmarkJean Wahl	Marcia Bennett
Louise Cockersham	Beatrice Winde
Young Rubin	Mitchell Taylor, Jr.
Paterson Judge	Bill Raymond
Judge Larner	Merwin Goldsmith
Man at Falls	John A. Mackay
Boy at the Falls	Donnique Privott
Tina Barbieri	Moynan King
Nite Spot Cabbie	Gary DeWitt Marshall
Reporter at Bar	John Christopher Jones
Nite Spot Woman	Gwendolyn Mulamba
Paterson Detective	Richard Davidson
Big Ed	George Odom
Woman at Prison	Tonye Patano
Paterson Policeman	Fulvio Cecere
Soldiers in U.S.O. Club	Phillip Jarrett, Rodney M. Jackson
Woman in U.S.O. Club	Judi Embden
Emilie Griffith	Terry Claybon
Joey Giordello	Ben Bray
Joey Cooper	Michael Justus

and Kenneth McGregor (Detective at Hospital), Frank Proctor (Pittsburgh Ring Announcer), Peter Wylie (Pittsburgh Referee), David Gray (Pittsburgh TV Announcer), Joe Matheson (Philadelphia Ring Announcer), Bill Lake (Philadelpia TV Announcer), Robin Ward (Reading, Pa. TV Announcer), Harry Davis (Reading, Pa. Referee), Pippa Pearthree (Patty Valentine), Jean Daigle (Detective), Robert Evans (Detective at Lafayette Bar), Scott Gibson (Reporter at Banquet), Ann Holloway (Cashier), Jim Bearden (Lieutenant), Bruce McFee, Conrad Bergschneider, Satori Shakoor, Zoran Radusinovic, Stephen Lee Wright, Michael Bodnar, Carson Mannin, Deborah Ellen Waller, Richard Litt, Adam Large, Douglas E. Hughes (Prison Guards), Peter Graham (Prisoner with Camera), George Masswohl (Mechanic), Lawrence Sacco, David Frisch (New Jersey Policemen), Ralph Brown (Federal Court Assistant Prosecutor), Dyron Holmes (Reporter), Ryan Williams (Elstan Martin), Bruce Vavrina (St. Joseph's Doctor), Brenda Braxton (Dancer with John Artis), Christopher Riordan (Jury Foreman)

The true story of how boxer Rubin "Hurricane" Carter was wrongly imprisoned for nearly twenty years for murders he did not commit, and how his supporters fought to see justice triumph. This film received an Oscar nomination for actor (Denzel Washington).

Denzel Washington

Deborah Kara Unger, Vicellous Reon Shannon

Denzel Washington

Deborah Kara Unger, Liev Schreiber, Vicellous Reon Shannon, John Hannah

THE THIRD MIRACLE

(SONY PICTURES CLASSICS) Producers, Fred Fuchs, Steven Haft, Elie Samaha; Executive Producers, Francis Ford Coppola, Ashok Amritraj, Andrew Stevens; Co-Producer, Don Carmody; Director, Agnieszka Holland; Screenplay, John Romano, Richard Vetere; Based on the novel by Richard Vetere; Photography, Jerzy Zielinski; Editor, David J. Siegel; Music, Jan A.P. Kaczmarak; Designer, Robert De Vico; Costumes, Denise Cronenberg; Special Effects, Michael Kavanaugh; Casting, Todd Thaler, Clare Walker; a Franchise Pictures presentation of an American Zoetrope and Haft Entertainment production; Dolby; Deluxe color; Rated R; 119 minutes; Release date: December 29, 1999

CAST

Father Frank Shore ....Ed Harris
Roxanna...Anne Heche
Archbishop Werner......................................Armin Mueller-Stahl
Bishop Cahill...Charles Haid
John Leone...Michael Rispoli
Helen O'Reagan ....Barbara Sukowa
Brother Gregory ....James Gallanders
Cardinal Sarrazin ....Jean-Louis Roux
Father Paul Panak ....Ken James
Maria Witkowski ....Caterina Scorsese
and Sofia Polanská (Young Helena), Pavol Simon (Helena's Father), Ivan Lujac (Young Priest), Patrik Minár (Young German Soldier), Kenny Robinson (Front Desk Manager), Rony Clanton (Higgins), Angela Fusco (Charity Woman), Susan Hinley (Sister Margaret), Jade Smith (Young Maria), Monique Mojica (Sister Mary Catherine), Gerard Ronan (One-Eyed Man), Alastair Moir (Boy in Wheelchair), Kay Hawtrey (Wheelchair Mother), Ron Gabriel (Dr. Farkas), Desmond Ellis (Card Playing Priest), Mark Huisman (Brother Thomas), Norma Dell'Agnese (Mrs. Witkowski), Rogue Johnson (Miller), Ian Ryan (Black Kid), Christopher Bolton (Wayne Stozzi), Natalie Urquhart (Backseat Girl), Ralph Small (Leo Lucker), Don Carmody (Jack DaSica), Rodger Barton (Detective Al Winston), Junior Williams (Officer Herman), Catherine Gouldier (Reporter), Lili Francks (Woman in Churchyard), Craig Eldridge (Father Burke), Michael Millar (Priest, Plaza Hotel), Aron Tager, Bob Jarvis (Cardinals), Arthur Eng (Doctor), Father Duaine Devereaux (Father at Mass), Steve Ferguson (Stevens), Ron Kennell (Spasmatic Man), Ned Vukovic (Father Castaldi), Mary Lu Zahalan (Jean), Trevor Lowden (Singing Boy)

A troubled priest, sent to Chicago to investigate the mystical phenomenon surrounding a recently deceased woman, finds himself becoming strongly attracted to the late woman's daughter, Roxanna, who firmly refuses to believe the mother she hated could be responsible for a modern miracle.

Anne Heche, Ed Harris

Caterina Scorsese

MR. DEATH: THE RISE AND FALL OF FRED A. LEUCHTER, JR.

(LIONS GATE) Producers, Michael Williams, David Collins, Dorothy Aufiero; Executive Producers, Jonathan Sehring, Caroline Kaplan, John Sloss; Director, Errol Morris; Photography, Peter Donohue; Additional Photography, Robert Richardson; Designer, Ted Bafaloukos; Music, Caleb Sampson; Editor, Karen Schmeer; an Independent Film Channel productions in association with Channel 4 presentation of a Fourth Floor/Scout production; U.S.-British; Dolby; Color; Rated PG-13; 92 minutes; Release date: December 29, 1999. Documentary on Fred A. Leuchter, Jr., a Massachusetts engineer and expert in the design and repair of more humane execution devices, who wound up testifying in favor of a Neo-Nazi group who claimed the Holocaust did not exist.

INTERVIEWS WITH

Fred A. Leuchter Jr., Robert Jan Van Pelt, David Irving, James Roth, Shelly Shapiro, Suzanne Tabasky, Ernst Zundel.

Fred A. Leuchter, Jr.

Jamie Lee Curtis, William Baldwin in *Virus* ©Universal Studios

VIRUS (**Universal**) Producer, Gale Anne Hurd; Director, John Bruno; Screenplay, Chuck Pfarrer, Dennis Feldman; Based on the Dark Horse Comic Book series Virus created by Chuck Pfarrer; Executive Producers, Mike Richardson, Chuck Pfarrer, Gary Levinsohn, Mark Gordon; Photography, David Eggby; Designer, Mayling Cheng; Editor, Scott Smith; Robotics Effects Designers, Steve Johnson, Eric Allard; Co-Producers, Todd Moyer, Dennis E. Jones, Bud Smith; Music, Joel McNeely; Visual Effects, Fantasy II Film Effects, Inc.; a Mutual Film Company presentation of a Dark Horse Entertainment/Valhalla Motion Pictures production; U.S.-Japanese-German; Dolby; Super 35 Widescreen; Deluxe color; Rated R; 99 minutes; Release date: January 15, 1999. CAST: Jamie Lee Curtis (Kit Foster), William Baldwin (Steve Baker), Donald Sutherland (Capt. Everton), Joanna Pacula (Nadia), Marshall Bell (J.W. Woods, Jr.), Julio Oscar Mechoso (Squeaky), Sherman Augustus (Richie), Cliff Curtis (Hiko), Yuri Chervotkin (Col. Kominski), Keith Flippen (Capt. Lonya Rostov), Olga Rzhepetskaya-Retchin (Cosmonaut), Levani (Capt. Alexi), David Eggby (Norfolk Captain)

INSIDE/OUT (**Parallel/Baltimore**) Producers, J.K. Eareckson, Tom Garvin; Co-Producer, Gill Holland; Director/Screenplay/Editor/Photography, Rob Tregenza; Music, J.K. Eareckson, Mary Tregenza; Costumes, Paula Stonestreet; a Parallel Pictures/Baltimore Film Factory production; Black and white; Not rated; 115 minutes; Release date: January 15, 1999. CAST: Frederic Pierrot (Jean Hammett), Stefania Rocca (Grace Patterson), Berangere Allaux (Monica Phillips), Tom Gilroy (David Shepard), Mikkel Gaup (Eric Johnson), Steven Watkins (Roger Freeman), David Roland Frank, Johanna Cox, Courtney Wilkenson, Jim Czarnecki, Brian Hemingson, David Beaudoin, Edgar Davis, Dominc Valentine, Branch Warfield.

Jean-Luke Figueroa, Sharon Stone in *Gloria* ©Mandalay Entertainment

GLORIA (**Columbia**) Producers, Gary Foster, Lee Rich; Executive Producers, G. Mac Brown, Chuck Binder; Director, Sidney Lumet; Screenplay, Steven Antin; Photography, David Watkin; Designer, Mel Bourne; Editor, Tom Swartwout; Costumes, Dona Granata; Music, Howard Shore; Co-Producer, Josie Rosen; Casting, Lou DiGiaimo; a Mandalay Entertainment presentation of an Eagle Point Production; Dolby; Technicolor; Rated R; 108 minutes; Release date: January 22, 1999. CAST: Sharon Stone (Gloria), Jean-Luke Figueroa (Nicky), Jeremy Northam (Kevin), Cathy Moriarty (Diane), George C. Scott (Ruby), Mike Starr (Sean), Barry McEvoy (Terry), Don Billett (Raymond), Jerry Dean (Mickey), Tony DiBenedetto (Zach), Teddy Atlas (Ian), Bobby Cannavale (Jack), Sarita Choudhury (Angela), Miriam Colon (Maria), Desiree F. Casado (Luz), Davenia McFadden, Chuck Cooper (Guards), Antonia Rey (Tenant), Sidney Armus (Pharmacist), John Heffernan (Hotel Clerk), James Lally (Freddie the Pawnbroker), Lillias White, Terry Alexander (Transit Cops), John Diresta (Radio Man), Lou Cantres, Jose Rabelo (Dominican Men), Lisa Louise Langford (Waitress), Ray Garvey (Police Detective), Nicole Brier (Young Blonde #1), Laura Wachal (Other Young Woman), Elle Alexander (Third Blonde), Donald J. Lee, Jr. (Father Paul), Don Clark Williams (Video Reporter), Nick Oddo (Uncle Manny), Timothy K. Rail (Priest with Students), Martha Rentas (Bus Driver), Bonnie Bedelia (Brenda)

Vince Vaughn, Joey Lauren Adams in *A Cool, Dry Place* © Twentieth Century Fox

A COOL, DRY PLACE (**20th Century Fox**) Producers, Katie Jacobs, Gail Mutrux; Co-Producer, David Coatsworth; Director, John N. Smith; Screenplay, Matthew McDuffie; Photography, Jean Lepine; Designer, Donald Graham Burt; Editor, Susan Shipton; Music, Curt Sobel; Costumes, Denise Cronenberg; Casting, Debra Zane; a Fox 2000 presentation of a Jacobs/Mutrux production; Dolby; Deluxe color; Rated PG-13; 97 minutes; Release date: January 29, 1999. CAST: Vince Vaughn (Russell Durrell), Joey Lauren Adams (Beth), Monica Potter (Kate), Bobby Moat (Calvin Durrell), Devon Sawa (Noah), Todd Louiso (Bob Harper), Jenny Robertson (Joyce Ives), Siobhan Fallon (Charlotte), Chris Bauer (Larry Ives), Nicholas Campbell (Frankie Cooland), Aleksa Palladino (Bonnie), Janet Kidder (Carol), Douglas Wert (Tom Johnson), Skipp Sudduth (Jack Newbauer), Dara Perlmutter (Meg), Jennifer Irwin (Connie Harper), Beth Littleford (Suzanne), Ben Bass (Placement Agent), Cale Sampson (Peter), Peter Costigan (Gas Station Attendant), John Nelles (Vet), Dean McDermott (Sheriff Pritchard), Kathryn Haggis (Days Inn Desk Clerk), John LeFebvre (Cob Whitman), Ron Payne (Councilman Thomas), Melanie Nicholls-King (Dallas Desk Clerk), Phil Lawn (Referee), Claudia Theriault (Answering Machine Voice)

FAME WHORE (**Apathy Prods.**) Producers, Jon Moritsugu, Andrea Sperling; Director/Screenplay/Editor, Jon Moritsugu; Photography, Sarah Leech; Designer, Jennifer Gentile; a Blurco production; Color; Not rated; 73 minutes; Release date: January 22, 1999. CAST: Peter Friedrich (Jody George), Amy Davis (Sophia), Victor of Aquitaine (George), Jason Rail, Michael Fitzpatrick, Izabela Wojcik

MY GIRLFRIEND'S BOYFRIEND (**Enlightenment Prods.**) Producers, Kenneth Shapiro, Evan Seplow; Director/Screenplay, Kenneth Shapiro; Photography, T.W. Li; Editor, Evan Seplow; Music, Deborah Gibson; Casting, Adrienne Stern; Color; Not rated; 80 minutes; Release date: January 22, 1999. CAST: Sean Runnette (Jake), Deborah Gibson (Melissa Stevens), Jill Novick (Liberty), Valerie Perrine (Rita Lindross), Chris Bruno (Cliff), Linda Larkin (Cory Lindross), Jack Koenig (Wes)

TINSELTOWN (**Goldwyn**) Producers, Randy Lippert, Tony Spiridakis; Director, Tony Spiridakis; Screenplay, Tony Spiridakis, Shem Bitterman; Based on their play Self Storage; Photography, Scott Henriksen; Music, Harry Spiridakis; Editor, Christopher Koefoed; Color; Rated R; 85 minutes; Release date: January 29, 1999. CAST: Tom Wood (Tiger), Rebecca Gray (Artists' Model), Arye Gross (Max), Joe Pantoliano (Arnie), Ron Perlman (Cliff), Bryan Pryor (Musician), Kristy Swanson (Nikki)

LEVITATION (**Northern Arts**) Producers, Shelly Strong, Scott D. Goldstein; Director/Screenplay, Scott D. Goldstein; Photography, Michael Wojciechowski; Editors, Fred Wardell, Scott D. Goldstein; Music, Leonard Rosenman; a Tenth Muse presentation of a Strong/Goldstein production; Dolby; Foto-Kem color; Not rated; 99 minutes; Release date: January 29, 1999. CAST: Sarah Paulson (Acey Rawlin), Ernie Hudson (Downbeat), Jeremy London (Bob), Ann Magnuson (Anna Rawlin/Sara Fulton), Antonio Fargas (Otis Hill), Grand Bush (Toby Banks), Christopher Boyer (Acey's Father), Karen Witter (Ranch Woman), Stephanie Hawkins (Elizabeth Fulton), Jim Kamm (Peter Fulton)

Sarah Michelle Gellar, Sean Patrick Flanery in *Simply Irresistible*
©Twentieth Century Fox

SIMPLY IRRESISTIBLE (**20th Century Fox**) Producers, John Fiedler, Jon Amiel, Joseph M. Caracciolo, Jr.; Executive Producers, Arnon Milchan, Elisabeth Robinson; Co-Producer, Brian Maas; Director, Mark Tarlov; Screenplay, Judith Roberts; Photography, Robert Stevens; Editor, Paul Karasick; Designers, John Kasarda, William Barclay; Music, Gil Goldstein; Casting, Billy Hopkins, Suzanne Smith, Kerry Barden; a Regency Entertainment presentation of a Polar production in association with Taurus Film; Dolby; Super 35 Widescreen; Deluxe; Rated PG-13; 96 minutes; Release date: February 5, 1999. CAST: Sarah Michelle Gellar (Amanda Shelton), Sean Patrick Flanery (Tom Bartlett), Patricia Clarkson

(Lois McNally, Tom's P.A.), Dylan Baker (Jonathan Bendel), Christopher Durang (Gene O'Reilly), Larry Gillard, Jr. (Nolan Traynor), Olek Krupa (Valderon), Amanda Peet (Chris, Tom's Girlfriend), Betty Buckley (Aunt Stella), Andrew Seear (Frank Rogers), Meg Gibson (Hannah Wallberg), Alex Draper (François), Drew Nieporent (Gil Shapiro), Anthony Ruivivar (Ramos), Andrew McLaren (The Poet), Steven Skybell (Herr Mueller, Chief Financier), Phyllis Somerville (Ruth), Bill Raymond (Howard), Yusef Bulos (Bill), Joseph Mosso (Abe), Harley Kaplan (Brian in Shoes Department), Molly Tarlow (Molly), Gabriel Macht (Charlie), Hal Robinson (Southern Cross Customer), Margaret Sophie Stein (Frau Mueller), Lily Semel (Lauren), Audrey Matson (Lauren's Mother), Debbon Ayer (Bendel's Sales Person), Marisa Zalabak (Reporter), Eric Rota (Sous Chef at Market), Kara Wethington (Singer), Leslie Lyles (T.J. Russo)

Dadon in *Windhorse* ©Shadow Distribution

WINDHORSE (**Shadow Distribution**) Producer/Director, Paul Wagner; Screenplay, Julia Elliott, Thupten Tsering, Paul Wagner; Co-Producer, Julia Elliott; Photography, Steven Schecter; Executive Producer, Ellen Casey Wagner; Editors, Paul Wagner, Tony Black; U.S.-Tibetan; Color; Not rated; 97 minutes; Release date: February 12, 1999. CAST: Tenzin Pema (Young Dolkar), Deepak Tserin (Young Dorjee), Pasang Dolma (Young Pema), Dadon (Dolkar), Name Withheld (Pema), Jampa Kelsang (Dorjee), Richard Chang (Duan-ping), Lu Yu (Mr. Du), Taije Silverman (Amy), Pema Choekyi (Amala), Nima Bhuti (Momola), Gorkyap (Pala), Dawa Tsering (Monk), Gelek (Mr. Li), Thupten Sherab (Samden), Lodoe Namgyal (Tashi), Sienna Craig (Julia), Abraham Zobloki (Sam)

UNCONDITIONAL LOVE (**Horne Entertainment**) Producer/Director/Screenplay, Steven Rush; Executive Producer, John Kennedy Horne; Photography, Ken Blakey; Designer, Fred Rassouli; Editor, Peregrine Beckman; Dolby; Color; Rated R; 105 minutes; Release date: February 12, 1999. CAST: John Kennedy Horne (Joe Kirkman), Tracey Ross (Patrice Sommers), Henry Silva (Ted Markham), Miles O'Keeffe (Juno), Sheryl Lee Ralph (Linda Cray), Leo Rossi (Martin Ward), Antonio Fargas (Bobby Chiclets), Robert Miano (Harry Peskel), Adrian Zmed (Mario), Mette Holt (Carolyn Thomassen), Robert Culp (Karl Thomassen)

BEST MAN: "BEST BOY" AND ALL OF US TWENTY YEARS LATER (**Independent**) Producer/Director/Screenplay, Ira Wohl; Photography, Tom McDonough; Designer, Tony Corbett; Videographer, Roman Fichman; Color; Not rated; 90 minutes; Release date: Feb. 12, 1999. Follow-up documentary to Ira Wohl's Academy Award-winning documentary "Best Boy" revisiting his retarded cousin Philly, twenty years later. Featuring Frances Reiss, Philip Wohl.

Mother, Michael Alig in *Party Monster* ©World of Wonder

PARTY MONSTER (World of Wonder) Producers/Directors, Fenton Bailey, Randy Barbato; Executive Producer, Sheila Nevins; Producer for HBO, John Hoffman; No other credits availble; Color; Not rated; 60 minutes; Release date: February 12, 1999. Documentary on Manhattan club promoter Michael Alig who was convicted of the murder of his roommate in 1997. (Note: This film originally aired on Cinemax in June of 1998).

Julie Benz, Rebecca Gayheart, Rose McGowan in *Jawbreaker*
©Columbia/TriStar

JAWBREAKER (TriStar) Producers, Stacy Kramer, Lisa Tornell; Director/Screenplay, Darren Stein; Photography, Amy Vincent; Designer, Jerry Fleming; Editor, Troy T. Takaki; Music, Stephen Endelman; Costumes, Vikki Brinkkord; Casting, Lisa Beach, Sarah Katzman; a Kramer-Tornell production in association with Crossroad Films; Dolby; CFI color; Rated R; 87 minutes; Release date: February 19, 1999. CAST: Rose McGowan (Courtney Shayne), Rebecca Gayheart (Julie Freeman), Julie Benz (Marcie Fox), Judy Evans Greer (Fern Mayo), Chad Christ (Zach Tartak), Ethan Erickson (Dane Sanders), Charlotte Roldan (Liz Purr), Pam Grier (Det. Vera Cruz), Carol Kane (Miss Sherman), Tatyana Ali (Brenda), Kall Harrington, Alexis Smart, Allison Thayer (Superstars), Alexandra Adl, Lisa Robin Kelly (Cheerleaders), Michael McClafferty (College Stud), Joni Allen, Vylette Fagerholm (Make-Up Mongers), Anna Zupa (Gothic Girl), Jan Linder (Customer), Brian Gattas, Claudine Claudio (Drama Students), Jessica Gaynes, Jane Connelly (Wannabes), Tommy McKay (Officer), Marita Black (Dreamgirl #1), Dan Gerrity (Dreamperson #2), Rebecca Street (Mom Freeman), Jeff Conaway (Marcie's Father), William Katt (Mr. Purr), P.J. Soles (Mrs. Purr), Sandy Martin (Nurse), Rachel Winfree (English Teacher), Sophia Abu Jamra (Biology Teacher), Donna Pieroni (Cooking Teacher), Rick Lindland (Auto Stud), Allison Robertson, Brett Anderson, Maya Ford, Torry Castellano (The Donnas), Billy Butler (High School Stud #2)

THE POET AND THE CON (Poet Prods.) Producer /Director/Screenplay/Editor, Eric Trules; Photography, Arnie Sirlan; Music, Ron Sures; Black and white/color; Not rated; 78 minutes; Release date: February 19, 1999. Documentary on poet-filmmaker Eric Trules relationship with his uncle, Harvey Rosenberg, a career criminal.

Francesca Faridany in *Conceiving Ada*
©Hotwire/ZDF/ARTE/Complex Corp.

CONCEIVING ADA (Fox Lorber) Producers, Lynn Hershman Leeson, Henry S. Rosenthal; Director, Lynn Hershman Leeson; Screenplay, Lynn Hershman Leeson, Eileen Jones; Photography, Hiro Narita, Bill Zarchy; Editor, Robert Dalva; Music, The Residents; a Hotwire/Complex Corporation production; Color; Not rated; 85 minutes; Release date: February 19, 1999. CAST: Tilda Swinton (Ada Byron King), Timothy Leary (Sims), Karen Black (Lady Byron/Mother Coer), Francesca Faridany (Emmy Coer), John O'Keefe (Charles Babbage), J.D. Wolfe (Nicholas Clayton), John Perry Barlow (John Crosse), Owen Murphy (William Lovelace), Esther Mulligan (Mary Shelley), R.U. Sirius (Barlow), Ellen Sebastian (Dr. Fury), Mark Capri (Dr. Locock), David Eppel (Simon), Pollyanna Jacobs (Cocktail Server), Lillian L. Malmberg (Anne Isabelle Byron), Cyrus Mare (Ralph Byron), David Brooks (Children's Tutor), Michael Oosterom (Lord Byron), Kashka Peck (Teenage Ada), Rose Lockwood (Child Ada/Claire), Charles Pinion (CD-ROM Byron), Jesse Talman Boss (Baby Ada), Chris Von Sneidern (Musician in the Elevator), Joe Wemple (Priest/Talk Show Host), Roger Shaw (Voice of Priest), Lavay Smith (Lead Singer—Club Band)

FREAKS UNCENSORED!: A HUMAN SIDESHOW (Bohemia Prods.) Producer, Vivian Forlander; Director/Editor, Ari Roussimoff; Screenplay, Ari Roussimoff, Vivian Forlander; Music, John Watts; Color; Not rated; 100 minutes; Release date: February 26, 1999. Documentary on human oddities, featuring Jeannie Tomaini (Half-Lady), Jack Dracula (Tattooed Wonder), Jennifer Miller (Bearded Woman Performance Artist), James Taylor (Author and publisher of Shocked and Amazed), Joe Petro III (Collector), David F. Friedman (Film Producer and Carnival Entrepreneur), Ari Roussimoff (The Jester)

Courtney B. Vance, Charles Dutton in *Blind Faith* ©Roxie Releasing

BLIND FAITH (Roxie Releasing) Producer, Nick Grillo; Executive Producers, Mace Neufeld, Robert Rehme; Director, Ernest Dickerson; Screenplay, Frank Military; Photography, Rodney Charters; Designer, Jeff Ginn; Editor, Stephen Lovejoy; Music, Ron Carter; Costumes, Martha Mann; Casting, Beth Klein, Alysa Wishingrad, Ross Clydesdale; Ultra-Stereo; Color; Not rated; 118 minutes; Release date: February 26, 1999. CAST: Charles Dutton (Charles Williams), Courtney B. Vance (John Williams), Kadeem Hardison (Eddie Williams), Lonette McKee (Carol Williams), Garland Whitt (Charles Williams Jr.), Karen Glave (Anna Huggins), Jeff Clarke (Timothy), Nancy Herard (Rose), Jim Jones (Philip), Alex Karzis (Frank), Dan Lett (Frank Minor), Aron Tager (Judge Aker), Birdie M. Hale (Mrs. Barry), Peter MacNeill (Captain McCully), Jeff Jones (Stanley Harris), Phillip Mackenzie (Anthony Grey) (Note: This film had its premiere on Showtime in 1998).

Myles Berkowitz, Elisabeth Wagner in *20 Dates*
©Fox Searchlight Pictures

20 DATES (Fox Searchlight) Producers, Elie Samaha, Mark McGarry, Jason Villard; Executive Producer, Tia Carrere; Director/Screenplay, Myles Berkowitz; Photography, Adam Biggs; Music, Steve Tyrell, Bob Mann; Editors, Michael Elliot, Lisa Cheek; Line Producer, Jeremy Gardiner; a Phoenician Films production; Dolby; Color; Rated R; 88 minutes; Release date: February 26, 1999. Filmmaker Myles Berkowitz films several dates in hopes of ending up with a girlfriend. With Myles Berkowitz, Elisabeth Wagner, Richard Arlook, Tia Carrere, Robert McKee; Elie Samaha (voice).

EIGHT DAYS A WEEK (Seventh Art) Producers, Martin Cutler, Michael Davis, Gary Preisler; Director/Screenplay, Michael Davis; Executive Producer, Dale Rosenbloom; Photographer, James Lawrence Spencer; Designer, Chuck Conner; Costumes, Sybil Mosely; Editor, David Carkhuff; Music, Kevin Bassinson; a Mayfair Entertainment International and Palisades Pictures presentation of a Michael Davis/Dale Rosenbloom production in association with Martin Cutler and Gary Preisler; Dolby; Color; Rated R; 93 minutes; Release date: February 26, 1999. CAST: Joshua Schaefer (Peter), Keri Russell (Erica), R.D. Robb (Matt), Mark Taylor (Peter's Father), Marcia Shapiro (Peter's Mother), Johnny Green (Nick), Buck Kartalian (Nonno), Catherine Hicks (Ms. Lewis), Patrick O'Brien (Erica's Father), Darleen Carr (Erica's Mother), Biff Manard (The Sad Man), Annie O'Donnell (Sad Man's Wife), Ernestine Mercer (Crazy Lady), Bill Hollis (Mr. Hatfield), Jean Pflieger (Ms. McCoy), Stephen Cserhalmi (Mister Mays), Van Epperson (Phil), Vinnie Buffolino (Young Nick), Jonathan Osser (Young Peter), Gabrielle Boni (Erica's Sister), Stephanie Sawyer (Young Erica), Taylor Nix (Robert), Steven Brotman (Bully), Jesse Hays (10 Year Old Peter), Jane Childerhose (Mrs. Olson), James Pappas (Key Man), Mary Helen Sifford (Permit Lady), Linda Ljoka (Mother), Robyn Fisch (Biblical Pursuit Lady), David Lind (Mailman), Marcia Knott (Matt's Mom), Peter Casey (Matt's Dad)

Dancemaker © Artistic License Films

DANCEMAKER (Artistic License) Producers, Jerry Kupfer, Matthew Diamond; Executive Producer, Walter Scheuer; Director/Screenplay, Matthew Diamond; Photography, Tom Hurwitz; Editor, Pam Wise; Associate Producer, Daisy Pommer; Produced in association with the Four Oaks Foundation; Color; Not rated; 98 minutes; Release date: March 3, 1999. Documentary on the Paul Taylor Dance Co., with Paul Taylor, Mauren Mansfield, Heather Berest, Terry Pexton, Ted Thomas, Takehiro Ueyama, Andy Lebeau, Silvia Nevjinsky, Jill Echo, Francie Huber, Kristi Egtvedt, Richard Chen See, Lisa Viola, Rachel Berman, Patrick Corban, Caryn Heilman, Thomas Patrick, Andrew Asnes

RELAX ... IT'S JUST SEX (Jour de Fete/Atlas) Producers, Steven J. Wolfe, Megan O'Neill, Harold Warren; Executive Producers, Eli Kabillio, Cevin D. Stoling; Co-Producers, David Cohn, Tom Seid, PJ Castellaneta; Director/Screenplay, PJ Castellaneta; Designer, Timm Bergen; Music, Lori Eschler Frystak; Editor, Tom Seid; Casting, Shevonne Durkin; Dolby; FotoKem color; Not rated; 110 minutes; Release date: March 5, 1999. CAST: Jennifer Tilly (Tara Ricotto), Mitchell Anderson (Vincey Sauris), Cynda Williams (Sarina Classer), Lori Petty (Robin Moon), Serena Scott Thomas (Megan Pillsbury), Eddie Garcia (Javi Rogero), Timothy Paul Perez (Gus Rogero), Chris Cleveland (Diego Tellez), T.C. Carson (Buzz Wagner), Billy Wirth (Jered Baroziak), Gibbs Toldsdorf (Dwight Bergman), Susan Tyrell (Alicia Pillsbury), Seymour Cassell (Emile Pillsbury), Paul Winfield (Auntie Miriam)

Norman Reedus, Deborah Harry in *Six Ways to Sunday*
©Stratosphere Entertainment

SIX WAYS TO SUNDAY (Stratosphere) Producers, Adam Bernstein, David Collins, Michael Naughton; Executive Producer, Charles Johnson; Director, Adam Bernstein; Screenplay, Adam Bernstein, Marc Gerald; Based upon the novel Portrait of a Young Man Drowning by Charles Perry; Photography, John Inwood; Co-Producers, Marc Gerald, Dorothy Aufiero, Michael Williams; Designer, Theresa Mastropierro; Costumes, Edi Giguere; Editor, Doug Abel; Music, Theodore Shapiro; Casting, Billy Hopkins, Suzanne Smith, Kerry Barden; a Jonathan Demme presentation of a Prosperity Electric production; Dolby; Widescreen; Color; Rated R; 97 minutes; Release date: March 5, 1999. CAST: Norman Reedus (Harry Odum), Deborah Harry (Kate Odum), Peter Appel (Abie "The Bug" Pinkwise), Elina Lowensöhn (Iris), Jerry Adler (Louis Varga), Holter Graham (Madden), Isaac Hayes (Bill Bennett), Adrien Brody (Arnie Finklestein), Paul Lazar (Hyman), Paul D'Amoto (Fishetti), Anna Thompson (Annibelle), Anna Marie Wieder (Madame Royce), Steve Itkin (Rudolph Sax), Clark Gregg (Benjamin Taft), Vincent Pastore (Uncle Max), Christopher Mackin (Necktie), Eugene Leong (Chinese Man), William Preston (Rabbi), Joseph Scott (Meat Chewer), Kathy Lee Hart (Waitress)

Rock the Boat ©Tell the Truth Pictures

ROCK THE BOAT (Tell the Truth Pictures) formerly The Human Race; Producer, Robert Hudson; Director/Photography, Bobby Houston; Editor, Michael Lorenzo; Music, Kevin Hayes; Sponsored by Boehringer Ingelheim-Roxane Laboratories; Color; Not rated; 84 minutes; Release date: March 5, 1999. Documentary about eleven H.I.V.-positive men who race the sloop, the Survivor, in the 1997 Trans-Pacific Yacht Race; featuring Robert Hudson, John Plander, Mike Schmidt, Ted Taylor, Dennis Boecker, Bill Kijovsky, Steve Kovacek, Mike Burelle, Richard Bartol, Keith Ericson, Bobby Houston.

Emily Bergl, Amy Irving in *The Rage: Carrie 2*
©United Artists Pictures Inc.

THE RAGE: CARRIE 2 (United Artists) Producer, Paul Monash; Executive Producer, Patrick Palmer; Director, Katt Shea; Screenplay, Rafael Moreu; Based on the character created by Stephen King; Photography, Donald M. Morgan; Designer, Peter Jamison; Editor, Richard Nord; Costumes, Theoni V. Aldredge; Music, Danny B. Harvey; Digital Visual Effects, Kleiser-Walczak Construction Company; Casting, Gretchen Rennell Court; a Red Bank Films production; from MGM Distribution; Dolby; Deluxe color; Rated R; 104 minutes; Release date: March 12, 1999. CAST: Emily Bergl (Rachel Lang), Jason London (Jesse Ryan), Dylan Bruno (Mark), J. Smith-Cameron (Barbara Lang), Amy Irving (Sue Snell), Zachery Ty Bryan (Eric), John Doe (Boyd), Gordon Clapp (Mr. Stark), Rachel Blanchard (Monica), Charotte Ayanna (Tracy), Justin Urich (Brad), Mena Suvari (Lisa), Elijah Craig (Chuck), Eddie Kaye Thomas (Arnie), Clint Jordan (Sheriff Kelton), Steven Ford (Coach Walsh), Kate Skinner (Emilyn), Rus Blackwell (Sheriff), Harold Surratt (School Principal), David Lenthall (English Teacher), Kayla Campbell (Little Rachel), Robert D. Raiford (Senior D.A.), Katt Shea (Deputy D.A.), Deborah Meschan (Party Girl), Robert Treveiler (Smiling Patient), Gina Stewart (Vet), Claire Hurst (Night Nurse), Albert E. Hayes (Head-Banging Patient), Colin Fickes (Tuba Player), Rhoda Griffis (Saleswoman), Eric Hill (Jesse's Spotter), Jennifer Nicole Parillo (Fleeing Party Girl), Jessica Cowart (Smoking Girl), Tiffany LeShani McMinn (Gardening Girl), Steven Culbertson (The Ref)

COOL CRIME (Phaedra) Director, Jerome Cohen-Olivar; No other credits given; Ultra-Stereo; Color; Not rated; 92 minutes; Release date: March 12, 1999. CAST: David Ackert (Nino), Ari Barak (Billardo), Kelly Bovino (India), Robert Cicchini (John), Melinda Hill (Melissa), John Mariano (Roberto), Robert Mariano (Uncle Bruce), Mirron E. Willis (Clive)

Dom DeLuise in *Baby Geniuses* ©TriStar Pictures Inc.

Matthew Lillard, Freddie Prinze Jr., Tchéky Karyo
in *Wing Commander* ©Wing Commander Productions

BABY GENIUSES (TriStar) Producer, Steven Paul; Executive Producer, David Saunders; Co-Executive Producers, Hank Paul, Jon Voight; Director, Bob Clark; Screenplay, Bob Clark, Greg Michael; Story, Steven Paul, Francisca Matos, Robert Grasmere; Photography, Stephen M. Katz; Designer, Francis J. Pezza; Editor, Stan Cole; Music, Paul Zaza; Visual Effects Supervisor, Jacques Stroweis; Costumes, Betty Pecha Madden; Baby Wardrobe, Baby Guess; Casting, Dorothy Koster-Paul; a Steven Paul/Crystal Sky production; Dolby; Super 35 Widescreen; CFI color; Rated PG; 94 minutes; Release date: March 12, 1999. CAST: Kathleen Turner (Elena), Christopher Lloyd (Heep), Kim Cattrall (Robin), Peter MacNicol (Dan), Dom DeLuise (Lenny), Ruby Dee (Margo), Kyle Howard (Dickie), Kaye Ballard (Mayor), Leo, Myles & Gerry Fitzgerald, Connor & Griffin Leggett (Sly & Whit), Megan & Gabrielle Robbins (Carrie), Breanna & Brittany McConnell (Lexi), Jacob Daniel & Zackery Handy (Deby), Amanda & Caitlin Fein (Teddie), Jim Hanks (Goon Ray), Sam McMurray (Goon Bob), Bill Wiley (Wino), Randy Travis (Control Room Technician), Judith Drake (911 Lady), Melissa Bickerton (Diaper Cart Nurse), Chip Heller (Baby Bunting), Dan Monahan (Reporter), Robin Klein, Russell Milton (Babyco Execs), Luis Esmenjaud (Santa Claus), Christopher Broughton (Clown), Mark Graciale, Thomas Crawford (Hypnotized Guards), Hank Garrett (Guard), Ariel Clark (Alien), Allyssa Herrmann (Wendy), Adam Koster (Male Nurse), Shepard Koster (Technician), Daniel Coulter Longcope (Habitat Guard), Eugene Osment (Cop on Hailer), Bonnie Paul (Headquarters Nurse), Randall Hall Senter (Security Guard); Babies' Voices: Miko Hughes (Sly/Whit), Scotty Leavenworth (Basil), Aaron Spann, Scarlett Pomers (Carrie), Ashli A. Adams (Teddy), Lexi Thomas (Lexi), Seth Adkins (Duby), Glenndon Chatman, Danielle Wiener (Joey/Malcolm)

ST. PATRICK'S DAY (Sceneries) Producers, Hope Perello, Kindra Anne Ruocco; Executive Producers, Philippe Diaz, Philippe Lenglet; Director/Screenplay, Hope Perello; Photography, Denise Brassard; Designer, Timothy Bride Keating; Editor, Ann Nervin Job; Music, Michael Muhlfriedel; a co-production of Sceneries Europe, Enrique Cerezo Producciones Cinematograficas and Marvel Movies; Color; Not rated; 105 minutes; Release date: March 12, 1999. CAST: Piper Laurie (Mary Pat), Redmond Gleeson (Thomas), Joanne Baron (Priss), Jim Metzler (Adam), Robert Evan Collins (Sean), Sandra Ellis Lafferty (Bridget), Martin Cassidy (Seamus), Sheila Grenham (Kate), Geraldine Hughes (Maeve), Marty McGuire (Fred), Colleen Fitzpatrick (Cassie), Chris Valenti (Patrick), David Ault (John Michael), Michelle Lawrence (Millicent), Denis O'Hare (Russell), Julie Strain (Molly), Ann Fairlie (Dorrie), J.D. Walsh (Michael John), Herta Ware (Aunt Delia), Gavin Atkins (Rory), Terence Atkins (Tory), Stephen O'Mahoney (Flann)

WING COMMANDER (20th Century Fox) Producer, Todd Moyer; Executive Producers, Joseph N. Cohen, Romain Schroeder, Jean-Martial LeFranc; Co-Executive Producer, Neil Young; Director/Story, Chris Roberts; Screenplay, Kevin Droney; Photography, Thierry Arbogast; Editor, Peter Davies; Music, Kevin Kiner; Designer, Peter Lamont; Costumes, Magali Guidasci; Visual Effects Supervisor, Chris Brown; Casting, Christian Kaplan; a No Prisoners Prods./Digital Anvil presentation, in association with Origin Systems and the Carousel Picture Co.; Dolby; Super 35 Widescreen; Technicolor; Rated PG-13; 99 minutes; Release date: March 12, 1999. CAST: Freddie Prinze, Jr. (Chris Blair), Saffron Burrows (Jeanette "Angel" Devereux), Matthew Lillard (Todd "Maniac" Marshall), Tchéky Karyo (Paladin), Jürgen Prochnow (Gerald), David Suchet (Sansky), David Warner (Tolwyn), Ginny Holder (Forbes), Hugh Quarshie (Obuta), Ken Bones (Wilson), John McGlynn (Belegarde), Richard Dillane (Hunter), Mark Powley (Polanski), David Fahm (Knight), Simon McCorkindale (Flight Boss), Fraser James (Helmsman), Craig Kelly (Radar Man Falk), Kieran Phipps (Peterson), Jamie Treacher (Pegasus Radar Man), Cyril Nri (Security Officer), Jari Kinnunen (Concordia Radar Man), Raph Taylor (Rodriguez), Paul Courtenay Hyu (Com Officer), Mark Jones (Kilrathi Admiral), Graham Riddell (Kilrathi Captain), Christopher P. Kibbey (Medic)

Park Overall in *Sparkler* ©Strand Releasing

SPARKLER (Strand) Producers, Jennifer Amerine, Kimberly Jacobs; Executive Producers, J. Herbert Niles III, John J. McDonnell III, Walter L. Threadgill, Pamela S. Calloway; Director, Darren Stein; Screenplay, Catherine Eads, Darren Stein; Photography, Rodney Taylor; Designer, Chris DiLeo; Costumes, Dalhia Schuette; Music, Dave Russo; Editor, Ryan Gold; Co-Producer/Casting, Joseph Middleton; a Sunshine Filmworks/Conspiracy Entertainment presentation; Color; Not rated; 96 minutes; Release date: March 19, 1999. CAST: Park Overall (Melba May), Veronica Cartwright (Dottie Delgato), Don Harvey (Flint), Jamie Kennedy (Trent), Steven Petrarca (Joel), Freddie Prinze, Jr. (Brad), Sandy Martin (Ed), Grace Zabriskie (Sherri), Sheila Tousey (Hurricane), Gloria Le Roy (Maxine), Glenn Shadix (Announcer), Jack Wallace (Jesse), Frances Bay (Raspy), Octavia Spencer (Wanda), Googy Gress (Big Stew), Chris Ellis, Robert Peters (Buddies), Wendy Worthington, William Hendry (Bar-Goers), Rhonda Dotson (Fawner), Catherine Rideout (Waitress), Judy Armstrong (Old Lady), Promise LeMarco (Card Dealer), Faith Johnson (Balloon Woman), Allison Jacobs (Charlene), Rachel Winfree (Beauty Client), Timi Prulhiere, Jackie Debatin (Showgirls), Mario Gardner (Captain Uhura), C.C. Carr (Sexy Face)

THE ROOK (Ecco Films) Producers, Eran Palatnik, Alan J. Abrams; Director, Eran Palatnik; Screenplay, Richard Lee Purvis; Photography, Zack Winestine; Music, Robert Een; 1994; Color; Not rated; 84 minutes; Release date: March 19, 1999. CAST: Martin Donovan (John Abbott), John A. MacKay (Bob Brice), Michael Finesilver (Donald Heller), Sean Clark (Fritz Fox), Harrison Baker (David P. Dawson), Diane Grotke (Dr. Abby Trent)

Noel Palomaria, Malcolm Moorman in *Hard* ©MPH Productions

HARD (Jour de Fête) Producers, John Matkowsky, Noel Palomaria, John Huckert; Director/Editor, John Huckert; Screenplay, John Huckert, John Matkowsky; Photography/Designer, John Matkowsky; Music, Phil Fettle, John Huckert; Designer, a M.P.H. Production; Color; Not rated; 102 minutes; Release date: March 26, 1999. CAST: Noel Palomaria (Det. Raymond Vates), Malcolm Moorman (Jack), Charles Lanyer (Det. Tom Ellis), Michael Waite (Andy), Steve Andrews (Det. Hendrickson), K.D. Jones (Det. Jenkins), Bob Hollander (Capt. Foster), Ken Narasaki (Det. Chyun), Steve Gonzales (Det. Dominguez), Chas Gray (Det. Kolletti), Brandi Garay (Cinnamon "Lockjaw" Smith), Marion M. Reed (Officer Bruin), Andrea Marcellus (Jenny), Alexandria Palomaria (Tracy), Paula Kay Perry (Bette), Alex DePedro (Andy Jr.), Marcie Harte (Forensics Expert), Vincent Bilancio (Lab Tech), Joshua Fitzgerald (Hitchhiker), Alex Boling (Tex), John Deleski (Hustler), Trish Elliott (Mrs. Hyatt), Charles Busser (Billy Hyatt), Cynthia Downey (Deputy Coroner), Brant Cotton, Miles Swain, Michael Vinton (Cops at Lake), Eric Heng (Bleeding Boy)

Giovanni Ribisi, Claire Danes, Omar Epps in *The Mod Squad*
©Metro-Goldwyn-Mayer Pictures Inc.

THE MOD SQUAD (MGM) Producers, Ben Myron, Alan Riche, Tony Ludwig; Executive Producers, Aaron Spelling, David Ladd; Director, Scott Silver; Screenplay, Stephen Kay, Scott Silver, Kay Lanier; Based upon characters created by Buddy Ruskin; Co-Producers, Michael Bennett, Richard Stenta; Photography, Ellen Kuras; Designer, Patrick Sherman; Editor, Dorian Harris; Costumes, Arianne Phillips; Music, BC Smith; Music Supervisor, Randy Gerston; Casting, Christine Sheaks; DTS Stereo; Deluxe color; Rated R; 94 minutes; Release date: March 26, 1999. CAST: Claire Danes (Julie Barnes), Giovanni Ribisi (Pete Cochrane), Omar Epps (Linc Hayes), Dennis Farina (Capt. Adam Greer), Josh Brolin (Billy), Steve Harris (Briggs), Richard Jenkins (Mothershed), Larry Brandenburg (Eckford), Lionel Mark Smith (Lanier), Sam McMurray (Tricky), Michael O'Neill (Greene), Stephen T. Kay (Bald Dude), Bodhi Pine Elfman (Gilbert, Skinny Freak), Holmes Osborne (Mr. Cochrane), Dey Young (Mrs. Cochrane), Toby Huss (Red), Michael Lerner (Howard), Monet Mazur (Howard's Girlfriend, Sally), Mariah O'Brien (Tiffany), Steve Chambers, Thomas J. Huff, Gary McLarty (Howard's Muscle), Jason Maves (Kirk), Casey Verst (Kevin), Ricky Lesser (Kris), Carmen Llywellyn (Alley Prostitute), Pilar Biggers (Pickup Girl), Khristian Lupo (Tiffany's Boyfriend), Joey Day (Billy's Other Girlfriend), Dean Marsico (Bartender), Skip Evans (Pilot), Eddie Griffin (Sonny)

Terumi Matthews, Belinda Becker in *The Sticky Fingers of Time*
© Strand Releasing

THE STICKY FINGERS OF TIME (Strand) Producers, Isen Robbins, Susan Stover; Executive Producers, Jean-Christophe Castelli, Steven G. Menkin, Ruth Robles, Louis Robles; Director/Screenplay, Hilary Brougher; Photography, Ethan Mass; Designer, Teresa Mastropierro; Editors, Sabine Hoffman, Hilary Brougher; Music, Miki Navazio; Costumes, Wendy Chuck; a Good Machine presentation; Color; Not rated; 81 minutes; Release date: March 26, 1999. CAST: Terumi Matthews (Tucker), Belinda Becker (Ofelia), James Urbaniak (Isaac), Amanda Vogel (Girl in Window), Nicole Zaray (Drew), Leo Marks (Dex), Samantha Buck (Gorge), Florence Meyer (Dental Clinic Receptionist), Thomas Pasley (J.L.), Julie Anderson (Dental Assistant of Death), Justin X. McAvoy (Cop), Amanda Cole (Rachel the Bartender), Tom Vought ("This Guy" in Bar), Alan Jerins (Drew's Mother), Rebeka Milkis (Little Drew)

MYSTERY'S CHOIR (Infinity Films) Producer/Director/Screen-play/Photography/Editor, Loan Do; Co-Producers, Hong Tran, Long Van Do; Color; Not rated; 65 minutes; Release date: April 5, 1999. CAST: Ciro Silva, Michel Tikhomiroff, Ilya Chaiken, Peter Kennedy (Film Crew at Lake), Deidre Currie (Daena), Jill Repplinger (Chelsea), Christopher Scappaticci, Ciro Silva (Shoe Sales Clerk), Jack Pretzer (Mother/Street Stranger "Virility"), William Hunt (Father), Frank Barrera (Cab Driver)

Master P, Eddie Griffin in *Foolish* ©Artisan Entertainment Inc.

Joe Carnahan in *Blood, Guts, Bullets & Octane* ©Lions Gate Films

BLOOD, GUTS, BULLETS & OCTANE (Lions Gate) Producers, Dan Leis, Joe Carnahan, Leon Corcos, Patrick M. Lynn; Director/Screen-play/Editor, Joe Carnahan; Executive Producers, Peter Broderick, Charles Leis; Photography, John A. Jimenez; Music, Mark Priolo, Martin Birke; a Short Fuse Films production in association with Next Wave Films; Dolby; Color/black and white; Rated R; 87 minutes; Release date: April 9, 1999. CAST: Dan Leis (Bob Melba), Ken Rudulph (FBI Agent Jared), Dan Harlan (Danny Woo), Joe Carnahan (Sid French), Hugh McChord (Mr. Reich), Kurt Johnson (Hillbilly Sniper), Michael Saumure (Vernon Cash), Mark S. Allen (FBI Agent Franks), Kelle Benedict (FBI Agent Little), Mike Maas (Victor Drub/Dumpster Bum), Nick Fenske (Mechanic), Mark Priolo (Frank Priolo), Andrew Fowler (Mike Carbuyer), Gloria Gomez (Julie Carbuyer), Josephina Arreola (Elda), Dave Booth (Jerry), Kevin Hale (Pinto Guy), Max Ancar (Frank Manzano), Leah Carnahan (Ginger), Scott Tyler (Dick Dupree, Sr.), Eric Lutes (Dick Dupree, Jr.), Carlos Hernandez (Diaz Carbajal), Karla Cave (Dottie Woo), Karen Olsen (Attendant), Matt Carnahan (Mitchell Wayne Richter), James Salter (Raymond Phelps), Jerry Rainbolt (Jerry Goldman), Carol Curry (Stripper), Rick Reinaldo, Dave Collagan (Inmates), Tanja Anguay, Priya Patel (Woo Cowgirls), Chuck Leis (Pete the Bartender), Shad Shelby (Paramedic), Spencer Mulcahy (Hick in Overalls), Dave Pierini (Bill the Mechanic)

FOOLISH (Artisan) Producers, Jonathan Heuer, Andrew Shack; Executive Producer/Screenplay, Master P; Director, Dave Meyers; Photography, Steve Gainer; Designer, Chuck Conner; Editor, Chris Davis; Music, Beats by the Pound, Wendy Melvoin, Lisa Coleman; Costumes, Jhane Isaacs; Casting, Megalarge; a Shooting Star Pictures production of a Master P/No Limit Film; Color; Rated R; 96 minutes; Release date: April 9, 1999. CAST: Eddie Griffin (Miles "Foolish" Waise), Master P (Quentin "Fifty Dollah" Waise), Amy Petersen (Desiree), Frank Sivero (Giovanni), Daphnee Lynn Duplaix (Charisse), Jonathan Banks (Numbers), Andrew Dice Clay (El Dorado Ron), Sven-Ole Thorsen (Paris), Marla Gibbs (Odetta), Traci Bingham (Simone), Bill Nunn (Jimmy Beck), John Marlo (Alabama Brown), Clifton Powell (Everette Washington), A.J. Johnson, Tommy Chunn, Chalante, Bob Baker, White Boy (Themselves), Anthony Bozwell (Walter), Marqel Lee (Shaun), Honest John (Manny), Bill Duke (Studio Producer), Nick Meany (Director), Dino Shortie (Card Player), Loni-Kaye Harkless (Miss Ida), Sebastian King (Minister), Tommy Rosales (Goon), Randy Harris (Lem), Brian Holtzman (Richie), Linda O'Neil (Nikeeta), Naomi Matsuda (Giovanni's Waitress), Lawrence Williams Jr., Mia X, Earl Carter (Hecklers), Leila Arcifri (Marissa), Pamela Paulshock (Monica), Essie Humphrey (Police Officer), Rebecca Holden (Rebecca the Waitress), Alicia Chavira (Young Desiree), Eddie Griffin Jr. (Young Foolish), Louis Coleman (Young Fifty), Lauren Peltz (Posh Hostess), Jeff Clanagan (Court Client), Lisa Patino (Rene), Ixchelle Marroquin (Bedsheet Girl), Gaetano LoGiudice (Tommy), Carlos Cervantes (Restaurant Owner), Orenda Waters (Flirtatious Woman), Lee Miller, Mark V. Smith-Sams (Bouncers), Jimmie Keller (Ticket Scalper), Fred Terrell (Valet), Derrell Cunegin (Fifty's Venue Patron), Atiim Benjamin (Cashier), Drew Powell (Man Next to White Boy), Darl Brown (Robin Harris), Fred Tatasciore (Redd Foxx), The Griff (Sammy Davis)

CALIFORNIA MYTH (Hollywood Independents) Producer/Editor, Arturo Escobar; Executive Producer, Stephen Strick; Director/Story, Michel Katz; Screenplay, T.J. Walsh, Michel Katz, Tony Martinez; Photography, Angelo Pacifici; Designer, Richard Jabardo; Music, Otmaro Ruiz; Color; Not rated; 90 minutes; Release date: April 16, 1999. CAST: Tyrone Power Jr., Laura Johnson, Sherry Hursey, John Posey, Patricia Charbonneau

THE JOYRIDERS (Providence Entertainment) Producers, Cindy Bond, Midge Sanford, Sarah Pillsbury; Director/Screenplay, Bradley Battersby; Photography, Steven Fierberg; Editor, Terilyn A. Shropshire; Designer, Amy Ancona; Dolby; Color; Rated PG-13; 90 minutes; Release date: April 16, 1999. CAST: Martin Landau (Gordon Trout), Kris Kristofferson (Eddie), Shawn Hatosy (Cam), Heather McComb (Crystal), Elizabeth Moss (Jodi), Diane Venora (Celeste), Debbie Bisno (Pancake

Waitress), Steve Bond (Highway Patrolman), Michael Chieffo (Res-Wel Manager), Kathleen S. Dunn (Wendy Trout), Satch Huizenga (Trucker), Jamielyn (Foster Sister), Jay Karnes (Donald Trout), Robert Knott (Cliff), Sage Leonard (Jodi's Brother), Al Mancini (Older Man at Movie), Jennifer Massey (Nurse), William Francis McGuire (Man in Movie Line), Peter Paige (Family Restaurant Waiter), Angela Paton (Rita Mae Tuttle), Onika Pointer (Pig Muffin), Tim Pulice (Fresno Cop), Mike Rademaekers (Foster Father), William Shockley (Pony Tail Trucker), Nils Allen Stewart (Biker), Dick Stilwell (Det. Osborne), David Vegh (Sales Clerk), Brandon Williams (Teen Thug), Francine Witkin (Elderly Lady)

David Spade in *Lost & Found* ©Lost & Found Productions

Stephen Baldwin, Claudia Schiffer in *Friends and Lovers*
©Lions Gate Films

FRIENDS AND LOVERS (**Lions Gate**) Producer, Josi W. Konski; Executive Producer, Gregory Cascante; Director/Screenplay, George Haas; Story, Neill Barry, George Haas; Co-Executive Producer, Eleanor Powell; Photography, Carlos Montaner; Designer, Ren Blanco; Editor, Barry Leirer; Music, Emilio Kauderer; Costumes, Diane Kranz; Casting, Mike Fenton, Allison Cowitt; a C.E.O. Films presentation of a Josi W. Konski production in association with Laguna Entertainment; Ultra-Stereo; Foto-kem color; Not rated; 104 minutes; Release date: April 16, 1999. CAST: Stephen Baldwin (Jon), Danny Nucci (David), George Newbern (Ian), Alison Eastwood (Lisa), Claudia Schiffer (Carla), Suzanne Cryer (Jane), David Rasche (Richard), Neill Barry (Keaton), Leon (Manny), Robert Downey, Jr. (Hans), Ann Magnuson (Katherine), Jamie Luner (Model), Courtney Bull (Little Girl), Ivo Lewis (Motel Clerk), Josi W. Konski (Tree Lot Owner)

CLUBLAND (**Seventh Art**) Director, Mary Lambert; Screenplay, Glen Ballard; No other credits available; Color; Rated R; 90 minutes; Release date: April 16, 1999. CAST: Lee Arenberg, Alexis Arquette, Terence Trent D'Arby, Rodney Eastman, Matt Gallini, Brad Hunt, Scot James, Lori Petty, Jon Sklaroff, Heather Stephens, Jimmy Tuckett

BEAUTOPIA (**Fox Lorber**) Producer/Director/Screenplay, Katharina Otto; Executive Producers, Tony Smith, Hilary Shor; Photography, Oliver Bokelberg; Editor, Bernadine Colish; Music, Hayley Moss, Frank Otto, Bernt Kohler-Adams; a Film Manufacturers presentation, in association with Hit & Run Prods.; Dolby; Color; Not rated; 104 minutes; Release date: April 16, 1999. Documentary on the fashion industry and four aspiring models from around the world on the verge of a career in the business, featuring Sarah Cookson, Dana Douglas, Susanne Hoppe, Petra Svabenska, Naomi Campbell, Cindy Crawford, Lauren Hutton, Elle Macpherson, Kate Moss, Claudia Schiffer, Oscar de la Renta, Isaac Mizrahi, Valentino.

LOST & FOUND (**Warner Bros.**) Producers, Wayne Rice, Morrie Eisenman, Andrew A. Kosove, Broderick Johnson; Director, Jeff Pollack; Screenplay, J.B. Cook, Marc Meeks, David Spade; Co-Producer, Todd P. Smith; Photography, Paul Elliott; Designer, Rusty Smith; Costumes, Susan Bertram; Editor, Christopher Greenbury; Music, John Debney; Casting, Jackie Burch; an Alcon Entertainment presentation of a Wayne Rice/Dinamo Entertainment production; Dolby; CFI color; Rated PG-13; 95 minutes; Release date: April 23, 1999. CAST: David Spade (Dylan Ramsey), Sophie Marceau (Lila Dubois), Patrick Bruel (René), Artie Lange (Wally), Mitchell Whitfield (Mark Glidewell), Martin Sheen (Millstone), Ever Carradine (Ginger), Stephanie Chang, Neal MacMillan (Restaurant Patrons), Lloyd Garroway (Waiter), Coby (Jack), Carole Cook (Sylvia), Estelle Harris (Mrs. Stubblefield), Marla Gibbs (Enid), Rose Marie (Clara), Natalie Barish, Phil Leeds (Elderly Couple), Christian Clemenson (Ray), Dee Dee Rescher (Sally), Faye DeWitt (Blind Lady), David Hartman (Cello Student), Larry Raben (Peter), Brett Banducci, Nicole Garcia, Mary Ingersal (Mall Quartet Players), Alessandra Toreson (Park Girl), Michelle Clunie (Gail), Abidah Viera (Vet), Shannon Dang (Girl at Pet Store), Carl Michael Lindner (Brat), Karen Rosin (Brat's Mother), Nicolas Greenbury, Andrew Greenbury (Rollerblade Kids), Frankie Muniz, David Garry (Joby the Valet), David Seewack (Valet at Millstone's), Wolf Muser (Ubermann), Della Miles, Erika Nann, Cynthia Bass (Singers), Garland Campbell, B.J. Clements, Mary Fukushima, Steve Griffin, Ermias Mesghenna, Tony Ruiz, Stefan Svensson (Millstone Party Band Members), Fred Golt (Table Guest), Pina De Rosa (Maria, the Cook), Danny Woodburn (Mover), Harper Roisman (Mr. Norton), Pearl Shear (Mrs. Norton), Robert Del, Robert "Schroe" Schroer (Construction Workers), Daphnee Lynn Duplaix (Flight Attendant), J.B. Cook (Jan-a-tor), Marc Lynn (Homeless Guy), Ovis (Pet Store Employee), Frankie Pace (Sal), "Skippy" (Flowbie), Hal Sparks (DJ), Don Perry (Guest at Millstone's), Jenniffer Farrell (Window Washer Girl), Audrey Wasilewski (Pet Store Saleswoman), Frankie Como (Stage Manager)

SO WRONG THEY'RE RIGHT (**8-TM**) Producer/Director/Editor, Russ Forster; Photography, Dan Sutherland; an 8-TM production, 1996; Color; Not rated; 94 minutes; Release date: April 23, 1999. Documentary on audiophiles devoted to and obsessed with the 8-track tape format.

Dean Stewart, Martin Donovan in *Heaven* ©Miramax Films

HEAVEN (Miramax) Producer, Sue Rogers; Executive Producers, Bob Weinstein, Harvey Weinstein; Director/Screenplay, Scott Reynolds; Based on the novel by Chad Taylor; Photography, Simon Raby; Designer, John Girdlestone; Editor, Wayne Cook; Music, Victoria Kelly; a Midnight Films production; Dolby; Super 35 Widescreen; Color; Rated R; 104 minutes; Release date: April 30, 1999. CAST: Martin Donovan (Robert Marling), Danny Edwards (Heaven), Richard Schiff (Stanner), Joanna Going (Jennifer Marling), Patrick Malahide (Melrose), Karl Urban (Sweeper), Michael Langley (Sean Marling), Jeremy Birchall (Tree), Clint Sharplin (Nicely), Barry Spring (Wibber), Jon Brazier (Billy), Dean Stewart (David), Jane Fullerton-Smith (Candy), Jean Hyland (Mrs. Daniels), Valerie Williams (Claire), James Cross, Leonard Sipill (Barmen), Andrew Iosefa (Bouncer), Kirsty Brown, Samantha Keen, Darren Taylor, Vanessa Green, Asa Lindh (Nightclub Dancers), Joy Watson, Johnny Bond (Diners), Nicholas Hayward (Tommy), Tanya Anderson (Nurse), Kate Walsh, Christine Cottle, Sally-Ann Brown (Restaurant Trio)

Elden Henson, Seth Green, Vivica A. Fox, Devon Sawa, Jessica Alba in *Idle Hands* ©Columbia Pictures Industires Inc.

IDLE HANDS (Columbia) Producers, Andrew Licht, Jeffrey A. Mueller, Suzanne Todd, Jennifer Todd; Executive Producer, Jeffrey Sudzin; Director, Rodman Flender; Screenplay, Terri Hughes, Ron Milbauer; Photography, Christopher Baffa; Designer, Greg Melton; Editor, Stephen E. Rivkin; Music, Graeme Revell; Special Make-up Effects

Designer/Creator, Greg Cannom; Casting, John Papsidera; a Licht/Mueller Film Corporation and a Team Todd production; Dolby; Deluxe color; Rated R; 92 minutes; Release date: April 30, 1999. CAST: Devon Sawa (Anton), Seth Green (Mick), Elden Henson (Pnub), Jessica Alba (Molly), Christopher Hart (The Hand), Vivica A. Fox (Debi), Jack Noseworthy (Randy), Katie Wright (Tanya), Sean Whalen (McMacy), Nick Sadler (Ruck), Fred Willard (Dad), Connie Ray (Mom), Steve Van Wormer (Curtis), Kelly Monaco (Tiffany), Timothy Stack (Principal Tidwell), Joey Slotnick (Burger Jungle Manager), Tom Delonge (Drive Thru Jockey), Sabrina Lu (News Reporter), Kyle Gass (Burger Jungle Guy), Mindy Sterling (Bowler), Donna Scott (Nurse), Randy Oglesby (Sheriff Buchanan), Molly Maslin, Carl Gabriel Yorke (Chaperones), Dexter Holland (Band Lead Singer), The Offspring (The Band)

Norman Rodway, Joel Grey in *The Empty Mirror* ©Lions Gate Films

THE EMPTY MIRROR (Lions Gate) Producers, David D. Johnson, M. Jay Roach, William Dance; Director/Story, Barry J. Hershey; Screenplay, Barry J. Hershey, R. Buckingham; Photography, Frederick Elmes; Editor, Marc Grossman; Music, John Frizzell; Designer, Tim Colohan; Costumes, Melinda Eshelman; Casting, Judy Courtney; a Walden Woods Film Co. Ltd. presentation; Dolby; Color; Not rated; 117 minutes; Release date: May 7, 1999. CAST: Norman Rodway (Adolf Hitler), Camilla Soeberg (Eva Braun), Peter Michael Goetz (Sigmund Freud), Doug McKeon (The Typist), Glenn Shadix (Hermann Goehring), Joel Grey (Josef Goebbels)

Isaac Agami in *Fare Games* ©Edison Agami Films

FARE GAMES (Edison Agami Films) Producer/Story, Isaac Agami; Director/Screenplay, Brian O'Hara; Photography, Larry Revene; Editor, Kevin O'Hara; Music, TAJ; Line Producer, Dave Steck; Color; Not rated; 90 minutes; Release date: May 7, 1999. CAST: Eddie Estefan (Jimmy), Russell Stewart (Martin), Elizabeth Curtain (Susie), Marina Morgan (Jennifer), Andre Leigh (Barbara)

A STRANGER IN THE KINGDOM (Whiskeyjack/Kingdom Come) Producer/Director, Jay Craven; Executive Producer, Matt Salinger; Co-Producers, Penny Perry, Lyman Orton; Screenplay, Don Bredes, Jay Craven; Based on the novel by Howard Frank Mosher; Photography, Philip Holahan; Editor, Elizabeth Schwartz; Music, The Horse Flies; Designer/Costumes, Stephanie Kerley Schwartz; Casting, Penny Perry; a Whiskeyjack Pictures/Kingdom Come Pictures presentation in association with Northflow Partners II; Dolby; DuArt color; Not rated; 112 minutes; Release date: May 7, 1999. CAST: David Lansbury (Charlie Kinneson), Ernie Hudson (Rev. Walter Andrews), Martin Sheen (Sigurd Moulton), Bill Raymond (Resolved Kinneson), Sean Nelson (Nat Andrews), Jean Louisa Kelly (Athena Allen), Jordan Bayne (Claire LaRivierre), Henry Gibson (Zack Burrows), Rusty DeWees (Harlan Kittredge), Larry Pine (Edward Kinneson), Michael Ryan Segal (Frenchie LaMott), Tom Aldredge (Elijah Kinneson), Carrie Snodgress (Ruth Kinneson), George Dickerson (Mason White)

Rene L. Moreno, Joey Lawrence in *Tequila Bodyshots*
© Heartland Releasing

TEQUILA BODY SHOTS (Heartland Releasing) Producers, Tony Shyu, Jong Shyu; Director/Screenplay, Tony Shyu; Photography, Lawrence Schweich; Designer, Peter Kanter; Editor, Pamela Raymer; Music, Shayne Fair, Larry Herbstritt; Visual Effects Supervisor, Roger Nall; Casting, Pam Gilles; a Showtown Films Inc. and Himalaya Entertainment production; Dolby; CFI color; Rated R; 95 minutes; Release date: May 7, 1999. CAST: Joey Lawrence (Johnny Orpheus), Dru Mouser (Tamlyn), Nathan Anderson (Paul), Josh Marchette (Al), Robert Patrick Benedict (Ted), Jennifer Lyons (Angela), Senta Moses (Linda), Henry Darrow (Doc), Rene L. Moreno (Hector), Stephanie Arellano (Tina), Richard Stay (Larry)

REVELATION (Penland) Producers, Paul Lalonde, Peter Lalonde; Director, Andre Van Heerden; Screenplay, Paul Lalonde; Photography, George Tirl; Music, Gary Koftinoff; Color; Not rated; 90 minutes; Release date: May 7, 1999. CAST: Jeff Fahey (Thorold Stone), Nick Mancuso (Franco Macalousso), Carol Alt (Cindy Bolton), Tony Nappo (Willie Spino), Leigh Lewis (Helen Hannah), David Roddis (Len Parker), Marium Carvell (Selma Davis), Rick Demas (David Nidd), Patrick Gallagher (Jake Goss), Rothaford Gray (Ron Spalding), Bruce McFee (Agent Spencer),

Corry Carpf (Wendy Stone), Chloe Randle-Reis (Maggie Stone), Melville White (Victor Davis), Neville Edwards (Agent Walker), Frank Proctor (TV/Radio News Reporter), Howard Hoover (O.N.E. Agent), Desmond Campbell (O.N.E. VR Guard #1), Barbara Mamabolo (Davis Daughter), Darrell Hicks (Boy), Andrew Dolha (World Post Courier), James Brinkley (O.N.E. Front Desk Guard), Paulino Nunes (Young Agent), Stephen McWade (Bomb Squad Agent), Lauren Spring (Injured Girl), Peter Schindelhauer (Terrorist), Richard Carmichael (O.N.E. Jail Guard)

Deon Richmond, Guy Torry, Donald Adeosun Faison
in *Trippin'* ©Rogue Pictures

TRIPPIN' (Rogue Pictures) Producers, Marc Abraham, Caitlin Scanlon; Executive Producer, Thomas A. Bliss; Co-Producer, Diane Batson-Smith; Director, David Raynr; Screenplay, Gary Hardwick; Designer, Aaron Osborne; Photography, John Aronson; Costumes, Jennifer Bryan; Music, Michel Columbier; Editor, Earl Watson; a Beacon Pictures presentation; Dolby; Color; Rated R; 94 minutes; Release date: May 12, 1999. CAST: Deon Richmond (Gregory Reed), Donald Adeosun Faison (June), Maia Campbell (Cinny Hawkins), Guy Torry (Fish), Aloma Wright (Louise Reed), Harold Sylvester (Willie Reed), Cleavon McClendon (Jamal), Bill Henderson (Gramps), Michael Warren (Shapic), Countess Vaughn (Anetta), Stoney Jackson (Kenyatta)

Corey Page, Ione Skye in *Mascara* ©Anamorph Films

MOMENT OF IMPACT (Independent) Producer, Melanie Judd; Director/Photography, Julia Loktev; Black and white; Not rated; 115 minutes; Release date: May 13, 1999. Documentary on how Russian-born computer analyst Leonid Loktev has coped after suffering a traumatic brain injury after being hit by a car; featuring Larisa Loktev, Leonid Loktev, and Julia Loktev.

MASCARA (Phaedra) Producer, Crocker Coulson; Director/Screenplay, Linda Kandel; Photography, Francois Dagenais; Co-Producer, Josie Wechsler; Editor, Jane Pia Abramowitz; Music, Steven Medina Hufsteter; an Anamorph Films production; Color; Rated R; 94 minutes; Release date: May 14, 1999. CAST: Ione Skye (Rebecca), Lumi Cavazos (Laura), Amanda de Cadenet (Jennifer), Steve Jones (Nick), Steve Schub (Donnie), Tara Subkoff (Daphne), Corey Page (Andrew), Clifton Gonzalez Gonzalez (Kyle), Karen Black (Aunt Eloise), Ivonne Coll (Laura's Mother), Larry Moss (Laura's Father), Barry del Sherman (Ken), Karen Wright (Hippie Hostess), Daniel Rivas (Rico), Ken Davitian (Rebecca's Boss), Richard Morrison (Bank Officer), Anthony Powers (Glen), Maya McLaughlin (Tracy Guttman), Megan Odabash (Yoga Woman), Holli Coleman (Ellie), Gladys Jimenez (Angelica), Joe Baiza (Jazz Musician), Sal Jenco (Hugh), Doug Spinuzza (Repo Man), Amanda Anka (Waitress), Jonathan Luria (Acting Teacher), Rick Dubov (Doctor), Rustam Branaman (Curtis), Blake Lindsley (Singer), Patrick Firpo (Rebecca's Father), Joyce Driscoll (Midwife)

Gabriel Köerner, Denise Crosby, Wil Wheaton
in *Trekkies* ©Paramount Classics

TREKKIES (Paramount Classics) Producer, W.K. Border; Executive Producers, Michael Leahy, Joel Soisson; Co-Executive Producer, Denise Crosby; Director/Editor, Roger Nygard; Photography, Harris Done; Music, Walter Werzowa, Jimmie Wood, J.J. Holiday, Billy Sullivan; a Neo Art & Logic Production; Foto-Kem color; Rated PG; 86 minutes; Release date: May 21, 1999. Documentary exploring the continuing phenomenon of Star Trek; featuring Denise Crosby, Barbara Adams, The Denis Bourguignon Family, David & Laurel & "Tammi" Greenstein, Gabriel & Richard Köerner, Richard Kronfeld, Joyce Mason & Evelyn De Biase, Anne Murphy, Majel Barrett Roddenberry, James Doohan, Walter Koenig, DeForest Kelley, Nichelle Nichols, Leonard Nimoy, William Shatner, George Takei, Grace Lee Whitney, LeVar Burton, John de Lancie, Michael Dorn, Terry Farrell, Jonathan Frakes, Chase Masterson, Kate Mulgrew, Robert O'Reilly, Ethan Phillips, Brent Spiner, Wil Wheaton, Buzz Aldrin, Brannon Braga, Erik Larson, Richard Arnold, Maria De Maci, Daryl & "Bones" Frazetti, James T. Kirk, Dr. Marc Okrand, Brian W. Phelps, Glen Proechel, Pat Rimington, Jeri Taylor, Mark Thompson, J. Trusk, Douglas Marcks, Deborah L. Warner, Michael Westmore, Frank D'Amico, Rick Overton, Jon Ross, Fred Travalena, Matt Weinhold.

Yonas Zergaw, Haile Gebrselassie in *Endurance* ©LaJunta, LLC

ENDURANCE (Walt Disney Pictures) Producers, Edward R. Pressman, Terrence Malick, Max Palevsky; Director/Screenplay, Leslie Woodhead; Co-Producer, Sally Roy; Executive Producer, Wallace Wolf; Associate Producer, Erin O'Rourke; Co-Executive Producers, Thomas Sumners, Werner Koenig; Photography, Ivan Strasburg; Editors, Saar Klein, Oral Norrie Ottey; Music, John Powell; Competition Director, Bud Greenspan; a La Junta LLC production, in association with Film Four and Helkon Media Filmvertrieb; U.S.-British; Dolby; Super 35 Widescreen; Deluxe Color; Rated G; 83 minutes; Release date: May 14, 1999. CAST: Present Day Gebrselassie Family: Haile Gebrselassie (Himself), Gebrselassie Bekele (Haile's Father), Assefa Gebrselassie (Haile's Brother), Alem Tellahun (Haile's Wife), Tizazu Mashresha (Haile's Police Trainer); Young Gebrselassie Family: Yonas Zergaw (Haile), Shawanness Gebrselassie (Haile's Mother), Tedesse Haile (Haile's Father), Winishet Tesfaye (Shawanness), Abinet Tedesse (Assefa), Berhane Tesfaye (Ayralem), Bekele Negash (Tekeya), Berhane Taye (Zergaw), Endale Workineh (Adenew), Zinash Workineh (Ydarawerk), Mengistu Workineh (Belay), Bashamyelesh Workineh (Yeshye)

Justin Theroux, Lisa Marie in *Frogs for Snakes* © TSG

FROGS FOR SNAKES (**Artisan**) Producer, Phyllis Freed Kaufman; Executive Producers, Larry Meistrich, Daniel J. Victor; Director/Screenplay, Amos Poe; Photography, Enrique Chediak; Designer, Michael Shaw; Costumes, Candice Donnelly; Editor, Jeff Kushner; Music, Lazy Boy; Casting, Lina Todd; Presented by The Shooting Gallery, in association with Rain Films Inc.; Dolby; Color; Rated R; 92 minutes; Release date: May 21, 1999. CAST: Nick Chinlund (Iggy), Robbie Coltrane (Al), David Deblinger (U.B.), Anthony DeSando (Rilke), Harry Hamlin (Klench), Ian Hart (Quint), Barbara Hershey (Eva), John Leguizamo (Zip), Lisa Marie (Myrna), Debi Mazar (Simone), Ron Perlman (Gascone), Mike Starr (Crunch), Justin Theroux (Flav), Clarence Williams III (Huck)

AMERICAN HOLLOW (**HBO**) Producer/Director, Rory Kennedy; Executive Producer, Sheila Nevins; Photography, Nick Doob; Editor, Adam Zucker; Music, Bill Frisell; a Moxie Films production; Color; Not rated; 86 minutes; Release date: May 26, 1999. Documentary on the Bowling Family who dwell in the Appalachian Mountains in Eastern Kentucky.

KEEPERS OF THE FRAME (**Fox Lorber/Winstar**) Producer, Randy Gitsch; Executive Producer, Earl McLaughlin; Co-Producer/Director, Mark McLaughlin; Photograph, Rich Lerner, David Emrich; Editor, Roderick Kent; Music, Steve Cornell; a Mount Pilot Prods. film; Technicolor; Not rated; 70 minutes; Release date: May 28, 1999. Documentary on film preservation, featuring Alan Alda, Laurence Austin, Stan Brakhage, Jean Picker Firstenberg, Leonard Maltin, Roddy McDowall, Debbie Reynolds, Kenneth Weissman, George Willeman.

Vincent D'Onofrio, Craig Bierko in *The Thirteenth Floor*
© Columbia Pictures Industries

THE THIRTEENTH FLOOR (**Columbia**) Producers, Roland Emmerich, Ute Emmerich, Marco Weber; Executive Producers, Michael Ballhaus, Helga Ballhaus; Director, Josef Rusnak; Screenplay, Josef Rusnak, Ravel Centeno-Rodriguez; Based upon the book Simulacron 3 by Daniel Galouye; Photography, Wedigo von Schultzendorff; Designer, Kirk M. Petruccelli; Music, Harald Kloser; Editor, Henry Richardson; Costumes, Joseph Porro; Co-Producer, Kelly Van Horn; Visual Effects Supervisor, Joe Bauer; Digital Visual Effects, Centropolis Effects; Casting, April Webster; a Centropolis Entertainment production; U.S.-German; Dolby; Super 35 Widescreen; Deluxe color; Rated R; 108 minutes; Release date: May 28, 1999. CAST: Craig Bierko (Douglas Hall), Armin-Mueller Stahl (Hannon Fuller), Gretchen Mol (Jane Fuller), Vincent D'Onofrio (Whitney/Ashton), Dennis Haysbert (Det. Larry

McBain), Steven Schub (Zev Bernstein), Jeremy Roberts (Tom Jones), Rif Hutton (Joe), Leon Rippy (Jane's Lawyer), Janet MacLachlan (Ellen), Brad Henke (Cop #1), Burt Bulos (Bellhop), Venessia Valentino (Concierge), Howard S. Miller (Chauffeur), Tia Texada (Natasha's Roommate), Shiri Appleby (Bridget Manilla), Robert Clendenin (Bank Manager), Rachel Winfree (Bank Customer), Meghan Ivey (Chanteuse), Alison Lohman (Honey Bear Girl), Hadda Brooks (Lounge Piano Player), Ron Boussom (Maitre'D), Ernie Lively (30's Cop), Toni Sawyer (Grierson's Wife), Brooks Almy (Bridget's Mom), Darryl Henriques (Cab Driver), Suzanne Harrer (Tired Dancer), Lee Weaver (30's Limo Driver), Geoffrey Rivas (Security Guard), Travis Tedford (Newspaper Boy), Jeff Blumenkrantz (Choreographer), Andrew Alden (Doorman), Johnny Crawford (Singer)

THE DELICATE ART OF THE RIFLE (**CLC Films**) Producer, T. Todd Flinchum; Director, D.W. Harper; Screenplay, Stephen Grant; Photography, Martin Brown; Designer, Alicia Kratzer; Color; Not rated; 93 minutes; Release date: May 28, 1999. CAST: David Grant (Jay), Stephen Grant (Walt Whitman), Joy Gewalt (Rachel), John Kessel (Dr. Maxwell T. Boaz), Will Shufort (Jack), Suzanne Kratzer (Sally), Jody Donkle (Samantha), Gabrielle Greigo (Hamlet, Prince of Denmark), Shannon Gelobter (Laertes), Bruce Sterling (Non-Linear Weatherman), Ryan Wilcox (John), Jamey Maness (Bob, the Econ Guy), Andrew Taylor (Tom), Brandon Whitsell (Pete)

Rebecca Chaney, Slash in *The Underground Comedy Movie*
©Phaedra Cinema

THE UNDERGROUND COMEDY MOVIE (**Phaedra**) Producer, Jeffrey Jaeger; Director/Screenplay, Vince Offer; Photography, Michael Hofstein; Designer, Wayne Holmes; Editor, Luis Ruiz; Music, David Rotter, Danny Rotter; Associate Producer, Skyler Andrew; Dolby; Color; Not rated; 87 minutes; Release date: May 28, 1999. Gena Lee Nolin (Marilyn), Slash (Himself), Michael Clarke Duncan (Gay Virgin), Joey Buttafuoco (Sonny), Lightfield Lewis (Virgin Hunter/Juror), Karen Black (Mother), Rebecca Chaney (Supermodel/Pregnant Girl), Jerry Mongo Brownlee (Juror), Michael Parisi (Godmother/Psychologist), Gloria Sperling (Granny), Bobby Lee (Sushi Papa)

Suzy Nakamura, Takayo Fischer in *Strawberry Fields*
©Phaedra Cinema

STRAWBERRY FIELDS (**Phaedra Cinema**) Producers, Jason Kliot, Rea Tajiri; Executive Producers, Joana Vicente, Michael Wolkowitz; Director, Rea Tajiri; Screenplay, Kerri Sakamoto; Story, Kerri Sakamoto, Rea Tajiri; Photography, Zack Winestine; Editors, James Lyons, Steve Hamilton; Music, Sooyoung Park, Bundy K. Brown; Art Director, Suzi Whaley; Costumes, Nanette Acosta, Lin Sanders; from Open City Films; Color; Not rated; 87 minutes; Release date: June 4, 1999. CAST: Suzy Nakamura (Irene), James Sie (Luke), Reiko Mathieu (Aura), Chris Tashima (Mark), Marilyn Tokuda (Alice), Peter Yoshida (Bill), Heather Yoshimura (Terri), Takayo Fischer (Takayo), Roger Smart (Teacher), Jose Lozano, Nathan Toan, Sarah McCaffrey, Larry Leopoldo (Students), Elise Nishiyama (Young Alice), Ashley Oshita (Young Irene), Chiye Tomihiro (Issei Woman), Chiyoko Yoshida (Folksinger), Wing Leung (Mr. Hatsumoto), Lola Lai Jong (Mrs. Hatsumoto)

Wendy Makkena, John Benjamin Hickey in *Finding North*
©Cowboy Booking International

FINDING NORTH (**Cowboy Booking**) Producers, Stephen Dyer, Steven A. Jones; Executive Producers, Hal "Corky" Kessler; Director, Tanya Wexler; Screenplay, Kim Powers; Photography, Michael Barrett; Designer, James B. Smythe; Co-Producer, Mike Dempsey; Editor, Thom Zimny; Costumes, Katelyn Burton; Casting, Brett Goldstein; a Stephen Dyer and Steven A. Jones production, presented in association with SoNo Pictures; Color; Not rated; 95 minutes; Release date: June 4, 1999. CAST: Wendy Makkena (Rhonda Portelli), John Benjamin Hickey (Travis Furlong), Jonathan Walker (Voice of Bobby), Anne Bobby (Debi), Rebecca Creskoff (Gina), Angela Pietropinto (Mrs. Portelli), Freddie Roman (Mr. Portelli), Molly McClure (Aunt Bonnie), Jay Michaelson

(Bud), Yusef Bulos (Taxi Driver), Garrett Moran (Stripper), Steven Jones (Funeral Director), Lynn Metrik (Bank Manager), Phyllis Cicero (Janice), Spiro Malas (Waiter), Amy Zimmerman (Ticket Agent), Lisa Peterson (Car Rental Agent), Bo Barron (Counter Boy), Cherami Leigh Kuehn (Gretchen), Matt Whitton (Young Bobby), Jody Napolotano (Young Dan Franklin), Gail Cronauer (Mrs. Penn), Lou Ann Stephens (Ethel/Bethel), R. Bruce Elliot (TV Salesman), Kermit Key, Richard Rogers, Russ Marker (Geezers), T.J. Morehouse (Drug Store Clerk), Mary Sheldon (Ellen), Westin Self (Young Bobby), Norman Bennett (Farmer McDonald), Marisa Perez (Baby Sitter), Jesse Plemmons (Hobo), Sara Proctor (Princess), Harrison Lindley (Cowboy)

William Shatner, Rafer Weigel, Eric McCormack
in *Free Enterprise* ©Mindfire Entertainment

FREE ENTERPRISE (**Regent Enterprises**) Producers, Dan Bates, Mark Altman, Allan Kaufman; Director/Editor, Robert Meyer Burnett; Screenplay, Mark A. Altman, Robert Meyer Burnett; Executive Producers, Mark Gottwald, Ellie Gottwald; Photography, Charles L. Barbee; Designer, Cynthia Halligan; Costumes, Ann Lambert; Line Producer, Ron Singer; Geek Magazine Concepts & Graphic Designs, Sean Fanning; Music, Scott Spock; Casting, Linda Francis; a Mindfire Entertainment production; Color; Rated R; 108 minutes; Release date: June 4, 1999. CAST: Rafer Weigel (Robert), Eric McCormack (Mark), Audie England (Claire), Patrick Van Horn (Sean), Jonathan Slavin (Dan Vebber), Phil LaMarr (Eric Wallace), William Shatner (Bill), Deborah Van Valkenberg (Marlena), Marilyn Kentz (Gail), Holly Gagnier (Laura), Jennifer Sommerfield (Tricia), Lori Lively (Leila), Russell Young (Andrew), Ellie Cornell (Suzanne Crawford), Joey D. Vieira (Hal Pittman), Spencer Klein (Young Robert), Ethan Glazer (Young Mark), Carl Bressler (Mort Burg), Annika Brindley (Astrid), Mandy Ingber ("The Munchkin" Beth)

THE LAST CIGARETTE (**New Yorker**) Producers, Gerd Hacker, Steve Hendel, Kevin Rafferty; Directors, Kevin Rafferty, Frank Keraudren; Editor, Frank Keraudren; Color; Not rated; 82 minutes; Release date: June 9, 1999. Documentary looking at the history of cigarette smoking.

OUT OF SEASON (**Jour de Fete**) Producer/Executive Producer/Director, Jeanette L. Buck; Screenplay/Co-Producer, Kim McNabb; Photography, Ed Talavera; Editor, Sharon Teo; Designer, Nadine Shamounki; Casting, Dorothy Neumann, Elizabeth Boykewich; an I.M.J. production; Color; Not rated; 96 minutes; Release date: June 11, 1999. CAST: Carol Moda (Micki), Joy Kelly (Roberta), Dennis Fecteau (Charlie), Nancy Daly (Shelley), Rusty Clauss (Jane), Gregory A. Reid, Jr. (Dexter), Holly Twyford (Lynn), Laura Carson (Cynthia), Victoria Lind (Sarah), Willette Thompson (Barbara), Marty Lodge (Glen), Al Faris (Clerk)

Lauren Hutton, William Ragsdale in *Just a Little Harmless Sex*
©Phaedra Cinema

Girl), Gordon Young (A-Bill), Loc Do (A-Hong), Kiem Thai (Fraudulent Father), Vicki Chan (Fraudulent Mother), Jackie Hart-Blanton (Counselor), Joel Bofman (Drug Dealer), Darren Dang (Tony at 8), Ricky Dang (Tony at 13), Terry Heinrich (Tien at 9)

JUST A LITTLE HARMLESS SEX (Phaedra) formerly *Isn't It Romantic?*; Producers, Deborah Capogrosso, Rick Rosenthal; Director, Rick Rosenthal; Screenplay, Marti Noxon, Roger Miller; Photography, Bruce Surtees; Editor, James Austin Stewart; Music, Tito Larriva; Designer, Amy Danger; Casting, Rene Haynes, Cathy Henderson-Martin, Don Zuckerman; a Miss Q production; Dolby; Foto-Kem color; Rated R; 98 minutes; Release date: June 11, 1999. CAST: Alison Eastwood (Laura), Robert Mailhouse (Alan), Rachel Hunter (Marilyn), Kimberly Williams (Alison), Lauren Hutton (Elaine), Tito Larriva (Chuey), Jonathan Silverman (Danny), Jessica Lundy (Terrianne), Michael Ontkean (Jeff), William Ragsdale (Brent), Robin Blazak (Cyndi the Drive-By Hooker), Nuno Bettencourt (Vince the Pizza Guy), Tom Pettit (Married Guy), Daniel O'Connor (Yoga Boy Matt), Tom Rhodes (Yoga Boy Jeremy)

AN AMERICAN LOVE STORY (American Playhouse) Producer/Director/Photography, Jennifer Fox; Editor, Jay Freund; Co-Producers, Jennifer Fleming, Vickie Kenny; Music, Marcus Miller; Associate Producer, Penelope Falk; Produced in association with American Playhouse & the Independent Television Service; a Zohé Film production; Color; Not rated; 540 minutes; Release date: June 23, 1999. A nine hour documentary on a thirty-year interracial marriage, featuring Karen Wilson, Bill Sims, Cicily Wilson, Chaney Sims.

Christopher Dalton, Tuan Tran in *Bastards* ©Margin

Will Arnett, Missy Yager in *The Broken Giant* ©Blue Guitar Films

BASTARDS (Margin) Producers, Tuan Tran, Luc Do; Director/Screenplay/Casting, Loc Do; Photography, Brett Webster; Associate Producer/Editor, Eric Yalkut Chase; Music, Tony Blondal; Descendents of War Productions, 1997; Color; Not rated; 100 minutes; Release date: June 11, 1999. CAST: Tuan Tran (Tony), Christopher Lance (Tien), Christopher Dalton (Red Rice), Tom Lui (Dat), Hiep Thi Le (Tony's Mother), Steve Cardwell (Tony's Father), Jeanne Chinn (Tien's Girlfriend), Long Nguyen (Communist Commander), Kelli Ratliff (Patty), Johnny Ly (Stinky), Tim Hundley (Utky), Melissa Chan (Dat's Girlfriend), Annie Herndon (Home Invasion Woman), Chau Nguyen (Home Invasion

THE BROKEN GIANT (Blue Guitar Films) Producers, Jeffrey Clifford, Jonathan Cohen; Director/Screenplay, Estep Nagy; Photography, Garrett Fisher; Editor, David Leonard; Designer, Michael Krantz; Music, Will Oldham; Costumes, Stephanie Maslansky; Casting, Carder Stout; 1996; Color; Not rated; 83 minutes; Release date: June 24, 1999. CAST: John Glover (Bennett Hale), Brooke Smith (Rosemary Smith), George Dickerson (Thomas Smith, the Mayor), Missy Yager (Clio Hale), Will Arnett (Ezra Caton), Chris Noth (Jack Frey), Joe Coleman (Sam Woodbridge)

Barbara Sonneborn in *Regret to Inform* ©Artistic License

REGRET TO INFORM (Artistic License) Producers, Barbara Sonneborn, Janet Cole; Director/Screenplay, Barbara Sonneborn; Executive Producer, Janet Cole; Editor, Lucy Massie Phenix; Music, Todd Boekelheide; Co-Producer, Ron Greenberg; Line Producer, Kathy Brew; Color; Not rated; 72 minutes; Release date: June 25, 1999. Filmmaker Barbara Sonneborn's account of her journey to Vietnam after finding out that her husband Jeff had been killed in action; featuring Barbara Sonneborn, April Burns, Lula Bia, Norma Banks, Phan Ngoc Dung, Diane C. Van Renselaar, Grace Castillo, Nguyen My Hien, Xuan Ngoc Evans, Charlotte Begay, Tran Nghia, Troung Thi Huoc, Phan Thi Thuan, Troung Thi Le, Le Thi Ngot, Nguyen Thi Hong.

AND BABY MAKES TWO (First Run Features) Producers/Directors, Judy Katz, Oren Rudavsky; Photography, Oren Rudavsky; Editor, Kate Taverna; Music, Joel Goodman; Color; Not rated; 60 minutes; Release date: June 25, 1999. Documentary on single motherhood.

Frannie, Zachary Browne in *Shiloh* 2: Shiloh Season
©Good DogII, LLC

SHILOH 2: SHILOH SEASON (Legacy) Producers, Carl Borack, Dale Rosenbloom; Director, Sandy Tung; Screenplay, Dale Rosenbloom; Based on the novel *Shiloh Season* by Phyllis Reynolds Naylor; Supervising Producers, Mark Yellen, Zane W. Levitt; Executive Producer, Seth Willenson; Photography, Troy Smith; Editor, Tom Seid; Music, Joel

Goldsmith; Designer, Joseph B. Tintfass; Costumes, Rikke Rosbaek; Casting, Laura Schiff; a Dale Rosenbloom/Carl Borack production in association with Utopia Pictures; Color; Rated PG; 96 minutes; Release date: June 25, 1999. CAST: Zachary Browne (Marty Preston), Scott Wilson (Judd Travers), Michael Moriarty (Ray Preston), Ann Dowd (Louise Preston), Caitlin Wachs (Dara Lynn Preston), Rachel David (Becky Preston), Rod Steiger (Doc Wallace), Marissa Leigh (Samantha), Joe Pichler (David Howard), Colin MacDonald (Michael), Dawn McMillan (Miss Talbot), John Short (Mr. Howard), Bonnie Bartlett (Mrs. Wallace), Kathleen Rose (Receptionist), Winfree (Sue Rachel), Elizabeth Karr (Jane), Shannon Marie Kies (Laurie), Eddie Mathers, Mark Vasconcellos (Rescuers), Frannie (Shiloh)

Paul Pena, Kongar-ol Ondar in *Genghis Blues* ©Roxie Releasing

GENGHIS BLUES (Roxie) Producers/Photography, Roko Belic, Adrian Belic; Director/Screenplay/Editor, Roko Belic; Original Concept/Associate Producer, Ralph Leighton; a Wadi Rum production; Color; Not rated; 88 minutes; Release date: July 1, 1999. Documentary about blind blues musician Paul Pena's journey to the republic of Tuva, where he competed in a throat-singing contest; featuring Paul "Earthquake" Pena, Kungar-ol Ondar, Richard Feynman, Ralph Leighton, B.B. King, Mario Casetta, Lemon DeGeorge, Tony DeCicco, Stephen Kent.

Don Handfield, Daniel Chilson in *Defying Gravity* ©Jour de Fete

DEFYING GRAVITY (Jour de Fete) Producers, David Clayton Miller, Jack Kroll; Director/Screenplay, John Keitel; Photography, Tom Harting; Editor, Matthew Yagle; Music, Jon T. Howard; Designer, Scott McPhail;

Costumes, Billy R. Miller; Casting, Patrick Baca; a Boom Pictures production; 1997; Dolby; Foto-Kem color; Not rated; 90 minutes; Release date: July 9, 1999. CAST: Daniel Chilson (John "Griff" Griffith), Niklaus Lange (Todd Bentley), Don Handfield (Pete Bradley), Linna Carter (Denetra Washington), Seabass Diamond (Matthew "Doogie" McDougal), Lesley Tesh (Heather), Ryan Tucker (Gary Buchanan), Nicki Lynn (Gretchen), Laura Fox (Mrs. Bradley), Kevin P. Wright (Mr. Bradley), Matt Steveley (Stewart "Stewy" Hanson), David Tuchman (Logan Franklin), Nick Fortunato Spano (Bozzy), Jess Martell (Scotty), Katrina Holden Bronson (Rachel), Jeffrey Hiner (Will), Michael Angelo (Sam), Marie Charles (Regina), Tammy Lynch (Tina), Erika Cohen (Det. Horne), Bob Peterson (Professor), Nita Genoveva (Doctor), Allyson Golob (Receptionist), Brendan Fleming (Murph), Brian Farber (Trip), Alan Olifson (Scooter), Casey F. O'Neill (Patrick), Peter Sanders (Tony), John Deleski (Travis), Hugh Warren (Jonesy), Eric Scott (Steinman), Chris Lehmann (Cooper), Larry Sullivan, Jr. (Oter), Mark Jodoin (Pauly), Bradley David (Garfield), Dan Butcher (Shep), Greg Money, Danny Roth (Pledges), Chuck Snay (Garrett), Erik Jirak (Wayne), Cameron Trousdale (Young Boy), Steven Burrill (Smitty), Brian Harris Krinsky (Edison), Renee Eloise (Loretta), Scott Roth (Field Reporter)

Vincent D'Onofrio, Thomas Jane in *The Velocity of Gary* ©Cineville

Julie Ariola, Rosanna Arquette in *I'm Losing You* ©Strand Releasing

THE VELOCITY OF GARY *(NOT HIS REAL NAME) (Cineville/Next Millennium) Producer, Dan Lupovitz; Executive Producers, Carl-Jan Colpaert, Kathryn Arnold, Ellen Wonder, Joe Simon, Vincent D'Onofrio, Dan Ireland; Director, Dan Ireland; Screenplay, James Still, based on his play; Photography, Claudio Rocha; Designer, Amy Ancona; Costumes, Tim Chappel; Editor, Louis Colina; Casting, Laurel Smith; a Dan Lupovitz/Joe Simon production in association with Ventanarosa Prods.; Dolby; Clairmont-Scope; Color; Rated R; 98 minutes; Release date: July 16, 1999. CAST: Vincent D'Onofrio (Valentino), Salma Hayek (Mary Carmen), Thomas Jane (Gary), Olivia d'Abo (Veronica), Chad Lindberg (Kid Joey), Lucky Luciano (The King), Shawn Michael Howard (Coco), Khalil Kain (Venus), Elizabeth D'Onofrio (Dorothy), Ethan Hawke (Nat), Jason Cutler (Romaine), Marion Eaton (Miss Sweetheart), Gloria Irizarry (Mrs. Sanchez), Rudy Rufus Isaacs (Sleeping Beauty), Cordelia Richards (Jana Roberts), Arielle Santos (Hope), Kimberly Scott (Nurse Adams), Jacob Sidney (Sean), Alex Sol (D.F.), Linda Wahl (Edna the Volunteer), Miss Monroe (Herself), Danny Aroyo, Ceaser Herrera (Thugs on Street), Bingo (Rodney), Hakan D'Onofrio (Running Boy), Keegan DeLancie (Choir Boy), Ravell Dameron (Receptionist in Clinic), Yvette Diaz (Young Mary Carmen), Phillip Esposito, Giovani Lampassi (Phone Sex Guys), Luchisha Evans (Waitress), Dan Lupovitz (Street Cruiser), Michael Mantell (Angry Customer), Stephen C. Marshal (Angry Boss), Hugh Palmer (Paramedic), John Panico (Saxophone Player), Sam Saletta (Boy #2, Tommy), Rachel Stires (Woman on Subway Bench)

I'M LOSING YOU (Lions Gate) Producers, Christine Vachon, Pamela Koffler; Executive Producers, David Cronenberg, Michael Paseornek, Jeff Sackman, John Dunning, Andre Link; Director/Screenplay, Bruce Wagner; Based on his novel; Photography, Rob Sweeney; Designer, Richard Sherman; Costumes, Theodora Van Runkle; Music, Daniel Catan; Editor, Janice Hampton; Line Producer, Dara Weintraub; a Killer Films production; Color; Not rated; 102 minutes; Release date: July 16, 1999. CAST: Andrew McCarthy (Bertie Krohn), Rosanna Arquette (Rachel Krohn), Frank Langella (Perry Needham Krohn), Salome Jens (Diantha Krohn), Buck Henry (Philip Dragom), Elizabeth Perkins (Aubrey), Gina Gershon (Lidia), Amanda Donohoe (Mona Deware), Laraine Newman (Casting Person), Aria Noelle Curzon (Tiffany), Julie Ariola (Melanctha), Norman Reedus (Toby), Ed Begley, Jr. (Zev), Don McManus (Jake Horowitz), Rick Zieff (The Dentist), J.B. Gaynor (Zephyr), Daniel von Bargen (Dr. Litvak), Phyllis Lyons (Dentist's Wife), Gary Watkins (Ted Kressler), Alexandria Sage (Perry's Assistant), Fred Sanders (Sam Melvin), August Amarino (Jean-Christophe), Lisa Edelstein (Diantha's Patient), Byron Jennings (Reginald), Adria Tennor (Assist. Director), Meher Tatna (Dr. Agarwal), Patrick Briston (Rico), Kevin Brophy (Conductor)

Ellen Barkin, Allison Janney, Kirsten Dunst in *Drop Dead Gorgeous* ©New Line Cinema

DROP DEAD GORGEOUS (**New Line Cinema**) Producers, Gavin Palone, Judy Hofflund; Executive Producers, Claire Rudnick Polstein, Donna Langley, Lona Williams; Director, Michael Patrick Jann; Screenplay, Lona Williams; Photography, Michael Spiller; Designer, Ruth Ammon; Editors, David Codron, Janice Hampton; Music, Mark Mothersbaugh; Costumes, Mimi Melgaard; Casting, John Papsidera; Presented in association with Capella/KC Medien; Dolby; Deluxe color; Rated PG-13; 99 minutes; Release date: July 23, 1999. CAST: Kirsten Dunst (Amber Atkins), Ellen Barkin (Annette Atkins), Allison Janney (Loretta), Denise Richards (Becky Leeman), Kirstie Alley (Gladys Leeman), Sam McMurray (Lester Leeman), Mindy Sterling (Iris Clark), Brittany Murphy (Lisa Swenson), Amy Adams (Leslie Miller), Laurie Sinclair (Michelle Johnson), Shannon Nelson (Tess Weinhaus), Tara Redepenning (Molly Howard), Sarah Stewart (Jenelle Betz), Alexandra Holden (Mary Johanson), Brooke Bushman (Tammy Curry), Matt Malloy (John Dough), Michael McShane (Harold Vilmes), Will Sasso (Hank Vilmes), Lona Williams (Jean Kangas), Jon T. Olson (Pat), Casey Tyler Garven (Brett), Ashley Dylan Bullard (Fry Girl), Jacy Dumermuth (Pregnant Fry Girl), Nora Dunn (Colleen), Mo Gaffney (Terry), Adam West (Himself), Mary Gillis (Chloris Klinghagen), Richard Narita (Mr. Howard), Patti Yasutake (Mrs. Howard), Seiko Matsuda (Tina/Seiko Howard), Allyson Kearns (Candy Striper), Tom Gilshannon (Lars Larson), Claudia Wilkens (Iona Hildebrandt), Dale Dunham (Mayor), Amanda Detmer (Miss Minneapolis), Thomas Lennon (Voice of Documentarian), Eric D. Howell (Sound Recordist), Matthew G. Park (Crew Guy), Terry Hempleman, Christopher Carlson (Cops), James Cada (Lisa Swenson's Father), Kristin Rudrüd (Pork Products Lady), Luke Ingles, Nick Ingles (Rocker Kids), Jimmie D. Wright (Doctor), Peter Aitchison (News Anchor), Mary Rehbein, Jeany Park (Reporters), Richard Ooms (Pastor), Robert-Bruce Brake (Mr. Melchoir), Bruce Linser (Ed), Tiffany Engen (Tap Dancer), Jennifer Baldwin Peden (Opera Singer), Annalise Nelson (Violinist), Samantha Harris (Miss Burnsville), Kari Ann Shiff (Miss Delluth), Mark Dahlen (Cops Crew Guy), Jeff Tatum (Fireman)

Sharon Houston, Adolph Dupree Brown, Adam Walden, Dante Salerno, Josh Kasselman, Richie Cohen, Rachelle Anthes, Marshall Dostal, Mark Flythe, Heather Bucha, Erica Bamforth, Stephanie Goldman, Steve O'Brien, M. Zickel, Fitz, Wendy Shanker, Heather Culton, Elizabeth Brady, Felicia Caplan, Jeff Catanese, Ethan Sandler, Derrick Manigo, Kathryn Hahn, Sherry Davey, Stephanie Kurtzuba, Candace Juman, Erin Cohen, Jeff Bond, Zach Galifianakis, Ben Davis, Lucia Marano, Jon Zack, Glen Cruz, Florence Mercier, Claudine Ohayon, Francesca Ferrara, Cooper Lawrence, Rebecca Roberts, Randy Eisenberg, Chris Spain, David Potischmann, Josh Berg, Risa Miller, Gabriel Harris, Randy Sklar, Jason Sklar, Emmy Laybourne, Erin Fotos, Lindsey Roberts, Rohana Kenin, Matt Price, Jason Nash, Diane Mercier, Scott Landsman, George Diehl, Megan Johnson, Ameenah Kaplan, Holly Rose, Marta Ravin, Nikki Arlyn, Rachel Arieff, Robyn Parsons, Josh Weinstein, Pete Labow, Gunslinger Tomas, Ilana Marcus, O. Susannah, Misty Greer, Robin Calloway, Mike Blieden, Matt Boline, Jay DiPietro, Mary Jo Winiarski, Amanda Bryan, Romel Henry, Yael Schuster, Saudia Young, Tom Cohen, Zack Eisenberg

James De Bello, Edward Furlong, Sam Huntington, Giuseppe Andrews in *Detroit Rock City* ©New Line Productions, Inc.

Jennifer Mayo, Dorothy Holland in *Summerspell* ©Margin

SUMMERSPELL (**Margin**) Producers, Lina Shanklin, Joanne D'Antonio; Director/Screenplay, Lina Shanklin; Photography, Robert Elswit; Editor, Gloria Whittemore; Music, Toni Marcus; a Films That Make a Difference production; Color; Not rated; 92 minutes; July release. CAST: Dorothy Holland (Bernice Wisdom), Jennifer Mayo (Eleanor Wisdom), Frank Whiteman (Lowell Wisdom), Michael Holmes (Uncle Ezra), Joan Crosby (Aunt Maggie), Kay Freeman (Aunt Lillian), Gay Hagen (Aunt Edna Mae), Ed Wright (Grandfather Wisdom), Coleman Creel (Cecil), Bert Tanswell (Rich)

FLUSHED (**First Run Features**) Producers, Carrie Ansell, Marshall Dostal, Ken Greenblatt; Director/Screenplay/Editor, Carrie Ansell; Photography, Scott Duncan Pauly; Designer, Shanya Tsao; 1998; Color; Not rated; 81 minutes; Release date: August 13, 1999. CAST: Miram Shor,

DETROIT ROCK CITY (**New Line Cinema**) Producers, Gene Simmons, Barry Levine, Kathleen Haase; Executive Producers, Michael De Luca, Brian Witten; Director, Adam Rifkin; Screenplay, Carl V. Dupré; Co-Producer, Art Schaefer; Photography, John R. Leonetti; Designer, Steve Hardie; Editors, Mark Goldblatt, Peter Schink; Music, J. Peter Robinson; Costumes, Rosanna Norton; Casting, Valerie McCaffrey; a Takoma Entertainment/Base-12 Productions/Kissnation production; Dolby; Super 35 Widescreen; Deluxe color; Rated R; 95 minutes; Release date: August 13, 1999. CAST: Edward Furlong (Hawk), Giuseppe Andrews (Lex), James De Bello (Trip), Sam Huntington (Jam), Lin Shaye (Mrs. Bruce), Melanie Lynskey (Beth), Natasha Lyonne (Christine), Miles Dougal (Elvis), Nick Scotti (Kenny), Emmanuelle Chriqui (Barbara), David Quane (Bobby), Rodger Barton (Mr. Bumsteen), Kathryn Haggis (Mrs. Bumsteen), David Gardner (Priest), Shannon Tweed (Amanda Finch), Kristin Booth (Cashier), Joe Flaherty (Father McNulty), Cody Jones (Little Kid), Matt Taylor (Chongo), Joan Heney (Study Hall Teacher), Rob Smith (Simple Simon), Aaron Berg (Bartender), Paul Brogren (Roadie #1), Allan Clow (Man with Coat), Chris Benson (Mr. Johansen), Colleen Williams (Nun), Richard Hillman (Scalper), Stephen Joffe, Ryan Letriard (Six Year Olds), Joseph Haase (Security Guard), Ron Jeremy Hyatt (MC), Kevin Corrigan, Steven Schirripa (Beefy Jerks), Lindy Booth (Girl #1), Christina Sicoli (Foxy Girl), Michael Barry (Nerd), Vic Rigler (Pizza Boy), Eileen Flood (Parishoner), Pamela Bowen (Matmok Lieutenant), Johnie Chase (Cop #1), Julian Richings (Ticket Taker), Gene Simmons, Paul Stanley, Ace Frehley, Peter Criss (KISS), Shane Daly, Noah Danby (Chong's Friends), Christopher Lee Clements, Jonathan Cuthill, Neno Vojic, Rich Coulson, Michael Kremko, Derek De Luis (Strippers), Tara Elliot, Elissa Bradley, Cherry Flatley, Leilene Onrade, Hazel K. Anderson, Jessica Kleiner, Nadia Dalchand, Kerri Michalica, Kerry Robinson (Babes), Dino M. Sicoli (Really Lucky Hot Tub Dude)

Harry Keitt and George Walton in *On the Ropes* ©Fox Lorber

ON THE ROPES (**Winstar Cinema**) Producers/Directors, Nanette Burstein, Brett Morgen; Executive Producers, Jennifer Fox, Jonathan Cohen; Photography, Brett Morgen; Editors, Nancy Baker, Nanette Burstein; Music, Theodore Shapiro; a Highway Films and The Learning Channel presentation; Dolby; Color; Not rated; 94 minutes; Release date: August 18, 1999. Documentary about the Bed-Stuy Boxing Center training boxers for the Golden Gloves Tournament, featuring Harry Keitt, Tyrene Manson, George Walton, Noel Santiago, Mickey Marcello, Randy Little, Ebony Pile, Equana Pile, Martin Goldman, Pastor James Pullings Jr., Eddie Mustafa Muhammed, Aida Santiago, Judge Finnegan.

Kiana Tom, Jean-Claude Van Damme in *Universal Soldier: The Return* ©TriStar Pictures Inc.

UNIVERSAL SOLDIER: THE RETURN (**TriStar**) Producers, Craig Baumgarten, Allen Shapiro, Jean-Claude Van Damme; Director, Mic Rodgers; Screenplay, William Malone, John Fasano; Based on characters created by Richard Rothstein, Christopher Leitch, Dean Devlin; Executive Producer, Michael Rachmil, Daniel Melnick; Photography, Michael A. Benson; Designer, David Chapman; Editor, Peck Prior; Music, Don Davis; Costumes, Jennifer L. Bryan; Casting, Rachel Abroms, Jory Weitz; a Baumgarten Prophet Entertainment/Indie Prod Company/Long Road production; Dolby; Deluxe color; Rated R; 82 minutes; Release date: August 20, 1999. CAST: Jean-Claude Van Damme (Luc), Michael Jai White (Seth), Heidi Schanz (Erin), Xander Berkeley (Dylan Cotner), Justin Lazard (Capt. Blackburn), Kiana Tom (Maggie), Daniel Von Bargen (Gen. Radford), James Black (Sgt. Morrow), Karis Paige Bryant (Hillary), Bill Goldberg (Romeo), Brent Anderson (2nd Technician), Brent Hinkley

(Squid), Woody Watson (RL Gate Guard), Jacqueline Klein (Betty Wilson), Maria Artita (Kitty Anderson), Sam Williamson (Hillary's Doctor), Dion Culberson (Drag Queen), Pam Dougherty (60 Year Old Woman), Heidi Franz (Erin's Stripper), Barbara Petricini Buxton (News Anchor), Molly Moroney (Pediatric Nurse), Josh Berry (Radio Man), Mic Rodgers (Big Biker), Mark Dalton (Lead RL Guard)

Katie Holmes, Marisa Coughlan, Barry Watson, Helen Mirren in *Teaching Mrs. Tingle* ©Dimension Films

TEACHING MRS. TINGLE (**Dimension**) formerly *Killing Mrs. Tingle*; Producer, Cathy Konrad; Executive Producers, Bob Weinstein, Harvey Weinstein, Cary Granat, Ted Field, Scott Kroopf, Erica Huggins; Director/Screenplay, Kevin Williamson; Photography, Jerzy Zielinski; Designer, Naomi Shohan; Costumes, Susie DeSanto; Music, John Frizzell; Casting, Lisa Beach; a Konrad Pictures/Interscope Communications production; Distributed by Miramax Films; Dolby; Panavision; Deluxe color; Rated PG-13; 96 minutes; Release date: August 20, 1999. CAST: Helen Mirren (Mrs. Tingle), Katie Holmes (Leigh Ann Watson), Jeffrey Tambor (Coach Wenchell), Barry Watson (Luke Churner), Marisa Coughlan (Jo Lynn Jordan), Liz Stauber (Trudie Tucker), Michael McKean (Principal Potter), Molly Ringwald (Miss Banks), Vivica A. Fox (Miss Gold), John Patrick White (Brian Berry), Robert Gant (Professor), Lesley Ann Warren (Leigh Ann's Mother)

A TIME TO DANCE: THE LIFE AND WORK OF NORMA CANNER (**Anthology/Independent**) Directors, Ian Brownell, Webb Wilcoxen; Narrator, Ruby Dee; No other credits available; Color; Not rated; 70 minutes; Release date: August 20, 1999. Documentary on dance therapist Norma Canner, who used movement to help disabled children.

WITH FRIENDS LIKE THESE ... (**Fine Line**) formerly *Mom's on the Roof*; Producers, Robert Greenhut, Amy Lemisch, Penny Marshall; Executive Producers, Jon Ein, Marty Feinberg, E.K. Gaylord II; Director/Screenplay, Philip Frank Messina; Photography, Brian J. Reynolds; Designer, Beth DeSort; Editor, Claudia Finkle; Music, John Powell; Casting, Rachel Abroms; Dolby; Color; Rated R; 105 minutes; Release date: Aug. 20, 1999. CAST: Adam Arkin (Steve Hersh), Robert Costanzo (Johnny DiMartino), Beverly D'Angelo (Theresa Carpenter), Elle Macpherson (Samantha Mastandrea), Amy Madigan (Hannah DiMartino), Laura San Giacomo (Joanne Hersh), David Strathairn (Armand Minetti), Jon Tenney (Dorian Mastandrea), Lauren Tom (Yolanda Chin), Carmine Costanzo (Nino DiMartino), Tom La Grua (Head Mob Guy), Garry Marshall (Frank Minetti), Michael McKean (Dr. Maxwell Hersh), Ashley Peldon (Marissa DiMartino), Jon Polito (Rudy Ptak), Armando Pucci (Dr. Puccini), Andrew Shaifer (Trent Rabinowitz), Heather Stephens (Babette), Bill Murray (Maurice Melnick), Martin Scorsese (Scorsese)

Candis Cayne in *Mob Queen* ©First Run Features

MOB QUEEN (First Run Features) Producer/Director, Jon Carnoy; Screenplay, Mike Horelick; Executive Producer, Marcin Czarnozyl; Photography, Nils Kenaston; Line Producer, Lisa Kolasa; Designers, Petra Barchi, Charlotte Bourke; Editor, Anton Salaks; Music, Jonathan Cossu; Costumes, Juliet Ouyoung; Casting, Eve Battaglia, Denise Fitzgerald; an Etoile Prods. presentation; Color; Not rated; 87 minutes; Release date: August 20, 1999. CAST: David Proval (George), Candis Cayne (Glorice), Tony Sirico (Joey "The Heart" Aorta), Dan Moran (Dip), Marlene Forte (Chica), Jerry Grayson (The Hitman), Gerry Cooney (Mickey the Baker), Bruno Iannone (Ruffo), Frank Adonis (Maderiaga), Nick Raio (Rivello), Frank Lombardi (Glasso), Marcus Powell (Gregory Kirk), William Russell (Swede), Will Hare (Father Doyle), Lee Wong (Chinese Cook), Lenny Steinline (Draft Detective), Ken Prymus (Friendly Sam), George Pollock (The Doctor), Lisa Thayer (Maria the Waitress), Mickey Smith (Messenger Boy)

Charlize Theron, Johnny Depp in *The Astronaut's Wife*
©New Line Cinema, Inc.

THE ASTRONAUT'S WIFE (New Line Cinema) Producer, Andrew Lazar; Executive Producers, Mark Johnson, Brian Witten, Donna Langley; Director/Screenplay, Rand Ravich; Photography, Allen Daviau; Designer, Jan Roelfs; Editors, Steve Mirkovich, Tim Alverson; Co-Producer, Diana Pokorny; Music, George S. Clinton; Costumes, Isis Mussenden; Casting, Rick Pagano, Debi Manwiller; a Mad Chance production; Dolby; Fotokem color; Rated R; 109 minutes; Release date: August 27, 1999. CAST: Johnny Depp (Spencer Armacost), Charlize Theron (Jillian Armacost), Joe Morton (Sherman Reese), Clea DuVall (Nan), Donna Murphy (Natalie Streck), Nick Cassavetes (Alex Streck), Samantha Eggar (Doctor), Gary

Grubbs (NASA Director), Blair Brown (Shelly McLaren), Tom Noonan (Jackson McLaren), Tom O'Brien (Allen Dodge), Lucy Lin (Shelly Carter), Michael Crider (Pat Elliot), Jacob Stein (Calvin), Timothy Wicker (Wide Eyed Kid #1), Brian Johnson (Excited Fourth Grader), Sarah Dampf (Paula), Charles Lanyer (Spencer's Doctor), Carlos Cervantes (Doctor), Conrad Bachman (Reporter), Rondi Reed (Dr. Conlin), Seth Barrish (Yuppie Shark), Ellen Lancaster (Dried Up Socialite), Julian Barnes (Waiter), Priscilla Shanks, Jennifer Burry, Susan Cella, Linda Powell (Women), Lyndsey Danielle Bonomolo (Screaming Girl), Elston Ridgle (Security Guard), Robert Sella (Maitre D'), Samantha Carpel (Reporter—Video), Lahai Fahnbulleh (Taxi Driver), Stephen Berger (Doorman), Michael Luceri (Doorman), Michael Luceri (Waiter at Party), Ben Van Bergen (Storage Facility Client), Edward Kerr (Pilot), Cole Mitchell Sprouse, Dylan Thomas Sprouse (Twins)

Jesse James, Jon Voight, Patrasche
in *A Dog of Flanders* ©Woods-Flanders California, Inc.

A DOG OF FLANDERS (Warner Bros.) Producer, Frank Yablans; Executive Producers, Martin J. Barab, Steven Paul, Mark Damon, Larry Mortorff; Director, Kevin Brodie; Screenplay, Kevin Brodie, Robert Singer; Based on the novel by Ouida (Marie Louise de la Ramée); Photography, Walther Vanden Ende; Designers, Hubert Pouille, Attila F. Kovacs; Editor, Annamaria Szanto; Music, Richard Friedman; Costumes, Beatrix Aruna Pasztor; a Woodbridge Films presentation; Dolby; Color; Rated PG; 100 minutes; Release date: August 27, 1999. CAST: Jack Warden (Jehan Daas), Jeremy James Kissner (Older Nello), Jesse James (Young Nello), Jon Voight (Michel La Grande), Cheryl Ladd (Anna Cogez), Bruce McGill (William, the Blacksmith), Steven Hartley (Carl Cogez), Andrew Bicknell (Stephens), Farren Monet (Aloise), Antje De Boeck (Millie), Madyline Sweeten (Young Aloise), Deborah Pollit (Mary Daas), James Garde (Steerns), Dirk Lavrysen (Peter Paul Rubens), Michael Vanderlinden (Peddler), Pierre Gerranio (Cathedral Priest), Jodie Scott (Fortune Teller), Jenny Tanghe (Gertrude), Fred Van Kuijk (Mayor), Jan Schulter-Stahlberg (Bernard), Frederick Oxby (Young Robert), Julien Bosman (Teenage Robert), Leo Burton Davies (Altar Boy), Bouli (Constable), Anne Grandhenry (Stephen's Wife), Jaak Van Assche (Heckler), Katarina Vercammen (Teacher), Gaston Bertin (Lovain Priest), Ariana Porcu (Baby Nello), Johan Reyman (Oil Miller)

CHILL FACTOR (Warner Bros.) Producer, James G. Robinson; Executive Producers, Jonathan A. Zimbert, Bill Bannerman; Director, Hugh Johnson; Screenplay, Drew Gitlin, Mike Cheda; Photography, David Gribble; Designer, Jeremy Conway; Editor, Pamela Power; Music, Hans Zimmer, John Powell; Costumes, Deborah Everton; Co-Producer, Jeff Neuman, Martin Wiley; Casting, Pam Dixon Mickelson; a James G. Robinson presentation of a Morgan Creek production; Dolby; Panavision; Technicolor; Rated R; 102 minutes; Release date: September 1, 1999. CAST: Cuba Gooding, Jr. (Arlo), Skeet Ulrich (Tim Mason), Peter Firth (Capt. Andrew Brynner), David Paymer (Dr. Richard Long), Hudson Leick (Vaughn), Daniel Hugh Kelly (Col. Leo Vitelli), Kevin J. O'Connor (Telstar), Judson Mills (Dennis), Jordan Mott (Carl), Dwayne Macopson

Cuba Gooding, Jr., Skeet Ulrich in *Chill Factor* ©Creek Productions, Inc.

(Burke), Jim Grimshaw (Deputy Pappas), Richard Todd Aguayo (Gomez), K. Addison Young (Ranger at Dam), James Van Harper (Ranger in Chopper), Tommy Smeltzer (Deputy Art Lewis), Geoff Palmer (Vitelli's Helicopter Pilot), Rhoda Griffis (Pregnant Woman), Johnny Cenicola (Little Boy), Larry Black (Fat Man in Tunnel), David Sharp Fralick (Blond Biker), Garrett Warren (Bearded Biker), Ron Clinton Smith (Hemmings), Stephen Robert (Vitelli's Lt.), Quint Von Canon, Bart Hansard (Crew Members), Howard Carroll (Volvo Driver), Lonnie Smith (Pumper), Johnell Gainy (Ranger Sgt. at Tech Site), Martin Valinsky (Big Ranger at Tech Site), Terry Loughlin (Courtroom General), Bob Penny (Motel Manager), Richie Dye (Ice Cream Andy), Mike Davis (Technician), Afemo Omilami (Courtroom Colonel), Steve Coulter (Sweeney), Phillip Devona (Young Guard), Suzi Bass (Darlene), Gordon A. Johnson (Hardware Store Owner), Tim Dabbs (Gomez's Pilot), Camden Dixon (Mailman), Peter MacKenzie (Technician), Wanda Acunda, Erin Daniels, Jason Cairns (Medics).

STATES OF CONTROL (**Phaedra**) Producers, Zack Winestine, Priscilla Guastavino, Joanne Pawlowski, Matt Janes; Director/Screenplay, Zack Winestine; Photography, Susan Starr; Editor, Jim Villone; Music, Richard Termini; Designer, Mario R. Ventenilla; Casting, Matthew Messinger; an Impulse Films Ltd. production; Ultra-Stereo; Color; Not rated; 84 minutes; Release date: Sept. 3, 1999. CAST: Jennifer van Dyck (Lisa), John Cunningham (Paul), Ellen Greene (Carol), Stephen Bogardus (Abel), Jennie Moreau (Suzanne), Stephen Gevedon (Alex), Nancy Giles (Volker), Matthew Sussman (Stage Manager), Jason Culp (Porn Store Customer)

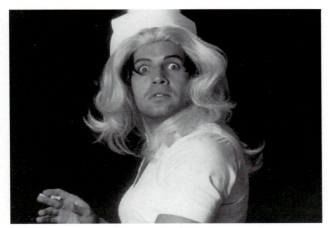

Billy Zane in *I Woke Up Early the Day I Died*
© Cinequanon Pictures International, Inc.

I WOKE UP EARLY THE DAY I DIED (Cinequanon Pictures Intl.) Producers, Chris Hanley, Billy Zane; Executive Producers, Jordan Gertner, Bradford L. Schlei; Director, Artis Iliopulos; Screenplay, Edward D. Wood Jr.; Photography, Michael F. Barrow; Editor, Dody Dorn; Music, Larry Groupe; Designer, Maia Javan; a Muse Prods.; Color; Not rated; 89 minutes; Release date: September 10, 1999. CAST: Billy Zane (The Thief), Sandra Bernhard (Sandy Sands), Ron Perlman (Cemetery Caretaker), Tippi Hedren (Maylinda), Andrew McCarthy, Rick Schroder, Steven Weber (Cops), Will Patton (Preacher), Carel Struycken (Undertaker), Max Perlich (Assistant Undertaker), John Ritter (Robert Forrest), Eartha Kitt (Singer), Ann Magnuson (Loan Secretary), Maila Nurmi (The Mysterious Woman), Christina Ricci (Teenage Hooker), Bud Cort (Salesman), Karen Black (Honey Child), Jonathan Taylor Thomas (Bystander), Abraham Benrubi (Bouncer), Conrad Brooks (Old Cop), Summer Phoenix (Girl at Beach), Nicolette Sheridan (Ballroom Woman), Kathy Wood, Lee Arenberg, Mark Boone Junior, Roberta Hanley, Taylor Negron, Rain Phoenix, Tara Reid, Joann Richter, Gregory Sporleder, David Ward

French Stewart, Bridgette Wilson in *Love Stinks* ©Independent Artists

LOVE STINKS (**Independent Artists**) Producers, Adam J. Merims, Todd Hoffman; Executive Producer, Craig Baumgarten, Jeff Franklin; Director/Screenplay, Jeff Franklin; Photography, Uta Briesewitz; Designer, Pamela A. Marcotte; Editor, Richard Candib; Costumes, Ileane Meltzer; Music, Bennett Salvay; Casting, Ferne Cassel; a Baumgarten/Prophet Entertainment production; Dolby; Color; Rated R; 94 minutes; Release date: September 10, 1999. CAST: French Stewart (Seth Winnick), Bridgette Wilson (Chelsea Turner), Bill Bellamy (Larry Garnett), Tyra Banks (Holly Garnett), Steve Hytner (Marty Mark), Jason Bateman (Jesse Travis), Tiffani-Amber Thiessen (Rebecca Melini), Ellis E. Williams (Minister), Boogie Knights (Wedding Band), Ivana Milavich (Amber), Montrose Hagins (Nana), Renata Scott (Mrs. Littlejohn), Warren Littlefield (Peter Bloomstein), Lisa Amsterdam, Tom Gammill, Tim Hightower, Hal Spear (The Writers), Shanna Moakler (Tawny), Julia Schultz (Tiffany), Bob Perlow (Warm-up Guy), Shae Marks (Jasmine), Colleen Camp (Monica Harris), John O'Hurley (Walter Drooz), Luis Avalos (Judge), Robyn Donny (Spa Receptionist), Jocelyne Kelly (Masseuse), Dale Raoul (Colonic Nurse), Brett Miller (Trainer), Kevin Farley (Sheriff), Jeff Franklin (Hotel Clerk), Carole Franklin (Real Estate Agent), Michael Caldwell (Dentist), Rachel Winfree (Dental Assistant), Dyllan Christopher (Young Boy), Terry Crisp (Reverend "E"), Darlene Dillinger, Gretchen Palmer, Meilani Paul (The Elvettes)

DEATH: A LOVE STORY (**Harken Prods.**) Producer/Director/Screenplay/Photography, Michelle Le Brun; Executive Producer, Mel Howard; Co-Producer, Tom Danon; Editor, Lisa Leeman; Music, Miriam Cutler; Color; Not rated; 61 minutes; Release date: September 10, 1999. Documentary in which filmmaker Michelle Le Brun chronicles the final months of her husband Mel Howard's battle with liver cancer.

Reese Witherspoon, Alessandro Nivola in *Best Laid Plans*
©Twentieth Century Fox

Danny Hoch, Dash Mihok, Piper Perabo, Mark Webber in *Whiteboyz*
©Fox Searchlight Pictures

BEST LAID PLANS (**Fox Searchlight**) Producers, Alan Greenspan, Betsy Beers, Chris Moore, Sean Bailey; Director, Mike Barker; Screenplay, Ted Griffin; Executive Producer, Mike Newell; Photography, Ben Seresin; Designer, Sophie Becher; Editor, Sloane Klevin; Costumes, Susan Matheson; Co-Producer, Nancy Paloian-Breznikar; Music, Craig Armstrong; Casting, Mali Finn; a Fox 2000 Pictures presentation of a Dogstar Films production; Dolby; FotoKem Color; Rated R; 92 minutes; Release date: September 10, 1999. CAST: Alessandro Nivola (Nick), Reese Witherspoon (Lissa), Josh Brolin (Bryce), Rocky Carroll (Bad Ass Dude), Michael G. Hagerty (Charlie the Proprietor), Terrence Howard (Jimmy), Jamie Marsh (Barry), Sean Nepita (Freddie), Jose Mendoza (Renaldo), Gene Wolande (Lawyer), Michael McCleery (Recycling Officer), Jonathan McMurtry (Vet), Terrance Sweeney (Priest), Teddy Vincent (Lawyer Secretary), Rebecca Klinger (Diner Waitress), Kate Hendrickson (Bar Waitress), Jody Wood (Brushfire Cop)

WHITEBOYZ (**Fox Searchlight**) Producers, Henri Kessler, Richard Stratton, Ezra Swerdlow; Executive Producers, David Peipers, John Sloss; Director, Marc Levin; Screenplay, Garth Belcon, Danny Hoch, Marc Levin, Richard Stratton; Story, Garth Belcon, Danny Hoch; Photography, Mark Benjamin; Designer, David Doernberg; Editor, Emir Lewis; Music, Che Guevara; Costumes, Carolyn Greco; Co-Producer, Paul Marcus; Casting, Kathleen Chopin, Sue Crystal; an Offline Entertainment Group production, presented in association with BAC Films and Le Studio Canal+; Dolby; Color; Rated R; 97 minutes; Release date: September 10, 1999. CAST: Danny Hoch (Flip), Dash Mihok (James), Mark Webber (Trevor), Piper Perabo (Sara), Eugene Byrd (Khalid), Bonz Malone (Darius), Dr. Dre, Fat Joe (Don Flip Crew), Rich Komenich (Flip's Dad), Annabel Armour (Flip's Mom), Lisa Jane Todd (Trevor's Mom), Brooke Byam (Country Western Singer), Diane Rinehart (Sara's Sister), Rick Snyder (Sara's Dad), Jacqueline Williams (Khalid's Mom), Reno Wilson (Mace), Dead Prez (Cornfield Rappers), Mic Geronimo (Friend of Mace), Slick Rick, Doug E. Fresh (Parking Lot Rappers), Snoop Dogg (Himself)

EXISTO (**Hometown Prods.**) Producers, J. Clarke Gallivan, Peter F. Kurland; Director, Coke Sams; Screenplay, Bruce Arntson, Coke Sams; Photography, Jim May; Editor, Scott Mele; Designer, Ruby Guidara; Casting, Kim Petrosky; Color; Not rated; 94 minutes; Release date: September 17, 1999. CAST: Bruce Arntson (Existo), Jackie Welch (Maxine), Mark Cabus (Roupen Dupree), Jim Varney (Marcel Horowitz), Gailard Sartain (Colette Watchuwill), Michael Montgomery (Armand Glasscock), David Alford (Dirk Beverage), Connye Florance (Ramona), Denice Hicks (Mo Deeks), Jenny Littleton (Penelope), Barry Scott (Bernard Ozak), Ray Thornton (Vigo)

Christina Fulton in *Lucinda's Spell* ©Golden Shadow

LUCINDA'S SPELL (**Golden Shadow**) Producer, Michael Kastenbaum; Executive Producer, Joe Chavez; Director/Screenplay, Jon Jacobs; Co-Producer, Truman Weatherly; Photography, Jaime Reynoso; Editor, Clayton Halsey; Music, Niki Jack; Costumes, Keith Sayer; Designers, Andy Peach, Jana Pesek; a Zero Pictures presentation, produced in association with Motion Picture Capital and developed in association with Bridge House; Color; Cinemascope; Not rated; 105 minutes; Release date: September 10, 1999. CAST: Jon Jacobs (Jason), Christina Fulton (Lucinda), Shannah Bettz (Beatrice), Leon Herbert (Maddison), Alix Koromzay (Natalie), J.C. Brandy (Betsy), John El (George), Fatt Natt (Jules), Brother Randy (Jim), Judy Garwood (Ms. Worth), Ajax Davis (Severain), Angie Green (Chickory)

Bruce Vilanch, Bette Midler in *Get Bruce* ©Miramax Films

GET BRUCE (Miramax) Producer/Director, Andrew J. Kuehn; Executive Producers, Gregory McClatchy, Susan B. Landau; Line Producer, Don Scotti; Co-Producers, Joan Hyler, Irwin M. Rappaport; Photography, Jose Luis Mignone; Music, Michael Feinstein; Editor, Maureen Nolan; Supervising Editor, Gregory McClatchy; an AJK Production; Dolby; Color; Rated R; 82 minutes; Release date: September 17, 1999. Documentary on comedy and joke writer Bruce Vilanch, featuring Whoopi Goldberg, Billy Crystal, Bette Midler, Roseanne, Lily Tomlin, Paul Reiser, Nathan Lane, Raquel Welch, Shirley MacLaine, Carol Burnett, Robin Williams, Florence Henderson, Michael Feinstein, Steven Seagal, Michael Douglas, Danny Harris, Jenifer Lewis, Jeff Margolis, Salma Hayek, Dora Mendoza, Paul Guerrero, Henne Vilanch, Michele Lee, George Schlatter, Stephen Pouliot, Susan Futterman, Marc Shaiman, Michael Smith, James Joyce, Don Scotti, Christine Baranski, Tim Curry, Traci Lords, Tom Vergron, David Copperfield, Margaret Cho, Beverly D'Angelo, Ali MacGraw, Lauren Bacall, Merry Clayton.

Damian Young in *Going Nomad* ©Great Jones Prod.

Matt Keeslar, Kathleen Robertson, Johnathon Schaech
in *Splendor* ©Goldwyn

SPLENDOR (Goldwyn) Producers, Damian Jones, Graham Broadbent, Gregg Araki; Executive Producers, Heidi Lester, William Tyrer, Chris Ball; Director/Screenplay/Editor, Gregg Araki; Line Producer, Dave Pomier; Photography, Jim Fealy; Designer, Patti Podesta; Music, Daniel Licht; Costumes, Susanna Puisto; Casting, Mary Margiotta, Karen Margiotta; a Summit Entertainment and Newmarket Capital Group presentation of a Desperate Pictures/Dragon Pictures production; Dolby; Color; Rated R; 93 minutes; Release date: September 17, 1999. CAST: Kathleen Robertson (Veronica), Johnathon Schaech (Abel), Matt Keeslar (Zed), Kelly Macdonald (Mike), Eric Mabius (Ernest), Dan Gatto (Mutt), Linda Kim (Alison), Audrey Ruttan (The Gloved One), Nathan Bexton (Waiter), Amy Stevens (Nana Kitty Cat), Adam Carola (Mike's Stupid Boss), Julie Millette (Supermarket Cashier), Jenica Bergere, Paige Dunn (Models), George Pennacchio (Newscaster), Wesley B (Himself)

GOING NOMAD (Cinema Guild) Producer/Director/Screenplay, Art Jones; Associate Producer, Angela Martenez; Photography, John Inwood; Editor, James Cozza; Music, Jim Papoulis; Line Producer, Luis Cubillos; Color; Not rated; 97 minutes; Release date: September 24, 1999. CAST: Damian Young (El Cid Rivera), Gregory Wolfe (Tully), Mason Pettit (Chuckles), Jamie C. Ward (Rev), Tom Oppenheim (Eddie), Jourdan Zayles (Officer Geraldine Fusco), Graciela Lecube (Voice of Cid's Mother), Victor Argo (Spiro), Chuck Patterson (Ray), Craig Smith (Spud), Bettina Mercado (Rosalita), Marilyn Brett (Estelle), Art Jones (Rilo), Nitza Wilon (Alice), José Yenque (Jose the Bodega Manager), Pietro Gonzalez (Pepe), Ralph Navarro (Ralph), Ted Coluca (Stanley the Steakhouse Manager), Mary Jane Wells (Marge, the Gun-Toting Tourist), Lou Lagalante (Bus Driver), Dicky Fine (Ralphie Dodd), Robert Amos (House the Wrestler), Daniel Lanzilotta (Leo the Bartender), Jennifer Summer (Little Girl on Street), Joe Sweet (Apartment Hunter), Jonathan Stahl (Toolbooth Customer), Steven Isola (Fusco's Perp)

SIMON SEZ (Independent Artists) Producer, Moshe Diamant; Director, Kevin Elders; Screenplay, Andrew Miller, Andrew Lowery; Story, Moshe Diamant, Rudy Cohen; Executive Producers, Rudy Cohen, Dan Frisch, Kevin Jones; Photography, Avraham Karpick; Designer, Damien Lanfranchi; Editor, Alain Jakubowicz; Music, Brian Tyler; Costumes, Jaleh Falk; Casting, Illana Diamant; a Signature Films production; Dolby; Color; Rated PG-13; 85 minutes; Release date: September 24, 1999. CAST: Dennis Rodman (Simon), Dane Cook (Nick), Natalia Cigliuti (Claire), Filip Nicolic (Michael), John Pinette (Macro), Jerome Pradon (Ashton), Ricky Harris (Micro), Henri Courseaux (Bernard), Xiong, Xin Xin (XIN-XIN), Emma Sjoberg (The Dancer), Igor De Savitch (Colonel Telore), Clayton Day (William Fence), Jean-Michel Dagory (Frenais), Pierre Madengar (Ethiopian Street Vendor), Cyrille Dufaut (Malcolm), Dario Andres, Jean-Elie-Pucci, Jamal Belhadj, Frederic Garcia, Claude Yurca, Mikael Meloul (Hooligans), Bernard Deloche, Sonny Stark, Versace Fortune (Henchmen)

Dennis Rodman, Filip Nicolic in *Simon Sez*
©Global Entertainment/GmbH & Co.

THE JAUNDICED EYE (Somford Entertainment) Producer, Dan Gifford; Executive Producer, Amy Sommer Gifford; Director/Screenplay/Co-Producer, Nonny De La Pena; Photography, Bestor Cram; Editor, Greg Byers; Music, Michael Brook; a Fifth Estate production, in association with Pyedog Prods.; Color; Not rated; 90 minutes; Release date: September 24, 1999. Documentary on a true criminal case in which a woman accused the gay father of her son and the boy's straight grandfather of molesting the child.

Daniela Romo, Tom Berenger in *One Man's Hero*
©MGM Entertainment, Inc

Robert Klein in *Suits* ©Taurus Entertainment

ONE MAN'S HERO (**Orion**) Producers, Lance Hool, William J. Macdonald, Conrad Hool; Director, Lance Hool; Screenplay, Milton S. Gelman; Photography, Joao Fernandes; Music, Ernest Troost; Editor, Mark Conte; Designer, Peter Wooley; Co-Producer, Paul L. Newman; Costumes, Matthew Jacobsen; Casting, Mary Jo Slater, Bruce Newberg; a Silver Lion Films presentation of a Hool/Macdonald production; Distributed by MGM; Dolby; Panavision; CFI color; Rated R; 121 minutes; Release date: September 24, 1999. CAST: Tom Berenger (John Reilly), Joaquim de Almeida (Cortina), Daniela Romo (Marta), Mark Moses (Col. Benton Lacey), Stuart Graham (Cpl. Kenneally), James Gammon (Gen. Zachary Taylor), Stephen Tobolowsky (Capt. Gaine), Carlos Carrasco (Dominguez), Patrick Bergin (Gen. Winfield Scott), Don Wycherley (Brian Athlone), Jorge Bosso (Col. Maximo Nexor), Rodolfo de Anda (Gen. Ampudia), Vanessa Bauche (Flor), Roger Cudney (Col. Harney), Guy De Saint Cyr (Lasher), Fernando Elizondo (2nd Guerilla), Gregg Fitzgerald (Paddy Noonan), Luke Hayden (Seamus McDougherty), Brett Hool (Army Recruiter), Jason Hool (Peter O'Neil), Perla De La Rosa (Juno), Steve Leone (John Daly), Luis Lorenzo (Padre Varga), Wolf Muser (Cpl. Schultz)

SUITS (**Taurus Entertainment**) Producer, Chris Giordano; Director/Screenplay, Eric Weber; Photography, Peter Nelson; Designer, Pamela Shamshiri; Costumes, Ivan Ingermann; Music, Pat Irwin; Editor, Nancy Novack; Casting, Lina Todd; an Eric Weber/Chris Giordano production; from the Tenafly Film Company; Color; Rated R; 88 minutes; Release date: September 24, 1999. CAST: Robert Klein (Tom Cranston), Tony Hendra (George Parkyn), Larry Pine (Peter Haverford), Paul Lazar (Mitchell Mitnick), Randy Pearlstein (Ken Tuttle), Ingrid Rogers (Anita Tanner), James Villemaire (Doug Humphrey), Mark Lake (Harson Covington), Joelle Carter (Heidi Wilson), Eben More (Rodney De Mole), Timothi-Jane Graham (Billie Weston), Frank Minucci (Robert Naylor, Sr.), Cary Prusa (Robert Naylor, Jr.), Marla Sucharetza (Taco Lady), Robert Whaley (Alain Godard), Edoardo Ballerini (Johnny Akida), Eliza Coyle (Mrs. Betsy Haverford), Tanya Pohlkotte (Anna), Alexandra Neil (Sally Parkyn), Ronald Guttman (Barry Hoffman), Michaline Babich (Regina Van Reich), Karen Williams (Penelope Brie), Irma St. Paul (Miss Volney), Chuck Montgomery (Dr. Glen Glenn), Jim Frangione, Steve Carrell (United Standards), Vanessa Dorman (Angelica), Steve Deighan (Tip), Sebastian Hendra (Parkyn's Son), Air Supply (Themselves)

UNCOMMON FRIENDS OF THE 20TH CENTURY (**Independent**) Producer/Director, John Biffar; Based on the autobiography by James D. Newton; Narrator, Walter Cronkite; Not other information available; Color; Not rated; 63 minutes; Release date: October 1, 1999. Documentary on James D. Newton's unlikely friendship with such notable Americans as Thomas Edison, Henry Ford, Harvey Firestone, and Charles Lindbergh.

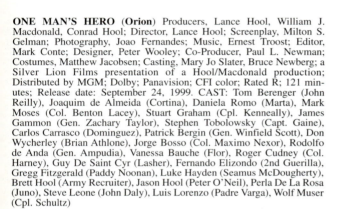

Nadja Salerno-Sonnenberg in *Speaking in Strings* ©Seventh Art Releasing

SPEAKING IN STRINGS (**Seventh Art**) Producers, Paola di Florio, Lilibet Foster; Director, Paola di Florio; Photography, Peter Rader; Music, Karen Childs; Editor, Ellen Goldwater; Associate Producers, Cindy Rosenberg, Julie Du Brow, Elizabeth Rodgers; a CounterPoint Films presentation; Color; Not rated; 73 minutes; Release date: September 24, 1999. Documentary of controversial classical violinist Nadja Salerno-Sonnenberg.

Asia Argento, Willem Dafoe in *New Rose Hotel* ©Avalanche

NEW ROSE HOTEL (Lions Gate) Producer, Edward R. Pressman; Executive Producers, Jay Cannold, Greg Woertz, Alessandro Camon; Director, Abel Ferrara; Screenplay, Abel Ferrara, Christ Zois; Based on a short story by William Gibson; Photography, Ken Kelsch; Designer, Frank De Curtis; Editors, Anthony Redman, Jim Moll; Music, Schoolly D; Co-Executive Producers, Christian Halsey, Lee Solomon; Co-Producers, Adam Brightman, Christopher Walken, Willem Dafoe; Costumes, David C. Robinson; an Edward R. Pressman production; Dolby; Color; Not rated; 92 minutes; Release date: October 1, 1999. CAST: Christopher Walken (Fox), Willem Dafoe (X), Asia Argento (Sandi), Annabella Sciorra (Mdm. Rosa), John Lurie (Distinguished Man), Naoko "Kimmy" Suzuki, Miou (Asian Girls), Yoshitaka Amano (Hiroshi), Gretchen Mol (Hiroshi's Wife), Phil Nielson (The Welshman), Ken Kelsch (The Expeditor), Andrew Fiscella (Sex Show Man), Rachel Glass, Roberta Orlan, Erin Jermaine Serrano, Micole Taggart (Sex Show Women), Ryuichi Sakamoto (Hosaka Executive), Victor Argo (Portuguese Business Man), Annamarie Wind (German Lady), Joel St. Bernard (Club Security), Harper Simon (Man at Table), William Webb (Bartender), George Smurra (One Eye George), John Ciarcia (Cha Cha), Frankie Cee (Frankie Fats), Echo Danon, Kyrie Tinch (Singers), Bridget Bernhart (Bar Lady), Dave Shelley (Maitre D'), Matthew Messina, Nick Guccione, Al Croseri, John Russo (Security), Vincent DiMarco, Walter Abraham, Sal Savino, Sam Canegallo, Tim Browning (Lab Scientists), M. Kelley Reynolds, Janine Glickman (Shower Girls), Ray DeFelita (Lab Security)

Norman Reedus, Chad Lowe in *Floating* ©Phaedra Cinema

FLOATING (Phaedra) Producers, Anaye Milligan, Mary Feuer; Director/Screenplay, William Roth; Photography, Wolfgang Held; Editor, Keith Reamer; Music, David Mansfield; Designer, Cheryl Dewardener; Costumes, Margaret Palmer; Casting, Patrick Cunningham; Color; Not rated; 90 minutes; Release date: October 8, 1999. CAST: Norman Reedus (Van), Chad Lowe (Doug), Will Lyman (Van's Father), Sybil Temchen (Julie), Jonathan Quint (Jason), Josh Marchette (Flip), Rachel Raposa (Sarah), Bruce Kenny (Coach), Adrienne Starrs (Doug's Mom), Rob Harriell (Steve), Casey Affleck, Jolyon Reese, Eddie Rutkowski (Preps), Ali Raizin, Angelica Nebbia, Sandra Iodice, Tracy Tobin (Girls), Linda Roth, Arnold Roth, Elsie Cotter, James Cotter, Jack W. Wolter (Screening People), Sean Biggins (Drug Buyer)

Tommy Blake, Tessa Blake in *Five Wives, Three Secretaries and Me*
©Castle Hill

FIVE WIVES, THREE SECRETARIES AND ME (Castle Hill) Producer, Jason Lyon; Director/Screenplay/Photography/Editor, Tessa Blake; Associate Producers, Gail Segal, Mary Weatherford, Laurie Williams; Music, Thomas W. Blake, Jr.; Color; Not rated; 80 minutes; Release date: October 8, 1999. Documentary on 87-year-old Texas serial monogomist Tommy Blake, featuring Muffet Criner Adickes Blake, Sandra Tessman Blake, Betty "Boop" Blake, Sharon Simons, Harriet Leasey, Louise Turner, Barbara Tucker, Virginia Keasling, Chelo Maris.

Valerie Red-Horse, Kimberly Norris Guerrero in *Naturally Native*

DILL SCALLION (Pedestrian Films) Producers, Joe Blake, Jennifer Amerine, Kimberly Jacobs; Executive Producers, Mark Herman, Jon Kittelsen; Director/Screenplay, Jordan Brady; Photography, Jonathan Brown; Editor, Sam Citron; Music, Sheryl Crow; Presented in association with Brady Oil Entertainment; Foto-Kem color; Not rated; 94 minutes; Release date: October 8, 1999. CAST: Billy Burke (Dill Scanlon), Peter Berg, Lauren Graham, Kathy Griffin, David Koechner, Jason Priestley, Henry Winkler, LeAnn Rimes, Willie Nelson.

NATURALLY NATIVE (Mashantucket Pequot Tribal Nation/Red-Horse Native Prods.) Producers, Valerie Red-Horse, Dawn Jackson, Yvonne Russo; Directors, Jennifer Wynne Farmer, Valerie Red-Horse; Screenplay, Valerie Red-Horse; Photography, Bruce Finn; Editor, Lorraine Salk; Music, Murielle Hamilton; Designer, Kee Miller; Costumes, Irene Fredericks; Color; Rated PG-13; 108 minutes; Release date: October 8, 1999. CAST: Valerie Red-Horse (Vickie Lewis Bighawk), Irene Bedard (Tanya Lewis), Kimberly Norris Guerrero (Karen Lewis), Pato Hoffmann (Steve Bighawk), Mark Abbott (Mark), Collin Bernsen (Craig), Mary Kay Place (Madam Celeste), Carol Potter (Rape Counselor), Floyd Red Crow Westerman (Chairman Pico), Max Gail (Carlson)

Mackenzie Astin, Carmen Electra in *The Mating Habits of the Earthbound Human* ©Earthbound Human Prods.

Chrissy Kobylak, Chloë Sevigny in *Julien Donkey-Boy* ©Fine Line

THE MATING HABITS OF THE EARTHBOUND HUMAN (Independent Artists) Producer, Larry Estes; Director/Screenplay, Jeff Abugov; Co-Producer, Victor Ho; Photography, Michael K. Bucher; Associate Producer, Sam Irvin; Music, Michael McCarty; Editor, Steven R. Myers; Designer, Helen Harwell; Costumes, Kristin M. Burke; a Welb Film Pursuits Ltd. presentation; Dolby; Color; Rated R; 88 minutes; Release date: October 8, 1999. CAST: Mackenzie Astin (The Male: Billy Waterston), Carmen Electra (The Female: Jenny Smith), David Hyde Pierce (The Narrator), Markus Redmond (The Male's Friend), Lucy Liu (The Female's Friend), Lisa Rotondi (Again, The Female's Friend), Sharon Wyatt (The Male's Mother), Jack Kehler (The Male's Father), Leo Rossi (The Female's Father), Antonette Saftler (The Female's Mother), Marc Blucas (The Female's Ex-Boyfriend), Anne Gee Byrd (The Female's Boss), Eric Kushnick (The Female's Brother), Linda Porter (The Wise Old Woman), Tyler Abugov (The Female's Fantasy Son), Lynn Ann Leveridge (The Large Female), Adam Abugov (The Male as a Cub), Billy Morts (The Ex-Boyfriend's Friend), Noah M. Breedon (The Baby)

JULIEN DONKEY-BOY (Fine Line) Producers, Scott Macaulay, Robin O'Hara, Cary Woods; Director/Screenplay, Harmony Korine; Photography, Anthony Dod Mantle; Editor, Valdis Oskarsdottir; Casting, Billy Hopkins, Suzanne Smith, Kerry Barden, Lori Eastside; an Independent Pictures presentation of an IP Production in association with Forensic/391 Films; Dolby; Color; Rated R; 94 minutes; Release date: October 8, 1999. CAST: Ewen Bremner (Julien), Chloë Sevigny (Pearl), Werner Herzog (Julien's Father), Evan Neumann (Chris), Joyce Korine (Grandmother), Chrissy Kobylak (Chrissy), Alvin Law (Card-Playing Neighbor), Brian Fisk (Pond Boy), Miriam Martinez (Teenage Girl), Edgar Erikkson (Bearded Man), James Moix (Dancing Man), Victor Varnado (Rapper), Oliver A. Bueno, Roger Harris, Josseph Padilla, Freddie Perez, Olivia Perez, Carmelo Rodriguez (Bowlers), Carmel Gayle (Clothing Store Cashier), Herman Reimmer (Man in Clothing Store), Virginia Reath (Gynecologist), Mary O'Hara (Nun), Donna Smith (Dancing Woman), Gary Bergman (Piano Player), Tom Mullica (Magician), Archie MacGregor, Jeanmarie Evans (Amnesiac Patients), Ricky Ashley (Hasidic Boy), Hy Richards, Barry Wernick, Clinton Wright (Doctors), Carmela Garcia (Nurse)

THE HAND BEHIND THE MOUSE (Walt Disney Pictures) Producer/Director/Screenplay, Leslie Iwerks; Photography, Shana Jagan; Editors, Stephen Myers, Seth Flaum; Music, John Debney, Louis Febre; Associate Producer, Ron Stark; Narrator, Kelsey Grammer; a Leslie Iwerks production; Distributed by Buena Vista Pictures; Dolby; Color; Rated G; 90 minutes; Release date: October 8, 1999. Documentary on one of Walt Disney's chief animators and the creator of Mickey Mouse, Ub Iwerks; featuring Russell Merritt, Mark Kausler, Leonard Maltin, John Lasseter, Roy E. Disney, Chuck Jones, Virginia Davis, Don Iwerks, Dave Smith, Tippi Hedren.

Steven Nelson in *Men Cry Bullets* ©Phaedra Cinema

MEN CRY BULLETS (Phaedra Cinema) Producers, Harry Ralston, Tamara Hernandez, Jessica Rains; Executive Producers, Bob Sturm, Harry Ralston, Tamara Hernandez; Director/Screenplay, Tamara Hernandez; Photography, Michael Grady; Designer, Ivana Letica; Editors, Scott Balcerek, Garth Grinde; Costumes, C.T. DeNelli; Music, The X-Friends; an ID Films production; Dolby; Color; Not rated; 106 minutes; Release date: October 8, 1999. CAST: Steven Nelson (Billy), Honey Lauren (Gloria), Jeri Ryan (Lydia), Michael Mangiamele (Paper Boy), Harry Ralston (Freddy Fishnets), Bob Sherer (Bootser), Sabrina Bertaccini (Colette), Trish Elliot (Gloria's Mother), Chanda (Tarty Tina), Dylan (Jack the Pig)

FIFTY (Warren Miller) Producer, Max Bervy Jr.; Executive Producers, Kurt Miller, Bailey Pryor, Peter Speek; Directors, Kurt Miller, Peter Speek; Screenplay, Warren Miller; Photography, Brian Sisselman; Editor, Kim Schneider; Color; Not rated; 90 minutes; Release date: October 1999. Skiing documentary, featuring J.P. Auclair, Jonny Moseley, Bob Rankin, Chris Anthony, Adrienne Gibbs, Mike Gibbs, Ted Gawthmey, Patty Kauf, Scott Kauf, Jason Lalla, Mike Thomas, Danny Caruso, Dan Gilchrist, Wendy Brookbank, Caleb Martin, Justin Patnode, Mickey Price, Megan Brown, Ben Hinkley, Suzanne Sawyer Montgomery, Curtis Tischler, Garrett Altmann, Vincent Dorion, Mike Douglas, Evan Dybvig, Tim McKeever, Philippe Poirier, Evan Raps, Adam Schrab, Luke Schrab, Anna Kanarowski, Josh Lieberman, Dustin Lindgren, Jason Toth, Will Garrow, Kina Pickett, Donna Weinbrecht, Youbi Ahmed, Stefen Gimpl, Nikke Gruenewaldt, Sebu Kuhlberg, Dave Richards, Michael Roddey, Jim Smith, Sean Smith (Athletes)

Norman Mailer, Anonymous in *Cremaster 2* ©Barbara Goldstone

CREMASTER 2 (Glacier Field, LLC) Producers, Barbara Gladstone, Matthew Barney; Director/Screenplay, Matthew Barney; Photography, Peter Strietmann; Designer, Matthew D. Ryle; Music, Jonathan Bepler; Prosthetic Makeup & Effects, Gabe Bartalos, Atlantic West Effects; Visual Effects Supervisor, Karen Ansel; Costumes, Linda Labelle, Laurence Esnault; Color; Not rated; 79 minutes; Release date: October 13, 1999. CAST: Norman Mailer (Harry Houdini), Matthew Barney (Gary Gilmore), Anonymous (Baby Face La Foe), Lauren Pine (Bessie Gilmore), Scott Ewalt (Frank Gilmore), Patty Griffin (Nicole Baker), Dave Lombardo, Bruce Steele, Steve Tucker (Johnny Cash), Cat Kubic, Sam Jalahej (Two-Step Dancers), #55 (Brahma Bull), Jacqueline Molasses (French Bulldog), Michael Thomson (Max Jensen), The Morman Tabernacle Choir

BELFAST, MAINE (Zipporah Films) Producer/Director/Editor, Frederick Wiseman; Photography, John Davey; a Belfast Inc. production; Color; Not rated; 248 minutes; Release date: Oct. 1999. Documentary looking at the activities and inhabitants of a small New England seaport town.

Michael York, Casper Van Dien in *The Omega Code*
©Providence Entertainment

THE OMEGA CODE (Providence Entertainment) Producers, Matthew Crouch, Rob Marcarelli, Lawrence Mortorff; Executive Producer, Paul Crouch; Director, Rob Marcarelli; Screenplay, Stephan Blinn, Hollis Barton; Co-Producer, Gary M. Bettman; Photography, Carlos Gonzalez; Editor, Peter Zinner; Designer, Mark Harper; Music, Harry Manfredini; a

TBN Films presentation of a Gener8xion Entertainment production; Dolby; Panavision; Fotokem color; Rated PG-13; 99 minutes; Release date: October 15, 1999. CAST: Casper Van Dien (Gillen Lane), Michael York (Stone Alexander), Catherine Oxenberg (Cassandra Barashe), Michael Ironside (Dominic), Jan Triska, Gregory Wagrowski (Prophets), Devon Odessa (Jennifer Lane), William Hootkins (Sir Percival Lloyd), Robert Ito (Shimoro Lin Che), Janet Carroll (Dorothy Thompson), George Coe (Senator Jack Thompson), Ravil Isyonov (Rykoff), Ayla Kell (Maddie Lane), Walter Williamson (Archbishop), Ross McKerras (Ferguson), Steve Franken (Jeffries), Alec Murdock (News Anchor), Jules Mandel (Rabbi), Nicole Forester (Student), Terry Rhoads (Reporter Matthews), Lise Simms (Talk Show Reporter), Drenda Spohnholtz (Coronation Reporter), Brett Miller (Sniper), Robert O'Reilly (Technician), Robert F. Lyons (General), Sabrina Marinucci (Italian Reporter), Stella Vordemann (Princess Gabrielle), Oded Teomi (Israeli Prime Minister), Mattia Castell (Alexander Aide), Liron Levo (Benjamin), Yehuda Efroni (Rostenberg)

Thomas Jane, Elisabeth Shue in *Molly*
©Metro-Goldwyn-Mayer Pictures Inc,

MOLLY (MGM) Producer, William J. MacDonald; Executive Producer, Amy Heckerling; Director, John Duigan; Screenplay, Dick Christie; Co-Producer, Frank Bodo; Photography, Gabriel Beristain; Designer, Sharon Seymour; Costumes, Carol Oditz; Music, Trevor Jones; Casting, Amanda Mackey Johnson, Cathy Sandrich; a Cockamamie/Absolute Entertainment production; Dolby; Deluxe color; Rated PG-13; 91 minutes; Release date: October 22, 1999. CAST: Elisabeth Shue (Molly McKay), Aaron Eckhart (Buck McKay), Jill Hennessy (Susan Brookes), Thomas Jane (Sam), D.W. Moffett (Mark Cottrell), Elizabeth Mitchell (Beverly Trehare), Robert Harper (Dr. Simmons), Elaine Hendrix (Jennifer Thomas), Michael Paul Chan (Domingo), Lucy Liu (Brenda), Jon Pennell (Gary McKay), Sarah Wynter (Julie McKay), Lauren Richter (Molly, 7 Years Old), Tanner Prairie (Buck, 8 Years Old), Nicholas Pryor (Dr. Prentice), Mark Phelan (Highway Patrolman), Jay Acovone (Jack), Julie Ariola (Joyce Lacy), Patricia Belcher (Margaret Duffy), Robert Neches (Randall Prescott), James Krag (Courtney Pratt), Michael Yama, Rachen Assapimonwait (Asian Clients), Musetta Vander (Maxine), Ana Christina (Fiona), Brian George (Director), Roger Davis (Sheriff), Erl (Sex Therapist), Vinny Argiro (Manager), Liz Lang, Kiki Susan Hall, Heather Bell (Nurses), Michelle Rock (Receptionist), Julio Oscar Mechoso (Fan), Athena Massey (Lauris), Lisa Mollick (Juliet), Terence Heuston (Romeo), Charles Hoyes (1st Base Umpire), Mark Christopher Lawrence (Angels' Manager), Irene Olga Lopez (Carmen), Jennifer O'Dell (Actress), Elisha Choice (Clerk), Kristina Malota (Small Girl), Joe Everett Michaels (Security Guard), Dick Christie (Maitre D'), Alexa Jago (Haughty Woman)

Jake Roberts in *Beyond the Mat* ©Lions Gate Films

BEYOND THE MAT (**Universal/Imagine**) Producers, Brian Grazer, Ron Howard, Michael Rosenberg, Barry Bloom, Barry W. Blaustein; Co-Producer, Debra Marie Simon; Director/Screenplay, Barry W. Blaustein; Photography, Michael Grady; Editor, Jeff Werner; Music, Nathan Barr; an Imagine Entertainment production; Dolby; FotoKem color; Rated R; 102 minutes; Release date: October 27, 1999. Documentary on the professional wrestling scene featuring Terry Funk, Mick Foley, Jake Roberts, Vince McMahon, Roland Alexander, Collette Foley, Dewey Foley, Noelle Foley, Brandy Smith, Paul Heyman, Tony Jones, Mike Modest, Darren Drozdov, Vicki Funk, Stacey Funk, Bradlee Funk, Chyna, Matt Hyson, Coco Bware, Jessie Ventura, New Jack, Dennis Stamp

Flea in *Liar's Poker* ©North Branch Entertainment

LIAR'S POKER (**North Branch Entertainment**) Producers, Billy Savino, Carlos H. Sanchez, Jeff Santo; Executive Producer, Billy Savino; Director/Screenplay, Jeff Santo; Photography, Giles M.I. Dunning; Editor, Kathryn Himoff; Music, Peter Himmelman; Designer, William Perretti; a Savino Brothers production; Dolby; Color; Rated R; 93 minutes; Release date: October 29, 1999. CAST: Richard Tyson (Jack), Caesar Luisi (Niko), Jimmy Blondell (Vic), Flea (Freddie), Neith Hunter (Brooke), Pamela Gidley (Linda), Amelia Heinie (Rebecca), Colin Patrick Lynch (Art), Paul Sloane (Niko), Jess King, Alan Steele, Frank Cavestani, Terry O'Brien, Dan Foley, Jim McCauley (Car Salesmen), Jonathan Black (Porkchop), Wells Rosales (Mexican Kid), Tanner Gill (Porkchop's Father), Melanie Pennell (Porkchop's Mother), Horacio LeDon (Manuel), Carlos A. Franco (Ruben), Chico (Latin #1), Roger Ontiveros, Darren Kennedy (Valets), Brian Petrich (Doorman), Kristi Frank, Hellena Schmied (Club Girls), Greggory Rogen (Hank the Waiter), Kinsey Ryan (Almost-Married Girl),

Shelly Six, Melissa Subel, Linda Santo, Elizabeth Gessaman (Bachelorettes), Simon Alexander (Flower Guy), Robert Bradley (Club Singer), Bruno Stempel (Club Cook), Calvin Levels (Bartender), Mary Ann Rounseville (911 Operator), Billy Savino, Jeff Santo (Cops), Jim Rafalin (Iron Worker), Googy Gress (Security Cop), Arthur Senzy, Marcus Aurelius (Detectives)

SLAVES OF HOLLYWOOD (**Filmopolis**) Directors/Screenplay, Terry Keefe, Michael J. Wechsler; No other credits available; Color; Not rated; 73 minutes; Release date: October 29, 1999. CAST: Amy Lyndon (Lydia Schnell), Tim Duquette (Sammy Stahr), Andre Barron (Dean Palermo), Hill Harper (Fisher Lovelace), Rob Hyland (Roman Sofine), Elliot Markman (George Pink), Katherin Morgan (Paulette Gittleman), Nicholas Worth (Sam Gittleman)

Terror Firmer ©Troma Entertainment

TERROR FIRMER (**Troma**) Producers, Lloyd Kaufman, Michael Herz; Director, Lloyd Kaufman; Screenplay, Patrick Cassidy, Douglas Buck, Lloyd Kaufman; Executive Producers, Kenneth B. Squire, Charles Berry Hill, David Berry Hill; Photography, Brendan Flynt; Editor, Gabriel Friedman; Designer, Jean Loscalzo; Creature Effects, Tim Considine; a Lloyd Kaufman & Michael Herz production in association with Santa Monica Holdings; Color; Not rated; 114 minutes; Release date: October 29, 1999. CAST: Will Keenan (Casey), Alyce LaTourelle (Jennifer), Lloyd Kaufman (Larry Benjamin), Trent Haaga (Jerry), Debbie Rochon (Christine), Sheri Wenden (Mysterious Woman), Eduardo Baer, Joseph Malerba (French Cool Cats), Ariel Wizman (Guy Beaten by Leg), Yaniv Sharon (Naked P.A.), Charlotte Kaufman (Audrey Benjamin), Gary Hrbek (Toddster), Joe Fleishaker (Jacob Gelman), Greg "G-Spot" Siebel (Ward), Mario Diaz (DJ), Mo Fischer (Andy), Lyle Derek (Asshole P.A.), Tracey Burroughs (Edgar Allan), Popo (Himself), Roy David (Jeff/Toxie), Sean Pierce (Moose), Barry Brisco (Stephen), Darko Malesh (Nikolai), Carla Burden (Sarah), Reverend Jen Miller (Tina), Eve Crosby (Jennifer's Mom), Stefanie Imhoff (Assia), Theo Kogan (Theodora), Michael Locascio (Old Man Phil), Wendy Adams (Toilet Plunger Police Gyno), Michael Levine (Police Detective), Gadi Harel (Cuntinuity Guy), Anthony Haden-Guest (Toxie's Father), Oakley Stevenson (Pregnant Woman), Ali Grossman (Homecoming Queen), Rik Slave, Lindsey Anderson (Two Sexed Freak), Maryse Pen (Elevator Screamer), Ileana Romero (Naked P.A. Lover), Joe Franklin (Himself)

THE SUBURBANS (**TriStar**) Producers, Michael Burns, Brad Krevoy, J.J. Abrams, Leanna Creel; Executive Producers, Marc Butan, Tim Foster, George Linardos; Director, Donal Lardner Ward; Screenplay, Donal Lardner Ward, Tony Guma; Photography, Michael Barrett; Music, Robbie Kondor; Designer, Usan Bolles; Editor, Kathryn Himoff; Casting, Sheila

Craig Bierko, Amy Brenneman, Donal Lardner Ward, Tony Guma in *The Suburbans* ©TriStar

Nancy St. Alban, Kevin Causey in *Some Fish Can Fly* ©Artistic License

Jaffe, Georgianne Walken, Julia Kim; an Ignite Entertainment production in association with Motion Picture Corporation of America; Dolby; Color; Rated R; 90 minutes; Release date: October 29, 1999. CAST: Amy Brenneman (Grace), Donal Lardner Ward (Danny), Tony Guma (Rory), Craig Bierko (Mitch), Will Ferrell (Gil), Jennifer Love Hewitt (Cate), Bridgette Wilson (Lara), Brian Chlebowski (Kenny), Perrey Reeves (Amanda), Willie Garson (Craig/Sponsor), Lisa Gerstein (Leslie Gonzalez), Antonio Fargas (Magee), Robert Loggia (Jules), Jerry Stiller (Speedo Silverberg), Ben Stiller (Jay Rose), Ben Kronen (Priest), Cleo Adell (Square Q Girl), Kurt Loder (MTV Personality), Emily Kuroda (Mrs. Lee Lee), David LaChapelle (Thorlakur), Karl A. D'Amico (MC), Matt Cedano (Tito), Mary Jane Lardner (Amelia), J.J. Abrams (Rock Journalist), Mary Porster (Mrs. Farley), Nikki Dion (Punk Rock Waitress)

SOME FISH CAN FLY (**Artistic License**) Producers, Joseph A. Zock, Miriam Foley; Executive Producer, Erik Henriksen; Director/Screenplay, Robert Kane Pappas; Line Producer, Scott Greenhaw; Photography, Jim Denny; Music, Edward B. Kessel, Marc R. Hoffman; Casting, Alan Greene, Craig Lechner; Dolby; Color; Not rated; 93 minutes; Release date: November 5, 1999. CAST: Nancy St. Alban (Nora), Kevin Causey (Kevin), Rik Nagel (Z), Clarke Bittner (Lyle), Nina Howie (Madeline), John Rowe (Chris), Bridget Barkan (Siobhan), Dorothea Hanrahan (Linda), Garland Hunter (Casting Director), Kirby Mitchell (The Marine), Jack Luceno (Irish Bouncer), Camilla Enders (Jilted Woman), Patty Croft (Aunt), Michael Gargano (Pushy Suitor), Leslie Bell, Maree Kniest (American Women), Jennifer Woodward (Ann), Robert Steffen (Nora's Dancing Partner), Rik Van Hunter (Investor), Andrea Mead (Patron), Stephanie Silverman (Waitress), Nancy Joyce Simmons (Lyle's Wife), Adrianne Martinez (Humping Man), Tiffany Shepis, Heather McKinney (Partiers), Miriam Foley (Kevin's Assistant), Robert Pappas (Narrator), Michael Ann Rowe (Sophisticated Woman), Con Horgan (Make-Out Man), Tom Blackburn (Patty), Susanna Tsyskin (Woman in Irish Bar), James Cunningham, Ciaran O'Reilly, Ciaran Sheehan (Local Irish Guys), H. Nicole Zock (Little Girl at Party), Brian Cole (Editor)

Fat Joe in *Thicker Than Water* ©Palm Pictures

THICKER THAN WATER (**Palm Pictures**) Producers, Darryl Taja, Andrew Shack; Director, Richard Cummings, Jr.; Screenplay, Ernest Nyle Brown; Executive Producer, Mack 10; Photography, Robert Benavides; Designer, Skip Weaver; Co-Executive Producer, Stavros Merjos; Music, QDIII; Editor, Danny Rafic; Casting, Star Entertainment; a Marshmedia production of a Hoo-Bangin'/Priority Film; Dolby; Color; Rated R; 91 minutes; Release date: October 29, 1999. CAST: Mack 10 (DJ), Fat Joe (Lonzo), Ice Cube (Slink), MC Eiht (Lil' Ant), CJ Mac (Gator), Big Pun (Punny), K-Mack (Tyree), Tom'ya Bowden (Leyla), Kidada Jones (Brandy), Krayzie Bone & Flesh 'n' Bone, B-Real, Bad Azz, WC

Adrien Brody, Maura Tierney in *Oxygen* ©Unapix Films, Inc.

OXYGEN (**Unapix Films**) Producers, Jonathan Stern, Richard Shepard, Carol Curb Nemoy, Mike Curb; Executive Producers, Karen J. Lauder, Marcus Ticotin; Director/Screenplay, Richard Shepard; Photography, Sarah Crawley; Designer, Rowena Rowling; Editor, Adam Lichtenstein; Music, Rolfe Kent; Costumes, Barbara Presar; Casting, Laura Rosenthal, Ali Farrell; a Curb Entertainment Intl. Corp. presentation in association with Abandon Pictures, of a Paddy Wagon Prods. production; Dolby; Color; Not Rated; 92 minutes; Release date: November 5, 1999. CAST: Maura Tierney (Madeline Foster), Adrien Brody (Harry), James Naughton (Clarke Hannon), Laila Robins (Frances Hannon), Paul Calderon (Jesse), Olek Krupa (Madeline's Lover), Dylan Baker (Jackson Lantham), Terry Kinney (Tim Kirkman), Frankie Faison (Phil Kline), Slavko Stimac (Jerome Jerzy), Michael Henderson (Handsome), Robert Shepard (Sal the Bartender), Eddie Perez (Scary Guy), Gene Canfield (Joe the Cop), Christopher James Quinn (Chris the Cop), Judy Goldschmidt (Judy the Cop), Bernard McClain (Byron the Cop), Edmond Genest (Sarcastic Dentist), Ernie Blackman (Dentist #2), Ted Neustadt, Bruno Gidello (FBI Agents) (This film premiered on HBO earlier in 1999).

Marvin Nelson (S.W.A.T. Team Member), Eriq F. Prince (Security Officer), Gary Anthony Ramsay (News Anchor #1), Dale Rivera (Security Guard—Bob), Sue Simmons (WNBC Anchor), Adam G. (Cop), LeShay N. Tomlinson (Student)

David Shackelford, Suzanne Mara, John Mykel Morse in *The Hungry Bachelors Club* ©Mama's Boys Prods.

Usher Raymond, Robert Ri'chard, Forest Whitaker in *Light It Up* ©Twentieth Century Fox

LIGHT IT UP (**20th Century Fox**) Producer, Tracey E. Edmonds; Executive Producer, Kenneth "Babyface" Edmonds; Director/Screenplay, Craig Bolotin; Photography Elliot Davis; Designer, Lawrence G. Paull; Editor, Wendy Greene Bricmont; Co-Executive Producer, David Starke; Costumes, Salvador Perez; Music, Harry Gregson-Williams; Casting, Robi Reed—Humes; a Fox 2000 Pictures presentation of an Edmonds Entertainment production; Dolby; Deluxe color; Rated R; 99 minutes; Release date: November 10, 1999. CAST: Usher Raymond (Lester Dewitt), Forest Whitaker (Officer Dante Jackson), Rosario Dawson (Stephanie Williams), Robert Ri'chard (Zacharias "Ziggy" Malone), Judd Nelson (Ken Knowles), Fredro Starr (Rodney J. Templeton), Sara Gilbert (Lynn Sabitini), Clifton Collins, Jr. (Robert "Rivers" Tremont), Glynn Turman (Principal Armstrong), Vic Polizos (Capt. Monroe), Vanessa L. Williams (Audrey McDonald), Gaddiel Otero (Arturo Orosco), Frank Dominelli (Sgt. Tortino), Reggie Theus, Jennifer Say Gan (Intel. Officers), Kevin Morrow (Boy—Gangbanger), Kevin Robert Kelly (O'Connor—Security Guard), LaTaunya Bounds (Bridget), Eric Hubbard, Melissa Gonzalez (Girls in Bathroom), Patrick Nugent (Police Officer Kelly), Sharif Atkins (Gunman), Stephen R. Key (Rookie Cop), Eric Avilis (Vernon), Shawn Isom (Straggler #1), Deborah J. Crable (WPIX Anchor), Amy Landecker (Reporter #2), Rengin Altay, Sam Samuelson (NY Post Reporters), Rhomeyn Johnson (Spotter—S.W.A.T.), Llou Johnson (Radio DJ), Daren Flam (Cop Shooting at Kids), Rick Johnson (Paul Miller—Sniper #1), Erick Garcia (Armondo), Olumiji Aina Olawumi (Student Council Secretary), Dan De Casual (Mr. Miller), Serena Altschul (Herself), Liza Cruzat (MTV Employee), Sabrina Dames Crutchfield (BET Reporter), Charles Brougham (Team Leader), Eddie Fernandez (Tactical Cop #2—Shooter), Donna Hanover (Fox News Anchor), Tara Hickey (Secretary), Darlene Komar (Principal Armstrong's Secretary), Velma Austin Massey (Lester's Mom), Robert Minor (Lester's Dad),

THE HUNGRY BACHELORS CLUB (**Mama's Boys Productions**) Producers, Dan Gifford, Amy Sommer Gifford; Executive Producer, Kimberly Becker; Director, Gregory Ruzzin; Screenplay, Fred Dresch, Ron Ratliff; Based on the book by Lynn Scott Myers; Photography, Robert Smith; Supervising Editors, Stephen Myers, Andrew Frank; Music, Larry Frank; a Taggart Transcontinental and Managed Passion Films presentation; Color; Rated PG-13; 93 minutes; Release date: November 12, 1999. CAST: Candice Azzara (Hannibal Youngblood), Michael Des Barres (Harold Spinner), Jorja Fox (Delmar Youngblood), Katherine Kendall (Missy Bainbridge), Suzanne Mara (Hortense), Peter Murnik (Jethro Youngblood), Bill Nunn (Moses Grady), Paul Provenza (Stanley Diggers), David Shackelford (Marlon), W. Morgan Sheppard (Mr. Ringold), Wendelin Harston (Sofia), Allorah Creevay (Betty Spinner), Rachel Bard (Mrs. Bainbridge), Leigh Ann Post (Dr. Woo), John Mykel Morse (Baron), Brian Morse (Habeeb), Dan Gifford (Dr. Berry), Ingrid Lambert Shea (Dolly), Christin Simon (Amy), Ben Fuhrman (Policeman), Heidi Morrow (Waitress), Erik Tieze (Attendant), Troy Joe Vincent, John Scott Clough (Men)

Mos Def, John Livingston. Miguel Ferrer in *Where's Marlowe?* ©Paramount Classics

WHERE'S MARLOWE? (**Paramount Classics**) Producer, Clayton Townsend; Executive Producers, Aaron Lipstadt, John Mankiewicz, Daniel Pyne; Director, Daniel Pyne; Screenplay, Daniel Pyne, John Mankiewicz; Photography, Greg Gardiner; Designer, Garreth Stover; Costumes, Mary Zophres; Music, Michael Convertino; Casting, Rick Pagano; a Western Sandblast Project; Dolby; Color/Black and white; Rated R; 99 minutes; Release date: November 12, 1999. CAST: Miguel Ferrer (Joe Boone), Mos Def (Wilton Crawley), John Livingston (A.J. Edison), Allison Dean (Angela), John Slattery (Murphy), Elizabeth Schofield (Monica Collins), Barbara Howard (Emma Huffington), Clayton Rohner (Beep Collins), Kirk Baltz (Rivers), Miguel Sandoval (Skip Pfeiffer), Brent Jennings (Funeral Director), Bill McKinney (Uncle Bill), Heather McComb (Trophy Wife), Wendy Crewson (Dr. Ninki Bregman), Joyce Guy (Wilt's Mom), Danny Ferrington (Ticket Taker), Brent Roam (Angry Man), Eyde Belasco (Art Woman), Miranda Gibson (Art Woman's Friend), Don Keith Opper (Composer), John Lavachiellei (Thoughtful Guy), Aaron Lipstadt (Festival Director), John Mankiewicz (Refreshment Man), Patrick Egan (A.J.'s Dad), Lisa Jane Persky (Jenny), Nicki Micheaux (Caroline), Kamala Dawson (Penny), Wendy Benson (Heather), Sarabeth Tucek (Rikki), Olivia Rosewood (Stacy/Fawn), Wilhelm (Wally), John Del Regno (Water Plant Worker), David Newsom (Jake Pierson), Maury Ginsberg (Surly Cop), David Vegh (Vouching Cop), Erich Anderson (Detective Simmons), Bok Yun Chon (Detective Hsu), John Hawkes (Earl), Julia Margaret Kruis (Beautiful Woman), David Richard (Lucky Man), Ken Jenkins (Linguist), Elizabeth Ruscio, Matt Roth (Clients), Kate Goehring (Maid), Connie Sawyer (Skip's Mom), Adam Setliff (EMT)

A FORCE MORE POWERFUL (**Santa Monica Pictures**) Producers, Steve York, Peter Ackerman; Executive Producers, Dalton Delan, Jack DuVall; Director/Screenplay, Steve York; Photography, Giulio Biccari, Peter Pearce, Dilip Varma; Editors, Joseph Wiedenmayer, Anny Lowery Meza; Music, John D. Keltonic; Narrator, Ben Kingsley; a Peter Ackerman-Steve York production; Dolby; Color; Not rated; 110 minutes; Release date: November 12, 1999. Documentary on nonviolent political movements of the 20th Century, featuring Prof. Devavrat Pathak, Alyque Padamsee, Rev. James Lawson, John Lewis, Diane Nash, Mikhuseli Jack, Prof. Janet Cherry, Tango Lamani.

HOME PAGE (**Copacetic Pictures**) Producers, Doug Block, Jane Weiner, Esther Robinson; Director/Photography, Doug Block; Screenplay, Doug Block, Deborah Rosenberg; Editor, Deborah Rosenberg; Music, Elephant Ears; Associate Producer, Christine Courtney; a co-presentation of Cinemax/ZDF-Arte; Color; Not rated; 99 minutes; Release date: November 19, 1999. Documentary on internet guru Justin Hall and various other cyberstars, featuring Lucy Block, Doug Block, Patrick Farley, Julie Petersen, Jim Petersen, Howard Rheingold, Judi Rose, John Seabrook, Marjorie Silver, Josh Silver, Carl Steadman, J. Carew Kraft.

2 BY 4 (**Strand**) Producers, John Hall, Ginny Biddle; Executive Producer, Darren Davy; Director, Jimmy Smallhorne; Screenplay, Jimmy Smallhorne, Terrence McGoff, Fergus Tighe; Photography, Declan Quinn; Designer, Hazel Mailloux; Costumes, Ivan Ingerman; Editors, Laure Sullivan, Scott Balcerek; Music, HuncaMunca Music Productions Ltd.; a Red Horse Films presentation; Color; Not rated; 80 minutes; Release date: November 26, 1999. CAST: Jimmy Smallhorne (Johnny Maher), Chris O'Neill (Uncle Trump), Bradley Fitts (Christian), Joe Holyoake (Joe), Terrence McGoff (Billy), Michael Liebmann (Eddie), Ronan Carr (Brains), Leo Hamill (Paddy), Seamus McDonagh (Conor), Kimberly Topper (Maria), Conor Foran (Paul), James Hanrahan (Taigh), Marian Quinn (Bibi)

BRAKHAGE (**Zeitgeist**) Producer/Editor, Alexa Frances-Shaw; Executive Producer, Ronn Mann; Director/Screenplay, Jim Shedden; Photography, Gerald Packer, Alexa-Frances Shaw; Music, James Tenney; a Sphinx Prods./Alexa Frances-Shaw production in association with Bravo!; Color/Black and white; Not rated; 73 minutes; Release date: December 1, 1999. Documentary on avant garde, experimental filmmaker Stan Brakhage.

Martin Donovan, Daphna Kastner in *Spanish Fly* ©Avalanche

SPANISH FLY (**Avalanche**) Producer, Juan Alexander; Director/Screenplay, Daphna Kastner; Photography, Arnaldo Catinari; Editor, Caroline Biggerstaff; Music, Mario de Benito; Designer, Alain Bainee; a Juan Alexander production in association with Portman Productions; Dolby; Color; Rated R; 91 minutes; Release date: December 1, 1999. CAST: Daphna Kastner (Zoe), Martin Donovan (Carl Livingston), Danny Huston (John), Toni Canto (Antonio Molina), Marianne Sagebrecht (Rosa), Antonio Castro (Julio), Maria de Medeiros (Rossy), Vernon Dobtcheff (Prof. Brittel), Cat Villiers (Julia), Mary McDonnell (Voice of Zoe's Mother), Felipe Velez (Taxi Driver), Chantal Rios (French Girl), Yoima, Giannina Facio (Antonio's Dates), Pablo Scola, Nieves De Medina (Bathroom Couples), Rebecca Broussard, Kim Manning, Wendell Calton (American Women), Andres Sanchez (Bullfighter), Jose Luis Mosquera (Transvestite), Juan Gonzales Gomez (Police Man), Hans Schiff (Barking Nugget), Richard Horowitz (Coyote), Daniel Green (Lancelot), Alejandro Van Rooy (Perceval), Mario Nerlich (Gregor from Hamburg), Fernando Trueba (Anthropologist), Ricardo Amador (Gypsy Boy), Alicia Agut (Julio's Mother), Maria Jurado (Zoe's Young Mother), Christian Molina (Zoe's Young Father)

Jimmy Smallhorne in *2 By 4* ©Strand Releasing

Angelina Jolie in *Hell's Kitchen* ©Cowboy Booking

John Wallowitch, Bertram Ross in *Wallowitch & Ross: This Moment*
©First Run Features

HELL'S KITCHEN (Cowboy Booking) Producers, Tony Cinciripini, Valarie Bienas, Randy Gardner; Executive Producer, Constantine Baris; Director/Screenplay, Tony Cinciripini; Photography, Michael Spiller, Derek Wiesehahn; Editor, Steve Silkensen; Music, Joseph Arthur, Mekhi Phifer; Casting, Meredith Jacobson Marciano; a Thomas DiGaetrano presentation; Dolby; Foto-Kem color; Rated R; 100 minutes; Release date: December 3, 1999. CAST: Rosanna Arquette (Liz McNeary), William Forsythe (Lou), Angelina Jolie (Gloria McNeary), Mekhi Phifer (Johnny Miller), Johnny Whitworth (Patty), Stephen Payne (Boyle), Jade Yorker (Ricky), Mike Nicolosi (Sean), Ryan Slater (Hayden), Sharif Rashid (Stevey), Martin Shakar (Warden), Ricky Tyberg (Jingo), Al Cayne (Sly), Stephon Fuller (Spike), Dan Musico (Hines), Don Wallace (Bulldozer), Larry Weiss, Heidi Coughlin (Bar Patrons), Thomas Patti ("BJ"), James Voight (Boyle's Bartender), Vito Antuofermo (Boyle's Thug), Paul Olden (Bulldozer Fight Announcer), Kenny McCabe (Bulldozer Referee), Antone Pagan (Drug Dealer), Golden Brooks (Gold), Bob Papa, Sal Marchiano (Hines Fight Announcers), Vinnie Ferguson (Hines Referee), Jack Lotz (Johnny's Corner Man), Rhoda Phifer (Johnny's Mother's Voice), Joseph Arthur (Musician), Matthew Bienas (Rasta Man)

LOVE GOD (Good Machine) Producer, Anthony Bregman; Director/Screenplay, Frank Grow; Photography, Terry Stacey; Editor, David Frankel; Music, Stuart Gray; Designer, Clay Brown; a Ted Hope and James Schamus presentation in association with Only Hearts and Chrystal Pictures; Color; Not rated; 95 minutes; Release date: December 3, 1999. CAST: Will Keenan (Larue), Shannon Burkett (Helen), Kymberli Ghee (Kathleen/Kali), Kerri Kenney (Darla), Michael Laurence (Victor), Dale Soules (Connie), Yukio Yamamoto (Dr. Noguchi)

CHERRY (Showcase Entertainment) Producers/Directors, Joseph Pierson, Jon Glascoe; Screenplay, Terry Reed; Photography, Phil Abraham; Designer, Sherri Adler; Editor, Susan Graef; Music, Joel Goodman; Costumes, Mary Ann McAlpin; a Cypress Films production; Color; Not Rated; 90 minutes; Release date: December 10, 1999. CAST: Shalom Harlow (Leila Sweet), Jake Weber (Dr. Beverly Kirk), David McCallum (Mammy), Gil Rogers (Uncle Ernest), Laurel Holloman (Evy Sweet), Isaach de Bankolé (Menu Man), Donovan Leitch (Eddie), Aleksa Palladino (Darcy), Heather Matarazzo (Dottie), Tim Bohn (Donald), Johann Carlo (Nurse), Jack Gilpin (Preacher), Matt Servitto (Customer), Caleb Archer (Jack), Kelly Singer (Red), John Dapolito (Bartender), John Richardson Hartmann, Robert Capelli Jr., Erik Jensen, Heath Jacob Baldwin, Mark Schulte (Men), Drenda Spohnholtz (Dog Woman), Jim Grollman (Man at Window), Francesca Di Mauro (Yumi Katsura Clerk), Jan Austell (Donald's Father), Beth McGuire (Donald's Mother), Joseph Pierson (Leila's Dad), Julie Robbins (Leila's Mom), Phebe Pierson (Little Leila), Helen Pierson (Little Evy), Io Tillet Wright (Timmy), Bernie Friedman (Drunk Guy), Marilyn (Paxil)

WALLOWITCH & ROSS: THIS MOMENT (First Run Features) Producer, Roberta Morris-Purdee; Executive Producer, Nathan Purdee; Director, Richard Morris; Co-Producer, Sue Gandy; Editors, Marsha Moore, Richard Morris; Music, John Wallowitch; Photography, Don Lenzer; a Karmic Release Ltd. production; Color; Not rated; 77 minutes; Release date: December 10, 1999. Documentary on cabaret performers John Wallowitch and Bertram Ross.

JEROME (Phaedra) Producers/Directors/Screenplay/Editors, Thomas Johnston, David Elton, Eric Tignini; Executive Producer, David Spade; Photography, Gina DeGirolamo; Designer, Linette Shorr; a JET Film Co. production; Color; Not rated; 91 minutes; Release date: December 10, 1999. CAST: Drew Pillsbury (Wade Hampton), Wendie Malick (Jane), Scott McKenna (Cal), Beth Kennedy (Pamela Hampton), James Keenley (Paul Hampton), Paul Marusich (Lonnie Dodson), Mike Traylor (Wingate Jones), Wes Norton (Hard Man in Bar), Linda Rae Jurgens (Waitress in Diner), Mark DeMichele (Cook in Diner), Richard Feld (Trucker in Diner), Jeff Haley (Bill Remus), Jay Holdeman (Sheriff Earl Combs)

Shalom Harlow, Jake Weber in *Cherry* ©Showcase Entertainment

PROMISING NEW ACTORS OF 1999

Ben Foster
(*Liberty Heights*)

Katie Holmes
(*Go, Teaching Mrs. Tingle*)

Samantha Morton
(*Dreaming of Joseph Lees, Sweet and Lowdown*)

Chris Klein
(*American Pie, Election*)

Frances O'Connor
(*A Little Bit of Soul, Mansfield Park*)

Haley Joel Osment
(*The Sixth Sense*)

Vicellous Reon Shannon
(*The Hurricane*)

Julia Stiles
(*10 Things I Hate About You*)

Mena Suvari
(*American Beauty, American Pie*)

Ben Silverstone
(*Get Real*)

Chris Stafford
(*Edge of Seventeen*)

Hilary Swank
(*Boys Don't Cry*)

TOP BOX OFFICE FILMS OF 1999

1. Star Wars Episode 1:
   The Phantom Menace (20th/May) $431,100,000
2. The Sixth Sense (BV/Aug) $293,450,000
3. Toy Story 2 (BV/Nov) $244,420,000
4. Austin Powers: The Spy
   Who Shagged Me (NLC/Jun) $206,000,000
5. The Matrix (WB/Mar) $171,420,000
6. Tarzan (BV/Jun) $170,610,000
7. Big Daddy (Col/Jun) $162,860,000
8. The Mummy (Univ/May) $155,280,000
9. Runaway Bride(Par-BV/Jul) $152,260,000
10. Stuart Little (Col/Dec) $140,120,000

Stuart Little in *Stuart Little* ©Columbia Pictures Industires, Inc.

Liam Neeson, Jake Lloyd, Ewan McGregor
in *The Phantom Menace* ©Lucasfilm Ltd.

11. The Blair Witch Project (Artisan/Jul) $138,620,000
12. The Green Mile(WB/Dec) $136,690,000
13. American Beauty (DW/Sep) $130,100,000
14. The World is Not Enough (MGM/Nov) $126,850,000
15. Double Jeopardy (Par/Sep) $116,750,000
16. Notting Hill (Univ/May) $115,930,000
17. Wild Wild West(WB/Jun) $113,660,000
18. Analyze This (WB/Mar) $106,840,000
19. The General's Daughter (Par/Jun) $102,430,000
20. American Pie (Univ/Jul) $101,210,000
21. Sleepy Hollow (Par/Nov) $100,920,000
22. Inspector Gadget (BV/Jul)...............................$97,300,000
23. The Haunting (DW/Jul) $89,770,000
24. Entrapment (20th/Apr)......................................$87,580,000
25. Pokémon: The First Movie (WB/Nov) $85,630,000
26. The Talented Mr. Ripley (Par-Mir/Dec) $81,260,000
27. Payback (Par/Feb) $80,980,000
28. Any Given Sunday (WB/Dec).............................$75,500,000
29. Deep Blue Sea (WB/Jul) $73,230,000
30. Galaxy Quest (DW/Dec) $70,990,000

31. The Thomas Crown Affair (MGM/Aug) $69,240,000
32. Blue Streak (Col/Sep) $68,000,000
33. End of Days (Univ/Nov)..................................$66,900,000
34. Bowfinger (Univ/Aug) $66,460,000
35. The Bone Collector (Univ-Col/Nov) $66,520,000
36. Deuce Bigalow: Male Gigolo (BV/Dec) $65,400,000
37. Life (Univ/Apr) $64,100,000
38. She's All That (Mir/Jan) $63,370,000
39. Three Kings (WB/Oct) $60,520,000
40. Bicentennial Man (BV/Dec) $58,100,000

Matt Damon, Jude Law, Philip Seymour Hoffman
in *The Talented Mr. Ripley* ©Paramount Pictures/Miramax Film Corp.

41. The Cider House Rules (Mir/Dec) $57,430,000
42. Eyes Wide Shut (WB/Jul) $55,600,000
43. Never Been Kissed (20th/Apr) $55,470,000
44. Varsity Blues (Par/Jan) $52,860,000
45. Message in a Bottle (WB/Feb) $52,830,000
46. South Park: Bigger... (Par-WB/Jun) $52,100,000
47. Forces of Nature (DW/Mar) $51,750,000
48. The Hurricane (Univ/Dec)................................$50,670,000
49. Stigmata (MGM/Sep) $49,970,000
50. House on Haunted Hill (WB/Oct).....................$40,850,000

51. Anna and the King (20th/Dec) $39,100,000
52. 10 Things I Hate About You (BV/Mar) $38,100,000
53. Cruel Intentions (Col/Mar)............................$37,640,000
54. Fight Club (20th/Oct)....................................$36,830,000
55. My Favorite Martian (BV/Feb) $36,810,000
56. 8MM (Col/Feb) $36,370,000
57. For Love of the Game (Univ/Sep) $35,190,000
58. Man on the Moon (Univ/Dec) $34,490,000
59. Instinct (BV/Jun) $34,100,000
60. The Best Man (Univ/Oct)...............................$34,000,000
61. Mickey Blue Eyes (WB/Aug) $33,830,000
62. The 13th Warrior (BV/Aug)............................$32,650,000
63. October Sky (Univ/Feb).................................$32,600,000
64. Lake Placid (20th/Jul) $31,610,000
65. Random Hearts(Col/Oct) $30,990,000

Hugh Grant, Jeanne Tripplehorn in *Mickey Blue Eyes* ©CR Films, LLC

Tom Cruise in *Eyes Wide Shut* ©Warner Bros.

66. Superstar (Par/Oct)......................................$30,600,000
67. Dogma (Lions/Nov) $30,420,000
68. Mystery Men (Univ/Aug) $29,540,000
69. The Insider (BV/Nov) $29,100,000
70. Girl, Interrupted (Col/Dec) $28,880,000
71. The Out-of-Towners (Par/Apr) $28,440,000
72. The Other Sister (BV/Feb).............................$27,580,000
73. The Story of Us (Univ/Oct) $27,110,000
74. Baby Geniuses (Col/Mar) $27,100,000
75. Blast From the Past (NLC/Feb) $26,520,000
76. The Wood (Par/Jul) $24,740,000
77. Arlington Road (SG/Jul) $24,400,000
78. The Iron Giant (WB/Aug) $23,120,000
79. Being John Malkovich (USA/Oct) $22,740,000
80. Edtv (Univ/Mar)..$22,390,000

81. At First Sight (MGM/Jan) $22,320,000
82. Magnolia (NLC/Dec) $22,210,000
83. The Bachelor (NLC/Nov) $21,590,000
84. Stir of Echoes (Artisan/Sep) $21,100,000
85. Doug's 1st Movie (BV/Mar) $19,350,000
86. Summer of Sam (BV/Jul) $19,280,000
87. Anywhere But Here (20th/Nov)............................$18,520,000
88. An Ideal Husband (Mir/Jun) $18,140,000
89. Drive Me Crazy (20th/Oct) $17,760,000
90. Bringing Out the Dead (Par-BV/Oct) $16,800,000
91. Go (Col/Mar) $16,720,000
92. True Crime (WB/Mar) $16,610,000
93. The Rage: Carrie 2 (MGM/Mar) $16,550,000
94. Muppets from Space (Col/Jul)............................$16,300,000
95. A Midsummer Night's Dream (FoxS/May) $15,980,000

William H. Macy in *Magnolia* ©New Line

96. The Corruptor (NLC/Mar) $15,100,000
97. Election (Par/Apr)..$14,910,000
98. Music of the Heart (Mir/Oct) $14,700,000
99. Tea With Mussolini (MGM/May).......................$14,180,000
100. The Messenger:
        The Story of Joan of Arc (Col/Nov) $14,110,000

ACADEMY AWARDS FOR 1999

PRESENTED SUNDAY, MARCH 26, 2000

ACADEMY AWARD WINNER FOR BEST PICTURE OF 1999

Kevin Spacey, Mena Suvari

Annette Bening

Kevin Spacey

AMERICAN BEAUTY

(**DREAMWORKS**) Producers, Bruce Cohen, Dan Jinks; Director, Sam Mendes; Screenplay, Alan Ball; Photography, Conrad L. Hall; Designer, Naomi Shohan; Editors, Tariq Anwar, Chris Greenbury; Music, Thomas Newman; Co-Producers, Stan Wlodkowski, Alan Ball; Costumes, Julie Weiss; Casting, Debra Zane; a Jinks/Cohen Company production; Dolby; Technicolor; Rated R; 118 minutes; Release date: September 15, 1999

CAST

Lester Burnham	Kevin Spacey
Carolyn Burnham	Annette Bening
Jane Burnham	Thora Birch
Ricky Fitts	Wes Bentley
Angela Hayes	Mena Suvari
Buddy Kane	Peter Gallagher
Barbara Fitts	Allison Janney
Colonel Fitts	Chris Cooper
Jim #1	Scott Bakula
Jim #2	Sam Robards
Brad	Barry Del Sherman
Sale House Woman #1	Ara Celi
Sale House Man #1	John Cho
Sale House Man #2	Fort Atkinson
Sale House Woman #2	Sue Casey
Sale House Man #3	Kent Faulcon
Sale House Women #4	Brenda Wehle, Lisa Cloud
Teenage Girls	Heather Joy Sher, Chelsea Hertford
Christy Kane	Amber Smith
Catering Boss	Joel McCrary
Mr. Smiley's Counter Girl (Janine)	Marissa Jaret Winokur
Mr. Smiley's Manager	Dennis Anderson
Firing Range Attendant	Matthew Kimbrough
Young Jane	Erin Cathryn Strubbe

and Alison Faulk, Krista Goodsitt, Lily Houtkin, Carolina Lancaster, Romana Leah, Chekesa Van Putten, Emily Zachary, Nancy Anderson, Reshma Gajjar, Stephanie Rizzo (Spartanette)

Middle-aged suburbanite Lester Burnham begins to question the empti-ness of his seemingly perfect life, becoming increasingly fed-up with his unhappy marriage and his alienated daughter.

Academy Award winner for Best Picture, Actor (Kevin Spacey), Director, Original Screenplay, and Cinematography. This film received additional nominations for actress (Annette Bening), editing, and original score.

©DreamWorks LLC

Kevin Spacey, Annette Bening

Kevin Spacey, Thora Birch

Wes Bentley, Thora Birch, Mena Suvari

Chris Cooper

Peter Gallagher

Thora Birch, Mena Suvari

KEVIN SPACEY

in *American Beauty* ©DreamWorks
ACADEMY AWARD FOR BEST ACTOR OF 1999

HILARY SWANK

in *Boys Don't Cry* ©Fox Searchlight Films
ACADEMY AWARD FOR BEST ACTRESS   OF 1999

MICHAEL CAINE

in *The Cider House Rules* ©Miramax
ACADEMY AWARD FOR BEST SUPPORTING ACTOR OF 1999

ANGELINA JOLIE

in *Girl, Interrupted* ©Columbia Pictures Industries, Inc.
ACADEMY AWARD FOR BEST SUPPORTING ACTRESS OF 1999

ACADEMY AWARD NOMINEES FOR BEST ACTOR

Russell Crowe in *The Insider*

Richard Farnsworth in *The Straight Story*

Sean Penn in *Sweet and Lowdown*

Denzel Washington in *The Hurricane*

ACADEMY AWARD NOMINEES FOR BEST ACTRESS

Annette Bening in *American Beauty*

Janet McTeer in *Tumbleweeds*

Julianne Moore in *The End of the Affair*

Meryl Streep in *Music of the Heart*

ACADEMY AWARD NOMINEES FOR BEST SUPPORTING ACTOR

Tom Cruise in *Magnolia*

Michael Clarke Duncan in *The Green Mile*

Jude Law in *The Talented Mr. Ripley*

Haley Joel Osment in *The Sixth Sense*

ACADEMY AWARD NOMINEES FOR BEST SUPPORTING ACTRESS

Toni Collette in *The Sixth Sense*

Catherine Keener in *Being John Malkovich*

Samantha Morton in *Sweet and Lowdown*

Chloë Sevigny in *Boys Don't Cry*

Antonia San Juan, Cecilia Roth

Marisa Paredes

ALL ABOUT MY MOTHER

(**SONY PICTURES CLASSICS**) Executive Producer, Agustín Almodóvar; Director/Screenplay, Pedro Almodóvar; Photography, Affonso Beato; Art Director, Antxón Gómez; Music, Alberto Iglesias; Eidtor, José Salcedo; Costumes, Jose Maria de Cossio, Sabine Daigeler; Director of Production, Esther García; an Agustin Almodóvar & Claude Berri presentation of an El Deseo S.A./Renn Productions/France 2 Cinema co-production; Spanish-French; Dolby; Color; Rated R; 99 minutes; American release date: November 19, 1999

CAST

Manuela ....Cecilia Roth
Huma Rojo ....Marisa Paredes
Sister Rosa ....Penélope Cruz
Agrado ....Antonia San Juan
Nina ....Candela Peña
Rosa's Mother ....Rosa María Sardá
Esteban ....Eloy Azorín
Lola, La Pionera ....Toni Cantó
and Fernando Fernán Gómez, Fernando Guillén, Carlos Lozano, Manuel Morón, Jose Luis Torrijo, Juan José Otegui, Carmen Balague, Malena Gutierrez, Yael Barnatán, Carmen Fortuny, Patxi Freytez, Juan Márquez, Michel Ruben, Daniel Lanchas, Rosa Manaut, Carlos Ga Cambero, Paz Sufrategui, Lola Garcia, Lluis Pascual

Following her beloved son's accidental death, Manuela vows to journey to Barcelona to find the boy's father, a transvestite who never knew of the boy's existence. There she meets a diverse group of women, all of whom are confronting emotional burdens of their own.

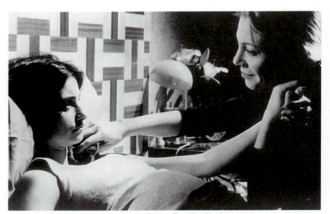

Penélope Cruz, Cecilia Roth

Penélope Cruz

ACADEMY AWARD WINNER FOR BEST FOREIGN LANGUAGE FILM

Cecilia Roth, Maria Sardá, Penélope Cruz

Cecilia Roth, Eloy Azorín

PRIVATE CONFESSIONS

(CASTLE HILL/FIRST RUN) Producer, Ingrid Dahlberg; Executive Producer, Kaj Larsen; Director, Liv Ullmann; Screenplay, Ingmar Bergman; Photography, Sven Nykvist; Designer, Mette Möller; Editor, Michal Leszczylowski; Costumes, Inger Pehrsson; a Sveriges Television Drama production, in association with NRK, DR, YLE-2, RUV-TV, and the Nordic TV Co-production Fund; Swedish, 1997; Dolby; Swelab color; Not rated; 125 minutes; American release date: January 6, 1999

CAST

Anna Bergman...Pernilla August
Henrik Bergman ....Samuel Fröler
Uncle Jacob...Max von Sydow
Maria ....Kristina Adolphson
Tomas Egerman ....Thomas Hanzon
Marta Gärdsjö..Gunnel Fred
The Bishop Agrell...Hans Alfredsson

Anna, a mother of three, who has been unfaithful to her clergyman husband, seeks the spiritual advice of a priest to help her cope with her collapsing life.

©Castle Hill Prods. Inc./First Run Features

Max von Sydow, Pernilla August

DR. AKAGI

(KINO) Producers, Hisa Ino, Koji Matsuda; Director, Shohei Imamura; Screenplay, Shohei Imamura, Daisuke Tengan; Based on the book *Doctor Liver* by Ango Sakaguchi; Photography, Shigeru Komatsubara; Art Director, Hisao Inagaki; Editor, Hajime Okayasu; Music, Yosuke Yamashita; an Imamura Production from Toei Co. Ltd./ Tohoku Shinsha Inc. Kadokawa Shoten/Comme des Cinemas/Catherine Dussart Productions/Le Studio Canal+; Japanese, 1998; Dolby; Color; Not rated; 128 minutes; American release date: January 15, 1999

CAST

Dr. Akagi ....Akira Emoto
Sonoko ....Kumiko Aso
Umemoto ....Jyuro Kara
Toriumi ....Masanori Sera
Piet ....Jacques Gamblin
Tomiko ....Keiko Matsuzaka
Gin...Misa Shimizu
Sankichi ....Yukiya Kitamura
Masuyo..Masa Yamada
Nosaka ....Tomoro Taniguchi
Sakashita...Kazuhiko Kanayama
Ikeda ....Masato Ibu
Hakamada..Hatsuo Yamaya

On the eve of the end of World War II, a doctor at a seaside village near Hiroshima attempts to find a cure for the hepatitis he believes is responsible for the much of the illness sweeping his community.

Akira Emoto, Kumiko Aso

MY NAME IS JOE

(**ARTISAN**) Producer, Rebecca O'Brien; Executive Producer, Ulrich Felsberg; Director, Ken Loach; Screenplay, Paul Laverty; Photography, Barry Ackroyd; Designer, Martin Johnson; Costumes, Rhona Russell; Music, George Fenton; Editor, Jonathan Morris; Casting, Gillian Berrie, Steven Mochrie; a Parallax Pictures/Road Movies Vierte Productions presentation, with the support of the Scottish Arts Council Lottery Fund, the Glasgow Film Fund and Filmstiftung Nordrhein-Westfalen, in collaboration with Channel Four Films, WDR/Arte/La Sept Cinema, ARD/DEGETO Film and BIM Distribuzione, Diaphana Distribution and Tornasol/Alta Films; British-German, 1998; Dolby; Color; Rated R; 105 minutes; American release date: January 22, 1999

Peter Mullan

CAST

Joe Kavanagh	Peter Mullan
Sarah Downey	Louise Goodall
Shanks	Gary Lewis
Maggie	Lorraine McIntosh
Liam	David McKay
Sabine	Anne-Marie Kennedy
Scott	Scott Hannah
Hooligan	David Peacock
Scrag	Gordon McMurray
Perfume	James McHendry
Zulu	Paul Clark
Mojo	Stephen McCole
Robbo	Simon Macallum

and Paul Gillan (Davy), Stephen Docherty (Doc), Paul Doonan (Tattie), Cary Carbin (Sepp Maier), David Hayman (McGowan), Martin McCardie (Alf), James McNeish (Shuggy), Kevin Kelly (Jake), Brian Timoney (Scooter), David Hough (Referee), Sandy West (DSS Investigator), John Comerford (DSS Supervisor), Carol Pyper Rafferty (Rhona), Elaine M. Ellis (Second Receptionist), Stewart Ennis (Doctor Boyle), Andy Townsley (Husband), Ann Marie Lafferty (Wife), Bill Murdoch (Postman), Kate Black (Kiosk Attendant), Rab Affleck (Lorry Driver)

Joe Kavanagh, attempting to restart his life after years of excessive drinking, falls in love with Sarah Downey, a health counselor.

Peter Mullan

Louise Goodall, Peter Mullan

237

CHILDREN OF HEAVEN

(MIRAMAX) Executive Producer, Seyed Saeed Seyed-zadeh; Director/Screenplay, Majid Majidi; Photography, Parviz Malek-zadeh; Editor, Hassan Hassan-doost; Art Director/Costumes, Asghar Nezhad Imani; Music, Keivan Jahan-shahi; a Production of the Institute for the Intellectual Development of Children and Young Adults; Iranian, 1997; Color; Rated PG; 88 minutes; American release date: January 22, 1999

CAST

Ali's Father	Amir Naji
Ali	Mir Farrokh Hashemian
Zahra	Bahareh Seddiqi
Roya	Nafiseh Jafar Mohammadi
Ali's Mother	Fereshteh Sarabandi
The Principal	Kamal Mir-karimi
The Coach	Behzad Rafi'i

When a young schoolboy loses the newly-repaired shoes of his younger sister, he comes up with a plan to keep the bad news from their impoverished family.

©Miramax Films

Mir Farrokh Hashemian

Bahareh Seddiqi

Stanislas Merhar

DRY CLEANING

(STRAND) Director, Anne Fontaine; Screenplay, Gilles Taurand, Anne Fontaine; Based on an original idea by Anne Fontaine, Claude Arnaud; Photography, Caroline Champetier; Set Designer, Antoine Platteau; Costumes, Elisabeth Tavernier; a co-production of Franco Espagnol, Cinea-Film Alain Sarde-Maestranza Films with the participation of CNC-Canal+-Region de Franche Comte-Sofinergie 4-Sofigram; French; Dolby; Color; Not rated; 97 minutes; American release date: February 5, 1999

CAST

Nicole Kunstler	Miou-Miou
Jean-Marie Kunstler	Charles Berling
Loic	Stanislas Merhar
Marylin	Mathilde Seigner
Yvette	Nanou Meister
Pierre	Noe Pflieger
Robert	Michel Bompoil
Steve	Christopher King
Bertrand	Gerard Blanc
Madame Bertrand	Betty Petristy

and Bobby Pacha (Patron Rach), Corinne Nejman (Josiane), Therese Gehin (Maryse), Joelle Gregorie (Travesti Banane), Pascal Allio, Caroline Galiani, Thomas Seiler (Dancers)

The routine lives of a married couple who run a dry cleaning shop are stirred up by a brother and sister who perform a provocative strip-tease drag act at a local nightclub.

©Strand Releasing

Isabelle Huppert, Vincent Martinez

Vincent Martinez

Isabelle Huppert

Vincent Martinez, Isabelle Huppert

THE SCHOOL OF FLESH

(**STRATOSPHERE**) a.k.a. *L'École de la Chair*; Producer, Fabienne Vonier; Executive Producer, Fabienne Tsaï; Director, Benoit Jacquot; Screenplay, Jacques Fieschi; Based on the novel by Yukio Mishima; Photography, Caroline Champetier; Designer, Katia Wyszkop; Editor, Luc Barnier; a Fabienne Vonier presentation of a co-production by Orsans Productions/V.M.P./La Sept Cinema/Les Films du Camelia/Artemis Productions/R.T.B.F./Samsa Film; French, 1998; Dolby; Panavision; Color; Rated R; 107 minutes; American release date: February 26, 1999

CAST

Dominique	Isabelle Huppert
Quentin	Vincent Martinez
Chris	Vincent Lindon
Madame Thorpe	Marthe Keller
Soukaz	François Berléand
Dominique's Friend	Danièle Dubroux
Cordier	Bernard Le Coq
Marine	Roxane Mesquida
Louis-Guy	Jean-Claude Daphin
Quentin's Mother	Michelle Goddet
Marcus	Jan-Michell
The Young Plumber	Laurent Jumeaucourt
Robert	Pierre Laroche
The Photographer	Richard Schroeder
Child Boxer	Jonathan Ubrette
The Man at the End	Nicolas Pignon

Dominique, a sophisticated career woman, becomes attracted to Quentin, a handsome young prostitute, and agrees to supply him with living quarters and money.

©Stratus Entertainment LLC

Nick Moran, Dexter Fletcher, Jason Statham, Jason Flemyng

Jason Statham, Dexter Fletcher, Jason Flemyng

LOCK, STOCK AND TWO SMOKING BARRELS

(**GRAMERCY**) Producer, Matthew Vaughn; Executive Producers, Steve Tisch, Peter Morton, Angad Paul, Stephen Marks, Trudie Styler; Director/Screenplay, Guy Ritchie; Line Producer, Ronaldo Vasconellos; Co-Producer, Georgia Masters; Photography, Tim Maurice-Jones; Designers, Iain Andrews, Eve Mavrakis; Costumes, Stephanie Collie; Editor, Niven Howie; Music, David A. Hughes, John Murphy; Casting, Celestia Fox, Guy Ritchie; a PolyGram Filmed Entertainment, Summit Entertainment, The Steve Tisch Company & SKA Films presentation of a Matthew Vaughn production; British, 1998; Dolby; Color; Rated R; 106 minutes; American release date: March 5, 1999

Nick Moran

CAST

Tom	Jason Flemyng
Soap	Dexter Fletcher
Eddie	Nick Moran
Bacon	Jason Statham
Winston	Steven Mackintosh
J	Nicholas Rowe
Charles	Nick Marcq
Willie	Charles Forbes
Big Chris	Vinnie Jones
Barry the Baptist	Lenny McLean
Little Chris	Peter McNicholl
Hatchet Harry	P.H. Moriarty
Dog	Frank Harper
Plank	Steve Sweeney
Paul	Huggy Leaver
Mickey	Ronnie Fox
John	Tony McMahon
Nick the Greek	Stephen Marcus
Rory Breaker	Vas Blackwood
JD	Sting
Dean	Jake Abraham
Traffic Warden	Robert Brydon
Lenny	Stephen Callender-Ferrier
Boxing Gym Bouncer	Steve Collins
Nathan	Elwin "Chopper" David
Tanya	Vera Day
Don	Jimmy Flint
Alan	Alan Ford
Phil	Sydney Golder
Slick	Alex Hall
Doorman	John Houchin
Barfly Jack	Danny John-Jules
Gordon	Bal Jusar
Gary	Victor McGuire
Serg	Mark Mooney
Gloria	Suzy Ratner
Samoan Joe	David "Disco" Reid
Policeman	Graham Stevens
John O'Driscoll	James Tarbuck
Man in Pub	Andy Tiernan
Frazer	Richard Vanstone
Yuppie in Car	Matthew Vaughn

Jason Flemyng, Jason Statham, Nick Moran, Dexter Fletcher

When Eddie finds himself owing $800,000 to gangster Hatchet Harry, he and his three friends come up with a scheme to lift stolen money from a gang of thieves who are plotting to rob some local marijuana sellers.

Vinnie Jones

THE HARMONISTS

(MIRAMAX) a.k.a. *The Comedian Harmonists*; Producers, Hanno Huth, Reinhard Kloos, Danny Krausz; Executive Producer/Director/ Photography, Joseph Vilsmaier; Screenplay, Klaus Richter; Based on an idea by Juergen Buescher; Line Producer, Peter Sterr; Editor, Peter R. Adam; Designer, Rolf Zehetbauer; Costumes, Ute Hofinger; Music, Harald Kloser; a Bavaria Film International and Betafilm presentation; German-Austrian, 1997; Dolby; Super 35 Widescreen; Color; Rated R; 116 minutes; American release date: March 12, 1999

CAST

Robert Biberti ....Ben Becker
Roman Cycowski ....Heino Ferch
Harry Frommermann ....Ulrich Noethen
Erich A. Collin ....Heinrich Schafmeister
Ari Leschnikoff ....Max Tidof
Erwin Bootz ....Kai Wiesinger
Erna Eggstein ....Meret Becker
Mary Cycowski ....Katja Riemann
Ursula Bootz ....Dana Vávrová
Chantal ....Noemi Fischer
Bob's Mother..Trude Ackermann
Young Boy ....Thommi Baake
Lola ....Anna-Kathrin Bleuler
Leila ....Tina Bordihn
and Martin Brambach (Comrade), Bob Brown, John Palmer (NBC Speakers), Liv Tullia, Veronika Neugebauer, Anika Decker (Young Girls), Klaus Nierhoff, Lance Girard (Policemen), Bettina Hirschberg (Woman at Keyboard), Rolf Hoppe (Nazi Officer "Gauleiter"), Suzanne Hoss (Rosa), Günter Larmprecht (Charell), Katy Lindner (Coat Check), Theresa Longoni, Janina Vilsmaier (Jewish Wedding Kids), Lukas Miko (Hans), Gerhard Naujoks (King Hanns's King), Jochen Nickel (Mr. Hagerer), Susi Nicoletti (Mrs. Grünbaum), Michaela Rosen (Madam Ramona), Emanuel Rund (Rabbi), Gérard Samaan (Roman's Father), Otto Sander (Bruno Levy), Jürgen Schomagel (The Reich's Music Programmer), Johannes Silberschneider (Stage Manager), Rudolph Wessely (Mr. Grünbaum), Frank Wieczorek (The Man in the Crowd), Judith Eberle, Margrita Fürnsinn, Melanie Gmeiner, Sabine Linhart, Karola Niederhuber, Stefanie Schwendy, Marianne Tarnowsky (Revue Girls), Giora Feidman (Solo Clarinet), The Pasadena Roof Orchestra

In late 1920s Germany, Harry Frommerman forms a singing group, The Comedian Harmonists, which becomes a great success on the eve of the Nazis' rise to power, a situation that poses a threat to the group's three Jewish members.

©Miramax Films

Rachel Griffiths, Pete Postlethwaite

©Fox Searchlight Pictures

AMONG GIANTS

(FOX SEARCHLIGHT) Producer, Stephen Garrett; Executive Producer, Jana Edelbaum; Co-Executive Producers, David M. Thompson, Jane Barclay, Sharon Harel; Director, Sam Miller; Screenplay, Simon Beaufoy; Line Producer, Joy Spink; Associate Producer, Lou Spain; Photography, Witold Stok; Designer, Luana Hanson; Editors, Elen Pierce Lewis, Paul Green; Costumes, Stephanie Collie; Music, Tim Atack; Casting, Di Carling; a Capitol Films presentation with the participation of British Screen, the Arts Council of England, BBC Films and the Yorkshire Media Production Agency of a Kudos production; British, 1998; Dolby; Rank color; Rated R; 96 minutes; American release date: March 26, 1999

CAST

Ray ....Pete Postlethwaite
Gerry ....Rachel Griffiths
Steve ....James Thornton
Shovel ....Lennie James
Bob ....Andy Serkis
Weasel ....Rob Jarvis
Frank ....Alan Williams
Barmaid..Emma Cunniffe
Derek ....Steve Huison
Lyn ....Sharon Bower
Billy ....David Webber
Steve's Dad ....Alvin Blossom
Ray's Son ....Sam Wilkinson
Ray's Daughter ....Jo Wilkinson

Ray and his team of electrical tower painters are hired to paint miles of pylons along the Yorkshire Moors, a task for which he hires Gerry, an Australian mountain climber with whom Ray falls in love.

Max Tidof, Heinrich Schafmeister, Ulrich Noethen,
Heino Ferch, Ben Becker

Elodie Bouchez, Natacha Régnier

Grégoire Colin, Natacha Régnier

Grégoire Colin, Natacha Régnier

THE DREAMLIFE OF ANGELS

(**SONY PICTURES CLASSICS**) Producer, Francois Marquis; Director, Erick Zonca; Screenplay, Erick Zonca, Roger Bohbot, Virginie Wagon; Photography, Agnés Godard; Designer, Jimmy Vansteenkiste; Costumes, François Clavel; Editor, Yannick Kergoat; Casting, Antoine Carrard; a Les Productions Bagheera, France 2 Cinema and Diaphana presentation with the participation of Centre National de la Cinematographie and Canal+; French, 1998; Dolby; Color; Rated R; 113 minutes; American release date: April 2, 1999

CAST

Isa..Elodie Bouchez
Marie..Natacha Régnier
Chriss...Grégoire Colin
Fredo...Jo Prestia
Charly ....Patrick Mercado
and Francine Massenhave (LaGardienne), Zivko Niklevski (Yugoslav Patron), Murielle Colvez (Shop Boss), Lyazid Ovelhadj (Ticket Vendor), Frédérique Hazard (Marie's Mother), Jean-Michael Lemayeux (Intern), Louise Motte (Sandrine), Rosa Maria, Mireille Bidon (Nurses), Corinne Masiero (Hollywood Girl), Juliette Richevaux (Solène), Stéphanie Delerue (Léa), Christian Cailleret (Monsieur Val), Gérard Beyrand (Foreman).

Elodie Bouchez

Factory worker Marie agrees to let drifter and fellow-employee Isa share her apartment, despite their diametrically opposed personalities.

©Sony Pictures Entertainment, Inc.

FOLLOWING

(ZEITGEIST) Producers, Emma Thomas, Christopher Nolan, Jeremy Theobald; Executive Producer, Peter Broderick; Director/Screenplay/Photography, Christopher Nolan; Designer, Tristan Martin; Editors, Gareth Heal, Christopher Nolan; Music, David Julyan; a Christopher Nolan production; British; Black and white; Not rated; 69 minutes; American release date: April 2, 1999

CAST

The Young Man (Bill)	Jeremy Theobald
Cobb	Alex Haw
The Blonde	Lucy Russell
The Policeman	John Nolan
The Bald Guy	Dick Bradsell
The Homeowner	Gillian El-Kadi
The Waitress	Jennifer Angel
Barman	Nicolas Carlotti
Accountant	Darren Ormandy

and Guy Greenway, Tasso Stevens (Heavies), Tristan Martin (Man at Bar), Rebecca James (Woman at Bar), Paul Mason (Homeowner's Friend), David Bovill (Homeowner's Husband)

Would-be writer Bill begins following people around London under the pretense of gathering material for his writing, until one of the people in question coaxes him into joining him in breaking into strangers' apartments.

©Zeitgeist Films

Jerry Theobald

Jackie Chan

Jackie Chan, Maggie Cheung

TWIN DRAGONS

(DIMENSION) a.k.a. *Seung Lung Wul*; Producer, Teddy Robin; Executive Producer, Ng Sze Yeun; Directors, Tsui Hark, Ringo Lam; Screenplay, Barry Wong, Tsui Hark, Cheung Tung Jo, Wong Yik; Editor, Mak Che Sin; Editorial Consultant, Rod Dean; Music, Michael Wandmacher, Phe Loung; Stunts, Jackie Chan, Yuan Wo Ping, Ching Siu Tung, Tung Wai, Tsui Siu Ming, Lee Kin San; English Post Production, Lloyd Chao; a Distant Horizon and Media Asia Distribution presentation of a film by Hong Kong Director's Guild; Distributed by Miramax; Hong Kong, 1992; Dolby; Technovision; Deluxe color; Rated PG-13; 89 minutes; American release date: April 9, 1999

CAST

Boomer/John Ma	Jackie Chan
Barbara	Maggie Cheung
Tyson	Teddy Robin
Tammy	Nina Li Chi
Hotel Staffer	Anthony Chan
Hotel Manager	Philip Chan
Twins Mother	Sylvia Chang
Boss Wing	Alfred Cheung
Cashier	Jacob Cheung
Orchestra Member	Cheung Tung Jo
Tammy's Father	Chor Yuen

and John Keung (Hotel Security), Ringo Lam (Car Mechanic), Lau Ka Leung (Doctor), Lai Ying Chow (Gang Leader), Jamie Luk (Rocky), Pa Shan (Thug), Ng Sze Yuen (Car Mechanic), John Wu (Priest), Eric Tsang (Man on Phone), Tsui Siu Ming (Car Mechanic), James Wong (Twins Father), Kirk Wong (Crazy Kung), Wong Lung Wai (Thug), David Wu (Waiter)

A pair of twins, one a famous maestro and one a martial arts specialist, find they must swap places when they are mistaken for one another by gangsters. This film was reedited and redubbed from the original 100 minute version.

©Dimension Films

Christian Bale, Emily Watson

Emily Watson

Christian Bale

METROLAND

(**LIONS GATE**) Producer, Andrew Bendel; Director, Philip Saville; Screenplay, Adrian Hodges; Based on the novel by Julian Barnes; Co-Producer, Antoine De Clermont-Tonnerre; Photography, Jean-Francois Robin; Music, Mark Knopfler; Costumes, Jenny Beavan; Editor, Greg Miller; Line Producer, Joy Spink; Casting, Deborah Brown; a Pandora Cinema presentation of a Blue Horizon/Mact/Filmania Production in association with the Arts Council of England with the participation of BBC Films, Canal+, the European Co-Production Fund (UK), Eurimages and Sogepaq; British-French, 1998; Dolby; Color; Not rated; 105 minutes; American release date: April 9, 1999

CAST

Chris	Christian Bale
Marion	Emily Watson
Toni	Lee Ross
Annick	Elsa Zylberstei
Henri	Rufus
Retired Commuter	John Wood
Joanna	Amanda Ryan
Dave	Jonathan Aris
Mickey	Ifan Meredith
Middle-Aged Commuter	Bill Thomas
Amy	Daisy & Bethan Fairban
Jacques	Boris Terrel
Punk Girl	Lucy Speed

and Del Bartle, Gareth Batson, Danny DeMatos, Braid Waisshan (The Subverts)

A visit from his old friend Toni causes Chris to think back on his wilder Bohemian days in Paris and wonder if perhaps he has settled for conformity as a married commuter.

©Lions Gate Films

Emily Watson, Christian Bale

Kate Winslet, Bella Rizza, Carrie Mullan

Carrie Mullan, Kate Winslet

HIDEOUS KINKY

(**STRATOSPHERE**) Producer, Ann Scott; Executive Producers, Simon Relph, Mark Shivas; Director, Gillies MacKinnon; Screenplay, Billy MacKinnon; Based on the novel by Esther Freud; Photography, John de Borman; Designers, Louise Marzaroli, Pierre Compertz; Editor, Pia Di Ciaula; Costumes, Kate Carin; Music, John Keane; Casting, Susie Figgis; a presentation of the Film Consortium and BBC Films, of a Greenpoint Films (UK)/L Films, AMLF (France) production; British-French; Dolby; CinemaScope; Color; Rated R; 99 minutes; American release date: April 16, 1999

CAST

Julia	Kate Winslet
Bilal	Saïd Taghmaoui
Bea	Bella Riza
Lucy	Carrie Mullan
Santoni	Pierre Clémenti
Charlotte	Abigail Cruttenden
Ben Said	Ahmed Boulane
Eva	Sira Stampe
Sufi Sheikh	Amidou
Patricia	Michelle Fairley
Henning	Kevin McKidd
Hippy	Peter Youngblood Hills
Aziz	Mohcine Barmouni
Hicham	Annouar Zrika
Hadaoui	Mohamed Cherkaoui
Doctor	Abderrahim Begache
Village Elder	Khaldi Cherif
Poet	Ahmed Madha
Translator	Frédérique Zepter
Bank Clerk	Salah-Dine Fenjirou
Bilal's Wife	Rouika Bent H'mad
Policeman	Hassan Bajja

and Abdellatif Jamal Saadi (Sufi Gate Man), Lisa Orgolini, David Baxt (Tourists), Fadila Benmoussa, Khadija Adly, Malika Khaldi, Khadija Belkiya (Hotel Ladies), Abdelkader Lotfi (Ticket Clerk)

Saïd Taghmaoui, Kate Winslet

Julia, seeking a more adventurous future for herself, takes her two young daughters out of London and travels to Morocco, where she becomes the lover of Bilal, a charismatic street performer.

©Stratosphere Entertainment

Carrie Mullan, Bella Riza

 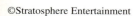

JEANNE AND THE PERFECT GUY

(**STRAND**) Producers, Cyriac Auriol, Pauline Duhault; Directors, Olivier Ducastel, Jacques Martineau; Lyrics/Dialogue, Jacques Martineau; Line Producer, Eric Zaouali; Photography, Mathieu Poirot-Delpech; Music, Philippe Miller; Editor, Sabine Mamou; Choreographer, Sylvie Giron; Casting, Antoinette Boulat; Co-Produced by Le Studio Canal+, France 2 Cinema, M6 Films, Orsans Productions, Pyramide; French; Color; Not rated; 98 minutes; American release date: April 16, 1999

Virginie Ledoyen

CAST

Jeanne	Virginie Ledoyen
Olivier	Mathieu Demy
François	Jacques Bonnaffe
Sophie	Valerie Bonneton
Jean-Baptiste	Frederic Gorny
The Messenger	Laurent Arcado
The Plumber	Michel Raskine
Jacques	Damien Dodane
Julien	Denis Podalydes
Rémi	David Saracino
Jeanne's Mother	Nelly Borgeaud
Jeanne's Father	Rene Morard

and Jean-Marc Rouleau (Friend Olivier), Sylvain Prunenec (Jérôme), Emmanuelle Goize (The Bookseller), Marief Guittier (The Nurse), Judith Guttier (The BDE Lady), Christiane Millet (The Night Nurse), Cedric Brenner (The BDE Guy), Nicolas Seguy (Edouard), Johanna Menuteau (Nathalie), Axelle Laffont (Hélène), Gregory Sauvion (Richard), My Linh Bui (Self Maid), Juliette Chanaud (Cinema Cashier), Philippe Mangeot (Act Up Militant)

Jeanne believes she has met the man of her dreams in Olivier, only to find out after their first encounter that he is H.I.V.-positive.

©Strand Releasing

Virginie Ledoyen, Mathieu Demy

EXISTENZ

(DIMENSION) Producers, Robert Lantos, Andras Hamori, David Cronenberg; Director/Screenplay, David Cronenberg; Photography, Peter Suschitzky; Designer, Carol Spier; Editor, Ronald Sanders; Music, Howard Shore; Visual and Special Effects Supervisor, Jim Isaac; Costumes, Denise Cronenberg; Co-Producers, Damon Bryant, Bradley Adams, Michael MacDonald; Associate Producer, Sandra Tucker; Casting, Deirdre Bowen; an Alliance Atlantis/Serendipity Point Films presentation in association with Natural Nylon Entertainment of a Robert Lantos production; Canadian-British; Dolby; Deluxe color; Rated R; 97 minutes; American release date: April 23, 1999

CAST

Allegra Geller	Jennifer Jason Leigh
Ted Pikul	Jude Law
Kiri Vinokur	Ian Holm
Gas	Willem Dafoe
Yevgeny Nourish	Don McKellar
Carlaw	Callum Keith Rennie
Seminar Leader	Christopher Eccleston
Merle	Sarah Polley
D'Arcy Nader	Robert A. Silverman
Chinese Waiter	Oscar Hsu
Noel Dichter	Kris Lemche
Assistants	Vik Sahay, Kirsten Johnson
Landry	James Kirchner
Volunteers	Balazs Koos, Stephanie Belding
Trout Farm Worker	Gerry Quigley

Game designer Allegra Geller, introducing her latest creation which successfully blurs the boundaries between realism and escapism, finds herself on the run with security guard Ted Pikul after an attempt on her life.

©Dimension Films

Jennifer Jason Leigh, Jude Law

Jennifer Jason Leigh

Jennifer Jason Leigh

Jude Law

Zhu Xu, Zhou Ren-ying

Zhu-Xu

Zhou Ren-ying, Zhu Xu

THE KING OF MASKS

(SAMUEL GOLDWYN) Producer/Director, Wu Tianming; Screenplay, Wei Minglun; Executive Producers, Mona Fong, Hon Pou Chu; Associate Producers, Law Shui Yin, Titus Ho, Lawrence Wong; Music, Zhao Jiping, Chen Wengui; Art Director, Wu Xujing; Photography, Mu Dayuan; a Shaw Brothers (H.K.) production; Chinese, 1997; Color; Not rated; 101 minutes; American release date: April 28, 1999

CAST

Bian Lian Wang	Zhu Xu
Doggie	Zhou Ren-ying
Tien Che	Zhang Riuyang
Liang Sao Lang	Zhao Zhigang

A lonely old street magician, adept in the art of "face-changing," befriends a 7-year-old girl who is being sold by her impoverished father.

©Samuel Goldwyn Films

Zhu Xu, Zhou Ren-ying

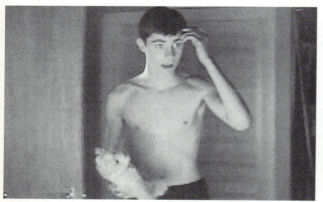
Ben Silverstone, Charlotte Brittain

Ben Silverstone

GET REAL

(PARAMOUNT CLASSICS) Producer, Stephen Taylor; Executive Producers, Anant Singh, Helena Spring; Director, Simon Shore; Screenplay, Patrick Wilde, based on his play *What's Wrong With Angry?*; Co-Producer, Patricia Carr; Photography, Alan Almond; Designer/Costumes, Bernard Lepel; Editor, Barrie Vince; Music, John Lunn; Casting, Di Carling; a Distant Horizon presentation of a Graphite Film with the participation of British Screen and the Arts Council of England; British; Dolby; Panavision; Rank color; Rated R; 110 minutes; American release date: April 30, 1999

CAST

Steven Carter	Ben Silverstone
John Dixon	Brad Gorton
Linda	Charlotte Brittain
Jessica	Stacy A. Hart
Wendy Bates	Kate McEnery
Mark Watkins	Patrick Nielsen
Kevin Granger	Tim Harris
Dave	James D. White
Christina Lindmann	Louise J. Taylor
Young Steven	James Perkins
Young Mark	Nicholas Hunter
Steven's Mother	Jacquetta May
Steven's Father	David Lumsden
Glen Armstrong	David Elliot
Linda's Brother	Morgan Jones
English Teacher	Richard Hawley
Cruising Man	Steven Mason
Glen's Wife	Charlotte Hanson
Crying Baby	Alina Hazeldine
Bob the Driving Instructor	Steven Elder
Aunt at Wedding	Leonie Thomas
Bridegroom	David Paul West
Policeman	Andy Rashleigh
John's Father	Ian Brimble
John's Mother	Judy Buxton
Woman Driving Instructor	Dorothy Clark
Julie	Amy Redler
Headmaster	Martin Milman
Roger McGregor	Andy Tungate

Sixteen-year-old Steven, who has come to accept his homosexuality, begins an affair with his school's number one academic achiever, John Dixon, who is far less comfortable about his own sexuality.

©Paramount Classics

Brad Gorton, Ben Silverstone

(back row) Ben Silverstone, Kate McEnery, Stacy A. Hart, Patrick Nielsen
(front row) James D. White, Brad Gorton, Tim Harris

Ben Silverstone, Charlotte Brittain

Brad Gorton (atop) Ben Silverstone

Ben Silverstone, David Elliot

Brad Gorton, Ben Silverstone

THE CASTLE

(MIRAMAX) Producer, Debra Choate; Executive Producer, Michael Hirsh; Director, Rob Sitch; Screenplay/Conceived by Santo Cilauro, Tom Gleisner, Jane Kennedy, Rob Sitch; Photography, Miriana Marusic; Designer, Carrie Kennedy; Music, Edmund Choi; Editor, Wayne Hyett; Casting, Jane Kennedy; Presented in association with Village Roadshow Pictures and Working Dog; Australian, 1997; Dolby; Color; Rated R; 85 minutes; American release date: May 7, 1999

Anthony Simcoe, Anne Tenney, Michael Caton, Sophie Lee, Eric Bana, Wayne Hope, Stephen Curry

CAST

Darryl Kerrigan	Michael Caton
Sal Kerrigan	Anne Tenney
Dale Kerrigan	Stephen Curry
Steve Kerrigan	Anthony Simcoe
Tracey Kerrigan	Sophie Lee
Wayne Kerrigan	Wayne Hope
Dennis Denuto	Tiriel Mora
Con Petropoulous	Eric Bana
Lawrence Hammill	Charles "Bud" Tingwell
Federal Court Judge	Robyn Nevin
Farouk	Costas Kilias
Ron Graham	Bryan Dawe
Jack	Monty Maizels
Evonne	Lynda Gibson
Mr. Lyle	John Benton
John Clifton	Laurie Dobson
Chairman	John Lee
Council Officer	Stephanie Daniel
Sergeant Mick Kennedy	John Flaus

and Les Toth (Heavy at Door), Erik Donnison (Barlow Representative), Roger Neave, Tony Evans, Robin Miller (High Court Judges), Julie Kulpinski (Kerry), Sam Gleisner (Steve & Kerry's Child), Sebastiano Liotta (Mr. Petropoulos), Josie Noviello (Mrs. Petropoulos), Linda Keane (Federal Court Lawyer), Marilyn Chestnut (High Court Stenographer), Julian Scarff (High Court Clerk of Courts), Marie-Therese Byrne (Assistant to Chairman), Clare O'Sullivan, Warwick Begg (High Court Lawyers), Maria Theodorakis (Federal Court Stenographer), John Evans (Federal Court Clerk of Courts), Michael Roland (High Court Lawyer), Matthew Giordanella (Con & Tracey's Son), Larry Emdur, Ian Ross (Themselves), Tony Martin (Adam Hammill)

When a multi-national company decides to buy the Kerrigan family's property, patriarch Darryl vows that he will rally his neighbors to fight the government to stay in the home he loves.

(right) Sophie Lee, Michael Caton

Michael Caton, Tiriel Mora

Sophie Lee, Anne Tenney (seated)

XIU XIU
THE SENT-DOWN GIRL

(**STRATOSPHERE**) Producers, Joan Chen, Alice Chan; Executive Producers, Joan Chen, Allison Liu, Cecile Shah Tsuei; Director, Joan Chen; Screenplay, Yang Geling, Joan Chen; Based on the novella *Tian Yu* by Yan Geling; Photography, Lu Yue; Designer, Pan Lai; Editor/Associate Producer, Ruby Yang; Music, Johnny Chen; a Whispering Steppes presentation; Taiwanese-Hong Kong-Chinese-U.S.; Dolby; Deluxe color; Rated R; 99 minutes; American release date: May 7, 1999

Lu Lu

CAST

Xiu Xiu ....Lu Lu
Lao Jin ....Lopsang
Mother ....Gao Jie
Sister..Li Qianqian
Father ....Lu Yue
Chen Li ....Qiao Qian
Peddler ....Gao Qiang
Motorcycle Man ....Qin Wenyuan
Headquarters Chief..Li Zhizhen
Three Toes ....Cao Jiong
Rider A ....Jiang Cheng
Hooligan ....Huzi
Accountant Cao ....Zhang Kun
Jeep Driver ....Li Shijin
and Jia Dong, Wang Yue (Yak Herders), Cao Xuelan (Honey Seller), Tan Xiaoying (Tractor Man), Lu Zhong (Belt Man), Hu Wenqi (Janitor), Li Yayu, Du Min (Nurses), Jia Dashui, Chen Yu (Patients), Wang Luoyong (Narrator), Yu Xiaolin (Jeep Driver Voice)

16-year-old Xiu Xiu, sent to the country to learn horse-herding so she might join the Girls' Iron Cavalry, completes her training with former prisoner of war Lao Jin only to find that she cannot return to her family without the proper permits.

Lopsang

Lu Lu

Moya Farrelly, Aidan Quinn

THIS IS MY FATHER

(SONY PICTURES CLASSICS) Producers, Nicolas Clermont, Philip King; Executive Producers, Elie Samaha, Kieran Corrigan; Director/Screenplay, Paul Quinn; Co-Producer, Stewart Harding; Co-Executive Producers, Aidan Quinn, Declan Quinn, Paul Quinn; Photography, Declan Quinn; Designer, Frank Conway; Editor, Glenn Berman; Costumes, Consolata Boyle; Music, Donal Lunny; Casting, John & Ros Hubbard, Nadia Rona & Rosina Bucci; a Filmline International and Hummingbird Communications production; Canadian-Irish; Dolby; Eastman color; Rated R; 120 minutes; American release date: May 7, 1999

CAST

Present Day
Kieran Johnson...James Caan
Jack, Kieran Johnson's Nephew ....Jacob Tierney
Seamus, Owner of the Bed-and-Breakfast...........Colm Meaney
Mrs. Kearney, Seamus' Mother ....Moira Deady
Betty...Susan Almgren
Maria..Pauline Hutton
Nuala..Fiona Glascott
Old Fiona..Françoise Graton
and Joel Gordon (Brian Winters), Alexandra Spunt, Victoria Sanchez (Students), Terrence Scammell (Chicago Radio DJ), Pat Leavy (Farmer Woman), Aidan Conron (Bartender), Peadar Lamb, Sean Madden (Men in Pub)

1939
Kieran O'Day ....Aidan Quinn
Fiona Flynn ....Moya Farrelly
Mrs. Maney...Maria McDermottroe
John Maney..Donal Donnelly
Widow Flynn...Gina Moxley
Father Mooney..Eamonn Morrissey
Father Quinn...Stephen Rea
Eddie Sharp, the Pilot ....John Cusack
Officer Jim...Brendan Gleeson
Officer Ben ....Pat Short
Liam Finneran ....John Kavanagh
and Sheila Flitton (Mrs. Madigan), Nevin Finegan (Petie Madigan), Oran Finegan (Davey Madigan), Karen Ardiff (Young Mrs. Kearney), Michael Byrne (Michael Finnegan), Marian Quinn (Concepta), Michael West (Nosey Nolan), Michael Devaney (Young Suitor), Karl Hayden, Gavin O'Connor (Town Lads), Kieran Hanrahan (Band Leader), Frank O'Dwyer (Dance Chaperone), Andrew Bennett (Mr. Kearney), Devan Murray (Christy), Brendan Conroy (Undertaker), Gary Merrigan (Child Finnegan)

A disillusioned Chicago teacher travels with his nephew to Ireland where the locals recount for him the story of his parents' love affair.

James Caan

Stephen Rea

John Cusack

Arata, Erika Oda, Susumu Terajima, Kei Tani, Takashi Naito

AFTER LIFE

(**ARTISTIC LICENSE**) a.k.a. *Wonderful Life*; Producers, Sato Shiho, Akieda Masayuki; Executive Producers, Shigenobu Yutaka, Yasuda Masahiro; Director/Screenplay/Editor, Kore-eda Hirokazu; Photography, Yamazaki Yutaka, Sukita Masayoshi; Art Directors, Isomi Toshihiro, Gunji Hideo; Music, Kasamatsu Yasuhiro; a TV Man Union Inc., Engine Film Inc. production; Japanese, 1998; Color; Not rated; 118 minutes; American release date: May 12, 1999

CAST

Takashi Mochizuki ....Arata
Shiori Satonaka ....Erika Oda
Takuro Sugie ....Takashi Naito
Ichiro Watanabe ....Taketoshi Naito
Ken-nosuke Nakamura ....Kei Tani
Satoru Kawashima ....Susumu Terajima
Yusuke Iseya ....Yusuke Iseya
Kyoko Watanabe ....Kyoko Kagawa
Ichiro Watanabe (Student Days) ....Sadao Abe
Kisuke Shoda ....Toru Yuri
Nobuko Amano ....Kazuko Shirakawa
Kiyo Nishimura ....Hisako Hara
Kana Yoshimoto ....Sayoka Yoshino
Kenji Yamamoto ....Kotaro Shiga
Kyoko Tsukamoto (Student Days)...Natsuo Ishido
Doorkeeper ....Akio Yokoyama

At a waystation for the newly dead, case workers interview their 22 new arrivals.

©Artistic License

Erika Oda, Arata

Cher, Lily Tomlin

Cher

TEA WITH MUSSOLINI

(G2 FILMS/MGM) Producers, Riccardo Tozzi, Giovannella Zannoni, Clive Parsons; Executive Producer, Marco Chimenz; Director, Franco Zeffirelli; Screenplay, John Mortimer, Franco Zeffirelli; Based on *The Autobiography of Franco Zeffirelli*; Photography, David Watkin; Art Directors, Carlo Centolavigna, Gioia Fiorella Mariani; Costumes, Jenny Beavan, Anna Anni, Alberto Spiazzi, Ermanno Daelli; Music, Alessio Vlad, Stefano Arnaldi; Associate Producer, Pippo Pisciotto; Editor, Tariq Anwar; Casting, Emma Style, Mirta Guarnaschelli; a Medusa Film—Cattleya—Cineritmo (Rome) Film and General Productions (London); Italian-British; Dolby; Cinecitta color; Rated PG; 117 minutes; American release date: May 14, 1999

CAST

Elsa Morganthal	Cher
Arabella Delancey	Judi Dench
Mary Wallace	Joan Plowright
Lady Hester Random	Maggie Smith
Georgie	Lily Tomlin
Luca Innocenti	Baird Wallace
Luca (child)	Charlie Lucas
Paolo	Massimo Ghini
Vittorio	Paolo Seganti
Mussolini	Claudio Spadaro
Cesare	Mino Bellei
Wilfred	Paul Chequer
Connie	Tessa Pritchard
British Consul	Michael Williams
Molly	Paula Jacobs
Edith	Bettine Milne
Hazel	Hazel Parsons
Ursula	Helen Stirling
Norma	Kathleen Doyle
Elderly Lady	Giselle Mathews
Signora Badaloni	Gianna Giachetti
Major Gibson	Chris Larkin
Sacristan	Giovanni Nannini
Dino Grandi	Pino Colizzi
Count Bernardini	Jack Basehart
Carabinieres	Giacomo Gonnella, Clemente Abete
Maurizio	Roberto Farnese
Carmelo	Chris Tattanelli
Anna	Claudia Piccoli
American Dealer	Allan Caister Pearce
German Officer	Herman Weiskopf
Giulia Meyer	Benedetta Magini
Menotti	Beppe Landini
Butler	Giuseppe Rossi Borghesano
Adrianna	Marcellina Ruocco
Professor Cassuto	Ferdinando Ferrini
Leading Facist	Massimo Salvianti

Luca Innocenti, born out of wedlock and left in the care of Mary Wallace, is raised by her and a group of eccentric British and American ladies living in Italy during the time that Mussolini rises to power, making the foreigners "enemy aliens."

Judi Dench, Charlie Lucas

Baird Wallace, Judi Dench, Lily Tomlin, Joan Plowright

Judi Dench

Maggie Smith

Joan Plowright

Lily Tomlin

BLACK MASK

(ARTISAN) Producer, Tsui Hark; Administrative Producer, Tiffany Chen; Director, Daniel Lee; Photography, Cheung Tung Leung; Music, Teddy Robin, Ben Vaughn; Martial Arts Director, Yuen Wo Ping; Editor, Cheung Ka Tai; a Distant Horizon presentation of a Charles Heung and Film Workshop Company Limited production; Hong-Kong, 1997; Dubbed in English; Dolby; Color; Rated R; 96 minutes; American release date: May 14, 1999

CAST

Tsui Chik ....Jet Li
Tracy ....Karen Mok
Rock ....Lau Ching Wan
Yeuk-lan...Francoise C.J. Yip
Commander Hung ....Patrick Long
King Kau...Anthony Wing Chau-Sang
and Lawrence Ah Mon, Moses Chan, Suk-yee Chan, King-fai Chung, Henry Fong, Michael Ian Lambert, Ken Lok, Mei-Yee Sze, Roy Szeto, Xin Xin Xiong

A biologically engineered super-soldier, trying to lead a normal life, realizes he must fight the military force that created him when he finds out it is trying to take over the Hong Kong drug empire.

©Artisan Entertainment Inc.

Jet Li

Francoise C.J. Yip

Thandie Newton

David Thewlis

BESIEGED

(FINE LINE FEATURES) Producer, Massimo Cortesi; Director, Bernardo Bertolucci; Screenplay, Clare Peploe, Bernardo Bertolucci; Photography, Fabio Cianchetti; Designer, Gianni Silvestri; Costumes, Metka Kosak; Editor, Jacopo Quadri; Music, Alessio Vlad; Piano Solos, Stefano Arnaldi; Associate Producer, Clare Peploe; a Fiction and Navert/Mediaset production, in association with BBC Films; Italian-British, 1998; Dolby; Technicolor; Rated R; 94 minutes; American release date: May 21, 1999

CAST

Shandurai...Thandie Newton
Jason Kinsky..David Thewlis
Agostino..Claudio Santamaria
and Additional Cast: John C. Owang, Paul Osul, Cyril Nri, Veronica Lazar, Gianfranco Mazzoni, Massimo DeRossi, Mario Mazzetti Di Pietralata; Children at Concert: Andrea Quercia (pianist), Alexander Menis, Natalia Mignosa, Lorenzo Mollica, Elena Perino, Fernando Trombetti, Veronica Visentin

Shandurai, an African woman working as a domestic in Rome for noted British pianist-composer Jason Kinsky, convinces the lovestruck artist to prove his love for her by helping to free her imprisoned husband back in her country.

© Fine Line Features

THE LOSS OF SEXUAL INNOCENCE

(SONY PICTURES CLASSICS) Producers, Mike Figgis, Annie Stewart; Director/Screenplay/Music, Mike Figgis; Executive Producer, Patrick Wachsberger; Co-Producer, Barney Reisz; Photography, Benoît Delhomme; Editor, Matthew Wood; Costumes, Florence Nicaise; a Summit Entertainment in association with Newmarket Capital Group presentation of a Red Mullet Film; British; Dolby; Color; Rated R; 106 minutes; American release date: May 28, 1999

Femi Ogumbanjo, Hanne Klintoe

CAST

Adult Nic	Julian Sands
Twins	Saffron Burrows
Lucca	Stefano Dionisi
Susan	Kelly MacDonald
Susan's Mum	Gina McKee
Nic (aged 16)	Jonathan Rhys-Meyers
Susan's Father	Bernard Hill
Blind Woman	Rossy De Palma
Nic (aged 5)	John Cowey
Mixed Race Girl	Nina McKay
Wangi	Dickson Osa-Omorogbe
Old Colonial Man	Jock Gibson Cowl
Flash Man	Justin Chadwick
Adam	Femi Ogumbanjo
Eve	Hanne Klintoe
Nic's Wife	Johanna Torrel
Nic's Son	Geraint Ellis
Nic (aged 12)	George Moktar
Detectives	Mark Long, Red Mullet
Policeman	Joe Cunningham
Nic's Brother (aged 3)	Wesley Kipling

and Anthony Cleckener, James Younger, Malcolm Holmes, Jeffrey Coulson (Four Boys), James Bradley, Nick Figgis, David Medleycott (Band Members), Mark Long (Man in Dream), Clare & Zoe Jones (Baby Twins), Marina Ilina, Fabrizia Farra (Novice Nuns), Roderic Leigh (Boring Businessman), Rachel Boss (Italian Woman), Bruno Bilotta (Italian Man), Rodney Charles (Charlie), Phil Swinburne (Games Teacher), Cite Chebbia (Blue Child), Neziha Youssef (Blue Mother), Rami Chebbi (Blue Father)

Various incidents that have made up the life of Nic from age five to his present adulthood, are interwoven with the story of Adam and Eve's fall from grace.

Julian Sands, Johanna Torrel

Saffron Burrows, Stefano Dionisi

Jonathan Rhys-Meyers, Kelly MacDonald

Julia Roberts, Hugh Grant

Hugh Grant, Julia Roberts

NOTTING HILL

(UNIVERSAL) Producer, Duncan Kenworthy; Executive Producers, Tim Bevan, Richard Curtis, Eric Fellner; Director, Roger Michell; Screenplay, Richard Curtis; Photography, Michael Coulter; Designer, Stuart Craig; Editor, Nick Moore; Costumes, Shuna Harwood; Music, Trevor Jones; Song: "She" by Charles Aznavour and Herbert Kretzmer/performed by Elvis Costello; Line Producer, Mary Richards; Casting, Mary Selway; a PolyGram Films presentation in association with Working Title Films from Notting Hill Pictures of a Duncan Kenworthy production; British; Dolby; Super 35 Widescreen; Deluxe color; Rated PG-13; 123 minutes; American release date: May 28, 1999

CAST

Anna Scott	Julia Roberts
William Thacker	Hugh Grant
Bernie	Hugh Bonneville
Honey	Emma Chambers
Spike	Rhys Ifans
Max	Tim McInnerny
Bella	Gina McKee
Tony	Richard McCabe
Martin	James Dreyfus
Rufus the Thief	Dylan Moran
Annoying Customer	Roger Frost
"Time Out" Journalist	Julian Rhind-Tutt
Anna's Publicist	Lorelei King
PR Chief	John Shrapnel
"Helix" Lead Actor	Clarke Peters
Foreign Actor	Arturo Venegas
Interpreter	Yolanda Vasquez
10-year-old Actress	Mischa Barton
Ritz Concierge	Henry Goodman
Tessa	Melissa Wilson
Keziah	Emma Bernard

and Dorian Lough, Sanjeev Bhaskar, Paul Chahidi, Matthew Whittle (Loud Men in Restaurant), Emily Mortimer (Perfect Girl), Tony Armatrading (Security Man), September Buckley (Third Assistant Director), Philip Manikum (Harry the Sound Man), Sam West (Anna's Co-Star), Dennis Matsuki (Japanese Business Man), Patrick Barlow (Savoy Concierge), Andy De La Tour, Maureen Hibbert, Rupert Proctor, David Sternberg (Journalists), Anna Beach (William's Mother), Alec Baldwin (Jeff), Matthew Modine (Anna's Co-Star—Black and White)

Bookstore owner William Thacker begins an affair with world famous actress Anna Scott until they both begin to wonder if it is possible for them to co-exist in each other's decidedly different worlds.

© PolyGram Filmed Entertainment, Inc.

Gina McKee

Rhys Ifans

Julia Roberts, Hugh Grant, Emma Chambers

Hugh Grant, Julia Roberts

Hugh Grant, Julia Roberts

Julia Roberts

Tim McInnerny

Hugh Bonneville

Emma Chambers

Julia Roberts, Hugh Grant, Roger Frost

TWICE UPON A YESTERDAY

(TRIMARK) formerly *The Man With Rain in His Shoes*; Producer, Juan Gordon; Executive Producers, Jon Slan, Gareth Jones; Director, Maria Ripoll; Screenplay, Rafa Russo; Line Producer, Sheila Fraser Milne; Photography, Javier Salmones; Designer, Grant Hicks; Editor, Nacho Ruiz-Capillas; Music, Luis Mendo, Bernardo Fuster, Angel Illarramendi; Costumes, John Krausa; Casting, Liora Reich, Camilla-Valentine Isola; a Paragon Entertainment Corporation & Handmade Films presentation in association with CLT-UFA International, Mandarin Films and Wild Rose Productions of an Esicma production; Spanish-British, 1998; Dolby; Color; Rated R: 89 minutes; American release date: May 28, 1999

CAST

Sylvia Weld	Lena Headey
Victor Bukowski	Douglas Henshall
Louise	Penélope Cruz
Rafael	Gustavo Salmerón
Dave Summers	Mark Strong
Don Miguel	Eusebio Lázaro
Alison Hayes	Charlotte Coleman
Freddy	Neil Stuke
Diane	Elizabeth McGovern
Director	Antonio Gil Martínez
Carol	Heather Weeks
Janice	Inday Ba
Simon	Paul Popplewell

and Dave Spinxs (Vendor), Dave Fishley (Pianist), Robert Oates (Driver), Toby Davies (James), Emily Hillier (Young Girl), Rafa Russo (Shoplifter), Tim Griggs (Bar Manager), Max Gold (Young Customer/Usher), Emma Freud (MC), Simon Meacock (Young Actor), Caprice Bourett (Presenter)

Victor, determined to woo back Sylvia before she marries another man, travels back in time in an effort to set things right.

©Trimark Pictures

Douglas Henshall, Lena Headey

Penélope Cruz, Douglas Henshall

ETERNITY AND A DAY

(ARTISTIC LICENSE) Producer/Director, Theo Angelopoulos; Screenplay, Theo Angelopoulos, Tonino Guerra, Petros Markaris; Executive Producer, Phoebe Economopoulos; Photography, Giorgos Arvanitis, Andreas Sinanos; Editor, Yannis Tsitsopoulos; Music, Eleni Karaindrou; Costumes, Giorgos Patsas; a Merchant Ivory Films presentation in association with Canal+, Classic SRL, Instituto Luce, WDR & ARTE; Greek, 1998; Dolby; Color; Not rated; 132 minutes; American release date: May 28, 1999

CAST

Alexandre	Bruno Ganz
The Poet	Fabrizio Bentivoglio
Anna	Isabelle Renauld
The Boy	Achilleas Skevis
Anna's Mother	Alexandra Ladikou
Alexandre's Mother	Despina Bebedeli
Urania	Eleni Gerassimidou
Alexandre's Daughter	Iris Hatziantoniou
Anna's Uncle	Nikos Kouros
Anna's Father	Alekos Oudinotis
The Doctor	Nikos Kolovos

A terminally ill poet finds a packet of letters from his long-dead wife which take him back to past events of his life.

©Merchant Ivory Films/Artistic License Films

Bruno Ganz, Isabelle Renauld

Eliades Ochoa, Orlando López, Joachim Cooder, Ibrahim Ferrer,
Juande Marcos González, Ry Cooder, Pio Leyva

Joachim Cooder, Ry Cooder

Ibrahim Ferrer, Omara Portuondo

BUENA VISTA SOCIAL CLUB

(ARTISAN ENTERTAINMENT) Producers, Ry Cooder, Ulrich Felsberg, Deepak Nayar; Executive Producers, Nick Gold, Ulrich Felsberg; Director, Wim Wenders; Photography, Jörg Widmer; Associate Producer, Rosa Bosch; Editor, Brian Johnson; a Road Movies production in association with Kintop Pictures and Arte, Channel 4; German-British-French-Cuban-U.S.; Dolby; Color; Rated G; 105 minutes; American release date: June 4, 1999. Documentary on the Cuban musicians and singers of the Buena Vista Social Club who came together to create a best-selling CD.

WITH

Company Segundo, Eliades Ochoa, Ry Cooder, Joachim Cooder, Ibrahim Ferrer, Omara Portuondo, Rubén González, Orlando "Cachao" López Vergara, Amadito Valdés, Manuel "Guajiro" Mirabal Vazquez, Barbarito Torres, Pío Leyva, Manuel "Punitillita" Licea, Juan de Marcos González, Raul Planas, Felix Valoy, Richard Egues, Joseantonio "Macto" Rodreiguez, Julienne Oviedo Sanchez

This film received an Oscar nomination for feature-length documentary.

©Artisan Entertainment Inc.

Orlando López, Company Segundo, Omara Portuondo, Ry Cooder

Jean-Luc Bideau, Christoph Koncz

Sylvia Chang

Samuel L. Jackson, Don McKellar

THE RED VIOLIN

(LIONS GATE) Producer, Niv Fichman; Director, François Girard; Screenplay, Don McKellar, François Girard; Co-Producers, Daniel Iron, Giannandrea Pecorelli; Line Producer, Barbara Shrier; Photography, Alain Dostie; Designer, François Seguin; Costumes, Renee April; Editor, Gaetan Huot; Music, John Corigliano; Solo Violin, Joshua Bell; Casting, Deirdre Bowen; a New Line International, Channel Four Films, Telefilm Canada presentation of a Rhombus Media/Mikado production; Canadian-Italian, 1998; Dolby; Color; Not rated; 131 minutes; American release date: June 11, 1999

CAST

Cremona
Nicolo Bussotti ....Carlo Cecchi
Anna Bussotti..Irene Grazioli
Cesca ....Anita Laurenzi
and Tommaso Puntelli (Apprentice), Aldo Brugnini (Assistant), Samuele Amighetti (Boy)

Vienna
Georges Poussin ....Jean-Luc Bideau
Kaspar Weiss ....Christoph Koncz
Antoinette Poussin ....Clothilde Mollet
Brother Christophe...Rainer Egger
and Wolgang Böck (Brother Michael),Anton Von Spielmann (Florentin Groll), Johannes Silberschneider (Father Richter), Arthur Denberg (Prince Mansfield) Paul Koeker (Brother Gustav), Josef Mairginter (Brother Franz), Johann Gotsch (Funeral Monk), Geza Hosszu-Legocky, David Alberman, Andrzej Matuszewski (Gypsy Violinists)

Oxford
Frederick Pope ....Jason Flemyng
Victoria...Greta Scacchi
Sara...Eva Marie Bryer
Gypsy Father ....Dimitri Andreas
and David Gant (Conductor), Stuart Ong (Manservant)

Shanghai
Xiang Pei ....Sylvia Chang
Chou Yuan..Liu Zi Feng
Comrade Chan Gong ....Tao Hong
Deputy...Cao Kun Qi
Young Ming ....Han Xio Fei
and Tan Zeng Wei (Guard), Zhou Zhi Qing (Senior Policeman), Wang Xiaoshuai (Junior Policeman), Qiao Zhi (Elderly Woman), Tang Ren (Young Ziang Pei), Lidou (Pawnbroker), Zhang Kai (Rally Speaker)

Montreal
Charles Morritz ....Samuel L. Jackson
Auctioneer ....Colm Feore
Madame Leroux ....Monique Mercure
Evan Williams ....Don McKellar
Mr. Ruselsky ....Ireneusz Bogajewicz
Nicolas Olsberg ....Julian Richings
Older Ming ....Russell Yuen
Madame Ming ....Sandra Oh
Suzanne ....Paula De Vasconcelos

When a legendary red violin shows up at a Montreal auction, Charles Morritz sets out to investigate its authenticity, tracing it through its 300-year journey from owner to owner.

1999 Academy Award-winner for Best Original Score.

©Lions Gate Films

Samuel L. Jackson

Jason Flemyng, Greta Scacchi

Carlo Cecchi

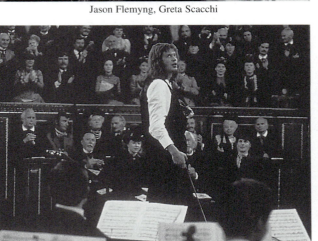

Jason Flemyng

Samuel L. Jackson, Don McKellar

Franka Potente

Franka Potente, Moritz Bleibtreu

RUN LOLA RUN

(SONY PICTURES CLASSICS) Producer, Stefan Arndt; Director/Screenplay, Tom Tykwer; Executive Producer, Maria Köpf; Photography, Frank Griebe; Editors, Mathilde Bonnefoy, Gebhard Henke, Andreas Schreitmüller; Set Designer, Alexander Manasse; Costumes, Monika Jacobs; Music, Tom Tykwer, Johnny Klimek, Reinhold Heil; a Bavaria Film International, X-Filme Creative Pool Production presentation; German, 1998; Dolby; Color; Rated R; 81 minutes; American release date: June 18, 1999

Franka Potente

CAST

Lola	Franka Potente
Manni	Moritz Bleibtreu
Lola's Father	Herbert Knaup
Norbert Von Au	Joachim Krol
Jutta Hansen	Nina Petri
Herr Schuster	Armin Rohde
Herr Meier	Ludger Pistor
Frau Jäger	Suzanne von Borsody
Mike	Sebastian Schipper
Doris	Julia Lindig
Herr Kruse	Lars Rudolph
Cleaner	Andreas Petri
Croupier	Klaus Müller
Casino Manager	Utz Krause
Casino Cashier	Beate Finckh
Ambulance Driver	Volkhard Buff
Ronnie	Heino Ferch
Mother	Ute Lubosch
Old Woman	Dora Raddy
Blind Woman	Monica Bleibtreu
Supermarket Security Guard	Peter Pauli
Policeman	Marc Bischoff

Three different dramatizations show what might occur when Lola is phoned by her boyfriend Manni and told to bring him 100,000 marks in 20 minutes, before the men to whom he owes the money show up.

Franka Potente

Franka Potente

Moritz Bleibtreu, Franka Potente

AN IDEAL HUSBAND

(MIRAMAX) Producers, Barnaby Thompson, Uri Fruchtmann, Bruce Davey; Executive Producers, Susan B. Landau, Ralph Kamp, Andrea Calderwood; Director/Screenplay, Oliver Parker; Based on the play by Oscar Wilde; Co-Producers, Nicky Kentish Barnes, Paul Tucker; Photography, David Johnson; Designer, Michael Howells; Editor, Guy Bensley; Music, Charlie Mole; Costumes, Caroline Harris; Casting, Celestia Fox; a Fragile Film in association with Icon Productions, Pathé Pictures, and the Arts Council of England; British; Dolby; Color; Rated PG-13; 96 minutes; American release date: June 18, 1999

Rupert Everett

CAST

Lady Gertrude Chiltern	Cate Blanchett
Mabel Chiltern	Minnie Driver
Lord Arthur Goring	Rupert Everett
Mrs. Cheveley	Julianne Moore
Sir Robert Chiltern	Jeremy Northam
Lady Markby	Lindsay Duncan
The Countess	Marsha Fitzalan
Phipps	Peter Vaughan
Lord Caversham	John Wood
Baron Arnheim	Jeroen Krabbé
Tommy Trafford	Ben Pullen
Mason	Neville Phillips
Vicounte de Nanjac	Nickolas Grace
Sir Edward	Simon Russell Beale
Miss Danvers	Anna Patrick
Lady Basildon	Delia Lindsay

Denise Stephenson (Gwendolen), Charles Edwards (Jack), Nancy Carroll (Cecily), Andy Harrison (Algernon), Jill Balcon (Lady Bracknell), Janet Henfrey (Miss Prism), Toby Robertson (Canon Chasuble), Michael Culkin (Oscar Wilde), Oliver Parker (Bunbury), Douglas Bradley (Brackpool), Susannah Wise (Young Mother), Peter Parker, Neil Mendoza (MPs), Oliver Ford Davies (Sir Hugo Danforth), John Thompson (The Speaker)

Sir Robert Chiltern's seemingly perfect marriage and career are in jeopardy when the scheming Mrs. Cheveley shows up threatening to reveal a secret from Robert's past, an incident that causes him to call on his womanizing friend, Arthur Goring, for assistance. Previous film version (British Lion, 1947) starred Paulette Goddard, Hugh Williams, Diana Wynyard, and Michael Wilding, and was released in the U.S. in 1948 by 20th Century-Fox.

©Miramax Films

Julianne Moore

Jeremy Northam, Cate Blanchett

Minnie Driver

MY SON THE FANATIC

(**MIRAMAX**) Producer, Chris Curling; Executive Producer, George Faber; Director, Udayan Prasad; Screenplay, Hanif Kureishi; Photography, Alan Almond; Designer, Grenville Horner; Editor, David Gamble; Line Producer, Anita Overland; Music, Stephen Warbeck; Costumes, Mary-Jane Reyner; a BBC Films presentation in association with Canal+, Image International and the Arts Council of Great Britain of a Zephyr Films production; British, 1997; Dolby; Color; Rated R; 89 minutes; American release date: June 25, 1999

CAST

Parvez	Om Puri
Bettina	Rachel Griffiths
Schitz	Stellan Skarsgard
Farid	Akbar Kurtha
Minoo	Gopi Desai
Fizzy	Harish Patel
Madeleine	Sarah Jane Potts
Mrs. Fingerhut	Judi Jones
Chief Inspector Fingerhut	Geoffrey Bateman
Drunk Man	Bernard Wrigley
Druggy Prostitute	Moya Brady
Man in Mosque	Badi Uzzaman
Comedian	Andy Devine
Walter	Shiv Grewal
Rashid	Omar Salimi
Maulvi	Bhasker Patel
Taxi Controller	Dev Sagoo
Margot	RowenaKing
Prostitutes	Olwen May, Alison Burrows
Acolytes	Parvez Qadir, Shakheil Bassi
Drivers	Balraj Singh Somal, Kez Kempton

When his son's obsession with religion begins tearing his homelife apart, taxi driver Parvez turns to steady customer Bettina, a prostitute, for friendship and understanding.

©Miramax Films

Om Puri, Rachel Griffiths

THE LOVERS ON THE BRIDGE

(**MIRAMAX ZOË**) Executive Producers, Hervé Truffaut, Albert Prévost; Director/Screenplay, Léos Carax; Photography, Jean-Yves Escoffier; Art Director, Michel Vandestien; Editor, Nelly Quettier; Production Supervisors, Charles Ferron, Nicolas Daguet; Associate Producer, Bernard Artigues; Paintings, Juliette Binoche; a Martin Scorsese presentation of a Christian Fechner presentation; French, 1991; Dolby; Color; Rated R; 120 minutes; American release date: July 2, 1999

CAST

Michèle Stalens	Juliette Binoche
Alex	Denis Lavant
Hans	Klause-Michael Grüber
Alex's Vagrant Friend	Daniel Buain
Marion	Marion Stalens
Julien	Chrichan Larson
Sailors	Paulette Berthonnier, Roger Berthonnier
The Couple in Car	Edith Scob, George Apperighis
The Fireman	Michael Vandestien
The Sleeping Man	Georges Castorp
Sleeping People	Marc Desclozeaux, Alain Dahan, Pierre Pessemesse, Maitre Bitoun, Johnny Aldama
Chief Police	Albert Prevost
The Judge	Marc Maurette
Sleeping Woman	Edith Mokomenede

Michèle, an artist who is losing her sight, falls in love with Alex, a street performer, who makes his home on the crumbling Pont-Neuf in Paris.

©Miramax Zoë

Denis Lavant, Juliette Binoche

Jacques Villeret, Daniel Prèvost, Thierry Lhermitte, Francis Huster

THE DINNER GAME

(LIONS GATE) Producer, Alain Poiré; Director/Screenplay, Francis Veber; Photography, Luciano Tovoli; Designer, Hugues Tissandier; Editor, Georges Klotz; Costumes, Jacqueline Bouchard; Music, Vladimir Cosma; a co-production of Gaumont, EFVE, TF1 Films Productions with the participation of TPS Cinéma; French, 1998; Dolby; Technovision; Color; Rated PG-13; 81 minutes; American release date: July 9, 1999

CAST

François Pignon	Jacques Villeret
Pierre Brochant	Thierry Lhermitte
Just LeBlanc	Francis Huster
Cheval	Daniel Prèvost
Christine	Alexandra Vandernoot
Marlene	Catherine Frot
Cordier	Edgar Givry
Sorbier	Christian Pereira
Louisette Blond	Pètronille Moss

Pierre Brochant feels certain that he will win the challenge of bringing the most boring dinner guest to his friends' party when he encounters an accountant who builds famous monuments with matchsticks.

©Lions Gate Films

(right) Jacques Villeret, Theirry Lhermitte

Jacques Villeret

AUTUMN TALE

(OCTOBER) formerly *A Tale of Autumn*; Producers, Françoise Etchegary, Margaret Menegoz, Eric Rohmer; Director/Screenplay, Eric Rohmer; Photography, Diane Baratier; Music, Claude Marti; Editor, Mary Stephen; a Les Films du Losange/La Sept Cionema production with the participation of Canal+, Sofilmka, Rhône-Alpes Cinema; French, 1998; Dolby; Color; Rated PG; 112 minutes; American release date: July 9, 1999

CAST

Isabelle ....Marie Rivière
Magali...Béatrice Romand
Gérald ....Alain Libolt
Étienne...Didier Sandre
Rosine...Alexia Portal
Léo...Stéphane Darmon
Émilia ....Aurélia Alcaïs
Grégoire ....Matthieu Davette
Jean-Jacques ....Yves Aclaïs

Both Isabelle and Rosine come up with schemes to find a suitable mate for the widowed Magali, only to realize that the selected men may not be willing to forsake their interests in Isabelle and Rosine.

Béatrice Romand, Marie Rivière

Marie Rivière, Alain Libolt, Béatrice Romand

271

Malcolm McDowell, Irene Jacob, Colin Firth

Mary Elizabeth Mastrantonio, Colin Firth

Robert Norman, Colin Firth

Kelly MacDonald, Irene Jacob, Robert Norman, Mary Elizabeth
Mastrantonio, Rosemary Harris

MY LIFE SO FAR

(MIRAMAX) Producers, David Puttnam, Steve Norris; Executive Producers, Bob Weinstein, Harvey Weinstein, Paul Webster; Director, Hugh Hudson; Screenplay, Simon Donald; Based on the book *Son of Adam* by Sir Denis Forman; Photography, Bernard Lutic; Editor, Scott Thomas; Co-Producer, Nigel Goldsack; Designer, Andy Harris; Music, Howard Blake; Costumes, Emma Porteous; Casting, Patsy Pollock; a presentation in association with the Scottish Arts Council Lottery Fund of an Enigma production in association with Hudson Film; British; Dolby; Color; Rated PG; 93 minutes; American release date: July 23, 1999

CAST

Edward Pettigrew ....Colin Firth
Gamma Macintosh ....Rosemary Harris
Heloise ....Irene Jacob
Moira Pettigrew ....Mary Elizabeth Mastrantonio
Uncle Morris Macintosh ....Malcolm McDowell
Fraser Pettigrew ....Robert Norman
Gabriel Chenoux..Tcheky Karyo
Elspeth Pettigrew..Kelly MacDonald
Rollo ....Roddy McDonald
Finlay ....Daniel Baird
Brenda ....Jennifer Fergie
Meg ....Kirsten Smith
Andrew Burns..Sean Scanlan
Uncle Crawford..John Bett
Aunt Eunice ....Anne Lacey
Debs Haig..Olivia Preston
Ruth Haig ....Sarah Turner
Jim Skelly ....Moray Hunter
Tom Skelly ....Jimmy Logan
Jim Menzies...Brendan Gleeson

Eileen McCallum (Mrs. Henderson), Carmen Pieraccini (Sissie), Elaine Ellis (Aggie), Julie Wilson Nimmo (Sarah), Elspeth McNaughton (Marnie), Freddie Jones (Reverend Finlayson), Stewart Forrest (Donald Burns), Caroline Spencer (Cassie Burns), Ralph Riach (Sir David Drummond), Andrea Hart (Lillian), Terry Neason (Hector), Jenni Keenan-Green (Caroline), Jenny Foulds (Frances), Clive Russell (The Tramp), Paul Young (Doctor Gebbie), Pamela Kelly (Euphemia Gebbie), Eric Barlow (Miner), Gordon McCorkell (Young Miner), Neil McMenemy (Miner's Son), Lorenzo Boni (Baby Fraser), Robyn Cochrane (Baby Brenda), Ross Anderson (Young Rollo), Joanne Turner (Young Debs Haig), Nicole O'Neill (Young Elspeth), Victoria Campbell (Young Meg), George Knight (Old Gardener)

In the Scottish Highlands, ten-year-old Fraser Pettigrew leads an idyllic life on the Kiloran House estate run by his level-headed mother and his eccentric, inventor father.

©Miramax Films

CABARET BALKAN

(PARAMOUNT CLASSICS) formerly *The Powder Keg*; Producers, Antoine de Clermont-Tonnerre, Goran Paskaljevic; Director, Goran Paskaljevic; Screenplay, Dejan Dukovski, Goran Paskaljevic, Filip David, Zoran Andric; Based on the play *Bure Baruta* by Dejan Dukovski; Photography, Milan Spasic; Art Director, Milenko Jeremic; Music, Zoran Simjanovic; Costumes, Zora Mojsilovic Popovic, Suna Ciftci; Editor, Petar Putnikovic; a MACT (France) - Ticket Productions (France) - Stefi S.A. (Greece) - Gradski Kina (Macedonia) - Mine Film (Turkey) - Vans (Yugoslavia) production; French-Greek-Macedonian-Turkish-Yugoslav, in Serbo-Croatian, 1998; Dolby; Color; Rated R; 100 minutes; American release date: July 23, 1999

CAST

Boris, the Esoteric Cabaret Artist	Nikola Ristanovski
The Boxer Who Takes the Train	Lazar Ristovski
Ana, the "Flirt" on the Bus	Mirjana Jokovic
The Young Man Chewing Gum Who Takes a Bus Hostage	Sergej Trifunovic
The Chain-Smoking Taxi Driver	Nebojsa Glogovac
Michael, the Homecoming Man	Miki Manojlovic
Alex, the "Reckless" Young Driver	Marko Urosevic
John, the VW Driver	Bogdan Diklic
John's Boxer Friend	Dragan Nikolic
The Bosnian Serb Mother	Mira Banjac
Viktor, Alex's Father	Danil Bata Stojkovic
The Bosnian Serb Father (Bus Driver)	Velimir Bata Zivojinovic

and Nebojsa Milovanovic (The Bosnian Serb Son Who Doesn't Want to End Up Like His Father), Aleksandar Bercek (Dimitri, the Crippled Ex-Cop from the Local Cafe), Vojislav Brajovic (Topi, the Ex-Student Revolutionary Trafficker), Ana Sofrenovic (The Desperate Young Woman on the Train), Ivan Bekjarev (The Man on the Bus Who Thinks He's Tough), Milena Dravic (The Lady on the Bus with the Hat and Fox Stole), Ljuba Tadic (The Orchestra Conductor Who Performs with Feeling), Toni Mihajlovski (George, the Eternal "Culprit," Ana's Boyfriend), Mirjana Karanoivc (Natalia, Michael's Ex-Fiancee), Dragan Jovanoic (Kosta, the Man with the Oar)

A series of connecting vignettes, all taking place on a freezing winter night in 1995 Belgrade, demonstrate the unrest of the Serbian people.

©Paramount Classics

Nikola Ristanovski

Dominic West, Luise Rainer

THE GAMBLER

(INDEPENDENT ARTISTS) Producers, Charles Cohen, Marc Vlessing; Director, Karoly Makk; Screenplay, Katharine Ogden, Charles Cohen, Nick Dear; Photography, Jules van den Stteenhoven; Designer, Ben van Os; Co-Producer, René Seegers; Music, Brian Lock; Costumes, Dien van Straalen; Editor, Kevin Whelan; Casting, Celestia Fox; a Channel Four Films and UGC DA International in association with Hungry Eye Pictures & KRO Drama presentation; British-Dutch-French-Hungarian, 1997; Dolby; Color; Not rated; 97 minutes; American release date: August 4, 1999

CAST

Fyodor Dostoyevsky	Michael Gambon
Anna Snitkina	Jodhi May
Grandmother	Luise Rainer
Polina	Polly Walker
Alexei	Dominic West
The General	John Wood
De Grieux	Johan Leysen
Mlle Blanche	Angeline Ball
Stellovsky	Tom Jansen
Pasha	William Houston
Ivan	Mark Lacey
Professor Ohlkin	Patrick Godfrey
Dunya	Lucy Davies

and Gijs Scholten van Asschat (Maikov), Marjon Brandsma (Mme. de Cominges), Ed de Bruin, József Pilissy (Croupiers), Vittoria de Bruin (Middle Aged Woman), András Fekete (Potapych), Zoltán Gera (Creditor), Greet Groot (Ustinya), Lajos István Hadjú (Dwarf), Zoltán Kamondy (Man in Rags), János Koltay (Casino Manager), Antal Konrád (Creditor), Antal Leisen (Butler), Nancy Manningham (Secretary), Károly Mécs (Hotel Manager), Peter Meikle (English Gentleman), Michael Mehlmann (Hanger-On), András Mész (Young Aristocrat), Ferenc Némethi (Doctor), Éva Papp (Grandmother's Maid), Géza Pártos (Pawnbroker), Milkós B. Székely (Anna's Father), Miklós Törkenczey (Shorthand Professor), Vera Venczel (Anna's Mother), János Xantus (Karl)

Anna goes to work as a stenographer for writer Fyodor Dostoyevsky, who is under pressure to deliver his new novel in twenty seven days to an unscrupulous publisher who has bought up all of the author's gambling debts.

©Independent Artists

THOSE WHO LOVE ME CAN TAKE THE TRAIN

(KINO) Producer, Charles Gassot; Director, Patrice Chéreau; Screenplay, Danièle Thompson, Patrice Chéreau, Pierre Trividic; Based on an original idea by Danièle Thompson; Photography, Eric Gautier; Set Designers, Richard Peduzzi, Sylvain Chauvellot; Costumes, Caroline de Vivaise; Editor, François Gedigier; Casting, Margot Capelier, Pascale Béraud; a Telema/Le Studio Canal+/France 2 Cinema/France 3 Cinema/Azor Films production; French, 1998; Color; Not rated; 122 minutes; American release date: August 4, 1999

Marie Daems, Vincent Perez

CAST

François	Pascal Greggory
Claire	Valéria Bruni-Tedeschi
Jean-Marie	Charles Berling
Lucien/Jean-Baptiste	Jean-Louis Trintignant
Louis	Bruno Todeschini
Bruno	Sylvain Jacques
Viviane	Vincent Perez
Thierry	Roschdy Zem
Catherine	Dominique Blanc
Elodie	Delphine Schlitz
Sami	Nathan Cogan
Lucie	Marie Daems
Geneviève	Chantel Neuwirth
Dominique	Thierry de Peretti
Bernard	Oliver Gourmet

A train carrying the friends, lovers and acquaintances of the deceased painter Jean-Baptiste makes its way to Limoges for his funeral, resulting in a most enlightening journey.

©Kino International

Valéria Bruni-Tedeschi, Vincent Perez

Jean-Louis Trintignant

THE ACID HOUSE

(ZEITGEIST) Producers, David Muir, Alex Usborne; Director, Paul McGuigan; Screenplay, Irvine Welsh, based on his short stories from the collection *The Acid House*; Photography, Alasdair Walker; Editor, Andrew Hulme; Costumes, Pam Tait, Lynn Aitken; Designers, Richard Bridgland, Mike Gunn; Associate Producer, Carolynne Sinclair Kidd; a FilmFour presentation of a Picture Palace North/Umbrella Production, produced in association with the Scottish Arts Council National Lottery Fund, the Glasgow Film Fund and the Yorkshire Media Production Agency; Scottish-British; Dolby; Color; Not rated; 112 minutes; American release date: August 6, 1999

Ewen Bremner, Arlene Cockburn

CAST

The Granton Star Cause
Boab...Stephen McCole
God ....Maurice Roëves
Kev...Garry Sweeney
Evelyn..Jenny McCrindle
Tambo..Simon Weir
Grant...Iain Andrew
Parkie..Irvine Welsh
and Pat Stanton (Barman), Alex Howden (Boab Snr.), Ann Louise Ross (Doreen), Dennis O'Connor (PC Cochrane), John Gardner (Sgt. Morrison), William Blair, Gary McCormack, Malcolm Shields (Workmates), Stewart Preston (Rafferty)

A Soft Touch
Johnny ....Kevin McKidd
Catriona ....Michelle Gomez
Alec...Tam Dean Burn
Larry ....Gary McCormack
Pool Player ....Scott Imrie
Alan ....Niall Greig Fulton
Deek ....William Blair
Skanko ....Cas Harkins
Drunk...Maurice Roëves
and Morgan Simpson (Chantel—Baby), Marnie Kidd (Chantel—Toddler), Alison Peebles (Mother), Joanne Riley (Diana), Sarah Gudgeon (New Girl), Katie Echlin (Wendy), William "Giggs" McGuigan (Pub Singer)

The Acid House
CoCo ....Ewen Bremner
Rory ....Martin Clunes
Jenny...Jemma Redgrave
Kirsty ....Arlene Cockburn
Emma ....Jane Stabler
Priest...Maurice Roëves
and Doug Eadie (CoCo's Father), Andrea McKenna (CoCo's Mother), Billy McElhaney (Felix the Paramedic), Ricky Callan (Tam the Driver), Barbara Rafferty (Dr. Callaghan), Stephen Docherty (Nurse Boyd), Ronnie McCann (Andy), Cas Harkins (Skanko)

Gary McCormack

A trilogy: The Granton Star Cause: a soccer player, dropped from his team, tossed out by his dad, dumped by his girlfriend and fired from his job meets a man who claims to be God; A Soft Touch: Johnny marries his pregnant girlfriend Catriona only to find that he is left holding the baby when his new wife begins carrying on with their arrogant neighbor Larry; The Acid House: Coco Bryce takes one acid trip too many and finds his adult mind transferred into the body of Rory and Jenny's new-born baby.

Alex Howden, Stephen McCole

BETTER THAN CHOCOLATE

(TRIMARK) Producer, Sharon McGowan; Director, Anne Wheeler; Screenplay/Co-Producer, Peggy Thompson; Photography, Gregory Middleton; Designer, David Roberts; Editor, Alison Grace; Costumes, Brad Gough; Associate Producers, Rosamond Norbury, Christopher Adkins; Music, Graeme Coleman; Casting, Lynne Carrow, Carole Tarlington, Claire Hewitt, Gail Carr; a Sharon McGowan and Peggy Thompson production; Canadian; Dolby; Color; Not rated; 103 minutes; American release date: August 13, 1999

CAST

Lila	Wendy Crewson
Maggie	Karyn Dwyer
Kim	Christina Cox
Frances	Ann-Marie MacDonald
Carla	Marya Delver
Paul	Kevin Mundy
Tony	Tony Nappo
Mr. Marcus	Jay Brazeau
Bernice	Beatrice Zeilinger
Judy/Jeremy	Peter Outerbridge
Skin Heads	Gerald Varga, Robert Parent
Safe Sex Advocate	Corrine Koslo
Religious Zealot	Veena Sood
Lila's Boss	Tony Marr
Woman in Real Estate Office	Colleen Wheeler
Woman in Washroom	Jenn Griffin
Courier	A.J. Bond

Nineteen year old Maggie meets Kim, the woman of her dreams, just before her brother and mother unexpectedly decide to move in with her.

Christina Cox, Karyn Dwyer

Julian Garner, Alex Dimitriades

HEAD ON

(STRAND) Producer, Jane Scott; Director, Ana Kokkinos; Screenplay, Ana Kokkinos, Andrew Bovell; Based on the book *Loaded* by Christos Tsiolkas; Photography, Jaems Grant; Designer, Nikki Di Falco; Editor, Jill Bilcock; Music, Ollie Olsen; Costumes, Anna Borghesi; a Great Scott production, in association with the Australian Film Finance Corp. and with the assistance of Film Victoria; Australian, 1998; Cinevex color; Not rated; 104 minutes; American release date: August 13, 1999

CAST

Ari	Alex Dimitriades
Johnny (Toula)	Paul Capsis
Sean	Julian Garner
Dimitri	Tony Nikolakopoulos
Betty	Elena Mandalis
Sophia	Eugenia Fragos
Joe	Damien Fotiou
Alex	Andrea Mandalis
Tasia	Maria Mercedes
Dina	Dora Kaskanis
Peter	Alex Pappas
Vassili	Vassili Zappa

and Chris Kaglaros (Groom), Ourania Sideropoulos (Bride), Anthony Lyritzis (Boy in Car), Ana Gonzalez (Woman Sweeping), Maya Stange (Janet), Aimee Robertson (Nose Ring Girl), Nathan Farinella (Young Ari), Paul Farinella (Young Peter), Allan Q (Vietnamese Man), Aris Gounaris (Dealer), Fiv Antoniou (Card Player), Nicholas Polites (Costa), Wasim Sabra (Charlie), Robert Henry Price (Fishing Cap Man), John Rakkas (Barman), Katerina Kotsonis (Ariadne), Nicholas Pantazopoulos (George), Michael Psomiadis (Grey Beard), Nikos Psaltopoulos (Stav), Chrystal Kyprianou (Mary), Diana Stathis (Woman), Marnie Statkus (Punk Girl), Costas Killas (Taxi Driver), Ayda Daher (Charlie's Mum), Nell Pigot (Senior Constable), Fonda Goniadis (Wog Cop), Gary McMahon (Thin Man), Okan Husnu (Rat), Blake Osborn (Good-Looking Guy), David Chisholm (Shaved Head).

Discontented 19-year-old Ari, the son of Greek immigrants living in Melbourne, confronts his homosexuality while trying to understand his relationship with his family and the aimlessness of his life.

STIFF UPPER LIPS

(COWBOY BOOKING INTERNATIONAL) Producers, Jeremy Bolt, Gary Sinyor; Director, Gary Sinyor; Screenplay, Paul Simpkin, Gary Sinyor; Co-Producers, Keith Richardson, Bobby Bedi; Co-Executive Producers, Andrew Cohen, Babs Thomas, Stephen Margolis; Executive Producer, Nigel Savage; Line Producers, Simon Hardy, Simon Scotland; Photography, Simon Archer; Designer, Mike Grant; Editor, Peter Hollywood; Music, David A. Hughes, John Murphy; Costumes, Stephanie Collie; Casting, Emma Style; a Cavalier Features and Impact Pictures presentation, in association with Yorkshire Films International, Kaleidoscope India Pvt, Filmania and the Isle of Man Film Commission; British, 1996; Dolby; Metrocolor; Not rated; 85 minutes; American release date: August 27, 1999

CAST

Horace	Peter Ustinov
Aunt Agnes	Prunella Scales
Emily	Georgina Cates
Edward	Samuel West
Cedric Trilling	Robert Portal
George	Sean Pertwee
Hudson Junior	Frank Finlay
Eric	Brian Glover
Mr. Tweeb	Richard Braine
Hurdlers	David Artus, Kevin Furlong
Don 1	Nicholas Selby
Don 2	John Boswell
Station Master	Jon Croft
Hudson Senior	Charles Simon

and Anna Livia Ryan (Rosie), Geoffrey Palmer (His Butler's Voice), David Ashton (Dr. Henry), Mac McDonald (American Husband), Kate Harper (American Wife), Rajendra Varman (Sitar Player), Miss Swati (Tea Server), Tigmanshu Dhulia (Stall Holder), Baron Baretto (Indian Boy), Sindhu Tolani (Indian Girl), Shri Vallabh Vyas (Defense Lawyer), John Winter (Prosecution Lawyer)

In 1908 England, Aunt Agnes's hopes to have her niece Emily married off to pompous Cedric are sidetracked when Emily finds her preferred mate in working class George.

©Cowboy Booking Intl.

Peter Ustinov, Prunella Scales

Sean Pertwee, Georgina Cates

THE VERY THOUGHT OF YOU

(MIRAMAX) a.k.a. *Martha, Meet Frank, Daniel, and Laurence*; Producer, Grainne Marmion; Director, Nick Hamm; Screenplay, Peter Morgan; Photography, David Johnson; Editor, Michael Bradsell; Associate Producer, Lesley Stewart; Designer, Max Gottlieb; Costumes, Anna Sheppard; Music, Ed Shearmur; Casting, Mary Selway, Victoria Thomas; a Channel Four Films presentation of a Banshee Production; British; Dolby; Color; Rated PG-13; 88 minutes; American release date: August 27, 1999

CAST

Martha	Monica Potter
Frank	Rufus Sewell
Daniel	Tom Hollander
Laurence	Joseph Fiennes
Pedersen	Ray Winstone
First Class Passenger	Debora Weston
Senior Partner	Jan Pearson
Information Officials	Steven O'Donnell, Rebecca Craig
Hotel Employee	Paul Bigley
Travel Agent	Geoffrey McGivern
Icelandair Official	Hamish Clarke
US Ground Stewardess	Lorelei King

and Steven Speirs (Taxi Driver), Robert Brydon (Bus Driver), Luke De Lacey, Sam Rumbelow, Stephen Mangan (Actors)

American airline employee Martha comes to London to establish a new life and winds up separately attracting the attention of three friends.

©Miramax Films

Joseph Fiennes, Monica Potter

BEDROOMS & HALLWAYS

(FIRST RUN FEATURES) Producers, Dorothy Berwin, Ceci Dempsey; Director, Rose Troche; Screenplay, Robert Farrar; Photography, Ashley Rowe; Editor, Chris Blunden; Designer, Richard Bridgland; Costumes, Annie Symons; Line Producer, Liz Bunton; Music, Alfredo D. Troche, Ian MacPherson; Casting, Gail Stevens; a Phaedra Cinema presentation in association with ARP, Pandora Film and BBC Films of a Berwin and Dempsey production; British, 1998; Color; Not rated; 96 minutes; American release date: September 3, 1999

CAST

Leo..Kevin McKidd
Jeremy ....Hugo Weaving
Sally..Jennifer Ehle
Keith..Simon Callow
Sybil..Harriet Walter
Darren..Tom Hollander
Angie...Julie Graham
Adam..Christopher Fulford
Brendan ....James Purefoy
John..Paul Higgins
Terry..Con O'Neill
and Merelina Kendall, Victoria Williams, Nicola McAuliffe (Lady Homeowners), Simon Green, Rowland Ogden (Gentlemen Homeowners)

Leo, a gay man seeking a meaningful relationship, is talked into joining a therapy group where he finds himself deeply attracted to ostensibly-straight Brendan, who is trying to get over his failed relationship with Sally.

© First Run Releases

Hugo Weaving

Rami Doueiri, Rola Al Amin, Mohamad Chamas

Rami Doueiri, Mohamad Chamas

Mahmoud Mabsout, Rola Al Amin, Rami Doueiri

WEST BEIRUT

(COWBOY BOOKING) Director/Screenplay, Ziad Doueiri; Line Producers, Rachid Bouchareb, Jean Brehat; Photography, Ricardo Jacques Gale; Music, Stewart Copeland; Designer, Hamze Nasrallah; Costumes, Pierre Matard; Editor, Dominique Marcombe; from La Sept Arte, 3B Productions; a co-production of Douri Films (Lebanon), Cine Libre Eliane Dubois (Belgium), Exposed Film Productions a.s., Bjorn Eivind Aarskog (Norway); Lebanese-Belgian-Norwegian-French, 1998; Color; Not rated; 105 minutes; American release date: September 3, 1999

CAST

Tarek ....Rami Doueiri
Omar..Mohamad Chamas
May ....Rola Al Amin
Hala...Carmen Lebbos
Riad...Joseph Bou Nassar
Neighbor ....Liliane Nemry
Oum Walid ....Leila Karam
Roadblock Militiaman.................................Hassan Farhat
Hassam (Baker) ....Mahmoud Mabsout
Papa Snake ....Fadi Abou Khalil

A group of teenagers in war-torn 1975 Beirut find that the political situation hasn't quite offered them the freedom they crave but instead has disrupted their rituals and daily adventures.

ALL THE LITTLE ANIMALS

(LIONS GATE) Producer/Director, Jeremy Thomas; Executive Producer, Chris Auty; Screenplay, Eski Thomas; Based on the novel by Walker Hamilton; Co-Producer, Denise O'Dell; Photography, Mike Molloy; Associate Producer, Hercules Bellville; Designer, Andrew Sanders; Editor, John Victor Smith; Music, Richard Hartley; Costumes, Louise Stjernsward; Casting, Celestia Fox; a Recorded Picture Company presentation in association with British Screen, J&M Entertainment, Isle of Man Film Commission, BBC Films, and Entertainment Film Distributors; British, 1998; Dolby; Widescreen; Technicolor; Rated R; 111 minutes; American release date: September 3, 1999

CAST

Mr. Summers	John Hurt
Bobby	Christian Bale
Bernard De Winter	Daniel Benzali
Mr. Whiteside	James Faulkner
Lorry Driver	John O'Toole
Des	Amanda Boyle
Bobby's Mother	Amy Robbins
Dean	John Higgins
Lepidopterist	Kaye Griffiths
Janet	Sevilla Delofski
Ice Cream Vendor	Helen Kluger

and Shane Barks (Young Bobby), Sjoerd Broeks (Mark), Elizabeth Earl (Child in Van), Andy Dixon (Philip), Michael Lewis (Vicar), Ruth Wright (Sandra)

Bobby, a brain damaged young man, escapes from his cruel stepfather and meets up with a nomad, Mr. Summers, who has left the world behind to spend his time burying animals thoughtlessly killed by humans.

©Lions Gate Films

John Hurt, Christian Bale

Christian Bale

WELCOME BACK, MR. McDONALD

(VIZ FILMS/TIDEPOINT PICTURES) Producers, Takashi Ishihara, Kanjiro Sakura; Executive Producers, Koichi Murakami, Hideyuki Takai; Director/Screenplay, Koki Mitani; Based on the play *The Radio Time* by Tokyo Sunshine Boys; Photography, Kenji Takama; Music, Takayuki Hattori; Editor, Hirohide Abe; a Fuji Television Network/Toho Co. production in association with Premier Intl.; Japanese, 1998; Dolby; Color; Not rated; 103 minutes; American release date: September 8, 1999

CAST

Kudo (Director)	Toshiaki Karasawa
Miyako Suzuki (Script Writer)	Kyoka Suzuki
Ushijima (Producer)	Masahiko Nishimura
Hiromitsu (Actor)	Jun Inoue
Security/Ex-Sound Effect Man	Shunji Fujimura
Nokko Senbon (Lead Actress)	Keiko Toda
Horinouchi (Executive Producer)	Akira Fuse
Hamamura Jo (Actor)	Toshiyuki Hosokawa

and Takehiko Ono (Ben Noda), Shiro Namiki (Suguru Hosaka), Yasukiyo Umeno (Furukawa), Yoshimasa Kondo (Miyako's Husband), Hiromasa Taguchi (Tatsumi), Moro Morooka (Bucky), Ken Watanabe (Truck Driver)

Five minutes before the premiere of the radio drama "The Women of Destiny" the leading lady suddenly demands script changes, resulting in a chaotic and tense evening for both cast and crew.

Jun Inoue

BLACK CAT, WHITE CAT

(USA FILMS) Producer, Karl Baumgartner; Executive Producer, Maksa C'atovic; Director, Emir Kusturica; Screenplay, Gordan Mihic, Emir Kusturica; Co-Producer, Marina Girard; Photography, Thierry Arbogast, Michel Amathieu; Editor, Svetolik Mica Zajc; Designer, Milenko Jeremic; Costumes, Nebojs'a Lipanovic; Music, Dr. Nelle Karajlic, Voja Aralica, Dejan Sparavalo, Emir Kusturica; an October Films release of a CIBY 2000/Pandora Film/Komuna Film co-production; French-German-Yugoslav, 1998; Dolby; Color; Rated R; 129 minutes; American release date: September 10, 1999

CAST

Matko Destanov	Bajram Severdzan
Zare Destanov	Florijan Ajdini
Grga Vellki	Ja'sar Destani
Little Grga	Adnan Bekir
Zarije Destanov	Zabit Mehmedovski
Grga Pitic	Sabri Sulejmani
Dadan	Srdan Todorovic
Afrodita	Salija Ibraimova
Bulgarian Customs Officer	Stojan Sotirov
Ida	Branka Katic
Uncle Sujka	Ljubica Adz'ovic
The Priest	Predrag Pepi Lakovic
Registry Officer	Predrag Miki Manojlovic

In order to pay a debt, gypsy Matko forces his son Zare into an arranged marriage to Afrodita, despite the fact that Zare prefers barmaid Ida.

©October Films

Rupert Everett, Asia Argento

Asia Argento, Jonathan Rhys Meyers

Florijan Ajdini, Zabit Mehmedovski

B. MONKEY

(MIRAMAX) Producers, Colin Vaines, Stephen Woolley; Executive Producer, Nik Powell; Director, Michael Radford; Screenplay, Michael Thomas, Chloe King; Based on the novel by Andrew Davies; Co-Executive Producers, Bob Weinstein, Harvey Weinstein; Co-Producer, Laurie Borg; Photography, Ashley Rowe; Designer, Sophie Becher; Editor, Joëlle Hache; Music, Jennie Muskett; Costumes, Valentine Breton Des Loys; Casting, Sharon Howard-Field, Karen Lindsay-Stewart; a Scala presentation of a Scala production and Synchronistic Pictures production of a Stephen Woolley production; British, 1998; Dolby; Technicolor; Rated R; 90 minutes; American release date: September 10, 1999

CAST

B. Monkey	Asia Argento
Alan	Jared Harris
Paul	Rupert Everett
Bruno	Jonathan Rhys Meyers
Mrs. Sturge	Juliet Wallace
Steve Davis	Ian Hart
Frank Rice	Tim Woodward
Goodchild	Bryan Pringle
Cherry	Clare Higgins
Angie	Simone Bowkett
Magnus	Michael Fitzgerald
Terence	Marc Warren
Barman (Conrans)	Camilo Gallardo
Carlo	Michael Carlin
Barman (Kings Head)	Paul Ireland
Nurse	Elisabeth Ash
Joy	Catherine Carter
Judith	Kate McGeever
Rudy	Jason Rose

and Amanda Boxer (Tory Lady), Vincent Regan (Johnny Hart), Kerry Shale (Texan), Serretta Wilson (Texan Wife), Eddie Marsan (Young Thug), Garry Catlin (Jim Arkwright), Jason Howard (Ricky Sturge), Tony Cyrus (Algerian Man), Paul Angelis (Gangster), Robin Lermitte (Manager), Dick Brannick (Mr. Gibson)

Armed robber Beatrice, known as "B. Monkey," believes she has escaped from her life of crime after falling in love with Alan, but her former criminal co-horts have no intention of seeing her shift over to a life of respectability.

©Miramax Films

EARTH

(ZEITGEIST) Producers, Deepa Mehta, Anne Masson; Director/Screenplay, Deepa Mehta; Based on the novel *Cracking India* by Bapsi Sidhwa; Executive Producers, David Hamilton, Jhamu Sughand; Photography, Giles Nuttgens; Designer, Aradhana Seth; Editor, Barry Farrell; Music, A.R. Rahman; India; Color; Not rated; 104 minutes; American release date: September 10, 1999

CAST

Dil Navaz, the Ice Candy Man	Aamir Khan
Shanta, the Ayah	Nandita Das
Hasan, the Masseur	Rahul Khanna
Lenny Sethna	Maia Sethna
Bunty Sethna	Kitu Gidwani
Imam Din	Kulbushan Kharbanda
Mr. Singh	Gulshan Grover
Rustom Sethna	Arif Zakaria
Butcher	Pavan Malhotra

The charmed life of eight-year-old Lenny comes to a halt when the 1947 partition of India takes place, leading to an eruption of violence between Hindus, Sikhs and Muslims.

©Zeitgeist Films

Nandita Das, Aamir Khan

Nandita Das, Rahul Khanna

Daniel Auteuil, child, Carole Bouquet

LUCIE AUBRAC

(USA FILMS) Producer/Director/Screenplay, Claude Berri; Based on the novel *Ils Partiront dans l'ivresse/Outwitting the Gestapo* by Lucie Aubrac; Executive Producer, Pierre Grunstein; Line Producer, Patrick Bordier; Photography, Vincenzo Marano; Costumes, Sylvie Gautrelet; Designer, Olivier Radot; Editor, Herve de Luze; Music, Philippe Sarde; Casting, Gerard Moulevrier; a Renn Productions, TF1 Films Productions, with the participation of Rhône-Alpes Cinéma, Pricel and D.A. Films, with the participation of Canal+ production French; Dolby; Technovision; Color; Rated R; 116 minutes; American release date: September 17, 1999

CAST

Lucie Bernard "Lucie Aubrac"	Carole Bouquet
Ramond Samuel "Raymond Aubrac"	Daniel Auteuil
Max	Patrice Chereau
Maurice	Jean-Roger Milo
Serge	Eric Boucher
Barbie	Heino Ferch
Charles-Henri	Bernard Verley
Paul Lardanchet	Jean Martin
Marie	Marie Pillet
Booboo	Maxime Henry
Lassagne	Alain Maratrat
Aubry	Franck de la Personne
Hardy	Pascal Greggory
Mr. Henry	Jean-Louis Richard
German Colonel	Hans Wyprachtiger
Lieutenant Schlondorff	Andrzej Seweryn
Pierrot the Forger	Gregoire Oestermann
Judith	Olga Grumberg

and Jacques Marchand (Justice of the Peace), Remy Darcy (Colonel Schwartzfeld), Hubert Saint Macrary (Dr. Dugoujon), Jean-Claude Bourbault (Colonel Lacaze), Yves Neff (Bruno), Jacques Bonnaffe (Pascal), Alain Sachs (Claude B.), Roland Amstutz (Attorney), Jean-Claude Grumberg (Raymond's Father), Daniele Goldmann (Raymond's Mother)

When French resistance fighter Raymond is captured and sentenced to death by the Nazis his wife Lucie risks her life to save him.

© October Films

ROMANCE

(TRIMARK) Producer, Jean-François Lepetit; Director/Screenplay, Catherine Breillat; Photography, Yorgos Arvanitis; Designer, Frédérique Belvaux; Costumes, Anne Dunsford Varenne; Editor, Agnès Guillemot; Music, D.J. Valentin, Raphaël Tidas; Casting, Michaël Weill, Estelle Bertrand, Nicolas Lublin, Guylène Péan, Jacques Grant, Catherine Hofer; a co-production of Flach Film , CB Films, Arte France Cinéma with the participation of Centre National de la Cinématographie, Canal+ and the support Procirep; French; Dolby; Color; Not rated; 97 minutes; American release date: September 17, 1999

Sagamore Stévenin, Caroline Ducey

François Berléand, Caroline Ducey

CAST

Marie ....Caroline Ducey
Paul ....Sagamore Stévenin
Robert Weil ....François Berléand
Paolo ....Rocco Siffredi
Ashley...Ashley Wanninger
Charlotte ....Emma Colberti
Claude ....Fabian de Jomaron
Man on Stairs...Reza Habouhossein
Scene in Arles
Model ....Carla
Photographer...Pierre Maufront
Hair Dresser...Antoine Amador
Hospital Scene
Echography Technician...Roman Rouzier
Head Doctor...Olivier Buchette
Midwife ....Emmanuelle N'Guyen
Nurse ....Nadia Latoui
Assistant Nurse ....Sylvie Drieu
and Samuel Chartier, Alexis Gignoux, Muriel Grégoire, Sébastien Jochmans, Emmanuel Salengro (Interns); Fantasy: Christian Potrasson (Lone Man), Melissa (Double for Maria)

When her lover Paul confesses his boredom with their relationship, Marie goes on a series of sexual adventures in a quest for self-knowledge.

©Trimark Pictures

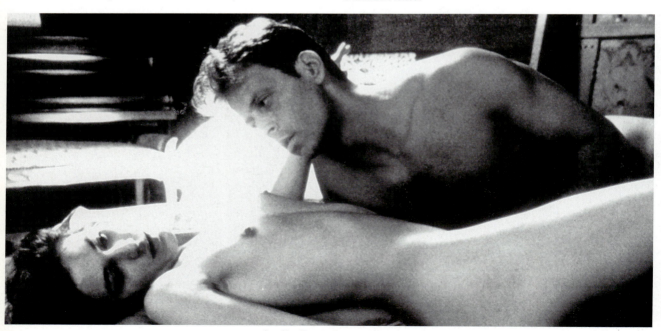

Caroline Ducey, Rocco Siffredi

PLUNKETT & MACLEANE

(USA FILMS) Producers, Tim Bevan, Eric Fellner, Rupert Harvey; Executive Producers, Gary Oldman, Douglas Urbanski, Selwyn Roberts, Matthew Stillman; Director, Jake Scott; Screenplay, Robert Wade, Neal Purvis, Charles McKeown; Based on an original screenplay by Selwyn Roberts; Photography, John Mathieson; Designer, Norris Spencer; Editor, Oral Norrie Ottey; Costumes, Janty Yates; Music, Craig Armstrong; Co-Producers, Jonathan Finn, Natascha Wharton; Casting, Jina Jay; a Gramercy Pictures presentation in association with The Arts Council of England of a Working Title production; British; Dolby; Super 35 Widescreen; Technicolor; Rated R; 102 minutes; American release date: October 1, 1999

Jonny Lee Miller, Robert Carlyle

CAST

Will Plunkett...Robert Carlyle
James Macleane...Jonny Lee Miller
Lady Rebecca Gibson ....Liv Tyler
Chance...Ken Stott
Lord Rochester ....Alan Cumming
Lord Gibson...Michael Gambon
Highwayman Rob...Iain Robertson
Eddie...Tommy Flanagan
Dennis...Stephen Walters
Catchpole ....James Thornton
Harrison...Terence Rigby
Lord Pelham..Christian Camargo
Newgate Priest..Karel Polisenky
Liz..Neve McIntosh
Sir Oswald...Matt Lucas
Viscount Bilston..David Williams

David Foxe (Lord Ketch), Jake Gavin (Newgate Gent), Alexander Armstrong (Winterburn), Ben Miller (Dixon), Jan Kuzelka (Peruquier), Vladimir Javorsky (Headbutted Tailor), Milena Sajdkova (Horse Dealer), Karel Dobry (Lewd Young Man), Daniel De La Falaise (MP), Tom Ward (Backbench Heckler), Nicholas Farrell (P.M.'s Secretary), Gordon Lovitt (Ranelagh MC), Claire Rushbrook (Lady Estelle), Tim McMullan (Bridegroom), Jeff Nuttal (Lord Morris), Dana Jurzova (Duchess of Stoke), Martin Serene (Josh), Dean Cook (Older Highwayman Kid), Jacob Yentob (Younger Highwayman Kid), Annabel Brooks (Widow with Garter), Tony Maudsley (Older Clergyman), Alex Palmer (Younger Clergyman), Victoria Harrison (Maria), Emma Faulkner (Young Girl Prostitute), Noel Fielding (Brothel Gent), Jack Walters (Duel Referee), Pavel Greg (Surgeon), Susan Porrett (Lady Newbold), Nichola McAuliffe (Lady Crombie), Anna Keaveney (Lady Marchant), Jacques Mathou (French Count), Michael Culkin (Judge Beresteade), Murray Lachlan Young (Gallows Priest), Dave Atkins (Landlord), Karel Augusta (Hangman), Drahomir Miraz (Hangman's Assistant)

Liv Tyler

Lower-class Will Plunkett, hoping to escape to America, and James Macleane, eager to advance in society, team for a life of crime to fulfill their ambitions.

Jonny Lee Miller, Liv Tyler

Alan Cumming

283

L'ENNUI

(PHAEDRA) Producer, Paulo Branco; Director, Cédric Kahn; Screenplay, Cédric Kahn, Laurence Ferreira Barbosa; Based on the novel *La Noia* by Alberto Moravia; Photography, Pascal Marti; Designer, François Abelanet; Costumes, Françoise Clavel; Editor, Yann Dedet; a co-production of Gemini Films, IMA Films, with the participation of Canal+ and CNC; French, 1998; Dolby; Color; Not rated; 120 minutes; American release date: October 8, 1999

CAST

Martin..Charles Berling
Cécilia ....Sophie Guillemin
Sophie ....Arielle Dombasle
Leopold Meyers ....Robert Kramer
Cécilia's Mother ....Alice Grey
Cécilia's Father ....Maurice Antoni
Maurice "Momo" Mayard................................. Tom Ouedraogo
Doctor...Patrick Arrachequesne
Meyers' Concierge...Mirtha Caputi Medeiros
University Dean ....Pierre Chevalier
Jean-Paul..Oury Milshtein
Agnès ....Anne-Sophie Morillon
Ferdinand ....Marc Chouppart

and Cécile Reigher (Ferdinand's Girlfriend), Antoine Beau (Pierre), Serge Bozon (Philosophy Student), Nicole Pescheux (Owner of Disreputable Bar), M'mah Maribe (Girl in Disreputable Bar), Seljko Zivanovic (Bouncer), Nathalie Besançon (Nurse), Gérard Arbeix (Owner of Momo's Cafe), Karim Grandi, Philippe Rebbot (Waiters at Momo's Cafe), Rosalie Coly (Woman in Telephone Booth), Estelle Perron (Voice of Prostitute), Karima Seddougui, Olga Zekova, Catherine Labbe, Aline Blondeau, Monique Le Mestre, Danielle Moro, Michelle Perrin, Sonia Mekoues, Alice Argentini, Marina de Luca, Catherine Chevalier, Catherine Contou, Bebita Bidounga (Prostitutes)

Martin, a philosophy teacher, bored with his married life, is driven to the brink of insanity by his desire for a young woman suspected of driving a colleague of Martin's to his death.

© Phaedra Cinema

Sophie Guillemin, Charles Berling

Fernando Fernán-Gómez

THE GRANDFATHER

(MIRAMAX) Producers, Luis María Delgado, Valentin Panero, Enrique Quintana; Director, José Luis Garci; Screenplay, José Luis Garci, Horacio Valcárcel; Based on the novel by Benito Peréz-Galdós; Photography, Raúl P. Cubero; Costumes, Gumersindo Andrés; Art Director, Gil Parrondo; Editor, Miguel G. Sinde; Make-up, Cristóbal Criado; a Nickelodeon production with the participation of Televisión Española; Spanish, 1998; Dolby; Color; Rated PG; 147 minutes; American release date: October 8, 1999

CAST

D. Rodrigo..Fernando Fernán-Gómez
D. Pío Coronado.....................................Rafael Alonso
Lucrecia ....Cayetana Guillén Cuervo
Senén ....Agustín González
Dolly ....Cristina Cruz
Nelly ....Alicia Rozas
Alcalde ....Fernando Guillén
Gregoria...María Massip
D. Carmelo...Francisco Algora
Alacaldesa ....Emma Cohen
Venancio ....José Caride
D. Salvador..Juan Calot
Consuelito ....Concha Gómez
Padre Maroto ....Francisco Piquer

A once wealthy and powerful count, now penniless, returns to Northern Spain to find out which of his granddaughters is his rightful heiress, a fact his one-time daughter-in-law hopes to keep him from finding out. This film received an Oscar nomination for best foreign-language film, 1998.

©Miramax Films

BEEFCAKE

(STRAND) Producers, Shandi Mitchell, Thom Fitzgerald; Direcor/Screenplay, Thom Fitzgerald; Photography, Thomas M. Harting; Designer, D'Arcy Poultney; Editors, Susan Shanks, Michael Weir; Music, John Roby; an Alliance/Atlantis production; Canadian; Dolby; Color; Not rated; 93 minutes; American release date: October 13, 1999

CAST

Bob Mizer ....Daniel MacIvor
Neil O'Hara ....Josh Peace
Mrs. Mizer ....Carroll Godsman

THEMSELVES

Jack LaLanne, Russ Warner, Dave Martin, Jim Lassiter, Joe Lietel, Joe Dallesandro, Valentine Hooven.

The story of physique photographer Bob Mizer, told through interviews with real-life muscle magazine participants from the 1950s, and interwoven with a dramatized story of a young man who comes to Hollywood to become an actor and winds up modeling for Mizer.

Ruth Gemmell, Colin Firth

Josh Peace

FEVER PITCH

(PHAEDRA) Producer, Amanda Posey; Executive Producers, Stephen Woolley, Nik Powell; Director, David Evans; Screenplay, Nick Hornsby, based on his book; Photography, Chris Seager; Designer, Michael Carlin; Editor, Scott Thomas; Music, Neill MacColl, Boo Hewerdine; Costumes, Mary-Jane Reyner; Casting, Liora Reich; a Channel Four presentation of a Wildgaze Films production; British, 1997; Dolby; Rank Film Labs color; Not rated; 102 minutes; American release date: October 15, 1999

CAST

Paul Ashworth ....Colin Firth
Sarah Hughes..Ruth Gemmell
Paul's Dad..Neil Pearson
Paul's Mum ....Lorraine Ashbourne
Steve..Mark Strong
Ted, the Headmaster..Ken Stott
Ray, the Governor ....Stephen Rea
Young Paul ....Luke Aikman
Paul's Sister..Bea Guard
Robert..Richard Claxton
Jo ....Holly Aird
Frank, Chip Shop..Peter Quince
Rex ....Charles Cork
Stan..Bob Curtiss
and Philip Bond (Turnstile Operator), Scott Baker (Man Behind), Annette Ekblom (Robert's Mother), Jackie Hyffes, Joe Reddington (Pupil's Parents), Graham Cull (Mr. Johnson), Mike Ingham (Radio Sports Commentator), Sam Dunbar Banks (Young Paul's Mate), Leigh Funnelle (Woman at Reading), David Hounslow (Man at Reading), Simon Bowen (Hillsborough Man), Silas Carson (Indian Waiter), Geoffrey Drew (House Owner), Liam Stapleton (2nd Governor), Emily Conway (Sasha), Tony Longhust (Taxi Driver), Shuli Morris-Evans (Party Baby), Brian Moore, David Pleat, Elton Welsby (Football Commentators)

Sarah finds herself competing with sports when she begins dating a fellow teacher, Paul Ashworth, a man obsessed with soccer in general and specifically a North London team, Arsenal, whose long losing streak is on the verge of being broken.

©Phaedra Cinema

Pierre Arditi, Agnès Jaoui, Lambert Wilson, André Dussollier, Sabine Azéma, Jean-Pierre Bacri

SAME OLD SONG
(ON CONNAÎT LA CHANSON)

(ARTISTIC LICENSE) Executive Producer, Bruno Pesery; Director, Alain Resnais; Screenplay, Agnès Jaoui, Jean-Pierre Bacri; Photography, Renato Berta; Set Designer, Jacques Saulnier; Editor, Hervé De Luze; Costumes, Jackie Budin; Music, Bruno Fontaine; from Merchant Ivory Films; an Arena Films, Camera One, France 2 Cinema, Vega Films, Greenpoint production, with the participation of Canal+, Cofimage 9, Sofineurope, Alla Film (Rome), Television Suisse Romande (SSR) and the European Coproduction Fund with the backing of Eurimages, the Centre National de la Cinematographie, the Procirep and the Office Federal de la Culture (Switzerland); French-Swiss-British, 1997; Dolby; Color; Not rated; 120 minutes; American release date: October 15, 1999

Agnès Jaoui, Sabine Azéma

CAST

Claude	Pierre Arditi
Odile Lalande	Sabine Azéma
Nicolas	Jean-Pierre Bacri
Simon	André Dussollier
Camille Lalande	Agnès Jaoui
Marc Duveyrier	Lambert Wilson
Jane	Jane Birkin
Father	Jean-Paul Roussillon

and Jacques Mauclair, Bonnafet Tarbouriech, Nelly Borgeaud (Doctors), Götz Burger (Von Choltitz), Jean-Pierre Darroussin (Young Man with Cheque), Charlotte Kady (Restaurant Customer), Pierre Meyrand (Cafe Owner), Claire Nadeau, Robert Bouvier; Frédérique Cantrel, Jérôme Chappatte, Nathalie Jeannet (Guests), Dominique Rozan (Elderly Man), Jean-Chrétien Sibertin Blanc (Young Fired Man), Wilfred Benaïche (Restaurant Waiter), Francoise Bertin (Little Lady on Tour), Romaine De Nando (Nurse), Delphine Quentin (Young Woman Kissing), Geoffroy Thiebaut (Marc's Colleague)

A roundelay of love complications involving various Parisians occur, with the characters expressing their feelings through lip-synched recordings.

©Artistic License

Pierre Arditi, Sabine Azéma

A GIRL CALLED ROSEMARIE

(CASTLE HILL) Producers, Bernd Eichinger, Uschi Reich; Executive Producers, Martin Moszkowicz, Robert Kulzer; Director, Bernd Eichinger; Screenplay, Bernd Eichinger; Photography, Gernot Roll; Art Directors, Harald Turzer, Thomas Freudenthal; Editor, Alex Berner; Costumes, Barbara Baum; Music, Norbert Schneider; a Hawkeye Entertainment presentation of a Constantin Film production for SAT-1 TV; German, 1997; Color; Not rated; 127 minutes; American release date: October 15, 1999

CAST

Rosemarie Nitribitt	Nina Hoss
Hartog	Heiner Lauterbach
Fribert	Mathieu Carrière
Bruster	Horst Krause
Marga	Hannelore Elsner
Christine	Katja Flint
Nadler	Til Schweiger
Von Oelsen	Heinrich Schafmeister

Rosemarie, an ambitious prostitute in 1950s West Germany, is persuaded by a French businessman to tape record the intimate conversations with her many important government clients.

©Castle Hill Prods./Hawkeye Entertainment

Rebecca Liljeberg, Alexandra Dahlström

Mathieu Carrière, Nina Hoss

Nina Hoss, Heiner Lauterbach

SHOW ME LOVE

(STRAND) formerly *Fucking Amal;* Producer, Lars Jonssön; Director/Screenplay, Lukas Moodysson; Photography, Ulf Brantås; Art Directors, Lina Strand, Heidi Saikkonen; Co-Producer, Peter Aalbæk Jensen; Editors, Michal Leszczylowski, Bernhard Winkler; Associate Producer, Anna Anthony; Produced by Memfis Film in co-operation with Zentropa Productions, Film i Väst, SVT Drama Götenborg and with support from the Swedish Film Institute/Charlotta Denward and the Danish Film Institute/Mikael Olsen; Swedish-Danish, 1998; Dolby; Color; Not rated; 89 minutes; American release date: October 15, 1999

CAST

Elin	Alexandra Dahlström
Agnes Ahlberg	Rebecca Liljeberg
Jessica	Erica Carlson
Johan Hult	Mathias Rust
Markus	Stefan Hörberg
Father Olof Ahlberg	Ralph Carlsson
Mother Karin Ahlberg	Maria Hedborg
Little Brother Oskar Ahlberg	Axel Widegren
Mother Birgitta	Jill Ung
Camilla	Lisa Skagerstam
Iktoria	Josefin Nyberg

and Johanna Larsson (Sara), Elinor Johansson (Jenny), Jessica Melkersson (Sabina), Lina Svantesson (Malin), Bo Lyckman (Man in Car), Daniel Teider (Johan's Little Brother), Nils Björkman (Bengtsson), Per Larsén, Kenneth Larsson (Teachers), Karl Strandlind (Ice Hockey Coach), Peter Teider (Marcus's Friend), Linda Malmquist (Sobbing Girl)

Fifteen-year old Elin, feeling trapped in her dead-end town and eager for experience, finds herself torn between her feelings for Johan and Agnes.

Lady Eboshi

San

Ashitaka, Yakul the Red Elk

PRINCESS MONONOKE

(MIRAMAX) Producer, Toshio Suzuki; Executive Producers, Yasuyoshi Tokuma, Bob Weinstein, Harvey Weinstein, Scott Martin; Director/Screenplay/Original Story, Hayao Miyazaki; English Language Adaptation, Neil Gaiman; Music, Joe Hisaishi; Voice Casting/Voice Direction, Jack Fletcher; Supervising Animators, Masahi Ando, Kitaro Kosaka, Yoshifumi Kondo; Telecom Animation Film, Atsuko Tanaka; Special Art Effects, Yoshikazu Fukutome; a Tokuma Shoten Nippon Television Network, Dentsu & Studio Ghibli presentation of a Studio Ghibli production; Japanese, 1997; Dolby; Panavision; Fujicolor; Rated PG-13; 115 minutes; American release date: October 29, 1999

VOICE CAST

Ashitaka	Billy Crudup
Jigo	Billy Bob Thornton
Lady Eboshi	Minnie Driver
Gonza	John Di Maggio
San, the Princess Mononoke	Claire Danes
Kohroku	John De Mita
Toki	Jada Pinkett-Smith
Moro	Gillian Anderson
Okkoto	Keith David

and Corey Burton, Tara Charandoff, Julia De Mita, Debi Derryberry, Alex Fernandez, Jack Fletcher, Patrick Fraley, John Hostetter, John Rafter Lee, Jessica Lynn, Sherry Lynn, Matt Miller, Marnie Mosiman, Tress MacNeille, Matt McKenzie, Michael McShane, Adam Paul, David Rasner, Dwight Schultz, Pamela Segall, K.T. Vogt (Additional Voices)

Ashitaka, on a journey to find the secret behind the curse placed upon him after inadvertently killing a protector-god, becomes involved in a bitter battle between two warring factions of humans and a race of forest-gods.

©Miramamx Films

Jigo

THE LEGEND OF 1900

(FINE LINE FEATURES) a.k.a. *The Legend of the Pianist of the Ocean*; Executive Producer, Laura Fattori; Director/Screenplay, Giuseppe Tornatore; Adapted from the stage monologue Novecento by Alessandro Baricco; Photography, Lajos Koltai; Designer, Francesco Frigeri; Music, Ennio Morricone; Editor, Massimo Quaglia; Costumes, Maurizio Millenotti; Visual Effects Supervisor, David Bush; Casting, Fabrizio Sergenti Castellani, Valeria McCaffrey, Jeremy Zimmermann; a Medusa Film production made by Sciarlo; Italian, 1998; Dolby; Technovision; Cinecitta color; Rated R; 116 minutes; American release date: October 29, 1999

Tim Roth

CAST

1900 (Danny Boodman T.D. Lemon 1900)	Tim Roth
Max Tooney	Pruitt Taylor Vince
Danny Boodman	Bill Nunn
Jelly Roll Morton	Clarence Williams III
The Girl	Mélanie Thierry
Music Shop Owner	Peter Vaughan
Plymouth Harbor Master	Niall O'Brien
Farmer	Gabriele Lavia
Mexican Stoker	Alberto Vasquez
The Young 1900 (age 4)	Easton Gage
The Young 1900 (age 8)	Cory Buck
Captain Smith	Harry Ditson
Disc Jockey	Norman Chancer
Black Guy	Sidney Cole
Napolitan Stoker	Luigi De Luca
Banjo Player	Agostino Di Giorgio
Black Stoker	Femi Elufowoju, Jr.
Chinese Stoker	Nigel Fan

Eamon Geoghegan (Sergeant), Piero Gimondo (Clarinetist), Kevin McNally (Senator Wilson), Luis Molteni (Commissioner), Roger Monk (Irish Stoker), Aida Noriko (Mattress Maker), Vernon Nurse (Fritz Hermann), Bernard Padden (Boatswain), Stefano Pagni (Bass/Tuba Player), Bryan Pringle (Ship's Recruiter), Michael Supnick (Trombonist), Ivan Truol Troncoso (Stowaway), Adriano Wajskol (Percussionist), Heathcote Williams (Doctor Klauserman), Wilson Du Bois (Radio Operator), Leonid Zaslavski (Polish Stoker), Steven Luotto ("Blind" Helmsman)

Jazz musician Max Tooney tells the unusual story of the world's greatest pianist, a foundling named 1900 who was born aboard an ocean liner and became that ship's entertainer, never setting foot on dry land.

©Fine Line Features

Mélanie Thierry

Pruitt Taylor Vince, Tim Roth

Clarence Williams III

DREAMING OF JOSEPH LEES

(FOX SEARCHLIGHT) Producer, Christopher Milburn; Executive Producer, Mark Thomas; Director, Eric Styles; Screenplay, Catherine Linstrum; Photography, Jimmy Dibling; Designer, Humphrey Jaeger; Editor, Caroline Limmer; Music, Zbigniew Preisner; Costumes, Maggie Chappelhow; Associate Producer, Chris Harris; Casting, Liora Reich, Carrie Hilton; a Christopher Milburn production in association with the Isle of Man Film Commission; British-U.S.; Deluxe; Dolby; Color; Rated R; 92 minutes; American release date: October 29, 1999

CAST

Eva Babbins	Samantha Morton
Joseph Lees	Rupert Graves
Harry Flyte	Lee Ross
Signora Caldoni	Miriam Margolyes
Father	Frank Finlay
Mr. Dian	Nick Woodeson
Maria Flyte	Holly Aird
Robert Babbins	Felix Billson
Janie Babbins	Lauren Richardson
Italian Doctor	Vernon Dobtcheff
Danny	Freddie Douglas
Nude Model	Richie Tonge

and Harry Selby, Julian Symmonds (Boxers), Juan Thomas (Referee), Emma Cunniffe (Red-Haired Girl), Siân James (Singer), Dyfan Jones (Double Bass Player), Doug Davidson (Saxophone Player), Terry Quayle (Trombonist), Don Elliott (Trumpet Player), Jim Caine (Pianist), Peter Gardner (Guitarist), Ken Ingham (Drummer), Anthony Hannan (Wedding Guest), Margaret John (Aunt Margaret).

Harry Flyte begins courting the sensuous Eva who agrees to move in with him but not marry him, due to her life-long infatuation with her cousin Joseph Lees, a man who has retreated from society after an accident has caused him to lose a leg.

©Fox Searchlight Pictures

Samantha Morton, Lee Ross

Rupert Graves

MY BEST FIEND: KLAUS KINSKI

(NEW YORKER) Producer, Lucki Stipetic; Executive Producers, André Singer, Christine Ruppert; Director/Screenplay/Narrator, Werner Herzog; Photography, Peter Zeitlinger; Editor, Joe Bini; Music, Popol Vuh; a Werner Herzog Filmproduktion/Cafe Production/Zephir Film co-production for the BBC, in collaboration with WDR, Arte, BR, YLE, with the participation of the Independent Film Channel; German-British; Dolby; Color; Not rated; 95 minutes; American release date: November 3, 1999. Documentary on director Werner Herzog's collaboration with the late actor Klaus Kinski.

WITH

Claudia Cardinale, Eva Mattes, Beat Presser, Guillermo Rios, Andrés Vicente, Justo Gonzalez, Benino Moreno Plácido, Baron v.d. Recke

©New Yorker Films

Werner Herzog, Klaus Kinski

ROSETTA

(USA FILMS) Producers, Luc Dardenne, Jean-Pierre Dardenne, Michele Petin, Laurent Petin; Directors/Screenplay, Luc Dardenne, Jean-Pierre Dardenne; Photography, Alain Marcoen; Designer, Igor Gabriel; Costumes, Monic Parelle; Editor, Marie-Helene Dozo; Associate Producer, Arlette Zylberberg; from October Films; a Les Films du Fleuve, RTBF (Belgium)/ARP Selection (France) production; Belgian-French; Dolby; Color; Rated R; 95 minutes; American release date: November 5, 1999

CAST

Rosetta	Emilie Dequenne
Riquet	Fabrizio Rongione
The Mother	Anne Yernaux
The Boss	Olivier Gourmet
The Campgrounds Manager	Bernard Marbaix
The Head of Personnel	Frederic Bodson
The Boss' Son	Florian Delain
Saleswomen	Christine Dorval, Mireille Bailly
The Mother's Boyfriend	Thomas Gollas
Policemen	Leon Michaux, Victor Marit
Madame Riga	Colette Regibeau
Girl in Locker Room	Claire Tefnin

and Sophia Leboutte (Fired Woman), Gaetano Ventura (Store Manager), Christian Neys, Valentin Traversi (Paramedics), Jean-Francois Noville (Hospital Worker)

17-year-old Rosetta, living in extreme poverty in a trailer park with her alcoholic mother, becomes determined to make a better life for herself.

©October Films

Sandra Oh

Don McKellar

LAST NIGHT

(LIONS GATE) Producers, Niv Fichman, Daniel Iron; Executive Producers, Caroline Benjo, Carole Scotta, Pierre Chevalier; Director/Screenplay, Don McKellar; Photography, Douglas Koch; Editor, Reginald Harkema; Designer, John Dondertman; Costumes, Lea Carlson; Co-Producer, Joseph Boccia; Casting, Diane Kerbel; a Rhombus Media presentation for Arte and the Canadian Broadcasting Corporation; French-Canadian, 1998; Dolby; Deluxe color; Rated R; 93 minutes; American release date: November 5, 1999

CAST

Patrick	Don McKellar
Sandra	Sandra Oh
Craig	Callum Keith Rennie
Jennifer	Sarah Polley
Duncan	David Cronenberg
Donna	Tracy Wright
Mrs. Carlton	Genevieve Bujold
Patrick's Mother	Roberta Maxwell
Patrick's Father	Robin Gammel
Alex, Jennifer's Boyfriend	Trent McMullen
Countdown Jogger	Jackie Burroughs

and Jessica Booker (Rose), Arsinée Khanjian (Streetcar Man), Charmion King (Grandmother), Bruce McDonald (Tough), Chandra Muszka (Streetcar Daughter)

A look at how various people prepare for the end of the world during the last remaining six hours of existence.

©Lions Gate Films

Emilie Dequenne

Pikachu, Ash

POKÉMON: THE FIRST MOVIE

(WARNER BROS.) Producers, Norman J. Grossfeld, Choji Yoshikawa, Tomoyuki Igarashi, Takemoto Mori; Executive Producers, Alfred R. Kahn, Masakazu Kubo, Takashi Kawaguchi; Director, Kunihiko Yuyama; English Adaptation Director, Michael Haigney; Screenplay, Takeshi Shudo; Adaptation Writers, Norman J. Grossfeld, Michael Haigney, John Touhey; Creator, Satoshi Tajiri; Photography, Hisao Shirai; Editor, Toshio Henmi; Art Director, Katsuyoshi Kanemura; Animation Production, Shogakukan Production Co. Ltd.; Animation Producers, Toshiaki Okuno, Shukichi Kanda; Music, Ralph Schuckett, John Loeffler, John Lissauer, Manny Corallo; Pokémon Theme, John Siegler, John Loeffler; Associate Producer, Kathy Borland; Chief Animator, Sayuri Ichiishi; Animation Supevisor, Yoichi Kotabe; Casting, Jim Malone; a Kids WB! presentation of a Pikachu Project '98-Shogakukan Inc. production in association with 4Kids Entertainment; Japanese; Dolby; Deluxe color; Rated G; 75 minutes; American release date, November 10, 1999

VOICE CAST

Veronica Taylor, Philip Bartlett, Rachael Lillis, Eric Stuart, Addie Blaustein, Ikue Otani, Ed Paul, Jimmy Zoppi, Michael Haigney, Kayzie Rogers, Ken Gates, Lee Quick, Lisa Ortiz, Amy Birnbaum, Megan Hollingshead, Eric Grossfeld, Tara Jayne

Ash Ketchum and his friends journey to New Island for the ultimate showdown between Pokemon Mew and the bio-engineered Mewtwo. Based on the video game, trading cards, and subsequent television series that premiered in the U.S. in 1998.

©Pikachu Projects '98

Mew

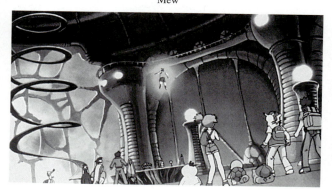

Mewtwo

Mew, Mewtwo

Bob Hoskins, Elaine Cassidy

FELICIA'S JOURNEY

(**ARTISAN**) Producer, Bruce Davey; Executive Producers, Paul Tucker, Ralph Kamp; Director/Screenplay, Atom Egoyan; Based on the novel by William Trevor; Co-Producer, Robert Lantos; Photography, Paul Sarossy; Designer, Jim Clay; Editor, Susan Shipton; Music, Mychael Danna; Costumes, Sandy Powell; Casting, Leo Davis; an Icon production, in association with Alliance Atlantis Pictures; British-Canadian; Dolby; Panavision; Deluxe color; Rated PG-13; 113 minutes; American release date: November 12, 1999

CAST

Joseph Ambrose Hilditch ....Bob Hoskins
Felicia ....Elaine Cassidy
Gala ....Arsinée Khanjian
Johnny Lysaght ....Peter McDonald
Felicia's Father ....Gerard McSorley
Mrs. Lysaght...Brid Brennan
Miss Calligary ....Claire Benedict
Young Hilditch..Danny Turner
Iris ....Sheila Reid
Sidney ....Nizwar Karani
and Ali Yassine (Customs Officer), Kriss Dosanjh (Salesman), Maire Stafford (Felicia's Great Grandmother), Gavin Kelty (Shay Mulroone), Mark Hadfield (Television Director), Susan Parry (Salome), Jean Marlow (Old Woman), Sidney Cole (Ethiopian), Barry McGovern (Gatherer), Sandra Voe (Jumble Sale Woman), Leila Hoffman (Bag Lady), Bob Mason (Jimmy), Emma Powell (Clinic Receptionist), Julie Cox (Marcia Tibbits), Nicki Murphy, Kelly Brailsford, Polly York, Gem Durham, Kerry Stacey, Laura Chambers, Bianaca McKenzie, Ladene Hall (The Lost Girls)

Felicia, a pregnant 17-year-old traveling through England to find her lover, crosses paths with Joseph Hilditch, a seemingly benign man who has murdered several women but has no conscious awareness of the crimes.

©Artisan Entertainment

Arsinée Khanjian

Bob Hoskins

Milla Jovovich

Milla Jovovich

THE MESSENGER: THE STORY OF JOAN OF ARC

(COLUMBIA) Producer, Patrice Ledoux; Director, Luc Besson; Screenplay, Andrew Birkin, Luc Besson; Photography, Thierry Arbogast; Designer, Hugues Tissandier; Costumes, Catherine Leterrier; Editor, Sylvie Landra; Co-Producer, Bernard Grenet; Music, Eric Serra; Casting, Lucinda Syson; a Gaumont production; French; Dolby; Technovision; Color; Rated R; 148 minutes; American release date: November 12, 1999

CAST

Joan ....Milla Jovovich
Charles VII ....John Malkovich
Yolande D'Aragon ....Faye Dunaway
The Conscience ....Dustin Hoffman
Alençon...Pascal Greggory
Gilles de Rais ....Vincent Cassel
Dunois..Tchéky Karyo
La Hire ....Richard Ridings
Aulon ....Desmond Harrington
Cauchon ....Timothy West
Talbot...Andrew Birkin
and Rab Affleck, Len Hibberd (Comrades), Stephane Algoud (Look Out), Edwin Apps (Bishop), David Bailie, David Barber, Timothy Bateson, Dominic Borrelli, Toby Jones, Philip Philmar, Brian Poyser, Ralph Riach, Peter Whitfield (English Judges), Christian Barbier, Christian Bergner, Patrice Cossoneau, Eric Tonetto (Captains), David Begg, Jerome Hankins (Noblemen—Rouen's Castle), John Boswall (Old Priest), Matthew Bowyer (The Bludgeoned French Soldier), Paul Brooke (Domremy's Priest), Bruce Byron (Joan's Father), Charles Cork (Vaucouleur's Priest), Tony D'Amario (Compiegne's Mayor), Daniel Daujon, Serge Fournier, Gerard Krawcyzk (Church's Peers—Coronation), Tonio Descanvelle (Xaintrailles), Philippe du Janerand (Dijon), Sylviane Duparc (Mary of Anjou's Lady's Companion), Barbara Elbourn (The Aunt), Christian Erickson (La Tremoille), Tara Flanagan (Woman—Rouen's Castle), David Gant (The Duke of Bedford), Sydney Golder (Cell's Guard), Jessica Goldman (Duchess of Bedford's Lady's Companion), Framboise Gommendy (Joan's Mother), Robert Goodman (Blackbeard), Jean Pierre Gos (Laxart), Joanne Greenwood (Catherine), Bernard Grenet (Senlis' Bishop), Valerie Griffiths (The Hag), Timothee Grimblat (Conscience—Child), Richard Guille (English Guard—Rouen's Castle), Thierry Guilmard, Didier Hoarau, Frank Lebreton (Assessors), Jacques Herlin (Orleans' Priest), Verka Jakob (Woman at the Cemetery), Michael Jenn (The Duke of Burgundy), Richard Leaf (Conscience—Young Man), Joseph Malerba (Beauvoir's Guard), Bruno Flender, Dominique Marcas, Joseph Rezwin, Frederic Witta (Poitiers' Inquisitors), Eric Mariotto (Young Monk), Rene Marquant (Rouen's Priest), Carl McCrystal (Glasdale), Gina McKee (The Duchess of Bedford), Phil McKee (RedBeard), Simon Meacock (The Teeth Soldier), John Merrick (Regnault De Chartres), Joseph O'Conor (Poitiers' Chief Inquisitor), Quentin Ogier (Louis), Kevin O'Neill (Scribe at Process), Melanie Page (Young Girl in Bath), Brian Pettifer (The Executioner), Enee Piat (Monk at Coronation), Irving Pomepui (Louis XI—5 years old), Olivier Rabourdin (Richemont), Vincent Regan (Buck), Rene Remblier (Dijon's Assistant), Mark Richards (Corridor's Guard in Rouen), Malcolm Rogers (Bishop), Tara Romer (Gamaches), Julie-Anne Roth (Young Girl in Bath), Olga Sekulic (Mary of Anjou), Joseph Sheridan (Canon), Vincent Tulli (Orleans' Physician), Jane Valentine (Joan—8 years old), Jemima West (Girl), Tat Whalley (Raymond)

The true story of how a 15th Century peasant girl, Joan of Arc, came to lead the French army in victorious battle against the English and ended up a matryr. Previous films about Joan of Arc include The Passion of Joan of Arc (1928, with Marie Falconetti); Joan of Arc (RKO, 1948, with Ingrid Bergman), and Saint Joan (UA, 1957, with Jean Seberg).

© Gaumont

Dustin Hoffman, Milla Jovovich

Faye Dunaway

Milla Jovovich

Tchéky Karyo, Desmond Harrington

Desmond Harrington, John Malkovich, John Merrick, Christian Erikson

Jackie, Lynn, Sue

42 UP

(FIRST RUN FEATURES) Producer/Director, Michael Apted; Co-Producer, Claire Lewis; Executive Producers, Ruth Pitt, Stephen Lambert; Editor, Kim Horton; Researcher, Melanie Archer; Photography, George Jesse Turner; a Granada Television production for the BBC; British; Color; Not rated; 139 minutes; American release date: November 17, 1999. The sixth enstallment in the documentary series that began with 7 Up in 1962, focusing on fourteen seven-year old children. The series has followed their lives at seven-year intervals under the titles *7 + 7 Up*, *21 Up*, *28 Up*, and *35 Up*. Of the original 14 children, 11 remain for this enstallment including Nick (physicist), Symon (ex-foster care boy), Jackie, Lynn and Susan (East End school mates), Tony (cab driver), Bruce (teacher), Paul (Aussie emigre), and Neil.

Alessandro Nivola, Frances O'Connor

Jonny Lee Miller, Embeth Davidtz

Embeth Davidtz, Alessandro Nivola

MANSFIELD PARK

(**MIRAMAX**) Producer, Sarah Curtis; Executive Producers, Trea Hoving, David Aukin, Colin Leventhal, David M. Thompson, Bob Weinstein, Harvey Weinstein; Director/Screenplay, Patricia Rozema; Based on the novel by Jane Austen, her letters and early journals; Photography, Michael Coulter; Designer, Christopher Hobbs; Editor, Martin Walsh; Music, Lesley Barber; Line Producer, Cathy Lord; Costumes, Andrea Galer; Casting, Gail Stevens; a BBC Films presentation in association with the Arts Council of England of a Miramax Hal Films production; British; Dolby; Deluxe color; Rated PG-13; 99 minutes; American release date: November 18, 1999

CAST

Fanny Price	Frances O'Connor
Mary Crawford	Embeth Davidtz
Edmund Bertram	Jonny Lee Miller
Henry Crawford	Alessandro Nivola
Sir Thomas Bertram	Harold Pinter
Lady Bertram	Lindsay Duncan
Mrs. Norris	Sheila Gish
Maria Bertram	Victoria Hamilton
Julia Bertram	Justine Waddell
Tom Bertram	James Purefoy
Mr. Rushworth	Hugh Bonneville
Fanny Price (age 10)	Hannah Taylor-Gordon
Yates	Charles Edwards
Young Susan	Talya Gordon
Carriage Driver	Bruce Byron
Young Maria	Elizabeth Eaton
Young Julia	Elizabeth Earl
Young Edmund	Philip Sarson
Teenage Fanny	Amelia Warner
Susan Price	Sophia Myles
Mr. Price	Hilton McRae
Betsey	Anna Popplewell
Boy with Bird Cart	Danny Worters
Dr. Winthrop	Gordon Reid
Ballroom Dancers	Jack Murphy, Peter Curtis, Emma Flett, Wendy Woodbridge

Fanny Price is taken from her life of poverty and sent to live with her wealthy relatives the Bertrams all of whom treat her as an inferior, except her cousin Edmund.

©Miramax Films

Alessandro Nivola, Embeth Davidtz, Sheila Gish

Lindsay Duncan, Frances O'Connor, Hugh Bonneville, Jonny Lee Miller, Victoria Hamilton, Justine Waddell, Sheila Gish

Alessandro Nivola, Jonny Lee Miller

Jonny Lee Miller, Frances O'Connor

Frances O'Connor, Harold Pinter

Frances O'Connor, Alessandro Nivola

Robert Carlyle

Sophie Marceau, Pierce Brosnan

Desmond Llewelyn, Pierce Brosnan, John Cleese

Maria Grazia Cucinotta

Denise Richards

Judi Dench

THE WORLD IS NOT ENOUGH

(MGM) Producers, Michael G. Wilson, Barbara Broccoli; Director, Michael Apted; Screenplay, Neal Purvis, Robert Wade, Bruce Feirstein; Story, Neal Purvis, Robert Wade; Photography, Adrian Biddle; Designer, Peter Lamont; Line Producer, Anthony Waye; Editor, Jim Clark; Costumes, Lindy Hemming; Music, David Arnold; Title song by David Arnold, Don Black/performed by Garbage; Second Unit Director, Vic Armstrong; Special Effects Supervisor, Chris Corbould; Main Title Designer, Daniel Kleinman; Casting, Debbie McWilliams; Stunts, Simon Crane; an Albert R. Broccoli's Eon Productions Limited presentation; British-U.S.; Dolby; Panavision; Deluxe color; Rated PG-13; 125 minutes; American release date: November 19, 1999

Pierce Brosnan, Desmond Llewelyn

CAST

James Bond ....Pierce Brosnan
Elektra King ....Sophie Marceau
Renard ....Robert Carlyle
Dr. Christmas Jones ....Denise Richards
Valentin Zukovsky ....Robbie Coltrane
M ....Judi Dench
Q..Desmond Llewelyn
R..John Cleese
Cigar Girl...Maria Grazia Cucinotta
Moneypenny ....Samantha Bond
Tanner ....Michael Kitchen
Charles Robinson ....Colin Salmon
Bull ....Goldie
Sir Robert King...David Calder
Dr. Holly Warmflash ....Serena Scott Thomas
Davidov ....Ulrich Thomsen
Gabor ....John Seru
Colonel Akakievich ....Claude-Oliver Rudolph
Lachaise ....Patrick Malahide
Foreman ....Omid Djalili
Dr. Arkov ....Jeff Nuttall
Coptic Priest ....Diran Meghreblian
Helicopter Pilot..John Albasiny
Pilot ....Patrick Romer
Pipeline Technicia ....Jimmy Roussounis
Captain Nikoli ....Justus Von Dohnanyi
Doctor ....Hassani Shapi
Trukhin ....Carl McCrystal
Newscaster..Martyn Lewis
Russian Radio Operator ....Kouroush Asad
Nina ....Daisy Beaumont
Verushka ....Nina Muschallik
Casino Thug...Daz Crawford
Casino Dealer...Peter Mehtab

Pierce Brosnan

James Bond is assigned to protect Elektra King who has inherited her father's vast holdings including an oil pipeline being built between Western Asia and Istanbul. The 19th official James Bond film and the third for Pierce Brosnan (Bond), Judi Dench (M), and Samantha Bond (Moneypenny). Robbie Coltrane repeats his role from GoldenEye while Desmond Llewelyn (who died on Dec. 19, 1999) appears for the 17th and final time as "Q."

Serena Scott Thomas, Pierce Brosnan

Baki Davrak, Jan Andres

Baki Davrak, Nisa Yildirim

Inge Keller

LOLA AND BILIDIKID

(PICTURE THIS! ENTERTAINMENT) Producer, Martin Hagemann; Executive Producer, James Schamus; Director/Screenplay, Kutlug Ataman; Co-Producers, Martin Wiebel, Zeynep Özbatur; Photography, Chris Squires; Designer, John Di Minico; Editor, Ewa J. Lind; Costumes, Ulla Gothe; Casting, Annette Borgmann, Cornelia Partmann (Germany), Yüzler Sesler, Elif Esin Cokünal; a Zero Film Production; German; Dolby; Color; Not rated; 91 minutes; American release date: November 19, 1999

CAST

Murat ....Baki Davrak
Lola ....Gandi Mukli
Bili..Erdal Yildiz
Kalipso ....Mesut Özdemir
Shehrazade...Celal Perk
Osman ....Hasan Ali Mete
Friedrich ....Michael Gerber
Ute ....Inge Keller
Iskender ....Murat Yilmaz
Hendryk ....Mario Irrek
Walter ....Jan Andres
Rudy ....Willi Herren
and Hakan Tandogan (Fatma Souad), Cihangir Gümüstürkmen (Lale Lokum), Nisa Yildirim (Fatma), Axel Pape (Dancing Man)

Osman, a 17-year-old Turkish taxi driver coming to terms with his homosexuality, runs away from his oppressive family life in Berlin and ends up in the Kruezberg section of the city where he meets up with his transvestite cousin Lola.

©Picture This! Entertainment

Gandi Mukli, Erdal Yildiz

HOLY SMOKE

(MIRAMAX) Producer, Jan Chapman; Executive Producers, Bob Weinstein, Harvey Weinstein, Julie Goldstein; Director, Jane Campion; Screenplay, Anna Campion, Jane Campion; Photography, Dion Beebee; Designer, Janet Patterson; Associate Producer, Mark Turnbull; Editor, Veronika Jenet; Music, Angelo Badalamenti; Casting, Alison Barrett, Billy Hopkins; Australian; Dolby; Color; Rated R; 114 minutes; American release date: December 3, 1999

Harvey Keitel, Kate Winslet

CAST

Ruth Barron	Kate Winslet
P.J. Waters	Harvey Keitel
Miriam (Mum)	Julie Hamilton
Gilbert (Dad)	Tim Robertson
Yvonne	Sophie Lee
Robbie	Dan Wyllie
Tim	Paul Goddard
Yani	George Mangos
Puss	Kerry Walker
Bill-Bill	Leslie Dayman
Prue	Samantha Murray
Stan	Austen Tayshus
Fabio	Simon Anderson
Carol	Pam Grier

and Eva Martin, Mira Wright, Polly Wright, Lior Aizenberg, S. Samaran, Michelle Abel, Adina Kumar, Jeff Silverman, Andreas Wagner, Vandana Mohinda (Devotees), Savrash, Saurabh Srinivasan (Dancing Boys), Dhritiman Chaterji (Chidaatma Baba), Genevieve Lemon (Rahi), Robert Joseph (Miriam's Taxi Driver), Arif (Boy Who Runs with Taxi), John Samaha (Chatiwali—Shiva's Diner), Jane Edwards (Priya), Miranda Cleary (Priya's Daughter), Tamsin Carroll (Jodie), T'Mara Buckmaster (Zoe), Ante Novakovic (Man with Trolley), Diana Kotatko, Patricia Lemon (Women with Trolley), Ethan Coker (Toddy Barron), Ellie Burchell (Tiffany Barron), Morgan Watt, Luke Testo, William Mackay, David Franco (Boyfriends), Eleanor Knox (Meryl), The Angels: Doc Neeson, Rick Brewster, John Brewster, Jim Hilburn, Brent Eccles (Band), Mark Gray (Dope Peddler), Cameron McAuliffe, Tim Rogers (Seducers), Johannes "Maddy" Brinkmann (Ruth's Boyfriend), Eric Schussler, Joan Bogden, Robert Lee (Cult Video Reporters)

Kate Winslet, Harvey Keitel

Ruth travels to India where she becomes part of a religious cult, prompting her concerned parents to hire a professional deprogrammer to bring her back to her traditional lifestyle.

©Miramax Films

Kate Winslet

Harvey Keitel

Julianne Moore, Ralph Fiennes

Julianne Moore

Ian Hart

Julianne Moore, Stephen Rea

THE END OF THE AFFAIR

(COLUMBIA) Producers, Stephen Woolley, Neil Jordan; Director/Screenplay, Neil Jordan; Based on the novel by Graham Greene; Photography, Roger Pratt; Designer, Anthony Pratt; Editor, Tony Lawson; Costumes, Sandy Powell; Co-Producer, Kathy Sykes; Music, Michael Nyman; Casting, Susie Figgis; a Stephen Woolley production; British; Dolby; Technicolor; Rated R; 109 minutes; American release date: December 3, 1999

CAST

Maurice Bendrix	Ralph Fiennes
Henry Miles	Stephen Rea
Sarah Miles	Julianne Moore
Henry's Maid	Heather Jay Jones
Mr. Savage	James Bolam
Mr. Parkis	Ian Hart
Lance Parkis	Samuel Bould
Waiter	Cyril Shaps
Bendrix' Landlady	Penny Morrell
Doctor Gilbert	Dr. Simon Turner
Father Smythe	Jason Isaacs
Miss Smythe	Deborah Findlay
Chief Warden	Nicholas Hewetson
Chief Engineer	Jack McKenzie

Two years after Sarah had ended her affair with Maurice, Maurice meets Sarah's husband Henry, an encounter which causes the former to have to confront his still-passionate feelings for Sarah. Previous film version was released by Columbia in 1955 and starred Deborah Kerr and Van Johnson. This film received Oscar nominations for actress (Julianne Moore) and cinematography.

©Columbia Pictures Industries Inc.

Julianne Moore, Ralph Fiennes

Julianne Moore, Samuel Bould

Ralph Fiennes, Stephen Rea

Stephen Rea

MISS JULIE

(UNITED ARTISTS) Producers, Mike Figgis, Harriet Cruickshank; Executive Producers, Annie Stewart, Willi Baer, Etchie Stroh; Director/Music, Mike Figgis; Screenplay, Helen Cooper; Based on the play by August Strindberg; Co-Producer, Jacquie Glanville, Photography, Benoît Delhomme; Designer, Michael Howells; Editor, Matthew Wood; Costumes, Sandy Powell; Casting, Jina Jay; a Moonstone Entertainment presentation of a Red Mullet production; Distributed by MGM; British; Dolby; Color; Rated R; 103 minutes; American release date: December 10, 1999

Saffron Burrows, Peter Mullan

CAST

Miss Julie..Saffron Burrows
Jean...Peter Mullan
Christine...Maria Doyle Kennedy
and Tam Dean Burn, Heathcote Williams, Eileen Walsh, Sue Maund, Joanna Page, Andrea Ollson, Sara Li Gustafsson, Bill Ellis, Duncan MacAskill, Katie Cohen, Helen Cooper, Flora Bradwell, Ernestine Hedger, Martin Gordon, Barbara Miles, Reg Beecham, Paul Duncan, Richard Burnett, Charlotte Mcleod (The Servants), Olivia Coles, Santi Rieser, Oliver Swan Jackson (Children), Sinead Jones, Griselda Sanderson, Christian Weaver (Musicians)

Miss Julie, the daughter of a wealthy count, sets out to seduce the Count's footservant, Jean, springing forth a confrontation between the two and Jean's lover, Christine.

Saffron Burrows

Lara Belmont, Tilda Swinton

Ray Winstone

THE WAR ZONE

(LOT 47) Producers, Sarah Radclyffe, Dixie Linder; Executive Producer, Eric Abraham; Director, Tim Roth; Screenplay, Alexander Stuart, based on his novel; Photography, Seamus McGarvey; Designer, Michael Carlin; Editor, Trevor Waite; Music, Simon Boswell; Costumes, Mary Jane Reyner; Casting, Jina Jay, Sharon Howard-Field; a Film Four presentation of a Sarah Radclyffe/Portobello Pictures production, in association with Fandango S.R.L. and Mikado S.R.L.; British-Italian; Dolby; Panavision; Color; Not rated; 98 minutes; American release date: December 10, 1999

CAST

Dad..Ray Winstone
Mum..Tilda Swinton
Jessie...Lara Belmont
Tom...Freddie Cunliffe
Lucy...Kate Ashfield
Carol...Aisling O'Sullivan
Nick..Colin J. Farrell
Nurse...Annabelle Apsion
Baby Alice..Megan Thorp
Barman...Kim Wall

A troubled fifteen-year old reclutantly moves with his family from London to Devonshire where he discovers a disturbing secret about his abusive dad and his older sister.

THE EMPEROR AND THE ASSASSIN

(SONY PICTURES CLASSICS) Producers, Chen Kaige, Shirley Kao, Satoru Iseki; Executive Producers, Han Sanping, Tsuguhiko Kadokawa, Hiromitsu Furukawa; Director, Chen Kaige; Screenplay, Wang Peigong, Chen Kaige; Photography, Zhao Fei; Designer, Tu Juhua; Costumes, Mo Xiaomin; Music, Zhao Jiping; Editor, Zhao Xinxia; Associate Producers, Philip Lee, Sunmin Park; a Shin Corporation and Le Studio Canal+ presentation of a New Wave Co. and Bejing Film Studio production in association with NDF; Japanese-Chinese-French; Dolby; Color; Rated R; 160 minutes; American release date: December 17, 1999

CAST

Lady Zhao ....Gong Li
Jing Ke ....Zhang Fengyi
Ying Zheng, King of Qin ....Li Xuejian
Dan, Prince of Yan..Sun Zhou
General Fan Yuqi ....Lu Xiaohe
Marquis Changxin ....Wang Zhiwen
Lu Buwei..Chen Kaige
Queen Mother ....Gu Yongfei
Gao Jianli ....Zhao Benshan
Qin Wuyang...Ding Haifeng
Prison Official...Pan Changjiang
Blind Girl ....Zhou Xun

In the third century B.C., King Ying Zheng, bent on unifying all of China, sets out on a rampage of terror, a goal his one-time lover Lady Zhao hopes to assist in by devising a fake assassination plot against him, giving him an excuse to invade his most potent obstacle, the kingdom of Yan.

©Sony Pictures Classics

Gong Li, Li Xuejian

Zhang Fengyi

Li Xuejian

TOPSY-TURVY

Allan Corduner, Jim Broadbent

Louise Gold, Timothy Spall

Jim Broadbent, Lesley Manville

(USA FILMS) Producer, Simon Channing-Williams; Director/Screenplay, Mike Leigh; Photography, Dick Pope; Designer, Eve Stewart; Editor, Robin Sales; Music, from Arthur Sullivan, Carl Davis; Costumes, Lindy Hemming; Make-Up & Hair Designer, Christine Blundell; Associate Producer, Georgina Lowe; Choreographer, Francesca Jaynes; Casting, Nina Gold; an October Films presentation in association with Thin Man Films/The Greenlight Fund/Newmarket Capital Group of a Simon Channing-Williams production; British; Dolby; Color; Rated R; 160 minutes; American release date: December 17, 1999

CAST

William Schwenck Gilbert...Jim Broadbent
Arthur Sullivan...Allan Corduner
Richard Temple ....Timothy Spall
Lucy Gilbert ("Kitty")...Lesley Manville
Richard D'Oyly Carte..Ron Cook
Helen Lenoir ....Wendy Nottingham
Durward Lely ....Kevin McKidd
Leonora Braham ....Shirley Henderson
Jessie Bond...Dorothy Atkinson
George Grossmith..Martin Savage
Mrs. Fanny Ronalds...Eleanor David
Madame Leon ....Alison Steadman
Richard Barker ....Sam Kelly
Louis..Dexter Fletcher
Clothilde ....Sukie Smith
Stage Doorkeeper..Roger Heathcott
Frank Cellier ....Stefan Bednarczyk
Armourer ....Geoffrey Hutchings
Butt ....Francis Lee
and Neenan (Cook), Adam Searle (Shrimp),Kate Doherty (Mrs. Judd), Kenneth Hadley (Pidgeon), Keeley Gainey (Maidservant), Gary Yershon (Pianist in Brothel), Gary Yershon (Madame), Julia Rayner (Mademoiselle Fromage), Jenny Pickering (Second Prostitute),Charles Simon (Gilbert's Father), Philippe Constantin (Paris Waiter), David Neville (Dentist), Matthew Mills (Walter Simmonds), Nicholas Woodeson (Mr. Seymour), Nick Bartlett, Gary Dunnington (Stagehands), Amanda Crossley (Emily), Kimi Shaw (Spinner), Toksan Takahashi (Calligrapher), Akemi Otani (Dancer), Kanako Morishita (Shamisen Player), Theresa Watson (Maude Gilbert), Lavinia Bertram (Florence Gilbert), Togo Igawa, Eiji Kusuhara (Kabuki Actors), Naoko Mori (Miss "Sixpence Please"), Eve Pearce (Gilbert's Mother), Neil Humphries (Boy Actor), Vincent Franklin (Rutland Barrington), Michael Simkins (Frederick Bovill), Cathy Sara (Sibyl Grey), Angela Curran (Miss Morton), Millie Gregory (Alice), Jonathan Aris (Wilhelm), Andy Serkis (John D'Auban), Mia Soteriou (Mrs. Russell), Louise Gold (Rosina Brandram), Shaun Glanville (Mr. Harris), Julian Bleach (Mr. Plank), Neil Salvage (Mr. Hurley), Matt Bardock (Mr. Tripp), Bríd Brennan (Madwoman); Ladies and Gentlemen of the Chorus: Mark Benton (Mr. Price), Heather Craney (Miss Russell), Julie Jupp (Miss Meadows), John Warnaby (Mr. Sanders), Kacey Ainsworth (Miss Fitzherbert), Ashley Artus (Mr. Marchmont), Richard Attlee (Mr. Gordon), Paul Barnhill (Mr. Flagstone), Nicholas Boulton (Mr. Conyngham), Lorraine Brunning (Miss Jardine), Simon Butteriss (Mr. Lewis), Wayne Cater (Mr. Rhys), Rosie Cavaliero (Miss Moore), Michelle Chadwick (Miss Warren), Debbie Chazen (Miss Kingsley), Richard Coyle (Mr. Hammond), Monica Dolan (Miss Barnes), Sophie Duval (Miss Brown), Anna Francolini (Miss Biddles), Teresa Gallagher (Miss Coleford), Sarah Howe (Miss Woods), Ashley Jensen (Miss Tringham), Gemma Page (Miss Langton-James), Paul Rider (Mr. Bentley), Mary Roscoe (Miss Carlyle), Steven Speirs (Mr. Kent), Nicola Wainwright (Miss Betts), Angie Wallis (Miss Wilkinson), Kevin Walton (Mr. Evans)

Following the failure of their latest operetta, librettist William Gilbert and composer Arthur Sullivan plan to dissolve their partnership but are contractually obligated to produce one more work for impressario Richard D'Oyly Carte, resulting in the creation of The Mikado. Previous film on Gilbert & Sullivan was The Story of Gilbert and Sullivan (released in the United States in 1953 as The Great Gilbert and Sullivan) starring Robert Morley and Maurice Evans.

1999 Academy Award-winner for Best Costume Design and Makeup. This film received additional Oscar nominations for original screenplay and art direction.

Katrin Cartlidge, Allan Corduner

Jim Broadbent

Jim Broadbent

Dorothy Atkinson, Shirley Henderson, Cathy Sara

Allan Corduner, Timothy Spall, Jim Broadbent

ONEGIN

(SAMUEL GOLDWYN) Producers, Ileen Maisel, Simon Bosanquet; Executive Producer, Ralph Fiennes; Director, Martha Fiennes; Screenplay, Michael Ignatieff, Peter Ettedgui; Based upon the verse novel by Alexander Pushkin; Photography, Remi Adefarasin; Designer, Jim Clay; Editor, Jim Clark; Music, Magnus Fiennes; Costumes, Chloe Obolensky, John Bright; Casting, Mary Selway; a Seven Arts Intl., Starz! Pictures, in association with Samuel Goldwyn Films/Canwest Entertainment presentation of a Baby Productions production; British; Dolby; Deluxe color; Not rated; 106 minutes; American release date: December 17, 1999

CAST

Evgeny Onegin	Ralph Fiennes
Tatyana Larin	Liv Tyler
Prince Nikitin	Martin Donovan
Vladimir Lensky	Toby Stephens
Olga Larin	Lena Headey
Guillot	Jason Watkins
Zaretsky	Alun Armstrong
Madame Larina	Harriet Walter
Princess Alina	Irene Worth
Katiusha	Francesca Annis
Anisia	Gwenllian Davies
Triquet	Simon McBurney
Andrey Petrovich	Geoff McGivern
Nanya	Margery Withers
Dandies	Tim McMullan, Tim Potter
Diplomat	Richard Bremmer
Mme. Volkonsky	Elizabeth Berrington

and Ian East (Executor), Chloe Elise Hanslip (Child Violinist), Marion Betzold (Ballerina), Chris Lee Wright (The Hussar), Tom Eastwood (Onegin's Uncle), Sophie Fiennes

Evgeny Onegin, a cynical, outspoken Russian sophisticate arrives in the country to claim an estate he has inherited and develops a relationship with his neighbor Lensky, Lensky's fiancee Olga, and Olga's sister Tatyana, who develops an attraction to the cold-hearted outsider.

© Samuel Goldwyn Films

Ralph Fiennes

Liv Tyler

Toby Stephens, Ralph Fiennes

Ralph Fiennes

Berl Senofsky in *The Winners* ©First Run Features

Paolo Massafra, Fabio Frascaro in *Pizzicata* ©Milestone Film

THE WINNERS (First Run Features) Producer, Nellie Kamer; Director/Photography, Paul Cohen; Screenplay, Paul Cohen, David van Tijn; Based on an original idea by David van Tijn; Editor, Ian Overweg; a VPRO/BRTN production; Dutch, 1998; Color; Not rated; 84 minutes; U.S. release: Jan. 20, 1999. Documentary looks at what happened to four musicians who had won prizes at Brussel's Queen Elizabeth Competition, featuring Philipp Hirschhorn, Berl Senofsky, Yevgeny Moguilevsky, Mikhail Bezverkhny, Mischa Maisky, Gidon Kremer.

GYPSY LORE (Bunyik) Director, Bence Gyöngyössy; Screenplay, Bence Gyöngyössy, András Nagy; Not other credits available; German-Hungarian-Bulgarian, 1997; Dolby; Color; Not rated; 93 minutes; U.S. release: Jan. 22, 1999. CAST: Djoko Rosic (Lover), Silvia Pincu (Sarolta), Mihály Szabados (Tamáska), János Derzsi, Diliana Dimitriova, Violetta Koleva.

THE MILKY WAY (Kino Intl.) Executive Producer, Muhammad Bakriah; Director, Ali Nassar; Screenplay, Ali Nassar, Ghalib Sha'ath; Photography, Amnon Salomon; Music, Nachum Heiman; Editors, Era Lapid, Tova Asher; a Sanabil production; Israeli, 1997; Color; Not rated; 104 minutes; U.S. release: Jan. 22, 1999. CAST: Muhammad Bakri (Mahmmud), Suheil Haddad (Mabruq), Mihaela Mitraki (Jamilah), Makram Khoury (The Mukhtar), Yussef Abu Warda (The Military Governor), Mahmmud Abu Jazi (Ahmad the Teacher)

PIZZICATA (Milestone) Producers, Edoardo Winspeare, Dieter Horres, Fratelli Guercia Sammarco; Director/Screenplay, Edoardo Winspeare; Photography, Paolo Carnera; Editor, Carlotta Cristiani; Costumes, Silvia Nebiolo; an Edoardo Winspeare, Classic SRL, Horres Film, Les Films du Paradoxe production; Italian, 1996; Color; Not rated; 93 minutes; U.S. release: Feb. 3, 1999. CAST: Cosimo Cinieri (Carmine Pantaleo), Fabio Frascaro (Tony Marciano), Chiara Torelli (Cosima Pantaleo), Anna Dimitri (Immacolata Pantaleo), Ines d'Anbrosio (Nzina Pantaleo), Paolo Massafra (Pasquale), Lamberto Probo (Donato Pantaleo)

THE TRIO (Attitude Films) Producers, Laurens Straub, Pia Frankenberg; Director, Hermine Huntgeburth; Screenplay, Horst Sczerba, Volker Einrauch, Hermine Huntgeburth; Photography, Martin Kukula; Art Director, Katharina Wöppermann; Costumes, Peri de Braganca; Editor, Ingrid Martell; Music, Niki Reiser; Casting, Risa Kes; a Next Film production in association with NDR, ORF and Arte; German, 1998; Dolby; Color; Not rated; 98 minutes; U.S. release: Feb. 12, 1999. CAST: Götz George (Zobel), Jeanette Hain (Lizzie), Felix Eitner (Rudolf), Christian Redl (Karl), Angelika Bartsch (Dorothee), Uwe Rohde (Police), Tana Schanzara (Wirtin)

PAULINA (Turbulent Arts) Producers/Editors, Jennifer Maytorena Taylor, Vicky Funari; Director, Vicky Funari; Screenplay, Vicky Funari, Paulina Cruz Suarez, Jennifer Maytorena Taylor; Photography, Marie Christine Camus; Music, Pauline Oliveros; a CineMamas production, in association with the Banff Centre for the Arts; Canadian-Mexican-U.S.; Color; Not rated; 88 minutes; U.S. release: Feb. 12, 1999. CAST: Paulina Cruz Suarez (Herself), Mathyselene Heredia Castillo (Paulina—young adult), Mariam Manzano Duran (Paulina—age 8), Erika Isabel de la Cruz Ramirez (Paulina, age 13), Emigdia Hernandez Suarez (Franca), Raul Amado (Facundo), Rene Pereyra (Mauro), Maira Sebulo (Placida), Alicia Ortega (Luz Maria), Lolo Navarro (Woman on Bus)

Suheil Haddad, Muhammad Bakri in *The Milky Way* ©Kino Intl.

Felix Eitner, Jeanette Hain in *The Trio* ©Attitude Films

Mirlan Abdykalykov in *Beshkempir: The Adopted Son* ©Fox Lorber

Baltasar Kormakur in *Devil's Island* ©Artistic License Films

BESHKEMPIR: THE ADOPTED SON (Fox Lorber) Producers, Irizaï Alibaev, Cedomir Kolar; Director, Aktan Abdykalykov; Screenplay, Aktan Abdykalykov, Avtandil Adikulov, Marat Sarulu; Photography, Hassan Kidirialev; Editor, Tilck Mambetova; Music, Nurlan Nishanov; from Kyrgyzfilm/Noé Productions; Kyrgyzstani-French, 1998; Color/black and white; Not rated; 81 minutes; U.S. release: Feb. 17, 1999. CAST: Mirlan Abdykalykov (Beshkempir), Albina Imasmeva, Adir Abilkassimov, Bakit Zilkieciev, Mirlan Cinkozoev

THE APPLE (New Yorker) Producers, Marin Karmitz, Veronique Cayla; Executive Producer, Iraj Sarbaz; Director, Samira Makhmalbaf; Screenplay/Editor, Mohsen Makhmalbaf; Photography, Ebrahim Ghafori, Mohamad Ahmadi; Iranian; Color; Not rated; 85 minutes; U.S. release: Feb. 19, 1999. CAST: Massoumeh Naderi (Massoumeh), Zahra Naderi (Zahra), Ghorbanali Naderi (Father), Soghra Behrozi (Mother), Azizeh Mohamadi (Social Worker)

FISTFUL OF FLIES (Southern Star) Producer, Julia Overton; Director/Screenplay, Monica Pellizzari; Photography, Jane Castle; Designer, Lissa Coote; Editor, James Manche; Music, Felicity Fox; Casting, Maura Fay Associates; Australian, 1997; Color; Not rated; 85 minutes; U.S. release: March 5, 1999. CAST: Dina Panozzo (Grace), Tasma Walton (Mars), John Lucantonio (Joe), Anna Volska (Nonna), Maria Venuti (Magda), Rachael Maza (Dr. Powers), Giordano Gangl (Ercole), Cathren Michalak (Innocentina)

DEVIL'S ISLAND (Artistic License) Producers, Fridrik Thor Fridriksson, Peter Rommel, Egil Odegaard, Peter Aalbaek Jenson; Director, Fridrik Thor Fridriksson; Screenplay, Einar Kárason; Photography/Line Producer, Ari Kristinsson; Designer, Arni Pall Johannsson; Editors, Steingrimur Karisson, Skule Eriksen; Costumes, Karl Aspelund; Music, Hilmar Örn Jilmarsson; an Icelandic Film Corporation, Reykjavik, Peter Rommel Film production (Berlin), Filmhuset, Osio and Zentropa Entertainments (Copenhagen); Icelandic-German; Color; Not rated; 103 minutes; U.S. release: March 12, 1999. CAST: Baltasar Kormakur (Baddi), Gisli Halldorsson (Thomas), Sigurveig Jonsdottir (Karolina), Halldora Geirhardsdottir (Dolly), Sveinn Geirsson (Danni), Guomudur Olafsson (Grettir), Ingvar E. Sigurdsson (Grjoni), Magnus Oafsson (Hreggvidur), Pallna Jonsdottir (Hveragerdur), Saga Jonsdottir (Gogo), Amijotur Sigurdsson (Bobo), Oskar Jonasson (Lul Lul), Ævar Orn Josepsson (Maggi Bjuti), Helga Braga Jonsdottir (Greta), Margaret Akadottir (Fia), Sigurdur Sigurjonsson (Toti), Gudrun Gisladottir (Porjunnur), Arni Tryggvason (Grjoni's Grandfather)

I STAND ALONE (Strand) Producer/Director/Screenplay, Gaspar Noe; Photography, Dominique Colin; Editors, Lucille Hadzihalilovic, Gaspar Noe; a Cinemas de La Zone/Lovestreams production with the participation of CNC; French; Color; Widescreen; Not rated; 93 minutes; U.S. release: March 17, 1999. CAST: Philippe Nahon (The Butcher), Frankye Pain (His Mistress), Blandine Lenoir (His Daughter, Cynthia), Martin Audrain (Mother-in-Law), Jean-Francois Rauger (Real Estate Agent), Guillaume Nicloux (Supermarket Manager), Olivier Doran (Narrator), Aissa Djbari (Dr. Choukroun), Serge Faurie (Hospital Director), Paule Abecassis (Junkie)

Massoumeh Naderi, Zahra Naderi in *The Apple* ©New Yorker Films

Philippe Nahon in *I Stand Alone* ©Strand Releasing

Dragon Urlic in *The Underground Orchestra* ©First Run/Icarus

Photographer ©Seventh Art

DOING TIME FOR PATSY CLINE (**Cowboy Booking**) Producers, John Winter, Chris Kennedy; Director/Screenplay, Chris Kennedy; Photography, Andrew Lesnie; Editor, Ken Sallows; Music, Peter Best; Designer, Roger Ford; Costumes, Louise Wakefield; Casting, Christine King; an Oilrag Prods. production, in association with the Australian Film Finance Corp., the NSW Film & Television Office, Southern Star; Australian, 1997; Dolby; Movielab color; Not rated; 93 minutes; U.S. release: March 19, 1999. CAST: Richard Roxburgh (Boy), Miranda Otto (Patsy), Matt Day (Ralph), Tony Barry, Kirk Paramore, Laurence Coy, Annie Byron, Roy Billing, Gus Mercurio, Betty Bobbitt, Frank Whitten, Tom Long, Wayne Pygram, Jeff Truman.

LILIAN'S STORY (**Phaedra**) Producer, Marian MacGowan; Executive Producers, David Court, Jeremy Bean; Co-Producer, Mike Wilcox; Director, Jerzy Domaradzki; Screenplay, Steve Wright; Based on the book by Kate Grenville; Photography, Slawomir Idziak; Editor, Lee Smith; Music, Cezary Skubiszewski; Designer, Roger Ford; Casting, Christine King; an Australian Film Finance Corp./Movieco Australia presentation of a CML production; Australian, 1996; Dolby; Atlab color; Not rated; 94 minutes; U.S. release: March 26, 1999. CAST: Ruth Cracknell (Lilian Singer), Barry Otto (John Singer/Albion Singer), Toni Collette (Young Lilian), John Flaus (Frank Stroud), Iris Shand (Aunt Kitty), Susie Lindeman (Jewel), Anne Louise Lambert (Lilian's Mother), Essie Davis (Zara), Morgan Smallbone (Young Frank), Mary Regan (Angelique), Jeff Truman (Riser), Bogdan Koca (Slav Taxi Driver), Bob Maza (Last Taxi Driver), David Argue (Spruiker)

MEETING PEOPLE IS EASY (**Seventh Art**) Director, Grant Gee; No other credits available; Color; Not rated; 94 minutes; U.S. release: March 26, 1999. Documentary follows the rock group Radiohead on their 1997 world tour, in the wake of their critically acclaimed album "OK Computer." Featuring Colin Greenwood, Ed O'Brien, Jonny Greenwood, Thom Yorke, Phil Selway (Radiohead)

THE UNDERGROUND ORCHESTRA (**First Run/Icarus Films**) Producer, Pieter van Huystee; Director, Heddy Honigmann; Screenplay/Reserach, Heddy Honigmann, Nosh van der Lely; Photography, Eric Guichard; Editor, Mario Steenbergen; Co-Producer, VPRO Televisie; French-Spanish, 1998; Color; Not rated; 108 minutes; U.S. release: March 31, 1999. Documentary about the musicians who play on the sidewalks of Paris and in the Metro.

PHOTOGRAPHER (**Seventh Art**) Producer/Director, Dariusz Jablonski; Screenplay, Andrzej Bodek, Arnold Mostowicz, Dariusz Jablonski; Co-Producer, Wolfgang Katzke; Photography, Tomasz Michalowski; Music, Michal Lorenc; Editor, Milenia Fiedler; an Apple Film Production; Polish-French, 1998; Dolby; Black & white/color; Not rated; 80 minutes; U.S. release: April 16, 1999. Documentary on how Walter Genewein kept a photographic account of the destruction of Polish Jews in the Lodz Ghetto from 1939 to 1944.

OPEN YOUR EYES (**Artisan**) Producer, José Luis Cuerda; Executive Producers, Fernando Bovaira, José Luis Cuerda; Director, Alejandro Amenábar; Screenplay, Alejandro Amenábar, Mateo Gil; Photography, Hans Burmann; Art Director, Wolfgang Burmann; Editor, Ma Elena Sainz de Rozas; Music, Alejandro Amenábar, Mariano Marín; a Summit Entertainment presentation for Sogetel, Las Prouciones del Escorpión, Les Films Alain Sarde and Lucky Red, with the participation of Sogepaq S.A. and the collaboration of Canal+ Spain; Spanish-French-Italian, 1997; Dolby; Color; Rated R; 110 minutes; U.S. release: April 16, 1999. CAST: Eduardo Noriega (César), Penélope Cruz (Sofia), Chete Lera (Antonio), Fele Martínez (Pelayo), Najwa Nimri (Nuria), Gerard Barray (Serge Duvernois, Man on TV), Jorge de Juan (Department Head), Miguel Palenzuela (Commisar), Pedro Miquel Martinez (Chief Doctor). Ion Gabella (Paranoid Recluse)

Penélope Cruz, Eduardo Noriega in *Open Your Eyes* ©Artisan Entertainment, Inc.

Marcello Mastroianni, Anouk Aimee, Michel Piccoli
in *Hundred and One Nights*

Paul Bowles in *Let It Come Down* ©Zeitgeist Films

HUNDRED AND ONE NIGHTS (Cinema Village Features) Producer, Cinema Tamaris; Director/Screenplay, Agnes Varda; Photography, Eric Gautier; Editor, Hugues Darmois; Art Director, Cyr Boitard, Cedric Simoneau; French, 1995; Color; Not rated; 101 minutes; U.S. release: April 16, 1999. CAST: Michel Piccoli (Simon Cinema), Marcello Mastroianni (The Italian Friend), Henri Garcin (Firmin, the Butler), Julie Gayet (Camille), Mathieu Demy (Mica), Emmanuel Salinger (Vincent), Anouk Aimee, Fanny Ardant, Jean-Paul Belmondo, Romane Bohringer, Sandrine Bonnaire, Jean-Claude Brialy, Patrick Bruel, Alain Delon, Catherine Deneuve, Robert De Niro, Gerard Depardieu, Harrison Ford, Gina Lollobrigida, Jeanne Moreau, Hanna Schygulla, Clint Eastwood.

NÔ (New Yorker) Producer, Bruno Jobin; Director, Robert Lepage; Screenplay, Robert Lepage, André Morency; Photography, Pierre Mignot; Designers, Claude Jacques, Jean Le Bourdais; Editor, Aube Foglia; Casting, Paul Cauffopé; from In Exteremis Images; French; Dolby; Black and white/color; Not rated; 83 minutes; U.S. release: April 23, 1999. CAST: Anne-Marie Cadieux (Sophie), Marie Brassard (Hanako), Alexis Martin (Michel), Marie Gignac (Patricia), Richard Frechette (Walter), Eric Bernier (Francois-Xavier)

LET IT COME DOWN: THE LIFE OF PAUL BOWLES (Zeitgeist) Producers, Nick de Pencier, Jennifer Baichwal; Director, Jennifer Baichwal; Photography, Nick de Pencier, Jim Allodi; Editor, David Wharnsby; Executive Producer, Daniel Iron; Readings, Tom McManus; Music, Paul Bowles; Canadian, 1998; Color; Not rated; 73 minutes; U.S. release: April 28, 1999. Documentary on author Paul Bowles, featuring Paul Bowles, Jane Bowles, William Burroughs, Phillip Ramey, Jonathan Sheffer, Ned Rorem, Marguerite McBey, Joseph McPhillips III, David Herbert, Mohammed Mrabet, Mohammed Choukri, Allen Ginsberg, Amina Bakalia

LOVERS OF THE ARCTIC CIRCLE (Fine Line Features) Producers, Fernando Bovaira, Enrique López Lavigne; Director/Screenplay, Julio Medem; Executive Producers, Txarli Llorente, Fernando de Garcillán; Photography, Kalo F. Berridi; Music, Alberto Iglesias; Editor, Iván Aledo; a Sogetel presentation of an Alicia Produce/Bailando en la Luna production; Spanish, 1998; Dolby; Super 35 Widescreen; Color; Rated R; 107 minutes; U.S. release: April 23, 1999. CAST: Fele Martínez (Otto), Najwa Nimri (Ana), Nancho Novo (Alvaro), Maru Valdivielso (Olga), Peru Medem (Otto as a Child), Sara Valiente (Ana as a Child), Victor Hugo Oliveira (Otto as a Teenager), Kristel Díaz (Ana as a Teenager), Pep Munné (Javier), Jaroslaw Bielski (Alvaro Midelman), Joost Siedhoff (Otto Midelman), Beate Jensen (Ula)

IN SEARCH OF KUNDUN WITH MARTIN SCORSESE (In Pictures) Producers, T. Celal, Jean Labib, Dale Ann Stieber, Michael H. Wilson; Director/Screenplay, Michael H. Wilson; Photography, Jean-Jacques Flori, Frederic Vassort; Editor, Rick Blue; Editorial Consultant,

Anne-Marie Cadieux, Marie Brassard in Nô ©New Yorker Films

Fele Martínez, Najwa Nimri in *Lovers of the Arctic Circle*
©Fine Line Features

Martin Scorsese in *In Search of Kundun*… ©In Pictures

Carlo Verdone, Andrea Ferreol in *Iris Blond* ©Miramax Films

Thelma Schoonmaker; Music, Ken Lauber; a Compagnie Panoptique production, in association with Ray Prods. with the participation of Canal+; French; Color; Not rated; 94 minutes; U.S. release: April 29, 1999. Documentary on the making of director Martin Scorese's 1997 film Kundun.

TESTAMENTO (SPIA Media Prods.) Executive Producer, Jose Luis Vasconcelos; Director, Francisco Manso; Screenplay, Mario Prata; Based on the novel Mr. Napumoceno's Last Will and Testament by Germano Almeida; Photography, Edgar Moura; Editor, Luis Sobral; Music, Tito Paris, Toy Vieira; Designer, Augusto Mayer; Casting, Francisco Manso, Joao Cayette, Joao Milagre; from Filmes Castello Lopes; Portuguese-Brazilian-Cape Verdean-French-Belgian; Dolby; Color; Not rated; 108 minutes; U.S. release: April 30, 1999. CAST: Nelson Xavier (Napumoceno), Maria Ceica (Graca), Chico Diaz (Carlos), Karla Leal (Adelia), Zeze Motta (Eduarda), Cesaria Evora (Arminda)

PUSHER (First Run Features) Producer, Henrik Danstrup; Executive Producers, Peter Aalbæk Jensen, Teddy Gerberg; Director, Nicolas Winding Refn; Screenplay, Nicolas Winding Refn, Jens Dahl; Photography, Morten Søborg; Designer, Kim Løvetand Julebæk; Editor, Anne Østerud; Music, Peter Peter, Povl Kristian Mortensen; from Balboa Enterprise ApS; Danish, 1996; Dolby; Color; Not rated; 105 minutes; U.S. release: May 7, 1999. CAST: Kim Bodnia (Frank), Zlatko Buric (Milo), Laura Drasbæk (Vic), Slavko Labovic (Radovan), Mads Mikkelsen (Tonny), Peter Anderson (Hasse), Vanja Bajicic (Branko), Lisbeth Rasmussen (Rita)

IRIS BLOND (Miramax) a.k.a. *Mad About Iris Blond*; Producers, Vittorio & Rita Cecchi Gori; Executive Producers, Bob Weinstein, Harvey Weinstein; Director, Carlo Verdone; Screenplay, Francesca Marciano, Pasquale Plastino, Carlo Verdone; Photography, Giuseppe Di Biase; Editor, Antonio Siciliano; Music, Lele Marchitelli; Art Director, Maurizio Marchitelli; Costumes, Tatiana Romanoff; a Mario & Vittorio Cecchi Gori presentation; Italian, 1997; Dolby; Cinecitt color; Rated R; 100 minutes; U.S. release: May 14, 1999. CAST: Carlo Verdone (Romeo Spera), Claudia Gerini (Iris Blond), Andrea Ferreol (Marguerite), Nello Mascia (Vincenzo Cecere), Nuccia Fumo (Fortune Teller), Mino Reitano (Himself), Didier De Neck (Julien), Alain Montoisy (Rene Discografico), Patrice De Mincke (Daniel), Liesbet Jammes (Jacqueline)

LEILA (First Run Features) Producers, Dariush Mehrjui, Faramarz Farazmand; Director, Dariush Mehrjui; Screenplay, Mahnaz Ansarian, Dariush Mahrjui; Photography, Mahmoud Kalari; Editor, Mustafa Kherqepush; Music, Keivan Jahanshahi; Iranian, 1997; Color; Not rated; 110 minutes; U.S. release: May 14, 1999. CAST: Leila Hatami (Leila), Ali Mosaffa (Reza), Jamileh Sheikhi (Reza's Mother), Amir Pievar (Reza's Father), Mohammad Reza Sharifinia (Leila's Uncle), Turan Mehrzad (Leila's Mother), Shaqayeq Farahani (Second Wife)

Kim Bodnia in *Pusher* ©First Run Features

Ali Mosaffa, Leila Hatami in *Leila* ©First Run Features

Riki Takeuchi, Masaya Katoh in *Nobody* ©Phaedra Cinema

Oda Akane in *Remembering the Cosmos Flower* ©Phaedra Cinema

WHEN LOVE COMES (Jour de Fete) a.k.a. *When Love Comes Along,* Producers, Jonathan Dowling, Michele Fanti; Director, Garth Maxwell; Screenplay, Garth Maxwell, Rex Pilgrim, Peter Wells; Photography, Darryl Ward; Editors, Cushla Dillon; Designer, Grace Mok; from MF Films, New Zealand; Color; Not rated; 94 minutes; U.S. release: June 4, 1999. CAST: Rena Owen (Katie), Dean O'Gorman (Mark), Simon Prast (Stephen), Nancy Brunning (Fig), Sophia Hawthorne (Sally), Simon Westaway (Eddie), Meighan Desmond (Shelley).

NOBODY (Phaedra) Producers, Toshifumi Ogura, Tsugio Hattori, Seiichi Kyoda; Director/Screenplay, Shundo Okawa; Photography, Hiroshi Ogata; Editor, Yoshio Kitazawa; Music, Kiyoshi Kakizawa; Japanese; Color; Not rated; 100 minutes; U.S. release: June 4, 1999. CAST: Masaya Katoh (Taki), Jimpachi Nezu (Detective Karaki), Riki Takeuchi (Nanbu), Hideo Nakano (Konishi), Hiromi Nakajima (Rika), Yumi Nishiyama (Reiko)

FLOATING LIFE (Cowboy Booking) Producer, Bridget Ikin; Director, Clara Law; Screenplay, Eddie Ling-Ching Fong, Clara Law; Photography, Dion Beebe; Designer, Chung Man Yee; Music, Davood A. Tabrizi; Editor, Suresh Ayyar; Australian, 1996; Color; Not rated; 95 minutes; U.S. release: June 11, 1999. CAST: Toby Chan, Cecilia Fong Sing Lee, Nina Liu, Edwin Pang, Annette Shun Wah, Toby Wong, Annie Yip

I WANT YOU (Gramercy) Producer, Andrew Eaton; Executive Producer, Stewart Till; Director, Michael Winterbottom; Screenplay, Eoin McNamee; Photography, Slavomir Idziak; Designers, David Bowes, David Bryan, Mark Tildesley; Music, Adrian Johnston; Editor, Trevor Waite; Casting, Rachael Fleming; British; Color; Not rated; 90 minutes; Release date: June 11, 1999. CAST: Rachel Weisz (Helen), Alessandro Nivola (Martin), Luka Petrusic (Honda), Labina Mitevska (Smokey), Carmen Ejogo (Amber), Ben Daniels (Bob), Dan Daniels (Bob), Graham Crowden (Old Man), Geraldine O'Raw (Sonja), Steve John Shepherd (Sam), Phyllida Law, Mary MacLeod (Women at Hairdresser's), Kenny Doughty (Smokey's Friend), Des McAleer (Flower Salesman), Julian Rivett (Billy), Julie Smith (Young Woman), Berwick Kaler (Taxi Driver)

REMEMBERING THE COSMOS FLOWER (Phaedra) Producers, Tetsutomo Kosugi, Kiichirou Yamazaki, Kenichi Hoyama, Junichi Suzuki, Kaz Tanaka; Director, Junichi Suzuki; Screenplay, Junichi Suzuki, Tetsutomo Kosugi; Photography, Kaz Tanaka; Designer, Hisao Inagaki; Editor, Shuichi Kakesu; Japanese; Color; Not rated; 103 minutes; U.S. release: June 11, 1999. CAST: Oda Akane (Akiko Sonoda), Mari Natsuki (Kiyomi Sonoda), Hisano Yamaoka (Kikuno Sonoda), Megumi Matsushita (Natsumi Yamakura), Kouichi Ishii (Shoukichi Yamakura), Satoya Matsuda (Daisuke Yamakura), Kai Shishido (Matsubara), Masahiro Noguchi (Nosaka), Joe Shishido (Soichiro Hakutsuru), Rumi Sakakibara (Kyoko Nihei), Eri Anzai (Naomi Onishi), Yoshie Kawada (Yoko), Saori Murata, Yukiyo Watanabe (Naomi's Friends), Yasuo Saito (Shuji Takada), Atsumi Hirohata (Delivery Woman), Sayuri Niita (Sanae Ono), Shuhei Hayashiya (Brewery Worker), Toshiya Fujita (High School Principal), Tamio Kawaji (High School Sub Principal), Miho Arai (Daisuke's Friend)

THE RED DWARF (Samuel Goldwyn) Producers, Yvan Le Moine, Alexandre Heylen; Director/Screenplay, Yvan Le Moine; Photography, Danny Elsen; Designer, Philipe Graff; Costumes, Pierre-Yves Gayraud; Editors, Ursula Lesiak, Ludo Troch; Music, Alexis Schelegin, Daniel Brandt; from A.A. les Films Belges (Brussels), Mainstream S.A. (Paris); French; Dolby; Color; Not rated; 102 minutes; U.S. release: June 11, 1999. CAST: Jean-Yves Thual (Lucien Lhotte), Dyna Gauzy (Isis Colombe), Michel Peyrelon (The Circus Director), Arno Chevrier (Bob), Anita Ekberg (Countess Paola Bendoni), Carlo Colombaioni (The Old Clown), Alain Flick (Picot), Alexandre von Sivers (Lambert), Dirk Lavryssen (Head of Office), Cyril Casmèze (Zoomorph)

SITCOM (Leisure Time Features) Producers, Olivier Delbosc, Marc Missonnier; Director/Screenplay, Francois Ozon; Photography, York Le Saux; Editor, Dominique Petrot; Music, Eric Neveux; Art Director, Angelique Puron; Costumes, Herve Poeydemenge; French; 1998; Color; Not rated; 85 minutes; U.S. release: June 18, 1999. CAST: Evelyne Dandry (Helen—Mother), Francois Martrhouret (Jean—Father), Marina

Anita Ekberg, Jean-Yves Thual in *The Red Dwarf* ©Samuel Goldwyn Films

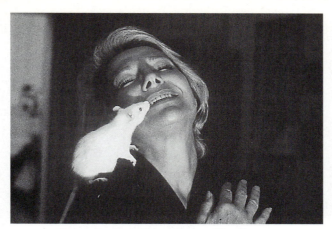

Evelyne Dandry in *Sitcom* ©Leisure Time Features

Virginie Ledoyen, Mathieu Amalric in *Late August, Early September*
©Zeitgeist Films

de Van (Sophie—Daughter), Adrien de Van (Nicholas—Son), Stephane Rideau (David), Lucia Sanchez (Maria), Julien-Emmanuel Eyoum Deido (Abdu), Jean Douchet (Psychiatrist)

LOVE ETC. (Phaedra) Producer, Patrick Godeau; Executive Producer, Francois Galfe; Director, Marion Vernoux; Screenplay, Marion Vernoux, Dodine Herry; Based on the novel *Talking It Over* by Julian Barnes; Photography, Eric Gautier; Editor, Jennifer Auge; Music, Alexandre Desplat, Leonard Cohen; Designer, Francois Emmanuelli; Costumes, Pierre-Yves Gayraud; an AliceLeo/France 3 Cinéma/Studio Canal+ co-production with Studio Images 3 and Cofimage 7 with the participation of the European Script Fund and Procirep; French, 1997; Dolby; Color; Not rated; 105 minutes; U.S. release: June 18, 1999. CAST: Charlotte Gainsbourg (Marie), Yvan Attal (Benoit), Charles Berling (Pierre), Susan Moncur (Susan), Thibault de Montalembert (Bernard), Elodie Navarre, Marie Adam, Charlotte Maury Sentier, Yvan Martin, Valerie Bonneton.

LATE AUGUST, EARLY SEPTEMBER (Zeitgeist) Producers, Georges Benayoun, Philippe Carcassonne; Director/Screenplay, Olivier Assayas; Line Producer, Françoise Guglielmi; Photography, Denis Lenoir; Designer, François Renaud Labarthe; Costumes, Françoise Clavel; Editor, Luc Barnier; a Dacia Films & Cinéa co-production, with the participation

of Canal+, the Centre National de la Cinématographie, Soficas Sonfinergie and Sofigram; French, 1998; Dolby; Color; Not rated; 112 minutes; U.S. release: July 7, 1999. CAST: Mathieu Amalric (Gabriel), Virginie Ledoyen (Anne), François Cluzet (Adrien), Jeanne Balibar (Jenny), Alex Descas (Jérémie), Arsinée Khanjian (Lucie), Mia Hansen-Løve (Véra), Nathalie Richard (Maryelle), Eric Elmosnino (Thomas), Olivier Cruveiller (Axel), Jean-Baptiste Malartre (Editeur), André Marcon (Hattou), Catherine Mouchet, Elli Medeiros

VIOLENT COP (WinStar) a.k.a. *Warning: This Man is Wild*; Producers, Shozo Ichiyama, Hisao Nabeshima, Takio Yoshida; Director, Takeshi Kitano; Screenplay, Hisashi Nozawa; Photography, Yasushi Sakakibara; Editor, Nobutake Kamiya; Co-produced by Bandai Co., Ltd. and Shochiku-Fuji Co., Ltd.; Japanese, 1989; Color; Not rated; 103 minutes; U.S. release: July 16, 1999. CAST: Takeshi Kitano (Azuma), Maiko Kawakami (Akari), Makoto Ashikawa (Kikuchi), Shiro Sano (Yoshinari), Shigeru Hiraizumi (Iwaki), Mikiko Otonashi (Iwaki's Wife), Hakuryu (Kiyoshiro), Ittoku Kishibe (Nindo), Ken Yoshizawa (Shinkai), Hiroyuki Katsube (Deputy Police Chief Higuchi), Noboru Hamada (Chief Det. Araki), Yuuki Kawai (Det. Honma), Ritsuko Amano (Honman's Fiancee), Taro Ishida (Det. Tashiro), Katsuki Muramatsu (Deputy Commissioner Anan), Kenichi Endo (Emoto), Ei Kawakami (Hashizume), Kiminari Natsumoto (Sakai), Zhao Fanghao (Psychiatrist Izumi)

Yvan Attal, Charlotte Gainsbourg, Charles Berling in *Love Etc.*
©Phaedra Cinema

Takeshi Kitano in *Violent Cop* ©WinStar Cinema

Aranka Coppens, Joost Wijnant in *Rosie* ©New Yorker Films

Marcello Mastroianni in *Marcello Mastrioanni: I Remember*
©First Look Pictures

MY BROTHER, MY SISTER, SOLD FOR A FISTFUL OF LIRE (**Jungle Films**) Director/Screenplay, Basile Sallustio; Photography, Marcello Montarsi, Olivier Pulinckx, Giuseppi Schifani; Editors, Evelyne Bertiau, Ann-Laure Guegan; Belgian-Italian, 1998; Color; Not rated; 90 minutes; U.S. release: July 21, 1999. Documentary about Pia Dilisa's efforts to find her brother and sister after they were shipped off to America from Italy in 1952.

ROSIE (**New Yorker**) Producer, Antonino Lombardo; Director/Screenplay, Patrice Toye; Photography Richard van Oosterhout; Costumes, An D'Huys; Art Director, Johan van Essche; Music, John Parish; Editor, Ludo Troch; a Prime Time, the Flemish Film Fund VRT, Nationale Loterij, Canal+ production; Belgian-Flemish, 1998; Dolby; Color; Not rated; 97 minutes; U.S. release: July 23, 1999. Cast: Aranka Coppens (Rosie), Sara De Roo (Irene), Dirk Roofthooft (Bernard), Joost Wijnant (Jimi), Frank Vercruyssen (Michel)

A LITTLE BIT OF SOUL (**Phaedra**) Producers, Peter Duncan, Simon Martin, Martin McGrath, Peter J. Voeten; Executive Producer, Tristam Miall; Director/Screenplay, Peter Duncan; Photography, Martin McGrath; Designer, Tony Campbell; Costumes, Terry Ryan; Music, Nigel Westlake; a Faust Film; Australian 1998; Dolby; Color; Rated R; 84 minutes; U.S.

release: Aug. 6, 1999. CAST: Geoffrey Rush (Godfrey Usher), David Wenham (Richard Shorkinghorn), Frances O'Connor (Kate Haslett), Heather Mitchell (Grace Michael), John Gaden (Dr. Sommerville), Iris Shand (Mrs. Crane), Kerry Walker (Eugenie Mason), Roy Billing (Judge), Jennifer Hagan (The Prosecution), Peter Duncan (The Defence), Paul Blackwell (Hungry Fred), Craig Rasmus (Bobby), Paul Livingston (Chicken Voices), Richard Roxburgh (Voice of Sir Samuel Michael)

MARCELLO MASTROIANNI: I REMEMBER (**First Look**) Executive Producer, Mario Di Biase; Director/Editor, Anna Maria Tatò; Photography, Giuseppe Rotunno; Line Producer, Loretta Bernabei; Music, Armando Trovaioli; a Mikado and Instituto Luce production in collaboration with Cinecitta-Rai Radiotelevisione Italiana and Tele+; Italian, 1997; Dolby; Color; Not rated; 199 minutes; U.S. release: Aug. 13, 1999. Documentary in which actor Marcello Mastroianni (1925-1996) reminisces about his life and film career.

PERFECT BLUE (**Manga**) Producers, Hiroaki Inoue, Masao Maruyama; Director, Satoshi Kon; Screenplay, Sadayuki Murai; Based on the novel by Yoshikazu Takeuchi; Based on character design by Hisashi Eguchi; Animation Director/Character Designer, Hideki Hamazu; Editor, Harutoshi Ogata; Photography, Hisao Shirai; Music, Masahiro Ikumi; Designer, Mitsusuke Hayakawa; a Rex Entertainment production; Japanese, 1997; Color; Not rated; 80 minutes; U.S. release: Aug. 20, 1999. Animated.

Geoffrey Rush, Heather Mitchell in *A Little Bit of Soul* ©Phaedra Cinema

Perfect Blue ©Palm Pictures

Miou-Miou, Marisa Berenson, Carmen Maura, Guesch Patti,
Marthe Keller in *Women* ©WinStar Cinema

Werner Schreyer, Nicolette Krebitz in *Bandits*
©Stratosphere Entertainment

KNOCKIN' ON HEAVEN'S DOOR (Myriad Pictures) Producers, Thomas Zickler, André Hennicke; Director/Screenplay, Thomas Jahn; Photography, Gero Steffen; Co-Producers, Wolfgang Braun, Christoph Ott; Designer, Monika Bauert; Costumes, Heike Weber; Editor, Alexander Berner; Music, Selig; a Mr. Brown Entertainment, Buena Vista International production; German; 1997; Color; Not rated; 89 minutes; U.S. release: Aug. 20, 1999. CAST: Til Schweiger (Martin Brest), Jan Josef Liefers (Rudi Wurlitzer), Thierry van Werveke (Henk), Moritz Bleibtreu (Abdul), Huub Stapel (Frankie "Boy" Beluga), Leonard Lansink (Kommissar Schneider), Ralph Herforth (Assistant Keller), Cornelia Froboess (Martins Mutter), Rutger Hauer (Curtiz), Willi Thomczyk (Autoverkaufer), Christiane Paul (Verkauferin in Boutique), Hannes Jaenicke (Motorradpolizist), Vladimir Weigl (Harald Rohwitz), Jenny Elvers (Schwester Labor A), Corinna Harfouch (Schwester Labor B)

THE WOUNDS (Leisure Time Features) Producer, Dragan Bjelogrlic; Director/Screenplay, Srdjan Dragojevic; Photography, Dusan Joksimovic; Editor, Petar Markovic; Music, Aleksandar Sasa Habic; a Cobra Film Department and Pandora Film production; Serbian; Dolby; Color; Not rated; 103 minutes; U.S. release: Aug. 27, 1999. CAST: Dusan Pekic (Pinki), Milan Maric (Kraut), Dragan Bjelogrlic (Dickie), Branka Katic (Suki), Predrag Miki Manojilovic (Stojan), Vesna Trivalic (Lidja), Andreja Jovanovic (Dijabola)

Janeane Garofalo, Bruce McCulloch in *Dog Park* ©Lions Gate

WOMEN (ELLES) (WinStar) Producer, Jani Thiltges; Director, Luis Galvão Teles; Screenplay, Luis Galvão Teles, Don Bohlinger; Photography, Alfredo Mayo; Designer, Véronique Sacrez; Music, Alejandro Massó; Editor, Regina Bärtschi; a Jani Thiltges and Claude Waringo presentation; French; Color; Not rated; 97 minutes; U.S. release: Sept. 17, 1999. CAST: Carmen Maura (Linda), Miou-Miou (Eva), Marisa Berenson (Chloé), Marthe Keller (Barbara), Guesch Patti (Branca), Joaquim De Almeida (Gigi), Morgan Perez (Luis), Didier Flamand (Edgar), Mapi Galan (Raquel), Florence Loiret (Tiago)

BANDITS (Stratosphere) Producers, Harry Kügler, Molly von Fürstenberg, Elvira Senft; Director, Katja von Garnier; Screenplay, Uwe Wilhelm, Katja von Garnier; From an idea by Ben Taylor, Katja von Garnier; Photography, Torsten Breuer; Designer, Susann Bieling; Editor, Hans Funck; Costumes, Claudia Bobsin; Music, The Bandits; Casting, Sabine Schroth; an Olga Film production, co-produced by Vela X in association with ProSieben and Flach Film/Jean-Francois Lepetit; German; Dolby; Color; Rated R; 109 minutes; U.S. release: Sept. 24, 1999. CAST: Katja Riemann (Emma), Jasmin Tabatabai (Luna), Nicolette Krebitz (Angel), Jutta Hoffmann (Marie), Hannes Jaenicke (Schwartz), Werner Schreyer (West), Andrea Sawatzki (Ludwig), Oliver Hasenfratz (Schneider), August Schmölzer (Gunther), Heio von Statten (Nick), Peter Sattmann (Gold), Peter Rühring (Prison Director), Irmhild Wagner (Prison Nun), Barbara Ahren (Congresswoman Roth), Helga Storck, Sarah Camp (Inspectors), Vicki Schmatolla (Elli), Erich Dierks, Peter Weiss (Poachers), Joseph Hannesschläger (Peasant), Edeltraud Schubert (Waitress), Claudia Ahrens (Secretary), Hillmer Meyer (Receptionist)

DOG PARK (Lions Gate) Producer, Susan Cavan; Director/Screenplay, Bruce McCulloch; Executive Producer, Jeff Sackman; Photography, David Makin; Designer, Marian Wihak; Editor, Christopher Cooper; Music, Craig Northey; Costumes, Linda Muir; an Accent Entertainment Corporation presentation; Canadian; Dolby; Deluxe color; Rated R; 90 minutes; U.S. release: Sept. 24, 1999. CAST: Natasha Henstridge (Lorna), Luke Wilson (Andy), Kathleen Robertson (Cheryl), Janeane Garofalo (Jeri), Bruce McCulloch (Jeff), Kristin Lehman (Keiran), Amie Carey (Rachel), Gordon Currie (Trevor), Harland Williams (Callum), Mark McKinney (Dog Psychologist), Jerry Schaefer (Norm), Zachary Bennett (Dougie), Peter MacNeill (Old Neighbor), Ron James, Albert Schultz (Dog Owners), Diane Flacks (Chirpy Dog Owner), Earl Pastko (Bartender), Nick Johne (Video Cashier), Jennifer Irwin (Woman), Myrna Sun (Hostess), Michael McManus (Derrick the Waiter), Tracy Wright (Dog Psychologist's Wife), Leisha Morais, Jason Arnott (Dog Psychologist's Children), Terri Hawkes (Announcer), Boyd Banks ("Go Away Stain" Host), Casey (Mogley), Blackie (Peanut)

Toni Collette, David Wenham in *The Boys* ©Stratosphere Entertainment

Adrian Pang in *That's the Way I Like It* ©Miramax Films

THE BOYS (Stratosphere) Producers, Robert Connolly, John Maynard; Executive Producer, Douglas Cummins; Director, Rowan Woods; Screenplay, Stephen Sewell; Based on the play by Gordon Graham; Photography, Tristan Milani; Designer, Luigi Pittorino; Costumes, Annie Marshall; Editor, Nick Meyers; Music, The Necks; Associate Producer, David Wenham; Casting, Lesley Burgess Casting; an Arena Film presentation; Australian; Dolby; Color; Rated R; 86 minutes; U.S. release: Oct. 15, 1999. CAST: David Wenham (Brett), Toni Collette (Michelle), Lynette Curran (Sandra), John Polson (Glenn), Jeanette Cronin (Jackie), Anthony Hayes (Stevie), Anna Lise (Nola), Pete Smith (George/Abo), Sal Sharah (Nick), Lawrence Woodward (Prison Officer), Peter Hehir (Graham Newton), Andrew Heys (Sparrow), Teo Gebert (Constable Zammit), Anthony Kierann (Constable Maguire), Stephen Leeder (Supervising Detective), Veronica Leave (Girl at the Bus Stop)

PUNITIVE DAMAGE (First Run/Icarus) Producers, Annie Goldson, Gaylene Preston; Director/Screenplay, Annie Goldson; Photography, Leon Narbey; Editor, John Gilbert; Music, Stephen Taberner; Line Producer, Catherine Madigan; Associate Producer, Penny Robins; a New Zealand Film Commission presentation of an Occasional Prods. production, in association with New Zealand on Air, U of Auckland; New Zealand; Dolby; Color; Not rated; 77 minutes; U.S. release: Oct. 1999. Documentary on Helen Todd's quest for justice for the death of her son Kamal Bamadhaj, one of the 270 unarmed demonstrators killed by the Indonesian military in the 1991 massacre in East Timor's capital of Dili.

THAT'S THE WAY I LIKE IT (Miramax) formerly *Forever Fever*; Producers, Glen Goei, Jeffrey Chiang, Tan Chih Chong; Director/Screenplay, Glen Goei; Photography, Brian Breheny; Designer, Laurence Eastwood; Costumes, Ashley Aeria; Editor, Jane Moran; Music, Guy Gross; Choreographer, Zaki Ahamad; a Tiger Tiger Films in association with Chinarunn Pictures presentation; Singaporean, 1998; Dolby; Color; Rated; 92 minutes; U.S. release: Oct. 15, 1999. CAST: Adrian Pang (Hock), Medaline Tan (Mei), Anna Belle Francis (Julie), Pierre Png (Richard), Steven Lim (Boon), Westley Wong (Bobby), Alaric Tay (Ah Seng), Dominic Page (Hock's Guardian Angel), Caleb Goh (Leslie/Ah Beng), Pamela Oei (Mui), Lim Kay Siu (Father), Margaret Chan (Mother), Lily Ong (Grandmother), Kumar (Mr. Larry), Lim Kay Tong (Mr. Tay), Koh Chieng Mun (Mrs. Chan Ai Ling), Jeffrey Tan, Cathy Kee, Aidil Bin Amin, Alicia Loo (Dancers), Andy Heng (Man in Kopi Tiam), Najip Ali (Cinema Patron), Jason Lam (Motorbike Salesman), Tan Kheng Hua, Michelle Chua, Jacqueline Pereira (Ticket Sellers), Irwan Bin Usop, Teo Kuan Soon (Richard's Gang Members), Jerrold Wong (Tranny in Cheong Sam), Moe Kassim (Tranny in Saron Kebaya), Ronald Chong (Young Hock), Brian Yu (Young Leslie), Shirui (Young Mei), Michelle Tan (Girl in Changing Room)

TO SPEAK THE UNSPEAKABLE: THE MESSAGE OF ELIE WIESEL (Independent) Director/Screenplay, Judit Elek; Narrator, William Hurt; Hungarian-French, 1996; Color; Not rated; 105 minutes; U.S. release: Oct. 1999. Documentary on Elie Wiesel.

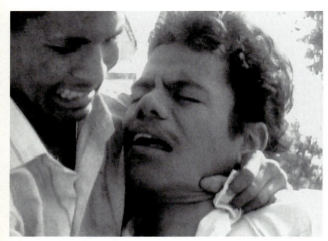

Punitive Damage ©First Run/Icarus

Firadus Kanga in *The Sixth Happiness* ©Regent Entertainment

Lionel Abelanski in *Train of Life* ©Paramount Classics

Helena Bonham Carter, Jean-Philippe Écoffey, Yvan Attal
in *Portrait Chinois* ©Phaedra Cinema

THE SIXTH HAPPINESS (Regent Entertainment) Producer, Tatiana Kennedy; Executive Producers, Frances-Anne Solomon, Ben Gibson; Director, Waris Hussein; Screenplay, Firdaus Kanga, based on his novel Trying to Grow; Photography, James Welland; Designer, Lynne Whiteread; Costumes, Amal Allana; Casting, Emma Style; a co-production of the British Film Institute/BBC; British; Dolby; Color; Not rated; 97 minutes; U.S. release: Oct. 22, 1999. CAST: Firdaus Kanga (Brit Kotwal), Souad Faress (Sera Kotwal), Khodus Wadia (Sam Kotwal), Nina Wadia (Dolly Kotwal), Ahsen Bhatti (Cyrus), Mahabanoo Mody-Kotwal (Jeroo), Nisha K. Nayar (Tina), Indira Varma (Amy), Roger Hammond (Father Ferre), Sabira Merchant (Madame Manekshaw), Noshirwan Jehangir (Doctor), Dara Madon (Old Parsee Man), Vijoo Khote (Wagh Baba), Firdausi Jussawalli (Plump Husband), Dolly Dotiwalla (Plump Wife), Pervin Wadia (Mother), Dilnaz Irani (Daughter), Goolistan Gandhi (Defarge), Meral Durlabhji (Batman Boy), Zubin Tatna (Dinsu Dinshaw), Meher Jehangir (Vera Dinshaw), Aloo Hirjee (Old Woman at Funeral), Arun Kannan (Rohit), Jamishi Shivjiani (Young Dolly), Zeenia Mirza (Young Tina), Pratima Kazmi (Wagh Baba's Woman)

TRAIN OF LIFE (Paramount Classics) Producers, Frederique Dumas, Marc Baschet, Cedomir Kolar, Ludi Boeken, Eric Dussart; Director/Screenplay, Radu Milhaileanu; Photography, Yorgos Arvanitis, Laurent Dailland; Editor, Monique Rysselinck; Music, Goran Bregovic; Designer, Cristi Niculescu; Costumes, Viorica Petrovici; a Noe Prods., Le Studio Canal+ (France)/Raphael Films (Belgium)/71A (Romania)/Hungry Eye Lowland Pictures (Netherlands) production; French-Belgian-Romanian-Dutch, 1998; Dolby; Widescreen; Color; Rated R; 102 minutes; U.S. release: Nov. 3, 1999. CAST: Lionel Abelanski (Shlomo), Rufus (Mordechai), Clement Harari (Rabbi), Michael Muller (Yossi), Bruno Abraham-Kremer (Yankele the Bookkeeper), Agathe de la Fontaine (Esther), Johan Leysen (Schmecht), Marie-Jose Nat (Sura), Gad Elmaleh (Manzatou), Bebe Bercovici (Joshua), Robert Borremans (Der Hauptsturmfuhrer), Mihai Calin (Sami), Constantin Codrescu, Theodor Danetti, Michel Israel, Savel Stiopul, Constantin Dinulescu (Wise Men), Ovidiu Cuncea (Moitl), Marius Drogeanu (Mendel), Daniel Decot, Michel Vanderlinden, Constantin Barbulescu (Resistants), Luminita Gheorghiu (Rivka), Vladimir Jurascu (Von Gluck), Zwi Kanar (Lilenfeld), Serge Kribus (Schtroul), Georges Siatidis (Itzik), Marian Stan (Man in Synagogue), Sanda Toma (Yossi's Mother), Rodica Sanda Tutuianu (Golda), Razvan Vasilescu (Tzigan Colonel)

PORTRAIT CHINOIS (SHADOW PLAY) (Phaedra Cinema) Producer, Georges Benayoun; Director, Martine Dugowson; Screenplay, Peter Chase, Martine Dugowson; Photography, Vincenzo Marano; Designer, Pierre Guffroy; Music, Peter Chase; Editor, Noëlle Boisson; British-French, 1996; Color; Not rated; minutes; U.S. release: November 5, 1999. CAST: Helena Bonham Carter (Ada), Romane Bohringer (Lise), Jean-Philippe Écoffey (Paul), Marie Trintignant (Nina), Elsa Zylberstein (Emma), Yvan Attal (Yves), Sergio Castellitto (Guido), Miki Manojlovic (Alphonse), Jean-Claude Brialy (René Sandre), Sophie Simon (Agnès), Emmanuelle Escourrou (Stéphanie), Mathilde Seigner (Fanny), Katia

Mechera (Emilia), Artus de Penguern (Gérard), Pierre Baillot (Monsieur Verdoux), Antoinette Moya (Christine Perridoux), Jean-Bernard Guillard (Thomas), Jacques Le Carpentier (Lise's Father), Florence Loiret (Emmanuelle), Catherine Sola (Yvonne), Marie-France Gantzer (Stationery Saleswoman), Jean Barney (Presenter), Marie Chevalier (Claire Destours), Yves Bonnen (Director), Claudine Delvaux (Emilienne), Joseph Falcucci (Locksmith), Rebecca Hampton (Sophie), Michèle Atlani (Young Girl), Léa Vigny, Stéphanie Cohen, Claire Bellar, Laly Meignan (Boutique Salesgirls), Lawrence Ledantec (Make-Up Artist), Magali De Jonckheere (Karine), Clément Sibony (Jean), Sébastien Culioli (Richard), Guillaume Watrinet (Bernard), Philippe Jutteau (Bob), Myriam Tadesse (Gladys), Raymonde Heudeline (Concierge), Bill Sanford (Simon), Michel Amphoux (Hervé Duru), Raphaël Bernard (Christian), Karine Roussel (Young Lise), Béatrice Dumas Fournier (Lise's Mother), Mathias Honoré (Loubard)

GRIZZLY FALLS (Providence Entertainment) Producers, Peter R. Simpson, Allan Scott; Executive Producers, Mark Damon, Raylan Jensen, Georges Campana; Director, Stewart Raffill; Screenplay, Richard Beattie; Story, Stuart Margolin; Photography, Thom Best; Designer, Tom Carnegie; Editor, Nick Rotundo; Music, David Reilly, Paul J. Zaza; Costumes, Minda Johansen; Ali Oop Provided by Ruth LaBarge; Casting, Ron Leach; a Behaviour Worldwide and Norstar Filmed Entertainment Inc. in association with Le Sabre presentation of a Peter Simpson and Allan Scott production; Canadian-British; Dolby; Color; Rated PG; 94 minutes; U.S. release: Nov. 5, 1999. CAST: Bryan Brown (Tyrone Bankston), Tom Jackson (Joshua), Oliver Tobias (Genet), Richard Harris (Old Harry), Daniel Clark (Young Harry), Chantal Dick (Young Jennifer), Trevor Lowden (Joshua, Jr.), Marnie McPhail (Mother), Ken Kramer (House Master), Brock Simpson (Lanky), Colin Simpson (Grits), Jim Bearden (Menke), John Tench (Wes), Ali Oop (Miz the Bear), Betty & Barney, Bonkers, Ursula, Whopper (Bears)

Daniel Clark, Ali Oop in *Grizzly Falls* ©Providence Entertainment

Tahmineh Normatova in *The Silence* ©New Yorker Films

Ammar Tafti, Marjam Mohamadamini, Ali Bakhshi
in *A Moment of Innocence* ©New Yorker Films

THE SILENCE (New Yorker) Producer, Marin Karmitz; Executive Producer, Mohamed Ahmadi; Director/Screenplay/Editor, Mohsen Makhmalbaf; Photography, Ebrahim Ghafouri; an MK2 Productions and Makhmalbaf Productions co-production; Iranian-French, 1998; Color; Not rated; 76 minutes; U.S. release: Nov. 10, 1999. CAST: Tahmineh Normatova (Khorshid), Nadereh Abdelahyeva (Nadereh), Golbibi Ziadolahyeva (Khorshid's Mother), Araz M. Mohamadli (Wandering Musician)

SECRET DEFENSE (Fabiano Canosa/Cineclub) Producers, Martine Marignac, Maurice Tinchant; Director, Jacques Rivette; Screenplay, Pascal Bonitzer, Emmanuelle Cuau, Jacques Rivette; Photography, William Lubtchansky; Art Director, Manu de Chauvigny; Editor, Nicole Lubtchansky; Music, Jordi Savall; a Pierre Grise production, from La Sept Cinema/T&C Film AG/Alia Films; French, 1998; Dolby; Color; Not rated; 170 minutes; U.S. release: Nov. 10, 1999. CAST: Sandrine Bonnaire (Sylvie), Jerzy Radziwilowicz (Walser), Laure Marsac (Veronique/Ludivine), Gregoire Colin (Paul), Francoise Fabian (Genevieve), Christine Vouilloz (Myriam), Mark Saporta (Jules), Sara Louis (Carole), Hermine Karagheuz (Nurse)

A MOMENT OF INNOCENCE (New Yorker) Producer, Mohamad Ahmadi; Director/Screenplay/Editor, Mohsen Makhmalbaf; Photography, Mahmoud Kalari; Music, Madjid Entezami; a co-production of Pakshiran, A. Alagheband, MK2 productions; Iranian, 1996; Color; Not rated; 78

minutes; U.S. release: Nov. 10, 1999. CAST: Ammar Tafti (The Young Policeman), Marjam Mohamadamini (The Young Woman), Ali Bakhshi (The Young Director), Mirhadi Tayebi (The Policeman), Mohsen Makhmalbaf (The Director)

YOU OR ME (Independent) Producer, Gyorgy Budai; Executive Producers, Peter Koltai, Zoltan Szedlacsko; Director/Photography, Tamas Sas; Screenplay, Istvan Nemes, Peter Geszti; Based on an original concept by Laszlo Des, Peter Geszti, Istvan Nemes; Editor, Zsuzsa Posan; Songs, Laszlo Des, Peter Geszti; an Axis Plusz/MTV production; Hungarian; Color; Not rated; 96 minutes; U.S. release: Nov. 12, 1999. CAST: Gabi Gubas, Attila Kiraly, Viktor Bodo, Karina Kecskes, Eszter Onodi, Gabor Mate, Andor Lukacs.

BOILING POINT (WinStar Cinema) Producer, Okuyama Kazuyoshi; Director/Screenplay, Takeshi Kitano; Photography, Yanagishima Katsumi; Editor, Taniguchi Toshio; Japanese, 1990; Color; Not rated; 98 minutes; U.S. release: Nov. 19, 1999. CAST: Masahiko Ono (Masaki), Takeshi Kitano (Uehara), Minoru Iizuka (Kazuo), Hisashi Igawa (Otomo, the Gang Boss), Koichi Akiyama (Gas Pump Attendant), Takahiko Aoki (Saburo), Makoto Ashikawa (Akira), Jennifer Baer (Woman on Beach), Bengal (Muto), Eri Fuse (Sumio), Naotaka Hanai (Rich Kid on Motorcycle), Hiroshi Ide (Hajime), Yuriko Ishada (Sayaka), Kenzo Matsuo (Naoya), Johnny Okura (Minamizaka)

Sandrine Bonnaire in *Secret Defense* ©Cineclub

Takeshi Kitano in *Boiling Point* ©WinStar Cinema

Goldie, David Bowie, Andrew Goth in *Everybody Loves Sunshine*
©Lions Gate

Angel Hamilton in *Wisconsin Death Trip*

EVERYBODY LOVES SUNSHINE (Lions Gate) a.k.a. *B.U.S.T.E.D.*; Producer, Joanne Reay; Executive Producers, Guy Collins, Heather Playford Denman, Bjorg Vceland, Simon Johnson; Director/Screenplay, Andrew Goth; Photography, Julian Morson; Designer, Paul Cross; Editor, Jeremy Gibbs; Music, Nicky Matthew; Costumes, Ffon Elinor; Casting, Sarah Bird; an IAC Holdings Ltd. presentation in association with the Isle of Man Film Commission and BV Films Intl. of a Gothic production; British; Dolby; Deluxe color; Not rated; 97 minutes; U.S. release: Nov. 19, 1999. CAST: Goldie (Terry), Andrew Goth (Ray), David Bowie (Bernie), Rachel Shelley (Clare), Clint Dyer (Leon), Sarah Shackleton (Helen), David Baker (Clinton), Paul Hawkyard (Ken), Graham Bryan (Pat), Danny Price (Spider), Tren (Nelson), Adrian Pang (Steven), Chooi Kheng-Beh (Mr. Chang), Doreen Ingleton (Ray's Mum), Sanchez Palmer (Carl), Kylie Smith (Joanne), Vicky Bennett (Claudette), Carl Learmond (Mo), Kevin John Harvey (Snake), Jamie Draven (Geeg), Vincent Davies (Simon), Paul Courtenay Hyu (Ian), Callum Courtey Kelly (Begon), Alicia Eyo (Sandra), Jonathan Chan-Pensley, Paul Chan (Chinese Attackers), Joanna Nata Sa Gara (Jane), Chicken Shop Girl (Sasha Fooks)

GOODBYE 20TH CENTURY (Salt City Prods.) Director/Screenplay, Aleksandar Popovski; Photography, Vladimir Samojlovsky; Music, Risto Vrtev; Macedonian, 1998; Color; Not rated; 83 minutes; Release date: Nov. 19, 1999. CAST: Dejan Acimovic, Vlado Javanovski, Sofija Kunovska, Toni Mihajlovski, Nikola Ristanovski, Irena Ristic, Lazar Ristovski, Emil Ruben, Petar Temelkovski

EXTRAORDINARY VISITOR (Cinema Esperanca) Producers, Jennice Ripley, Paul Pope; Director/Screenplay, John W. Doyle; Photography, Brian Hebb; Designer, Pam Hall; Editor, Lara Mazur; Music, Eric Cadesky, Nick Dyer; a Film East production; Canadian; Color; Not rated; 90 minutes; U.S. release: Nov. 26, 1999. CAST: Mary Walsh (Marietta), Andy Jones (Rick), Raoul Bhaneja (John the Baptist), Jordan Canning (Alison), Rick Boland (Pope Innocent XVI), Greg Malone (Cardinal Vignetti), Bryan Hennessy (Archbishop Devine), Ken Campbell, Maisie Rillie, Roger Maunder, Janet Michael, Bill Rowe.

WISCONSIN DEATH TRIP (Cinemax Reel Life/BBC Arena) Producers, Maureen A. Ryan, James Marsh; Director/Screenplay, James Marsh; Adapted from the book by Michael Lesy; Executive Producer, Anthony Wall; Supervising Producer for Cinemax, Nancy Abraham; Executive Producer for Cinemax, Sheila Nevins; Photography, Eigil Bryld; Editor, Jinx Godfrey; Narrator, Ian Holm; British-U.S.; Color; Not rated; 76 minutes; U.S. release: Dec. 1, 1999. A combination documentary-dramatization of the mysterious events in 1890's Black River Falls, Wisconsin, that resulted in multiple cases of murder and madness. CAST: Jo Vukelich (Mary Sweeney), Marilyn White (Pauline L'Allemand), Jeff Golden (The Newspaper Editor), Marcus Monroe (Young Anderson), John Schneider (Asylum Clerk), John Bates (Undertaker), Raeleen McMillion (Crying Woman), Krista Grambow (Mourning Woman), Clay Anton, Bobby Jo Westphal (Eloping Couple), Scott Hulber (Pouch), Zeke Dasko (Edgar L'Allemand)

BEYOND THE CLOUDS (Sceneries Entertainment) Producers, Stephane Tchal Gadjieff, Philippe Carcassonne; Executive Producers, Wim Wenders, Vittorio Cecchi Gori; Directors, Michelangelo Antonioni, Wim Wenders (Prologue/Intertitles/Epilogue); Screenplay, Michelangelo Antonioni, Wim Wenders, Tonino Guerra; Based on Antonioni's journals and his short story collection Bowling on the Tiber; Photography, Alfio Contini, Robby Muller; Editors, Claudio DiMauro, Michelangelo Antonioni, Peter Przygodda; a Sunshine, Cine b, Cecchi Gori Group, Road Movies production; French-Italian-German, 1995; Color; Not rated; 104 minutes; U.S. release: Dec. 1, 1999. CAST: *Chronicle of a Love That Never Was*: Ines Sastre (Carmen), Kim Rossi-Stuart (Silvano); *The Girl, The Crime*: Sophie Marceau (The Girl), John Malkovich (The Director); *This Body of Mud*: Irene Jacob (The Girl), Vincent Perez (The Boy); *Don't Try to See Me Again*: Fanny Ardant (Patricia), Peter Weller (Husband), Chiara Caselli (Mistress), Jean Reno (Carlo), Marcello Mastroianni (The Man of All Vices), Jeanne Moreau (Friend)

WRAPPED REICHSTAG (Ventura Film) Producers/Directors/Screenplay, Jörg Daniel Hissen, Wolfram Hissen; Photography, Michael Hammon, Albert Maysles, Eric Turpin, Jörg Widmer; Editor, Götz Filenius, Dirk Grau; French-German, 1996; Dolby; Color; 98 minutes; U.S. release: Dec. 3, 1999. Documentary on artists Christo & Jeanne-Claude's 1995 project of wrapping fabric around the Reichstag in Berlin.

Vincent Perez, Irene Jacob in *Beyond the Clouds* ©Sceneries Distribution

Virtual Sexuality ©Columbia/TriStar

Hossain Sabzian in *Close-Up* ©Zeitgeist Films

VIRTUAL SEXUALITY (TriStar) Producer, Christopher Figg; Executive Producers, Kevin Loader, Jonathan Darby, Charles Armitage; Director, Nick Hurran; Screenplay, Nick Fisher; Based on the novel by Chloe Rayban; Photography, Brian Tufano; Designer, Chris Edwards; Editor, John Richards; Music, Rupert Gregson-Williams; Casting, Janey Fothergill, Jane Davies; a Noel Gay Motion Picture Company production, presented by The Bridge; British; Dolby; Color; Rated R; 92 minutes; U.S. release: Dec. 3, 1999. CAST: Laura Fraser (Justine), Rupert Penry-Jones (Jake), Luke De Lacey (Chas), Kieran O'Brien (Alex), Marcelle Duprey (Fran), Natasha Bell (Hoover), Steve John Shepherd (Jason), Laura Macaulay (Monica), Roger Frost (Frank), Ruth Sheen (Jackie), Laura Aikman (Lucy), Ram John Holder (Declan), Amanda Holden (Shoe Shop Assist.), Alan Westaway (Geoff), William Osborne (Sex Shop Assist.), Philip Bird (Justine's Dad), Judith Scott (Sharon), Stewart Harwood, Nicholas Pry (Labourers), Alison Garland (Scary Nurse), Robert Oates (Cabbie), Caroline Chikezie (Gushy Assist.), Trish Bertram (Reporter), Toby Cockerell (Wiry Lad), Keeley Gainey (Receptionist), Melinda Messenger (Superbra Girl), Jake Curran (Nick), James Daley (Maggot), Monty Fromant (Taylor), Martin Hutson (Rory), Joseph Kpobie (Knobhead), Peter McCabe (Spriggs), Ozdemir Mamodeally (Rex), Carl Pizzie (Floyd), Del Synott (Carter), Freddie White (Giblet), James D. White (Matt), Zoe Hodges (Lily), Preeya Kalidas (Charlotte), Samantha Levelle (Louise), Tracey Murphy (Helen), Emma Jane Pierson (Fiona), Ania Sowinski (Vicky), Ebony Thomas (Rachel), Lynne Wilmot (Laura)

GENESIS (Kino) Executive Producers, Jacques Atlan, Chantal Bagilishya; Director, Cheick Oumar Sissoko; Screenplay, Jean-Louis Sagot-Duvauroux; Photography, Lionel Cousin; Editor, Alio Auguste; Music, Décor Sonore; a co-production of Kora Films, Balanzan, CNPC and Cinéma Public Films; French-Mali; Color; Not rated; 102 minutes; U.S. release: Dec. 3, 1999. CAST: Sotigui Kouyaté (Jacob), Salif Keita (Esaü), Balla Moussa Keita (Hamor), Fatoumata Diawara (Dina), Maïmouna Hélène Diarra (Lea)

THE PORT OF LAST RESORT (National Center for Jewish Film) Producers/Directors/Screenplay/Editors, Joan Grossman, Paul Rosdy; Music, John Zorn; Co-Producer, Lukas Stepanik; Photography, Wolfgang Lehner; Austrian; 1998; Color-black and white; Not rated; 79 minutes; December release. Documentary on how some 20,000 European Jews escaped the Nazis and fled to Shanghai, China. With the voices of Barbara Sukowa (Annie Witting), Otto Tausig (A.J. Storfer), and Jaromir Borek, Erika Deutinger, Fritz von Friedl, Brigitta Furgler, Dietrich Hollinderbäumer, Peter Kybart, Gen Seto, Michael Scheidl, Matty O'Shea, Keenan Shimizu, Sabine Thomson, Maria Urban; Interviewers: Fred Fields, Ernest Heppner, Illo Heppner, Siegmar Simon.

BLACK AND WHITE IN COLOR (Film Forum/Independent) Producers, David Charap, Cestmir Kopecky; Director, Mira Erdevicki-Charap; Photography, Marek Jicha; Editor, David Charap; Music, Vera Bílá and Kale; Czech; Color; Not rated; 60 minutes; U.S. release: Dec. 15, 1999. Documentary on Czech Romany singer Vera Bílá

CLOSE-UP (Zeitgeist) Executive Producer, Ali Reza Zarrin; Director/Screenplay/Editor, Abbas Kiarostami; Photography, Ali Reza Zarrin-Dast; Produced by the Institute for the Intellectual Development of Children and Young Adults; Iranian, 1990; Color; Not rated; 90 minutes; U.S. release: Dec. 31, 1999. CAST: Hossain Sabzian, Mohsen Makhmalbaf (Themselves), Abolfazl Ahankhah (Father of the Family), Mehrdad Ahankhah, Manoochehr Ahankhah (Family Sons), Mahrokh Ahankhah, Nayer Mohseni Zonoozi (Family Daughters), Ahmed Reza Moayed Mohseni (Family Friend), Hossain Farazmand (Reporter), Hooshang Shamaei (Taxi Driver), Mohammad Ali Barrati (Soldier), Davood Goodarzi (Sergeant), Haji Ali Reza Ahmadi (Judge), Hassan Komaili, Davood Mohabbat (Court Reporters), Abbas Kiarostami (Himself)

Vera Bílá in *Black and White in Color*

F. Murray Abraham

Alan Alda

Joan Allen

Woody Allen

Biographical Data
(Name, real name, place and date of birth, school attended)

AAMES, WILLIE (William Upton): Los Angeles, CA, July 15, 1960.

AARON, CAROLINE: Richmond, VA, Aug. 7, 1954. Catholic U.

ABBOTT, DIAHNNE: NYC, 1945.

ABBOTT, JOHN: London, June 5, 1905.

ABRAHAM, F. MURRAY: Pittsburgh, PA, Oct. 24, 1939. UTx.

ACKLAND, JOSS: London, Feb. 29, 1928.

ADAMS, BROOKE: NYC, Feb. 8, 1949. Dalton.

ADAMS, CATLIN: Los Angeles, Oct. 11, 1950.

ADAMS, DON: NYC, Apr. 13, 1926.

ADAMS, EDIE (Elizabeth Edith Enke): Kingston, PA, Apr. 16, 1927. Juilliard, Columbia.

ADAMS, JOEY LAUREN: Little Rock, AR, Jan. 6, 1971.

ADAMS, JULIE (Betty May): Waterloo, IA, Oct. 17, 1926. Little Rock, Jr. College.

ADAMS, MASON: NYC, Feb. 26, 1919. UWi.

ADAMS, MAUD (Maud Wikstrom): Lulea, Sweden, Feb. 12, 1945.

ADJANI, ISABELLE: Germany, June 27, 1955.

AFFLECK, BEN: Berkeley, CA, Aug. 15, 1972.

AGAR, JOHN: Chicago, IL, Jan. 31, 1921.

AGUTTER, JENNY: Taunton, England, Dec. 20, 1952.

AIELLO, DANNY: NYC, June 20, 1933.

AIMEE, ANOUK (Dreyfus): Paris, France, Apr. 27, 1934. Bauer-Therond.

AKERS, KAREN: NYC, Oct. 13, 1945, unter College.

ALBERGHETTI, ANNA MARIA: Pesaro, Italy, May 15, 1936.

ALBERT, EDDIE (Eddie Albert Heimberger): Rock Island, IL, Apr. 22, 1908. U of Minn.

ALBERT, EDWARD: Los Angeles, Feb. 20, 1951. UCLA.

ALBRIGHT, LOLA: Akron, OH, July 20, 1925.

ALDA, ALAN: NYC, Jan. 28, 1936. Fordham.

ALEANDRO, NORMA: Buenos Aires, Dec. 6, 1936.

ALEJANDRO, MIGUEL: NYC, Feb. 21, 1958.

ALEXANDER, JANE (Quigley): Boston, MA, Oct. 28, 1939. Sarah Lawrence.

ALEXANDER, JASON (Jay Greenspan): Newark, NJ, Sept. 23, 1959. Boston U.

ALICE, MARY: Indianola, MS, Dec. 3, 1941.

ALLEN, DEBBIE (Deborah): Houston, TX, Jan. 16, 1950. Howard U.

ALLEN, JOAN: Rochelle, IL, Aug. 20, 1956. EastIllU.

ALLEN, KAREN: Carrollton, IL, Oct. 5, 1951. UMd.

ALLEN, NANCY: NYC, June 24, 1950.

ALLEN, STEVE: NYC, Dec. 26, 1921.

ALLEN, TIM: Denver, CO, June 13, 1953. W. MI. Univ.

ALLEN, WOODY (Allan Stewart Konigsberg): Brooklyn, Dec. 1, 1935.

ALLEY, KIRSTIE: Wichita, KS, Jan. 12, 1955.

ALLYSON, JUNE (Ella Geisman): Westchester, NY, Oct. 7, 1917.

ALONSO, MARIA CONCHITA: Cuba, June 29, 1957.

ALT, CAROL: Queens, NY, Dec. 1, 1960. HofstraU.

ALVARADO, TRINI: NYC, Jan. 10, 1967.

AMIS, SUZY: Oklahoma City, OK, Jan. 5, 1958. Actors Studio.

AMOS, JOHN: Newark, NJ, Dec. 27, 1940. Colo. U.

ANDERSON, GILLIAN: Chicago, IL, Aug. 9, 1968. DePaul U.

ANDERSON, KEVIN: Waukeegan, IL, Jan. 13, 1960.

ANDERSON, LONI: St. Paul, MN, Aug. 5, 1946.

ANDERSON, MELISSA SUE: Berkeley, CA, Sept. 26, 1962.

ANDERSON, MELODY: Edmonton, Canada, 1955. Carlton U.

ANDERSON, MICHAEL, JR.: London, England, Aug. 6, 1943.

ANDERSON, RICHARD DEAN: Minneapolis, MN, Jan. 23, 1950.

ANDERSSON, BIBI: Stockholm, Sweden, Nov. 11, 1935. Royal Dramatic Sch.

ANDES, KEITH: Ocean City, NJ, July 12, 1920. Temple U., Oxford.

ANDRESS, URSULA: Bern, Switzerland, Mar. 19, 1936.

ANDREWS, ANTHONY: London, Dec. 1, 1948.

ANDREWS, JULIE (Julia Elizabeth Wells): Surrey, England, Oct. 1, 1935.

ANGLIM, PHILIP: San Francisco, CA, Feb. 11, 1953.

ANISTON, JENNIFER: Sherman Oaks, CA, Feb. 11, 1969.

ANN-MARGRET (Olsson): Valsjobyn, Sweden, Apr. 28, 1941. Northwestern U.

ANSARA, MICHAEL: Lowell, MA, Apr. 15, 1922. Pasadena Playhouse.

ANSPACH, SUSAN: NYC, Nov. 23, 1945.

ANTHONY, LYSETTE: London, 1963.

ANTHONY, TONY: Clarksburg, WV, Oct. 16, 1937. Carnegie Tech.

ANTON, SUSAN: Yucaipa, CA, Oct. 12, 1950. Bemardino College.

ANTONELLI, LAURA: Pola, Italy, Nov. 28, 1941.

ANWAR, GABRIELLE: Lalehaam, England, Feb. 4, 1970

APPLEGATE, CHRISTINA: Hollywood CA, Nov. 25, 1972.

ARCHER, ANNE: Los Angeles, Aug. 25, 1947.

ARCHER, JOHN (Ralph Bowman): Osceola, NB, May 8, 1915. USC.

ARDANT, FANNY: Monte Carlo, Mar 22, 1949

Jennifer Aniston

ARKIN, ADAM: Brooklyn, NY, Aug. 19, 1956.
ARKIN, ALAN: NYC, Mar. 26, 1934. LACC.
ARMSTRONG, BESS: Baltimore, MD, Dec. 11, 1953.
ARNAZ, DESI, JR.: Los Angeles, Jan. 19, 1953.
ARNAZ, LUCIE: Hollywood, July 17, 1951.
ARNESS, JAMES (Aurness): Minneapolis, MN, May 26, 1923. Beloit College.
ARQUETTE, DAVID: Winchester, VA, Sept. 8, 1971.
ARQUETTE, PATRICIA: NYC, Apr. 8, 1968.
ARQUETTE, ROSANNA: NYC, Aug. 10, 1959.
ARTHUR, BEATRICE (Frankel): NYC, May 13, 1924. New School.
ASHER, JANE: London, Apr. 5, 1946.
ASHLEY, ELIZABETH (Elizabeth Ann Cole): Ocala, FL, Aug. 30, 1939.
ASHTON, JOHN: Springfield, MA, Feb. 22, 1948. USC.
ASNER, EDWARD: Kansas City, KS, Nov. 15, 1929.
ASSANTE, ARMAND: NYC, Oct. 4, 1949. AADA.
ASTIN, JOHN: Baltimore, MD, Mar. 30, 1930. U Minn.
ASTIN, MacKENZIE: Los Angeles, May 12, 1973.
ASTIN, SEAN: Santa Monica, Feb. 25, 1971.

Christina Applegate

ATHERTON, WILLIAM: Orange, CT, July 30, 1947. Carnegie Tech.
ATKINS, CHRISTOPHER: Rye, NY, Feb. 21, 1961.
ATKINS, EILEEN: London, June 16, 1934.
ATKINSON, ROWAN: England, Jan. 6, 1955. Oxford.
ATTENBOROUGH, RICHARD: Cambridge, England, Aug. 29, 1923. RADA.
AUBERJONOIS, RENE: NYC, June 1, 1940. Carnegie Tech.
AUDRAN, STEPHANE: Versailles, France, Nov. 8, 1932.
AUGER, CLAUDINE: Paris, France, Apr. 26, 1942. Dramatic Cons.
AULIN, EWA: Stockholm, Sweden, Feb. 14, 1950.
AUMONT, JEAN PIERRE: Paris, France, Jan. 5, 1909. French Nat'l School of Drama.
AVALON, FRANKIE (Francis Thomas Avallone): Philadelphia, PA, Sept. 18, 1939.
AYKROYD, DAN: Ottawa, Canada, July 1, 1952.
AZARIA, HANK: Forest Hills, NY, Apr. 25, 1964. AADA, Tufts Univ.
AZNAVOUR, CHARLES (Varenagh Aznourian): Paris, France, May 22, 1924.
AZZARA, CANDICE: Brooklyn, NY, May 18, 1947.
BACH, CATHERINE: Warren, OH, Mar. 1, 1954.
BACALL, LAUREN (Betty Perske): NYC, Sept. 16, 1924. AADA.
BACH, BARBARA: Queens, NY, Aug. 27, 1946.
BACKER, BRIAN: NYC, Dec. 5, 1956. Neighborhood Playhouse.
BACON, KEVIN: Philadelphia, PA, July 8, 1958.
BAIN, BARBARA: Chicago, IL, Sept. 13, 1934. U Ill.
BAIO, SCOTT: Brooklyn, NY, Sept. 22, 1961.
BAKER, BLANCHE: NYC, Dec. 20, 1956.
BAKER, CARROLL: Johnstown, PA, May 28, 1931. St. Petersburg, Jr. College.
BAKER, DIANE: Hollywood, CA, Feb. 25, 1938. USC.
BAKER, JOE DON: Groesbeck, TX, Feb.12, 1936.
BAKER, KATHY: Midland, TX, June 8, 1950. UC Berkley.
BAKULA, SCOTT: St. Louis, MO, Oct. 9, 1955. KansasU.
BALABAN, BOB: Chicago, IL, Aug. 16, 1945. Colgate.
BALDWIN, ADAM: Chicago, IL, Feb. 27, 1962.
BALDWIN, ALEC: Massapequa, NY, Apr. 3, 1958. NYU.
BALDWIN, STEPHEN: Long Island, NY, 1966.
BALDWIN, WILLIAM: Massapequa, NY, Feb. 21, 1963.
BALE, CHRISTIAN: Pembrokeshire, West Wales, Jan. 30, 1974.
BALK, FAIRUZA: Point Reyes, CA, May 21, 1974.
BALLARD, KAYE: Cleveland, OH, Nov. 20, 1926.
BANCROFT, ANNE (Anna Maria Italiano): Bronx, NY, Sept. 17, 1931. AADA.
BANDERAS, ANTONIO: Malaga, Spain, Aug. 10, 1960.
BANERJEE, VICTOR: Calcutta, India, Oct. 15, 1946.

Alan Arkin

BANES, LISA: Chagrin Falls, OH, July 9, 1955. Juilliard.
BARANSKI, CHRISTINE: Buffalo, NY, May 2, 1952. Juilliard.
BARBEAU, ADRIENNE: Sacramento, CA, June 11, 1945. Foothill College.
BARDOT, BRIGITTE: Paris, France, Sept. 28, 1934.
BARKIN, ELLEN: Bronx, NY, Apr. 16, 1954. Hunter College.
BARNES, CHRISTOPHER DANIEL: Portland, ME, Nov. 7, 1972.
BARR, JEAN-MARC: San Diego, CA, Sept. 1960.
BARRAULT, JEAN-LOUIS: Vesinet, France, Sept. 8, 1910.
BARRAULT, MARIE-CHRISTINE: Paris, France, Mar. 21, 1944.
BARREN, KEITH: Mexborough, England, Aug. 8, 1936. Sheffield Playhouse.
BARRETT, MAJEL (Hudec): Columbus, OH, Feb. 23, 1939. Western Reserve U.
BARRIE, BARBARA: Chicago, IL, May 23, 1931.
BARRY, GENE (Eugene Klass): NYC, June 14, 1919.
BARRY, NEILL: NYC, Nov. 29, 1965.
BARRYMORE, DREW: Los Angeles, Feb. 22, 1975.
BARRYMORE, JOHN DREW: Beverly Hills, CA, June 4, 1932. St. John's Military Academy.

Kevin Bacon

BARTEL, PAUL: Brooklyn, NY, Aug. 6, 1938. UCLA.

BARTY, BILLY: (William John Bertanzetti) Millsboro, PA, Oct. 25, 1924.

BARYSHNIKOV, MIKHAIL: Riga, Latvia, Jan. 27, 1948.

BASINGER, KIM: Athens, GA, Dec. 8, 1953. Neighborhood Playhouse.

BASSETT, ANGELA: NYC, Aug. 16, 1958.

BATEMAN, JASON: Rye, NY, Jan. 14, 1969.

BATEMAN, JUSTINE: Rye, NY, Feb. 19, 1966.

BATES, ALAN: Allestree, Derbyshire, England, Feb. 17, 1934. RADA.

BATES, JEANNE: San Francisco, CA, May 21, 1918. RADA.

BATES, KATHY: Memphis, TN, June 28, 1948. S. Methodist U.

BAUER, STEVEN (Steven Rocky Echevarria): Havana, Cuba, Dec. 2, 1956. U Miami.

BAXTER, KEITH: South Wales, England, Apr. 29, 1933. RADA.

BAXTER, MEREDITH: Los Angeles, June 21, 1947. Intelochen Acad.

BAYE, NATHALIE: Mainevile, France, July 6, 1948

BEACHAM, STEPHANIE: Casablanca, Morocco, Feb. 28, 1947.

BEALS, JENNIFER: Chicago, IL, Dec. 19, 1963.

BEAN, ORSON (Dallas Burrows): Burlington, VT, July 22, 1928.

BEAN, SEAN: Sheffield, Yorkshire, England, Apr. 17, 1958.

BEART, EMMANUELLE: Gassin, France, Aug. 14, 1965.

BEATTY, NED: Louisville, KY, July 6, 1937.

BEATTY, WARREN: Richmond, VA, Mar. 30, 1937.

BECK, JOHN: Chicago, IL, Jan. 28, 1943.

BECK, MICHAEL: Memphis, TN, Feb. 4, 1949. Millsap College.

BECKINSALE, KATE: England, July 26, 1974.

BEDELIA, BONNIE: NYC, Mar. 25, 1946. Hunter College.

BEGLEY, ED, JR.: NYC, Sept. 16, 1949.

BELAFONTE, HARRY: NYC, Mar. 1, 1927.

BEL GEDDES, BARBARA: NYC, Oct. 31, 1922.

BELL, TOM: Liverpool, England, 1932.

BELLER, KATHLEEN: NYC, Feb. 10, 1957.

BELLWOOD, PAMELA (King): Scarsdale, NY, June 26, 1951.

BELMONDO, JEAN PAUL: Paris, France, Apr. 9, 1933.

BELUSHI, JAMES: Chicago, IL, June 15, 1954.

BELZER, RICHARD: Bridgeport, CT, Aug. 4, 1944.

BENEDICT, DIRK (Niewoehner): White Sulphur Springs, MT, March 1, 1945. Whitman College.

BENEDICT, PAUL: Silver City, NM, Sept. 17, 1938.

BENIGNI, ROBERTO: Tuscany, Italy, Oct. 27, 1952.

BENING, ANNETTE: Topeka, KS, May 29, 1958. SFSt. U.

BENJAMIN, RICHARD: NYC, May 22, 1938. Northwestern U.

BENNENT, DAVID: Lausanne, Sept. 9, 1966.

Alec Baldwin

Scott Bakula

Christian Bale

BENNETT, ALAN: Leeds, England, May 9, 1934. Oxford.

BENNETT, BRUCE (Herman Brix): Tacoma, WA, May 19, 1909. U Wash.

BENNETT, HYWEL: Garnant, So. Wales, Apr. 8, 1944.

BENSON, ROBBY: Dallas, TX, Jan. 21, 1957.

BERENGER, TOM: Chicago, IL, May 31, 1950, U Mo.

BERENSON, MARISA: NYC, Feb. 15, 1947.

BERG, PETER: NYC, March 11, 1964. Malcalester College.

BERGEN, CANDICE: Los Angeles, May 9, 1946. U PA.

BERGEN, POLLY: Knoxville, TN, July 14, 1930. Compton, Jr. College.

BERGER, HELMUT: Salzburg, Austria, May 29, 1942.

BERGER, SENTA: Vienna, Austria, May 13, 1941. Vienna Sch. of Acting.

BERGER, WILLIAM: Austria, Jan. 20, 1928. Columbia.

BERGERAC, JACQUES: Biarritz, France, May 26, 1927. Paris U.

BERGIN, PATRICK: Dublin, Feb. 4, 1951.

BERKLEY, ELIZABETH: Detroit, MI, July 28, 1972.

BERKOFF, STEVEN: London, England, Aug. 3, 1937.

BERLE, MILTON (Berlinger): NYC, July 12, 1908.

BERLIN, JEANNIE: Los Angeles, Nov. 1, 1949.

BERLINGER, WARREN: Brooklyn, Aug. 31, 1937. Columbia.

BERNHARD, SANDRA: Flint, MI, June 6, 1955.

BERNSEN, CORBIN: Los Angeles, Sept. 7, 1954. UCLA.

BERRI, CLAUDE (Langmann): Paris, France, July 1, 1934.

BERRIDGE, ELIZABETH: Westchester, NY, May 2, 1962. Strasberg Inst.

BERRY, HALLE: Cleveland, OH, Aug. 14, 1968.

BERRY, KEN: Moline, IL, Nov. 3, 1933.

BERTINELLI, VALERIE: Wilmington, DE, Apr. 23, 1960.

BEST, JAMES: Corydon, IN, July 26, 1926.

BETTGER, LYLE: Philadelphia, PA, Feb. 13, 1915. AADA.

BEY, TURHAN: Vienna, Austria, Mar. 30, 1921.

BEYMER, RICHARD: Avoca, IA, Feb. 21, 1939.

BIALIK, MAYIM: San Diego, CA, Dec. 12, 1975.

BIEHN, MICHAEL: Anniston, AL, July 31, 1956.

BIGGS, JASON: Pompton Plains, NJ, May 12, 1978.

BIKEL, THEODORE: Vienna, May 2, 1924. RADA.

BILLINGSLEY, PETER: NYC, Apr. 16, 1972.

BINOCHE, JULIETTE: Paris, France, Mar. 9, 1964.

BIRCH, THORA: Los Angeles, Mar. 11, 1982.

BIRKIN, JANE: London, Dec. 14, 1947

BIRNEY, DAVID: Washington, DC, Apr. 23, 1939. Dartmouth, UCLA.

BIRNEY, REED: Alexandria, VA, Sept. 11, 1954. Boston U.

Fairuza Balk

Kathy Bates

Annette Bening

Tom Berenger

BISHOP, JOEY (Joseph Abraham Gotllieb): Bronx, NY, Feb. 3, 1918.

BISHOP, JULIE (Jacqueline Wells): Denver, CO, Aug. 30, 1917. Westlake School.

BISSET, JACQUELINE: Waybridge, England, Sept. 13, 1944.

BLACK, KAREN (Ziegler): Park Ridge, IL, July 1, 1942. Northwestern.

BLACKMAN, HONOR: London, Aug. 22, 1926.

BLADES, RUBEN: Panama City, July 16, 1948. Harvard.

BLAIR, BETSY (Betsy Boger): NYC, Dec. 11, 1923.

BLAIR, JANET (Martha Jane Lafferty): Blair, PA, Apr. 23, 1921.

BLAIR, LINDA: Westport, CT, Jan. 22, 1959.

BLAKE, ROBERT (Michael Gubitosi): Nutley, NJ, Sept. 18, 1933.

BLAKELY, SUSAN: Frankfurt, Germany, Sept. 7, 1950. U TX.

BLAKLEY, RONEE: Stanley, ID, 1946. Stanford U.

BLANCHETT, CATE: Melbourne, Australia, May 14, 1969.

BLETHYN, BRENDA: Ramsgate, Kent, Eng., Feb. 20, 1946.

BLOOM, CLAIRE: London, Feb. 15, 1931. Badminton School.

BLOOM, VERNA: Lynn, MA, Aug. 7, 1939. Boston U.

BLOUNT, LISA: Fayettville, AK, July 1, 1957. UAk.

BLUM, MARK: Newark, NJ, May 14, 1950. UMinn.

BLYTH, ANN: Mt. Kisco, NY, Aug. 16, 1928. New Waybum Dramatic School.

BOCHNER, HART: Toronto, Canada, Oct. 3, 1956. U San Diego.

BOCHNER, LLOYD: Toronto, Canada, July 29, 1924.

BOGOSIAN, ERIC: Woburn, MA, Apr. 24, 1953. Oberlin College.

BOHRINGER, RICHARD: Paris, France, Jan. 16, 1941.

BOLKAN, FLORINDA (Florinda Soares Bulcao): Ceara, Brazil, Feb. 15, 1941.

BOLOGNA, JOSEPH: Brooklyn, NY, Dec. 30, 1938. Brown U.

BOND, DEREK: Glasgow, Scotland, Jan. 26, 1920. Askes School.

BONET, LISA: San Francisco, CA, Nov. 16, 1967.

BONHAM-CARTER, HELENA: London, England, May 26, 1966.

BOONE, PAT: Jacksonville, FL, June 1, 1934. Columbia U.

BOOTHE, JAMES: Croydon, England, Dec.19, 1930

BOOTHE, POWERS: Snyder, TX, June 1, 1949. So. Methodist U.

BORGNINE, ERNEST (Borgnino): Hamden, CT, Jan. 24, 1917. Randall School.

BOSCO, PHILIP: Jersey City, NJ, Sept. 26, 1930. CatholicU.

BOSLEY, TOM: Chicago, IL, Oct. 1, 1927. DePaul U.

BOSTWICK, BARRY: San Mateo, CA, Feb. 24, 1945. NYU.

BOTTOMS, JOSEPH: Santa Barbara, CA, Aug. 30, 1954.

BOTTOMS, SAM: Santa Barbara, CA, Oct. 17, 1955.

BOTTOMS, TIMOTHY: Santa Barbara, CA, Aug. 30, 1951.

BOULTING, INGRID: Transvaal, So. Africa, 1947.

BOUTSIKARIS, DENNIS: Newark, NJ, Dec. 21, 1952. CatholicU.

BOWIE, DAVID (David Robert Jones): Brixton, South London, England, Jan. 8, 1947.

BOWKER, JUDI: Shawford, England, Apr. 6, 1954.

BOXLEITNER, BRUCE: Elgin, IL, May 12, 1950.

BOYLE, LARA FLYNN: Davenport, IA, Mar. 24, 1970.

BOYLE, PETER: Philadelphia, PA, Oct. 18, 1933. LaSalle College.

BRACCO, LORRAINE: Brooklyn, NY, 1955.

BRACKEN, EDDIE: NYC, Feb. 7, 1920. Professional Children's School.

BRAEDEN, ERIC (Hans Gudegast): Kiel, Germany, Apr. 3, 1942.

BRAGA, SONIA: Maringa, Brazil, June 8, 1950.

BRANAGH, KENNETH: Belfast, No. Ireland, Dec. 10, 1960.

BRANDAUER, KLAUS MARIA: Altaussee, Austria, June 22, 1944.

BRANDIS, JONATHAN: CT, Apr. 13, 1976.

BRANDO, JOCELYN: San Francisco, Nov. 18, 1919. Lake Forest College, AADA.

BRANDO, MARLON: Omaha, NB, Apr. 3, 1924. New School.

BRANDON, CLARK: NYC, Dec. 13, 1958.

BRANDON, MICHAEL (Feldman): Brooklyn, NY, Apr. 20, 1945.

BRANTLEY, BETSY: Rutherfordton, NC, Sept. 20, 1955. London Central Sch. of Drama.

BRENNAN, EILEEN: Los Angeles, CA, Sept. 3, 1935. AADA.

BRIALY, JEAN-CLAUDE: Aumale, Algeria, 1933. Strasbourg Cons.

BRIDGES, BEAU: Los Angeles, Dec. 9, 1941. UCLA.

BRIDGES, JEFF: Los Angeles, Dec. 4, 1949.

BRIMLEY, WILFORD: Salt Lake City, UT, Sept. 27, 1934.

BRINKLEY, CHRISTIE: Malibu, CA, Feb. 2, 1954.

BRITT, MAY (Maybritt Wilkins): Sweden, Mar. 22, 1936.

BRITTANY, MORGAN (Suzanne Cupito): Los Angeles, Dec. 5, 1950.

BRITTON, TONY: Birmingham, England, June 9, 1924.

BRODERICK, MATTHEW: NYC, Mar. 21, 1962.

BRODY, ADRIEN: NYC, Dec. 23, 1976,

BROLIN, JAMES: Los Angeles, July 18, 1940. UCLA.

BROLIN, JOSH: Los Angeles, Feb. 12, 1968.

BROMFIELD, JOHN (Farron Bromfield): South Bend, IN, June 11, 1922. St. Mary's College.

BRON, ELEANOR: Stanmore, England, Mar. 14, 1934.

BRONSON, CHARLES (Buchinsky): Ehrenfield, PA, Nov. 3, 1920.

BROOKES, JACQUELINE: Montclair, NJ, July 24, 1930. RADA.

BROOKS, ALBERT (Einstein): Los Angeles, July 22, 1947.

Kenneth Branagh

Beau Bridges

Sandra Bullock

Gabriel Byrne

BROOKS, MEL (Melvyn Kaminski): Brooklyn, NY, June 28, 1926.

BROSNAN, PIERCE: County Meath, Ireland. May 16, 1952.

BROWN, BLAIR: Washington, DC, Apr. 23, 1947. Pine Manor.

BROWN, BRYAN: Panania, Australia, June 23, 1947.

BROWN, GARY (Christian Brando): Hollywood, CA, 1958.

BROWN, GEORG STANFORD: Havana, Cuba, June 24, 1943. AMDA.

BROWN, JAMES: Desdemona, TX, Mar. 22, 1920. Baylor U.

BROWN, JIM: St. Simons Island, NY, Feb. 17, 1935. Syracuse U.

BROWNE, LESLIE: NYC, 1958.

BROWNE, ROSCOE LEE: Woodbury, NJ, May 2, 1925.

BUCHHOLZ, HORST: Berlin, Germany, Dec. 4, 1933. Ludwig Dramatic School.

BUCKLEY, BETTY: Big Spring, TX, July 3, 1947. TxCU.

BUJOLD, GENEVIEVE: Montreal, Canada, July 1, 1942.

BULLOCK, SANDRA: Arlington, VA, July 26, 1964.

BURGHOFF, GARY: Bristol, CT, May 24, 1943.

BURGI, RICHARD: Montclair, NJ, July 30, 1958.

BURKE, PAUL: New Orleans, July 21, 1926. Pasadena Playhouse.

BURNETT, CAROL: San Antonio, TX, Apr. 26, 1933. UCLA.

BURNS, CATHERINE: NYC, Sept. 25, 1945. AADA.

BURNS, EDWARD: Valley Stream, NY, Jan. 28, 1969.

BURROWS, DARREN E.: Winfield, KS, Sept. 12, 1966

BURSTYN, ELLEN (Edna Rae Gillhooly): Detroit, MI, Dec. 7, 1932.

BURTON, LeVAR: Los Angeles, CA, Feb. 16, 1958. UCLA.

BUSCEMI, STEVE: Brooklyn, NY, Dec. 13, 1957.

BUSEY, GARY: Goose Creek, TX, June 29, 1944.

BUSFIELD, TIMOTHY: Lansing, MI, June 12, 1957. E. Tenn. St. U.

BUTTONS, RED (Aaron Chwatt): NYC, Feb. 5, 1919.

BUZZI, RUTH: Westerly, RI, July 24, 1936. Pasadena Playhouse.

BYGRAVES, MAX: London, Oct. 16, 1922. St. Joseph's School.

BYRNE, DAVID: Dumbarton, Scotland, May 14, 1952.

BYRNE, GABRIEL: Dublin, Ireland, May 12, 1950.

BYRNES, EDD: NYC, July 30, 1933.

CAAN, JAMES: Bronx, NY, Mar. 26,1939.

CAESAR, SID: Yonkers, NY, Sept. 8, 1922.

CAGE, NICOLAS (Coppola): Long Beach, CA, Jan.7, 1964.

CAINE, MICHAEL (Maurice Micklewhite): London, Mar. 14, 1933.

CAINE, SHAKIRA (Baksh): Guyana, Feb. 23, 1947. Indian Trust College.

CALLAN, MICHAEL (Martin Calinieff): Philadelphia, Nov. 22, 1935.

CALLOW, SIMON: London, June 15, 1949. Queens U.

CALVERT, PHYLLIS: London, Feb. 18, 1917. Margaret Morris School.

CALVET, CORRINE (Corinne Dibos): Paris, France, Apr. 30, 1925. U Paris.

CAMERON, KIRK: Panorama City, CA, Oct. 12, 1970.

CAMP, COLLEEN: San Francisco, CA, 1953.

CAMPBELL, BILL: Chicago, IL, July 7, 1959.

CAMPBELL, GLEN: Delight, AR, Apr. 22, 1935.

CAMPBELL, NEVE: Guelph, Ontario, Canada, Oct. 3, 1973.

CAMPBELL, TISHA: Oklahoma City, OK, Oct. 13, 1968.

CANALE, GIANNA MARIA: Reggio Calabria, Italy, Sept. 12, 1927.

CANNON, DYAN (Samille Diane Friesen): Tacoma, WA, Jan. 4, 1937.

CAPERS, VIRGINIA: Sumter, SC, Sept. 25, 1925. Juilliard.

CAPSHAW, KATE: Ft. Worth, TX, Nov. 3, 1953. UMo.

CARA, IRENE: NYC, Mar. 18, 1958.

CARDINALE, CLAUDIA: Tunis, N. Africa. Apr. 15, 1939. College Paul Cambon.

CAREY, HARRY, JR.: Saugus, CA, May 16, 1921. Black Fox Military Academy.

CAREY, PHILIP: Hackensack, NJ, July 15, 1925. U Miami.

CARIOU, LEN: Winnipeg, Canada, Sept. 30, 1939.

CARLIN, GEORGE: NYC, May 12, 1938.

CARLYLE, ROBERT: Glasgow, Scotland, Apr. 14, 1961.

CARMEN, JULIE: Mt. Vernon, NY, Apr. 4, 1954.

CARMICHAEL, IAN: Hull, England, June 18, 1920. Scarborough College.

CARNE, JUDY (Joyce Botterill): Northampton, England, 1939. Bush-Davis Theatre School.

CARNEY, ART: Mt. Vernon, NY, Nov. 4, 1918.

CARON, LESLIE: Paris, France, July 1, 1931. Nat'l Conservatory, Paris.

CARPENTER, CARLETON: Bennington, VT, July 10, 1926. Northwestern.

CARRADINE, DAVID: Hollywood, Dec. 8, 1936. San Francisco State.

CARRADINE, KEITH: San Mateo, CA, Aug. 8, 1950. Colo. State U.

CARRADINE, ROBERT: San Mateo, CA, Mar. 24, 1954.

CARREL, DANY: Tourane, Indochina, Sept. 20, 1936. Marseilles Cons.

CARRERA, BARBARA: Managua, Nicaragua, Dec. 31, 1945.

CARRERE, TIA (Althea Janairo): Honolulu, HI, Jan. 2, 1965.

CARREY, JIM: Jacksons Point, Ontario, Canada, Jan. 17, 1962.

CARRIERE, MATHIEU: Hannover, West Germany, Aug. 2, 1950.

CARROLL, DIAHANN (Johnson): NYC, July 17, 1935. NYU.

CARROLL, PAT: Shreveport, LA, May 5, 1927. Catholic U.

CARSON, JOHN DAVID: California, Mar. 6, 1952. Valley College.

CARSON, JOHNNY: Corning, IA, Oct. 23, 1925. U of Neb.

James Caan

Dana Carvey

Jackie Chan

CARSTEN, PETER (Ransenthaler): Weissenberg, Bavaria, Apr. 30, 1929. Munich Akademie.

CARTER, NELL: Birmingham, AL, Sept. 13, 1948.

CARTLIDGE, KATRIN: London, 1961.

CARTWRIGHT, VERONICA: Bristol, England, Apr 20, 1949.

CARUSO, DAVID: Forest Hills, NY, Jan. 7, 1956.

CARVEY, DANA: Missoula, MT, Apr. 2, 1955. SFST.CoI.

CASELLA, MAX: Washington D.C, June 6, 1967

CASEY, BERNIE: Wyco, WV, June 8, 1939.

CASSAVETES, NICK: NYC, 1959, Syracuse U, AADA.

CASSEL, JEAN-PIERRE: Paris, France, Oct. 27, 1932.

CASSEL, SEYMOUR: Detroit, MI, Jan. 22, 1935.

CASSIDY, DAVID: NYC, Apr. 12, 1950.

CASSIDY, JOANNA: Camden, NJ, Aug. 2, 1944. Syracuse U.

CASSIDY, PATRICK: Los Angeles, CA, Jan. 4, 1961.

CATES, PHOEBE: NYC, July 16, 1962.

CATTRALL, KIM: Liverpool, England, Aug. 21, 1956. AADA.

CAULFIELD, MAXWELL: Glasgow, Scotland, Nov. 23, 1959.

CAVANI, LILIANA: Bologna, Italy, Jan. 12, 1937. U Bologna.

CAVETT, DICK: Gibbon, NE, Nov. 19, 1936.

CHAKIRIS, GEORGE: Norwood, OH, Sept. 16, 1933.

CHAMBERLAIN, RICHARD: Beverly Hills, CA, March 31, 1935. Pomona.

CHAMPION, MARGE (Marjorie Belcher): Los Angeles, Sept. 2, 1923.

CHAN, JACKIE: Hong Kong, Apr. 7, 1954

CHANNING, CAROL: Seattle, WA, Jan. 31, 1921. Bennington.

CHANNING, STOCKARD (Susan Stockard): NYC, Feb. 13, 1944. Radcliffe.

CHAPIN, MILES: NYC, Dec. 6, 1954. HB Studio.

CHAPLIN, GERALDINE: Santa Monica, CA, July 31, 1944. Royal Ballet.

CHAPLIN, SYDNEY: Los Angeles, Mar. 31, 1926. Lawrenceville.

CHARISSE, CYD (Tula Ellice Finklea): Amarillo, TX, Mar. 3, 1922. Hollywood Professional School.

CHARLES, JOSH: Baltimore, MD, Sept. 15, 1971.

CHARLES, WALTER: East Strousburg, PA, Apr. 4, 1945. Boston U.

CHASE, CHEVY (Cornelius Crane Chase): NYC, Oct. 8, 1943.

CHAVES, RICHARD: Jacksonville, FL, Oct. 9, 1951. Occidental College.

CHAYKIN, MAURY: Canada, July 27, 1954

CHEN, JOAN (Chen Chung): Shanghai, Apr. 26, 1961. CalState.

CHER (Cherilyn Sarkisian): El Centro, CA, May 20, 1946.

CHILES, LOIS: Alice, TX, Apr. 15, 1947.

CHONG, RAE DAWN: Vancouver, Canada, Feb. 28, 1962.

CHONG, THOMAS: Edmonton, Alberta, Canada, May 24, 1938.

CHRISTIAN, LINDA (Blanca Rosa Welter): Tampico, Mexico, Nov. 13, 1923.

CHRISTIE, JULIE: Chukua, Assam, India, Apr. 14, 1941.

CHRISTOPHER, DENNIS (Carrelli): Philadelphia, PA, Dec. 2, 1955. Temple U.

CHRISTOPHER, JORDAN: Youngstown, OH, Oct. 23, 1940. Kent State.

CILENTO, DIANE: Queensland, Australia, Oct. 5, 1933. AADA.

CLAPTON, ERIC: London, Mar. 30, 1945.

CLARK, CANDY: Norman, OK, June 20, 1947.

CLARK, DICK: Mt. Vernon, NY, Nov. 30, 1929. Syracuse U.

CLARK, MATT: Washington, DC, Nov. 25, 1936.

CLARK, PETULA: Epsom, England, Nov. 15, 1932.

CLARK, SUSAN: Sarnid, Ont., Canada, Mar. 8, 1943. RADA.

CLAY, ANDREW DICE (Andrew Silverstein): Brooklyn, NY, Sept. 29, 1957, Kingsborough College.

CLAYBURGH, JILL: NYC, Apr. 30, 1944. Sarah Lawrence.

CLEESE, JOHN: Weston-Super-Mare, England, Oct. 27, 1939, Cambridge.

CLOONEY, ROSEMARY: Maysville, KY, May 23, 1928.

CLOSE, GLENN: Greenwich, CT, Mar. 19, 1947. William & Mary College.

COBURN, JAMES: Laurel, NB, Aug. 31, 1928. LACC.

COCA, IMOGENE: Philadelphia, Nov. 18, 1908.

CODY, KATHLEEN: Bronx, NY, Oct. 30, 1953.

COFFEY, SCOTT: HI, May 1, 1967.

COLE, GEORGE: London, Apr. 22, 1925.

COLEMAN, GARY: Zion, IL, Feb. 8, 1968.

COLEMAN, DABNEY: Austin, TX, Jan. 3, 1932.

COLEMAN, JACK: Easton, PA, Feb. 21, 1958. Duke U.

COLIN, MARGARET: NYC, May 26, 1957.

COLLET, CHRISTOPHER: NYC, Mar. 13, 1968. Strasberg Inst.

COLLETTE, TONI: Sydney, Australia, Nov. 1, 1972.

COLLINS, JOAN: London, May 21, 1933. Francis Holland School.

COLLINS, PAULINE: Devon, England, Sept. 3, 1940.

COLLINS, STEPHEN: Des Moines, IA, Oct. 1, 1947. Amherst.

COLON, MIRIAM: Ponce, PR., 1945. UPR.

COLTRANE, ROBBIE: Ruthergien, Scotland, Mar. 30, 1950.

COMER, ANJANETTE: Dawson, TX, Aug. 7, 1942. Baylor, Tex. U.

CONANT, OLIVER: NYC, Nov. 15, 1955. Dalton.

CONAWAY, JEFF: NYC, Oct. 5, 1950. NYU.

CONNELLY, JENNIFER: NYC, Dec. 12, 1970

CONNERY, SEAN: Edinburgh, Scotland, Aug. 25, 1930.

CONNERY, JASON: London, Jan. 11, 1963.

CONNICK, HARRY, JR.: New Orleans, LA, Sept. 11, 1967.

CONNOLLY, BILLY: Glasgow, Scotland, Nov. 24, 1942.

CONNORS, MIKE (Krekor Ohanian): Fresno, CA, Aug. 15, 1925. UCLA.

CONRAD, ROBERT (Conrad Robert Falk): Chicago, IL, Mar. 1, 1935. Northwestern U.

Joan Chen

Tom Cruise

Joan Cusack

John Cusack

CONSTANTINE, MICHAEL: Reading, PA, May 22, 1927.

CONTI, TOM: Paisley, Scotland, Nov. 22, 1941.

CONVERSE, FRANK: St. Louis, MO, May 22, 1938. Carnegie Tech.

CONWAY, GARY: Boston, Feb. 4, 1936.

CONWAY, KEVIN: NYC, May 29, 1942.

CONWAY, TIM (Thomas Daniel): Willoughby, OH, Dec. 15, 1933. Bowling Green State.

COOGAN, KEITH (Keith Mitchell Franklin): Palm Springs, CA, Jan. 13, 1970.

COOK, RACHEL LEIGH: Minneapolis, MN, Oct. 4, 1979.

COOPER, BEN: Hartford, CT, Sept. 30, 1930. Columbia U.

COOPER, CHRIS: Kansas City, MO, July 9, 1951. UMo.

COOPER, JACKIE: Los Angeles, Sept. 15, 1921.

COPELAND, JOAN: NYC, June 1, 1922. Brooklyn College, RADA.

CORBETT, GRETCHEN: Portland, OR, Aug. 13, 1947. Carnegie Tech.

CORBIN, BARRY: Dawson County, TX, Oct. 16, 1940. Texas Tech. U.

CORCORAN, DONNA: Quincy, MA, Sept. 29, 1942.

CORD, ALEX (Viespi): Floral Park, NY, Aug. 3, 1931. NYU, Actors Studio.

CORDAY, MARA (Marilyn Watts): Santa Monica, CA, Jan. 3, 1932.

COREY, JEFF: NYC, Aug. 10, 1914. Fagin School.

CORNTHWAITE, ROBERT: St. Helens, OR, Apr. 28, 1917. USC.

CORRI, ADRIENNE: Glasgow, Scot., Nov. 13, 1933. RADA.

CORT, BUD (Walter Edward Cox): New Rochelle, NY, Mar. 29, 1950. NYU.

CORTESA, VALENTINA: Milan, Italy, Jan. 1, 1924.

COSBY, BILL: Philadelphia, PA, July 12, 1937. Temple U.

COSTER, NICOLAS: London, Dec. 3, 1934. Neighborhood Playhouse.

COSTNER, KEVIN: Lynwood, CA, Jan. 18, 1955. CalStaU.

COURTENAY, TOM: Hull, England, Feb. 25, 1937. RADA.

COURTLAND, JEROME: Knoxville, TN, Dec. 27, 1926.

COX, BRIAN: Dundee, Scotland, June 1, 1946. LAMDA.

COX, COURTENEY: Birmingham, AL, June 15, 1964.

COX, RONNY: Cloudcroft, NM, Aug. 23, 1938.

COYOTE, PETER (Cohon): NYC, Oct. 10, 1941.

CRAIG, MICHAEL: Poona, India, Jan. 27, 1929.

CRAIN, JEANNE: Barstow, CA, May 25, 1925.

CRAVEN, GEMMA: Dublin, Ireland, June 1, 1950.

CRAWFORD, MICHAEL (Dumbel-Smith): Salisbury, England, Jan. 19, 1942.

CREMER, BRUNO: Paris, France, 1929.

CRENNA, RICHARD: Los Angeles, Nov. 30, 1926. USC.

CRISTAL, LINDA (Victoria Moya): Buenos Aires, Feb. 25, 1934.

CROMWELL, JAMES: Los Angeles, CA, Jan. 27, 1940.

CRONYN, HUME (Blake): Ontario, Canada, July 18, 1911.

CROSBY, DENISE: Hollywood, CA, Nov. 24, 1957.

CROSBY, HARRY: Los Angeles, CA, Aug. 8, 1958.

CROSBY, MARY FRANCES: Los Angeles, CA, Sept. 14, 1959.

CROSS, BEN: London, Dec. 16, 1947. RADA.

CROSS, MURPHY (Mary Jane): Laurelton, MD, June 22, 1950.

CROUSE, LINDSAY: NYC, May 12, 1948. Radcliffe.

CROWE, RUSSELL: New Zealand, Apr. 7, 1964.

CROWLEY, PAT: Olyphant, PA, Sept. 17, 1932.

CRUDUP, BILLY: Manhasset, NY, July 8, 1968. UNC/Chapel Hill.

CRUISE, TOM (T. C. Mapother, IV): July 3, 1962, Syracuse, NY.

CRYER, JON: NYC, Apr. 16, 1965, RADA.

CRYSTAL, BILLY: Long Beach, NY, Mar. 14, 1947. Marshall U.

CULKIN, KIERAN: NYC, Sept. 30, 1982.

CULKIN, MACAULAY: NYC, Aug. 26, 1980.

CULLUM, JOHN: Knoxville, TN, Mar. 2, 1930. U Tenn.

CULLUM, JOHN DAVID: NYC, Mar. 1, 1966.

CULP, ROBERT: Oakland, CA, Aug. 16, 1930. U Wash.

CUMMING, ALAN: Perthshire, Scotland, 1964.

CUMMINGS, CONSTANCE: Seattle, WA, May 15, 1910.

CUMMINGS, QUINN: Hollywood, Aug. 13, 1967.

CUMMINS, PEGGY: Prestatyn, N. Wales, Dec. 18, 1926. Alexandra School.

CURRY, TIM: Cheshire, England, Apr. 19, 1946. Birmingham U.

CURTIN, JANE: Cambridge, MA, Sept. 6, 1947.

CURTIS, JAMIE LEE: Los Angeles, CA, Nov. 22, 1958.

CURTIS, KEENE: Salt Lake City, UT, Feb. 15, 1925. U Utah.

CURTIS, TONY (Bernard Schwartz): NYC, June 3, 1924.

CUSACK, JOAN: Evanston, IL, Oct. 11, 1962.

CUSACK, JOHN: Chicago, IL, June 28, 1966.

CUSACK, SINEAD: Dalkey, Ireland, Feb. 18, 1948

DAFOE, WILLEM: Appleton, WI, July 22, 1955.

DAHL, ARLENE: Minneapolis, Aug. 11, 1928. U Minn.

DALE, JIM: Rothwell, England, Aug. 15, 1935.

Beverly D'Angelo   Ellen DeGeneres   Danny DeVito   Clint Eastwood

DALLESANDRO, JOE: Pensacola, FL, Dec. 31, 1948.

DALTON, TIMOTHY: Colwyn Bay, Wales, Mar. 21, 1946. RADA.

DALTREY, ROGER: London, Mar. 1, 1944.

DALY, TIM: NYC, Mar. 1, 1956. Bennington College.

DALY, TYNE: Madison, WI, Feb. 21, 1947. AMDA.

DAMON, MATT: Cambridge, MA, Oct. 8, 1970.

DAMONE, VIC (Vito Farinola): Brooklyn, NY, June 12, 1928.

DANCE, CHARLES: Plymouth, England, Oct. 10, 1946.

DANES, CLAIRE: New York, NY, Apr. 12, 1979.

D'ANGELO, BEVERLY: Columbus, OH, Nov. 15, 1953.

DANGERFIELD, RODNEY (Jacob Cohen): Babylon, NY, Nov. 22, 1921.

DANIELS, JEFF: Athens, GA, Feb. 19, 1955. EMichSt.

DANIELS, WILLIAM: Brooklyn, NY, Mar. 31, 1927. Northwestern.

DANNER, BLYTHE: Philadelphia, PA, Feb. 3, 1944. Bard College.

DANNING, SYBIL (Sybille Johanna Danninger): Vienna, Austria, May 4, 1949.

DANSON, TED: San Diego, CA, Dec. 29, 1947. Stanford, Carnegie Tech.

DANTE, MICHAEL (Ralph Vitti): Stamford, CT, 1935. U Miami.

DANZA, TONY: Brooklyn, NY, Apr. 21, 1951. UDubuque.

D'ARBANVILLE-QUINN, PATTI: NYC, 1951.

DARBY, KIM (Deborah Zerby): North Hollywood, CA, July 8, 1948.

DARCEL, DENISE (Denise Billecard): Paris, France, Sept. 8, 1925. U Dijon.

DARREN, JAMES: Philadelphia, PA, June 8, 1936. Stella Adler School.

DARRIEUX, DANIELLE: Bordeaux, France, May 1, 1917. Lycee LaTour.

DAVENPORT, NIGEL: Cambridge, England, May 23, 1928. Trinity College.

DAVID, KEITH: NYC, June 4, 1954. Juilliard.

DAVIDOVICH, LOLITA: Toronto, Ontario, Canada, July 15, 1961.

DAVIDSON, JAYE: Riverside, CA, 1968.

DAVIDSON, JOHN: Pittsburgh, Dec. 13, 1941. Denison U.

DAVIES, JEREMY (Boring): Rockford, IA, Oct. 28, 1969.

DAVIS, CLIFTON: Chicago, IL, Oct. 4, 1945. Oakwood College.

DAVIS, GEENA: Wareham, MA, Jan. 21, 1957.

DAVIS, HOPE: Tenafly, NJ, 1967.

DAVIS, JUDY: Perth, Australia, Apr. 23, 1955.

DAVIS, MAC: Lubbock, TX, Jan. 21,1942.

DAVIS, NANCY (Anne Frances Robbins): NYC, July 6, 1921. Smith College.

DAVIS, OSSIE: Cogdell, GA, Dec. 18, 1917. Howard U.

DAVIS, SAMMI: Kidderminster, Worcester-shire, England, June 21, 1964.

DAVISON, BRUCE: Philadelphia, PA, June 28, 1946.

DAWBER, PAM: Detroit, MI, Oct. 18, 1954.

DAY, DORIS (Doris Kappelhoff): Cincinnati, Apr. 3, 1924.

DAY, LARAINE (Johnson): Roosevelt, UT, Oct. 13, 1917.

DAY LEWIS, DANIEL: London, Apr. 29, 1957. Bristol Old Vic.

DAYAN, ASSI: Israel, Nov. 23, 1945. U Jerusalem.

DEAKINS, LUCY: NYC, 1971.

DEAN, JIMMY: Plainview, TX, Aug. 10, 1928.

DEAN, LOREN: Las Vegas, NV, July 31, 1969.

DeCAMP, ROSEMARY: Prescott, AZ, Nov. 14, 1913.

DeCARLO, YVONNE (Peggy Yvonne Middleton): Vancouver, B.C., Canada, Sept. 1, 1922. Vancouver School of Drama.

DEE, FRANCES: Los Angeles, Nov. 26, 1907. Chicago U.

DEE, JOEY (Joseph Di Nicola): Passaic, NJ, June 11, 1940. Patterson State College.

DEE, RUBY: Cleveland, OH, Oct. 27, 1924. Hunter College.

DEE, SANDRA (Alexandra Zuck): Bayonne, NJ, Apr. 23, 1942.

DeGENERES, ELLEN: New Orleans, LA, Jan. 26, 1958.

DeHAVEN, GLORIA: Los Angeles, July 23, 1923.

DeHAVILLAND, OLIVIA: Tokyo, Japan, July 1, 1916. Notre Dame Convent School.

DELAIR, SUZY (Suzanne Delaire): Paris, France, Dec. 31, 1916.

DELANY, DANA: NYC, March 13, 1956. Wesleyan U.

DELPY, JULIE: Paris. Dec. 21, 1969.

DELON, ALAIN: Sceaux, France, Nov. 8, 1935.

DELORME, DANIELE: Paris, France, Oct. 9, 1926. Sorbonne.

DEL TORO, BENICIO: Santurce, Puerto Rico, Feb. 19, 1967.

DeLUISE, DOM: Brooklyn, NY, Aug. 1, 1933. Tufts College.

DeLUISE, PETER: NYC, Nov. 6, 1966.

DEMONGEOT, MYLENE: Nice, France, Sept. 29, 1938.

DeMORNAY, REBECCA: Los Angeles, Aug. 29, 1962. Strasberg Inst.

DEMPSEY, PATRICK: Lewiston, ME, Jan. 13, 1966.

DeMUNN, JEFFREY: Buffalo, NY, Apr. 25, 1947. Union College.

DENCH, JUDI: York, England, Dec. 9, 1934.

DENEUVE, CATHERINE: Paris, France, Oct. 22, 1943.

DeNIRO, ROBERT: NYC, Aug. 17, 1943. Stella Adler.

DENNEHY, BRIAN: Bridgeport, CT, Jul. 9, 1938. Columbia.

DENVER, BOB: New Rochelle, NY, Jan. 9, 1935.

DEPARDIEU, GERARD: Chateauroux, France, Dec. 27, 1948.

DEPP, JOHNNY: Owensboro, KY, June 9, 1963.

DEREK, BO (Mary Cathleen Collins): Long Beach, CA, Nov. 20, 1956.

DERN, BRUCE: Chicago, IL, June 4, 1936. UPA.

DERN, LAURA: Los Angeles, Feb. 10, 1967.

DeSALVO, ANNE: Philadelphia, Apr. 3.

DEVANE, WILLIAM: Albany, NY, Sept. 5, 1939.

DeVITO, DANNY: Asbury Park, NJ, Nov. 17, 1944.

DEXTER, ANTHONY (Walter Reinhold Alfred Fleischmann): Talmadge, NB, Jan. 19, 1919. U Iowa.

DEY, SUSAN: Pekin, IL, Dec. 10, 1953.

DeYOUNG, CLIFF: Los Angeles, CA, Feb. 12, 1945. Cal State.

DIAMOND, NEIL: NYC, Jan. 24, 1941. NYU.

DIAZ, CAMERON: Long Beach, CA, Aug. 30, 1972.

DiCAPRIO, LEONARDO: Hollywood, CA, Nov.11, 1974.

DICKINSON, ANGIE (Angeline Brown): Kulm, ND, Sept. 30, 1932. Glendale College.

DIGGS, TAYE (Scott Diggs): Rochester, NY, 1972.

DILLER, PHYLLIS (Driver): Lima, OH, July 17, 1917. Bluffton College.

DILLMAN, BRADFORD: San Francisco, Apr. 14, 1930. Yale.

DILLON, KEVIN: Mamaroneck, NY, Aug. 19, 1965.

DILLON, MATT: Larchmont, NY, Feb. 18, 1964. AADA.

DILLON, MELINDA: Hope, AR, Oct. 13, 1939. Goodman Theatre School.

DIXON, DONNA: Alexandria, VA, July 20, 1957.

DOBSON, KEVIN: NYC, Mar. 18, 1944.

DOBSON, TAMARA: Baltimore, MD, May 14, 1947. MD Inst. of Art.

DOHERTY, SHANNEN: Memphis, TN, Apr. 12, 1971.

DOLAN, MICHAEL: Oklahoma City, OK, June 21, 1965.

DONAHUE, TROY (Merle Johnson): NYC, Jan. 27, 1937. Columbia U.

DONAT, PETER: Nova Scotia, Jan. 20, 1928. Yale.

DONNELLY, DONAL: Bradford, England, July 6, 1931.

D'ONOFRIO, VINCENT: Brooklyn, NY, June 30, 1959.

DONOHOE, AMANDA: London, June 29 1962.

DONOVAN, MARTIN: Reseda, CA, Aug. 19, 1957.

DONOVAN, TATE: NYC, Sept. 25, 1963.

DOOHAN, JAMES: Vancouver, BC, Mar. 3, 1920. Neighborhood Playhouse.

DOOLEY, PAUL: Parkersburg WV, Feb. 22, 1928. U WV.

DORFF, STEPHEN: CA, July 29, 1973.

DOUG, DOUG E. (Douglas Bourne): Brooklyn, NY, Jan. 7, 1970.

DOUGLAS, DONNA (Dorothy Bourgeois): Baywood, LA, Sept. 26, 1935.

DOUGLAS, ILLEANA: MA, July 25, 1965.

DOUGLAS, KIRK (Issur Danielovitch): Amsterdam, NY, Dec. 9, 1916. St. Lawrence U.

DOUGLAS, MICHAEL: New Brunswick, NJ, Sept. 25, 1944. U Cal.

DOUGLASS, ROBYN: Sendai, Japan, June 21, 1953. UCDavis.

DOURIF, BRAD: Huntington, WV, Mar. 18, 1950. Marshall U.

DOWN, LESLEY-ANN: London, Mar. 17, 1954.

DOWNEY, ROBERT, JR.: NYC, Apr. 4, 1965.

DRAKE, BETSY: Paris, France, Sept. 11, 1923.

DRESCHER, FRAN: Queens, NY, Sept. 30, 1957.

Jenna Elfman

Harvey Fierstein

Nina Foch

DREW, ELLEN (formerly Terry Ray): Kansas City, MO, Nov. 23, 1915.

DREYFUSS, RICHARD: Brooklyn, NY, Oct. 19, 1947.

DRILLINGER, BRIAN: Brooklyn, NY, June 27, 1960. SUNY/Purchase.

DRIVER, MINNIE (Amelia Driver): London, Jan. 31, 1971.

DUCHOVNY, DAVID: NYC, Aug. 7, 1960. Yale.

DUDIKOFF, MICHAEL: Torrance, CA, Oct. 8, 1954.

DUGAN, DENNIS: Wheaton, IL, Sept. 5, 1946.

DUKAKIS, OLYMPIA: Lowell, MA, June 20, 1931.

DUKE, BILL: Poughkeepsie, NY, Feb. 26, 1943. NYU.

DUKE, PATTY (Anna Marie): NYC, Dec. 14, 1946.

DUKES, DAVID: San Francisco, June 6, 1945.

DULLEA, KEIR: Cleveland, NJ, May 30, 1936. SF State College.

DUNAWAY, FAYE: Bascom, FL, Jan. 14, 1941, Fla. U.

DUNCAN, SANDY: Henderson, TX, Feb. 20, 1946. Len Morris College.

DUNNE, GRIFFIN: NYC, June 8, 1955. Neighborhood Playhouse.

DUNST, KIRSTEN: Point Pleasant, NJ, Apr. 30, 1982.

DUPEREY, ANNY: Paris, France, 1947.

DURBIN, DEANNA (Edna): Winnipeg, Canada, Dec. 4, 1921.

DURNING, CHARLES S. : Highland Falls, NY, Feb. 28, 1923. NYU.

DUSSOLLIER, ANDRE: Annecy, France, Feb. 17, 1946.

DUTTON, CHARLES: Baltimore, MD, Jan. 30, 1951. Yale.

DUVALL, ROBERT: San Diego, CA, Jan. 5, 1931. Principia College.

DUVALL, SHELLEY: Houston, TX, July 7, 1949.

DYSART, RICHARD: Brighton, ME, Mar. 30, 1929.

DZUNDZA, GEORGE: Rosenheim, Germ., July 19, 1945.

EASTON, ROBERT: Milwaukee, WI, Nov. 23, 1930. U Texas.

EASTWOOD, CLINT: San Francisco, May 31, 1931. LACC.

EATON, SHIRLEY: London, 1937. Aida Foster School.

EBSEN, BUDDY (Christian, Jr.): Belleville, IL, Apr. 2, 1910. U Fla.

ECKEMYR, AGNETA: Karlsborg, Sweden, July 2. Actors Studio.

EDELMAN, GREGG: Chicago, IL, Sept. 12, 1958. Northwestern U.

EDEN, BARBARA (Huffman): Tucson, AZ, Aug. 23, 1934.

EDWARDS, ANTHONY: Santa Barbara, CA, July 19, 1962. RADA.

EDWARDS, LUKE: Nevada City, CA, Mar. 24, 1980.

EGGAR, SAMANTHA: London, Mar. 5, 1939.

EICHHORN, LISA: Reading, PA, Feb. 4, 1952. Queens Ont. U RADA.

EIKENBERRY, JILL: New Haven, CT, Jan. 21, 1947.

EILBER, JANET: Detroit, MI, July 27, 1951. Juilliard.

EKBERG, ANITA: Malmo, Sweden, Sept. 29, 1931.

EKLAND, BRITT: Stockholm, Sweden, Oct. 6, 1942.

ELDARD, RON: Long Island, NY, Feb. 20, 1965.

ELFMAN, JENNA (Jennifer Mary Batula): Los Angeles, Sept. 30, 1971.

ELIZONDO, HECTOR: NYC, Dec. 22, 1936.

ELLIOTT, ALISON: San Francisco, CA, 1969.

ELLIOTT, CHRIS: NYC, May 31, 1960.

ELLIOTT, PATRICIA: Gunnison, CO, July 21, 1942. UCol.

ELLIOTT, SAM: Sacramento, CA, Aug. 9, 1944. U Ore.

ELWES, CARY: London, Oct. 26, 1962.

ELY, RON (Ronald Pierce): Hereford, TX, June 21, 1938.

EMBRY, ETHAN (Ethan Randall): Huntington Beach, CA, June 13, 1978.

ENGLUND, ROBERT: Glendale, CA, June 6, 1949.

ERBE, KATHRYN: Newton, MA, July 2, 1966.

ERDMAN, RICHARD: Enid, OK, June 1, 1925.

ERICSON, JOHN: Dusseldorf, Ger., Sept. 25, 1926. AADA.

ERMEY, R. LEE (Ronald): Emporia, KS, Mar. 24, 1944

ESMOND, CARL (Willy Eichberger): Vienna, June 14, 1906. U Vienna.

ESPOSITO, GIANCARLO: Copenhagen, Denmark, Apr. 26, 1958.

ESTEVEZ, EMILIO: NYC, May 12, 1962.

ESTRADA, ERIK: NYC, Mar. 16, 1949.

EVANS, DALE (Francis Smith): Uvalde, TX, Oct. 31, 1912.

EVANS, JOSH: NYC, Jan. 16, 1971.

EVANS, LINDA (Evanstad): Hartford, CT, Nov. 18, 1942.

EVERETT, CHAD (Ray Cramton): South Bend, IN, June 11, 1936.

EVERETT, RUPERT: Norfolk, England, 1959.

EVIGAN, GREG: South Amboy, NJ, Oct. 14, 1953.

FABARES, SHELLEY: Los Angeles, Jan. 19, 1944.

FABIAN (Fabian Forte): Philadelphia, Feb. 6, 1943.

FABRAY, NANETTE (Ruby Nanette Fabares): San Diego, Oct. 27, 1920.

FAHEY, JEFF: Olean, NY, Nov. 29, 1956.

FAIRBANKS, DOUGLAS, JR.: NYC, Dec. 9, 1907. Collegiate School.

FAIRCHILD, MORGAN (Patsy McClenny): Dallas, TX, Feb. 3, 1950. UCLA.

FALK, PETER: NYC, Sept. 16, 1927. New School.

FARENTINO, JAMES: Brooklyn, NY, Feb. 24, 1938. AADA.

FARGAS, ANTONIO: Bronx, NY, Aug. 14, 1946.

FARINA, DENNIS: Chicago, IL, Feb. 29, 1944.

FARINA, SANDY (Sandra Feldman): Newark, NJ, 1955.

FARNSWORTH, RICHARD: Los Angeles, Sept. 1, 1920.

FARR, FELICIA: Westchester, NY, Oct. 4. 1932. Penn State College.

FARROW, MIA (Maria): Los Angeles, Feb. 9, 1945.

FAULKNER, GRAHAM: London, Sept. 26, 1947. Webber-Douglas.

FAVREAU, JON: Queens, NY, Oct. 16, 1966.

FAWCETT, FARRAH: Corpus Christie, TX, Feb. 2, 1947. TexU.

FEINSTEIN, ALAN: NYC, Sept. 8, 1941.

FELDMAN, COREY: Encino, CA, July 16, 1971.

FELDON, BARBARA (Hall): Pittsburgh, Mar. 12, 1941. Carnegie Tech.

FELDSHUH, TOVAH: NYC, Dec. 27, 1953, Sarah Lawrence College.

FELLOWS, EDITH: Boston, May 20, 1923.

FENN, SHERILYN: Detroit, MI, Feb. 1, 1965.

FERRELL, CONCHATA: Charleston, WV, Mar. 28, 1943. Marshall U.

FERRELL, WILL: Irvine, CA, July 16, 1968.

FERRER, MEL: Elbeton, NJ, Aug. 25, 1912. Princeton U.

FERRER, MIGUEL: Santa Monica, CA, Feb. 7, 1954.

FERRIS, BARBARA: London, 1943.

FIEDLER, JOHN: Plateville, WI, Feb. 3, 1925.

FIELD, SALLY: Pasadena, CA, Nov. 6, 1946.

FIELD, SHIRLEY-ANNE: London, June 27, 1938.

FIELD, TODD (William Todd Field): Pomona, CA, Feb. 24, 1964.

FIENNES, JOSEPH: Salisbury, Wiltshire, England, May 27, 1970.

FIENNES, RALPH: Suffolk, England, Dec. 22, 1962. RADA.

FIERSTEIN, HARVEY: Brooklyn, NY, June 6, 1954. Pratt Inst.

FINCH, JON: Caterham, England, Mar. 2, 1941.

FINLAY, FRANK: Farnworth, England, Aug. 6, 1926.

FINNEY, ALBERT: Salford, Lancashire, England, May 9, 1936. RADA.

FIORENTINO, LINDA: Philadelphia, PA, Mar. 9, 1960.

FIRTH, COLIN: Grayshott, Hampshire, England, Sept. 10, 1960.

FIRTH, PETER: Bradford, England, Oct. 27, 1953.

FISHBURNE, LAURENCE: Augusta, GA, July 30, 1961.

FISHER, CARRIE: Los Angeles, CA, Oct. 21, 1956. London Central School of Drama.

FISHER, EDDIE: Philadelphia, PA, Aug. 10, 1928.

FISHER, FRANCES: Orange, TX, 1952.

FITZGERALD, TARA: London, Sept. 17, 1968.

FITZGERALD, GERALDINE: Dublin, Ireland, Nov. 24, 1914. Dublin Art School.

FLAGG, FANNIE: Birmingham, AL, Sept. 21, 1944. UAl.

FLANAGAN, FIONNULA: Dublin, Dec. 10, 1941.

FLANNERY, SUSAN: Jersey City, NJ, July 31, 1943.

FLEMING, RHONDA (Marilyn Louis): Los Angeles, Aug. 10, 1922.

FLEMYNG, ROBERT: Liverpool, England, Jan. 3, 1912. Haileybury College.

FLETCHER, LOUISE: Birmingham, AL, July 22 1934.

Bridget Fonda   Edward Furlong   Sarah Michelle Gellar   Balthalzar Getty

Hugh Grant

Rachel Griffiths

Woody Harrelson

Ed Harris

FLOCKHART, CALISTA: Stockton, IL, Nov. 11, Rutgers U.

FOCH, NINA: Leyden, Holland, Apr. 20, 1924.

FOLEY, DAVE: Toronto, Canada, Jan. 4, 1963.

FOLLOWS, MEGAN: Toronto, Canada, Mar. 14, 1968.

FONDA, BRIDGET: Los Angeles, Jan. 27, 1964.

FONDA, JANE: NYC, Dec. 21, 1937. Vassar.

FONDA, PETER: NYC, Feb. 23, 1939. U Omaha.

FONTAINE, JOAN: Tokyo, Japan, Oct. 22, 1917.

FOOTE, HALLIE: NYC, 1953. UNH.

FORD, GLENN (Gwyllyn Samuel Newton Ford): Quebec, Canada, May 1, 1916.

FORD, HARRISON: Chicago, IL, July 13, 1942. Ripon College.

FOREST, MARK (Lou Degni): Brooklyn, NY, Jan. 1933.

FORLANI, CLAIRE: London, July 1, 1972.

FORREST, FREDERIC: Waxahachie, TX, Dec. 23, 1936.

FORREST, STEVE: Huntsville, TX, Sept. 29, 1924. UCLA.

FORSLUND, CONNIE: San Diego, CA, June 19, 1950. NYU.

FORSTER, ROBERT (Foster, Jr.): Rochester, NY, July 13, 1941. Rochester U.

FORSYTHE, JOHN (Freund): Penn's Grove, NJ, Jan. 29, 1918.

FORSYTHE,WILLIAM: Brooklyn, NY, June 7, 1955

FOSSEY, BRIGITTE: Tourcoing, France, Mar. 11, 1947.

FOSTER, JODIE (Ariane Munker): Bronx, NY, Nov. 19, 1962. Yale.

FOSTER, BEN: Boston, MA, Oct. 29, 1980.

FOSTER, MEG: Reading, PA, May 14, 1948.

FOX, EDWARD: London, Apr. 13, 1937. RADA.

FOX, JAMES: London, May 19, 1939.

FOX, MICHAEL J.: Vancouver, BC, June 9, 1961.

FOXWORTH, ROBERT: Houston, TX, Nov. 1, 1941. Carnegie Tech.

FRAKES, JONATHAN: Bethlehem, PA, Aug. 19, 1952. Harvard.

FRANCIOSA, ANTHONY (Papaleo): NYC, Oct. 25, 1928.

FRANCIS, ANNE: Ossining, NY, Sept. 16, 1932.

FRANCIS, ARLENE (Arlene Kazanjian): Boston, Oct. 20, 1908. Finch School.

FRANCIS, CONNIE (Constance Franconero): Newark, NJ, Dec. 12, 1938.

FRANCKS, DON: Vancouver, Canada, Feb. 28, 1932.

FRANKLIN, PAMELA: Tokyo, Feb. 4, 1950.

FRANZ, ARTHUR: Perth Amboy, NJ, Feb. 29, 1920. Blue Ridge College.

FRANZ, DENNIS: Chicago, IL, Oct. 28, 1944.

FRASER, BRENDAN: Indianapolis, IN, Dec. 3, 1968.

FRAZIER, SHEILA: NYC, Nov. 13, 1948.

FRECHETTE, PETER: Warwick, RI, Oct. 1956. URI.

FREEMAN, AL, JR.: San Antonio, TX, Mar. 21, 1934. CCLA.

FREEMAN, KATHLEEN: Chicago, IL, Feb. 17, 1919.

FREEMAN, MONA: Baltimore, MD, June 9, 1926.

FREEMAN, MORGAN: Memphis, TN, June 1, 1937. LACC.

FREWER, MATT: Washington, DC, Jan. 4, 1958, Old Vic.

FRICKER, BRENDA: Dublin, Ireland, Feb. 17, 1945.

FRIELS, COLIN: Glasgow, Sept. 25, 1952.

FRY, STEPHEN: Hampstead, London, Eng., Aug. 24, 1957.

FULLER, PENNY: Durham, NC, 1940. Northwestern U.

FUNICELLO, ANNETTE: Utica, NY, Oct. 22, 1942.

FURLONG, EDWARD: Glendale, CA, Aug. 2, 1977.

FURNEAUX, YVONNE: Lille, France, 1928. Oxford U.

GABLE, JOHN CLARK: Los Angeles, Mar. 20, 1961. Santa Monica College.

GABOR, ZSA ZSA (Sari Gabor): Budapest, Hungary, Feb. 6, 1918.

GAIL, MAX: Derfoil, MI, Apr. 5, 1943.

GAINES, BOYD: Atlanta, GA, May 11, 1953. Juilliard.

GALLAGHER, PETER: NYC, Aug. 19, 1955. Tufts U.

GALLIGAN, ZACH: NYC, Feb. 14, 1963. ColumbiaU.

GALLO, VINCENT: Buffalo, NY, Apr. 11, 1961.

GAM, RITA: Pittsburgh, PA, Apr. 2, 1928.

GAMBLE, MASON: Chicago, IL, Jan. 16, 1986.

GAMBON, MICHAEL: Dublin, Ireland, Oct. 19, 1940.

GANZ, BRUNO: Zurich, Switzerland, Mar. 22, 1941.

GARBER, VICTOR: Montreal, Canada, Mar. 16, 1949.

GARCIA, ANDY: Havana, Cuba, Apr. 12, 1956. FlaInt.

GARFIELD, ALLEN (Allen Goorwitz): Newark, NJ, Nov. 22, 1939. Actors Studio.

GARFUNKEL, ART: NYC, Nov. 5, 1941.

GARLAND, BEVERLY: Santa Cruz, CA, Oct. 17, 1926. Glendale College.

GARNER, JAMES (James Baumgarner): Norman, OK, Apr. 7, 1928. Okla. U.

GAROFALO, JANEANE: Newton, NJ, Sept. 28, 1964.

GARR, TERI: Lakewood, OH, Dec. 11, 1949.

GARRETT, BETTY: St. Joseph, MO, May 23, 1919. Annie Wright Seminary.

GARRISON, SEAN: NYC, Oct. 19, 1937.

GARY, LORRAINE: NYC, Aug. 16, 1937.

GASSMAN, VITTORIO: Genoa, Italy, Sept. 1,1922. Rome Academy of Dramatic Art.

GAVIN, JOHN: Los Angeles, Apr. 8, 1935. Stanford U.

GAYLORD, MITCH: Van Nuys, CA, Mar. 10, 1961. UCLA.

GAYNOR, MITZI (Francesca Marlene Von Gerber): Chicago, IL, Sept. 4, 1930.

GAZZARA, BEN: NYC, Aug. 28, 1930. Actors Studio.

GEARY, ANTHONY: Coalsville, UT, May 29, 1947. UUt.

GEDRICK, JASON: Chicago, IL, Feb. 7, 1965. Drake U.

GEESON, JUDY: Arundel, England, Sept. 10, 1948. Corona.

Goldie Hawn

Hal Holbrook

GELLAR, SARAH MICHELLE: NYC, Apr. 14, 1977.

GEOFFREYS, STEPHEN: Cincinnati, OH, Nov. 22, 1964. NYU.

GEORGE, SUSAN: West London, England, July 26, 1950.

GÉRARD, GIL: Little Rock, AR, Jan. 23, 1940.

GERE, RICHARD: Philadelphia, PA, Aug. 29, 1949. U Mass.

GERROLL, DANIEL: London, Oct. 16, 1951. Central.

GERSHON, GINA: Los Angeles, June 10, 1962.

GERTZ, JAMI: Chicago, IL, Oct. 28, 1965.

GETTY, BALTHAZAR: Los Angeles, CA, Jan. 22, 1975.

GETTY, ESTELLE: NYC, July 25, 1923. New School.

GHOLSON, JULIE: Birmingham, AL, June 4, 1958.

GHOSTLEY, ALICE: Eve, MO, Aug. 14, 1926. Okla U.

GIANNINI, GIANCARLO: Spezia, Italy, Aug. 1, 1942. Rome Acad. of Drama.

GIBB, CYNTHIA: Bennington, VT, Dec. 14, 1963.

GIBSON, HENRY: Germantown, PA, Sept. 21, 1935.

GIBSON, MEL: Peekskill, NY, Jan. 3, 1956. NIDA.

GIBSON, THOMAS: Charleston, SC, July 3, 1962.

GIELGUD, JOHN: London, Apr. 14, 1904. RADA.

GIFT, ROLAND: Birmingham, England, May 28 1962.

GILBERT, MELISSA: Los Angeles, CA, May 8, 1964.

GILES, NANCY: NYC, July 17, 1960, Oberlin College.

GILLETTE, ANITA: Baltimore, MD, Aug. 16, 1938.

GILLIAM, TERRY: Minneapolis, MN, Nov. 22, 1940.

GILLIS, ANN (Alma O'Connor): Little Rock, AR, Feb. 12, 1927.

GINTY, ROBERT: NYC, Nov. 14, 1948. Yale.

GIRARDOT, ANNIE: Paris, France, Oct. 25, 1931.

GISH, ANNABETH: Albuquerque, NM, Mar. 13, 1971. DukeU.

GIVENS, ROBIN: NYC, Nov. 27, 1964.

GLASER, PAUL MICHAEL: Boston, MA, Mar. 25, 1943. Boston U.

GLASS, RON: Evansville, IN, July 10, 1945.

GLEASON, JOANNA: Winnipeg, Canada, June 2, 1950. UCLA.

GLEASON, PAUL: Jersey City, NJ, May 4, 1944.

GLENN, SCOTT: Pittsburgh, PA, Jan. 26, 1942. William and Mary College.

GLOVER, CRISPIN: NYC, Sept 20, 1964.

GLOVER, DANNY: San Francisco, CA, July 22, 1947. SFStateCol.

GLOVER, JOHN: Kingston, NY, Aug. 7, 1944.

GLYNN,CARLIN: Cleveland, Oh, Feb. 19, 1940. Actors Studio.

GOLDBERG, WHOOPI (Caryn Johnson): NYC, Nov. 13, 1949.

GOLDBLUM, JEFF: Pittsburgh, PA, Oct. 22, 1952. Neighborhood Playhouse.

GOLDEN, ANNIE: Brooklyn, NY, Oct. 19, 1951.

GOLDSTEIN, JENETTE: Beverly Hills, CA, 1960.

GOLDTHWAIT, BOB: Syracuse, NY, May 1, 1962.

GOLDWYN, TONY: Los Angeles, May 20, 1960. LAMDA.

GOLINO, VALERIA: Naples, Italy, Oct. 22, 1966.

GONZALEZ, CORDELIA: Aug. 11, 1958, San Juan, PR. UPR.

GONZALES-GONZALEZ, PEDRO: Aguilares, TX, Dec. 21, 1926.

GOODALL, CAROLINE: London, Nov. 13, 1959. BristolU.

GOODING, CUBA, JR.: Bronx, N.Y., Jan. 2, 1968.

GOODMAN, DODY: Columbus, OH, Oct. 28, 1915.

GOODMAN, JOHN: St. Louis, MO, June 20, 1952.

GORDON, KEITH: NYC, Feb. 3, 1961.

GORDON-LEVITT, JOSEPH: Los Angeles, Feb. 17, 1981.

GORMAN, CLIFF: Jamaica, NY, Oct. 13, 1936. NYU.

GORSHIN, FRANK: Pittsburgh, PA, Apr. 5, 1933.

GORTNER, MARJOE: Long Beach, CA, Jan. 14, 1944.

GOSSETT, LOUIS, JR.: Brooklyn, NY, May 27, 1936. NYU.

GOULD, ELLIOTT (Goldstein): Brooklyn, NY, Aug. 29, 1938. Columbia U.

GOULD, HAROLD: Schenectady, NY, Dec. 10, 1923. Cornell.

GOULD, JASON: NYC, Dec. 29, 1966.

GOULET, ROBERT: Lawrence, MA, Nov. 26, 1933. Edmonton.

GRAF, DAVID: Lancaster, OH, Apr. 16, 1950. OhStateU.

GRAFF, TODD: NYC, Oct. 22, 1959. SUNY/ Purchase.

GRAHAM, HEATHER: Milwauke, WI, Jan. 29, 1970.

GRANGER, FARLEY: San Jose, CA, July 1, 1925.

GRANT, DAVID MARSHALL: Westport, CT, June 21, 1955. Yale.

GRANT, HUGH: London, Sept. 9, 1960. Oxford.

GRANT, KATHRYN (Olive Grandstaff): Houston, TX, Nov. 25, 1933. UCLA.

GRANT, LEE: NYC, Oct. 31, 1927. Juilliard.

GRANT, RICHARD E: Mbabane, Swaziland, May 5, 1957. Cape Town U.

Jennifer Love Hewitt

Dennis Hopper

Elizabeth Hurley

GRAVES, PETER (Aurness): Minneapolis, Mar. 18, 1926. U Minn.
GRAVES, RUPERT: Weston-Super-Mare, England, June 30, 1963.
GRAY, CHARLES: Bournemouth, England, 1928.
GRAY, COLEEN (Doris Jensen): Staplehurst, NB, Oct. 23, 1922. Hamline.
GRAY, LINDA: Santa Monica, CA, Sept. 12, 1940.
GRAY, SPALDING: Barrington, RI, June 5, 1941.
GRAYSON, KATHRYN (Zelma Hedrick): Winston-Salem, NC, Feb. 9, 1922.
GREEN, KERRI: Fort Lee, NJ, Jan. 14, 1967. Vassar.
GREEN, SETH: Philadelphia, PA, Feb. 8, 1974.
GREENE, ELLEN: NYC, Feb. 22, 1950. Ryder College.
GREENE, GRAHAM: Six Nations Reserve, Ontario, June 22, 1952
GREENWOOD, BRUCE: Quebec, Canada, Aug. 12, 1956.
GREER, JANE: Washington, DC, Sept. 9, 1924.
GREER, MICHAEL: Galesburg, IL, Apr. 20, 1943.
GREIST, KIM: Stamford, CT, May 12, 1958.

GREY, JENNIFER: NYC, Mar. 26, 1960.
GREY, JOEL (Katz): Cleveland, OH, Apr. 11, 1932.
GREY, VIRGINIA: Los Angeles, Mar. 22, 1917.
GRIECO, RICHARD: Watertown, NY, Mar. 23, 1965.
GRIEM, HELMUT: Hamburg, Germany, Apr. 6, 1932. HamburgU.
GRIER, DAVID ALAN: Detroit, MI, June 30, 1955. Yale.
GRIER, PAM: Winston-Salem, NC, May 26, 1949.
GRIFFITH, ANDY: Mt. Airy, NC, June 1, 1926. UNC.
GRIFFITH, MELANIE: NYC, Aug. 9, 1957. Pierce Col.
GRIFFITH, THOMAS IAN: Hartford, CT, Mar. 18, 1962.
GRIFFITHS, RACHEL: Melbourne, Australia, 1968.
GRIMES, GARY: San Francisco, June 2, 1955.
GRIMES, SCOTT: Lowell, MA, July 9, 1971.
GRIMES, TAMMY: Lynn, MA, Jan. 30, 1934. Stephens College.
GRIZZARD, GEORGE: Roanoke Rapids, NC, Apr. 1, 1928. UNC.
GRODIN, CHARLES: Pittsburgh, PA, Apr. 21, 1935.
GROH, DAVID: NYC, May 21, 1939. Brown U, LAMDA.
GROSS, MARY: Chicago, IL, Mar. 25, 1953.
GROSS, MICHAEL: Chicago, IL, June 21, 1947.
GUEST, CHRISTOPHER: NYC, Feb. 5, 1948.
GUEST, LANCE: Saratoga, CA, July 21, 1960. UCLA.
GUILLAUME, ROBERT (Williams): St. Louis, MO, Nov. 30, 1937.
GUINNESS, ALEC: London, Apr. 2, 1914. Pembroke Lodge School.
GULAGER, CLU: Holdenville, OK, Nov. 16 1928.
GUTTENBERG, STEVE: Massapequa, NY, Aug. 24, 1958. UCLA.
GUY, JASMINE: Boston, Mar. 10, 1964.
HAAS, LUKAS: West Hollywood, CA, Apr. 16, 1976.
HACK, SHELLEY: Greenwich, CT, July 6, 1952.
HACKETT, BUDDY (Leonard Hacker): Brooklyn, NY, Aug. 31, 1924.
HACKMAN, GENE: San Bernardino, CA, Jan. 30, 1930.
HAGERTY, JULIE: Cincinnati, OH, June 15, 1955. Juilliard.
HAGMAN, LARRY (Hageman): Weatherford, TX, Sept. 21, 1931. Bard.
HAID, CHARLES: San Francisco, June 2, 1943. CarnegieTech.
HAIM, COREY: Toronto, Canada, Dec. 23, 1972.
HALE, BARBARA: DeKalb, IL, Apr. 18, 1922. Chicago Academy of Fine Arts.
HALEY, JACKIE EARLE: Northridge, CA, July 14, 1961.
HALL, ALBERT: Boothton, AL, Nov. 10, 1937. Columbia.
HALL, ANTHONY MICHAEL: Boston, MA, Apr. 14, 1968.
HALL, ARSENIO: Cleveland, OH, Feb. 12, 1959.

Don Johnson

HAMEL, VERONICA: Philadelphia, PA, Nov. 20, 1943.
HAMILL, MARK: Oakland, CA, Sept. 25, 1952. LACC.
HAMILTON, CARRIE: NYC, Dec. 5, 1963.
HAMILTON, GEORGE: Memphis, TN, Aug. 12, 1939. Hackley.
HAMILTON, LINDA: Salisbury, MD, Sept. 26, 1956.
HAMLIN, HARRY: Pasadena, CA, Oct. 30, 1951.
HAMPSHIRE, SUSAN: London, May 12, 1941.
HAMPTON, JAMES: Oklahoma City, OK, July 9, 1936. NTexasStU.
HAN, MAGGIE: Providence, RI, 1959.
HANDLER, EVAN: NYC, Jan. 10, 1961. Juillard.
HANKS, TOM: Concord, CA, Jul. 9, 1956. CalStateU.
HANNAH, DARYL: Chicago, IL, Dec. 3, 1960. UCLA.
HANNAH, PAGE: Chicago, IL, Apr. 13, 1964.
HARDEN, MARCIA GAY: LaJolla, CA, Aug. 14, 1959.
HARDIN, TY (Orison Whipple Hungerford, II): NYC, June 1, 1930.

Val Kilmer

Ice Cube

Nastassja Kinski   Kris Kristofferson   Diane Lane   Jessica Lange

HAREWOOD, DORIAN: Dayton, OH, Aug. 6, 1950. U Cinn.

HARMON, MARK: Los Angeles, CA, Sept. 2, 1951. UCLA.

HARPER, JESSICA: Chicago, IL, Oct. 10, 1949.

HARPER, TESS: Mammoth Spring, AK, 1952. SWMoState.

HARPER, VALERIE: Suffern, NY, Aug. 22, 1940.

HARRELSON, WOODY: Midland, TX, July 23, 1961. Hanover College.

HARRINGTON, PAT: NYC, Aug. 13, 1929. Fordham U.

HARRIS, BARBARA (Sandra Markowitz): Evanston, IL, July 25, 1935.

HARRIS, ED: Tenafly, NJ, Nov. 28, 1950. Columbia.

HARRIS, JULIE: Grosse Point, MI, Dec. 2, 1925. Yale Drama School.

HARRIS, MEL (Mary Ellen): Bethlehem, PA, 1957. Columbia.

HARRIS, RICHARD: Limerick, Ireland, Oct. 1, 1930. London Acad.

HARRIS, ROSEMARY: Ashby, England, Sept. 19, 1930. RADA.

HARRISON, GEORGE: Liverpool, England, Feb. 25, 1943.

HARRISON, GREGORY: Catalina Island, CA, May 31, 1950. Actors Studio.

HARRISON, NOEL: London, Jan. 29, 1936.

HARROLD, KATHRYN: Tazewell, VA, Aug. 2, 1950. Mills College.

HARRY, DEBORAH: Miami, IL, July 1, 1945.

HART, ROXANNE: Trenton, NJ, 1952, Princeton.

HARTLEY, MARIETTE: NYC, June 21, 1941.

HARTMAN, DAVID: Pawtucket, RI, May 19, 1935. Duke U.

HASSETT, MARILYN: Los Angeles, CA, Dec. 17, 1947.

HATCHER, TERI: Sunnyvale, CA, Dec. 8, 1964.

HATOSY, SHAWN: Fredrick, MD, Dec. 29, 1975.

HAUER, RUTGER: Amsterdam, Holland, Jan. 23, 1944.

HAVER, JUNE: Rock Island, IL, June 10, 1926.

HAVOC, JUNE (Hovick): Seattle, WA, Nov. 8, 1916.

HAWKE, ETHAN: Austin, TX, Nov. 6, 1970.

HAWN, GOLDIE: Washington, DC, Nov. 21, 1945.

HAWTHORNE, NIGEL: Coventry, Eng., Apr. 5, 1929.

HAYEK, SALMA: Coatzacoalcos, Veracruz, Mexico, Sept. 2, 1968.

HAYES, ISAAC: Covington, TN, Aug. 20, 1942.

HAYS, ROBERT: Bethesda, MD, July 24, 1947, SD State College.

HEADLY, GLENNE: New London, CT, Mar. 13, 1955. AmCollege.

HEALD, ANTHONY: New Rochelle, NY, Aug. 25, 1944. MIStateU.

HEARD, JOHN: Washington, DC, Mar. 7, 1946. Clark U.

HEATHERTON, JOEY: NYC, Sept. 14, 1944.

HECHE, ANNE: Aurora, OH, May 25, 1969.

HECKART, EILEEN: Columbus, OH, Mar. 29, 1919. Ohio State U.

HEDAYA, DAN: Brooklyn, NY, July 24, 1940.

HEDISON, DAVID: Providence, RI, May 20, 1929. Brown U.

HEDREN, TIPPI (Natalie): Lafayette, MN, Jan. 19, 1931.

HEGYES, ROBERT: Metuchen, NJ, May 7, 1951.

HELMOND, KATHERINE: Galveston, TX, July 5, 1934.

HEMINGWAY, MARIEL: Ketchum, ID, Nov. 22, 1961.

HEMMINGS, DAVID: Guilford, England, Nov. 18, 1941.

HEMSLEY, SHERMAN: Philadelphia, PA, Feb. 1, 1938.

HENDERSON, FLORENCE: Dale, IN, Feb. 14, 1934.

HENDRY, GLORIA: Jacksonville, FL, 1949.

HENNER, MARILU: Chicago, IL, Apr. 6, 1952.

HENRIKSEN, LANCE: NYC, May 5, 1940.

HENRY, BUCK (Henry Zuckerman): NYC, Dec. 9, 1930. Dartmouth.

HENRY, JUSTIN: Rye, NY, May 25, 1971.

HEPBURN, KATHARINE: Hartford, CT, May 12, 1907. Bryn Mawr.

HERMAN, PEE-WEE (Paul Reubenfeld): Peekskill, NY, Aug. 27, 1952.

HERRMANN, EDWARD: Washington, DC, July 21, 1943. Bucknell, LAMDA.

HERSHEY, BARBARA (Herzstein): Hollywood, CA, Feb. 5, 1948.

HESSEMAN. HOWARD: Lebanon, OR, Feb. 27, 1940.

HESTON, CHARLTON: Evanston, IL, Oct. 4, 1922. Northwestern U.

HEWITT, JENNIFER LOVE: Waco, TX, Feb. 21, 1979.

HEWITT, MARTIN: Claremont, CA, Feb. 19, 1958. AADA.

HEYWOOD, ANNE (Violet Pretty): Birmingham, England, Dec. 11, 1932.

HICKMAN, DARRYL: Hollywood, CA, July 28, 1933. Loyola U.

HICKMAN, DWAYNE: Los Angeles, May 18, 1934. Loyola U.

HICKS, CATHERINE: NYC, Aug. 6, 1951. Notre Dame.

HIGGINS, ANTHONY (Corlan): Cork City, Ireland, May 9, 1947. Birmingham Sch. of Dramatic Arts.

HIGGINS, MICHAEL: Brooklyn, NY, Jan. 20, 1926. AmThWing.

HILL, ARTHUR: Saskatchewan, Canada, Aug. 1, 1922. U Brit. College.

HILL, BERNARD: Manchester, England, Dec. 17, 1944.

HILL, STEVEN: Seattle, WA, Feb. 24, 1922. U Wash.

HILL, TERRENCE (Mario Girotti): Venice, Italy, Mar. 29, 1941. U Rome.

HILLER, WENDY: Bramhall, Cheshire, England, Aug. 15, 1912. Winceby House School.

HILLERMAN, JOHN: Denison, TX, Dec. 20, 1932.

HINES, GREGORY: NYC, Feb.14, 1946.

HINGLE, PAT: Denver, CO, July 19, 1923. Tex. U.

HIRSCH, JUDD: NYC, Mar. 15, 1935. AADA.

HOBEL, MARA: NYC, June 18, 1971.

HODGE, PATRICIA: Lincolnshire, England, Sept. 29, 1946. LAMDA.

HOFFMAN, DUSTIN: Los Angeles, Aug. 8, 1937. Pasadena Playhouse.

HOFFMAN, PHILIP SEYMOUR: Fairport, NY, July 23, 1967.

HOGAN, JONATHAN: Chicago, IL, June 13, 1951.

HOGAN, PAUL: Lightning Ridge, Australia, Oct. 8, 1939.

HOLBROOK, HAL (Harold): Cleveland, OH, Feb. 17, 1925. Denison.

HOLLIMAN, EARL: Tennesas Swamp, Delhi, LA, Sept. 11, 1928. UCLA.

HOLM, CELESTE: NYC, Apr. 29, 1919.

HOLM, IAN: Ilford, Essex, England, Sept. 12, 1931. RADA.

HOLMES, KATIE: Toledo, OH, Dec. 18, 1978.

HOMEIER, SKIP (George Vincent Homeier): Chicago, IL, Oct. 5, 1930. UCLA.

HOOKS, ROBERT: Washington, DC, Apr. 18, 1937. Temple.

HOPE, BOB (Leslie Townes Hope): London, May 26, 1903.

HOPKINS, ANTHONY: Port Talbot, So. Wales, Dec. 31, 1937. RADA.

HOPPER, DENNIS: Dodge City, KS, May 17, 1936.

HORNE, LENA: Brooklyn, NY, June 30, 1917.

HORSLEY, LEE: Muleshoe, TX, May 15, 1955.

HORTON, ROBERT: Los Angeles, July 29, 1924. UCLA.

HOSKINS, BOB: Bury St. Edmunds, England, Oct. 26, 1942.

HOUGHTON, KATHARINE: Hartford, CT, Mar. 10, 1945. Sarah Lawrence.

HOUSER, JERRY: Los Angeles, July 14, 1952. Valley, Jr. College.

HOWARD, ARLISS: Independence, MO, 1955. Columbia College.

HOWARD, KEN: El Centro, CA, Mar. 28, 1944. Yale.

HOWARD, RON: Duncan, OK, Mar. 1, 1954. USC.

HOWARD, RONALD: Norwood, England, Apr. 7, 1918. Jesus College.

HOWELL, C. THOMAS: Los Angeles, Dec. 7, 1966.

HOWELLS, URSULA: London, Sept. 17, 1922.

HOWES, SALLY ANN: London, July 20, 1930.

HOWLAND, BETH: Boston, MA, May 28, 1941.

HUBLEY, SEASON: NYC, May 14, 1951.

HUDDLESTON, DAVID: Vinton, VA, Sept. 17, 1930.

HUDSON, ERNIE: Benton Harbor, MI, Dec. 17, 1945.

HUGHES, BARNARD: Bedford Hills, NY, July 16, 1915. Manhattan College.

HUGHES, KATHLEEN (Betty von Gerkan): Hollywood, CA, Nov. 14, 1928. UCLA.

HULCE, TOM: Plymouth, MI, Dec. 6, 1953. N.C. Sch. of Arts.

HUNNICUT, GAYLE: Ft. Worth, TX, Feb. 6, 1943. UCLA.

HUNT, HELEN: Los Angeles, June 15, 1963.

HUNT, LINDA: Morristown, NJ, Apr. 1945. Goodman Theatre.

HUNT, MARSHA: Chicago, IL, Oct. 17, 1917.

HUNTER, HOLLY: Atlanta, GA, Mar. 20, 1958. Carnegie-Mellon.

HUNTER, KIM (Janet Cole): Detroit, Nov. 12, 1922.

HUNTER, TAB (Arthur Gelien): NYC, July 11, 1931.

HUPPERT, ISABELLE: Paris, France, Mar. 16, 1955.

HURLEY, ELIZABETH: Hampshire, Eng., June 10, 1965.

HURT, JOHN: Lincolnshire, England, Jan. 22, 1940.

HURT, MARY BETH (Supinger): Marshalltown, IA, Sept. 26, 1948. NYU.

HURT, WILLIAM: Washington, DC, Mar. 20, 1950. Tufts, Juilliard.

HUSSEY, RUTH: Providence, RI, Oct. 30, 1917. U Mich.

HUSTON, ANJELICA: Santa Monica, CA, July 9, 1951.

HUTTON, BETTY (Betty Thornberg): Battle Creek, MI, Feb. 26, 1921.

HUTTON, LAUREN (Mary): Charleston, SC, Nov. 17, 1943. Newcomb College.

HUTTON, TIMOTHY: Malibu, CA, Aug. 16, 1960.

HYER, MARTHA: Fort Worth, TX, Aug. 10, 1924. Northwestern U.

ICE CUBE (O'Shea Jackson): Los Angeles, June 15, 1969.

IDLE, ERIC: South Shields, Durham, England, Mar. 29, 1943. Cambridge.

INGELS, MARTY: Brooklyn, NY, Mar. 9, 1936.

IRELAND, KATHY: Santa Barbara, CA, Mar. 8, 1963.

IRONS, JEREMY: Cowes, England, Sept. 19, 1948. Old Vic.

IRONSIDE, MICHAEL: Toronto, Canada, Feb. 12, 1950.

IRVING, AMY: Palo Alto, CA, Sept. 10, 1953. LADA.

IRWIN, BILL: Santa Monica, CA, Apr. 11, 1950.

ISAAK, CHRIS: Stockton, CA, June 26, 1956. UofPacific.

IVANEK, ZELJKO: Lujubljana, Yugo., Aug. 15, 1957. Yale, LAMDA.

IVEY, JUDITH: El Paso, TX, Sept. 4, 1951.

JACKSON, ANNE: Alleghany, PA, Sept. 3, 1926. Neighborhood Playhouse.

JACKSON, GLENDA: Hoylake, Cheshire, England, May 9, 1936. RADA.

JACKSON, JANET: Gary, IN, May 16, 1966.

JACKSON, KATE: Birmingham, AL, Oct. 29, 1948. AADA.

JACKSON, MICHAEL: Gary, IN, Aug. 29, 1958.

JACKSON, SAMUEL L.: Atlanta, Dec. 21, 1948.

JACKSON, VICTORIA: Miami, FL, Aug. 2, 1958.

JACOBI, DEREK: Leytonstone, London, Oct. 22, 1938. Cambridge.

Frank Langella

Martin Lawrence

Delroy Lindo

Andie MacDowell

JACOBI, LOU: Toronto, Canada, Dec. 28, 1913.

JACOBS, LAWRENCE-HILTON: Virgin Islands, Sept. 14, 1953.

JACOBY, SCOTT: Chicago, IL, Nov. 19, 1956.

JAGGER, MICK: Dartford, Kent, England, July 26, 1943.

JAMES, CLIFTON: NYC, May 29, 1921. Ore. U.

JANNEY, ALLISON: Dayton, OH, Nov. 20, 1960. RADA.

JARMAN, CLAUDE, JR.: Nashville, TN, Sept. 27, 1934.

JASON, RICK: NYC, May 21, 1926. AADA.

JEAN, GLORIA (Gloria Jean Schoonover): Buffalo, NY, Apr. 14, 1927.

JEFFREYS, ANNE (Carmichael): Goldsboro, NC, Jan. 26, 1923. Anderson College.

JEFFRIES, LIONEL: London, June 10, 1926. RADA.

JERGENS, ADELE: Brooklyn, NY, Nov. 26, 1922.

JETER, MICHAEL: Lawrenceburg, TN, Aug. 26, 1952. Memphis St.U.

JILLIAN, ANN (Nauseda): Cambridge, MA, Jan. 29, 1951.

JOHANSEN, DAVID: Staten Island, NY, Jan. 9, 1950.

JOHN, ELTON (Reginald Dwight): Middlesex, England, Mar. 25, 1947. RAM.

JOHNS, GLYNIS: Durban, S. Africa, Oct. 5, 1923.

JOHNSON, DON: Galena, MO, Dec. 15, 1950. UKan.

JOHNSON, PAGE: Welch, WV, Aug. 25, 1930. Ithaca.

JOHNSON, RAFER: Hillsboro, TX, Aug. 18, 1935. UCLA.

JOHNSON, RICHARD: Essex, England, July 30, 1927. RADA.

JOHNSON, ROBIN: Brooklyn, NY, May 29, 1964.

JOHNSON, VAN: Newport, RI, Aug. 28, 1916.

JOLIE, ANGELINA (Angelina Jolie Voight): Los Angeles, June 4, 1975.

JONES, CHRISTOPHER: Jackson, TN, Aug. 18, 1941. Actors Studio.

JONES, DEAN: Decatur, AL, Jan. 25, 1931. Actors Studio.

JONES, GRACE: Spanishtown, Jamaica, May 19, 1952.

JONES, JACK: Bel-Air, CA, Jan. 14, 1938.

JONES, JAMES EARL: Arkabutla, MS, Jan. 17, 1931. U Mich.

JONES, JEFFREY: Buffalo, NY, Sept. 28, 1947. LAMDA.

JONES, JENNIFER (Phyllis Isley): Tulsa, OK, Mar. 2, 1919. AADA.

JONES, L.Q. (Justice Ellis McQueen): Aug 19, 1927.

JONES, SAM J.: Chicago, IL, Aug. 12, 1954.

JONES, SHIRLEY: Smithton, PA, March 31, 1934.

JONES, TERRY: Colwyn Bay, Wales, Feb. 1, 1942.

JONES, TOMMY LEE: San Saba, TX, Sept. 15, 1946. Harvard.

JOURDAN, LOUIS: Marseilles, France, June 9, 1920.

JOVOVICH, MILLA: Kiev, Ukraine, Dec. 7, 1975.

JOY, ROBERT: Montreal, Canada, Aug. 17, 1951. Oxford.

Kyle MacLachlan

Shirley MacLaine

William H. Macy

JUDD, ASHLEY: Los Angeles, CA, Apr. 19, 1968.

JURADO, KATY (Maria Christina Jurado Garcia): Guadalajara, Mex., Jan. 16, 1927.

KACZMAREK, JANE: Milwaukee, WI, Dec. 21, 1955.

KANE, CAROL: Cleveland, OH, June 18, 1952.

KAPLAN, MARVIN: Brooklyn, NY, Jan. 24, 1924.

KAPOOR, SHASHI: Calcutta, India, Mar. 18, 1938.

KAPRISKY, VALERIE (Cheres): Paris, France, Aug. 19, 1962.

KARRAS, ALEX: Gary, IN, July 15, 1935.

KARTHEISER, VINCENT: Minneapolis, MN, May 5, 1979.

KATT, WILLIAM: Los Angeles, CA, Feb. 16, 1955.

KAUFMANN, CHRISTINE: Lansdorf, Graz, Austria, Jan. 11, 1945.

KAVNER, JULIE: Burbank, CA, Sept. 7, 1951. UCLA.

KAZAN, LAINIE (Levine): Brooklyn, NY, May 15, 1942.

KAZURINSKY, TIM: Johnstown, PA, March 3, 1950.

KEACH, STACY: Savannah, GA, June 2, 1941. U Cal., Yale.

KEATON, DIANE (Hall): Los Angeles, CA, Jan. 5, 1946. Neighborhood Playhouse.

KEATON, MICHAEL: Coraopolis, PA, Sept. 9, 1951. KentStateU.

KEDROVA, LILA: Leningrad, 1918.

KEEL, HOWARD (Harold Leek): Gillespie, IL, Apr. 13, 1919.

KEENER, CATHERINE: Miami, FL, 1960.

KEESLAR, MATT: Grand Rapids, MI, 1972.

KEITEL, HARVEY: Brooklyn, NY, May 13, 1939.

KEITH, DAVID: Knoxville, TN, May 8, 1954. UTN.

KELLER, MARTHE: Basel, Switzerland, 1945. Munich Stanislavsky Sch.

KELLERMAN, SALLY: Long Beach, CA, June 2, 1936. Actors Studio West.

KELLY, MOIRA: Queens, NY, Mar. 6, 1968.

KEMP, JEREMY (Wacker): Chesterfield, England, Feb. 3, 1935. Central Sch.

KENNEDY, GEORGE: NYC, Feb. 18, 1925.

KENNEDY, LEON ISAAC: Cleveland, OH, 1949.

KENSIT, PATSY: London, Mar. 4, 1968.

KERR, DEBORAH: Helensburg, Scotland, Sept. 30, 1921. Smale Ballet School.

KERR, JOHN: NYC, Nov. 15, 1931. Harvard, Columbia.

KERWIN, BRIAN: Chicago, IL, Oct. 25, 1949.

KEYES, EVELYN: Port Arthur, TX, Nov. 20, 1919.

KIDDER, MARGOT: Yellow Knife, Canada, Oct. 17, 1948. UBC.

KIDMAN, NICOLE: Hawaii, June 20, 1967.

KIEL, RICHARD: Detroit, MI, Sept. 13, 1939.

KIER, UDO: Koeln, Germany, Oct. 14, 1944.

KILMER, VAL: Los Angeles, Dec. 31, 1959. Juilliard.

KINCAID, ARON (Norman Neale Williams, III): Los Angeles, June 15, 1943. UCLA.

KING, ALAN (Irwin Kniberg): Brooklyn, NY, Dec. 26, 1927.

KING, PERRY: Alliance, OH, Apr. 30, 1948. Yale.

Steve Martin

Frances McDormand

KINGSLEY, BEN (Krishna Bhanji): Snaiton, Yorkshire, England, Dec. 31, 1943.
KINNEAR, GREG: Logansport, IN, June 17, 1963.
KINSKI, NASTASSJA: Berlin, Ger., Jan. 24, 1960.
KIRBY, BRUNO: NYC, Apr. 28, 1949.
KIRK, TOMMY: Louisville, KY, Dec.10 1941.
KIRKLAND, SALLY: NYC, Oct. 31, 1944. Actors Studio.
KITT, EARTHA: North, SC, Jan. 26, 1928.
KLEIN, CHRIS: Hinsdale, IL, March 14, 1979.
KLEIN, ROBERT: NYC, Feb. 8, 1942. Alfred U.
KLEMPERER, WERNER: Cologne, Mar. 22, 1920.
KLINE, KEVIN: St. Louis, MO, Oct. 24, 1947. Juilliard.
KLUGMAN, JACK: Philadelphia, PA, Apr. 27, 1922. Carnegie Tech.
KNIGHT, MICHAEL E.: Princeton, NJ, May 7, 1959.
KNIGHT, SHIRLEY: Goessel, KS, July 5, 1937. Wichita U.
KNOX, ELYSE: Hartford, CT, Dec. 14, 1917. Traphagen School.
KOENIG, WALTER: Chicago, IL, Sept. 14, 1936. UCLA.

KOHNER, SUSAN: Los Angeles, Nov. 11, 1936. U Calif.
KORMAN, HARVEY: Chicago, IL, Feb. 15, 1927. Goodman.
KORSMO, CHARLIE: Minneapolis, MN, July, 1978.
KOTEAS, ELIAS: Montreal, Quebec, Canada, 1961. AADA.
KOTTO, YAPHET: NYC, Nov. 15, 1937.
KOZAK, HARLEY JANE: Wilkes-Barre, PA, Jan. 28, 1957. NYU.
KRABBE, JEROEN: Amsterdam, The Netherlands, Dec. 5, 1944.
KREUGER, KURT: St. Moritz, Switzerland, July 23, 1917. U London.
KRIGE, ALICE: Upington, So. Africa, June 28, 1955.
KRISTEL, SYLVIA: Amsterdam, The Netherlands, Sept. 28, 1952.
KRISTOFFERSON, KRIS: Brownsville, TX, June 22, 1936, Pomona College.
KRUGER, HARDY: Berlin, Germany, April 12, 1928.
KRUMHOLTZ, DAVID: NYC, May 15, 1978.
KUDROW, LISA: Encino, CA, July 30, 1963.
KURTZ, SWOOSIE: Omaha, NE, Sept. 6, 1944.
KWAN, NANCY: Hong Kong, May 19, 1939. Royal Ballet.
LaBELLE, PATTI: Philadelphia, PA, May 24, 1944.
LACY, JERRY: Sioux City, IA, Mar. 27, 1936. LACC.
LADD, CHERYL (Stoppelmoor): Huron, SD. July 12, 1951.
LADD, DIANE (Ladner): Meridian, MS, Nov. 29, 1932. Tulane U.
LAHTI, CHRISTINE: Detroit, MI, Apr. 4, 1950. U Mich.
LAKE, RICKI: NYC, Sept. 21, 1968.
LAMARR, HEDY (Hedwig Kiesler): Vienna, Sept. 11, 1913.
LAMAS, LORENZO: Los Angeles, Jan. 28, 1958.
LAMBERT, CHRISTOPHER: NYC, Mar. 29, 1958.
LANDAU, MARTIN: Brooklyn, NY, June 20, 1931. Actors Studio.
LANDRUM, TERI: Enid, OK, 1960.
LANE, ABBE: Brooklyn, NY, Dec. 14, 1935.
LANE, DIANE: NYC, Jan. 22, 1963.
LANE, NATHAN: Jersey City, NJ, Feb. 3, 1956.
LANG, STEPHEN: NYC, July 11, 1952. Swarthmore College.
LANGE, HOPE: Redding Ridge, CT, Nov. 28, 1931. Reed College.
LANGE, JESSICA: Cloquet, MN, Apr. 20, 1949. U Minn.
LANGELLA, FRANK: Bayonne, NJ, Jan. 1, 1940. SyracuseU.
LANSBURY, ANGELA: London, Oct. 16, 1925. London Academy of Music.
LaPAGLIA, ANTHONY: Adelaide, Australia. Jan 31, 1959.
LARROQUETTE, JOHN: New Orleans, LA, Nov. 25, 1947.
LASSER, LOUISE: NYC, Apr. 11, 1939. Brandeis U.
LATIFAH, QUEEN (Dana Owens): East Orange, NJ, 1970.
LAUGHLIN, JOHN: Memphis, TN, Apr. 3.
LAUGHLIN, TOM: Minneapolis, MN, 1938.

LAUPER, CYNDI: Astoria, Queens, NYC, June 20, 1953.
LAURE, CAROLE: Montreal, Canada, Aug. 5, 1951.
LAURIE, HUGH: Oxford, Eng., June 11, 1959.
LAURIE, PIPER (Rosetta Jacobs): Detroit, MI, Jan. 22, 1932.
LAUTER, ED: Long Beach, NY, Oct. 30, 1940.
LAVIN, LINDA: Portland, ME, Oct. 15 1939.
LAW, JOHN PHILLIP: Hollywood, CA, Sept. 7, 1937. Neighborhood Playhouse, U Hawaii.
LAW, JUDE: Lewisham, Eng., Dec. 29, 1972.
LAWRENCE, BARBARA: Carnegie, OK, Feb. 24, 1930. UCLA.
LAWRENCE, CAROL (Laraia): Melrose Park, IL, Sept. 5, 1935.
LAWRENCE, VICKI: Inglewood, CA, Mar. 26, 1949.
LAWRENCE, MARTIN: Frankfurt, Germany, Apr. 16, 1965.
LAWSON, LEIGH: Atherston, England, July 21, 1945. RADA.
LEACHMAN, CLORIS: Des Moines, IA, Apr. 30, 1930. Northwestern U.
LEARY, DENIS: Boston, MA, Aug. 18, 1957.
LEAUD, JEAN-PIERRE: Paris, France, May 5, 1944.

Mary McDonnell

Malcolm McDowell

LeBLANC, MATT: Newton, MA, July 25, 1967.

LEDERER, FRANCIS: Karlin, Prague, Czech., Nov. 6, 1906.

LEE, CHRISTOPHER: London, May 27, 1922. Wellington College.

LEE, MARK: Australia, 1958.

LEE, MICHELE (Dusiak): Los Angeles, June 24, 1942. LACC.

LEE, PEGGY (Norma Delores Egstrom): Jamestown, ND, May 26, 1920.

LEE, SHERYL: Augsburg, Germany, Arp. 22, 1967.

LEE, SPIKE (Shelton Lee): Atlanta, GA, Mar. 20, 1957.

LEGROS, JAMES: Minneapolis, MN, Apr. 27, 1962.

LEGUIZAMO, JOHN: Columbia, July 22, 1965. NYU.

LEIBMAN, RON: NYC, Oct. 1l, 1937. Ohio Wesleyan.

LEIGH, JANET (Jeanette Helen Morrison): Merced, CA, July 6, 1926. ColofPacific.

LEIGH, JENNIFER JASON: Los Angeles, Feb. 5, 1962.

LeMAT, PAUL: Rahway, NJ, Sept. 22, 1945.

LEMMON, CHRIS: Los Angeles, Jan. 22, 1954.

LEMMON, JACK: Boston, Feb. 8, 1925. Harvard.

LENO, JAY: New Rochelle, NY, Apr. 28, 1950. Emerson College.

LENZ, KAY: Los Angeles, Mar. 4, 1953.

LENZ, RICK: Springfield, IL, Nov. 21, 1939. U Mich.

LEONARD, ROBERT SEAN: Westwood, NJ, Feb. 28, 1969.

LERNER, MICHAEL: Brooklyn, NY, June 22, 1941.

LESLIE, JOAN (Joan Brodell): Detroit, Jan. 26, 1925. St. Benedict's.

LESTER, MARK: Oxford, England, July 11, 1958.

LETO, JARED: Bossier City, LA, Dec. 26, 1971.

LEVELS, CALVIN: Cleveland. OH, Sept. 30, 1954. CCC.

LEVIN, RACHEL: NYC, 1954. Goddard College.

LEVINE, JERRY: New Brunswick, NJ, Mar. 12, 1957, Boston U.

LEVY, EUGENE: Hamilton, Canada, Dec. 17, 1946. McMasterU.

LEWIS, CHARLOTTE: London, Aug.7, 1967.

LEWIS, GEOFFREY: San Diego, CA, Jan. 1, 1935.

LEWIS, JERRY (Joseph Levitch): Newark, NJ, Mar. 16, 1926.

LEWIS, JULIETTE: Los Angeles CA, June 21, 1973.

LIGON, TOM: New Orleans, LA, Sept. 10, 1945.

LILLARD, MATTHEW: Lansing, MI, Jan. 24, 1970.

LINCOLN, ABBEY (Anna Marie Woolridge): Chicago, IL, Aug. 6, 1930.

LINDEN, HAL: Bronx, NY, Mar. 20, 1931. City College of NY.

LINDO, DELROY: London, Nov. 18, 1952.

LINDSAY, ROBERT: Ilketson, Derbyshire, England, Dec. 13, 1951, RADA.

LINN-BAKER, MARK: St. Louis, MO, June 17, 1954, Yale.

LINNEY, LAURA: New York, NY, Feb. 5, 1964.

LIOTTA, RAY: Newark, NJ, Dec. 18, 1955. UMiami.

LISI, VIRNA: Rome, Nov. 8, 1937.

LITHGOW, JOHN: Rochester, NY, Oct. 19, 1945. Harvard.

LL COOL J (James Todd Smith): Queens, NY, Jan. 14, 1968.

LLOYD, CHRISTOPHER: Stamford, CT, Oct. 22, 1938.

LLOYD, EMILY: London, Sept. 29, 1970.

LOCKE, SONDRA: Shelbyville, TN, May, 28, 1947.

LOCKHART, JUNE: NYC, June 25, 1925. Westlake School.

LOCKWOOD, GARY: Van Nuys, CA, Feb. 21, 1937.

LOGGIA, ROBERT: Staten Island, NY, Jan. 3, 1930. UMo.

LOLLOBRIGIDA, GINA: Subiaco, Italy, July 4, 1927. Rome Academy of Fine Arts.

LOM, HERBERT: Prague, Czechoslavakia, Jan. 9, 1917. Prague U.

LOMEZ, CELINE: Montreal, Canada, May 11, 1953.

LONDON, JULIE (Julie Peck): Santa Rosa, CA, Sept. 26, 1926.

LONE, JOHN: Hong Kong, Oct 13, 1952. AADA.

LONG, NIA: Brooklyn, NY, Oct. 30, 1970.

LONG, SHELLEY: Ft. Wayne, IN, Aug. 23, 1949. Northwestern U.

LOPEZ, JENNIFER: Bronx, NY, July 24, 1970.

LOPEZ, PERRY: NYC, July 22, 1931. NYU.

LORDS, TRACY (Nora Louise Kuzma): Steubenville, OH, May 7, 1968.

LOREN, SOPHIA (Sophia Scicolone): Rome, Italy, Sept. 20, 1934.

LOUIS-DREYFUS, JULIA: NYC, Jan. 13, 1961.

LOUISE, TINA (Blacker): NYC, Feb. 11, 1934, Miami U.

LOVE, COURTNEY (Love Michelle Harrison): San Francisco, July 9, 1965.

LOVETT, LYLE: Klein, TX, Nov. 1, 1957.

LOVITZ, JON: Tarzana, CA, July 21, 1957.

LOWE, CHAD: Dayton, OH, Jan. 15, 1968.

LOWE, ROB: Charlottesville, VA, Mar. 17, 1964.

LOWITSCH, KLAUS: Berlin, Apr. 8, 1936, Vienna Academy.

LUCAS, LISA: Arizona, 1961.

LUCKINBILL, LAURENCE: Fort Smith, AK, Nov. 21, 1934.

LUFT, LORNA: Los Angeles, Nov. 21, 1952.

LULU (Marie Lawrie): Glasgow, Scotland, Nov. 3, 1948.

LUNA, BARBARA: NYC, Mar. 2, 1939.

LUNDGREN, DOLPH: Stockolm, Sweden, Nov. 3, 1959. Royal Inst.

LuPONE, PATTI: Northport, NY, Apr. 21, 1949, Juilliard.

LYDON, JAMES: Harrington Park, NJ, May 30, 1923.

LYNCH, KELLY: Minneapolis, MN, Jan. 31, 1959.

LYNLEY, CAROL (Jones): NYC, Feb. 13, 1942.

LYON, SUE: Davenport, IA, July 10, 1946.

LYONNE, NATASHA: NYC, 1978.

MacARTHUR, JAMES: Los Angeles, Dec. 8, 1937. Harvard.

MACCHIO, RALPH: Huntington, NY, Nov. 4, 1961.

MacCORKINDALE, SIMON: Cambridge, England, Feb. 12, 1953.

MacDOWELL, ANDIE (Rose Anderson MacDowell): Gaffney, SC, Apr. 21, 1958.

MacGINNIS, NIALL: Dublin, Ireland, Mar. 29, 1913. Dublin U.

MacGRAW, ALI: NYC, Apr. 1, 1938. Wellesley.

MacLACHLAN, KYLE: Yakima, WA, Feb. 22, 1959. UWa.

MacLAINE, SHIRLEY (Beaty): Richmond, VA, Apr. 24, 1934.

MacLEOD, GAVIN: Mt. Kisco, NY, Feb. 28, 1931.

MacNAUGHTON, ROBERT: NYC, Dec. 19, 1966.

MACNEE, PATRICK: London, Feb. 1922.

MacNICOL, PETER: Dallas, TX, Apr. 10, 1954. UMN.

MacPHERSON, ELLE: Sydney, Australia, 1965.

MacVITTIE, BRUCE: Providence, RI, Oct. 14, 1956. BostonU.

MACY, W. H. (William): Miami, FL, Mar. 13, 1950. Goddard College.

MADIGAN, AMY: Chicago, IL, Sept. 11, 1950. Marquette U.

MADONNA (Madonna Louise Veronica Cicone): Bay City, MI, Aug. 16, 1958. UMi.

MADSEN, MICHAEL: Chicago, IL, Sept. 25, 1958.

MADSEN, VIRGINIA: Winnetka, IL, Sept. 11, 1963.

MAGNUSON, ANN: Charleston, WV, Jan. 4, 1956.

MAGUIRE, TOBEY: Santa Monica, CA, June 27, 1975.

MAHARIS, GEORGE: Astoria, NY, Sept. 1, 1928. Actors Studio.

MAHONEY, JOHN: Manchester, England, June 20, 1940, WUIll.

MAILER, STEPHEN: NYC, Mar. 10, 1966. NYU.

MAJORS, LEE: Wyandotte, MI, Apr. 23, 1940. E. Ky. State College.

MAKEPEACE, CHRIS: Toronto, Canada, Apr. 22, 1964.

MAKO (Mako Iwamatsu): Kobe, Japan, Dec. 10, 1933. Pratt.

MALDEN, KARL (Mladen Sekulovich): Gary, IN, Mar. 22, 1914.

MALKOVICH, JOHN: Christopher, IL, Dec. 9, 1953, IllStateU.

MALONE, DOROTHY: Chicago, IL, Jan. 30, 1925.

MANN, TERRENCE: KY, 1945. NCSchl Arts.

MANOFF, DINAH: NYC, Jan. 25, 1958. CalArts.

MANTEGNA, JOE: Chicago, IL, Nov. 13, 1947. Goodman Theatre.

MANZ, LINDA: NYC, 1961.

MARAIS, JEAN: Cherbourg, France, Dec. 11, 1913, St. Germain.

MARCEAU, SOPHIE (Maupu): Paris, Nov. 17, 1966.

MARCHAND, NANCY: Buffalo, NY, June 19, 1928.

MARCOVICCI, ANDREA: NYC, Nov. 18, 1948.

MARGULIES, JULIANNA: Spring Valley, NY, June 8, 1966.

MARIN, CHEECH (Richard): Los Angeles, July 13, 1946.

Anne Meara

Helen Mirren

Matthew Modine

Julianne Moore

MARIN, JACQUES: Paris, France, Sept. 9, 1919. Conservatoire National.

MARINARO, ED: NYC, Mar. 31, 1950. Cornell.

MARS, KENNETH: Chicago, IL, 1936.

MARSH, JEAN: London, England, July 1, 1934.

MARSHALL, KEN: NYC, 1953. Juilliard.

MARSHALL, PENNY: Bronx, NY, Oct. 15, 1942. UN. Mex.

MARSHALL, WILLIAM: Gary, IN, Aug. 19, 1924. NYU.

MARTIN, ANDREA: Portland, ME, Jan. 15, 1947.

MARTIN, DICK: Battle Creek, MI Jan. 30, 1923.

MARTIN, GEORGE N.: NYC, Aug. 15, 1929.

MARTIN, MILLICENT: Romford, England, June 8, 1934.

MARTIN, PAMELA SUE: Westport, CT, Jan. 15, 1953.

MARTIN, STEVE: Waco, TX, Aug. 14, 1945. UCLA.

MARTIN, TONY (Alfred Norris): Oakland, CA, Dec. 25, 1913. St. Mary's College.

MASON, MARSHA: St. Louis, MO, Apr. 3, 1942. Webster College.

MASSEN, OSA: Copenhagen, Denmark, Jan. 13, 1916.

MASTERS, BEN: Corvallis, OR, May 6, 1947. UOr.

MASTERSON, MARY STUART: Los Angeles, June 28, 1966, NYU.

MASTERSON, PETER: Angleton, TX, June 1, 1934. Rice U.

MASTRANTONIO, MARY ELIZABETH: Chicago, IL, Nov. 17, 1958. UIll.

MASUR, RICHARD: NYC, Nov. 20, 1948.

MATHESON, TIM: Glendale, CA, Dec. 31, 1947. CalState.

MATHIS, SAMANTHA: NYC, May 12, 1970.

MATLIN, MARLEE: Morton Grove, IL, Aug. 24, 1965.

MATTHAU, WALTER (Matuschanskaya-sky): NYC, Oct. 1, 1920.

MATTHEWS, BRIAN: Philadelphia, Jan. 24. 1953. St. Olaf.

MAY, ELAINE (Berlin): Philadelphia, Apr. 21, 1932.

MAYO, VIRGINIA (Virginia Clara Jones): St. Louis, MO, Nov. 30, 1920.

MAYRON, MELANIE: Philadelphia, PA, Oct. 20, 1952. AADA.

MAZURSKY, PAUL: Brooklyn, NY, Apr. 25, 1930. Bklyn College.

MAZZELLO, JOSEPH: Rhinebeck, NY, Sept. 21, 1983.

McCALLUM, DAVID: Scotland, Sept. 19, 1933. Chapman College.

McCAMBRIDGE, MERCEDES: Jolliet, IL, Mar. 17, 1918. Mundelein College.

McCARTHY, ANDREW: NYC, Nov. 29, 1962. NYU.

McCARTHY, KEVIN: Seattle, WA, Feb. 15, 1914. Minn. U.

McCARTNEY, PAUL: Liverpool, Eng-land, June 18, 1942.

McCLANAHAN, RUE: Healdton, OK, Feb. 21, 1934.

McCLORY, SEAN: Dublin, Ireland, Mar. 8, 1924. U Galway.

McCLURE, MARC: San Mateo, CA, Mar. 31, 1957.

McCLURG, EDIE: Kansas City, MO, July 23, 1950.

McCOWEN, ALEC: Tunbridge Wells, England, May 26, 1925. RADA.

McCRANE, PAUL: Philadelphia, PA, Jan. 19. 1961.

McCRARY, DARIUS: Walnut, CA, May 1, 1976.

McDERMOTT, DYLAN: Waterbury, CT, Oct. 26, 1962. Neighborhood Playhouse.

McDONALD, CHRISTOPHER: NYC, 1955.

McDONNELL, MARY: Wilkes Barre, PA, Apr. 28, 1952.

McDORMAND, FRANCES: Illinois, June 23, 1957.

McDOWELL, MALCOLM (Taylor): Leeds, England, June 19, 1943. LAMDA.

McELHONE, NATASCHA (Natasha Taylor): London, Mar. 23, 1971.

McENERY, PETER: Walsall, England, Feb. 21, 1940.

McENTIRE, REBA: McAlester, OK, Mar. 28, 1955. SoutheasternStU.

McGAVIN, DARREN: Spokane, WA, May 7, 1922. College of Pacific.

McGILL, EVERETT: Miami Beach, FL, Oct. 21, 1945.

McGILLIS, KELLY: Newport Beach, CA, July 9, 1957. Juilliard.

McGINLEY, JOHN C.: NYC, Aug. 3, 1959. NYU.

McGOOHAN, PATRICK: NYC, Mar. 19, 1928.

McGOVERN, ELIZABETH: Evanston, IL. July 18, 1961. Juilliard.

McGOVERN, MAUREEN: Youngstown, OH, July 27, 1949.

McGREGOR, EWAN: Perth, Scotland, March 31, 1971

McGUIRE, BIFF: New Haven, CT, Oct. 25. 1926. Mass. Stale College.

McGUIRE, DOROTHY: Omaha, NE, June 14, 1918.

McHATTIE, STEPHEN: Antigonish, NS, Feb. 3. Acadia U AADA.

McKAY, GARDNER: NYC, June 10, 1932. Comell.

McKEAN, MICHAEL: NYC, Oct. 17, 1947.

McKEE, LONETTE: Detroit, MI, July 22, 1955.

McKELLEN, IAN: Burnley, England, May 25, 1939.

McKENNA, VIRGINIA: London, June 7, 1931.

McKEON, DOUG: Pompton Plains, NJ, June 10, 1966.

McKERN, LEO: Sydney, Australia, Mar. 16, 1920.

McKUEN, ROD: Oakland, CA, Apr. 29, 1933.

McLERIE, ALLYN ANN: Grand Mere, Canada, Dec. 1, 1926.

McMAHON, ED: Detroit, MI, Mar. 6, 1923.

McNAIR, BARBARA: Chicago, IL, Mar. 4, 1939. UCLA.

McNAMARA, WILLIAM: Dallas, TX, Mar. 31, 1965.

McNICHOL, KRISTY: Los Angeles. CA, Sept. 11, 1962.

McQUEEN, ARMELIA: North Carolina, Jan. 6, 1952. Bklyn Consv.

Cathy Moriarty

Jeremy Northam

Chris O'Donnell

Lena Olin

McQUEEN, CHAD: Los Angeles, CA, Dec. 28, 1960. Actors Studio.

McRANEY, GERALD: Collins, MS, Aug. 19, 1948.

McSHANE, IAN: Blackburn, England, Sept. 29, 1942. RADA.

McTEER, JANET: York, England, 1961.

MEADOWS, JAYNE (formerly Jayne Cotter): Wuchang, China, Sept. 27, 1924. St. Margaret's.

MEANEY, COLM: Dublin, May 30, 1953.

MEARA, ANNE: Brooklyn, NY, Sept. 20, 1929.

MEAT LOAF (Marvin Lee Aday): Dallas, TX, Sept. 27, 1947.

MEDWIN, MICHAEL: London, 1925. Instut Fischer.

MEKKA, EDDIE: Worcester, MA, June 14, 1952. Boston Cons.

MELATO, MARIANGELA: Milan, Italy, 1941. Milan Theatre Acad.

MEREDITH, LEE (Judi Lee Sauls): Oct. 22, 1947. AADA.

MERKERSON, S. EPATHA: Saganaw, MI, Nov. 28, 1952. Wayne St. Univ.

MERRILL, DINA (Nedinia Hutton): NYC, Dec. 29, 1925. AADA.

MESSING, DEBRA: Brooklyn, NY, Aug. 15, 1968.

METCALF, LAURIE: Edwardsville, IL, June 16, 1955., IIIStU.

METZLER, JIM: Oneonda, NY, June 23. Dartmouth.

MICHELL, KEITH: Adelaide, Australia, Dec. 1, 1926.

MIDLER, BETTE: Honolulu, HI, Dec. 1, 1945.

MILANO, ALYSSA: Brooklyn, NY, Dec. 19, 1972.

MILES, JOANNA: Nice, France, Mar. 6, 1940.

MILES, SARAH: Ingatestone, England, Dec. 31, 1941. RADA.

MILES, SYLVIA: NYC, Sept. 9, 1934. Actors Studio.

MILES, VERA (Ralston): Boise City, OK, Aug. 23, 1929. UCLA.

MILLER, ANN (Lucille Ann Collier): Chireno, TX, Apr. 12, 1919. Lawler Professional School.

MILLER, BARRY: Los Angeles, CA, Feb. 6, 1958.

MILLER, DICK: NYC, Dec. 25, 1928.

MILLER, JASON: Long Island City, NY, Apr. 22, 1939. Catholic U.

MILLER, JONNY LEE: Surrey, England, Nov. 15, 1972.

MILLER, LINDA: NYC, Sept. 16, 1942. Catholic U.

MILLER, PENELOPE ANN: Santa Monica, CA, Jan. 13, 1964.

MILLER, REBECCA: Roxbury, CT, 1962. Yale.

MILLS, DONNA: Chicago, IL, Dec. 11, 1945. Ull.

MILLS, HAYLEY: London, Apr. 18, 1946. Elmhurst School.

MILLS, JOHN: Suffolk, England, Feb. 22, 1908.

MILLS, JULIET: London, Nov. 21, 1941.

MILNER, MARTIN: Detroit, MI, Dec. 28, 1931.

MIMIEUX, YVETTE: Los Angeles, Jan. 8, 1941. Hollywood High.

MINNELLI, LIZA: Los Angeles, Mar. 19, 1946.

MIOU-MIOU (Sylvette Henry): Paris, France, Feb. 22, 1950.

MIRREN, HELEN (Ilynea Mironoff): London, July 26, 1946.

MITCHELL, JAMES: Sacramento, CA, Feb. 29, 1920. LACC.

MITCHELL, JOHN CAMERON: El Paso, TX, Apr. 21, 1963. NorthwesternU.

MITCHUM, JAMES: Los Angeles, CA, May 8, 1941.

MODINE, MATTHEW: Loma Linda, CA, Mar. 22, 1959.

MOFFAT, DONALD: Plymouth, England, Dec. 26, 1930. RADA.

MOFFETT, D. W.: Highland Park, IL, Oct. 26, 1954. Stanford U.

MOHR, JAY: New Jersey, Aug. 23, 1971.

MOKAE, ZAKES: Johannesburg, So. Africa, Aug. 5, 1935. RADA.

MOLINA, ALFRED: London, May 24, 1953. Guildhall.

MOLL, RICHARD: Pasadena, CA, Jan. 13, 1943.

MONK, DEBRA: Middletown, OH, Feb. 27, 1949.

MONTALBAN, RICARDO: Mexico City, Nov. 25, 1920.

MONTENEGRO, FERNADA (Arlete Pinheiro): Rio de Janiero, Brazil, 1929.

MONTGOMERY, BELINDA: Winnipeg, Canada, July 23, 1950.

MONTGOMERY, GEORGE (George Letz): Brady, MT, Aug. 29, 1916. U Mont.

MOODY, RON: London, Jan. 8, 1924. London U.

MOOR, BILL: Toledo, OH, July 13, 1931. Northwestern.

MOORE, CONSTANCE: Sioux City, IA, Jan. 18, 1919.

MOORE, DEMI (Guines): Roswell, NM, Nov. 11, 1962.

MOORE, DICK: Los Angeles, Sept. 12, 1925.

MOORE, DUDLEY: Dagenham, Essex, England, Apr. 19, 1935.

MOORE, JULIANNE (Julie Anne Smith): Fayetteville, NC, Dec. 30, 1960.

MOORE, KIERON: County Cork, Ireland, 1925. St. Mary's College.

MOORE, MARY TYLER: Brooklyn, NY, Dec. 29, 1936.

MOORE, ROGER: London, Oct. 14, 1927. RADA.

MOORE, TERRY (Helen Koford): Los Angeles, Jan. 7, 1929.

MORALES, ESAI: Brooklyn, NY, Oct. 1, 1962.

MORANIS, RICK: Toronto, Canada, Apr. 18, 1954.

MOREAU, JEANNE: Paris, France, Jan. 23, 1928.

MORENO, RITA (Rosita Alverio): Humacao, P.R., Dec. 11, 1931.

MORGAN, HARRY (HENRY) (Harry Bratsburg): Detroit, Apr. 10, 1915. U Chicago.

MORGAN, MICHELE (Simone Roussel): Paris, France, Feb. 29, 1920. Paris Dramatic School.

MORIARTY, CATHY: Bronx, NY, Nov. 29, 1960.

MORIARTY, MICHAEL: Detroit, MI, Apr. 5, 1941. Dartmouth.

MORISON, PATRICIA: NYC, Mar. 19, 1915.

MORITA, NORIYUKI "PAT": Isleton, CA, June 28, 1932.

MORRIS, GARRETT: New Orleans, LA, Feb. 1, 1937.

MORRIS, HOWARD: NYC, Sept. 4, 1919. NYU.

Bill Paxton

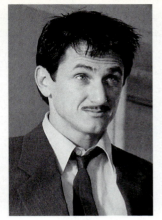
Sean Penn

Joan Plowright

Sarah Polley

MORROW, ROB: New Rochelle, NY, Sept. 21, 1962.

MORSE, DAVID: Hamilton, MA, Oct. 11, 1953.

MORSE, ROBERT: Newton, MA, May 18, 1931.

MORTENSEN, VIGGO: New York, NY, 1958.

MORTON, JOE: NYC, Oct. 18, 1947. Hofstra U.

MORTON, SAMANTHA: Nottingham, England, 1977.

MOSES, WILLIAM: Los Angeles, Nov. 17, 1959.

MOSTEL, JOSH: NYC, Dec. 21, 1946. Brandeis U.

MOUCHET, CATHERINE: Paris, France, 1959. Ntl. Consv.

MUELLER-STAHL, ARMIN: Tilsit, East Prussia, Dec. 17, 1930.

MULDAUR, DIANA: NYC, Aug. 19, 1938. Sweet Briar College.

MULGREW, KATE: Dubuque, IA, Apr. 29, 1955. NYU.

MULHERN, MATT: Philadelphia, PA, July 21, 1960. Rutgers Univ.

MULL, MARTIN: N. Ridgefield, OH, Aug. 18, 1941. RISch. of Design.

MULLIGAN, RICHARD: NYC, Nov. 13, 1932.

MULRONEY, DERMOT: Alexandria, VA, Oct. 31, 1963. Northwestern.

MUMY, BILL (Charles William Mumy, Jr.): San Gabriel, CA, Feb. 1, 1954.

MURPHY, DONNA: Queens, NY, March 7, 1958.

MURPHY, EDDIE: Brooklyn, NY, Apr. 3, 1961.

MURPHY, MICHAEL: Los Angeles, CA, May 5, 1938. UAz.

MURRAY, BILL: Wilmette, IL, Sept. 21, 1950. Regis College.

MURRAY, DON: Hollywood, CA, July 31, 1929.

MUSANTE, TONY: Bridgeport, CT, June 30, 1936. Oberlin College.

MYERS, MIKE: Scarborough, Canada, May 25, 1963.

NABORS, JIM: Sylacauga, GA, June 12, 1932.

NADER, GEORGE: Pasadena, CA, Oct. 19, 1921. Occidental College.

NADER, MICHAEL: Los Angeles, CA, 1945.

NAMATH, JOE: Beaver Falls, PA, May 31, 1943. UAla.

NAUGHTON, DAVID: Hartford, CT, Feb. 13, 1951.

NAUGHTON, JAMES: Middletown, CT, Dec. 6, 1945.

NEAL, PATRICIA: Packard, KY, Jan. 20, 1926. Northwestern U.

NEESOM, LIAM: Ballymena, Northern Ireland, June 7, 1952.

NEFF, HILDEGARDE (Hildegard Knef): Ulm, Germany, Dec. 28, 1925. Berlin Art Acad.

NEILL, SAM: No. Ireland, Sept. 14, 1947. U Canterbury.

NELL, NATHALIE: Paris, France, Oct. 1950.

NELLIGAN, KATE: London, Ont., Canada, Mar. 16, 1951. U Toronto.

NELSON, BARRY (Robert Nielsen): Oakland, CA, Apr. 16, 1920.

NELSON, CRAIG T.: Spokane, WA, Apr. 4, 1946.

NELSON, DAVID: NYC, Oct. 24, 1936. USC.

NELSON, JUDD: Portland, ME, Nov. 28, 1959, Haverford College.

NELSON, LORI (Dixie Kay Nelson): Santa Fe, NM, Aug. 15, 1933.

NELSON, TRACY: Santa Monica, CA, Oct. 25, 1963.

NELSON, WILLIE: Abbott, TX, Apr. 30, 1933.

NEMEC, CORIN: Little Rock, AK, Nov. 5, 1971.

NERO, FRANCO (Francisco Spartanero): Parma, Italy, Nov. 23, 1941.

NESMITH, MICHAEL: Houston, TX, Dec. 30, 1942.

NETTLETON, LOIS: Oak Park, IL, 1931. Actors Studio.

NEUWIRTH, BEBE: Dec. 31, 1958.

NEWHART, BOB: Chicago, IL, Sept. 5, 1929. Loyola U.

NEWMAN, BARRY: Boston, MA, Nov. 7, 1938. Brandeis U.

NEWMAN, LARAINE: Los Angeles, Mar. 2, 1952.

NEWMAN, NANETTE: Northampton, England, 1934.

NEWMAN, PAUL: Cleveland, OH, Jan. 26, 1925. Yale.

NEWMAR, JULIE (Newmeyer): Los Angeles, Aug. 16, 1933.

NEWTON, THANDIE: Zambia, 1972.

NEWTON-JOHN, OLIVIA: Cambridge, England, Sept. 26, 1948.

NGUYEN, DUSTIN: Saigon, Vietnam, Sept. 17, 1962.

NICHOLAS, DENISE: Detroit, MI, July 12, 1945.

NICHOLAS, PAUL: London, 1945.

NICHOLS, NICHELLE: Robbins, IL, Dec. 28, 1933.

NICHOLSON, JACK: Neptune, NJ, Apr. 22, 1937.

NICKERSON, DENISE: NYC, 1959.

NICOL, ALEX: Ossining, NY, Jan. 20, 1919. Actors Studio.

NIELSEN, BRIGITTE: Denmark, July 15, 1963.

NIELSEN, LESLIE: Regina, Saskatchewan. Canada, Feb. 11, 1926. Neighborhood Playhouse.

NIMOY, LEONARD: Boston, MA, Mar. 26, 1931. Boston College, Antioch College.

NIXON, CYNTHIA: NYC, Apr. 9, 1966. Columbia U.

NOBLE, JAMES: Dallas, TX, Mar. 5, 1922, SMU.

NOIRET, PHILIPPE: Lille, France, Oct. 1, 1930.

NOLAN, KATHLEEN: St. Louis, MO, Sept. 27, 1933. Neighborhood Playhouse.

NOLTE, NICK: Omaha, NE, Feb. 8, 1940. Pasadena City College.

NORRIS, BRUCE: Houston, TX, May 16, 1960. Northwestern.

NORRIS, CHRISTOPHER: NYC, Oct. 7, 1943. Lincoln Square Acad.

NORRIS, CHUCK (Carlos Ray): Ryan, OK,Mar. 10, 1940.

NORTH, HEATHER: Pasadena, CA, Dec. 13, 1950. Actors Workshop.

NORTH, SHEREE (Dawn Bethel): Los Angeles. Jan. 17, 1933. Hollywood High.

NORTHAM, JEREMY: Cambridge, Eng., Dec. 1, 1961.

NORTON, EDWARD: Boston, MA, Aug. 18, 1969.

NORTON, KEN: Jacksonville, Il, Aug. 9, 1945.

NOURI, MICHAEL: Washington, DC, Dec. 9, 1945.

NOVAK, KIM (Marilyn Novak): Chicago, IL, Feb. 13, 1933. LACC.

NOVELLO, DON: Ashtabula, OH, Jan. 1, 1943. UDayton.

NUYEN, FRANCE (Vannga): Marseilles, France, July 31, 1939. Beaux Arts School.

O'BRIAN, HUGH (Hugh J. Krampe): Rochester, N,. Apr. 19, 1928. Cincinnati U.

O'BRIEN, CLAY: Ray, AZ, May 6, 1961.

O'BRIEN, MARGARET (Angela Maxine O'Brien): Los Angeles, Jan. 15, 1937.

O'BRIEN, VIRGINIA: Los Angeles, Apr. 18, 1919.

O'CONNELL, JERRY (Jeremiah O'Connell): New York, NY, Feb. 17, 1974.

O'CONNOR, CARROLL: Bronx, NY, Aug. 2, 1924. Dublin National Univ.

O'CONNOR, DONALD: Chicago, IL, Aug. 28, 1925.

O'CONNOR, GLYNNIS: NYC, Nov. 19, 1955. NYSU.

O'DONNELL, CHRIS: Winetka, IL, June 27, 1970.

O'DONNELL, ROSIE: Commack, NY, March 21, 1961.

O'HARA, CATHERINE: Toronto, Canada, Mar. 4, 1954.

O'HARA, MAUREEN (Maureen Fitz-Simons): Dublin, Ireland, Aug. 17, 1920.

O'HERLIHY, DAN: Wexford, Ireland, May 1, 1919. National U.

O'KEEFE, MICHAEL: Larchmont, NY, Apr. 24, 1955. NYU, AADA.

OLDMAN, GARY: New Cross, South London, England, Mar. 21, 1958.

OLIN, KEN: Chicago, IL, July 30, 1954. UPa.

OLIN, LENA: Stockholm, Sweden, Mar. 22, 1955.

OLMOS, EDWARD JAMES: Los Angeles, Feb. 24, 1947. CSLA.

O'LOUGHLIN, GERALD S.: NYC, Dec. 23, 1921. U Rochester.

OLSON, JAMES: Evanston, IL, Oct. 8, 1930.

OLSON, NANCY: Milwaukee, WI, July 14, 1928. UCLA.

O'NEAL, GRIFFIN: Los Angeles, 1965.

O'NEAL, RON: Utica, NY, Sept. 1, 1937. Ohio State.

O'NEAL, RYAN: Los Angeles, Apr. 20, 1941.

O'NEAL, TATUM: Los Angeles, Nov. 5, 1963.

O'NEIL, TRICIA: Shreveport, LA, Mar. 11, 1945. Baylor U.

O'NEILL, ED: Youngstown, OH, Apr. 12, 1946.

O'NEILL, JENNIFER: Rio de Janeiro, Feb. 20, 1949. Neighborhood Playhouse.

ONTKEAN, MICHAEL: Vancouver, B.C., Canada, Jan. 24, 1946.

O'QUINN, TERRY: Newbury, MI, July 15, 1952.

ORBACH, JERRY: Bronx, NY, Oct. 20, 1935.

O'SHEA, MILO: Dublin, Ireland, June 2, 1926.

OSMENT, HALEY JOEL: Los Angeles, Apr. 10, 1988.

O'TOOLE, ANNETTE (Toole): Houston, TX, Apr. 1, 1953. UCLA.

O'TOOLE, PETER: Connemara, Ireland, Aug. 2, 1932. RADA.

OVERALL, PARK: Nashville, TN, Mar. 15, 1957. Tusculum College.

OWEN, CLIVE: Coventry, Eng., 1965.

Kelly Preston

Freddie Prinze, Jr.

Stephen Rea

OZ, FRANK (Oznowicz): Hereford, England, May 25, 1944.

PACINO, AL: NYC, Apr. 25, 1940.

PACULA, JOANNA: Tamaszow Lubelski, Poland, Jan. 2, 1957. Polish Natl. Theatre Sch.

PAGET, DEBRA (Debralee Griffin): Denver, Aug. 19, 1933.

PAIGE, JANIS (Donna Mae Jaden): Tacoma, WA, Sept. 16, 1922.

PALANCE, JACK (Walter Palanuik): Lattimer, PA, Feb. 18, 1920. UNC.

PALIN, MICHAEL: Sheffield, Yorkshire, England, May 5, 1943, Oxford.

PALMER, BETSY: East Chicago, IN, Nov. 1, 1926. DePaul U.

PALMER, GREGG (Palmer Lee): San Francisco, Jan. 25, 1927. U Utah.

PALMINTERI, CHAZZ (Calogero Lorenzo Palminteri): New York, NY, May 15, 1952.

PAMPANINI, SILVANA: Rome, Sept. 25, 1925.

PANEBIANCO, RICHARD: NYC, 1971.

PANKIN, STUART: Philadelphia, Apr. 8, 1946.

PANTOLIANO, JOE: Jersey City, NJ, Sept. 12, 1954.

PAPAS, IRENE: Chiliomodion, Greece, Mar. 9, 1929.

PAQUIN, ANNA: Winnipeg, Manitoba, Canada, July, 24, 1982.

PARE, MICHAEL: Brooklyn, NY, Oct. 9, 1959.

PARKER, COREY: NYC, July 8, 1965. NYU.

PARKER, ELEANOR: Cedarville, OH, June 26, 1922. Pasadena Playhouse.

PARKER, FESS: Fort Worth, TX, Aug. 16, 1925. USC.

PARKER, JAMESON: Baltimore, MD, Nov. l8, 1947. Beloit College.

PARKER, JEAN (Mae Green): Deer Lodge, MT, Aug. 11, 1912.

PARKER, MARY-LOUISE: Ft. Jackson, SC, Aug. 2, 1964. Bard College.

PARKER, NATHANIEL: London, 1963.

PARKER, SARAH JESSICA: Nelsonville, OH, Mar. 25, 1965.

PARKER, SUZY (Cecelia Parker): San Antonio, TX, Oct. 28, 1933.

PARKER, TREY: Auburn, AL, May 30, 1972.

PARKINS, BARBARA: Vancouver, Canada, May 22, 1943.

PARKS, MICHAEL: Corona, CA, Apr. 4, 1938.

PARSONS, ESTELLE: Lynn, MA, Nov. 20, 1927. Boston U.

PARTON, DOLLY: Sevierville, TN, Jan. 19, 1946.

PATINKIN, MANDY: Chicago, IL, Nov. 30, 1952. Juilliard.

PATRIC, JASON: NYC, June 17, 1966.

PATRICK, DENNIS: Philadelphia, Mar. 14, 1918.

PATTERSON, LEE: Vancouver, Canada, Mar. 31, 1929. Ontario College.

PATTON, WILL: Charleston, SC, June 14, 1954.

PAULIK, JOHAN: Prague, Czech., 1975.

PAVAN, MARISA (Marisa Pierangeli): Cagliari, Sardinia, June 19, 1932. Torquado Tasso College.

PAXTON, BILL: Fort Worth, TX, May. 17, 1955.

PAYMER, DAVID: Long Island, NY, Aug. 30, 1954.

PAYS, AMANDA: Berkshire, England, June 6, 1959.

PEACH, MARY: Durban, S. Africa, 1934.

PEARCE, GUY: England, Oct. 5, 1967.

PEARSON, BEATRICE: Dennison, TX, July 27, 1920.

PECK, GREGORY: La Jolla, CA, Apr. 5, 1916. U Calif.

PEÑA, ELIZABETH: Cuba, Sept. 23, 1961.

PENDLETON, AUSTIN: Warren, OH, Mar. 27, 1940. Yale U.

PENHALL, BRUCE: Balboa, CA, Aug. 17, 1960.

PENN, SEAN: Burbank, CA, Aug. 17, 1960.

PEREZ, JOSE: NYC, 1940.

PEREZ, ROSIE: Brooklyn, NY, Sept. 6, 1964.

PERKINS, ELIZABETH: Queens, NY, Nov. 18, 1960. Goodman School.

PERKINS, MILLIE: Passaic, NJ, May 12, 1938.

PERLMAN, RHEA: Brooklyn, NY, Mar. 31, 1948.

PERLMAN, RON: NYC, Apr. 13, 1950. UMn.

PERREAU, GIGI (Ghislaine): Los Angeles, Feb. 6, 1941.

PERRINE, VALERIE: Galveston, TX, Sept. 3, 1943. U Ariz.

PERRY, LUKE (Coy Luther Perry, III): Fredricktown, OH, Oct. 11, 1966.

PESCI, JOE: Newark, NJ. Feb. 9, 1943.

PESCOW, DONNA: Brooklyn, NY, Mar. 24, 1954.

PETERS, BERNADETTE (Lazzara): Jamaica, NY, Feb. 28, 1948.

PETERS, BROCK: NYC, July 2, 1927. CCNY.

PETERS. JEAN (Elizabeth): Caton, OH, Oct. 15, 1926. Ohio State U.

PETERSEN, PAUL: Glendale, CA, Sept. 23, 1945. Valley College.

PETERSEN, WILLIAM: Chicago, IL, Feb. 21, 1953.

PETERSON, CASSANDRA: Colorado Springs, CO, Sept. 17, 1951.

PETTET, JOANNA: London, Nov. 16, 1944. Neighborhood Playhouse.

PETTY, LORI: Chattanooga, TN, 1964.

PFEIFFER, MICHELLE: Santa Ana, CA, Apr. 29, 1958.

PHILLIPPE, RYAN (Matthew Phillippe): New Castle, DE, Sept. 10, 1975.

PHILLIPS, LOU DIAMOND: Phillipines, Feb. 17, 1962, UTx.

PHILLIPS, MacKENZIE: Alexandria, VA, Nov. 10, 1959.

PHILLIPS, MICHELLE (Holly Gilliam): Long Beach, CA, June 4, 1944.

PHILLIPS, SIAN: Bettws, Wales, May 14, 1934. UWales.

PHOENIX, JOAQUIN: Puerto Rico, Oct. 28, 1974.

PICARDO, ROBERT: Philadelphia, PA, Oct. 27, 1953. Yale.

PICERNI, PAUL: NYC, Dec. 1, 1922. Loyola U.

PIDGEON, REBECCA: Cambridge, MA, 1963.

PIERCE, DAVID HYDE: Saratoga Springs, NY, Apr. 3, 1959.

Vanessa Redgrave

Burt Reynolds

Christina Ricci

PIGOTT-SMITH, TIM: Rugby, England, May 13, 1946.

PINCHOT, BRONSON: NYC, May 20, 1959. Yale.

PINE, PHILLIP: Hanford, CA, July 16, 1920. Actors' Lab.

PISCOPO, JOE: Passaic. NJ, June 17, 1951.

PISIER, MARIE-FRANCE: Vietnam, May 10, 1944. U Paris.

PITILLO, MARIA: Mahwah, NJ, 1965.

PITT, BRAD (William Bradley Pitt): Shawnee, OK, Dec. 18, 1963.

PIVEN, JEREMY: NYC, July 26, 1965.

PLACE, MARY KAY: Tulsa OK, Sept. 23, 1947. U Tulsa.

PLATT, OLIVER: Oct. 10, 1960.

PLAYTEN, ALICE: NYC, Aug. 28, 1947. NYU.

PLESHETTE, SUZANNE: NYC, Jan. 31, 1937. Syracuse U.

PLIMPTON, MARTHA: NYC, Nov. 16, 1970.

PLOWRIGHT, JOAN: Scunthorpe, Brigg, Lincolnshire, England, Oct. 28, 1929. Old Vic.

PLUMB, EVE: Burbank, CA, Apr. 29, 1958.

PLUMMER, AMANDA: NYC, Mar. 23, 1957. Middlebury College.

PLUMMER, CHRISTOPHER: Toronto, Canada, Dec. 13, 1927.

PODESTA, ROSSANA: Tripoli, June 20, 1934.

POITIER, SIDNEY: Miami, FL, Feb. 27, 1927.

POLANSKI, ROMAN: Paris, France, Aug. 18, 1933.

POLITO, JON: Philadelphia, PA, Dec. 29, 1950. Villanova U.

POLITO, LINA: Naples, Italy, Aug. 11, 1954.

POLLACK, SYDNEY: South Bend, IN, July 1, 1934.

POLLAK, KEVIN: San Francisco, Oct. 30, 1958.

POLLAN, TRACY: NYC, June 22, 1960.

POLLARD, MICHAEL J.: Passaic, NJ, May 30, 1939.

POLLEY, SARAH: Jan. 8, 1979.

PORTMAN, NATALIE; Jerusalem, June 9, 1981.

POSEY, PARKER: Baltimore, MD, Nov. 8, 1968.

POSTLETHWAITE, PETE: London, Feb. 7, 1945.

POTTS, ANNIE: Nashville, TN, Oct. 28, 1952. Stephens College.

POWELL, JANE (Suzanne Burce): Port-land, OR, Apr. 1, 1928.

POWELL, ROBERT: Salford, England, June 1, 1944. Manchester U.

POWER, TARYN: Los Angeles, CA, Sept. 13, 1953.

POWER, TYRONE, IV: Los Angeles, CA, Jan. 22, 1959.

POWERS, MALA (Mary Ellen): San Francisco, CA, Dec. 29, 1921. UCLA.

POWERS, STEFANIE (Federkiewicz): Hollywood, CA, Oct. 12, 1942.

PRENTISS, PAULA (Paula Ragusa): San Antonio, TX, Mar. 4, 1939. Northwestern U.

PRESLE, MICHELINE (Micheline Chassagne): Paris, France, Aug. 22, 1922. Rouleau Drama School.

PRESLEY, PRISCILLA: Brooklyn, NY, May 24, 1945.

PRESNELL, HARVE: Modesto, CA, Sept. 14, 1933. USC.

345

Tim Robbins   Paul Rudd   Susan Sarandon   Annabella Sciorra

PRESTON, KELLY: Honolulu, HI, Oct. 13, 1962. USC.

PRESTON, WILLIAM: Columbia, PA, Aug. 26, 1921. PaStateU.

PRICE, LONNY: NYC, Mar. 9, 1959. Juilliard.

PRIESTLEY, JASON: Vancouver, Canada, Aug, 28, 1969.

PRIMUS, BARRY: NYC, Feb. 16, 1938. CCNY.

PRINCE (P. Rogers Nelson): Minneapolis, MN, June 7, 1958.

PRINCIPAL, VICTORIA: Fukuoka, Japan, Jan. 3, 1945. Dade, Jr. College.

PRINZE, JR., FREDDIE: Los Angeles, March 8, 1976.

PROCHNOW, JURGEN: Berlin, June 10, 1941.

PROSKY, ROBERT: Philadelphia, PA, Dec. 13, 1930.

PROVAL, DAVID: Brooklyn, NY, May 20, 1942.

PROVINE, DOROTHY: Deadwood, SD, Jan. 20, 1937. U Wash.

PRYCE, JONATHAN: Wales, UK, June 1, 1947, RADA.

PRYOR, RICHARD: Peoria, IL, Dec. 1, 1940.

PULLMAN, BILL: Delphi, NY, Dec. 17, 1954. SUNY/Oneonta, UMass.

PURCELL, LEE: Cherry Point, NC, June 15, 1947. Stephens.

PURDOM, EDMUND: Welwyn Garden City, England, Dec. 19, 1924. St. Ignatius College.

QUAID, DENNIS: Houston, TX, Apr. 9, 1954.

QUAID, RANDY: Houston, TX, Oct. 1, 1950. UHouston.

QUINLAN, KATHLEEN: Mill Valley, CA, Nov. 19, 1954.

QUINN, AIDAN: Chicago, IL, Mar. 8, 1959.

QUINN, ANTHONY: Chihuahua, Mex., Apr. 21, 1915.

RAFFERTY, FRANCES: Sioux City, IA, June 16, 1922. UCLA.

RAFFIN, DEBORAH: Los Angeles, Mar. 13, 1953. Valley College.

RAGSDALE, WILLIAM: El Dorado, AK, Jan. 19, 1961. Hendrix College.

RAILSBACK, STEVE: Dallas, TX, 1948.

RAINER, LUISE: Vienna, Austria, Jan. 12, 1910.

RALSTON, VERA (Vera Helena Hruba): Prague, Czech., July 12, 1919.

RAMIS, HAROLD: Chicago, IL, Nov. 21, 1944. WashingtonU.

RAMPLING, CHARLOTTE: Surmer, England, Feb. 5, 1946. U Madrid.

RAMSEY, LOGAN: Long Beach, CA, Mar. 21, 1921. St. Joseph.

RANDALL, TONY (Leonard Rosenberg): Tulsa, OK, Feb. 26, 1920. Northwestern U.

RANDELL, RON: Sydney, Australia, Oct. 8, 1920. St. Mary's College.

RAPAPORT, MICHAEL: March 20, 1970.

RAPP, ANTHONY: Chicago, Oct. 26, 1971.

RASCHE, DAVID: St. Louis, MO, Aug. 7, 1944.

REA, STEPHEN: Belfast, No. Ireland, Oct. 31, 1944.

REAGAN, RONALD: Tampico, IL, Feb. 6, 1911. Eureka College.

REASON, REX: Berlin, Ger., Nov. 30, 1928. Pasadena Playhouse.

REDDY, HELEN: Melbourne, Australia, Oct. 25, 1942.

REDFORD, ROBERT: Santa Monica, CA, Aug. 18, 1937. AADA.

REDGRAVE, CORIN: London, July 16, 1939.

REDGRAVE, LYNN: London, Mar. 8, 1943.

REDGRAVE, VANESSA: London, Jan. 30, 1937.

REDMAN, JOYCE: County Mayo, Ireland, 1919. RADA.

REED, PAMELA: Tacoma, WA, Apr. 2, 1949.

REEMS, HARRY (Herbert Streicher): Bronx, NY, 1947. U Pittsburgh.

REES, ROGER: Aberystwyth, Wales, May 5, 1944.

REESE, DELLA: Detroit, MI, July 6, 1932.

REEVE, CHRISTOPHER: NYC, Sept. 25, 1952. Cornell, Juilliard.

REEVES, KEANU: Beiruit, Lebanon, Sept. 2, 1964.

REEVES, STEVE: Glasgow, MT, Jan. 21, 1926.

REGEHR, DUNCAN: Lethbridge, Canada, Oct. 5, 1952.

REID, ELLIOTT: NYC, Jan. 16, 1920.

REID, TIM: Norfolk, VA, Dec. 19, 1944.

REILLY, CHARLES NELSON: NYC, Jan. 13, 1931. UCt.

REILLY, JOHN C.: Chicago, IL, May 24, 1965.

REINER, CARL: NYC, Mar. 20, 1922. Georgetown.

REINER, ROB: NYC, Mar. 6, 1947. UCLA.

REINHOLD, JUDGE (Edward Ernest, Jr.): Wilmington, DE, May 21, 1957. NCSchool of Arts.

REINKING, ANN: Seattle, WA, Nov. 10, 1949.

REISER, PAUL: NYC, Mar. 30, 1957.

REMAR, JAMES: Boston, MA, Dec. 31, 1953. Neighborhood Playhouse.

RENFRO, BRAD: Knoxville, TN, July 25, 1982.

RENO, JEAN (Juan Moreno): Casablanca, Morocco, July 30, 1948.

REVILL, CLIVE: Wellington, NZ, Apr. 18, 1930.

REY, ANTONIA: Havana, Cuba, Oct. 12, 1927.

REYNOLDS, BURT: Waycross, GA, Feb. 11, 1935. Fla. State U.

REYNOLDS, DEBBIE (Mary Frances Reynolds): El Paso, TX, Apr. 1, 1932.

RHOADES, BARBARA: Poughkeepsie, NY, Mar. 23, 1947.

RHODES, CYNTHIA: Nashville, TN, Nov. 21, 1956.

RHYS-DAVIES, JOHN: Salisbury, England, May 5, 1944.

RHYS-MEYERS, JONATHAN: Cork, Ireland, July 27, 1977.

RIBISI, GIOVANNI: Los Angeles, CA, Dec. 17, 1974.

RICCI, CHRISTINA: Santa Monica, CA, Feb. 12, 1980.

RICHARD, CLIFF (Harry Webb)**:** India, Oct. 14, 1940.

RICHARDS, DENISE: Downers Grove, IL, Feb. 17, 1972.

RICHARDS, MICHAEL: Culver City, CA, July 14, 1949.

RICHARDSON, JOELY: London, Jan. 9, 1965.

RICHARDSON, MIRANDA: Southport, England, Mar. 3, 1958.

RICHARDSON, NATASHA: London, May 11, 1963.

RICKLES, DON: NYC, May 8, 1926. AADA.

RICKMAN, ALAN: Hammersmith, England, Feb. 21, 1946.

RIEGERT, PETER: NYC, Apr. 11, 1947. U Buffalo.

RIFKIN, RON: NYC, Oct. 31, 1939.

RIGG, DIANA: Doncaster, England, July 20, 1938. RADA.

RINGWALD, MOLLY: Rosewood, CA, Feb. 16, 1968.

RITTER, JOHN: Burbank, CA, Sept. 17, 1948. US. Cal.

RIVERS, JOAN (Molinsky)**:** Brooklyn, NY, NY, June 8, 1933.

ROACHE, LINUS: Manchester, England, 1964.

ROBARDS, JASON: Chicago, IL, July 26, 1922. AADA.

ROBARDS, SAM: NYC, Dec. 16, 1963.

ROBBINS, TIM: NYC, Oct. 16, 1958. UCLA.

ROBERTS, ERIC: Biloxi, MS, Apr. 18, 1956. RADA.

ROBERTS, JULIA: Atlanta, GA, Oct. 28, 1967.

ROBERTS, RALPH: Salisbury, NC, Aug. 17, 1922. UNC.

ROBERTS, TANYA (Leigh)**:** Bronx, NY, Oct. 15, 1954.

ROBERTS, TONY: NYC, Oct. 22, 1939. Northwestern U.

ROBERTSON, CLIFF: La Jolla, CA, Sept. 9, 1925. Antioch College.

ROBERTSON, DALE: Oklahoma City, July 14, 1923.

ROBINSON, CHRIS: West Palm Beach, FL, Nov. 5, 1938. LACC.

ROBINSON, JAY: NYC, Apr. 14, 1930.

ROBINSON, ROGER: Seattle, WA, May 2, 1940. USC.

ROCHEFORT, JEAN: Paris, France, 1930.

ROCHON, LELA (Staples)**:**

ROCK, CHRIS: Brooklyn, NY, Feb. 7, 1966.

ROGERS, MIMI: Coral Gables, FL, Jan. 27, 1956.

ROGERS, WAYNE: Birmingham, AL, Apr. 7, 1933. Princeton.

RONSTADT, LINDA: Tucson, AZ, July 15, 1946.

ROOKER, MICHAEL: Jasper, AL, Apr. 6, 1955.

ROONEY, MICKEY (Joe Yule, Jr.)**:** Brooklyn, NY, Sept. 23, 1920.

ROSE, REVA: Chicago, IL, July 30, 1940. Goodman.

ROSEANNE (Barr)**:** Salt Lake City, UT, Nov. 3, 1952.

ROSS, DIANA: Detroit, MI, Mar. 26, 1944.

ROSS, JUSTIN: Brooklyn, NY, Dec. 15, 1954.

ROSS, KATHARINE: Hollywood, Jan. 29, 1943. Santa Rosa College.

ROSSELLINI, ISABELLA: Rome, June 18, 1952.

ROSSOVICH, RICK: Palo Alto, CA, Aug. 28, 1957.

ROTH, TIM: London, May 14, 1961.

ROUNDTREE, RICHARD: New Rochelle, NY, Sept. 7, 1942. Southern Ill.

ROURKE, MICKEY (Philip Andre Rourke, Jr.)**:** Schenectady, NY, Sept. 16, 1956.

ROWE, NICHOLAS: London, Nov. 22, 1966, Eton.

ROWLANDS, GENA: Cambria, WI, June 19, 1934.

RUBIN, ANDREW: New Bedford, MA, June 22, 1946. AADA.

RUBINEK, SAUL: Fohrenwold, Germany, July 2, 1948.

RUBINSTEIN, JOHN: Los Angeles, CA, Dec. 8, 1946. UCLA.

RUCK, ALAN: Cleveland, OH, July 1, 1960.

RUCKER, BO: Tampa, FL, Aug. 17, 1948.

RUDD, PAUL: Boston, MA, May 15, 1940.

RUDD, PAUL: Passaic, NJ, Apr. 6, 1969.

RUDNER, RITA: Miami, FL, Sept. 17, 1955.

RUEHL, MERCEDES: Queens, NY, Feb. 28, 1948.

RULE, JANICE: Cincinnati, OH, Aug. 15, 1931.

RUPERT, MICHAEL: Denver, CO, Oct. 23, 1951. Pasadena Playhouse.

RUSH, BARBARA: Denver, CO, Jan. 4, 1927. U Calif.

RUSH, GEOFFREY: Toowoomba, Queensland, Australia, July 6, 1951. Univ. of Queensland.

RUSSELL, JANE: Bemidji, MI, June 21, 1921. Max Reinhardt School.

RUSSELL, KURT: Springfield, MA, Mar. 17, 1951.

RUSSELL, THERESA (Paup)**:** San Diego, CA, Mar. 20, 1957.

RUSSO, JAMES: NYC, Apr. 23, 1953.

RUTHERFORD, ANN: Toronto, Canada, Nov. 2, 1920.

RYAN, JOHN P.: NYC, July 30, 1936. CCNY.

RYAN, MEG: Fairfield, CT, Nov. 19, 1961. NYU.

RYAN, TIM (Meineslschmidt)**:** Staten Island, NY, 1958. Rutgers U.

RYDER, WINONA (Horowitz)**:** Winona, MN, Oct. 29, 1971.

SACCHI, ROBERT: Bronx, NY, 1941. NYU.

SÄGEBRECHT, MARIANNE: Starnberg, Bavaria, Aug. 27, 1945.

SAINT, EVA MARIE: Newark, NJ, July 4, 1924. Bowling Green State U.

SAINT JAMES, SUSAN (Suzie Jane Miller)**:** Los Angeles, Aug. 14, 1946. Conn. College.

ST. JOHN, BETTA: Hawthorne, CA, Nov. 26, 1929.

ST. JOHN, JILL (Jill Oppenheim)**:** Los Angeles, Aug. 19, 1940.

SALA, JOHN: Los Angeles, CA, Oct. 5, 1962.

SALDANA, THERESA: Brooklyn, NY, Aug. 20, 1954.

SALINGER, MATT: Windsor, VT, Feb. 13, 1960. Princeton, Columbia.

SALT, JENNIFER: Los Angeles, Sept. 4, 1944. Sarah Lawrence College.

SAMMS, EMMA: London, Aug. 28, 1960.

SAN GIACOMO, LAURA: Orange, NJ, Nov. 14, 1961.

SANDERS, JAY O.: Austin, TX, Apr. 16, 1953.

Kristin Scott Thomas

Ben Silverstone

Jada Pinkett Smith

SANDLER, ADAM: Bronx, NY, Sept. 9, 1966. NYU.

SANDS, JULIAN: Yorkshire, England, Jan 15, 1958.

SANDS, TOMMY: Chicago, IL, Aug. 27, 1937.

SAN JUAN, OLGA: NYC, Mar. 16, 1927.

SARA, MIA (Sarapocciello): Brooklyn, NY, June 19, 1967.

SARANDON, CHRIS: Beckley, WV, July 24, 1942. U WVa., Catholic U.

SARANDON, SUSAN (Tomalin): NYC, Oct. 4, 1946. Catholic U.

SARRAZIN, MICHAEL: Quebec City, Canada, May 22, 1940.

SAVAGE, FRED: Highland Park, IL, July 9, 1976.

SAVAGE, JOHN (Youngs): Long Island, NY, Aug. 25, 1949. AADA.

SAVIOLA, CAMILLE: Bronx, NY, July 16, 1950.

SAVOY, TERESA ANN: London, July 18, 1955.

SAXON, JOHN (Carmen Orrico): Brooklyn, NY, Aug. 5, 1935.

SBARGE, RAPHAEL: NYC, Feb. 12, 1964.

SCACCHI, GRETA: Milan, Italy, Feb. 18, 1960.

SCALIA, JACK: Brooklyn, NY, Nov. 10, 1951.

SCARWID, DIANA: Savannah, GA, Aug. 27, 1955. AADA. Pace U.

SCHEIDER, ROY: Orange, NJ, Nov. 10, 1932. Franklin-Marshall.

SCHEINE, RAYNOR: Emporia, VA, Nov. 10. VaCommonwealthU.

SCHELL, MARIA: Vienna, Jan. 15, 1926.

SCHELL, MAXIMILIAN: Vienna, Dec. 8, 1930.

SCHLATTER, CHARLIE: Englewood, NJ, May 1, 1966. Ithaca College.

SCHNEIDER, JOHN: Mt. Kisco, NY, Apr. 8, 1960.

SCHNEIDER, MARIA: Paris, France, Mar. 27, 1952.

SCHREIBER, LIEV: San Francisco, CA, Oct. 4, 1967.

SCHRODER, RICK: Staten Island, NY, Apr. 13, 1970.

SCHUCK, JOHN: Boston, MA, Feb. 4, 1940.

SCHULTZ, DWIGHT: Milwaukee, WI, Nov. 10, 1938. MarquetteU.

SCHWARZENEGGER, ARNOLD: Austria, July 30, 1947.

SCHWARTZMAN, JASON: Los Angeles, June 26, 1980.

SCHWIMMER, DAVID: Queens, NY, Nov. 12, 1966.

SCHYGULLA, HANNA: Katlowitz, Germany, Dec. 25, 1943.

SCIORRA, ANNABELLA: NYC, Mar. 24, 1964.

SCOFIELD, PAUL: Hurstpierpoint, England, Jan. 21, 1922. London Mask Theatre School.

SCOGGINS, TRACY: Galveston, TX, Nov. 13, 1959.

SCOLARI, PETER: Scarsdale, NY, Sept. 12, 1956. NYCC.

SCOTT, CAMPBELL: South Salem, NY, July 19, 1962. Lawrence.

SCOTT, DEBRALEE: Elizabeth, NJ, Apr. 2, 1953

SCOTT, GORDON (Gordon M. Werschkul): Portland, OR, Aug. 3, 1927. Oregon U.

SCOTT, LIZABETH (Emma Matso): Scranton, PA, Sept. 29, 1922.

SCOTT, MARTHA: Jamesport, MO, Sept. 22, 1914. U Mich.

SCOTT THOMAS, KRISTIN: Redruth, Cornwall, Eng., May 24, 1960.

SEAGAL, STEVEN: Detroit, MI, Apr. 10, 1951.

SEARS, HEATHER: London, Sept. 28, 1935.

SECOMBE, HARRY: Swansea, Wales, Sept. 8, 1921.

SEDGWICK, KYRA: NYC, Aug. 19, 1965. USC.

SEGAL, GEORGE: NYC, Feb. 13, 1934. Columbia.

SELBY, DAVID: Morganstown, WV, Feb. 5, 1941. UWV.

SELLARS, ELIZABETH: Glasgow, Scotland, May 6, 1923.

SELLECK, TOM: Detroit, MI, Jan. 29, 1945. USCal.

SERBEDZIJA, RADE: Bunic, Yugoslavia, July 27, 1946.

SERNAS, JACQUES: Lithuania, July 30, 1925.

SERRAULT, MICHEL: Brunoy, France. Jan. 24, 1928. Paris Consv.

SETH, ROSHAN: New Delhi, India. 1942.

SEWELL, RUFUS: Twickenham, Eng., Oct. 29, 1967.

SEYMOUR, JANE (Joyce Frankenberg): Hillingdon, England, Feb. 15, 1952.

SHALHOUB, TONY: Oct. 7, 1953.

SHARIF, OMAR (Michel Shalhoub): Alexandria, Egypt, Apr. 10, 1932. Victoria College.

SHANDLING, GARRY: Chicago, IL, Nov. 29, 1949.

SHATNER, WILLIAM: Montreal, Canada, Mar. 22, 1931. McGill U.

SHAVER, HELEN: St. Thomas, Ontario, Canada, Feb. 24, 1951.

SHAW, FIONA: Cork, Ireland, July 10, 1955. RADA.

SHAW, STAN: Chicago, IL, 1952.

SHAWN, WALLACE: NYC, Nov. 12, 1943. Harvard.

SHEA, JOHN: North Conway, NH, Apr. 14, 1949. Bates, Yale.

SHEARER, HARRY: Los Angeles, Dec. 23, 1943. UCLA.

SHEARER, MOIRA: Dunfermline, Scotland, Jan. 17, 1926. London Theatre School.

SHEEDY, ALLY: NYC, June 13, 1962. USC.

SHEEN, CHARLIE (Carlos Irwin Estevez): Santa Monica, CA, Sept. 3, 1965.

SHEEN, MARTIN (Ramon Estevez): Dayton, OH, Aug. 3, 1940.

SHEFFER, CRAIG: York, PA, Apr. 23, 1960. E. StroudsbergU.

SHEFFIELD, JOHN: Pasadena, CA, Apr. 11, 1931. UCLA.

SHELLEY, CAROL: London, England, Aug. 16, 1939.

SHEPARD, SAM (Rogers): Ft. Sheridan, IL, Nov. 5, 1943.

SHEPHERD, CYBILL: Memphis, TN, Feb. 18, 1950. Hunter, NYU.

SHER, ANTONY: England, June 14, 1949.

SHERIDAN, JAMEY: Pasadena, CA, July 12, 1951.

SHIELDS, BROOKE: NYC, May 31, 1965.

SHIRE, TALIA: Lake Success, NY, Apr. 25, 1946. Yale.

SHORT, MARTIN: Toronto, Canada, Mar. 26, 1950. McMasterU.

Mira Sorvino

David Spade

Ben Stiller

Eric Stoltz

Donald Sutherland

Jonathan Taylor Thomas

Emma Thompson

Lily Tomlin

SHOWALTER, MAX (formerly Casey Adams): Caldwell, KS, June 2, 1917. Pasadena Playhouse.

SHUE, ELISABETH: S. Orange, NJ, Oct. 6, 1963. Harvard.

SIEMASZKO, CASEY: Chicago, IL, March 17, 1961.

SIKKING, JAMES B.: Los Angeles, Mar. 5, 1934.

SILVA, HENRY: Brooklyn, NY, 1928.

SILVER, RON: NYC, July 2, 1946. SUNY.

SILVERMAN, JONATHAN: Los Angeles, CA, Aug. 5, 1966. USC.

SILVERSTONE, ALICIA: San Francisco, CA, Oct. 4, 1976.

SILVERSTONE, BEN: London, Eng, Apr. 4, 1979.

SIMMONS, JEAN: London, Jan. 31, 1929. Aida Foster School.

SIMON, PAUL: Newark. NJ, Nov. 5, 1942.

SIMON, SIMONE: Bethune, France, Apr. 23, 1910.

SIMPSON, O. J. (Orenthal James): San Francisco, CA, July 9, 1947. UCLA.

SINBAD (David Adkins): Benton Harbor, MI, Nov. 10, 1956.

SINCLAIR, JOHN (Gianluigi Loffredo): Rome, Italy, 1946.

SINDEN, DONALD: Plymouth, England, Oct. 9, 1923. Webber-Douglas.

SINGER, LORI: Corpus Christi, TX, May 6, 1962. Juilliard.

SINISE, GARY: Chicago, Mar. 17. 1955.

SIZEMORE, TOM: Detroit, MI, Sept. 29, 1964.

SKARSGÅRD, STELLAN: Gothenburg, Vastergotland, Sweden, June 13, 1951.

SKERRITT, TOM: Detroit, MI, Aug. 25, 1933. Wayne State U.

SKYE, IONE (Leitch): London, England, Sept. 4, 1971.

SLATER, CHRISTIAN: NYC, Aug. 18, 1969.

SLATER, HELEN: NYC, Dec. 15, 1965.

SMITH, CHARLES MARTIN: Los Angeles, CA, Oct. 30, 1953. CalState U.

SMITH, JACLYN: Houston, TX, Oct. 26, 1947.

SMITH, JADA PINKETT: Baltimore, MD, Sept. 18, 1971.

SMITH, KEVIN: Red Bank, NJ, Aug. 2, 1970.

SMITH, KURTWOOD: New Lisbon, WI, Jul. 3, 1942.

SMITH, LANE: Memphis, TN, Apr. 29, 1936.

SMITH, LEWIS: Chattanooga, TN, 1958. Actors Studio.

SMITH, LOIS: Topeka, KS, Nov. 3, 1930. U Wash.

SMITH, MAGGIE: Ilford, England, Dec. 28, 1934.

SMITH, ROGER: South Gate, CA, Dec. 18, 1932. U Ariz.

SMITH, WILL: Philadelphia, PA, Sept. 25, 1968.

SMITHERS, WILLIAM: Richmond, VA, July 10, 1927. Catholic U.

SMITS, JIMMY: Brooklyn, NY, July 9, 1955. Cornell U.

SNIPES, WESLEY: NYC, July 31, 1963. SUNY/Purchase.

SNODGRESS, CARRIE: Chicago, IL, Oct. 27, 1946. UNI.

SOBIEKSI, LEELEE (Liliane Sobieski): NYC, June 10, 1982.

SOLOMON, BRUCE: NYC, 1944. U Miami, Wayne State U.

SOMERS, SUZANNE (Mahoney): San Bruno, CA, Oct. 16, 1946. Lone Mt. College.

SOMMER, ELKE (Schletz): Berlin, Germany, Nov. 5, 1940.

SOMMER, JOSEF: Greifswald, Germany, June 26, 1934.

SORDI, ALBERTO: Rome, Italy, June 15, 1920.

SORVINO, MIRA: Tenafly, NJ, Sept. 28, 1967.

SORVINO, PAUL: NYC, Apr. 13, 1939. AMDA.

SOTHERN, ANN (Harriet Lake): Valley City, ND, Jan. 22, 1909.

SOTO, TALISA (Miriam Soto): Brooklyn, NY, Mar. 27, 1967.

SOUL, DAVID: Chicago, IL, Aug. 28, 1943.

SPACEK, SISSY: Quitman, TX, Dec. 25, 1949. Actors Studio.

SPACEY, KEVIN: So. Orange, NJ, July 26, 1959. Juilliard.

SPADE, DAVID: Birmingham, MS, July 22, 1964.

SPADER, JAMES: Buzzards Bay, MA, Feb. 7, 1960.

SPANO, VINCENT: Brooklyn, NY, Oct. 18, 1962.

SPENSER, JEREMY: Ceylon, 1937.

SPINELLA, STEPHEN: Naples, Italy, Oct. 11, 1956. NYU.

SPRINGFIELD, RICK (Richard Spring Thorpe): Sydney, Australia, Aug. 23, 1949.

STACK, ROBERT: Los Angeles, Jan. 13, 1919. USC.

STADLEN, LEWIS J.: Brooklyn, NY, Mar. 7, 1947. Neighborhood Playhouse.

STAHL, NICK: Dallas, TX, Dec. 5, 1979.

STALLONE, FRANK: NYC, July 30, 1950.

STALLONE, SYLVESTER: NYC, July 6, 1946. U Miami.

STAMP, TERENCE: London, July 23, 1939.

STANG, ARNOLD: Chelsea, MA, Sept. 28, 1925.

STANLEY, KIM (Patricia Reid): Tularosa, NM, Feb. 11, 1925. U Tex.

STANTON, HARRY DEAN: Lexington, KY, July 14, 1926.

STAPLETON, JEAN: NYC, Jan. 19, 1923.

STAPLETON, MAUREEN: Troy, NY, June 21, 1925.

STARR, RINGO (Richard Starkey): Liverpool, England, July 7, 1940.

STEEL, ANTHONY: London, May 21, 1920. Cambridge.

STEELE,BARBARA: England, Dec. 29, 1937.

STEELE, TOMMY: London, Dec. 17, 1936.

STEENBURGEN, MARY: Newport, AR, 1953. Neighborhood Playhouse.

STEIGER, ROD: Westhampton, NY, Apr. 14, 1925.

STERLING, JAN (Jane Sterling Adriance): NYC, Apr. 3, 1923. Fay Compton School.

STERLING, ROBERT (William Sterling Hart): Newcastle, PA, Nov. 13, 1917. UPittsburgh.

STERN, DANIEL: Bethesda, MD, Aug. 28, 1957.

STERNHAGEN, FRANCES: Washington, DC, Jan. 13, 1932.

STEVENS, ANDREW: Memphis, TN, June 10, 1955.

Rip Torn

Jeanne Tripplehorn

Liv Tyler

Liv Ullmann

STEVENS, CONNIE (Concetta Ann Ingolia): Brooklyn, NY, Aug. 8, 1938. Hollywood Professional School.
STEVENS, FISHER: Chicago, IL, Nov. 27, 1963. NYU.
STEVENS, STELLA (Estelle Eggleston): Hot Coffee, MS, Oct. 1, 1936.
STEVENSON, PARKER: Philadelphia, PA, June 4, 1953. Princeton.
STEWART, ALEXANDRA: Montreal, Canada, June 10, 1939. Louvre.
STEWART, ELAINE (Elsy Steinberg): Montclair, NJ, May 31, 1929.
STEWART, FRENCH (Milton French Stewart): Albuquerque, NM, Feb. 20, 1964.
STEWART, JON (Jonathan Stewart Liebowitz): Trenton, NJ, Nov. 28, 1962.
STEWART, MARTHA (Martha Haworth): Bardwell, KY, Oct. 7, 1922.
STEWART, PATRICK: Mirfield, England, July 13, 1940.
STIERS, DAVID OGDEN: Peoria, IL, Oct. 31, 1942.
STILES, JULIA: NYC, Mar. 28, 1981.
STILLER, BEN: NYC, Nov. 30, 1965.
STILLER, JERRY: NYC, June 8, 1931.
STING (Gordon Matthew Sumner): Wallsend, England, Oct. 2, 1951.
STOCKWELL, DEAN: Hollywood, Mar. 5, 1935.
STOCKWELL, JOHN (John Samuels, IV): Galveston, TX, Mar. 25, 1961. Harvard.
STOLTZ, ERIC: Whittier, CA, Sept. 30, 1961. USC.
STONE, DEE WALLACE (Deanna Bowers): Kansas City, MO, Dec. 14, 1948. UKS.
STORM, GALE (Josephine Cottle): Bloomington, TX, Apr. 5, 1922.
STOWE, MADELEINE: Eagle Rock, CA, Aug. 18, 1958.
STRAIGHT, BEATRICE: Old Westbury, NY, Aug. 2, 1916. Dartington Hall.
STRASSMAN, MARCIA: New Jersey, Apr. 28, 1948.
STRATHAIRN, DAVID: San Francisco, Jan. 26, 1949.
STRAUSS, PETER: NYC, Feb. 20, 1947.
STREEP, MERYL (Mary Louise): Summit, NJ, June 22, 1949. Vassar, Yale.
STREISAND, BARBRA: Brooklyn, NY, Apr. 24, 1942.

STRITCH, ELAINE: Detroit, MI, Feb. 2, 1925. Drama Workshop.
STROUD, DON: Honolulu, HI, Sept. 1, 1937.
STRUTHERS, SALLY: Portland, OR, July 28, 1948. Pasadena Playhouse.
STUDI, WES (Wesley Studie): Nofire Hollow, OK, Dec. 17, 1947.
SUMMER, DONNA (LaDonna Gaines): Boston, MA, Dec. 31, 1948.
SUTHERLAND, DONALD: St. John, New Brunswick, Canada, July 17, 1935. U Toronto.
SUTHERLAND, KIEFER: Los Angeles, CA, Dec. 18, 1966.
SUVARI, MENA: Newport, RI, Feb. 9, 1979.
SVENSON, BO: Goreborg, Sweden, Feb. 13, 1941. UCLA.
SWANK, HILARY: Bellingham, WA, July 30, 1974.
SWAYZE, PATRICK: Houston, TX, Aug. 18, 1952.
SWEENEY, D. B. (Daniel Bernard Sweeney): Shoreham, NY, Nov. 14, 1961.
SWINBURNE, NORA (Elinore Johnson): Bath, England, July 24, 1902. RADA.
SWIT, LORETTA: Passaic, NJ, Nov. 4, 1937. AADA.
SYLVESTER, WILLIAM: Oakland, CA, Jan. 31, 1922. RADA.
SYMONDS, ROBERT: Bistow, AK, Dec. 1, 1926. TexU.
SYMS, SYLVIA: London, June 1, 1934. Convent School.
SZARABAJKA, KEITH: Oak Park, IL, Dec. 2, 1952. UChicago.
T, MR. (Lawrence Tero): Chicago, IL, May 21, 1952.
TABORI, KRISTOFFER (Siegel): Los Angeles, Aug. 4, 1952.
TAKEI, GEORGE: Los Angeles, CA, Apr. 20, 1939. UCLA.
TALBOT, NITA: NYC, Aug. 8, 1930. Irvine Studio School.
TAMBLYN, RUSS: Los Angeles, Dec. 30, 1934.
TARANTINO, QUENTIN: Knoxville, TN, Mar. 27, 1963.
TATE, LARENZ: Chicago, IL, Sept. 8, 1975.
TAYLOR, ELIZABETH: London, Feb. 27, 1932. Byron House School.
TAYLOR, LILI: Glencoe, IL, Feb. 20, 1967.
TAYLOR, RENEE: NYC, Mar. 19, 1935.

TAYLOR, ROD (Robert): Sydney, Aust., Jan. 11, 1929.
TAYLOR-YOUNG, LEIGH: Washington, DC, Jan. 25, 1945. Northwestern.
TEEFY, MAUREEN: Minneapolis, MN, 1954, Juilliard.
TEMPLE, SHIRLEY: Santa Monica, CA, Apr. 23, 1927.
TENNANT, VICTORIA: London, England, Sept. 30, 1950.
TERZIEFF, LAURENT: Paris, France, June 25, 1935.
TEWES, LAUREN: Braddock, PA, Oct. 26, 1954.
THACKER, RUSS: Washington, DC, June 23, 1946. Montgomery College.
THAXTER, PHYLLIS: Portland, ME, Nov. 20, 1921. St. Genevieve.
THELEN, JODI: St. Cloud, MN, 1963.
THERON, CHARLIZE: Benoni, So. Africa, Aug. 7, 1975.
THEWLIS, DAVID: Blackpool, Eng., 1963.
THOMAS, HENRY: San Antonio, TX, Sept. 8, 1971.
THOMAS, JAY: New Orleans, July 12, 1948.
THOMAS, JONATHAN TAYLOR (Weiss): Bethlehem, PA, Sept. 8, 1981.
THOMAS, MARLO (Margaret): Detroit, Nov. 21, 1938. USC.
THOMAS, PHILIP MICHAEL: Columbus, OH, May 26, 1949. Oakwood College.
THOMAS, RICHARD: NYC, June 13, 1951. Columbia.
THOMPSON, EMMA: London, England, Apr.15, 1959. Cambridge.
THOMPSON, FRED DALTON: Sheffield, AL, Aug. 19, 1942
THOMPSON, JACK (John Payne): Sydney, Australia, Aug. 31, 1940.
THOMPSON, LEA: Rochester, MN, May 31, 1961.
THOMPSON, REX: NYC, Dec. 14, 1942.
THOMPSON, SADA: Des Moines, IA, Sept. 27, 1929. Carnegie Tech.
THORNTON, BILLY BOB: Hot Spring, AR, Aug. 4, 1955.
THORSON, LINDA: Toronto, Canada, June 18, 1947. RADA.
THULIN, INGRID: Solleftea, Sweden, Jan. 27, 1929. Royal Drama Theatre.
THURMAN, UMA: Boston, MA, Apr. 29, 1970.

James Van Der Beek

Jean-Claude Van Damme

Jon Voight

Denzel Washington

TICOTIN, RACHEL: Bronx, NY, Nov. 1, 1958.

TIERNEY, LAWRENCE: Brooklyn, NY, Mar. 15, 1919. Manhattan College.

TIFFIN, PAMELA (Wonso): Oklahoma City, OK, Oct. 13, 1942.

TIGHE, KEVIN: Los Angeles, Aug. 13, 1944.

TILLY, JENNIFER: Los Angeles, CA, Sept. 16, 1958.

TILLY, MEG: Texada, Canada, Feb. 14, 1960.

TOBOLOWSKY, STEPHEN: Dallas, Tx, May 30, 1951. So. Methodist U.

TODD, BEVERLY: Chicago, IL, July 1, 1946.

TODD, RICHARD: Dublin, Ireland, June 11, 1919. Shrewsbury School.

TOLKAN, JAMES: Calumet, MI, June 20, 1931.

TOMEI, MARISA: Brooklyn, NY, Dec. 4, 1964. NYU.

TOMLIN, LILY: Detroit, MI, Sept. 1, 1939. Wayne State U.

TOPOL (Chaim Topol): Tel-Aviv, Israel, Sept. 9, 1935.

TORN, RIP: Temple, TX, Feb. 6, 1931. UTex.

TORRES, LIZ: NYC, Sept. 27, 1947. NYU.

TOTTER, AUDREY: Joliet, IL, Dec. 20, 1918.

TOWSEND, ROBERT: Chicago, IL, Feb. 6, 1957.

TRAVANTI, DANIEL J.: Kenosha, WI, Mar. 7, 1940.

TRAVIS, NANCY: Astoria, NY, Sept. 21, 1961.

TRAVOLTA, JOEY: Englewood, NJ, 1952.

TRAVOLTA, JOHN: Englewood, NJ, Feb. 18, 1954.

TREMAYNE, LES: London, Apr. 16, 1913. Northwestern, Columbia, UCLA.

TREVOR, CLAIRE (Wemlinger): NYC, March 8, 1909.

TRINTIGNANT, JEAN-LOUIS: Pont-St. Esprit, France, Dec. 11, 1930. DullinBalachova Drama School.

TRIPPLEHORN, JEANNE: Tulsa, OK, 1963.

TSOPEI, CORINNA: Athens, Greece, June 21, 1944.

TUBB, BARRY: Snyder, TX, 1963. AmConsv Th.

TUCCI, STANLEY: Katonah, NY, Jan. 11, 1960.

TUCKER, CHRIS: Atlanta, GA, 1972.

TUCKER, MICHAEL: Baltimore, MD, Feb. 6, 1944.

TUNE, TOMMY: Wichita Falls, TX, Feb. 28, 1939.

TURNER, JANINE (Gauntt): Lincoln, NE, Dec. 6, 1963.

TURNER, KATHLEEN: Springfield, MO, June 19, 1954. UMd.

TURNER, TINA (Anna Mae Bullock): Nutbush, TN, Nov. 26, 1938.

TURTURRO, JOHN: Brooklyn, NY, Feb. 28, 1957. Yale.

TUSHINGHAM, RITA: Liverpool, England, Mar. 14, 1940.

TUTIN, DOROTHY: London, Apr. 8, 1930.

TWIGGY (Lesley Hornby): London, Sept. 19, 1949.

TWOMEY, ANNE: Boston, MA, June 7, 1951. Temple U.

TYLER, BEVERLY (Beverly Jean Saul): Scranton, PA, July 5, 1928.

TYLER, LIV: Portland, ME, July 1, 1977.

TYRRELL, SUSAN: San Francisco, 1946.

TYSON, CATHY: Liverpool, England, June 12, 1965. Royal Shake. Co.

TYSON, CICELY: NYC, Dec. 19, 1933. NYU.

UGGAMS, LESLIE: NYC, May 25, 1943. Juilliard.

ULLMAN, TRACEY: Slough, England, Dec. 30, 1959.

ULLMANN, LIV: Tokyo, Dec. 10, 1938. Webber-Douglas Acad.

ULRICH, SKEET (Bryan Ray Ulrich): North Carolina, Jan. 20, 1969.

UMEKI, MIYOSHI: Otaru, Hokaido, Japan, Apr. 3, 1929.

UNDERWOOD, BLAIR: Tacoma, WA, Aug. 25, 1964. Carnegie-Mellon U.

UNGER, DEBORAH KARA: Victoria, British Columbia, 1966.

URICH, ROBERT: Toronto, Canada, Dec. 19, 1946.

USTINOV, PETER: London, Apr. 16, 1921. Westminster School.

VACCARO, BRENDA: Brooklyn, NY, Nov. 18, 1939. Neighborhood Playhouse.

VALANDREY, CHARLOTTE (Anne Charlone Pascal): Paris, France, 1968.

Robin Wiliams

Treat Williams

351

Vanessa L. Williams

Renée Zellweger

VALLI, ALIDA: Pola, Italy, May 31, 1921. Academy of Drama.

VALLONE, RAF: Riogio, Italy, Feb. 17, 1916. Turin U.

VAN ARK, JOAN: NYC, June 16, 1943. Yale.

VAN DAMME, JEAN-CLAUDE (J-C Vorenberg): Brussels, Belgium, Apr. 1, 1960.

VAN DE VEN, MONIQUE: Netherlands, 1952.

VAN DER BEEK, JAMES: Chesire, CT, March 8, 1977.

VAN DEVERE, TRISH (Patricia Dressel): Englewood Cliffs, NJ, Mar. 9, 1945. Ohio Wesleyan.

VAN DIEN, CASPER: Ridgefield, NJ, Dec. 18, 1968.

VAN DOREN, MAMIE (Joan Lucile Olander): Rowena SD, Feb. 6, 1933.

VAN DYKE, DICK: West Plains, MO, Dec. 13, 1925.

VANITY (Denise Katrina Smith): Niagara, Ont., Can, Jan. 4, 1959.

VAN PALLANDT, NINA: Copenhagen, Denmark, July 15, 1932.

VAN PATTEN, DICK: NYC, Dec. 9, 1928.

VAN PATTEN, JOYCE: NYC, Mar. 9, 1934.

VAN PEEBLES, MARIO: NYC, Jan. 15, 1958. Columbia U.

VAN PEEBLES, MELVIN: Chicago, IL, Aug. 21, 1932.

VANCE, COURTNEY B.: Detroit, MI, Mar. 12, 1960.

VARNEY, JIM: Lexington, KY, June 15, 1949.

VAUGHN, ROBERT: NYC, Nov. 22, 1932. USC.

VAUGHN, VINCE: Minneapolis, MN, Mar. 28, 1970.

VEGA, ISELA: Mexico, 1940.

VELJOHNSON, REGINALD: NYC, Aug. 16, 1952.

VENNERA, CHICK: Herkimer, NY, Mar. 27, 1952. Pasadena Playhouse.

VENORA, DIANE: Hartford, CT, 1952. Juilliard.

VERDON, GWEN: Culver City, CA, Jan. 13, 1925.

VERNON, JOHN: Montreal, Canada, Feb. 24, 1932.

VEREEN, BEN: Miami, FL, Oct. 10, 1946.

VICTOR, JAMES (Lincoln Rafael Peralta Diaz): Santiago, D.R., July 27, 1939. Haaren HS/NYC.

VINCENT, JAN-MICHAEL: Denver, CO, July 15, 1944. Ventura.

VIOLET, ULTRA (Isabelle Collin-Dufresne): Grenoble, France, 1935.

VITALE, MILLY: Rome, Italy, July 16, 1928. Lycee Chateaubriand.

VOHS, JOAN: St. Albans, NY, July 30, 1931.

VOIGHT, JON: Yonkers, NY, Dec. 29, 1938. Catholic U.

VON BARGEN, DANIEL: Cincinnati, OH, June 5, 1950. Purdue.

VON DOHLEN, LENNY: Augusta, GA, Dec. 22, 1958. UTex.

VON SYDOW, MAX: Lund, Sweden, July 10, 1929. Royal Drama Theatre.

WAGNER, LINDSAY: Los Angeles, June 22, 1949.

WAGNER, NATASHA GREGSON: Los Angeles, CA, Sept. 29, 1970.

WAGNER, ROBERT: Detroit, Feb. 10, 1930.

WAHL, KEN: Chicago, IL, Feb. 14, 1953.

WAITE, GENEVIEVE: South Africa, 1949.

WAITE, RALPH: White Plains, NY, June 22, 1929. Yale.

WAITS, TOM: Pomona, CA, Dec. 7, 1949.

WALKEN, CHRISTOPHER: Astoria, NY, Mar. 31, 1943. Hofstra.

WALKER, CLINT: Hartfold, IL, May 30, 1927. USC.

WALLACH, ELI: Brooklyn, NY, Dec. 7, 1915. CCNY, U Tex.

WALLACH, ROBERTA: NYC, Aug. 2, 1955.

WALLIS, SHANI: London, Apr. 5, 1941.

WALSH, M. EMMET: Ogdensburg, NY, Mar. 22, 1935. Clarkson College, AADA.

WALSTON, RAY: New Orleans, Nov. 22, 1917. Cleveland Playhouse.

WALTER, JESSICA: Brooklyn, NY, Jan. 31, 1944 Neighborhood Playhouse.

WALTER, TRACEY: Jersey City, NJ, Nov. 25, 1942.

WALTERS, JULIE: London, Feb. 22, 1950.

WALTON, EMMA: London, Nov. 1962. Brown U.

WARD, BURT (Gervis): Los Angeles, July 6, 1945.

WARD, FRED: San Diego, CA, Dec. 30, 1942.

WARD, RACHEL: London, Sept. 12, 1957.

WARD, SELA: Meridian, MS, July 11, 1956.

WARD, SIMON: London, Oct. 19, 1941.

WARDEN, JACK (Lebzelter): Newark, NJ, Sept. 18, 1920.

WARNER, DAVID: Manchester, England, July 29, 1941. RADA.

WARNER, MALCOLM-JAMAL: Jersey City, NJ, Aug. 18, 1970.

WARREN, JENNIFER: NYC, Aug. 12, 1941. U Wisc.

WARREN, LESLEY ANN: NYC, Aug. 16, 1946.

WARREN, MICHAEL: South Bend, IN, Mar. 5, 1946. UCLA.

WARRICK, RUTH: St. Joseph, MO, June 29, 1915. U Mo.

WASHINGTON, DENZEL: Mt. Vernon, NY, Dec. 28, 1954. Fordham.

WASSON, CRAIG: Ontario, OR, Mar. 15, 1954. UOre.

WATERSTON, SAM: Cambridge, MA, Nov. 15, 1940. Yale.

WATLING, JACK: London, Jan. 13, 1923. Italia Conti School.

WATSON, EMILY: London, Jan. 14, 1967.

WAYANS, DAMON: NYC, Sept. 4, 1960.

WAYANS, KEENEN, IVORY: NYC, June 8, 1958. Tuskegee Inst.

WAYNE, PATRICK: Los Angeles, July 15, 1939. Loyola.

WEATHERS, CARL: New Orleans, LA, Jan. 14, 1948. Long Beach CC.

WEAVER, DENNIS: Joplin, MO, June 4, 1924. U Okla.

WEAVER, FRITZ: Pittsburgh, PA, Jan. 19, 1926.

WEAVER, SIGOURNEY (Susan): NYC, Oct. 8, 1949. Stanford, Yale.

WEBER, STEVEN: Queens, NY, March 4, 1961.

WEDGEWORTH, ANN: Abilene, TX, Jan. 21, 1935. U Tex.

WELCH, RAQUEL (Tejada): Chicago, IL, Sept. 5, 1940.

WELD, TUESDAY (Susan): NYC, Aug. 27, 1943. Hollywood Professional School.

WELDON, JOAN: San Francisco, Aug. 5, 1933. San Francisco Conservatory.

WELLER, PETER: Stevens Point, WI, June 24, 1947. AmThWing.

WENDT, GEORGE: Chicago, IL, Oct. 17, 1948.

WEST, ADAM (William Anderson): Walla Walla, WA, Sept. 19, 1929.

WETTIG, PATRICIA: Cincinatti, OH, Dec. 4, 1951. TempleU.

WHALEY, FRANK: Syracuse, NY, July 20, 1963. SUNY/Albany.

WHALLEY-KILMER, JOANNE: Manchester, England, Aug. 25, 1964.
WHEATON, WIL: Burbank, CA, July 29, 1972.
WHITAKER, FOREST: Longview, TX, July 15, 1961.
WHITAKER, JOHNNY: Van Nuys, CA, Dec. 13, 1959.
WHITE, BETTY: Oak Park, IL, Jan. 17, 1922.
WHITE, CHARLES: Perth Amboy, NJ, Aug. 29, 1920. Rutgers U.
WHITELAW, BILLIE: Coventry, England, June 6, 1932.
WHITMAN, STUART: San Francisco, Feb. 1, 1929. CCLA.
WHITMORE, JAMES: White Plains, NY, Oct. 1, 1921. Yale.
WHITNEY, GRACE LEE: Detroit, MI, Apr. 1, 1930.
WHITTON, MARGARET: Philadelphia, PA, Nov. 30, 1950.
WIDDOES, KATHLEEN: Wilmington, DE, Mar. 21, 1939.
WIDMARK, RICHARD: Sunrise, MN, Dec. 26, 1914. Lake Forest.
WIEST, DIANNE: Kansas City, MO, Mar. 28, 1948. UMd.
WILBY. JAMES: Burma, Feb. 20, 1958.
WILCOX, COLIN: Highlands, NC, Feb. 4, 1937. U Tenn.
WILDER, GENE (Jerome Silberman): Milwaukee, WI, June 11, 1935. UIowa.
WILLIAMS, BILLY DEE: NYC, Apr. 6, 1937.
WILLIAMS, CARA (Bernice Kamiat): Brooklyn, NY, June 29, 1925.
WILLIAMS, CINDY: Van Nuys, CA, Aug. 22, 1947. KACC.
WILLIAMS, CLARENCE, III: NYC, Aug. 21, 1939.
WILLIAMS, ESTHER: Los Angeles, Aug. 8, 1921.
WILLIAMS, JOBETH: Houston, TX, Dec 6, 1948. Brown U.
WILLIAMS, MICHELLE: Kalispell, MT, Sept. 9, 1980.
WILLIAMS, PAUL: Omaha, NE, Sept. 19, 1940.
WILLIAMS, ROBIN: Chicago, IL, July 21, 1951. Juilliard.
WILLIAMS, TREAT (Richard): Rowayton, CT, Dec. 1, 1951.
WILLIAMS, VANESSA L.: Tarrytown, NY, Mar. 18, 1963.
WILLIAMSON, FRED: Gary, IN, Mar. 5, 1938. Northwestern.
WILLIAMSON, NICOL: Hamilton, Scotland, Sept. 14, 1938.
WILLIS, BRUCE: Penns Grove, NJ, Mar. 19, 1955.
WILLISON, WALTER: Monterey Park, CA, June 24, 1947.
WILSON, DEMOND: NYC, Oct. 13, 1946. Hunter College.
WILSON, ELIZABETH: Grand Rapids, MI, Apr. 4, 1925.
WILSON, LAMBERT: Paris, France, 1959.
WILSON, LUKE: Dallas, TX, Sept. 21, 1971.
WILSON, SCOTT: Atlanta, GA, 1942.

WINCOTT, JEFF: Toronto, Canada, May 8, 1957.
WINCOTT, MICHAEL: Toronto, Canada, Jan. 6, 1959. Juilliard.
WINDE, BEATRICE: Chicago, IL, Jan. 6.
WINDOM, WILLIAM: NYC, Sept. 28, 1923. Williams College.
WINDSOR, MARIE (Emily Marie Bertelson): Marysvale, UT, Dec. 11, 1924. Brigham Young U.
WINFIELD, PAUL: Los Angeles, May 22, 1940. UCLA.
WINFREY, OPRAH: Kosciusko, MS, Jan. 29, 1954. TnStateU.
WINGER, DEBRA: Cleveland, OH, May 17, 1955. Cal State.
WINKLER, HENRY: NYC, Oct. 30, 1945. Yale.
WINN, KITTY: Washington, D.C., Feb. 21, 1944. Boston U.
WINNINGHAM, MARE: Phoenix, AZ, May 6, 1959.
WINSLET, KATE: Reading, Eng., Oct. 5, 1975.
WINSLOW, MICHAEL: Spokane, WA, Sept. 6, 1960.
WINTER, ALEX: London, July 17, 1965. NYU.
WINTERS, JONATHAN: Dayton, OH, Nov. 11, 1925. Kenyon College.
WINTERS, SHELLEY (Shirley Schrift): St. Louis, Aug. 18, 1922. Wayne U.
WITHERS, GOOGIE: Karachi, India, Mar. 12, 1917. Italia Conti.
WITHERS, JANE: Atlanta, GA, Apr. 12, 1926.
WITHERSPOON, REESE (Laura Jean Reese Witherspoon): Nashville, TN, Mar. 22, 1976.
WOLF, SCOTT: Newton, MA, June 4, 1968.
WONG, B.D.: San Francisco, Oct. 24, 1962.
WONG, RUSSELL: Troy, NY, 1963. SantaMonica College.
WOOD, ELIJAH: Cedar Rapids, IA, Jan 28, 1981.
WOODARD, ALFRE: Tulsa, OK, Nov. 2, 1953. Boston U.
WOODLAWN, HOLLY (Harold Ajzen-berg): Juana Diaz, PR, 1947.
WOODS, JAMES: Vernal, UT, Apr. 18, 1947. MIT.
WOODWARD, EDWARD: Croyden, Surrey, England, June 1, 1930.
WOODWARD, JOANNE: Thomasville, GA, Feb. 27, 1930. Neighborhood Playhouse.
WORONOV, MARY: Brooklyn, NY, Dec. 8, 1946. Cornell.
WORTH, IRENE (Hattie Abrams): Nebraska, June 23, 1916. UCLA.
WRAY, FAY: Alberta, Canada, Sept. 15, 1907.
WRIGHT, AMY: Chicago, IL, Apr. 15, 1950.
WRIGHT, MAX: Detroit, MI, Aug. 2, 1943. WayneStateU.
WRIGHT, ROBIN: Dallas, TX, Apr. 8, 1966.
WRIGHT, TERESA: NYC, Oct. 27, 1918.
WUHL, ROBERT: Union City, NJ, Oct. 9, 1951. UHouston.
WYATT, JANE: NYC, Aug. 10, 1910. Barnard College.
WYLE, NOAH: Los Angeles, June 2, 1971.
WYMAN, JANE (Sarah Jane Fulks): St. Joseph, MO, Jan. 4, 1914.

WYMORE, PATRICE: Miltonvale, KS, Dec. 17, 1926.
WYNN, MAY (Donna Lee Hickey): NYC, Jan. 8, 1930.
WYNTER, DANA (Dagmar): London, June 8. 1927. Rhodes U.
YORK, MICHAEL: Fulmer, England, Mar. 27, 1942. Oxford.
YORK, SUSANNAH: London, Jan. 9, 1941. RADA.
YOUNG, ALAN (Angus): North Shield, England, Nov. 19, 1919.
YOUNG, BURT: Queens, NY, Apr. 30, 1940.
YOUNG, CHRIS: Chambersburg, PA, Apr. 28, 1971.
YOUNG, LORETTA (Gretchen): Salt Lake City, UT, Jan. 6, 1912. Immaculate Heart College.
YOUNG, SEAN: Louisville, KY, Nov. 20, 1959. Interlochen.
YULIN, HARRIS: Los Angeles, Nov. 5, 1937.
ZACHARIAS, ANN: Stockholm, Sweden, Sweden, 1956.
ZADORA, PIA: Hoboken, NJ, 1954.
ZELLWEGER, RENEE: Katy, TX, Apr. 25, 1969.
ZERBE, ANTHONY: Long Beach, CA, May 20, 1939.
ZETA-JONES, CATHERINE: Swansea, Wales, Sept. 25, 1969.
ZIMBALIST, EFREM, JR.: NYC, Nov.30, 1918. Yale.
ZUNIGA, DAPHNE: Berkeley, CA, Oct. 28, 1963. UCLA.

Catherine Zeta-Jones

OBITUARIES - 1999

REX ALLEN, 77, Arizona-born cowboy star died on Dec. 17, 1999 after being accidentally run over in his driveway at his home in Tucson, AZ. He made his debut in 1949 in *The Arizona Cowboy* and continued to appear in some twenty Republic westerns including *Under Mexicali Stars, Hills of Oklahoma, The Old Overland Trail, Down Laredo Way,* and *South Pacific Senorita.* He also served as narrator of such films as *The Incredible Journey* and *Charlotte's Web.* No reported survivors.

KIRK ALYN (John Fego, Jr.), 88, New Jersey-born actor who played comic book hero Superman in the Columbia serials *Superman* and *Atom Man vs. Superman,* died on March 14, 1999 in Woodlands, TX. His feature-length motion pictures included *Blackhawk, A Guy Named Joe, Call of the Rockies, Forty Thieves, G-Men vs. the Underworld, Little Miss Broadway, Daughter of Don Q,* and *Radar Patrol.* Survived by his daughter from his marriage to actress Virginia O'Brien, as well as two other children.

HOYT AXTON, 61, Oklahoma-born songwriter, actor and singer died at his home in Victor, MT, on Oct. 26, 1999, having recently suffered two heart attacks. The writer of such hits as "Heartbreak Hotel," "Joy to the World" and "The No No Song," he also acted in such movies as *Smoky* (1966), *The Black Stallion, Heart Like a Wheel, Gremlins,* and *Disorganized Crime.* He is survived by his wife and five children.

Ian Bannen

Hillary Brooke

IAN BANNEN, 71, Scottish screen, stage and theatre actor, who received an Oscar nomination for the 1965 film *The Flight of the Phoenix,* was killed on Nov. 3, 1999 in a car crash near Loch Ness, Scotland while on location for a film. His other film credits include *Private's Progress* (his 1956 debut), *A Tale of Two Cities* (1958), *Man in a Cocked Hat* (Carlton Browne of the F.O.), *Station Six Sahara, Psyche 59, Rotten to the Core, The Hill, Penelope, Sailor from Gibraltar, Lock Up Your Daughters!, Too Late the Hero, The Offence, The Mackintosh Man, Bite the Bullet, From Beyond the Grave, The Watcher in the Woods, Eye of the Needle, Night Crossing, Gandhi, Gorky Park, Hope and Glory, Crossing the Line (The Big Man), Damage, Braveheart,* and *Waking Ned Devine.* Survived by his wife.

LIONEL BART, 68, British song-writer who composed the score for the musical *Oliver!,* which was made into the 1968 Academy Award-winner for Best Picture, died of cancer on April 3, 1999 in London. His other credits include writing the title song for the James Bond film *From Russia With Love.* Survived by two sisters.

Dirk Bogarde

JOHN BERRY, 82, Bronx-born screen and stage director died on Nov. 29, 1999 at his home in Paris. After having directed such Hollywood movies as *Cross My Heart, Miss Susie Slagle's, Casbah, Tension,* and *He Ran All the Way,* he moved to Europe to avoid the blacklist. There he directed such movies as *C'est Arrive a Paris* and *The Great Lover* (Don Juan) then returned to American filmmaking with such pictures as *Maya, Claudine, Thieves,* and *The Bad News Bears Go to Japan.* His final movie, *Boesman and Lena,* was released posthumously. He is survived by his wife, two sons and a daughter.

BILLY BENEDICT, 82, Oklahoma-born character player, best known for playing "Whitey" in the Bowery Boys comedies, died on Nov. 25, 1999 in Los Angeles. Among his many films are *Steamboat Round the Bend, Way Down East* (1935), *College Scandal, The Country Doctor, Libeled Lady, King of the Newsboys, Lucky Partners, My Little Chickadee, Adventures of Captain Marvel, The Talk of the Town, The Ox-Bow Incident, The Story of G.I. Joe, Road to Utopia, The Hucksters,* and *Hello Dolly!* No reported survivors.

DIRK BOGARDE (Derek Niven Van den Bogaerde), 78, one of England's leading motion picture actors during the 1950s and 60s in such films as *The Blue Lamp, Doctor in the House, Victim, I Could Go on Singing, The Servant,* and *Darling,* died of a heart attack at his London home on May 8, 1999. Following his 1947 debut in *Esther Waters* he was seen in such other pictures as *Quartet, So Long at the Fair, Appointment in London, The Sea Shall Not Have Them, The Sleeping Tiger, Doctor at Sea, Cast a Giant Shadow, The Spanish Gardener, Ill Met By Moonlight, Campbell's Kingdom, A Tale of Two Cities* (1958), *The Doctor's Dilemma, Libel, Song Without End, The Singer Not the Song, Damn the Defiant!* (*HMS Defiant*), *The Mind Benders, Agent 8 3/4 (Hot Enough for June), McGuire Go Home!* (*The High Bright Sun*), *King and Country, Accident, Our Mother's House, The Fixer, Justine, Oh! What a Lovely War, The Damned, Death in Venice, The Night Porter, Providence, A Bridge Too Far, Despair,* and *Daddy Nostalgia*. He had been knighted in 1992. No reported survivors.

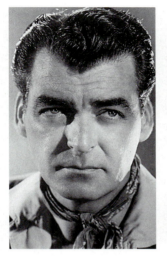

Rory Calhoun   Peggy Cass

BETTY BOX, 83, British producer died on Jan. 15, 1999 in London. Her credits include *Miranda, So Long at the Fair, Appointment with Venus* (*Island Rescue*), *Doctor in the House, Doctor at Sea, The Iron Petticoat, A Tale of Two Cities* (1958), *Doctor in Distress, No Love for Johnnie, Agent 8 3/4 (Hot Enough for June), Deadlier Than the Male,* and *Percy.* Survived by her husband, writer Peter Rogers.

ROBERT BRESSON, 98, French writer-director of such notable films as *Diary of a Country Priest* and *Pickpocket*, died a this home in Droué-sur-Drouette, France on Dec. 18, 1999. Among his other films are *Angels of the Streets* (his 1943 debut), *A Man Escaped, The Trial of Joan of Arc, Balthazar, Lancelot of the Lake, The Devil Probably,* and *Money.* Survived by his second wife.

HILLARY BROOKE (Beatrice Peterson), 84, Queens-born screen and television actress died on May 25, 1999 in Fall Brook, CA. Following her 1937 debut in *New Faces of 1937,* she was seen in such movies as *The Philadelphia Story, New Moon* (1940), *Dr. Jekyll and Mr. Hyde* (1941), *Mr. and Mrs. North, Born to Sing, To the Shores of Tripoli, Wake Island, Sherlock Holmes and the Voice of Terror, Lady in the Dark, And the Angels Sing, Jane Eyre* (1944), *Ministry of Fear, The Enchanted Cottage, Road to Utopia, Monsieur Beaucaire, The Gentleman Misbehaves, Big Town, The Fuller Brush Man, Africa Screams, Abbott and Costello Meet Captain Kidd, Never Wave at a WAC, Invaders from Mars* (1953), and *The Man Who Knew Too Much* (1956). She is survived by a son, a stepdaughter, a brother, 17 grandchildren, and 11 great-grandchildren.

VANESSA BROWN (Smylia Brind), 71, Vienna-born American actress died of cancer on May 21, 1999 in Los Angeles, CA. She was seen in such motion pictures as *Margie, The Late George Apley, Mother Wore Tights, The Ghost and Mrs. Muir, The Foxes of Harrow, The Heiress, Tarzan and the Slave Girl, The Bad and the Beautiful, Rosie!,* and *Bless the Beasts and Children.* Survived by her son and a daughter.

RORY CALHOUN (Francis Timothy Durgin), 76, Los Angeles-born screen and television actor died on April 28, 1999 in Burbank, CA, where he was being treated for diabetes and emphysema. Having made his movie debut in 1944, billed as "Frank McCown," in *Something for the Boys,* he became "Rory Calhoun" in 1947 and thereafter was seen in such titles as *The Red House, That Hagen Girl, Massacre River, A Ticket to Tomahawk, I'd Climb the Highest Mountain, Meet Me After the Show, With a Song in My Heart, The Silver Whip, How to Marry a Millionaire, River of No Return, A Bullet is Waiting, Four Guns to the Border, The Looters, The Treasure of Pancho Villa, The Spoilers* (1956), *Flight to Hong Kong, Apache Territory, The Colossus of Rhodes, Young Fury, Apache Uprising, Night of the Lepus, Won Ton Ton the Dog Who Saved Hollywood, The Main Event, Motel Hell, Angel,* and *Pure Country.* Survived by four daughters.

CANDY CANDIDO (Jonathan Joseph Candido), 85, New Orleans-born actor died of natural causes on May 19, 1999 in Los Angeles. He was seen in such movies as *Sadie McKee, Roberta, The Cowboy from Brooklyn, Rhythm Parade, The Great Rupert,* and *The Plunderers of Painted Flats.* His voice, which could fluctuate between a deep bass and a high pitched squeak, was heard in such features as *Peter Pan, Sleeping Beauty, Robin Hood,* and *The Great Mouse Detective.*

Marguerite Chapman   Ellen Corby

ALLAN CARR, 62, motion picture and stage producer, died of liver cancer on June 29, 1999 at his home in Beverly Hills, CA. His film credits include *Survive!, Grease, Can't Stop the Music, Grease 2,* and *Where the Boys Are '84.* No reported survivors.

PEGGY CASS (Mary Margaret Cass), 74, Boston-born character actress, best known for her Tony Award-winning and Oscar-nominated portrayal of the frumpish secretary Agnes Gooch in *Auntie Mame,* died of heart failure on March 8, 1999 in New York City. Her other movies include *The Marrying Kind, Gidget Goes Hawaiian,* and *If It's Tuesday This Must Be Belgium.* On television she was well-known for appearing on such game shows as "Match Game" and "To Tell the Truth." Survived by her husband.

MARGUERITE CHAPMAN, 81, New York-born screen and television actress died on August 31, 1999 in Burbank, CA. Among her movie credits are *Charlie Chan at the Wax Museum, Navy Blues, Submarine Raider, Appointment in Berlin, Pardon My Past, Mr. Disrict Attorney, Coroner Creek, Kansas Raiders, Flight to Mars, Bloodhounds of Broadway, The Seven Year Itch,* and *The Amazing Transparent Man.* No reported survivors.

PIERRE CLEMENTI, 57, French motion picture actor died of liver cancer in Paris on Dec. 27, 1999. Among his credits are *The Leopard, Belle Du Jour, Benjamin, The Milky Way* (1969), *The Conformist, Steppenwolf, L'Amour des Femmes, Le Pont du Nord, Quartet, Exposed,* and *Hideous Kinky.* No reported survivors.

IRON EYES CODY, 94, American Indian character actor died on January 4, 1999 at his home in Los Angeles. His many films include *The Rainbow Trail, Texas Pioneers, Rose Marie* (1936), *Union Pacific, Green Hell, Ride 'em Cowboy, Bowery Buckaroos, The Paleface, Blood on the Moon, The Cowboy and the Indians, Broken Arrow, Sitting Bull, The Great Sioux Massacre,* and *El Condor.* He was perhaps most widely known for his appearance in an early 1970s "Keep America Beautiful" commerical promoting Earth Day in which he shed a tear after seeing garbage dumped on the landscape. Survived by a son, three grandchildren, and a niece.

ELLEN CORBY (Ellen Hansen), 87, Wisconsin-born screen, stage and television actress who earned an Oscar nomination for *I Remember Mama* and later became well-known for playing the Grandmother on the long-running series "The Waltons," died on April 14, 1999 in Woodland Hills, CA. Following her debut in 1946 in *The Dark Corner* she was seen in such motion pictures as *It's a Wonderful Life, Till the End of Time, Cuban Pete, The Spiral Staircase, Born to Kill, Forever Amber, They Won't Believe Me, Fighting Father Dunne, The Noose Hangs High, Little Women* (1949), *Mighty Joe Young, Madame Bovary, The Gunfighter, Caged, Peggy, Harriet Craig, Goodbye My Fancy, The Mating Season, Angels in the Outfield* (1951), *On Moonlight Bay, Fearless Fagan, Shane, About Mrs. Leslie, Sabrina* (1954), *Susan Slept Here, Night Passage, Macabre, Vertigo, Visit to a Small Planet, Pocketful of Miracles, Hush...Hush Sweet Charlotte, The Family Jewels,* and *The Gnome-Mobile.* No reported survivors.

Charles Crichton

Quentin Crisp

CHARLES CRICHTON, 89, British director who helmed the Ealing Studios classics *The Lavender Hill Mob* and *The Titfield Thunderbolt,* and later received a pair of Oscar nominations for directing and co-scripting *A Fish Called Wanda,* died on Sept. 14, 1999 in London. His other credits as director include *Hue and Cry, Against the Wind, Dance Hall, Love Lottery, The Man in the Sky, Law and Disorder, The Battle of the Sexes,* and *The Third Secret.* Survived by his wife and two sons from a previous marriage.

QUENTIN CRISP (Denis Pratt), 90, British author whose book "The Naked Civil Servant" documented his life as an openly gay man in London, died in Manchester, England on Nov. 21, 1999 while preparing his latest one-man show. He was also seen in such movies as *The Bride, Resident Alien, Orlando,* and *To Wong Foo Thanks for Everything Julie Newmar.* No reported survivors.

EDWARD DMYTRYK, 90, Canadian-born director of such American films as *Crossfire,* for which he received an Oscar nomination, *The Caine Mutiny* and *Raintree County,* died on July 1, 1999 at his home in Encino, CA. Starting with *The Hawk* in 1935 he went on to directed such other pictures as *The Devil Commands, Sweetheart of the Campus, Secrets of the Lone Wolf, Hitler's Children, Behind the Rising Sun, Tender Comrade, Murder My Sweet, Back to Bataan, Till the End of Time, The Juggler, Broken Lance, The End of the Affair* (1954), *Soldier of Fortune, The Left Hand of God, The Mountain, The Young Lions, Warlock* (1959), *A Walk on the Wild Side, The Carpetbaggers, Where Love Has Gone, Mirage, Alvarez Kelly, Anzio,* and *Bluebeard* (1972). As one of the most famous of the blacklist victims of the Communist Witch Hunts, he became one of the Hollywood Ten, but garnered notoriety as the only member who recanted and named names. Survived by his wife, actress Jean Porter, two sons, two daughters, and three grandchildren.

Anne Francine

Huntz Hall

FAITH DOMERGUE, 74, New Orleans-born screen actress discovered by Howard Hughes, died on April 4, 1999 in Santa Barbara, CA, of cancer. Among her movies were *Young Widow, Vendetta, Where Danger Lives, Duel at Silver Creek, The Atomic Man, The Great Sioux Uprising, Cult of the Cobra, It Came from Beneath the Sea, This Island Earth,* and *Track of Thunder.*

ROBERT DOUGLAS (Robert Douglas Finlayson), 89, British character actor died on Jan. 11, 1999 at his home in Encinitas, CA. Following his 1936 debut in *Over the Moon* he was seen in such movies as *The Decision of Christopher Blake, The Adventures of Don Juan, The Fountainhead, Kim At Sword's Point, Ivanhoe, Target Unknown, The Desert Rats, The Prisoner of Zenda* (1952), *Fair Wind to Java, King Richard and the Crusaders, The Virgin Queen, The Scarlet Coat,* and *The Young Philadelphians.* He also directed the 1964 feature *Night Train to Paris.* Survived by his son and a daughter.

ROSS ELLIOTT, 82, New York City-born movie and television character actor died of cancer on Aug. 12, 1999 in Los Angeles. Among his films are *Woman on the Run, Chinatown at Midnight, I Can Get It for You Wholesale, Dragnet, Tarantula, D-Day the Sixth of June, Monster on Campus, Tammy Tell Me True, Kelly's Heroes,* and *The Towering Inferno.* He is survived by his wife and a sister.

GEORGE "CHET" FORREST (George Forrest Chichester, Jr.), 84, Brooklyn-born songwriter who co-wrote such tunes as "Stranger in Paradise" and "The Donkey Serenade" died in Miami on Oct. 10, 1999. Collaborating with Robert Wright he wrote the score for the Broadway musical *Kismet* among others and songs/lyrics for such films as *Maytime, Sweethearts, Let Freedom Ring, Broadway Serenade, Balalaika, Music in*

My Heart (earning an Oscar nomination for the song "It's a Blue World"), *Blondie Goes Latin, Flying With Music* (Oscar nomination for "Pennies for Peppino"), *Swing Out the Blues,* and *Everything I Have is Yours.* No reported survivors.

HELEN FORREST (Helen Fogel), 82, Atlantic City-born singer of the 1940s, best known for the tune "I Had the Craziest Dream," died of congestive heart failure on July 11, 1999 in Los Angeles. As vocalist with the Harry James orchestra she was seen in such movies as *Private Buckaroo, Bathing Beauty* and *Best Foot Forward.* Survived by a son.

ANNE FRANCINE, 82, Philadelphia born actress-singer died in London, CT, on Dec. 3, 1999. Among her movie credits are *Juliet of the Spirits, Stand Up and Be Counted, Savages,* and *Crocodile Dundee.* No immediate survivors.

ALLEN FUNT, 84, New York City-born television host and creator of "Candid Camera" died at his home in Pebble Beach, CA, of complications from a stroke he had suffered in 1993. In addition to directing, producing, editing and creating the hidden camera series which had spawned from its radio counterpart, "Candid Microphone," he directed-wrote-produced the feature spinoffs *What Do You Say to a Naked Lady?* and *Money Talks.* Survived by his son Peter, who co-hosted some "Candid Camera" specials with him; four other children and four grandchildren.

Madeline Kahn

ERNEST GOLD, 77, Vienna-born composer, best known for his Academy Award-winning score for *Exodus,* died from complications from a stroke on March 17, 1999. He received additional Oscar nominations for *On the Beach, It's a Mad Mad Mad Mad World,* and *The Secret of Santa Vittoria.* His other scores include *The Pride and the Passion, Inherit the Wind, Judgment at Nuremberg, A Child is Waiting, Ship of Fools, Fun with Dick and Jane,* and *Tom Horn.* Survived by his wife, two daughters, a son, and a stepson.

JAMES GOLDSTONE, 68, Los Angeles-born screen and television director died of cancer on Nov. 5, 1999 at his home in Shaftsbury, VT. His theatrical features include *Winning, Red Sky at Morning, They Only Kill Their Masters, The Gang That Couldn't Shoot Straight, Swashbuckler, Rollercoaster,* and *When Time Ran Out.* On television he won an Emmy Award for the movie *Kent State.* Survived by his wife, his mother, a sister, two sons, a daughter, and six grandchildren.

Garson Kanin

DeForest Kelley

SANDRA GOULD, 73, Brooklyn-born character actress, best remembered for taking over the role of "Gladys Kravitz" from Alice Pearce on the series "Bewitched," died of a stroke in Burbank, CA, on July 20, 1999. Among her movie credits were *Romance on the High Seas, It's a Great Feeling, The Ghost and Mr. Chicken,* and *The Barefoot Executive.* Survived by a son.

NANCY GUILD, 73, died on Aug. 16, 1999 at her home in East Hampton, Long Island, NY, after a long battle with emphysema. She was seen in such movies as *Somewhere in the Night, The Brasher Doubloon,* and *Black Magic,* before retiring from acting and becoming a writer. She is survived by three daughters, and three granddaughters.

TITO GUIZAR (Federico Arturo Guizar Tolentino), 91, Mexican singer-actor died in San Antonio, TX, on Dec. 24, 1999 of unspecified causes. After making his name as a popular nightclub singer he was seen in such films as *Big Broadcast of 1938, Tropic Holiday, St. Louis Blues* (1939), *Blondie Goes Latin, Brazil* (1944), *Mexicana,* and *Thrill of Brazil.* Survived by a son, two daughters and five grandchildren.

HUNTZ HALL (Henry Hall), 78, Boston-born actor-comedian, a leading member of the group that was variously known as the Dead End Kids, the East Side Kids, and the Bowery Boys, died of cardiac disease on Jan. 30, 1999 in Los Angeles. He made his motion picture debut in 1937, repeating his stage role from *Dead End.* Afterwards he was seen in such movies as *Crime School, Angels with Dirty Faces, Hell's Kitchen, They Made Me a Criminal, Invisible Stripes, East Side Kids, Spooks Run Wild, Mr. Wise Guy, 'Neath Brooklyn Bridge, Private Buckaroo, Mr. Muggs Steps Out, Docks of New York, Mr. Hex, Bowery Bombshell, Jinx Money, Master Minds, Bowery Battalion, Hold That Line, Jalopy, Dig That Uranium, Hold That Hypnotist, Gentle Giant, The Phynx, Herbie Rides Again, Won Ton Ton the Dog Who Saved Hollywood, Valentino* (1977), and *The Escape Artist.* Survived by a son and a grandson.

ED HERLIHY, 89, Boston-born radio and television announcer (most prominently for Kraft Foods), died at his Manhattan home on Jan. 30, 1999. He was heard or seen in such movies as *The King of Comedy, Zelig, Pee-wee's Big Adventure, Hannah and Her Sisters,* and *Radio Days.* Survived by his wife, two daughters, two sons, five grandchildren, and one great-grandchild.

AL HIRT (Alois Maxwell Hirt), 76, world famous New Orleans-born Dixieland jazz trumpeter died at his home in New Orleans on Apr. 27, 1999, having suffered from liver ailments. He was seen in such movies as *Rome Adventure* and *Number One.* Survivors include his wife and six children.

BRION JAMES, 54, California-born screen and television character actor, who specialized in villain roles, died at his Malibu, CA, home on Aug. 7, 1999 after suffering a heart attack. He was seen in such movies as *Corvette Summer, The Postman Always Rings Twice* (1981), *Southern Comfort, Blade Runner, 48 HRS, Silverado, Enemy Mine, Red Heat, Tango & Cash, The Horror Show, The Player, Cabin Boy,* and *The Fifth Element.* Survived by two brothers.

Richard Kiley   Desmond Llewelyn

HENRY JONES, 86, Philadelphia-born screen, stage and television character actor died in Los Angeles on May 17, 1999 from injuries suffered in a fall at his Santa Monica home. Among his many movies are *Taxi* (1951), *The Bad Seed* (repeating his Broadway role as the handyman), *The Girl He Left Behind, The Girl Can't Help It, Will Success Spoil Rock Hunter?, 3:10 to Yuma, Vertigo, Cash McCall, Angel Baby, Stay Away Joe, Support Your Local Sheriff!, Rascal, Butch Cassidy and the Sundance Kid, Dirty Dingus Magee, Skin Game, Napoleon and Samantha, Pete 'n' Tillie, Tom Sawyer* (1973), *Nine to Five, Deathtrap, Dick Tracy, Arachnophobia,* and *The Grifters.* Survived by his daughter and son.

MADELINE KAHN, 57, Boston-born screen, stage and television actress, who earned Oscar nominations for her roles as "Trixie Delight" in *Paper Moon* and as "Lilly von Shtupp" in *Blazing Saddles,* died of ovarian cancer on Dec. 3, 1999 in Manhattan. She made her film debut in 1972 in *What's Up Doc?,* after which she appeared in such motion pictures as *Young Frankenstein, At Long Last Love, The Adventures of Sherlock Holmes' Smarter Brother, Won Ton Ton the Dog Who Saved Hollywood, High Anxiety, The Cheap Detective, The Muppet Movie, Simon, Happy Birthday Gemini, History of the World Part 1, Yellowbeard, City Heat, Clue, Betsy's Wedding, Mixed Nuts, Nixon,* and her last, *Judy Berlin,* released posthumously. She is survived by her husband and her brother.

GARSON KANIN, 86, Rochester-born screen and stage director-writer died on March 13, 1999 at his Manhattan home, following a lengthy illness. His film credits include, as director, *The Great Man Votes, Bachelor Mother, Tom Dick & Harry, My Favorite Wife,* and *They Knew What They Wanted;* as co-director: *The True Glory,* a documentary for which he shared an Academy Award with Carol Reed; as director-writer: *Where It's At* and *Some Kind of a Nut;* and as writer *The Rat Race* (from his play) and *It Should Happen to You;* plus the following co-scripted with his wife of 43 years, Ruth Gordon (who died in 1985): *A Double Life* (Oscar nomination), *Adam's Rib* (Oscar nomination), *The Marrying Kind,* and *Pat and Mike* (Oscar nomination). His best known play, *Born Yesterday,* was adapted for the screen in 1950 and 1993. He is survived by his second wife, actress Marian Seldes, and his sister.

DeFOREST KELLEY, 79, Atlanta-born screen and television actor, best known for his role as "Dr. Leonard "Bones" McCoy" on the television series "Star Trek" and in six *Star Trek* feature films, died of unspecified causes on June 11, 1999 in Los Angeles. His other films include *Fear in the Night, Variety Girl, The Men, House of Bamboo, The Man in the Gray Flannel Suit, Gunfight at the O.K. Corral, Raintree County, The Law and Jake Wade, Warlock, Where Love Has Gone, Marriage on the Rocks,* and *Night of the Lepus.* Survived by his wife of fifty-four years.

RICHARD KILEY, 76, Chicago-born screen, stage and television actor-singer, best remembered for his Tony Award-winning performance as Don Quixote in *Man of La Mancha,* died of a blood disorder on March 5, 1999 in Middletown, NY. He was seen in such motion pictures as *The Mob, Eight Iron Men, Pick-Up on South Street, Blackboard Jungle, The Phenix City Story, Pendulum, The Little Prince, Looking for Mr. Goodbar, Endless Love,* and *Patch Adams.* Survived by his wife, six children, twelve grandchildren, and one great-grand child.

MABEL KING, 66, Charleston-born screen, stage and television character actress and singer, best known for playing the Wicked Witch of the West on Broadway and in the 1978 film version of *The Wiz,* died on Nov. 9, 1999 in Woodland Hills, CA, after a long illness and complications from diabetes. Among her other movies were *The Bingo Long Traveling All-Stars and Motor Kings, The Jerk, The Gong Show Movie,* and *Scrooged.* On television she starred in the series "What's Happening!" Survived by her mother and a sister.

STANLEY KUBRICK, 70, Bronx-born motion picture director-writer-producer, one of the most original and acclaimed of all filmmakers, died on March 7, 1999 at his home in Hertfordshire, England. His thirteen features were *Fear and Desire, Killer's Kiss, The Killing, Paths of Glory, Spartacus, Lolita, Dr. Strangelove: Or How I Learned to Stop Worrying and Love the Bomb* (Oscar nominations as director, writer, producer), *2001: A Space Odyssey* (Oscar nominations as director and writer; Academy Award for Best Special Visual Effects), *A Clockwork Orange* (Oscar nominations as director, writer, producer), *Barry Lyndon* (Oscar nominations as director, writer, producer), *The Shining, Full Metal Jacket* (Oscar nomination as writer), and his last, *Eyes Wide Shut,* released posthumously. Survived by his fourth wife and three daughters.

BETHEL LESLIE, 70, New York City-born screen, stage and television actress, died of cancer on Nov. 28, 1999 at her Manhattan home. Her film credits include *Captain Newman M.D., A Rage to Live, The Molly Maguires, Old Boyfriends, Ironweed,* and *Message in a Bottle.* She is survived by a daughter, a brother, and two grandchildren.

DESMOND LLEWELYN, 85, British character actor, best known for playing "Q," the gadgetry expert, in 17 of the James Bond movies, died on Dec. 19, 1999 from injuries sustained in a car accident. He had been driving in East Sussex, south of London, on his way back from a book signing when his car collided head-on with another. He made his first appearance as "Q" in *From Russia with Love* in 1964 while his last, *The World is Not Enough,* was currently in theatres at the time of his death. His other credits included small roles in such movies as *Knights of the Round Table, A Night to Remember, Only Two Can Play,* and *Chitty Chitty Bang Bang.* He is survived by his wife and two sons.

VICTOR MATURE, 86, Kentucky-born motion picture actor, best known for his portrayal of the Biblical strongman Samson in the 1949 epic *Samson and Delilah*, died of cancer on Aug. 4, 1999 in Rancho Santa Fe, CA. Cashing in on his muscular physique, he became a star with the Prehistoric adventure *One Million B.C.*, thereafter appearing in such movies as *No No Nanette*, *I Wake Up Screaming*, *The Shanghai Gesture*, *Song of the Islands*, *My Gal Sal*, *Seven Days Leave*, *My Darling Clementine* (as Doc Holliday), *Kiss of Death* (1947), *Cry of the City*, *Red Hot and Blue*, *Wabash Avenue*, *Stella* (1950), *The Last Vegas Story*, *Androcles and the Lion*, *Something for the Birds*, *Million Dollar Mermaid*, *Affair With a Stranger*, *The Robe*, *Veils of Baghdad*, *Demetrius and the Gladiators*, *The Egyptian*, *Chief Crazy Horse*, *Violent Saturday*, *Zarak*, *The Big Circus*, *Hannibal*, *The Tartars*, *After the Fox*, *Head*, *Every Little Crook and Nanny*, and *Won Ton Ton the Dog Who Saved Hollywood*. Survivors include his fifth wife and a daughter.

Stanley Kubrick

DONAL McCANN, 56, one of Ireland's foremost stage actors, died in Dublin of cancer of the pancreas on July 17, 1999. Among his motion picture credits were *The Fighting Prince of Donegal*, *Hedda Gabler*, *Out of Africa*, *Cal*, *The Dead* (his best-known film role, as Gabriel Conroy, in this adaptation of the James Joyce story), *The Miracle* (1991), and *Illuminata*, released posthumously.

GRACE McDONALD, 81, Boston-born dancer-actress died of pneumonia in Scottsdale, AZ on Oct. 30, 1999. She started as a dancer in an act with her brother, Ray McDonald (who died in 1959), before appearing in such motion pictures as *Dancing on a Dime*, *Give Out Sisters*, *It Ain't Hay*, *Always a Bridesmaid*, *Murder in the Blue Room*, *Follow the Boys*, *See My Lawyer*, and *Honeymoon Ahead*. Survived by her husband, three sons, and seven grandchildren.

BUZZ MILLER (Vernal Miller), 75, Arizona-born dancer, best known for appearing with Carol Haney and Peter Gennaro in the classic "Steam Heat" number in the original Broadway version of *The Pajama Game* as well as the 1957 film adaptation, died of emphysema on Feb. 23, 1999 at his home in Manhattan. He also danced in such movies as *On the Riviera*, *There's No Business Like Show Business*, and *Anything Goes* (1956). Survived by two brothers and a sister.

GUY MITCHELL (Al Cernick), 72, Detroit-born singer-actor died from complications following surgery in Las Vegas, NV on July 1, 1999. In addition to recording such hits as "Singing the Blues" and "My Heart Cries for You" he appeared in such movies as *Those Redheads from Seattle*, *Red Garters*, and *The Wild Westerners*. He is survived by his wife, two sons, and five grandchildren.

CLAYTON MOORE (Jack Carlton Moore), 85, Chicago-born screen and television actor, who entered Western lore by portraying the Lone Ranger on television from 1949 to 1957, died on Dec. 28, 1999 in West Hills, CA, after suffering a heart attack at his home in Calabasas. He also played the Ranger in two theatrical features, *The Lone Ranger* and *The Lone Ranger and the Lost City of Gold*, in addition to appearing in such serials as *The Perils of Nyoka*, *G-Men Never Forget*, and *The Ghost of Zorro*. Survived by his daughter, and his fourth wife.

Victor Mature   Anthony Newley

ANTHONY NEWLEY, 67, London-born screen, stage and television actor-singer-writer-director-producer-composer, died of cancer on Apr. 14, 1999 at his home in Jensen Beach, FL. As a teenager he made his debut in the serial *The Adventures of Dusty Bates*, and continued his acting career in such films as *Oliver Twist* (as the Artful Dodger), *Above Us the Waves*, *Cockleshell Heroes*, *X the Unknown*, *Fire Down Below*, *How to Murder a Rich Uncle*, *Idol on Parade*, *Killers of Kilimanjaro*, *Jazzboat*, *The Small World of Sammy Lee*, *Doctor Dolittle* (1967), *Sweet November*, *Can Hieronymus Merkin Ever Forget Mercy Humppe and Find True Happiness?* (which he also directed, wrote, produced, and collaborated on songs for), *Mr. Quilp* (also songs), and *The Garbage Pail Kids Movie*. His most notable achievements were serving as star, director, co-writer and song writer (with Leslie Bricusse) on the stage musicals *Stop the World— I Want to Get Off* (for which he composed what would become his theme song, "What Kind of Fool Am I?") and *The Roar of the Greasepaint— Smell of the Crowd* (where he wrote and introduced "Who Can I Turn To?"). With Bricusse he received Oscar nominations for collaborating on the songs "Goldfinger" (from the film of the same name) and "The Candy Man" (from *Willy Wonka and the Chocolate Factory*). All four of his marriages (including one to actress Joan Collins) ended in divorce. He is survived by his mother and four children.

BERNADETTE O'FARRELL, 75, Irish screen and television actress, best known for portraying Maid Marian on the 1950s series "The Adventures of Robin Hood," died in September 1999 in England of unspecified causes. She was seen in such movies as *The Happiest Days of Your Life, Lady Godiva Rides Again, The Story of Gilbert and Sullivan,* and *The Bridal Path,* many of which were directed by her husband (1950-97), Frank Launder (who died in 1997). She retired in 1959. Survived by two daughters.

BOB PECK, 53, British screen and stage actor, whose most prominent movie role was as the game warden in the 1993 blockbuster hit *Jurassic Park,* died of cancer in London on Apr. 4, 1999. Among his other film credits were *The Kitchen Toto, On the Black Hill, Slipstream,* and *Lord of the Flies* (1990). Survived by his wife, two daughters, and a son.

Oliver Reed

ABRAHAM POLONSKY, 88, New York City-born director-writer died at his home in Beverly Hills on Oct. 26, 1999. He scripted such movies as *Golden Earrings, Body and Soul* (1947), *I Can Get It for Your Wholesale,* and *Madigan.* He made his debut as director-screenwriter on the 1949 film *Force of Evil* but did not direct another picture for twenty years after being blacklisted during the McCarthy era. He returned to direct and write *Tell Them Willie Boy is Here* and *Romance of a Horse Thief.* Polonsky also co-wrote the script for *Odds Against Tomorrow* under the pseudonymn "John O. Killens." He is survived by his son, a daughter, and two granddaughters.

MARIO PUZO, 78, Manhattan-born novelist-screenwriter who penned the best seller *The Godfather,* which became the basis for the classic 1972 film of the same name, died of heart failure at his home in Bay Shore, NY, on July 2, 1999. He collaborated with Francis Ford Coppola on the screenplays for all three *Godfather* movies winning Academy Awards for *The Godfather* and *The Godfather Part II.* He was also credited on the scripts of such movies as *Earthquake, Superman,* and *The Cotton Club.* Survivors include his companion of many years, five children, nine grandchildren, his sister, and his brother.

IRVING RAPPER, 101, London-born director, perhaps best known for helming the 1942 Bette Davis classic *Now, Voyager,* died on Dec. 20, 1999 at the Motion Picture and Television Fund home in Los Angeles. Among his other credits are *One Foot in Heaven, The Gay Sisters, The Adventures of Mark Twain, Rhapsody in Blue, The Corn is Green, Deception, The Voice of the Turtle, The Glass Menagerie* (1950), *Another Man's Poison, Forever Female, The Brave One, Marjorie Morningstar, The Miracle* (1959), *The Christine Jorgensen Story,* and *Born Again.* No reported survivors.

OLIVER REED, 61, London-born screen and television actor, who starred in such motion pictures as the Oscar-winning *Oliver!* (as Bill Sykes) and *Women in Love,* died of a heart attack on May 2, 1999 in Valetta on the island of Malta where he was filming a role in *Gladiator.* Starting as an extra and bit player in such movies as *Beat Girl, The League of Gentlemen,* and *The Angry Silence,* he had his breathrough as a leading man with *The Curse of the Werewolf* and *The System (The Girl-Getters).* He went on to appear in such movies as *The Trap* (1966), *The Shuttered Room, The Jokers, I'll Never Forget What's 'is Name, The Assassination Bureau, Hannibal Brooks, The Lady in the Car with Glasses and a Gun, The Hunting Party, Z.P.G., The Devils, The Triple Echo, The Three Musketeers* (1974; as Athos), *The Four Musketeers, Tommy, Royal Flash, The Great Scout and Cathouse Thursday, Burnt Offerings, The Big Sleep* (1978), *The Class of Miss MacMichael, The Brood, Condorman, Lion of the Desert, Two of a Kind, Castaway, Gor,* and *Funny Bones.* Survived by his wife and a daughter.

Bert Remsen   Lee Richardson

BERT REMSEN, 74, Long Island-born screen, stage and television character actor who appeared in many of director Robert Altman's movies including *Brewster McCloud, Thieves Like Us, Nashville,* and *A Wedding,* died of natural causes at his home in the San Fernando Valley on Apr. 22, 1999. His many other movies include *Pork Chop Hill, Baby Blue Marine, The Rose, Carny, Inside Moves, Looking to Get Out, Places in the Heart, Code of Silence, South of Reno, Miss Firecracker, Daddy's Dyin'... Who's Got the Will?, Dick Tracy, Only the Lonely, The Bodyguard, Jack the Bear, Maverick,* and *Forces of Nature.* Survived by his wife, two daughters, a brother, and two grandchildren.

LEE RICHARDSON, 73, Chicago-born screen, stage, and television character actor, died of cardiac arrest after complications from a perforated ulcer, on Oct. 2, 1999 at his Manhattan home. His movies include *Prince of the City, Daniel, Prizzi's Honor, Sweet Lorraine, Q & A,* and *A Stranger Among Us.* Survived by his daughter, a son, and a sister.

George C. Scott

Buddy Rogers

Ruth Roman

GEORGE C. SCOTT, 71, Virginia-born screen, stage and television actor, whose towering performance in the title role of *Patton* brought him an Academy Award, which he, in turn, refused, died of a ruptured abdominal aortic aneurysm on Sept. 22, 1999 in Westlake Village, CA. Having made a name for himself on the New York stage as one of the most exciting young actors of the 1950s, he came to Hollywood to make his debut there in 1959 in *The Hanging Tree*. That same year he earned his first Osar nomination for *Anatomy of a Murder*. Two years later he made history by being the first actor on record to refuse his nomination, for his work in *The Hustler*. In 1971 he received his fourth and final nomination for *The Hospital*. His other motion pictures are *The List of Adrian Messenger, Dr. Strangelove: Or How I Learned to Stop Worrying and Love the Bomb, The Yellow Rolls-Royce, The Bible, Not With My Wife You Don't, The Flim-Flam Man, Petulia, They Might Be Giants, The Last Run, The New Centurions, Rage* (which he also directed), *Oklahoma Crude, The Day of the Dolphin, Bank Shot, The Savage is Loose* (also director, producer), *The Hindenburg, Crossed Swords, Islands in the Stream, Movie Movie, Hardcore, The Changeling, The Formula, Taps, Firestarter, The Exorcist III, The Rescuers Down Under* (voice), *Malice, Angus,* and *Gloria* (1999). He is survived by his wife, actress Trish Van Devere, with whom he had acted in several films; a daughter from his first marriage; a son and a daughter from his second marriage; and two sons (one of whom is actor Campbell Scott) from his two marriages to actress Colleen Dewhurst.

CHARLES "BUDDY" ROGERS, 94, Kansas-born screen actor who starred in the first film to win the Academy Award for Best Picture, *Wings*, died at his home in Rancho Mirage, CA, on Apr. 21, 1999. He was launched by Paramount Pictures as the lead in the 1926 release *Fascinating Youth*, and went on to appear in such features as *So's Your Old Man, Abie's Irish Rose* (1928), *Varsity, Red Lips, Close Harmony, Half-Way to Heaven, Heads Up, Paramount on Parade, Safety in Numbers, Follow Thru, Young Eagles, Along Came Youth, This Reckless Age, Dance Band, Old Man Rhythm, This Way Please, Mexican Spitfire's Baby, Mexican Spitfire at Sea,* and his last, *The Parson and the Outlaw,* in 1957. He appeared opposite Mary Pickford in the 1927 film *My Best Girl* and the two were married ten years later, remaining wed until Pickford's death in 1979. In 1986 he was given the Jean Hersholt Humanitarian Award. Survived by his second wife.

RUTH ROMAN, 75, Massachusetts-born screen and television actress, died in her sleep on Sept. 9, 1999 at her home in Laguna Beach, CA. Her films include *Stage Door Canteen* (her debut, in 1943), *Since You Went Away, The Affairs of Susan, Incendiary Blonde, A Night in Casablanca, The Big Clock, Night Has a Thousand Eyes, Good Sam, The Window, Champion, Beyond the Forest, Always Leave Them Laughing, Colt .45, Three Secrets, Dallas, Strangers on a Train, Mara Maru, Young Man with Ideas, Blowing Wild, Down Three Dark Streets, The Far Country, The Bottom of the Bottle, Joe Macbeth, Look in Any Window, Love Has Many Faces, The Baby, The Killing Kind,* and *Day of the Animals.* Survived by a son.

NORMAN ROSSINGTON, 70, British character actor, probably best known to American audiences for portraying the Beatles' manager "Norm" in the 1964 classic *A Hard Day's Night*, died of cancer on May 21, 1999 in Manchester, England. His other film credits include *Saint Joan, A Night to Remember, Carry on Sergeant, The League of Gentlemen, Saturday Night and Sunday Morning, No Love for Johnnie, Lawrence of Arabia, The Longest Day, Those Magnificent Men in Their Flying Machines, The Wrong Box, Double Trouble* (1967), *The Charge of the Light Brigade* (1968), *Man in the Wilderness, Young Winston, The Krays,* and *Let Him Have It.* He is survived by his wife.

STEFAN SCHNABEL, 87, Berlin-born screen, stage, radio and television character player, died of a heart attack on March 11, 1999 at his home in Rogaro, Italy. Perhaps best known for his role of "Dr. Stephen Jackson" on the long-running soap opera "Guiding Light," he was also seen in such movies as *Houdini, The Iron Curtain, Diplomatic Courier, The Counterfeit Traitor, Two Weeks in Another Town, Rampage, Lovesick,* and *Anna.* Survived by his wife, two sons, a daughter, and three grandchildren.

Sylvia Sidney

DOUGLAS SEALE, 85, British actor-director-producer died in Manhattan on June 13, 1999. Outside of his varied work on stage including *Noises Off*, for which he received a Tony nomination, his movie credits included *Amadeus, Heaven Help Us, Ernest Saves Christmas* (as Santa Claus), *Mr. Destiny, Almost an Angel, Aladdin* (as the voice of the Sultan), and *Palookaville.* Survived by two sons, and two grandchildren.

SAM SHAW, 87, Manhattan-born photojournalist and movie producer died on April 5, 1999 in Westwood, NJ. Best known for his famous photo of Marilyn Monroe standing over a subway grate with her skirt billowing around her, taken during the filming of *The Seven Year Itch*, he later produced such movies as *Paris Blues* and several John Cassavetes films including *Husbands, A Woman Under the Influence*, and *Gloria* (1980). Survivors include two daughters, seven grandchildren, and a great-grandchild.

RICHARD B. SHULL, 70, Illinois-born screen, stage and television character actor, died of a heart attack on Oct. 14, 1999 in Manhattan. He had been appearing in the Broadway production *Epic Proportions* at the time of his death. Among the movies in which he was seen were *The Anderson Tapes, Such Good Friends, Slither, Cockfighter, The Fortune, Hearts of the West, The Big Bus, Wholly Moses, Spring Break, Unfaithfully Yours, Splash, Garbo Talks, Housesitter, Trapped in Paradise*, and *Private Parts* (1997). He is survived by his fourth wife.

SYLVIA SIDNEY (Sophia Kossow), 88, Bronx-born screen, stage and television actress, who became a major presence in 1930s films ranging from *Street Scene* to *Dead End*, died of throat cancer on July 1, 1999 in Manhattan. Following a bit role in the 1927 film *Broadway Lights*, she became a star in 1931 with her performance in *City Streets* opposite Gary Cooper. Her other films thereafter included *Confessions of a Co-Ed, An American Tragedy, Ladies of the Big House, Merrily We Go to Hell, Madame Butterfly, Jennie Gerhardt, Good Dame, 30 Day Princess, Behold My Wife, Accent on Youth, Mary Burns—Fugitive, The Trail of the Lonesome Pine, Fury, Sabotage, You Only Live Once, You and Me* (1938), *...One Third of a Nation, The Wagons Roll at Night, Blood on the Sun, The Searching Wind, Les Miserables* (1952), *Violent Saturday, Summer Wishes Winter Dreams* (for which she received an Oscar nomination), *Hammett, Beetlejuice*, and *Mars Attacks!* Her three marriages (including those to publisher Bennett Cerf and actor Luther Adler) ended in divorce. No immediate survivors.

JOHN STEARS, 64, British special effects artist, who won Oscars for his work on *Thunderball* and *Star Wars*, died of a stroke on June 28, 1999 in Los Angeles. His other credits included *Dr. No, Goldfinger, Chitty Chitty Bang Bang, On Her Majesty's Secret Service*, and *FX*. Survived by his wife, two daughters, and three brothers.

DONALD STEWART, 69, Detroit-born screenwriter, who won an Academy Award for collaborating with Costa-Gavras on the script for *Missing*, died of a cancer on Apr. 28, 1999 at his Los Angeles home. Among his other credits were *Jackson County Jail, The Hunt for Red October*, and *Clear and Present Danger*. Survived by his wife, two sons, a daughter, and four grandchildren.

SHIRLEY STOLER, 69, Brooklyn-born screen, stage and television character actress, best remembered for playing the serial murderer in *The Honeymoon Killers* and the imposing concentration camp commandant in *Seven Beauties*, died of heart failure on Feb. 17, 1999 in Manhattan. Her other films include *The Deer Hunter, Sticky Fingers, Miami Blues*, and *Frankenhooker*. She is survived by two brothers, and a sister.

SUSAN STRASBERG, 60, Manhattan-born actress who became a star with her portrayal of Anne Frank in the original 1955 production of *The Diary of Anne Frank*, died of cancer at her home in Manhattan on Jan. 21, 1999. Following her 1955 film debut in *The Cobweb*, she was seen in such other movies as *Picnic, Stage Struck, Hemingway's Adventures of a Young Man, McGuire Go Home (The High Bright Sun), The Trip, Chubasco, Psych-Out, The Brotherhood, Rollercoaster, The Manitou, In Praise of Older Women, The Delta Force*, and *The Runnin' Kind*. She was the daughter of noted acting teacher Lee Strasberg and acting coach Paula Miller. She is survived by her daughter from her marriage to actor Christopher Jones, her brother, and two half-brothers.

MEL TORME, 73, Chicago-born singer-actor-songwriter who, in time, became one of the most noted jazz singers of his day, died of complications from a stroke at the Los Angeles Medical Center on June 5, 1999. As an actor he was seen in such movies as *Higher and Higher* (his debut, in 1944), *Janie Gets Married, Junior Miss, Good News, Words and Music, The Big Operator, Girls Town, Walk Like a Dragon, The Private Lives of Adam and Eve, A Man Called Adam*, and *The Naked Gun 2 1/2: The Smell of Fear*. His most famous composition as a songwriter was his collaboration with Robert Wells, "The Christmas Song" which became a hit for Nat King Cole. Survivors include his fourth wife, five children, and two stepchildren.

Susan Strasberg   Mel Torme

BOBS WATSON, 68, former child actor, who starred with Lionel Barrymore in the 1938 film *On Borrowed Time*, died of cancer on June 26, 1999 at his home in Laguna Beach, CA. His other films include *In Old Chicago, Kentucky, Boys' Town, Dr. Kildare's Crisis, Men of Boys' Town, The Bold and the Brave*, and *First to Fight*. Survived by his wife, three sons, a sister, and five brothers.

NORMAN WEXLER, 73, screenwriter, best known for penning *Serpico* (for which he received an Oscar nomination) and *Saturday Night Fever*, died of a heart attack on Aug. 23, 1999 in Washington, D.C. His other credits include *Joe* (Oscar nomination), *Mandingo, Staying Alive*, and *Raw Deal* (1986). Survived by his sister, and his two daughters.

ALBERT WHITLOCK, 84, London-born special effects artist, who won Academy Awards for his work on *Earthquake* and *The Hindenburg*, died in Santa Barbara, CA on Oct. 26, 1999 after a long illlness. He also worked on such movies as *The Birds, Marnie, Torn Curtain, The Sting, Bound for Glory, History of the World Part 1*, and *Greystoke: The Legend of Tarzan Lord of the Apes*. Survivors include his wife, two sons, and two grandsons.

SIR JOHN WOOLF, 86, British producer who won an Academy Award for the 1968 Best Picture winner *Oliver!*, died at his home in London on June 28, 1999. As the co-founder of Romulus Films, he was responsible for such movies as *The African Queen, Moulin Rouge, Beat the Devil, Richard III* (1956), and *Room at the Top*. Survived by his wife and his son.

INDEX

Battaglia, Eve, 206
Battersby, Bradley, 194
Bauchau, Patrick, 80
Bauche, Vanessa, 210
Bauer, Chris, 19, 149-150, 152, 187
Bauer, Joe, 199
Bauer, Laura Cunningham, 150
Bauer, Richard, 43
Bauert, Monika, 317
Baum, Barbara, 287
Baum, Brent, 125
Baum, Carol, 174
Baum, Kimberly, 92
Baumgarten Prophet Entertainment, 205, 207
Baumgarten, Alan, 112
Baumgarten, Craig, 205, 207
Baumgartner, Karl, 280
Bavan, Yolande, 96
Bavaria Film International, 242, 267
Baxt, David, 246
Bay, Frances, 42, 78, 193
Bay, Michael, 87
Bayeux, Carole, 150
Bayla, Cleo, 170
Bayne, Jordan, 197
Bays, Joe, 18, 163
BBC, 290, 295, 319
BBC Arena, 321
BBC Films, 242, 245-246, 258, 269, 278-279, 296
Beach, Adam, 113
Beach, Anna, 260
Beach, Gary, 129
Beach, Lisa, 45, 73, 169, 189, 205
Beacham, Frank, 152
Beacon Pictures, 103, 145, 184, 197
Beale, Simon Russell, 268
Bean, Jeremy, 311
Bean, Orson, 132-133, 325
Bean, Steve, 14, 37
Bearde, Nicolas, 31
Bearden, Jim, 184, 319
Beasley, Allyce, 163
Beasley, John, 62, 124
Beason, Eric L., 103
Beat, Jackie, 149
Beato, Affonso, 234
Beats by the Pound, 194
Beattie, Richard,319
Beatty, Lou, Jr., 120
Beatty, Ned, 38, 41, 325
Beau, Antoine, 284
Beaucaire, J.E., 150
Beauchemin, Scott, 102
Beaudoin, David, 187
Beaufoy, Simon, 242
Beaumont, Daisy, 299
Beautopia, 195
Beauvais, Garcelle, 41, 64
Beavan, Jenny, 164, 245, 256
Beaver, Jim, 166
Bebedeli, Despina, 262

Becerra, Veronica, 175
Becerril, Fernando, 30
Becher, Sophie, 208, 280
Beck, Bill, 87
Beck, Christophe, 108
Beckel, Graham, 31, 101
Becker, Belinda, 193-194
Becker, Ben, 242
Becker, Gerry, 87, 93, 113, 173
Becker, Jan, 105
Becker, Jurek, 105
Becker, Kimberly, 216
Becker, Meret, 242
Beckett, Warren, 113
Beckinsale, Kate, 91, 325
Beckman, Peregrine, 188
Bedard, Irene, 211
Bedelia, Bonnie, 144, 187, 325
Bedi, Bobby, 277
Bednarczyk, Stefan, 306
Bedrooms & Hallways, 278
Beebe, Dick, 129
Beebe, Dion, 301, 314
Beecham, Reg, 304
Beecher, Robert, 80
Beecroft, Jeffrey, 16
Beefcake, 285
Beeman, Shann, 39
Beers, Betsy, 20, 208
Begache, Abderrahim, 246
Begay, Charlotte, 202
Begg, David, 294
Begg, Warwick, 252
Begley, Ed, Jr., 203, 325
Behar, Henri, 90
Behaviour Worldwide, 319
Behrman, Lorne, 66
Behrozi, Soghra, 310
Beigelman, Mark, 77
Being John Malkovich, 133, 223, 233
Beisner, Michelle, 170
Bejing Film Studio, 305
Bekele, Gebrselassie, 198
Bekir, Adnan, 280
Bekjarev, Ivan, 273
Belack, Doris, 32
Bel-Air Entertainment, 16
Belasco, Eyde, 217
Belcher, Patricia, 16, 73, 213
Belcon, Garth, 208
Belcourt, Emile, 43
Belding, Stephanie, 125, 248
Belfast, M., 213
Belfast, Maine, 213
Belhadj, Jamal, 209
Belic, Adrian, 202
Belic, Roko, 202
Belkiya, Khadija, 246
Bell, Alan Edward, 119
Bell, Bob, 78
Bell, Cecil, 149
Bell, Heather, 213
Bell, Joshua, 130, 264
Bell, Leslie, 215
Bell, Marshall, 187

Bell, Natasha, 322
Bell, Robert N., 78
Bell, Ross Grayson, 120
Bella, Ullses, 40
Bellamy, Bill, 170, 207
Bellamy, Ned, 87, 125, 133, 152
Bellan, Joe, 33, 161
Bellar, Claire 319
Bellei, Mino, 256
Bellin, Thomas, 156
Bello, Gregg, 89, 105
Bello, Maria, 13
Bellville, Hercules, 279
Belmondo, Jean-Paul, 312
Belmont, Lara, 304
Belson, Kristine, 72
Beltrami, Marco, 99
Belvaux, Frédérique, 282
Belvin, Jackie, 18
Belzer, Richard, 173, 325
Benaïche, Wilfred, 286
Benassi, Justin Michael, 29
Benavides, Robert, 215
Benayoun, Georges, 315, 319
Benazzo, Maurizio, 90
Ben-David, Tal, 50
Bendel, Andrew, 245
Bender, Chris, 69
Bender, Lawrence, 164
Benedict, Billy, 354
Benedict, Claire, 293
Benedict, Kelle, 194
Benedict, Robert Patrick, 197
Benedict, Tannis, 163
Benedicto, Lourdes, 112
Bengal, 320
Bening, Annette, 4, 10, 24, 224-225, 231, 325-326
Benjamin, Alessandra, 76
Benjamin, Atiim, 194
Benjamin, Mark, 208
Benjamin, Nashom, 149
Benjo, Caroline, 291
Benmoussa, Fadila, 246
Benn, Krystal, 10
Benner, Al, 175
Bennes, John, 17
Bennet, Brian, 117
Bennett, Andrew, 180, 254
Bennett, Elizabeth Ann, 140
Bennett, Fran, 19
Bennett, Gail, 15
Bennett, Marcia, 184
Bennett, Matthew, 43, 152
Bennett, Michael, 193
Bennett, Nathan, 95
Bennett, Norman, 200
Bennett, Tony, 23
Bennett,Vicki, 321
Bennett, Zachary, 317
Benniman, Rosalyn, 130
Benoit, Jacqueline, 133
Benrubi, Abraham, 207
Benshan, Zhao, 305
Bensley, Guy, 268

Benson, Bruce, 62
Benson, Chris, 204
Benson, Jodi, 146
Benson, Martin, 180
Benson, Michael A., 205
Benson, Peter, 75
Benson, Wendy, 217
Bentivoglio, Fabrizio, 262
Bentley, Wes, 224-225
Benton, Ephraim, 93
Benton, John, 252
Benton, Mark, 306
Ben-Victor, Paul, 28, 124
Benz, Julie, 189
Benzali, Daniel, 279
Bepler, Jonathan, 213
Berard, Jillian, 109
Béraud, Pascale, 274
Bercek, Aleksandar, 273
Bercovici, Bebe, 319
Berenbaum, Michael, 90
Berenger, Tom, 210, 325-326
Berenson, Marisa, 317, 325
Beresford, Bruce, 106
Berest, Heather, 190
Berg, Aaron, 204
Berg, Barry, 97
Berg, Charles, 33
Berg, Josh, 204
Berg, Peter, 211, 325
Bergen, Robert, 60
Bergen, Timm, 190
Bergenstock, Rob, 123
Berger, Albert, 45, 73
Berger, Howard, 129
Berger, Mel, 33
Berger, Roger, 102
Berger, Stephen, 206
Bergere, Jenica, 209
Bergesio, Dario, 177
Bergin, Joan, 149
Bergin, Patrick, 210, 325
Bergl, Emily, 191
Bergman, Alan, 9
Bergman, Gary, 212
Bergman, Ingmar, 236
Bergman, Jaime, 170
Bergman, Marilyn, 9
Bergman, Mary Kay, 65, 79
Bergner, Christian, 294
Bergschneider, Conrad 184
Bergstrom, Christina, 16
Beristain, Gabriel, 213
Berkeley, Xander, 205
Berkley, Elizabeth, 102, 170, 325
Berkowitz, Myles, 190
Berléand, François, 239, 282
Berliner, Roshelle, 128
Berling, Charles, 238, 274, 284, 315
Berman, Bruce, 23, 35, 79, 110, 125
Berman, Glenn, 254
Berman, Lloyd, 92
Berman, Rachel, 190
Bern, Mina, 149
Bernabei, Loretta, 316

Bernard, Emma, 260
Bernard, Michelle, 170
Bernard, Raphaël, 319
Bernardi, Barry, 15, 78, 156
Bernat, Eric, 77
Berner, Alexander, 287, 317
Bernhard, Sandra, 207, 325
Bernhart, Bridget, 211
Bernier, Eric, 312
Bernier, Kristian, 104
Bernsen, Collin, 211
Bernstein, Adam, 191
Bernstein, Al, 175
Bernstein, Armyan, 103, 145, 184
Bernstein, Charles, 57
Bernstein, Elmer, 26, 64, 127
Bernstein, Michael "Moe", 102
Bernstein, Steven L., 20
Bernstein, Steven, 73
Berra, Stephen, 144
Berreondo, Christian, 130
Berri, Claude, 234, 281, 325
Berridi, Kalo F., 312
Berrie, Gillian, 237
Berrington, Elizabeth, 308
Berry, Bill, 173
Berry, Don, 127
Berry, Jennifer, 10
Berry, John, 354
Berry, Josh, 205
Berry, Kasey, 158
Berry, Michael, 101
Berry, Vincent, 104
Berta, Renato, 286
Bertaccini, Sabrina, 212
Berthier, Gabriel, 30
Berthonnier, Paulette, 269
Berthonnier, Roger, 269
Bertiau, Evelyne, 316
Bertin, Francoise, 286
Bertin, Gaston, 206
Bertish, Suzanne, 96
Bertolini, Christopher, 62
Bertolucci, Bernardo, 258
Bertram, Lavinia, 306
Bertram, Susan, 195
Bertram, Trish, 322
Bertrand, Estelle, 282
Bervy, Max, 212
Berwin, Dorothy, 278
Besançon, Nathalie, 284
Beshkempir: The Adopted Son, 310
Besieged, 258
Besser, Stuart M., 130
Besson, Luc, 294
Best Laid Plans, 208
Best Man, The, 126, 223
Best Man: "Best Boy" And All Of Us Twenty Years Later, 188
Best, Ahmed, 52
Best, Peter, 311
Best, Thom. 319
Bestrop, Juel, 59
Betafilm, 242

239

Chan, Alice, 253
Chan, Anthony, 244
Chan, Jackie, 244, 328
Chan, Kim, 28
Chan, Margaret, 318
Chan, Melissa, 201
Chan, Michael Paul, 136, 213
Chan, Moses, 258
Chan, Paul, 321
Chan, Peter Ho-Sun, 54
Chan, Philip, 244
Chan, Suk-yee, 258
Chan, Toby, 314
Chan, Vicki, 201
Chanaud, Juliette, 247
Chancer, Norman, 289
Chanchani, Dhruv, 52
Chanda, 212
Chandler, Jared, 62
Chaney, Rebecca, 199
Chang, Betsy, 173
Chang, Christina, 116
Chang, Lia, 102
Chang, Richard, 188
Chang, Stephanie, 195
Chang, Sylvia, 244, 264
Chang, Terence, 28, 164
Changjiang, Pan, 305
Channel Four Films, 237, 264, 273, 277
Channel Four, 285
Channing-Williams, Simon, 306
Chan-Pensley, Jonathan, 321
Chao, Lloyd, 244
Chapin, Miles, 173, 328
Chapman, Andi, 42
Chapman, David, 205
Chapman, Jan, 301
Chapman, Kevin, 94
Chapman, Lia, 124
Chapman, Marguerite, 355
Chapman, Michael, 119
Chapman, Teresa, 173
Chappatte, Jérôme, 286
Chappel, Tim, 203
Chappelhow, Maggie, 290
Chappell, Katsy, 78
Chappelle, Dave, 20, 101
Chappelle, Tommy, 29
Charap, David, 322
Charandoff, Tara, 288
Charbonneau, Patricia, 11, 194
Charles, Aude, 97
Charles, Glen, 43
Charles, Josh, 72, 328
Charles, Les, 43
Charles, Marie, 203
Charles, Rodney, 259
Charman, Kathryn, 75
Charoenpura, Indhira, 91
Charters, Rodney, 190
Chartier, Samuel, 282
Chase, Carl, 49
Chase, Christopher, 60

Chase, Eric Yalkut, 201
Chase, Johnie, 204
Chase, Peter 319
Chasin, Emma, 59
Chaterji, Dhritiman, 301
Chatman, Glenndon, 192
Chau-Sang, Anthony Wing, 258
Chauvellot, Sylvain, 274
Chavarria, Jennifer, 173
Chavez, Joe, 208
Chavira, Alicia, 194
Chaykin, Maury, 48, 113, 328
Chazen, Debbie, 306
Cheatham, Maree, 134, 195
Chebbi, Rami, 259
Chebbia, Cite, 259
Cheburin, Alexei, 102
Cheda, Mike, 206
Chediak, Enrique, 57, 199
Cheek, Lisa, 190
Cheek, Molly, 69
Cheeseman, Ken, 10
Chen, Joan, 253, 328-329
Chen, Johnny, 253
Chen, Tiffany, 258
Chen, Zidu, 33
Cheng, Diane, 37
Cheng, Jiang, 253
Cheng, Mayling, 187
Chenoweth, Ellen, 23, 70, 140
Chequer, Paul, 256
Cher, 256, 328
Chéreau, Patrice, 274, 281
Cherif, Khaldi, 246
Cherkaoui, Mohamed, 246
Chernov, Jeffrey, 36
Cherry, 218
Cherry, Prof. Janet, 217
Cherry, Maj. Fred, 57
Chertok, Jack, 15
Chervotkin, Yuri, 187
Cheshier, Lydell M., 134
Chester, Vanessa Lee, 11
Chestnut, Marilyn, 252
Chestnut, Morris, 126
Cheung, Alfred, 244
Cheung, George Kee, 59
Cheung, Jacob, 244
Cheung, Maggie, 244
Chevalier, Catherine, 284
Chevalier, Pierre, 284, 291
Chevrier, Arno, 149, 314
Chi, Nina Li, 244
Chianese, Dominic, 89, 152
Chiang, Jeffrey, 318
Chiate, Debra, 40
Chico, 214, 313
Chieffo, Michael, 15, 87, 195
Chikezie, Caroline 322
Chiklis, Michael, 102
Childerhose, Jane, 190
Children Of Heaven, 238
Childress, Mark, 124
Childs, Karen, 210

Chilson, Daniel, 202-203
Chimenz, Marco, 256
Chin, Keith, 164
Chin, Stephen, 175
Chinarunn Pictures, 318
Chinlund, Nick, 199
Chinn, Jeanne, 201
Chinn, Lori Tan, 93
Chiong, Roddy, 13
Chiquette, Shawn Elaine Brown, 101
Chirbas, James, 29
Chisholm, David, 276
Chiu, Lynda, 28
Chlebowski, Brian, 215
Cho, John, 69, 92, 224
Cho, Margaret, 209
Choate, Debra, 252
Choekyi, Pema, 188
Choi, Edmund, 252
Choice, Elisha, 213
Chon, Bok Yun, 217
Chong, Marcus, 35
Chong, Ronald 318
Chong, Tan Chih, 318
Chopin, Kathleen, 208
Chotikasupa, Somsuda, 91
Chott, Bill, 182
Choudhury, Sarita, 187
Choukri, Mohammed, 312
Chouppart, Marc, 284
Chow, Ho, 28, 125
Chow, Lai Ying, 244
Chow, Robert, 87
Chriqui, Emmanuelle, 204
Christ, Chad, 189
Christie, Dick, 213
Christiansen, Christian J., 101
Christina, Ana, 213
Christner, Gil, 87
Christo, 322
Christofferson, Debra, 15, 64
Christopher, Dyllan, 207
Christopher, Faith, 99
Christy, George, 89
Chu, Hon Pou, 249
Chua, Michelle, 318
Chuck, Wendy, 8, 45, 194
Chula, Babz, 106
Chun, Alice Lee, 28
Chun, Charles, 15
Chung, King-fai, 258
Chunn, Tommy, 194
Church, Austin B., 106
Church, Jeannie Grelier, 106
Church, Mike, 113
Churgin, Lisa Zeno, 20, 158
Chye, Kee Thuan, 164
Chyna, 214
Ci Fam, Ghia, 46
Cianchetti, Fabio, 258
Ciarcia, John, 211
Ciarfalio, Carl N., 120
Ciarflio, Carl, 117
Cibelli, Christopher, 20
CIBY 2000, 280
Cicchini, Robert, 26, 191

Cicco, Johnny, 98
Ciccolella, Jude, 149
Cicero, Phyllis, 200
Cider House Rules, The, 158, 222, 228
Ciftci, Suna, 273
Cigliuti, Natalia, 209
Cilauro, Santo, 252
Cimino, Leonardo, 152
Cinciripini, Tony, 218
Cinehaus, 173
Cine Libre Eliane Dubois, 278
Cinéa, 315
Cinea-Film Alain Sarde-Maestranza Films, 238
Cinecitta-Rai Radiotelevisione Italiana and Tele+, 316
Cinema Esperanca, 321
Cinema Guild, 209
Cinema Tamaris, 312
Cinema Village Features, 312
CineMamas, 309
Cinemas de La Zone, 310
Cinemax, 189, 217, 321
Cinequanon Pictures Intl, 207
CineSon, 20
Cineville, 203
Cinieri, Cosimo, 309
Cinkozoev, Mirlan, 310
Ciornei, Frank, 127
Citer, Leonid, 127
Citron, Sam, 211
City (La Ciudad), The, 128
City, Alex, 55
Claire, Alison, 169
Clanagan, Jeff, 194
Clanton, Rony, 186
Clapp, Gordon, 191
Clapton, Eric, 119, 328
Clark, Ariel, 192
Clark, Bob, 192
Clark, Daniel, 319
Clark, Dave Allen, 70
Clark, Dorothy, 250
Clark, Jason, 109, 163
Clark, Jim, 299, 308
Clark, John, 170, 333
Clark, Oliver, 37, 87, 124
Clark, Paul, 237
Clark, Sean, 193
Clark, Spencer Treat, 70, 106
Clark, Victoria, 152
Clarke, Ashley, 33
Clarke, Caitlin, 123
Clarke, Christian, 75
Clarke, Daisy, 33
Clarke, Gin, 52
Clarke, Hamish, 277
Clarke, Jeff, 190
Clarke, Matt, 113
Clarke-Robert, 118
Clarke, Ron, 56
Clarke, Shirley, 95
Clarke, Stanley, 126

Clarke-Hill, Tom, 48
Clarkson, Patricia, 155, 188
Clash, Kevin, 72, 112
Classic SRL, 262, 309
Claudio, Claudine, 189
Claus, Marc, 170
Clauss, Rusty, 200
Clavel, François, 243
Clavel, Françoise, 284, 315
Claxton, Richard, 285
Clay, Andrew Dice, 194, 328
Clay, Jenny White Buffalo, 65
Clay, Jim, 293, 308
Claybon, Terry, 184
Clayton, Curtiss, 91
Clayton, Gina, 43
Clayton, Merry, 209
CLC Films, 199
Cleary, Miranda, 301
Cleckener, Anthony, 259
Cleese, John, 37, 298-299, 328
Cleland-Hura, Rikki, 146
Clem, Frank, 59
Clemenson, Christian, 195
Clement, Jennifer, 95
Clémenti, Pierre, 246, 356
Clements, B.J., 195
Clements, Christopher Lee, 204
Clendenin, Robert, 199
Clermont, Nicolas, 254
Cleveland, Chris, 190
Clifford, Francesca, 65
Clifford, Jeffrey, 201
Clifford, Brian, 180
Clifton Collins, Jr., 216
Clinton, George S., 59, 206
Clinton, Mildrid, 66
Clooney, George, 65, 110-111
Close, Bryan, 107
Close, Glenn, 24, 38, 60, 328
Close-Up, 322
Closs, Ashleigh, 66
Clotworthy, Robert, 26
Cloud, Lisa, 224
Clough, John Scott, 216
Clow, Allan, 204
CLT-UFA International, 262
Clubland, 195
Clunes, Martin, 275
Clunie, Michelle, 195
Cluzet, François, 315
Clydesdale, Ross, 190
Cmiral, Elia, 99
CML, 311
CNC, 284, 310
CNC-Canal+-Region de Franche Comte-Sofinergie 4-Sofigram, 238
Coates, Bill, 29
Coates, Nelson, 100
Coatsworth, David, 82, 187
Cobbs, Bill, 116
Cobra Film Department, 317
Coburn, Arthur, 103

373

Francine, Anne, 357
Francis, Freddie, 122
Francis-Bruce, Richard, 55, 155
Francks, Lili, 186
Franco Espagnol, 238
Franco, Carlos A., 214
Franco, David, 145, 301
Franco, James Edward, 40
Franco, Larry, 17, 143
Franco, Olympio D., 91
Francolini, Anna, 306
Frandsen, Jessica, 112
Frangione, Jim, 210
Frank, Andrew, 216
Frank, Brian, 108
Frank, David Roland, 187
Frank, Joe, 182
Frank, Kristi, 214
Frank, Larry, 216
Frank, Tony, 8
Frankel, Art, 166
Frankel, David, 218
Franken, Steve, 213
Frankenberg, Pia, 309
Frankenheimer, John, 62
Franklin, Carole, 207
Franklin, Jeff, 163, 207
Franklin, Joe, 214
Franklin, Vincent, 306
Franks, Steve, 63
Frannie, 202
Franz, Heidi, 205
Frascaro, Fabio, 309
Fraser, Brendan, 14, 49, 95, 333
Fraser, Brent David, 65
Fraser, Cameron, 36
Fraser, Erin, 118
Fraser, Genevieve, 113
Fraser, Laura, 178, 322
Frazel, Cheryl, 81
Frazen, Diane, 81
Frazetti, Daryl "Bones", 198
Frazier, Gibson, 129
Frazier, Joe, 20
Freaks Uncensored!: A Human Sideshow, 189
Freberg, Stan, 163
Frechette, Richard, 312
Fred, Gunnel, 236
Frederic, Patrick, 20
Fredericks, David, 95, 106
Fredericks, Irene, 211
Fredericks, Neal, 71
Free Enterprise, 200
Freeman, David, 93, 187
Freeman, J.E., 39
Freeman, Jeff, 24, 189
Freeman, K. Todd, 158
Freeman, Kay, 204
Freeman, Matt, 39
Freeman, Morgan J., 57
Frehley, Ace, 204
French, Arthur, 37, 130
Fresh, Doug E., 208
Freud, Emma, 262
Freud, Esther, 246

Freudenthal, Thomas, 287
Freund, Jay, 201
Frey, Darcy, 43
Freytez, Patxi, 234
Fridriksson, Fridrik Thor, 310
Friedberg, Mark, 81, 148
Friedman, Bernie, 102, 127, 218
Friedman, Brian, 11
Friedman, Bud, 173
Friedman, David F., 189
Friedman, David, 77
Friedman, Gabriel, 214
Friedman, Louis G., 69
Friedman, Mark, 15, 116
Friedman, Richard, 206
Friedman, Steven Mark, 116
Friedrich, Peter, 188
Friel, Anna, 51
Friends and Lovers, 195
Frigeri, Francesco, 289
Frisch, Dan, 209
Frisch, David, 184
Frisell, Bill, 199
Fritz, Nikki, 39
Frizzell, John, 18, 196, 205
Froboess, Cornelia, 317
Frogley, Louise, 99, 117
Frogs For Snakes, 198-199
Fröler, Samuel, 236
Fromant, Monty, 322
Frost, Damon, 29
Frost, Roger, 260-261, 322
Frot, Catherine, 270
Fruchtmann, Uri, 268
Frutkoff, Gary, 117
Fryar, Irving, 170
Fryer, Jeff, 50
Frystak, Lori Eschler, 190
Fuchs, Fred, 186
Fucile, Tony, 83
Fucking Amal, 287
Fugate, Tony, 11
Fuhrman, Ben, 216
Fuji Television Network, 279
Fuji, J.A., 32
Fujii, Mika, 174
Fujimoto, Tak, 84
Fujimura, Shunji, 279
Fujita, Toshiya, 314
Fukushima, Mary, 195
Fulford, Christopher, 278
Fulford, Wendji, 94
Fuller, Kurt, 43, 157
Fuller, Stephon, 218
Fullerton, Olivia, 170
Fullerton, Richard, 72
Fullerton-Smith, Jane, 196
Fulton, Christina, 208
Fulton, Larry, 84
Fulton, Niall Greig, 275
Fumo, Nuccia, 313
Funari, Vicky, 309
Funck, Hans, 317
Funk, Bradlee, 214
Funk, Stacey, 214
Funk, Terry, 214

Funk, Vicki, 214
Funnelle, Leigh, 285
Funt, Allen, 357
Furgler, Brigitta, 322
Furlong, Brian, 94
Furlong, Edward, 204, 332-333
Furlong, Kevin, 277
Fürnsinn, Margrita, 242
Furth, George, 42
Furukawa, Hiromitsu, 305
Fusco, Angela, 186
Fuse, Akira, 279
Fuse, Eri, 320
Fuster, Bernardo, 262
Futterman, Susan, 209
G., Adam, 216
G2 FILMS, 256
Gabella, Ian, 311
Gabriel, Ana, 26
Gabriel, Igor, 291
Gabriel, Ron, 186
Gabrych, Andersen, 50
Gaden, John, 316
Gadjieff, Stephane Tchal, 321
Gadoury, Odette, 138
Gaeta, John, 35
Gaffigan, Jim, 110
Gaffney, Mo, 37, 109, 204
Gage, Ali, 21
Gage, Easton, 289
Gage, Melanie, 173
Gagnier, Holly, 200
Gail, Max, 211, 333
Gaiman, Neil, 288
Gainer, Steve, 194
Gainer, Tia, 73
Gainey, Keeley, 306, 322
Gainey, M.C., 76, 109
Gainor, Glenn S., 109
Gains, Herbert W., 8
Gainsbourg, Charlotte, 315
Gainy, Johnell, 207
Gaither, Jamala, 166
Gajjar, Reshma, 224
Galan, Mapi, 317
Galante, Maria, 128
Galanti, Lt. Paul, 57
Galanti, Phyllis, 57
Galasso, Victoria, 66
Galaxy Quest, 182, 222
Galbreath, Jessica, 66
Gale, David, 8, 20, 45, 73
Gale, Ricardo Jacques, 278
Galer, Andrea, 296
Galfe, Francois, 315
Galiani, Caroline, 238
Galifianakis, Zach, 204
Gallagher, Bronagh, 52
Gallagher, Gina, 23
Gallagher, Joe, 149
Gallagher, Michael, 14
Gallagher, Patrick, 197
Gallagher, Peter, 129, 224-225, 333
Gallagher, Teresa, 306
Gallanders, James, 186
Gallardo, Camilo, 280

Gallini, Matt, 145, 195
Gallivan, Christopher, 65
Gallivan, J. Clarke, 208
Gallo, Carla, 12
Gallo, Michaela, 117
Galouge, Daniel, 199
Galt, Nigel, 75
Gamba, Gichi, 87
Gamble, David, 269
Gamble, Mason, 70, 333
Gambler, The, 273
Gamblin, Jacques, 236
Gamboa, Joonee, 91
Gambon, Michael, 136, 142-143, 273, 283, 333
Gammel, Robin, 291
Gammell, Josie, 169
Gammill, Tom, 207
Gammon, James, 83, 210
Gan, Jennifer Say, 216
Ganapoler, Louis, 134
Ganatra, Ravin, 48
Gandara, Liz, 157
Gandolfini, James, 19
Gandhi, Goolistan, 319
Gandy, Sue, 218
Ganey, Catrina, 127
Gangl, Giordano, 310
Ganis, Sid, 63, 156
Gannascoli, Joseph R., 93
Gant, David, 264, 294
Gant, Mtume, 127
Gantzer, Marie-France, 319
Gant, Robert, 205
Ganz, Bruno, 262, 333
Ganz, Lowell, 33
Gaoat, Sudarat L., 91
Garay, Brandi, 193
Garbage, 299
Garber, Dennis, 136
Garci, José Luis, 284
Garcia, Andy, 20, 333
Garcia, Carmela, 212
Garcia, Cipriano, 128
Garcia, Eddie, 190
Garcia, Erick, 216
García, Esther, 234
Garcia, Frederic, 209
Garcia, Jerry, 95
Garcia, Joe, 109
Garcia, Jose Angel, 149
Garcia, Julio, 175
Garcia, Lola, 234
Garcia, Marcos Martinez, 128
Garcia, Moises, 128
Garcia, Nicole, 195
Garcia, Rich, 103
Garcia, Risa Bramon, 20, 42
Garcia, Rodrigo, 128
Garcia, Ron, 129
Garcia-Lorido, Daniella, 20
Garcin, Henri, 312
Garde, James, 206
Gardiner, Greg, 217
Gardiner, Jeremy, 190
Gardner, David, 204
Gardner, John, 275

Gardner, Mario, 193
Gardner, Peter, 290
Gardner, Randy, 218
Gardos, Eva, 149
Garefino, Anne, 65
Gargano, Michael, 215
Garito, Ken, 66-67
Garland, Alison, 322
Garland, Glenn, 125
Garlin, Jeff, 59
Garner, Julian, 276
Garner, Natalie, 156
Garofalo, Janeane, 20, 87, 99, 139, 317, 333
Garr, Teri, 82, 333
Garrett, Brad, 150
Garrett, Brooke, 21
Garrett, Hank, 192
Garrett, Joe, 15
Garrett, Stephen, 242
Garrido, Augie, 103
Garrison, Grant, 70
Garrow, Will, 212
Garroway, Lloyd, 145, 195
Garry, David, 195
Garson, Willie, 133, 175, 215
Gartner, Karen, 113
Garven, Casey Tyler, 204
Garvey, Ray, 150, 187
Garvin, Tom, 187
Garwood, Judy, 208
Garwood, Norman, 48
Gascogne, Geoff, 177
Gaskins, Emilie, 126
Gaskins, Willie, 126
Gaspari, Christopher, 66
Gass, Kyle, 152, 196
Gasser, Jim, 170
Gasser, Mary, 77
Gassot, Charles, 274
Gasteyer, Ana, 82
Gaston, Michael, 106
Gates, Jean, 29
Gates, Ken, 292
Gates, Mark, 50
Gates, Spencer, 169
Gati, Kathleen, 105
Gatins, John, 8
Gattas, Brian, 189
Gatto, Dan, 209
Gaudreault, Emile, 33
Gaumont, 270, 294
Gaup, Mikkel, 187
Gautier, Eric, 274, 312, 315
Gautrelet, Sylvie, 281
Gauzy, Dyna, 314
Gavin, Jake, 283
Gavin, James, 101
Gawthmey, Ted, 212
Gay, Amanda, 138
Gay, Lu, 87
Gayet, Julie, 312
Gayheart, Rebecca, 189
Gayle, Carmel, 212
Gaylord, E.K., II, 205
Gaynes, Jessica, 189
Gaynor, J.B., 203

Paddock, Josh, 39
Padilla, Carlos, 175
Padilla, Josseph, 212
Padilla, Rhency, 91
Pagán, Antone, 127, 218
Pagano, Alfred, 65
Pagano, Eugene, 65
Pagano, Rick, 206, 217
Page, Bobbi, 60
Page, Charles, 152
Page, Corey, 197-198
Page, David, 78
Page, Dominic, 318
Page, Gemma, 306
Page, Joanna, 304
Page, Melanie, 294
Paget, Lou, 128
Pagni, Stefano, 289
Paige, Gabriel, 59
Paige, Jason, 45
Paige, Jennifer, 147
Paige, Peter, 195
Paiment, Mahee, 34
Pain, Frankye, 310
Pais, Josh, 130
Paisley, Ray, 43
Pakshiran, 320
Palagonia, Al, 66
Palahniuk, Chuck, 120
Palatnik, Eran, 193
Palenzuela, Miguel, 311
Palermo, Eddy, 177
Palermo, George, 20
Palevsky, Max, 198
Palisades Pictures, 190
Pallad, Pete, 69
Palladino, Aleksa, 86, 187, 218
Palladino, Jack, 136
Palm Pictures, 215, 316
Palmer, Alex, 283
Palmer, Alyson, 37
Palmer, Geoff, 207
Palmer, Geoffrey, 164, 277
Palmer, Gretchen, 207
Palmer, Hayley, 91
Palmer, Hugh, 203
Palmer, John, 242
Palmer, K.P., 173
Palmer, Margaret, 211
Palmer, Patrick, 191
Palmer, Sanchez, 321
Palmer-Smith, Glenn, 102
Palmieri, Tom, 149
Palminteri, Chazz, 23, 163, 344
Paloian-Breznikar, Nancy, 208
Palomaria, Alexandria, 193
Palomaria, Noel, 193
Palone, Gavin, 204
Paltrow, Gwyneth, 176-177
Pandora Cinema, 245
Pandora Film, 278, 280, 317
Panero, Valentin, 284
Panettiere, Hayden, 16
Pang, Adrian, 318

Pang, Andrew, 28
Pang, Edwin, 314
Panico, John, 203
Pankow, Joanne, 29
Pannelli, Nicola, 177
Panozzo, Dina, 310
Pantazopoulos, Nicholas, 276
Pantoliano, Joe, 35, 102, 188, 344
Paolino, T.J., 98
Papa, Bob, 218
Papadopoulos, Chris, 90
Papajohn, Michael, 103
Paparazzo, Janet, 66
Paparone, Joe, 90
Pape, Axel, 300
Papoulis, Jim, 209
Papp, Éva, 273
Pappas, James, 190
Pappas, Robert Kane, 215
Pappas, Robert, 215
Papsidera, John, 196, 204
Paquin, Anna, 11, 34, 344
Paquin, Bethany M., 10
Parada, Dan, 157
Paradiso, Roger, 9, 89
Paragon Entertainment, 262
Parallax Pictures, 237
Parallel Pictures, 187
Paramore, Kirk, 311
Paramount, 5, 8, 13, 20, 37, 45, 62, 65, 73, 81, 86, 106, 118, 127, 143, 177, 180, 198, 216-217, 222, 250, 273, 319, 362
Parati, Tim, 112
Pare, Chris, 75
Paredes, Marisa, 234
Parelle, Monic, 291
Parent, Robert, 276
Parillo, Jennifer Nicole, 191
Parilo, Markus, 43
Paris, Julie, 21, 81, 330
Paris, Tito, 313
Parish, John, 316
Parisi, Carmine, 93
Parisi, Heather Elizabeth, 51
Parisi, Michael, 199
Parisot, Dean, 182
Park, Jeany, 204
Park, Kris, 112
Park, Matthew G., 204
Park, Ray, 52
Park, Sooyoung, 200
Park, Sunmin, 305
Parke, Evan Dexter, 158
Parker, Alan, 180
Parker, Anthony Ray, 35
Parker, Chad, 78
Parker, Daniel T., 37, 182
Parker, Gary, 110
Parker, Mary-Louise, 42, 344
Parker, Nicole Ari, 101, 151
Parker, Nicole, 20
Parker, Oliver, 268
Parker, Peter, 268
Parker, Sarah Jessica, 95,

344
Parker, Trey, 65, 344
Parks, Joel, 45
Parriott, Sara, 81
Parrish, Paula, 150
Parrondo, Gil, 284
Parry, Susan, 293
Parsons, Clive, 256
Parsons, George R., 136
Parsons, Hazel, 256
Parsons, Jennifer, 40
Parsons, Jenny, 43
Parsons, Michael, 33
Parsons, Robyn, 204
Partmann, Cornelia, 300
Pártos, Géza, 273
Party Monster, 189
Pasadena Roof Orchestra, 242
Pascal, Adam, 42
Pascual, Lluis, 234
Paseornek, Michael, 203
Pashalinski, Lola, 150
Paskaljevic, Goran, 273
Pasley, Thomas, 194
Pass, Cyndi, 33
Pastko, Earl, 317
Pastore, Vincent, 93, 184, 191
Pastoriza, Robert, 33
Pasztor, Beatrix Aruna, 206
Patano, Tonye, 184
Patch, Karen, 160
Patel, Bhasker, 269
Patel, Harish, 269
Patel, Priya, 194
Paterson, Owen, 35
Pathak, Prof. Devavrat, 217
Pathé Pictures, 268
Patinkin, Mandy, 112, 344
Patino, Alejandro, 92
Patino, Lisa, 194
Patnode, Justin, 212
Paton, Angela, 195
Paton, Julia, 43
Patrick O'Brien, 163, 190
Patrick O'Hara, 170
Patrick O'Neal Jones, 110
Patrick, Anna, 268
Patrick, Emily, 19
Patrick, Thomas, 24-25, 190
Patsas, Giorgos, 262
Patsavas, Alex, 109
Pattamadilok, Parinya, 91
Patterson, Barbara June, 122
Patterson, Brian, 110
Patterson, Chuck, 209
Patterson, J.P., 9
Patterson, Janet, 301
Patterson, Jenny, 17
Patti, Guesch, 317
Patti, Thomas, 218
Patton, Jody, 178
Patton, Will, 48, 102, 207, 344
Pattur, Karla, 81
Paul, Adam, 288
Paul, Angad, 241

Paul, Bonnie, 192
Paul, Christiane, 317
Paul, Ed, 292
Paul, Hank, 192
Paul, Meilani, 207
Paul, Nathan, 33
Paul, Randall, 75
Paul, Richard, 66
Paul, Steven, 192, 206
Pauli, Peter, 267
Paulina, 309
Paull, Lawrence G., 216
Pauls, Marcus, 32
Paulsen, Tiffany, 81
Paulshock, Pamela, 107, 194
Paulson, Jay, 39
Paulson, Sarah, 21, 188
Pauly, Scott Duncan, 204
Pavlinovic, Zeljka, 129
Pawk, Michele, 152
Pawlowski, Joanne, 207
Payakkapong, Ayutthaya A., 91
Payback, 13, 222
Paymer, David, 13, 107, 184, 206, 345
Payne, Alexander, 45
Payne, Christian, 147
Payne, Dean, 113
Payne, Ron, 187
Payne, Stephen, 218
Payton-Wright, Pamela, 10
Peabody, Dossy, 10
Peace, Josh, 285
Peach, Andy, 208
Peaco, Bobby, 77
Peacock, David, 237
Peacock, Ross, 42
Péan, Guylène, 282
Pearce, Allan Caister, 256
Pearce, Eve, 306
Pearce, Guy, 30, 345
Pearce, Natasha, 112
Pearce, Peter, 217
Pearce, Scott, 110
Pearce, Steve, 149
Pearl, Barry, 15
Pearlstein, Randy, 210
Pearson, Gil, 122
Pearson, Jan, 277
Pearson, Jim, 146
Pearson, Neil, 285
Pearson, Richard, 72, 92
Pearthree, Pippa, 184
Peck, Bob, 360
Peck, Brian, 173
Peck, George, 144
Peck, Kashka, 189
Pecorelli, Giannandrea, 264
Peden, Jennifer Baldwin, 204
Pedersen, Bjorn Ove, 96
Pedestrian Films, 211
Peduzzi, Richard, 274
Peebles, Alison, 275
Peer, Joe, 107
Peer, Ron, 42
Peet, Amanda, 128, 188
Peigong, Wang, 305

Peipers, David, 208
Peipmann, Jason, 113
Peirce, Kimberly, 115
Peirce, Todd, 120
Peitzman, Hailey, 78
Pekic, Dusan, 317
Peldon, Ashley, 205
Pellegrino, Frank, 28, 93
Pellington, Mark, 70
Pellizzari, Monica, 310
Pelman, Yoram, 20
Peloso, Glen, 125
Peltier, Leroy, 113
Peltz, Lauren, 194
Pema, Tenzin, 188
Pen, Maryse, 214
Peña, Candela, 234
Pena, Nonny De La, 209
Pena, Paul "Earthquake", 202
Penacoli, Jerry, 182
Pencier, Nick de, 312
Pender, Janaya, 35
Pender, Paul, 70
Pendleton, Austin, 123, 345
Pendry, Greyson, 173
Penman, Sarah, 170
Penn, Richard, 78
Penn, Sean, 133, 150, 230, 343, 345
Penn, Zak, 78
Pennacchio, George, 209
Pennell, Jon, 213
Pennell, Melanie, 214
Penny, Bob, 207
Penotti, John, 90
Penry-Jones, Rupert, 322
Penton, Adam, 50
Pepe, Neil, 23, 166
Pepi, Kyle, 98
Pepi, Ryan, 98
Peploe, Clare, 258
Pepper, Barry, 155
Perabo, Piper, 208
Peralta, Antonio, 128
Peranio, Vincent, 140
Percy, Lee, 115
Perdomo, Gustavo A., 62
Pe're', Wayne, 117
Pereira, Christian, 270
Pereira ,Jacqueline, 318
Pereira, Virginia, 166
Perella, Marco, 8
Perello, Hope, 192
Perensky, Tonie, 8
Peretti, Thierry de, 274
Pereyra, Rene, 309
Perez, Alex, 117
Perez, Eddie, 216
Perez, Freddie, 212
Perez, Jose, 117, 345
Perez, Marisa, 200
Perez, Miguel, 166
Perez, Morgan, 317
Perez, Olivia, 212
Perez, Rosie, 12, 345
Perez, Salvador, 216
Perez, Timothy Paul, 134,